SOFTWARE FOR USE

A Practical Guide
to the Models and Methods
of Usage-Centered Design

LARRY L. CONSTANTINE
LUCY A. D. LOCKWOOD

ACM Press
New York, New York

ADDISON-WESLEY
An imprint of Addison Wesley Longman, Inc.

Reading, Massachusetts • Harlow, England • Menlo Park, California
Berkeley, California • Don Mills, Ontario • Sydney
Bonn • Amsterdam • Tokyo • Mexico City

The publisher offers discounts on this book when ordered in quantity for special sales. For more information, please contact:

Corporate, Government, and Special Sales
Addison Wesley Longman, Inc.
One Jacob Way
Reading, Massachusetts 01867
(781) 944-3700

Library of Congress Cataloging-in-Publication Data

Constantine, Larry L.
   Software for use : a practical guide to the models and methods
of usage-centered design / Larry L. Constantine, Lucy A.D.
Lockwood.
   p. cm.
  Includes bibliographical references and index.
  ISBN 0-201-92478-1
  1. Application software—Development. I. Lockwood, Lucy A. D. II.
Title.
  QA76.76.A65 C665 1999
  005.1—dc21

                                                    98–46573
                                                       CIP
                                                        AC

Text printed on recycled and acid-free paper.

ISBN 0201924781

3 4 5 6 7 8   CR   02 01 00

3rd Printing   January 2000

*To Betty and Roy Lockwood, who late in life
took up the challenges of modern computers
and who continue to inspire us.*

Contents

Acknowledgments

This book has been a long time coming. Too long, many would say, and we would have to include ourselves in the chorus. The concepts and techniques of usage-centered design evolved slowly over the entire six years we have been working together. They have flowed from many fonts, emerging from our own work on user interface design problems, from the work of our many clients, from our attempts as teachers to communicate ideas, and from the efforts of our countless students to learn what we were communicating.

The book itself has taken about twice as long to write as it should have. We apologize to our clients and students and colleagues who have waited so long, but for all the frustrations there is also compensation: It is a much better book for having had the extra review and input and revision and refinement.

Along the way, there have been many contributors, believers, and supporters whom we would like to acknowledge. It began with Ivar Jacobson, who not only contributed a cornerstone of the foundation on which our work is built but also has been a supportive colleague throughout the evolution of our models and methods.

It has been said that consulting is a form of paid education. Every good consulting engagement is a learning experience, and as we have helped clients we have also learned from them. Among our many clients have been visionaries who recognized usability as a critical problem in delivering quality service and products and who saw in usage-centered design a practicable solution. It has been our privilege to work with people like Werner Hoefler, Franz Petz, and Helmut Windl of Siemens AG in Germany and Bryan Luke at Westpac Bank in Australia and to help them turn visions into realities.

We are grateful to numerous colleagues who have engaged in a dialogue with us that helped shape and refine our thinking, among them Hugh Beyer, Ian Graham, Karen Holtzblatt, Hermann Kaindl, Meilir Page-Jones, and Rebecca

Wirfs-Brock. Special thanks go also to Jared Spool, whose affectionate antagonism has often led us to tighten our concepts and streamline our methods.

We are particularly grateful to James Noble, who joined with us to teach usage-centered design and brought new energy and insight at a stage when everything seemed settled. In insisting we practice what we preach and calling on us to simplify and generalize, he helped make fundamental improvements in both the approach and how it is taught.

We also want to thank Roy Lockwood, who at the age of 87 started learning to use computers and in the process gave us new insights into the shortcomings of modern graphical user interfaces.

The book would not be in your hands now were it not for the faith and fortitude of our long-suffering editor, Peter Gordon, who said at the outset that he wanted a work of lasting value, even if it took longer to deliver. We look forward to the long-promised celebratory dinner with him. Our appreciation also goes to associate editor Helen Goldstein and production coordinator Genevieve Rajewski, who alternately cajoled, pestered, and pleaded with us in an effort to bring this work to print. And thanks also to Jean Peck, our vigilant, thorough, and unfailingly correct copy editor, who saved us from numerous small embarrassments and helped polish the final work to an acceptable patina.

The greatest debt, not surprisingly, is owed to our students. Those thousands of students in the seminars, workshops, lectures, and tutorials we have taught have also taught us. Every time we teach, we discover something new that causes us to refine the concepts, polish the presentation, and revise our thinking. Thank you, all of you. We will try to keep up with you.

Preface

Software for Use is a book for professionals under pressure, for those who work under the dual demands for high-quality software-based systems on the one hand and faster delivery with fewer resources on the other. This book shows how to use streamlined techniques to make software-based systems significantly more usable and useful regardless of whether these systems are installed on desktop computers, ensconced on large mainframe servers, embedded in industrial electronics, or accessed via the World Wide Web. It is written primarily for computer software and applications developers—the analysts, designers, engineers, and programmers who are responsible for producing software systems. In concept, perhaps, usability ought to be the bailiwick of usability specialists. In practice, however, developers of various stripes make the vast majority of the myriad decisions that shape and determine the ultimate usability of software-based products; it is for these frontline troops of the industry that this book was conceived.

Usage-centered design, the approach taken in this book, originated with our own frustrating experiences as users of software and our recurring dissatisfaction with software that was unnecessarily awkward and difficult to use. The wealth of established knowledge about human–computer interaction was somehow not being fully translated into more usable products. As we studied how software-based products were being developed, we began to understand where things were going wrong and what needed to be changed in order to deliver better systems.

Usage-centered design is a streamlined but systematic approach for devising software closely fitted to the genuine needs of users—software that is not only more useful and easier to use but also simpler and easier to construct. Usage-centered design is tailored to the high-pressure realities of modern software development. Using a few simple but powerful models, it provides a scheme for quickly understanding users in relation to systems, their working intentions in carrying out tasks, and the support they need from the system to perform those tasks. Its methods and models can be applied within almost any software development life cycle (SDLC) model and incorporated into almost any modern development practices, including various object-oriented (OO) approaches such as the Unified Modeling Language (UML). Usage-centered design is not partial to any one language or platform, being equally effective with rapid iterative development using the latest integrated visual development environments or with character-based control systems running on specialized hardware.

A major part of our message to designers and developers of every ilk is simple: Usability is not rocket science. It is often hard work and invariably requires great attention to detail, but, given a few basic conceptual tools, you, too, can learn how to recognize problems in usability and how to improve the usability of the systems you develop. Professor Woody Flowers of the Massachusetts Institute of Technology has given cameras to middle-school students, who then must photograph hard-to-use things and explain the problems. If untrained teenagers can manage the basics of usability, competent adults ought to be able to master the essentials.

Quite honestly, we think the model-driven approaches explained in this book can be of value to almost any professional with responsibility for product design and development, and that includes a full range of design specialists, from user interface and interaction designers to ergonomicists and human factors engineers, from graphic artists and industrial designers to human–computer interaction specialists and usability testers. In our experience, the most important prerequisite is not a particular academic degree or level of applied experience, but the willingness and ability to approach the material with an open mind.

In our own design work and teaching, our emphasis has always been on simple, powerful techniques that can be quickly learned and applied. For example, a free-lance designer specializing in Web-based applications learned about usage-centered design techniques in a short conference presentation and was able to apply them immediately in her work. After attending a one-hour lecture, a project leader at a computer peripherals company taught his group how to improve the user interfaces of their software through use case models. Around the world are companies successfully applying these techniques to problems as diverse as banking applications, industrial automation controls, and commercial software development tools.

We should not give the impression that usage-centered design is for everyone or for all problems. We use models as a kind of vaulting pole, to gain leverage and height in hurdling the problems of user interface design. In our experience, using simple models to understand a problem and potential solutions speeds up the process, but some newcomers to such techniques will find it difficult not to just skip up to the bar and leap before they look.

Although we both have backgrounds heavy in the human sciences, we draw a sharp distinction between interesting research issues and the realities of everyday decision making. Among academics and professionals are those who seem to believe that human–machine interaction can be understood only through cognitive and perceptual psychology, that a thorough grounding in the academic literature is a prerequisite for doing effective interaction design. Our own views are that many of the complexities and subtleties that loom so large for researchers and research laboratories are of lesser consequence in everyday decision making.

We consider the creative urge a vital force in good design, but we base it on a platform of sound engineering. Some professionals who think of user interfaces as a form of theater or consider design to be based primarily on artistic inspiration have had to struggle with the methodical nature of usage-centered design. On the other hand, the enthusiastic converts to our model-driven approach include designers and artists who have found that abstract models can inspire greater creativity.

In organizing the book, we have striven to live up to our subtitle, creating a practical guide that is more than an introduction even if perhaps less than a handbook. To this end, the book is organized into distinct sections. Of course, they are written with the expectation that most readers who want to understand the material thoroughly will take them in sequence. In particular, most of the later chapters depend to a substantial degree on the conceptual foundation laid in the first six chapters. In fact, if all you seek is a general understanding of usage-centered design, Sections I and II cover the core material. In Sections III and IV, we shift to the sundry and sometimes messy details of practical application. This is likely to be of particularly keen interest to developers, especially those with limited background in user interface design, but we would not recommend beginning with these sections.

In keeping with the practical, applied focus of the book, numerous small specific examples are used throughout the text. In addition, we have included two completely worked-out applications of usage-centered design. One, introduced in Chapter 4, is used for illustration throughout the middle chapters and concludes in Chapter 10; the other forms the whole of Chapter 15. If you are one of those "get-down-and-dirty" detail-oriented developers who cannot resist seeing how it all works out in the end, you might begin with the applied example in Chapter 15 before going back to build the necessary background by working through Chapters 4 through 14.

Because we see on-line documentation to be an integral feature of the user interface and a major factor in usability, we have devoted an entire chapter to help systems. Once familiar with the basics in Chapters 2 and 3 plus Section II, technical writers and documentation specialists should find much of interest in Chapter 11.

Professionals who already have a thorough background in human–computer interaction and user interface design and who are most interested in what makes usage-centered design unique may want to skip directly to the core material on the models and modeling techniques in Section II. Other material that has proved to be of particular interest to such professionals can be found in Chapter 12 on the progressive usage model and in Chapter 17 on usability metrics.

Managers, project leaders, and others who might be more interested in the management and organizational implications of usage-centered design than in its technical details might start with the first two chapters, then skim Section V on assessment and improvement, and finish off with Section VI on organizing and managing the process.

Despite its long gestation period, the material herein is still a work in progress. Just as it has been enhanced and extended through the contributions of our many students and clients, we anticipate it will also be advanced by you, our readers. As we tell every class we have ever taught, we want to hear from you. So, please tell us about your experiences in putting usage-centered design into practice, and we will keep improving on the usability of the process. You can contact us through our Web site: www.foruse.com.

TOWARD MORE USABLE SOFTWARE

1

SOFTWARE FOR USE: Usage, Usability, and User Interfaces

UPGRADING USABILITY

We were headed for Australia via San Francisco, and the limo was already 20 minutes late picking us up. A quick call to the limousine service got us a simple but unwelcome explanation. The wrong date had been entered into their computer, so they were all prepared to pick us up on Monday instead of Sunday. We hurriedly piled our luggage into the back of our car and took off. Some adept driving combined with light Sunday traffic meant that we still made it to Boston's Logan Airport with nearly an hour to spare.

"I just need to reissue these tickets to include the upgrade from your banked miles," the agent at the ticket counter told us as she began typing away into her computer terminal. "Don't worry, you have plenty of time." Ah, but there was a problem. The system would not accept the fare code. The fare on which our complex itinerary had been calculated, having expired, was no longer recognized by the system, even though countless valid tickets, ours among them, were still outstanding. Not to worry, we were told, there were ways around this problem. "Happens all the time," the agent said with a pleasant smile as she began copying information from our tickets, manually reentering data the system had only a minute earlier displayed in full detail. Besides all our personal details and the legs of our itinerary, dozens of obscure codes had to be flawlessly copied, character for character, from the printed tickets. On several occasions, the agent would navigate her way to one screen, scroll through data, write down a code or identification number on a scrap of paper, and then navigate to another screen where she typed the same code again into another part of the system.

We told her that we were software usability consultants and commiserated with her as she suffered good naturedly at the hands of a punishing user interface.

Some 45 minutes and countless keyboard operations later, we had our new tickets and boarding passes and were headed for the gate. It had taken us longer to check in at the airport than to drive there from 32 miles away.

On a later occasion, we watched another agent complete this unexceptional task that "happens all the time." It took some 446 keystrokes worth of interactions with half a dozen separate subsystems to process one ticket, and that, we were told, was one of the relatively easy cases. So much for the power of modern computer systems. One agent remarked that it would take less time to write out new tickets in longhand than to process them through the computer software.

What was most amazing to us was that every shred of information these hard-working agents had to laboriously retype was already known to the reservation system, having been previously entered by the travel agent and validated, accepted, and stored by the system. The sundry manual operations and work-arounds needed by the agent to trick the system into reissuing identical tickets at the right fare basis could have been readily automated. It seemed fairly obvious that no one had ever considered this normal interaction—reissuing a ticket with valid upgrade—as a discrete task to be supported by the user interface. What should have involved a single, simple operation was extended into a feature-length on-screen drama. How many passengers each month were annoyed rather than bemused by this fiasco? Not only was the airline embarrassing itself and frustrating its best passengers, but it also was wasting the time of highly trained staff—all because of a system that was not designed for use.

This well-known airline reservation system for one of the world's largest airlines illustrates a number of important points about software usability and its myriad facets. It shows that usability can be a function of policy as well as programming. Encoded in the system was a business rule of questionable legitimacy—namely, that discontinued fare bases and their codes would not be kept in the system once they expired. This example also illustrates that small decisions at the detail level can have a profound effect on efficiency and ease of use. Even a fairly unsophisticated clipboard facility allowing the agent to copy raw text from one part of the system into a clipboard or holding bin and then paste it elsewhere would have reduced entry errors and dramatically cut the time to complete the transaction. Even better would have been an object-based facility for grabbing a ticket record in one place and then plunking it in another.

Much software is designed and built with little consideration for how it will be used and how it can best support the work its users will be doing.

Most importantly, this experience illustrates the significance of organizing the user interface to fit with the actual tasks for which a system will be used. The users of the reservation and ticketing system had been given a tool that was ill-suited for many of the tasks at hand. Clever and persistent people, they had found ways to make it do the work they needed to accomplish, but a better tool could have made these same tasks much simpler. In truth, much software is designed and built with little consideration for how it will be used and how it can best support the work its users will be doing.

Many systems, including some of the most complex and costly, have been constructed with development focused almost entirely on internals, on processing logic and data organization to fulfill narrow concepts of functional objectives. If it works, some would argue, that is enough. If the airline reservation system helps to sell seats and fill planes, that is enough. At what cost, though, to the airline and its customers? What would it have cost to do it right, to have given the counter agents and other users of the system a better tool? As we will see, by focusing first on use and usability rather than on features or functionality, on users and usage more than on user interfaces, systems can be turned into better tools for the job that are smaller, simpler, and ultimately less expensive.

HOMO HABILIS

Humans are tool users. We use tools to extend our grasps, to see beyond the horizon and beneath the soil, to build things and to tear them down. We use tools to carry things and to move ourselves. We use them to make goods and even to make other tools.

All software systems are tools, and software developers are, therefore, tool builders. Whether we are writing routine business applications for internal use by our employers or we are part of a team developing shrink-wrap software for sale, whether our programs are only new twists on old standards or we are devising exotic control programs for a new generation of peripherals, we are building tools. It is fashionable to speak of the "art" of computer programming and to emphasize the creative elements of design, but Avram Miller of Intel once said, "We are toolmakers, not artists." This

> *All software systems are tools, and software developers are, therefore, tool builders.*

strikes us as a noble undertaking. Tools help people accomplish things. Good tools help people achieve what they want to or need to in less time or with less effort or more simply. Even computer games can be thought of as tools in that they help people have fun or learn or improve eye–hand coordination or just relax.

This book is a toolkit for toolmakers, a collection of tools devised and assembled to help the professionals who develop computer software and applications. These tools are conceptual levers for making it easier to pry loose essential ideas about how software is to be used and for manipulating designs into proper shape to fit that usage. Many of these conceptual tools were crafted to help design **user interfaces**—those points of contact between systems and their users. However, this book is about more than just the layout of screens or the sequencing of interaction.

It is about designing user interfaces and the systems to which they give access so that these are more useful and more usable to the companies and customers who depend on them.

THE QUALITY OF USE

What makes a thing useful? In one tax office in Australia, a completely computerized system had been created merely to control the queuing of people making inquiries. For each patron, the computer printed a sequentially numbered slip of paper and then displayed on full-color monitors the number to be served next and the window at which it was to be served. The simple ticket-dispensing machine commonly used at delicatessens and bakeries probably would have sufficed, but it would not have blended as well with the elegant decor of the office nor, perhaps, have justified quite so convincingly the need for more tax dollars. Ironically, impressive though the system was, it failed to fulfill completely its intended if inappropriate purpose. Patrons seemed unable to read or correctly interpret the monitor display, so a uniformed attendant watching the monitor announced aloud each number as it appeared and directed its holder to the appropriate window.

> *Even software that is capable, in theory, of performing desired tasks will not be fully useful if we cannot make it perform those tasks in practice.*

Utility means that a system does something worthwhile, something that is, in itself, of sufficient value to justify the investment in equipment and programming. In other words, to make useful software, we have to choose appropriate problems to solve. Sadly, all too many software systems, like the tax office dispatcher, are sorely lacking in elementary utility.

Utility may seem to be more a matter of management and policy-making than of software engineering, but software developers have an important role in increasing utility. By better understanding the real requirements and supplying systems to support what users truly need, systems analysts and designers stand to deliver more useful systems. Recognizing the importance of utility as a component of usefulness, they are in a better position to steer projects toward appropriate problems or the most utilitarian portions of problems.

Capability is also required for usefulness. A system must be capable, at least in principle, of doing what it is supposed to do. Whatever problem we choose to solve, the functionality for performing the necessary tasks must be coded somewhere within the system. A communications program that will not link through a server modem will be of little use in a networked environment, for example. As with utility, here, too, developers have a contribution to make by better understanding real requirements and more directly supporting them in software.

Both capability and utility are essential but are not sufficient for usefulness. Software that does not include necessary features or that solves the wrong problem is not going to be terribly useful. But even software that is capable, in theory, of performing desired tasks will not be fully useful if we cannot make it perform those tasks in practice. Users must be able to get the software to do its thing—to process the data or perform whatever feats it was intended to perform. In other words, systems must be usable to be most useful. The airline ticketing software, for example, may have had utility and capability—it solved important problems and provided necessary functions—but it fell short when it came to usability.

Usability is the central subject of this book. It is a more complicated matter than utility and capability because it is about systems in interaction with people, a point where matters become muddier and messier. It is not possible to talk about usability without thinking in terms of people and the impact a system has on the people who use it. Usability is influenced by many factors. Highly usable systems are easy for people to learn how to use and easy for people to use productively. They make it easy to remember from one use to another how they are used. Highly usable systems help people to work efficiently while making fewer mistakes. Like a finely crafted woodworking tool, a beautifully bound book, or a superbly engineered set of golf clubs, the best systems give pleasure and satisfaction; they make people feel good about using them.

We can think of these characteristics as five facets of usability, as different aspects of a system and its user interface that contribute to usability [compare Nielsen, 1993: 25 ff.]:

- Learnability
- Rememberability
- Efficiency in use
- Reliability in use
- User satisfaction

Software should be easy to learn how to use, and, once learned, remembering how to use it should be easy as well. Software should also be efficient to use, leading to greater productivity on the part of its users. Often, of course, there is a trade-off between making software easy to learn and to remember on the one hand and making it efficient to use on the other. Systems that walk a user slowly, step-by-step through a complex task are sometimes easier to learn, but the same approach can prevent the well-trained user from working quickly. Effectively resolving this engineering trade-off is one of the more

> *Systems that walk a user slowly, step-by-step through a complex task are sometimes easier to learn, but the same approach can prevent the well-trained user from working quickly.*

interesting challenges in designing usable software, one to which we will return in later chapters.

Unlike computers, which often seem nearly infallible, people are inherently and highly error-prone. Software that leads its users to make fewer mistakes will be more reliable in use—that is, in how it functions in combination with its users and in how it promotes reliable human performance. Such software is clearly more usable than software that leads its users into error or merely leaves them to their own devices. Of course, software should be reliable in itself as well. Both internal reliability and reductions in human error may contribute to usability, but reliability in use is more closely tied with user interface design than with coding and debugging. The design of the airline ticketing system, for example, may have been highly reliable in itself, but it greatly multiplied the number of user errors by requiring the manual reentering of complex codes copied from one part of the user interface to another.

> *Users who are annoyed or unhappy, bored or fatigued, are likely to make more mistakes and to work less efficiently.*

Finally, software that satisfies users, leaving them subjectively pleased about their experience using it, is more useful than software that irritates or displeases users. User satisfaction is not just a sales slogan. Satisfying software is likely to be used more often and used more effectively. Users who are annoyed or unhappy, bored or fatigued, are likely to make more mistakes and to work less efficiently. User satisfaction, elusive though it may be, can also make a contribution to usability.

Usable software is quality software, and usability is one measure of software quality. The classic view of software quality, reinforced in recent times by the so-called Total Quality Management movement, has focused primarily on internal efficiency and reliability—that is, on the efficiency and reliability of the code in operation. Other aspects of software quality have sometimes been considered, including generality, flexibility, maintainability, and modifiability *of code* [Yourdon and Constantine, 1979: 8–13]. However, when the view of software begins to shift outward from a limited internal perspective to an external one that more fully considers customers and end users, usability, along with utility and capability, are clearly seen as key factors in software quality.

ECONOMICS OF USABILITY

Users and usability are important for developers to understand because the way developers deal with users and with their need for useful tools can dramatically affect the cost of development and the time it takes to deliver new systems. One study [Lederer and Prasad, 1992] found that the four most frequently cited reasons for cost overruns in software development projects all concerned users and the uses of software. The foremost cause of cost overruns was frequent requests for changes from users, which is not surprising, considering that the second leading cause was overlooked but necessary tasks. Third rated was the users' own lack of understanding of their requirements. Fourth highest was insufficient user–analyst communication.

These causes of cost overruns are clearly interconnected. As analysts and designers, we are not talking enough with our users. Often, users do not understand their own problems, and, since we are not communicating sufficiently with them, we are not helping them to understand or to articulate their needs. Consequently, important tasks are being overlooked, and systems are being designed without needed features and facilities. As a result, users make frequent requests for changes that delay delivery and drive up costs. Better communication between users and developers, with particular emphasis on building an understanding of the real requirements of users, produces adequate systems more cheaply and efficiently.

The usability of the delivered product also has important economic implications. It takes time to learn how to use software effectively, and the harder it is to use a system, the longer it will take users to learn to use it well. Time spent climbing the learning curve is time that users are not being fully productive. Moreover, training itself takes time and costs money. An entire industry thrives on the challenges of learning to use modern software tools by conducting pricey seminars, publishing fat how-to books, and producing dazzling multimedia training

> *Time spent climbing the learning curve is time that users are not being fully productive.*

materials. Internal software training has also become a major cost of doing business within some sectors, such as banking, telecommunications, and insurance, which rely particularly heavily on information technology.

Trying to use complex, hard-to-use software can be a frustrating, tiresome experience that leaves users dissatisfied. Perhaps these effects may seem unimportant, but tired, frustrated, unhappy users make more mistakes. Fatigued users who are more prone to error are less productive. It costs money and time to find and correct mistakes, and undiscovered errors that enter a database or propagate through a system may be the most costly of all.

Technical support for software products has become a major cost of information technology. Software vendors are increasingly finding it necessary to charge for technical support because the cost of providing telephone help lines staffed by trained operators continues to rise. Some companies have been inundated by calls for technical support after the release of new products with major usability problems. Internally operated help desks for software created in-house are becoming a substantial budget item within many companies. It can be difficult to track the cost of the support provided informally by colleagues, but the economic impact of ad hoc and unofficial technical support may also be sizable. Such informal peer support involves all those times you turn to your office mate to ask how to do something with a piece of software or all those occasions when you walk down the hall to get the local tool guru to show you, once more, the trick for opening auxiliary files without switching windows. A 1995 *ComputerWorld* survey in Australia found these informal and usually undocumented costs to be running between A\$6,000 and A\$20,000 per year for each workstation. Even without accounting for the lost productivity due to work being interrupted and taking time to resume, these costs are not difficult to understand once you add up the salaries and overhead for at least two well-paid professionals every time an informal consultation occurs.

The costs of poorly designed, hard-to-use software are incurred not only by the ultimate users but also by the original developers. Unusable features or facilities that are difficult to master lead to requests for changes. Reworks and revisions are often precipitated by usability problems. Instead of moving on to work on new systems, developers remain chained to old ones that must be revised to correct usability defects. They end up having to solve the same problems again and again, reconsidering the same user interface design issues because they lack standard solutions, systematic approaches, or effective guidelines. In the process, relationships with customers and users worsen. For the in-house developers of software destined for use within the same company, usability problems can add significantly to the strain and stress in relations with end users and internal clients. In the long run, the cost to internal developers can be their jobs, as more and more companies and institutions consider outsourcing information systems development as a way to cut costs and obtain better products and service.

> *Usability problems can add significantly to the strain and stress in relations with end users and clients. In the long run, the cost to developers can be their jobs.*

For companies producing software to sell, usability problems no doubt account for a significant portion of returns and lost sales, although these proportions are difficult to quantify. Even in the worst cases, customers are unlikely to cite user interface or usability issues when returning software since very few are likely to admit they could not figure out how to use a package. Instead, they will report that the software was incompatible with their systems or unsuited to their problems. And lost sales due to inferior usability or the superiority of a competitor's product are likely to remain a manifest but unfathomable mystery in most cases.

Over the long run, producing hard-to-use products with inferior user interfaces has another effect on developers. In our experience, almost no professional wants to produce shoddy systems. Most programmers and analysts prefer to take pride in their work. When impossible schedules, incomplete analyses, or lack of knowledge, skills, or tools repeatedly force developers to deliver inferior software, morale is eroded. When morale declines, so does productivity.

In short, low usability costs money. Both software developers and software users alike have a substantial economic stake in improving the usability of software.

SELLING INFORMATION TECHNOLOGY

To succeed, software has to sell. Management has to be convinced of the value of a proposed application. Potential customers have to see a package as meeting a perceived need. Users have to be persuaded to use a program. The hard rule of economic advantage ultimately governs success, whether the software is sold to a single sponsor who foots the entire bill or is burned onto CD-ROMs and mass-marketed to the general public.

Usability has not always been a selling factor for software. Programs of prodigious difficulty have achieved wide distribution and use; ugly and obscure user interfaces have survived over long periods. In every area of computer application, there is a primitive stage where the mere capability for doing something useful, however crudely accomplished, is enough for success in the marketplace or with management. Consultant Jared Spool refers to this as the "raw iron" phase of product life. The first word processors, for example, were beasts, but they still beat typing and retyping documents by hand. Users put up with the pain of interpreting format codes and memorizing arbitrary function keys because the payoff was being able to save, edit, reformat, and reprint material on demand. Besides, these systems were the only game in town.

> *There is a primitive stage where the mere capability for doing something useful, however crudely accomplished, is enough for success.*

But applications evolve. Designers and developers keep designing and developing, and basic facilities become augmented and elaborated. Users start wanting more functions and features, and, as the attention of clients and consumers shifts from *mere* capability to *more* capability, developers comply. Marketing then centers on feature lists because every added feature has value in convincing someone to buy a product or to buy into a project. Amar Bose, of stereo speaker fame, aptly summarized this phase of product evolution by saying that, to the marketing mind, the "perfect product is something that has one more knob and is one dollar cheaper" [*Wall Street Journal*, December 31, 1996].

The trend to add more knobs cannot continue indefinitely, however. Systems do not typically become cheaper as they become more complex; they become more costly. Eventually, too, there comes a point where additional knobs and features just make a system more unwieldy, not more capable.

As users and customers grow accustomed to using computer applications, they grow less patient with them. They and their bosses expect steady improvement in efficiency and productivity, but there comes a time when improvements can no longer be achieved through additional features. Usability then assumes greater and greater salience in decisions regarding which piece of software to buy, which to build, and which to use. Software developers and software sellers thus have to pay closer attention to usability as their users and their markets mature.

APPROACHING USABILITY

How can we satisfy the expanding need for more usable software? The usability of software can be improved through a variety of means, but a handful of well-established approaches account for most attempts. The best accepted and most widely used approaches include usability testing, style guides and standards, expert consultation, and iterative prototyping. Unfortunately, although sometimes effective, these techniques all have significant shortcomings.

TESTING, TESTING

Far and away the most popular and widely practiced approach for improving software usability is usability testing. To some people, usability laboratories and usability testing are virtually synonymous with software usability engineering. One Australian firm even has a trademarked technique called "Usability by Design" that is, on close examination, more a matter of repeated testing and review than of design.

Usability testing is based on standard techniques that are well known and widely taught. Testing can be conducted either under controlled conditions in a usability testing laboratory or under more or less normal working conditions in field tests at work sites. Laboratory and field techniques for usability testing have somewhat different strengths and weaknesses and are probably best used in combination whenever time and budget permit. Many companies also look to beta-testing, in which a preliminary version of a system is released to selected customers and users, as a major source of information about usability problems. Beta-testing can be thought of as an uncontrolled and usually unsupervised variation of field techniques for usability testing. Done well, usability testing in one form or another can be an effective tool to improve the usability of software, but both laboratory and field approaches have major limitations.

For good reason, one of the axioms of software quality is that you cannot test your way to quality. This applies to software usability as much as to any other aspect of software quality. The biggest problem with all testing techniques is that they tend to come late in the product development process. To conduct tests, you have to have something to test, and that typically requires either a working version of the system under development, a relatively complete simulation, or a fully functional prototype. By the time most forms of testing, including usability testing, become practical, a substantial amount of development has already been completed, and much or most of the design will have been committed to code in one form or another.

The cost of finding and fixing any form of software defect increases with time. The cost curve looks something like that of Figure 1-1. If we spot a misspelled variable name when we first type it, the cost of correction is the time it takes to hit the backspace key and retype the name. If we compile and run the component without catching the error, it may take some sleuthing to uncover the reason for incorrect output. If the problem should slip through until we have integrated the various components and are testing the system as a whole, it can take some serious and protracted detective work to find the problem. Once a system has been delivered, the cost of identifying and correcting a defect can jump sharply. One laser printer manufacturer determined that a single defect in the embedded programming, such that it required upgrading printers already in the field, would cost more than all of the expected profit over the product's entire market life. Better to get it right in the first place. To improve quality, defect prevention—through better methods applied more effectively—is far more efficient and cost effective than defect detection and removal.

> *Usability testing can be an effective tool to improve the usability of software, but you cannot test your way to quality.*

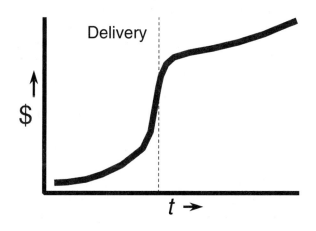

FIGURE 1-1 *The rising cost of corrections.*

A common outcome of usability testing, however refined and successful, is that many of the findings from the tests end up being ignored. The same can often be said for the recommendations of usability and user interface design experts when their opinions are sought relatively late in the development process. In either case, the problems uncovered often do not get corrected because the necessary changes are deemed to be too extensive or expensive. Those changes that do get made are likely to be the more superficial ones because those are the easiest to effect in completed code. The end result is that relatively superficial or cosmetic changes are made to solve deeper problems that are actually architectural in nature.

Some professionals would argue that usability testing can be conducted early in the development process by carrying out "tests" with designs in the form of drawings or pictures. Clearly, user tests conducted through pretended interactions with a nonworking prototype are quite different in kind from having a user perform real work with a functioning system. Such investigations can be very worthwhile, but they are best thought of as a form of inspection or review rather than as a variant of genuine laboratory or field testing. We do not call it a test when two programmers look over an outline for a program component or when consumers are asked to react to a model of a new automobile. In all of engineering, testing invariably refers to experimentation or trial use of working systems, prototypes, or simulations that function to some degree.

Another limitation of usability testing is the coverage problem common to all forms of testing. No test plan can be expected to cover all the possible combinations of interaction with a typical software system. Testing is based on probabilities and can uncover only some fraction of existing problems. Laboratory usability testing, despite advantages in revealing problems that may otherwise be difficult to recognize, may be especially inefficient relative to its cost for finding most usability defects.

> *Usability testing becomes more efficient and cost effective when applied selectively to a well-thought-out design that is already basically sound.*

One can also argue that all testing approaches are inherently inefficient for reducing defects. Testing rests implicitly on a model of development that begins with designing and coding a system incorrectly, then proceeds to identifying the defects and finding their causes, and finally finishes with correcting the defects and testing those corrections. This model, which permeates software development, in some sense charges three times for a single job.

Our central argument throughout this book is that it is always better to design and build a system right in the first place. In fact, usability testing becomes more efficient and cost effective when applied selectively to a well-thought-out design that is already basically sound. We will have more to say about the most effective uses of usability testing in Chapter 18.

POPULAR STYLE

In terms of popularity, user interface style guides and standards manuals probably come a close second behind testing as a route for those seeking improved usability. All the major platform vendors promulgate standard styles for the user interfaces of software to run on their systems, and many companies also commission or create their own guidelines for in-house software development.

The rationale for style guides and standards manuals as contributors to improved software usability is twofold. First, standards promote consistency, and consistency is a significant factor in making user interfaces easier to learn and to remember. Standards appeal especially to the corporate mentality that desires set solutions to set problems. Second, well-conceived standards and style guidelines can reflect the best practices in user interface design. Adhering to best-practice solutions, as reflected in available standards, can lead to better software. User interface standards and style guides can also save developers time. Referring to them can replace continued rethinking of old issues and coming up with unique solutions to every superficially different problem.

Unfortunately, the field of standards and style guides is riddled with potholes and pitfalls. Industry standards are often ignored, even by the very software companies that developed them and that call for others to adhere to them. In truth, it may be all but impossible to follow the published standards and guidelines in practice. Advice on one page is contradicted by rules on another, and there are more pages than any ordinary developer can be expected to understand and recall. Despite their encyclopedic appearance, published standards and style guides may leave the majority of questions unanswered. Jared Spool has reported that only about 10% of the user interface design questions raised by developers over the course of a typical project can be answered by reference to platform-based published guides. Another 10% or so may be covered by the corporate standards developed in-house by particular companies. In other words, even if used well and used consistently, user interface standards manuals and style guides will leave developers in the dark or on their own most of the time.

> *Often, the standards are ignored, even by the companies that developed them.*

BUILD IT AGAIN

Rapid iterative prototyping and refinement are at the heart of many modern software development life cycle (SDLC) models. The basic idea is to build something small and relatively simple as quickly as possible, initially as a prototype, then try it out, and then revise the system based on information gained from trial usage.

Building a system is generally more difficult than building a prototype. Building a new shopping plaza takes a lot more time and resources than does assembling an architect's scale model for the project. In software design, unlike in the construction trades, prototypes are often used as a substitute for design, the attitude being that there is no need to design, since it is merely a prototype being coded. Only slightly more refined is the view that the prototype can serve as a design or that repeated prototyping can serve as the sole design process. Prototypes and prototyping are not substitutes for analysis and design, not excuses for sloppy thinking. Even the most thoroughgoing prototype can obscure important issues, such as database organization or partitioning between client and server.

> *Prototypes and prototyping are not substitutes for analysis and design, not excuses for sloppy thinking.*

Software prototypes of all kinds do have their uses. Prototyping can test the feasibility of an approach, and prototypes can serve as a proof of concept for radically new software. Most importantly, prototypes can be an effective tool for communication between developers and users. Prototypes convey in clear and concrete terms what designers have in mind for a system and can evoke rich reactions from users. However, prototypes must not be confused with finished systems, and many users have some tendency to look at more sophisticated working prototypes as if they were the next thing to final products. Developers, too, may, on occasion, try to fob off a prototype as a substitute for the real thing. It is worth noting that software engineering is the only engineering discipline that tries to sell prototypes as finished goods.

House construction offers a classic analogue for modern iterative software prototyping: the New England farmhouse. The typical New England farmhouse may have started as a modest cottage, but, over generations of remodeling and expansion, it evolves into a sprawling collage of buildings and additions in disparate styles. It is, at best, a practical kludge with no real architecture, no plan, no design, and hence no consistency. While uneven floorboards and odd-sized rooms may appeal to some home owners as quaint or even charming, software users are seldom charmed by quaint designs in computer software.

> *The lack of overall planning in iterative refinement means that a point is reached when the underlying code in the software fails whenever a change or enhancement is attempted.*

An iterative model of construction does allow for large projects to be completed in small steps with shorter planning horizons. Unfortunately, the lack of overall planning that often comes with iterative refinement means that a point is reached when the farmhouse foundation will not support another balcony or dormer or when the underlying code in the software fails whenever a change or enhancement is attempted. In the exceptional case, where such problems remain manageable over the long term, the result may be perpetual revision to a system that is never quite finished.

TAKE A LOOK AT THIS

Many developers who are concerned about the usability of the software they develop rely on design reviews in one form or another to identify usability problems and improve user interfaces. User interface reviews, especially if done informally, are simple and straightforward to introduce into almost any software development environment or process. All that may be needed is to encourage designers and programmers to show their work to their colleagues for comments and suggestions. Reviews, unless they break down into all-out warfare among developers with divergent opinions, will, with reasonable luck, promote collaboration. Even the least effective review process can spread ideas and contribute to information-sharing among developers. Reviews are appealing to many managers and developers because they need not take a lot of time. An hour or two poring over a set of screen layouts can lead to major improvements in a user interface.

The biggest problem with peer reviews is that they have some tendency to lead to long, unproductive debates and discussions. Software professionals often have strong opinions and little hesitance to support their views. Take any two programmers, goes the popular wisdom, and you will get three strong opinions. An hour of vigorous debate over the merits of floating, dockable toolbars may be interesting, even entertaining, but it is not likely to be the best use of time for a team of six professionals. Informal peer reviews, especially when not well organized or carefully structured, may be relatively inefficient even if they are relatively inexpensive.

The quality of a peer review may also be sharply limited by the quality of the experience of the peers. Developers with little or no knowledge of the subtleties of software usability are unlikely to succeed as critical reviewers, regardless of how highly motivated and concerned about usability they may be. The secret to success is to involve knowledgeable developers in inspections that are well organized and conducted for efficient discovery of usability defects. How to do this is the subject of Chapter 16.

EXPERT OPINION

Experts and specialists in user interface design, usability engineering, and human–computer interaction have become an important resource in the software field. Whether hired or retained under contract, usability experts offer instant capability without having to climb the learning curve. Trained usability specialists can be cost effective in some capacities, such as for expert evaluation of designs, even when they are relatively expensive (as they are likely to be).

Unfortunately, there are not enough adequately trained experts to meet the needs of all the world's software development projects. Even when appropriate, using experts to solve usability problems can leave developers as much in the dark as ever. In many cases, there is little or no transfer of skills or knowledge. A project team may get a full accounting of usability problems in its design, along with a set of recommendations for improving the software, but team members can remain clueless as to why one thing is a problem while another is not and ignorant of how conclusions or solutions were reached. They may see the problems but do not learn how to avoid them in the next project.

CHANGING CONTEXTS

Almost continuously over its brief history, the process of software development has been changing. It has changed in almost every dimension and aspect. Where once coding was an eremitic practice, it now is a team process. Where once programmers made conversions from decimal to octal addresses in their heads, they now connect program objects by drawing a line from one box on a screen to another.

The social and economic context in which software and computer applications are developed has also changed dramatically in recent years. In areas as diverse as consumer products, video games, and satellite communications technology, engineers are being challenged to deliver new products in less and less time. Both the viable life span of products in the marketplace and the time available in which to produce the next generation have been shortening. Newly reengineered cell phones are being paraded off assembly lines every six months, and radically redesigned versions of major software products are being expected almost as quickly. Where once new business applications might have been developed in programming projects lasting many months or even years, more and more developers are finding themselves working within development "time boxes," with new systems scheduled for completion in 90 or 120 days. Under the pressure of competition that is spread around the globe, management is expecting us all to produce better software in less time. At the same time as the twin demands for higher-quality systems in less time have been growing, the demand for professional developers has outstripped the supply. Many understaffed development teams are coping with oversized projects.

Increasingly, in almost every corner of the marketplace, product development is becoming client-centered and customer-driven. The "voice of the customer" has grown louder and is being listened to with greater care and attention. Customers expect systems to fit their needs more closely than ever, and they have grown used to having their input solicited and heeded.

While socioeconomic conditions have been changing, the technology of development has also continued to evolve. Object technology, client-server architecture, and graphical user interfaces (GUIs) and other new techniques and technology have all placed new demands on developers. The advent of visual programming and visual development environments, such as Visual Basic and Delphi, while offering solutions to some problems, has placed further challenges in front of developers. In short, software and applications development is being called on to deliver more and better systems, more quickly, using new technologies, but with fewer resources.

Effective strategies for improving software usability must take all these pressures and constraints into account, and they must recognize

> *Most decisions regarding the user interface or affecting the usability of software are made by ordinary developers—systems analysts, designers, even programmers—not by experts in human–computer interaction or trained usability professionals.*

how systems become as usable or unusable as they are. The majority of decisions about usability and user interfaces are not made by experts in human–computer interaction or trained usability professionals. They are not even being made in consultation with such experts. Most decisions regarding the user interface or affecting the usability of software are made by ordinary developers—systems analysts, designers, even programmers—with no special training or experience regarding software usability or user interface design. Developers determine the placement of visual components on the user interface; they write the code that determines how the user interface behaves; they determine the contents of messages and the conditions under which these will be displayed.

Developers, the frontline troops of software, need to be empowered by better tools and techniques if they are to deliver highly usable software on restricted schedules and budgets. They will need simple and highly efficient methods for fitting systems to usage. This book is about just such methods. Usage-centered design helps developers focus on the essential core of tasks that need to be supported by software. Using simple yet powerful

> *Developers, the frontline troops of software, need to be empowered by better tools and techniques to deliver usable software.*

tools and concepts that are easy to learn and apply, usage-centered design offers solutions to the usability challenges confronting software developers.

2

BUILT-IN USABILITY:
A Usage-Centered Design Approach

INTERFACING WITH USERS

Computer programming and software development did not always have a concern for users or a focus on the usability of systems. In the 1950s and 1960s, when modern business and scientific computing began to come into its own as an industry and a profession, **users**—that is, the ultimate end users of the results of computations—did not typically get anywhere near computers. The machines—large, expensive, and often more than a little bit temperamental—were attended like electronic idols by duly anointed operators and fed their programs and data by properly initiated programmers. Only the operators, the service technicians, and a few select others actually flipped switches or pressed buttons on the control console of one of those sluggish giants. The users of information were handed a report or a table of numbers and considered themselves lucky if the columns were formatted so that the numbers could be easily read.

In the strictest sense, the input fields of punched cards and the lines and columns of printed reports could be said to have constituted the user interface for early applications, but these physical artifacts of data processing were seldom thought of as an interface with users. They were considered to be merely the inputs and the outputs of the program; the layout of input fields or the formatting of printed reports was just another part of the programming. Customers, clients, managers, and supervisors always factored into the programming equation—somebody had to approve the results or pay the invoice—but users, as such, did not exist. True, keypunch operators had to cope with the arrangement of input fields or manage the conversion from printed forms to machinable data, but they were hardly thought of as users. Managers might study a monthly printout, but they were not considered users of the software, only users of the report.

MOTHERS OF USABILITY

The first real users of electronic computers were programmers, and the first programmers were women. Betty Holberton and Jean Bartik headed the all-female team of programmers for the original Eniac built in 1945. Convinced that computers needed to be made easier to program and operate in order to become effective and widely used tools, the women introduced a number of innovations to improve the usability of early machines.

Bartik collaborated with mathematician Adele Goldstine to make the Eniac easier to reprogram by reworking it to function as a stored program machine. Holberton, highly concerned with what she referred to as "human engineering," would first figure out what people needed and then convince her male engineering colleagues that the ideas were theirs. She later developed the first primitive assembly language for Univac, basing it on the radical human-oriented scheme of mnemonic op-codes. In her efforts to make the Univac friendlier to its users, the programmers and operators, she designed the control panel with what was to become an all-but-universal feature of modern computer interfaces—a numeric keypad next to a typewriter keyboard.

Men may have claimed the patents and dominated the headlines in those early days of computing, but the pioneers of computer usability were women [Petzinger, 1996].

User interfaces became a major issue in most software development only when people other than programmers or operators began to have direct, hands-on access to computers. By the early 1960s, several developments conspired to shift the attention of programmers from a complete preoccupation with internals, the insides of machines and programs, to those points where the systems met the outside world. The modern concept of user interfaces in computing effectively dates from the arrival of terminals connected directly or indirectly with computers. As more people could interact with computers directly, the interface between these users and the computer with its programs became a subject of increasing importance for the designers and developers of programs. Minicomputers—small and cheap by comparison to their mainframe ancestors—made it possible for a programmer or a nuclear physicist or someone else with a computational problem to sit beside a box not much bigger than a large refrigerator and type the details of a problem on a typewriter keyboard. Under control of the program, the results could be typed back on the typewriter device or even displayed on an oscilloscope screen. Time-sharing, the forerunner of network and client-server computing, gave dozens of people, dozens of *users*, simultaneous access to one large computer through scattered terminals.

What began as a strictly technical issue—how does the computer program interact with the user through devices such as typewriter terminals—only gradually evolved into a concern with users themselves. The slow rise of **user-centered design** [Norman and Draper, 1986] represented a gradual shift from a focus on technology (user interfaces) to a focus on people (users). User-centered design, if truly and faithfully practiced, placed people at the very heart of the system design process. As it evolved, user-centered design was redubbed "user-centric" design by a profession obsessed with technical neologisms. Under either title, it has become the dominant force in user interface design for software in recent decades.

Users may feel better for the attention they receive through user-centered design, but placing them at the center of the development process does not necessarily give them better systems. Good systems are good tools, and good tools are designed to fit the purposes for which they will be used. Good tools make work easier, simpler, faster, or more enjoyable, or they make it possible to accomplish what otherwise could not be accomplished. To design dramatically more usable tools, it is not users who must be understood, but usage—how and for what ends software tools will be employed. Appropriately, this emerging view of systems as tools is referred to as **usage-centered design** [Constantine, 1996d]. Usage-centered design focuses on the work that users are trying to accomplish and on what the software will need to supply via the user interface to help them accomplish it.

> *User-centered design represents a shift of focus from technology to people, from user interfaces to users. To design dramatically more usable tools, however, it is not users who must be understood, but usage.*

ELEMENTS OF A USAGE-CENTERED APPROACH

The approach to usage-centered design covered in this book is the product of repeated refinement and redesign, honed by our experience and the experiences of our many students and clients. It is based on what works—what has most consistently and expeditiously yielded the best results for real developers working on real problems. We have tried to keep applying the philosophy and principles of usability to the improvement of the design process itself, maintaining a pragmatic focus, streamlining activities for efficiency, and simplifying the techniques and explanations. We have devised techniques as needed to solve problems and incorporated concepts when these helped to organize our thinking. We have abandoned methods that proved inefficient, and we have condensed and reorganized ideas whenever it made them more understandable.

Usage-centered design incorporates five key elements that, taken together, can lead to significant improvements in the usability of software. These elements include

- Pragmatic design guidelines
- Model-driven design process
- Organized development activities
- Iterative improvement
- Measures of quality

Although these elements combine to form a coherent approach, they can also be considered separately as techniques for improving software usability and user interface design. After the five elements are described briefly, two of them, model-driven design and organized development processes, will be discussed in considerably more detail in this chapter.

PRINCIPAL PRINCIPLES

Usage-centered design is founded on a set of basic guidelines to help designers make reasonable decisions that lead to highly usable systems. These guidelines contribute to the goals of designing systems that are learnable, rememberable, efficient, reliable, and satisfying to use—the aspects of usability introduced in Chapter 1. The guidelines include both usability rules and design principles. The "rules" of usability define the general character of what constitutes well-designed, usable systems. These rules provide broad, overall directions for user interface design, pointing designers toward generally superior solutions. In contrast, the design principles in usage-centered design provide narrower guidance on more specific issues in software usability.

MODELS AND MODELING

Because of its focus on understanding the work and the working objectives of users, usage-centered design has evolved into a model-driven process. Through models, developers can better understand usage and more readily represent their understanding in ways that assist communication with users and guide the work of programmers. Usage-centered design employs a set of simple, interrelated models to model both the nature of the uses to which a system will be put and the organization of a user interface that effectively supports those uses.

DEVELOPMENT PROCESSES

Although some software developers prefer to work in a wholly personal and spontaneous manner, most modern software and applications development projects are completed in accord with some form of procedure or organized process. The activities of usage-centered design can be incorporated into almost any software development life cycle model, however elaborate or Spartan, however rigorous or informal. Usage-centered design is a streamlined process that can be scaled to suit projects of varying size and scope. Its activities can be flexibly rearranged to suit various objectives or constraints, and many of the activities can be carried out concurrently for greater efficiency and faster delivery of software.

ITERATIVE IMPROVEMENT

Getting a system exactly right the first time is very difficult, if not impossible. The usage-centered approach incorporates successive refinements based on the findings from usability inspections and tests. Actual implementation can be completed in a series of iterations, starting with a central core of most needed features and facilities and expanding outward. In this manner, a working and usable system can be quickly deployed and then steadily improved with further work.

QUALITY MEASURES

The usage-centered design process is supported by an innovative suite of software metrics that allow developers to assess the quality of user interface designs. These metrics can augment usability inspections, reviews, and testing by giving early indications of the relative quality of designs. Usable with visual designs or with paper prototypes, the metrics allow comparisons of design alternatives without requiring them to be first reduced to practice in the form of simulations, working systems, or functioning prototypes.

DRIVING MODELS

Modeling has always been a part of software development, beginning with the use of flowcharts and their sundry descendants to model the procedures and algorithms that were coded in early programming languages. Modeling for analysis and design came into its own with the rise of structured design [Stevens, Myers, and Constantine, 1974; Yourdon and Constantine, 1979] and the panoply of later approaches to software engineering. Analysis and design models, from structure charts to object-communication diagrams, data flow diagrams to finite state machines, have since become integral to the core curricula in computing science and software engineering and part of the everyday practice of legions of programming professionals.

Models have many uses and advantages in the development process [Constantine, 1994f], foremost in helping developers to organize their thinking. Through models, analysts and designers can put their understanding "out there," on paper or in a computer file, where it can be examined by others, tested, reviewed, and refined. Models can also serve as a succinct and unambiguous language for communication among developers.

Not all software developers make explicit use of models, in part because modeling has gained an unfortunate reputation as a drag on the process of development, as a make-work nuisance to appease customers or satisfy contract obligations or conform to government regulations. To many, models are not a means

> *Models help developers to organize their thinking.*

to better software but a form of advanced documentation that keeps programmers from getting down to work on the "real stuff"—the coding itself. An oft-mentioned consequence of modeling is "analysis paralysis," an all-too-common common malady in which developers become preoccupied with and mired in their models without producing programs. In truth, of course, analysis paralysis is not a shortcoming of models but of how they are used by some developers in some environments. Any activity in the course of software development that becomes an end in itself will hinder rather than hasten development.

Modeling is often the most efficient way to quickly build an understanding of a problem and map out the speediest resolution. Even under the pressure of severely restricted development schedules, teams that take the time to model the problem domain and plan their programming ultimately deliver more complete and better systems than those that plunge directly into coding [Constantine, 1995e]. In many cases, they do so as quickly as or even more quickly than had they skipped over model building altogether.

ATTRACTIVE ABSTRACTIONS

One of the innovations of usage-centered design is the way it employs abstract models to solve concrete problems. Rather than representing the literal actions of users or the concrete objects they manipulate, these models represent abstractions—the concepts and core ideas out of which work is composed and from which supporting systems will be constructed.

There are many advantages to abstractions and abstract models [Constantine, 1996b]. Abstraction is at the very foundation of modern software development practice, from abstract data types to abstract classes. Abstraction gives us the power to think large, to construe the unconstructed and the unconstructible, and to explore the avenues of possible programs without having to walk them all first. Models based on abstractions are necessarily simpler than the things they represent. They hide detail and ignore information selectively and, consequently, are easier to construct than the things they represent. It costs less and takes less time to model the forces and stresses on a bridge than to build the bridge.

Abstract models have, however, played a lesser role among user interface designers and usability professionals. Interaction designers and user interface engineers have tended to do their thinking on paper or on-screen with representations that almost invariably look much like the screens and components they are designing. They do sketches or careful drawings, mock-ups or prototypes. The pictures may sometimes be crude and hastily drawn, they may be monochromatic and even unaesthetic, but they still look like screens and forms and dialogue boxes populated with menus and toolbars, selection lists and option buttons. The most dedicated usability specialists and graphics designers may draft concrete scenarios and paper their offices with elaborate storyboards illustrating the succession of scenes as users interact with proposed software.

Abstract models, by contrast, allow us to defer thinking about such details and keep our attention fixed on the larger picture. Through them, we can see the forest without becoming too distracted by the trees. Abstract user interface models facilitate what has been termed **bifocal modeling** [Muller et al., 1995]. Just as bifocal glasses allow those of us who are over forty to appreciate the scenery and yet to see the subtleties in a small blossom, bifocal modeling helps designers and users move between a panoramic overview and close-in, detailed views of designs and design artifacts.

Abstract models also encourage innovation. By leaving open more options, they invite us to fill in the blanks in imaginative ways. As soon as we draw a pair of scrollbars on a sketch for a window, we have locked ourselves into one way of moving around on a drawing. If, instead, we place an abstract tool called a

> *Abstract models encourage innovation. By leaving open more options, they invite us to fill in the blanks in imaginative ways.*

"drawing navigator" on a model, we start thinking in terms of other possibilities, perhaps a navigation window with a bird's-eye view or a cameralike pan-and-zoom mode. When the time is right, we can consider the alternatives and fill in the blanks, but the longer we resist committing to an easy or a conventional solution, the more likely we are to find a better way.

In our experience, abstract models are a powerful aid to designing better user interfaces. They can help ordinary developers to devise extraordinary interfaces that work dramatically better in practice.

DOWN TO ESSENTIALS

Essential models, a particularly effective form of abstraction, are at the heart of usage-centered design. The roots of essential modeling trace back at least to structured design [Stevens, Myers, and Constantine, 1974], in which data flow diagrams were introduced for defining and describing application requirements apart from the data structures and algorithms by which these requirements might be implemented in software. Essential modeling continued to be refined and improved, eventually becoming a cornerstone of modern structured systems analysis [McMenamin and Palmer, 1984]

Essential models are intended to capture the essence of problems through technology-free, idealized, and abstract descriptions. By assuming perfect technology, such as infinitely fast computers, arbitrarily large displays, keyless input from users, or whatever might most expeditiously realize necessary functions, models can be constructed that are free of unnecessary limitations or restrictive assumptions. The resulting design models are more flexible, leaving open more options and more readily accommodating changes in technology. Technology changes constantly and rapidly; what is not technically or economically feasible today may become so next year or even next month. For example, bar coding, which was once expensive and inaccurate, is now cheap and practical for many uses. Essential models are more robust than concrete representations simply because they are more likely to remain valid in the face of both changing requirements and changes in the technology of implementation.

> *Essential models are more robust than concrete models because they are more likely to remain valid in the face of changing requirements and technology.*

In usage-centered design, essential models can also serve another end. Compared to conventional models based in physical actions or concrete details, essential models of usage highlight purpose—what it is that users are trying to accomplish and why they are doing it—in terms of both the immediate work and the larger context in which interactions are conducted. Essential models help us screen out steps or activities that are artifacts of the concrete implementation or of specific technological assumptions. By identifying and representing the essential aspects of user requirements—the uses to which a system may be put and the interrelationships among these—essential models enable us to design better user interfaces that more simply and straightforwardly meet basic user needs and better support the work that users are trying to accomplish. Systems that support the work with fewer elements and features can actually be smaller and simpler and thus easier to learn, easier to use, and easier to design and build in the first place.

THE ARCHITECTURE OF INTERFACES

The goal of all user interface design is an effective plan or organization for the user interface. An effective plan is not just a matter of selecting visual components—user interface *widgets*, as they are often called—and placing them someplace on a screen or dialogue box. The user interface needs to be organized and to make sense as a whole. The various small pieces need to be collected together in ways that support work and make sense to users, and the various collections need to be interconnected in ways that communicate effectively with users. It is not enough to place the right widgets on a screen if the user cannot figure out which widget to use next. It is not enough to have an attractive and acceptable layout for each screen if the user gets lost in going from one screen to another. What is needed is a good architecture.

The term **user interface architecture** refers to the overall structure, the total organization of the user interface, not merely its detailed appearance. User interface architecture is not about the individual buttons and drop-down lists or even the sundry screens and dialogues on which they appear, but rather about how all these things are integrated into a complete system that makes sense to the user.

Most user interface designers design screens, windows, and widgets; the best ones design user interface architectures.

In modern practice, the final design for a graphical user interface is most often represented by a picture or collection of pictures showing how the various visible components will be arrayed on the screens, dialogue boxes, windows, and panels of the user interface. This picture is referred to as a *visual design* or *paper prototype*. The completed visual design is the guide or pattern from which the actual software user interface will be constructed. It can take many forms,

> *Most user interface designers design screens, windows, and widgets; the best ones design user interface architectures.*

from a rough, hand-drawn sketch to a complete but nonfunctional layout created using an appropriate software tool. (We will have much more to say about prototypes and the alternative ways in which designs can be embodied in later chapters.)

Many design approaches start immediately with a visual design or paper prototype and, through trial and error or successive refinements, arrive at a final design for the user interface and its parts. Usage-centered design takes what may appear to be a more indirect route, but which ultimately proves to be a more efficient and effective way to design good user interface architectures.

MULTIPLE VIEWS

Just as we would not build a house solely on the basis of a sketch of how it looked from the street, we cannot expect to do good user interface design based on a single view. For the house, we would expect to have multiple views from different angles, including specialized views, such as floor plans showing the location of electrical outlets and plumbing fixtures. For the user interface, a sketch of the main screen is not enough. We also need to be able to picture, for example, how different parts of the user interface are interconnected.

A good user interface design is based on a sound user interface architecture, and a sound architecture is one that supports easy and efficient usage. Usage-centered design constructs detailed designs for user interfaces from architectural models of the overall interface organization. Because good user interface architecture is fitted to the structure of usage, usage-centered design, in turn, bases user interface architecture on models of usage.

The set of distinct but interrelated models in usage-centered design allows us to look at our users, their work, and the user interface that will support them from varied viewpoints; it enables us to explore problems and solutions from different angles. The views offered by these models help developers frame the issues and focus on the most vital matters in user interface design. In our experience, three basic models, sometimes supplemented by an additional model, are needed to do

> *The models in usage-centered design help developers frame the issues and focus on the most vital matters in user interface design.*

a thorough job of answering the most vital design questions concerning users, usage, and user interfaces. This may seem like a surfeit of models, but the models are all quite simple and closely related. The process of constructing the interrelated set of models is also made easy and efficient by the way the modeling activities are organized within usage-centered design.

In order to be successful in designing usage-centered software, a number of key questions need to be answered:

- Who are the users and how will they relate to the system?
- What tasks are users trying to accomplish through the system we are designing?
- What do they need from the system in order to accomplish their tasks and how should it be organized?
- What are the operating conditions under which the system will be used?
- What should the user interface look like (or feel like or sound like) and how should it behave?

Models help us represent efficiently and succinctly our answers to these questions. Usage-centered design employs a central core of three simple models that address the first three of these questions relating to users, usage, and architecture, respectively:

- **role model**—the relationships between users and the system
- **task model**—the structure of tasks that users will need to accomplish
- **content model**—the tools and materials to be supplied by the user interface, organized into useful collections and the interconnections among these collections

Each of these core models consists of two parts: a collection of descriptions and a map of the interrelationships among those descriptions. To complete the specification of the user interface design, we employ two additional models:

- **operational model**—the operational context in which the system is deployed and used
- **implementation model**—the visual design of the user interface and description of its operation

To understand what kind of users will be making use of the system, we construct a role model in the form of a collection of **user roles** and a **user role map** defining their interrelationships; to understand what users will be doing with the system, we build a task model in the form of **essential use cases** and a **use case map**. The role model and task model are models of the problem to be solved. To represent what tools and materials will be supplied to support those essential use cases, we employ an **interface context model** along with a **navigation map** defining the interconnections among the various interaction spaces of user interface architecture. These three two-part models will be discussed in detail in Chapters 4, 5, and 6, respectively.

To represent how the design will need to be adapted to the operating context in which it will be deployed and used, we create an operational model. Finally, the implementation model refers to the concrete model in the form of a paper prototype or visual design that shows what the various parts of the implemented user interface are intended to look like. Each of these five models will be explored at length in later chapters.

The three core models are surprisingly simple, yet together they allow us to represent complex problems and sophisticated uses with relative ease.

At the core of usage-centered design are the three abstract models by which we represent the structure of usage and the architecture of the user interface that will support that usage: the role model, task model, and content model. Each of these core models is surprisingly simple, with a minimum of notation and very few conventions to master, yet together they allow us to represent complex problems and sophisticated applications with relative ease.

The role model identifies the roles which users can play. That is, it represents the various forms and patterns of relationships possible between a system and its users. The task model is based on essential use cases that represent specific cases of use in terms of the sundry goals that users can undertake in using a system to accomplish work. In a logical sense, we cannot understand what users will be trying to do with our system until we know who the users are and what manner of relationships they will assume with our system, so essential use cases can be thought of as deriving from user roles. In a similar vein, we cannot know what the right facilities and features to supply are until we know what users are trying to do, so the content model, which represents what the interface contains and how it is organized, is considered to be a logical consequence of the task model.

The final visual design needs to be based on the architectural models and adapted to the actual environment in which the system will be used. The operational model helps adapt the final visual design to the conditions and constraints of the **operational contexts** within which the system will be deployed and used.

Figure 2-1 outlines the principal logical relationships among all five models. (The principal logical dependencies are shown by heavy arrows.) To the right are the models that are primarily focused on design; to the left are those more concerned with problem definition. The three core models are in the top half of the

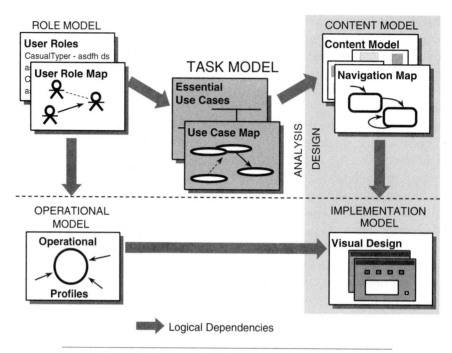

FIGURE 2-1 *Essential models, logical relationships.*

diagram, with the task model in the middle to emphasize its central role as the heart of usage-centered design.

This diagram should not be taken as a kind of flowchart for usage-centered design, however. As we will see, the actual process of usage-centered modeling is more flexible and less formal than the diagram may seem to suggest. In practice, the models are often developed concurrently, with analysts or designers moving back and forth among the alternative views presented by the models. Very often, in the course of modeling use cases, additional user roles will be recognized or aspects of the content model will become clearer. With experience, developers will find it easier to think in terms of these models as interconnected representations and will become adept at switching views in order to work on a problem from the perspective of the model that best suits the moment. However, in our experience as trainers, most people find it much easier to learn usage-centered modeling as a sequential rather than concurrent process, building one model at a time before moving on to the next logical model. For this reason, the presentation in this book is organized as if the models were derived in logical sequence rather than simultaneously.

The models that are the central theme of this book are focused on user interface and interaction design. For the complete design of a software system, other models already familiar to software developers are also necessary. Perhaps most important among these other models is the *data model*, whether in the form of an entity relationship diagram or an object class model. The data model defines the kinds of data that will be recognized by and maintained within the system. Data models and data modeling are sometimes closely tied to certain aspects of user interface design, but task models have proved more central to user interface design. A detailed discussion of data modeling and data-oriented software design is beyond the scope of this book; the curious reader is referred to any of the many excellent books on these topics. Our attention to data models will be limited to those points where they most closely touch user interface design.

GENERALLY SIMPLE

Abstract models of the kind employed in usage-centered design encourage simplification and promote thinking in more general rather than more specific terms. Simplification and generalization are justifiable activities in themselves. Repeated simplification and generalization reduce models and the interfaces designed from them to their essential cores. We find that developers who return again and again to their work, simplifying it and making it more general-purpose, produce smaller, simpler systems that deliver more value to users without being more complicated or more costly.

> *Developers who return again and again to their work, simplifying it and making it more general-purpose, produce smaller, simpler systems that deliver more to users.*

Simplification and generalization are intermediary steps that link the models of the usage-centered design process. So important are these interspersed bouts of simplification and generalization that the words "simplify, generalize" have become a virtual mantra to the designers we have trained. The mantra reminds us all that, rather than building bigger and bigger systems, a worthier goal of software design is to build systems that accomplish more with less. The slogan "More through less!" may be an appropriate technological update of architect Miës van der Rohe's famous dictum "Less is more."

COORDINATED ACTIVITY

It would be misleading to call usage-centered design a methodology; it is more of a collection of coordinated activities that contribute to software usability. These activities can be thought of as being like game pieces—dominoes might be an appropriate metaphor—that can be assembled in different ways to chart a path from conception to well-constructed software. As in the game of dominoes, there are logical relationships that require some pieces—some activities—to be arranged in a particular order, yet there are many possible orderings. After a four-six domino is played, for instance, a six-two or six-five or even a double-six is allowed, but a double-three piece will not work.

Figure 2-2 presents an overview of the usage-centered design process showing its key activities and some of the relationships among the tasks it comprises. Here, we will take only a quick tour of the process—just enough to describe briefly the various activities in usage-centered design and how they are interconnected. The figure also represents some closely related activities (shaded in the diagram) that are part of the larger software design and development process. Later chapters will cover details of the various pieces of the process, and the closing chapters will return to the larger organizational and management context.

> *The activities of usage-centered design are like game pieces that can be assembled in different ways to chart a path from conception to well-constructed software.*

In the diagram, time flows from top to bottom, but it should not be confused with a conventional "waterfall" software development life cycle. In the waterfall model, the process is divided into a succession of separate steps or phases carried out in sequence. Usage-centered design is a **concurrent engineering** process, in which independent or separable activities are carried out in parallel whenever practical. Concurrent engineering approaches have been successfully applied within many areas of modern design, engineering, construction, and manufacturing to deliver completed products more quickly and efficiently. Concurrent engi-

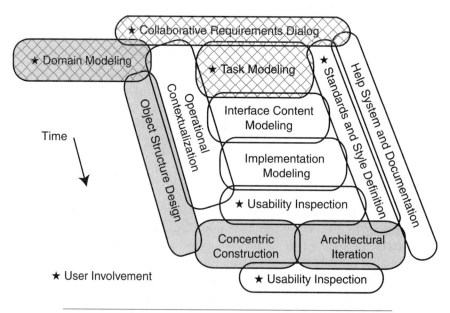

FIGURE 2-2 *Usage-centered design activity model.*

neering develops various models, descriptions, and subsystems at the same time. Where the work products are largely independent of one another, their development can be carried out in independent, parallel activities; where they are significantly related or interconnected, concurrent activities will need to be coordinated through effective communication linkages of one form or another.

The overlapping shapes in the figure—the dominoes of the process—represent the activities of usage-centered design, each with its own focus and purpose. As the diagram suggests, the boundaries separating activities are not always sharply delineated; activities can overlap to some greater or lesser degree and often proceed in parallel.

The process begins with a trio of activities (crosshatched in the figure) aimed at establishing the basic nature of the requirements for the system. A **Collaborative Requirements Dialogue** is a specialized conversation and negotiation between developers and their users and clients to establish the requirements of the system to be constructed. At the heart of this trio, and the very core of the usage-centered design process, is **Task Modeling**. The aim of this activity is to develop a clear and complete picture of the work to be supported through role and task models. Task Modeling interacts with another design and development activity that is, strictly speaking, outside of the immediate scope of usage-centered design: **Domain Modeling**. Domain Modeling develops a representation of all the interrelated concepts and constructs in the application domain, either in the form of an entity-relationship model or, more commonly these days, a domain class model. Domain Modeling establishes the vocabulary of the system and its operation.

Task Modeling is followed by and overlaps with **Interface Content Modeling**. As already stated, experienced designers may actually develop both task models and content models together in concurrent modeling activities. These modeling activities feed into and overlap with Implementation Modeling, the process of detailed design and prototyping. **Usability Inspection** appears in two places in the process model, both preceding and following the implementation activities of Concentric Construction and Architectural Iteration.

Running in parallel with all the modeling and design activities, beginning with the Collaborative Requirements Dialogue, are two somewhat complex and specialized activities with rather big names: **Operational Contextualization** and **Standards and Style Definition**. Operational Contextualization is aimed at adapting the design to the actual operational conditions and environment in which the system will be deployed, a topic that is explored at some length in Chapter 13. Conducting this activity as a parallel process is a radical departure from many older approaches to user interface design, which often begin by focusing quite early on aspects of the operating environment, such as lighting, noise, vibration, and any special needs among users. In our experience, superior designs result by focusing initially on the nature and structure of the work and then later adapting the user interface to operating conditions and constraints as the design details emerge. In other words, task organization needs to be the primary factor shaping the interface architecture, with operating context as a secondary influence, rather than the other way around.

Similarly, many user interface design approaches begin with user interface standards and style guides, either as documents to be specified at the outset or as established definitions within which to carry out the design. In our view, it is illogical to try to set standards for something when you do not yet know what it is that you are doing and what you need to standardize. Appropriate standards and guidelines for style should follow from an understanding of the work and design requirements. In practice, of course, some standards and definitions of style will already be established before a typical project begins. The activity of Standards and Style Definition is a concurrent activity shaping and being shaped by other activities, from the Collaborative Requirements Dialogue right through to Usability Inspection. User interface standards and style guides must exert a continuous influence on design, but, at the same time, they will also be reviewed and revised as determined by the outcomes of modeling and design activities.

> *Standards and guidelines for style should follow from an understanding of the work and design requirements.*

Because the final goal of software development is a working and usable system, the design and refinement activities must eventually lead to actual construction and testing of a working system. The parallel and interactive activities of Concentric Construction and Architectural Iteration constitute the implementation phase of usage-centered development. Concentric Construction is a process for developing working systems in layers, as guided by essential use case models. Architectural Iteration is a method for maintaining a sound internal software architecture as successive layers are added to a system. Just how these implementation activities are carried out is discussed in Chapter 19.

Users play an important part in usage-centered design even if they are not at the very center of the process. Users or user representatives are involved in several activities within the process—in the Collaborative Requirements Dialogue, Domain Modeling, Task Modeling, Standards and Style Definition, and Usability Inspections. These activities can be conducted conjointly, with users and developers working together, or with users reviewing and providing feedback on work completed by developers. In this light, the process might be characterized as user-involved rather than user-centered.

FLEXIBLE STAGING

The activity model in Figure 2-2 represents an overview of the complete usage-centered design process, although not all projects will require all of the activities in their fullest and most detailed form. As with dominoes, activities can be staged in various ways as suited to a particular project or design problem. For some projects, one or more activities might assume much greater importance or extend over a greater portion of the total life cycle than is represented in the diagram. In other projects, particular activities may become unimportant or even superfluous. Activities are intended to be rearranged, expanded, compressed, or even omitted altogether as needed. The irreducible minimum for a usage-centered approach is task modeling with essential use cases. Under exceptionally tight deadlines or extremely limited resources or for very simple systems, just identifying and developing the essential use case model can be better than nothing in helping to guide developers toward improved user interfaces.

> *The irreducible minimum for a usage-centered approach is task modeling with essential use cases.*

Certain of the activities can be considered to be more or less autonomous for some purposes, capable of being incorporated into other software development life cycles or process models. For example, Usability Inspections can be plugged into just about any software development project to good effect. Similarly, some of the components of usage-centered design can be used independently of other parts of the process. For example, it is certainly possible to apply the rules and principles of software usability independent of what models or methods might be used for a given project.

The activities of usage-centered design can also be dynamically reconfigured to suit changing conditions over the course of a project. An inspection might be dropped because results from early reviews are particularly favorable. A review and revision of standards and style guides might be initiated once a particular subsystem is to be constructed. As unanticipated problems arise and deadlines approach, resources can be reallocated to emphasize some activities over others.

ORDER AND CHAOS

Some years ago, in the course of working on a user interface design problem, we had an experience that changed our views on how best to organize development activities. Our backgrounds in data modeling and structured design meant that we were both convinced of the value of orderly and methodical development. On this one occasion, however, we were particularly determined to try to follow a rigorous and logical sequence of analysis and design. Each phase of the process was to be carried to absolute completion before beginning the following phase. Such discipline may seem a worthy objective, but we found it almost impossible to sustain, despite our commitment to the approach. When we were supposed to be developing abstract task models, we were getting distracted with ideas for new user interface widgets; when we should have been organizing the major interaction contexts of the interface, we would get an inspiration for a clever icon for some toolbar. In short, try as we might, we could not stick to a strict sequence of systematic modeling and design. We kept getting ahead of ourselves.

Our frustration was hardly remarkable; most developers could report similar experiences. The nice, neat diagrams that portray a logical progression of analyses and models bear little resemblance to how developers practice the art and craft of software development. Even those who are convinced of the value of thorough analysis and careful model building are nearly always carrying out a much more disorderly and undisciplined process than the ideal to which they aspire. They get ahead of themselves; they forget things. They skip around, moving back and forth between alternate views and among various parts of the problem. There is no orderly progression from high-level, abstract overview toward low-level, concrete detail. Designers bounce between abstraction and detail, from analysis to implementation, almost on a moment-to-moment basis.

> *There is no orderly progression from high-level, abstract overview toward low-level, concrete detail. Designers bounce between abstraction and detail, from analysis to implementation, almost on a moment-to-moment basis.*

Our experience inspired us to reconsider the problem of process. Instead of taking the usual view that our failure to keep to the regimen meant there was something wrong with us, we considered, for the sake of argument, an alternative view. Maybe there was nothing particularly wrong with us as designers nor, for that matter, with thousands of others who had tried and failed to keep to a rigorous procedure. Maybe the problem was with the procedures themselves; maybe the processes were not designed to fit the way humans solve problems or design solutions.

This analysis led us to devise a simple scheme for making design and development processes better suited to the way real people do real work. We called this scheme **feed-forward/work-back** [Constantine, 1994i]. Feed-forward/work-back can simplify most any software development approach and make it better suited to the way mere mortals solve real-world problems. It offers a way to maintain orderly progress without ignoring or losing good ideas that occur out of sequence. It can support creative problem solving and collaboration without turning the development process into chaos.

The keys to making the scheme work are what we call *feed-forward bins*. A feed-forward bin is a holding place for keeping ideas that occur out of sequence. A bin is just a piece of paper, a tray, or a file or folder on a computer that holds information of one kind or associated with one particular activity. Bins are a general-purpose technique for facilitating smooth and efficient group problem solving [Doyle and Strauss, 1982]. They can save a group from getting completely distracted or mired down in prolonged or pointless debate. Whenever a discussion reaches a point where it seems to be going nowhere or whenever a subject arises that is off the topic or out of order, a note is placed in a bin for later attention.

For software development, one bin is established for each phase or activity in the analysis and design process. If the software development life cycle being used has five steps, then five feed-forward bins are created, each one designated for a specific process. Alternatively, a bin can be designated for each of the major work products or deliverables in the process. For example, in usage-centered design, we typically establish feed-forward bins for each of the various models: user roles, use cases, interface contents, navigation, operational context, and visual design details.

In the feed-forward/work-back scheme, whenever we find we are getting ahead of ourselves, we pause to record the idea or issue that has arisen and then feed it forward into the appropriate bin. We then return to the task of whatever activity was under way. When we begin a new stage or activity, we start by looking in the feed-forward bin for usable ideas or issues to be resolved. In this way, feed-forward bins help maintain continuity in the design process and reduce the chances of important matters being overlooked. They allow groups to be spontaneous in solving problems creatively without chasing butterflies at every turn.

In addition to bins associated with each of the models or activities of usage-centered design, other, more generic bins can be useful. We often find use for a *deferred-decisions bin*, for example. Another particularly useful bin is for unanswered questions, a place for matters we are not sure of or that require additional information or more analysis before they can be resolved. A *questions bin* can be especially useful as input for subsequent meetings with users or clients. By setting aside issues in bins, we can keep the design process moving forward even when key information is missing.

The other half of the feed-forward/work-back scheme is what we do when we recognize, too late, that we missed something important in an earlier activity. At that point, we go back to the earlier activity and finish the uncompleted work and then carry the consequences forward to the point where we left off. This is the *work-back* part of the scheme. As the effects of the corrected or completed work are propagated forward again, the relevant models are updated so that all views are maintained in sync.

Feed-forward bins and the flexible process they support are not required to do usage-centered design, but they can make life easier for designers and project teams. As with the rest of the usage-centered approach, the goal is to produce better systems through working more efficiently, not just working harder.

3

IN PRINCIPLE:
Rules and Principles
of Usage-Centered Design

DESIGN AS DIALOGUE

Effective user interface design is a dialogue—a dialogue between designers and users. The dialogue is founded on the realization that there are real people on the other side of the user interface and that good designs communicate effectively with them. Unfortunately, the software developers and the users on the other side of the screen are not in the same room and do not even speak the same language. The only available translator is the user interface itself.

The design dialogue begins with the users and their problems, which the designer seeks to understand by some means or another. On the basis of this understanding, the designer builds a conceptual model of the users and the work they intend to accomplish. This conceptual model becomes a plan for the design and organization of the system and its interfaces. Through an effective design, the designer conveys this conceptual model, which is ultimately based on insight into users and their problems, back to the users through a well-organized user interface. Through interaction with the user interface, users will construct their own mental models of the system, how it is organized, and how it behaves. If all has gone well in the design dialogue, the user interface and the models on which it is organized will seem familiar and understandable to the user because they have been presented clearly and simply through the user interface and because, ultimately, they are based upon how the users work and understand their own work.

Throughout this dialogue, models are the essential material. Donald Norman [1988] distinguishes three models: the **designer's model**, which guides the developer in creating the system and its user interface; the **system model**, which the developer embodies in the system itself; and the **user's model**, which the user builds up through interaction with the user interfaces.

The user, of course, never sees the system model, much less the designer's conceptual model on which it was based. Users see screens and buttons and data fields and menus. They see the keyboard and other devices with which they interact with the system, but of the heart and substance of the system itself, they see nothing. They do not see that clever loop some programmer coded or the efficient way the pointers are organized or the clean separation of the program into highly cohesive, reusable modules. To users, the user interface is the system.

> *Of the heart and substance of the system itself, users see nothing. To users, the user interface is the system.*

In truth, the user interface is the only system users see, and, through interaction with it, they build up their own mental images of the total system and how it works [Norman, 1988]. Typically, the user's model is not methodically thought out, but instead grows rather organically and spontaneously from the process of interaction with the user interface. The user slowly develops a picture of what is in the system, what it is capable of doing, and how it responds to various actions. Most users will not even be conscious of their mental models, though they draw upon them continually to understand a system, navigate through its features, and anticipate what will happen when they take certain actions. One office worker, for example, had cluttered her hard disk with files named **Y** and **YY** and **YNY**. Her mental model considered all error messages and dialogue boxes as inscrutable intrusions to be dealt with in the same simpleminded manner. Whenever such messages appeared, she would just keep typing "y" and "n" until they all went away and her screen looked comfortably familiar again.

Without the initial input from the user, the exchange between user and designer becomes a monologue; the designer is just holding forth to an audience of users who are presented with a system as fait accompli. In many projects, the design dialogue derails before it is begun because developers do not turn to users as resources.

The goal of the design dialogue is, in every case, clear communication, which begins with the designer's mental model based on some understanding of what is needed to support the users of a system. All too often, developers avoid the inconvenience and tedium of actual meetings or discussions with users by simply making things up as they go along, fantasizing what they think users might want or need. Under some circumstances, daydreaming the users' end of the dialogue can work fairly well, especially if the end users are other programmers or if the application domain is otherwise well known to the designers. Most of the time, however, building a useful understanding of what the system is to be used for and how it will be used requires interaction with users.

In the end, the designer wants to present a user interface that models to users what the system is and does and how this relates to the tasks users are trying to accomplish. This model should be explicit and easily understood by users. Ideally, it should be familiar or resemble familiar ideas or models in terms of the uses to which the system will be put. In other words, the system should "speak" to users in ways they can understand. It should convey a clear and evident image of itself.

If the user interface fails to communicate clearly to the user, the user may end up building an incorrect or inaccurate mental model. The wrong mental model can lead to mistakes in usage. For example, the user of an email application will need to understand how sent messages are handled. One possible user's model might be the postal metaphor: When you post a letter, you no longer have it; if you want a copy for your files, you have to make one before you send the letter. An alternative model is the fax metaphor: When you transmit a fax, you still have the fax you sent without having to make a copy; it is the recipient who gets a copy—or *facsimile*—of the original. An email system can be based on either approach. Copies of sent email could, by default, be either saved locally or deleted automatically. Either way, if the user's mental model does not match the system model, there will be problems. Users mistakenly thinking in terms of the postal model could end up running out of storage space with double copies of everything sent, while those misconstruing a fax-like model could wrongly assume that copies of past messages are available somewhere in their systems.

In practice, communication with the user often breaks down because designers are not thinking in terms of how to present their own understanding of the system model to users in a way that will help users understand what is "really going on." Users often end up with wildly inaccurate and incongruous notions of the systems they use. If designers do not pay

DATA À LA DISNEY

Not everyone views the relationship between system builders, systems, and system users as a dialogue. To some designers, the objective is not clear and direct communication in order to make the system model and the designer's model available and understandable to users; the objective is to hide the system model from users while making it unnecessary for them to know anything about the underlying model. In this approach, users are not to be offered real access to or control over a system, but only a carefully mediated and regulated illusion. The goal is to disguise the system and its underlying models as much as possible behind a facade that seems real to users.

This view might be called the *Disney–Apple model* because it characterizes not only Walt Disney theme parks but also the user interface philosophy Apple pioneered with the Macintosh. In the Disney–Apple view, system designers are not in the business of communicating, but of creating illusions; they are show-business artists as much as or more than they are engineers. Staffers at Disney World are told not to "break the magic," not to expose the technical realities behind the attractive fantasy; developers of Macintosh software are admonished to design interfaces that sustain the illusion of control for users.

We would wholeheartedly agree that users should be protected from the raw realities of internal programming and data structures. The system models as they are presented to users should take familiar form and communicate in terms of the users' world. People do, indeed, like to feel in control of the world around them, including the systems they use as tools in their work. The illusion of control, however, is frequently no substitute for the real thing, especially as users progress in knowledge and abilities. Of course, in certain cases, such as a security system, the goal of good design must be neither control nor the illusion of control, but the restriction of access, knowledge, and control. There are no universal answers in user interface design, only those that fit or fail to fit with the task at hand and the hands performing the task.

attention to making the underlying models evident and understandable, even the most determined users may be left confused.

A few years ago, a leading consultant, one of the brightest men in the computer field, posted a message on GuildNet, a cyberspace gathering place for consultants. He was making the switch to Microsoft's Word for Windows and was having trouble understanding its behavior. He wanted a simple explanation of the underlying model that relates documents, templates, and styles in Word. Numerous consultants and experts willingly offered their views and explanations, but no sooner was a model put forth than it would be unceremoniously punctured by exceptions and counterexamples contributed by others in the forum. The brightest and best informed minds in the field could not articulate what the underlying model was. The consensus reached through the long thread of email messages was simply that, whatever the underlying model was, it was not conveyed to users in a clear enough and consistent enough manner through the user interface. Even the most intelligent and motivated users had difficulty building a dependable and accurate mental model of how the software functioned.

> *Communication often breaks down because designers are not thinking in terms of how to present their own understanding of the system in a way that will help users understand what is "really going on."*

This incident illustrates a common way in which the design dialogue gets derailed. The designer's model was not being simply and directly communicated to the users through the user interface. For example, styles in Word depend on other styles, forming a hierarchy. But the dependencies and the resulting hierarchy are not readily apparent or visible in normal use, so changes in one style seem to unexpectedly precipitate changes in others, while mysteriously leaving still others untouched. This design no doubt made sense to the original programmers, who might well protest that the user can trace out the hierarchy through various buried menus and dialogue boxes. Unfortunately, it does not necessarily make sense to the end users. Users of such software can be observed resorting to risk avoidance or even superstitious patterns of usage. Some, for example, simply give up completely on defining or using any but a few basic styles. Others define every new style to be independent of existing styles. And many just try various actions and techniques until they stumble on ones that work, without knowing why or learning how to recreate the results. Users do not reap much benefit from features they fail to fathom. In their efforts to avoid or overcome or work around the unfathomable, they can end up working less efficiently and less effectively than if those mysterious features had never been implemented.

RULES AND PRINCIPLES

Knowing that you are a participant in an important dialogue is not enough to make you a good communicator. You need to understand how to communicate effectively based on the rules of grammar and the principles of good construction. The first step to more usable systems is the recognition that user interface design is a dialogue with users carried out through the medium of the user interface itself. The next step is to understand the basic rules and principles of good user interface design.

Over the years, in our own design work, in teaching, and through the efforts of our clients, we have compiled a set of basic guidelines that help designers devise better user interfaces. Other lists of rules and guidelines have been devised and used successfully [see, for example, Nielsen, 1993; 1994b], and we will have more to say about some of these a little later. The principles that have become part of our approach to usage-centered design are a core set of fairly broad, simple, and easy-to-remember rules that, in practice, seem to offer the most usable guidance to ordinary developers trying to make everyday user interface design decisions. They embody much of the theoretical underpinnings of good user interface design, yet they are readily applied to practical design issues and offer the added advantage of being easy to learn and remember.

The guidelines are divided into five "rules" of usability and six design principles. Usability rules point out the general direction toward usability; design principles map the route to take. Strictly speaking, all of these, rules and principles alike, are mere heuristics. That is, they are simple rules of thumb that generally point the way to better designs but without any general guarantee of good results. Heuristics will not resolve design issues on their own and are no substitute for thoughtful analysis or inspired creativity on the part of the designer. The best of rules can be applied ignorantly or indiscriminately, but the ones offered here improve the odds of making sound decisions and producing solid results. Keep them in mind as you work your way through the user interface design process, and you have a good shot at producing more usable systems.

USABILITY RULES

Some principles of usability are sufficiently general and broad in scope to warrant being referred to as *usability rules*. These rules can be thought of as being like a compass, establishing a general direction for software developers aiming for greater usability.

IN THEORY

Some books on human–computer interaction or user interface design devote considerable space to the theoretical underpinnings of interaction and interface design in terms of cognitive psychology and the psychology of learning and perception. This will no doubt be of interest to some readers, and those who would like to know more are referred to excellent discussions in standard textbooks [for example, Preece et. al., 1994]. However, in our experience, this understanding is generally not of great immediate value to practicing professionals trying to design software user interfaces. For one thing, a tremendous gap separates the concerns of research psychologists and those of software designers. It is seldom clear how the distribution of error rates in short-term memory or the reliability of color discrimination might relate to deciding whether to use a scrolling pick list or a set of option buttons. Making matters even more difficult for practitioners, the theories and models of psychology are moving targets, with accumulating new research findings continuously challenging established theories and driving the evolution of new models.

Good design is not, however, merely a matter of the rote repetition of mechanical rules. If designers are to produce better than ho-hum human interfaces, they need some theoretical understanding of the human side of the interaction. Much of this more abstract perspective is reflected in the rules and principles introduced in this chapter. Some of the more basic concepts about the characteristics and limitations of the human processor can also be useful for the designer to understand and keep in mind when designing user interfaces. Here, we offer half a dozen of the most salient:

1. **To err is human.** Human information processing is strikingly error-prone. Making mistakes is the norm, and people generate errors at remarkably high rates. Reducing errors is more than a matter of motivation or practice on the part of the human user. Ill-formed systems can make it easier to make mistakes or harder to avoid them; well-formed systems make it harder to make mistakes and easier to do the right thing. In effective user interface design, errors and error handling are prominent considerations receiving careful attention.

2. **The speed of thought.** The human CPU and its attached peripherals are much slower than most people would guess. It typically takes about a tenth of a second merely to recognize an object on the screen, nearly a quarter second to shift the gaze and attention from one object to another, and a full 1.25 seconds on average to make a simple choice between two alternatives methods [Olson and Olson, 1990].

3. **The hand is slower than the eye.** Put manual operations in the loop, and activity can get even slower. Typing can take anywhere from under 0.1 second to as much as 1.25 seconds per character, depending on the material, the context, and the typist. One mouse click takes about as long as one keystroke, but pointing to something by moving the mouse from one place to another on the screen averages around 1.5 seconds. In general, the longer the move and the smaller the target, the longer it takes. Formulas exist for predicting the time [Fitts, 1954], but the important point is that it is almost always a lot longer than you might think. Switching from keyboard to mouse or back typically adds another 0.36 second [Olson and Olson, 1990]. Total up these numbers over hundreds of steps per task and thousands of tasks per day, and you realize why careful user interface design can make a big difference in productivity.

4. **Small numbers.** Thanks to the pioneers of structured analysis and design, hardly a programmer alive has not heard of psychologist George Miller's magical number 7 ±2, which represents the number of "chunks" of information the average person can typically hold in short-term memory [Miller, 1956]. Although the full story is complicated by many exceptions and qualifiers, the important thing to remember is that none of us can mentally juggle more than a handful of things at once without dropping a few figurative balls.

5. **The face is familiar but the name escapes.** As a rule, humans recognize things more readily than they can recall information unaided by cues. Picking the right code from a list of them is far easier and more reliable than typing in a code from memory.

6. **Up the learning curve.** Learning anything new or different, however easy or reasonable it might be, takes time. Performing any new task or using new tools to perform an old task, humans start out slow and error-prone, building speed and accuracy only over time. This seems obvious, but it is often ignored by software developers and their managers.

FIRST RULE: ACCESS

> *The system should be usable, without help or instruction, by a user who has knowledge and experience in the application domain but no prior experience with the system.*

This first rule, sometimes referred to as *The Great Law of Usability*, states simply that, if you know your job, you ought to be able to use software intended to support you in your work without first having to read a 500-page manual or take a 2-day course. For the designer, the goal is a system so closely fitted to the work and to how users think about it and perform it, so naturally presenting itself to the user, that it can be put to use immediately without the user's having to learn anything new or different.

Clearly, immediate accessibility is a difficult though desirable objective. In a sense, the Access Rule represents a sort of "Holy Grail" of software usability, a gleaming ideal, glimpsed in the distance, forever sought but always beyond reach. Nevertheless, the Access Rule establishes a standard of excellence against which user interface designs can be judged, a continuous reminder to designers regarding the goal for which they are aiming.

Usability rules point out the general direction toward usability; design principles map the route to take.

It has become popular in recent years to try to eliminate paper documentation by putting software manuals or even training materials on-line in the form of built-in help files. This is not what is meant by the Access Rule. Ideally, a well-designed system should enable the user who knows how to perform some task to accomplish it with the system without consulting even an on-line help system.

Highly accessible interfaces are sometimes referred to as *intuitive*. It would be more accurate to describe them as **intuitable** [Raskin, 1994], meaning that the guesses and presuppositions of users are more likely to be right than wrong and that, even when wrong, the results are reasonable responses from the system that are readily understood by the users. The design goal is interfaces that instruct—that, by their very organization and construction, guide users in how to use them. In Chapter 7, we will look at some specific methods for making user interfaces intrinsically instructive.

Immediate usability by the inexperienced user represents a sort of "Holy Grail" of software usability, a gleaming ideal, glimpsed in the distance, forever sought but always beyond reach.

The Access Rule is primarily directed at supporting beginners, first-time users unfamiliar with a given piece of software. The field of human–computer interaction understands such users and their needs in terms of user interfaces quite well.

In many respects, the Apple Macintosh was optimized for such users. But you are only a first-time user once, and beginners do not typically stay beginners for long. No matter how simple you make a system for first-time users, across-the-board usability requires something more. Well-designed systems need to support all their users, including those who have extensive experience in working with a system.

SECOND RULE: EFFICACY

> *The system should not interfere with or impede efficient use by a skilled user who has substantial experience with the system.*

The Efficacy Rule is stated in the negative because that is how it often comes into play in actual user interfaces. In many cases, the very design practices that make things easiest for beginners make things harder for everyone else. Designers will find it very challenging to serve both the user who is just learning a system and the user who has already learned it well.

It is not enough for designers simply to throw a few crumbs to the experts in the form of keyboard shortcuts that provide alternatives to mousing around the interface or to offer a few "advanced" options grafted onto basic dialogue boxes. Good interfaces do not punish power users by assuming they will put up with and master almost anything. Features to support the expert user need to be as well conceived and as well organized as those to support the rank beginner.

THIRD RULE: PROGRESSION

> *The system should facilitate continuous advancement in knowledge, skill, and facility and accommodate progressive change in usage as the user gains experience with the system.*

Inexperienced users do not wake up one morning and suddenly find themselves metamorphosed into experts. Learning the layout of a user interface and becoming adept at using it constitute a continuous process in which skill and ability are improved steadily but incrementally. The Progression Rule means that some connection is needed between the simpler and the more advanced facilities, that the organization and details of the user interface should actively aid the user in understanding and using additional features and acquiring new skills.

Instead of leaving users on their own to cope with advanced but arbitrary features that are difficult to learn, good designs help users become power users—for example, by furnishing shortcuts that are naturally related to the longer means preferred by beginners. The Progression Rule also suggests that the various features and facilities supporting newcomers, old hands, and everyone in between need to be integrated and meaningfully related. This objective is hard to achieve without systematic design that addresses the overall user interface architecture as a unified whole.

To design good user interfaces that support continuous learning and advancement by users, developers need to understand how the patterns of usage change as users progress in knowledge and skill. As we will see in Chapter 12, the needs of users and the typical ways in which they interact with systems change predictably over time as they progress from initial use toward expertise. Things that are encouraging and comforting to beginners can become annoying impediments

Instead of leaving users on their own to master advanced features, good designs help users become power users.

for advanced users; facilities that advanced users employ with confidence may be daunting or even frightening for those just starting out. Yet, all these things need to be smoothly integrated into a seamless interface. Discontinuities that force users who are used to working in one mode or style to suddenly shift to a different interface or style of interaction do not support progressive learning.

FOURTH RULE: SUPPORT

> *The system should support the real work that users are trying to accomplish by making it easier, simpler, faster, or more fun or by making new things possible.*

The Support Rule is the very heart of usage-centered design. It is based on the notion that all software systems are tools, and good tools support work. It exhorts designers to understand what users will need to do with a system and how they will need to do it in order to perform their work better.

Designers, like good managers, need to be able to tell the difference between real work and mere activity. For example, consider the design of a system for managing personal information, such as addresses, contact details, lists of things to do, and the like—a *personal information manager* (PIM), as it is usually called. Developers of software PIMs have not only taken their inspiration from paper-based systems, such as DayTimer and FiloFax, but also, in some cases, have slavishly imitated these systems by simulating the behavior of pocket organizers and other physical systems on-screen. Is this bad design?

The problem with these approaches is that they mistake activity for work. The activities of using a paper-based organizer are not the real work that a software PIM should support. The real work is not "using a DayTimer" but organizing and coordinating personal activities and information. The producers of paper-based systems like the DayRunner or FiloFax carefully designed these systems to support the real work within the constraints of print, paper, and binders. Computer

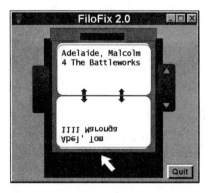

FIGURE 3-1 *Misused metaphors: simulated reality.*

software offers many more capabilities but also suffers from limitations not found in the tangible forms of personal information managers.

Consider, for example, a software PIM that organizes contact information with a rotary file metaphor, such as the one illustrated in Figure 3-1. Turning the knob on a real rotary index file is a quick and facile way to locate a particular address, but using a mouse to turn the simulated knob in an on-screen representation is an exercise in inefficiency.

The very best tools enable us to accomplish entirely new things or to carry out work in radically different ways. When possible, we want software that goes beyond merely supporting established ways of working; we want it to open new possibilities. Every software engineering effort should be seen as an opportunity for reengineering the work itself. Supporting the real work that users are trying to accomplish may mean changing that work. The best tools, from microscopes to software spreadsheets, transform the work they were intended to support. The cut-and-paste capabilities of word-processing programs, to take but one example, make it possible for people to write in new, nonlinear ways, building up a linear narrative from small pieces written totally out of order, for instance.

FIFTH RULE: CONTEXT

> *The system should be suited to the real conditions and actual environment of the operational context within which it will be deployed and used.*

The Context Rule emphasizes that the best design intentions are inadequate if they do not take into account where and under what circumstances systems will actually be used. For example, the control panel for a video cassette recorder may be elegantly designed and even sensibly laid out, but if the gray labels on the black buttons are too faint to read in the reduced room lighting of most television viewing, usability will be reduced. Differences in the work environment, the flow of information into and out of the system, the expected population of users, and numerous other factors can all be important to take into account in designing good user interfaces.

Every context is different. A bank is not a commodities trading floor, and a retail store is another context altogether. A kiosk for use by an untrained and unprepared tourist in a noisy mall poses design problems that may be dramatically different from a system supplying much the same information to a trained operator working for a telephone-based concierge service. The basic tasks may be quite similar, but how best to support them in software can be quite different.

Following the Context Rule is a challenge for designers because operational context covers an assortment of issues and areas of concern, some of which are related to the users of systems and some to the working environment in which systems are used. Operational context needs to be a background concern throughout much of the design process in order to produce systems well suited to the context in which they will be used. We will go into more detail on this subject in Chapter 13.

USER INTERFACE DESIGN PRINCIPLES

The five rules of usability frame the philosophy of usage-centered design but do not in themselves offer designers enough in the way of specific direction when it comes to resolving practical problems in user interface design. For that, more focused design principles are needed. The set of six principles offered here summarizes a great deal of what is known about effective user interface design. Each principle incorporates a number of closely related, more detailed considerations within a general class of issues. These issues are structure, simplicity, visibility, feedback, tolerance, and reuse.

STRUCTURE PRINCIPLE

> *Organize the user interface purposefully, in meaningful and useful ways based on clear, consistent models that are apparent and recognizable to users, putting related things together and separating unrelated things, differentiating dissimilar things and making similar things resemble one another.*

The Structure Principle is concerned with the overall user interface architecture and directly reflects the notion of user interface design as a dialogue between designers and users. Good user interfaces are deliberately organized in ways that reflect the structure of the work being supported and the way in which users think about that work. All too often, especially using modern visual development tools, the placement of visual components within forms or dialogues and their distribution among these is almost haphazard, reflecting little more than the order in which things came up in conversation or were considered by programmers. Features that are used together and thought of together by users ought to appear together on the user interface or at least be clearly and closely associated. Those things that in terms of the work and the thinking of users, are unrelated ought to be separated or distinguished on the user interface. Similar arrangements ought to be used for similar information, and features with similar or related behavior ought to have some commonality in appearance.

In keeping with the notion of design as dialogue, good user interfaces present to the user a clear and consistent model that is readily apparent and recognizable to the user. In many cases, achieving good structure requires drawing on objects or actions that are familiar to users or that resemble familiar things. This should not become an excuse for silly or simplistic simulations of tangible systems from the real world. As often as not, like the on-screen Roladex, these are inefficient and ineffective.

Metaphors from the real world, such as file folders, cabinets, and rooms by which to organize data, can be useful for structuring user interfaces and making them more accessible to users, especially first-time users. Metaphors are immensely popular with usability specialists and the software-buying public, but they are not the universal answer for user interface design. Strained metaphors can make a user interface harder to understand, and simplistic simulations can make them harder to use.

> *Strained metaphors can make a user interface harder to understand, and simplistic simulations can make them harder to use.*

During one of our classes, a team working on the design of software for processing conference registrations was stalled in a heated discussion. Under the leadership of a man who had once taken a course in human–computer interaction, they were agonizing over trying to find the right visual metaphor. He had been taught the overly simplified idea that good user interface design always started with a suitable metaphor.

The important issue is not whether there is a metaphor or even a whole set of metaphors incorporated into the user interface but whether the interface is well organized and suited to the work at hand. If a metaphor is readily apparent from an understanding of the work, then consider using it, but you should not feel compelled to find metaphors where there may be none or none that are helpful. The point of reference for the appropriate structure of a user interface is always the users: how they think, how they work, and what they are trying to accomplish.

To illustrate how the Structure Principle applies to evaluating user interface design alternatives, consider the dialogue box shown in Figure 3-2. This dialogue

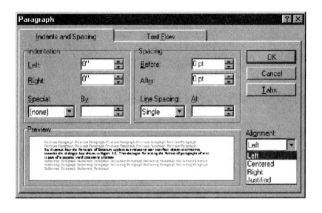

FIGURE 3-2 *Tabbed dialogue for paragraph formatting.*
(MICROSOFT WORD 95)

for setting the format of paragraphs of text is part of a popular word-processing program. Before reading further, you might study the layout of the dialogue for a minute to see whether you can identify some problems based on the Structure Principle.

In the lower right corner of the dialogue box is an obvious problem in structure. The selections for left-aligned, right-aligned, and centered text are arranged in a way that does not make sense in terms of their meaning. The vertical arrangement represents an inappropriate visual metaphor. Most of us think of "left" being to the left, "right" being to the right, and "centered" being in the center. Arranging options according to their meanings makes it easier to recognize and select the one you want. The same problem reappears in the settings for indentation. In either case, the user must read the words in order to make the correct selection; an inherently spatial task has been forced into a verbal mold. Furthermore, both indentation and alignment are concerned with the edges or margins of the text, yet these visually and logically interrelated facilities are separated on the interface. On the other hand, all of the controls for line spacing have been grouped into a single panel on the dialogue, which is an example of good structure.

Yet another example from the same word-processing software is that not all aspects of formatting are found where one would expect—namely, under the **Format** menu. Page layout requires going through the **File** menu, and footnotes are incongruously accessed through the **View** menu. Changing from identical headers on every page to alternating odd-even headers is not achieved through **View|Header and Footer**, but through the **File|Page Setup**... dialogue. Inconsistencies of this sort make it harder to learn how to find things and harder to remember what you learned. They can lead to mistakes even by more experienced users.

SIMPLICITY PRINCIPLE

> *Make simple, common tasks simple to do, communicating clearly and simply in the user's own language and providing good shortcuts that are meaningfully related to longer procedures.*

Saying that simple user interfaces are better is a little like saying that sunny days are brighter. Naturally, we would like to make all our user interfaces simple and easy to use, but, unfortunately, neither everything about a user interface nor every task to be performed can be made simple. Design is always a matter of trade-offs. Making some things simpler will, all but inevitably, make others more complicated. If the number of menus is reduced, the number of items per menu will likely be increased. If each dialogue box is kept small, with few features, any given interaction is apt to take the user through more of them.

You cannot make everything simple. Following the Simplicity Principle requires that you know what tasks are more common and what tasks are simpler from the user's perspective. These tasks should be kept short and simple when performed with the software.

> *You cannot make everything simple. Common tasks and tasks that are simple from the user's perspective should be made short and simple within the user interface.*

Knowing what tasks are most common does not necessarily require conducting a survey or undertaking extensive research. Often, just some extra thought will make clear what tasks are likely to be the most frequent. Consider, for example, a utility for formatting floppy disks. Such utilities are often loaded with a variety of capabilities related to formatting disks. Standard 3½-inch disks can be formatted in three different densities, with or without a copy of system files, and optionally labeled. Some formatting programs also allow for a "quick format" that merely erases files by marking them as deleted within the disk's directory.

A case can be made that the basic reason for having a formatting utility at all is to be able to format an unformatted disk. Nowadays, nearly all floppy disks are "high density," and few users are likely to format them to less than maximum capacity. The format routine can be used to erase all contents of a disk, but this is an ancillary function, and many users may not even think of this application of the utility. With all this in mind, consider this interaction with the formatting utility of a popular desktop productivity tool.

You insert a blank disk, select **Disk|Format Diskette** from a menu, and the dialogue box of Figure 3-3a appears. The cursor stays in "wait" mode for an unexpectedly long time as the system tries, unsuccessfully, to read the disk as if it were formatted. Finally, the message in Figure 3-3b appears. You have already inserted

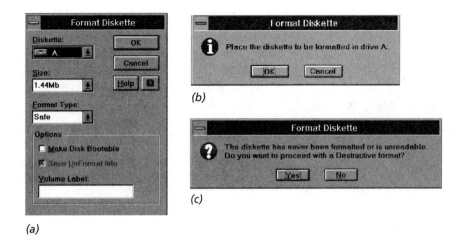

FIGURE 3-3 *Simple disk formatting?*
(NORTON DESKTOP)

the disk, which the system should know since it already has tried to read it. Nevertheless, you obediently click on **OK** to tell the system to go ahead. You are simply returned to the original dialogue box. A click on **OK** and another delay yields the message in Figure 3-3c. Of course, there is only one sensible thing to do with an unformatted disk that you have asked to be formatted, yet the system insists on making you say it again. By this time, you are ready to scream, "Just format the darned disk, you bloody idiot!" To add further insult, once the utility finishes, it imposes another message, asking if you want to format any more disks. You don't, but clicking on **No** is not enough; that just returns you to the original dialogue box, where you have to tell it—again—to go away.

All these elements of the interaction may have seemed perfectly reasonable from the programmer's viewpoint, but they make clear that nobody thought about what the utility was really being used for and what the simplest, most common, and most central tasks are. Unnecessary confirmations and ancillary features have been allowed to interfere with the swift and simple completion of a common task.

VISIBILITY PRINCIPLE

> *Keep all needed options and materials for a given task visible without distracting the user with extraneous or redundant information.*

The Visibility Principle is about designing user interfaces that make things visible and available to users based on what they are trying to accomplish. The goal is to go beyond WYSIWYG (What You See Is What You Get) to WYSIWYN (What You

See Is What You Need). WYSIWYN interfaces make visible all and only those things the user must have to complete the task at hand.

On the one hand, the design objective is to make all the needed and relevant options visible and explicit. On the other hand, good designs do not overwhelm users with too many alternatives or confuse them with unneeded information. WYSIWYN interfaces are better because they fit with the limited capacity of human working memory and because people can recognize more things than they can recall and recognize them more readily. (See sidebar, In Theory.) The load on long-term memory is reduced by always presenting users with the available options and alternatives. The load on short-term memory is reduced by not requiring users to remember and reproduce information from one part of the interface to another.

> *Good designs do not overwhelm users with too many alternatives or confuse them with unneeded information.*

Many times, we have waited at the front desk of a major hotel as the clerk copied information from one screen onto a slip of paper and then reentered the same information through the keyboard after switching to another screen. You do not need to know anything more about the application to recognize this as a failure in software design. The programmers were not thinking about how the system would be used and what information would be needed at various points. They were most likely thinking in terms of databases and rows and columns and datagrids, without regard for the harried desk clerk who is trying to find a nonsmoking room ready for occupancy.

Consider using a fax management program. Often times, you may have sent a fax, for example, only to find out that your client or colleague did not receive it

FIGURE 3-4 *How to resend a fax?*
(DELRINA WINFAX PRO)

and that you must therefore send it again. In the user interface of Figure 3-4, where do you go to send the same fax all over again? Perhaps you first try the big button prominently labeled **Send**. No, that just brings up the dialogue to assemble and send a new fax. Under the **Send** menu, we find only **Fax**... and **Log**..., which seem to replicate the menu bar choices. However, this is deceptive because **Send|Fax**... just replicates the **Send** button, and **Send|Log**... does the same thing as clicking on the **Send Log** button (which is nothing in this instance, since the **Send Log** is already showing). A further hunt through the **Fax** menu reveals a motley miscellany of selections, but none to resend a fax. No, in this case, what you need is hidden under the **Log** menu, of all illogical places, where it is called, obscurely, **Resubmit**. The term "**Resend**" or "**Send Again**" might be reasonable, but no ordinary fax user is going to say, "I need to *resubmit* this fax to the fax manager queue." **Resubmit** is clearly geek-speak, not user-speak. Its name and location on the user interface suggest that this was an inside-out design, where detailed programming decisions rather than usability dictated the design.

After presenting this example to several thousand people in our classes, we were pleased to find that the next release of this software had moved the option for resending a fax to the **Send** menu. Alas, it was still called **Resubmit**.

FEEDBACK PRINCIPLE

> *Keep users informed of actions or interpretations, changes of state or condition, and errors or exceptions that are relevant and of interest to the user through clear, concise, and unambiguous language familiar to users.*

Good user interfaces are good conversationalists, telling the user what is happening inside the system. The Feedback Principle tells designers some of the rules of this conversation.

We have all had the experience of telling someone something only to have them later say they did not hear. A message that is not seen or heard communicates nothing, so part of successful feedback is to present information in such a way that it is noticed, read, and interpreted correctly.

Where on the screen is the user most likely to notice feedback? Wherever the user is looking. And where is that most likely to be? Wherever the pointer or cursor is at the moment.

Aside from the spot on the screen where they happen to be working, users are most likely to attend to feedback at the center of the screen or at the top and are least likely to notice it at the bottom edge. The standard practice of putting information about changes in state on a status line at the bottom of a window is particularly unfortunate, especially if the style guide calls for lightweight type on a gray background. Most of us have had the experience of failing to notice a message at the bottom of the screen and then wondering why the software was not doing what we expected.

If you are forced by convention, by a client, or by a stubborn boss to put important information on the status line, you can take advantage of other characteristics of human visual processing to increase the likelihood that your users will notice. Motion and color attract attention. Briefly blinking the status bar message or flashing it first in a bright color will increase its chances of being seen. You do not want to go wild, with blinking yellow and blue that does not quit until the next phase is finished, but you may find that a brief flash or two can reduce user errors.

Usable systems keep users informed about a lot of things. Systems should let users know how input from the user was interpreted. Every time a system changes its internal state in ways that affect the user, the user should be informed, especially whenever the change is in how the system interprets user actions, including which actions will be disallowed or ignored. The Feedback Principle should not become an excuse for creating a plethora of message boxes, however. The goal is to find a way of communicating that is succinct and natural.

Good feedback does not require being wordy. In fact, it does not even require words. A police officer directing traffic does not need to hold up a message board to indicate that cross-traffic has stopped and it is okay to proceed. A wave of the hand will do the trick. On screen, the mouse pointer changing from an arrow to a slash-and-circle "no" symbol communicates swiftly and succinctly to the software user that something is prohibited. Wordy messages, especially "cutesy" ones that talk down to users, are not good feedback.

> *Good feedback does not require words. A police officer directing traffic does not need to hold up a message board to indicate that it is okay to proceed.*

Users also need feedback on errors and exception conditions. In many programs, errors are reported to users in ways that are uninformative or misleading. Some abusive messages even make users feel inadequate. A user is unlikely to be encouraged by a message box that reads "`Improper input. Retype data correctly.`" Not only does such a message seem to imply that the user has been a bad person, but it also is not very instructive. It does not indicate which input is the problem and why.

Good error messages are just another example of good communication. The best are succinct, expressed in user language, and easy to understand. They start with a heading or caption or capsule description that immediately identifies the problem to the user and then go on to explain the problem specifically and precisely and to suggest problem solutions or corrective courses of action.

Alan Cooper [1995] has suggested the radical view that error messages are unnecessary and are a symptom of poor user interface design; good programming should all but eliminate them. In this view, an error condition is not the result of a user doing something wrong; it comes from a failure on the part of the developers to handle all cases properly. This perspective reverses the usual programming approach to errors and exceptions. An "invalid format" does not mean that the user typed incorrectly, for example; it means that the programmer failed to successfully parse the input.

Our own view is less extremist but of similar leanings. Many of the messages in typical software are redundant, uninformative, distracting, irritating, or without justification when considered from the user's perspective. The worst are the gratuitously injected "confirmation" messages that ask users, in effect, to repeat what they have already said to the system. The topic of messages and message design does not reduce to a simple ban or an easy formula, however, so we will have to return to the subject in Chapter 11.

TOLERANCE PRINCIPLE

> *Be flexible and tolerant, reducing the cost of mistakes and misuse by allowing undoing and redoing while also preventing errors wherever possible by tolerating varied inputs and sequences and by interpreting all reasonable actions reasonably.*

Even better than good error messages are fewer errors. More usable systems help users make fewer mistakes. There are a number of strategies for reducing user errors, and these are embodied in the Tolerance Principle.

Good software can be thought of as both flexible and forgiving. Not only does it accept varied input and actions from users, but, when something unexpected arrives, it also does not punish them. Systems that simply hang or become lost at the first unexpected code are the worst examples, but less extreme cases of intolerant software are everywhere. Errors need to be anticipated and planned for. Experienced programmers and designers assume that users are human and will make mistakes; they even assume that other programs, having been written by humans, will be faulty as well.

Not everything that programmers think of as an error is really an error. In many cases, programming imposes a rigid logic or enforces an unnecessarily narrow concept of acceptable input. This is Cooper's point when he talks about eliminating error messages; he is really talking about tolerant programming. Good software interprets reasonably any reasonable action by the user. It is not necessary to anticipate every possible input or action or to always do the best or right thing when something out of the ordinary arrives, but software should at least not do something stupid when confronted with unexpected input or actions. For many tasks, different users will find different sequences or arrangements easier, and tolerant software allows for such individual variation.

Many software systems—even standard operating systems—routinely refuse to accept very reasonable actions by users. A common, everyday scenario finds the user several levels down in nested dialogue boxes before realizing that this is not where he or she wanted to be or what he or she wanted to do. A click on the intended tool or menu rewards the user with an annoying chirp or ping, a reminder that, before trying something else, he or she has to back out of all those nested dialogues, clicking a whole series of **Cancel**, **Close**, and **OK** buttons. Observations of this common "error" suggest that it is probably a very natural thing to do. In almost all cases, the system could itself safely cancel each of the open dialogues in turn, which would be exactly what the user's action meant anyway: "I don't want to be down here or doing this; I want to be back up here and do this instead."

> *Software should at least not do something stupid when confronted with unexpected input or actions.*

Perhaps because computers are so strictly logical and literal, programmers tend to think similarly in linear logic, often imposing on users a strict, sequential ordering that may or may not make sense from a task standpoint. Consider the dialogue box in Figure 3-5, used to control animation of displayed objects in a presentation package. Often, the user wants to animate a static object with a particular effect, such as a wipe or fade-in. You might want to make an object "fly in" from the right side of the screen, for example, but you cannot simply select **Effects** or click on the appropriate drop-down list because these are inactive and thus grayed-out. You have to first change the **Don't Build** to **Build** under **Build Options** before the other controls become active. This makes perfectly logical sense from the programmer's view, but it is intolerant. To the user, simply selecting **Fly From Right** under **Effects** should work since it clearly and unambiguously implies that the user wants the object to "build." A tolerant system designed

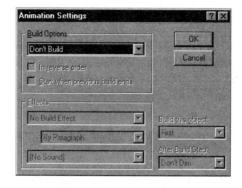

FIGURE 3-5 *Animating objects.*
(MICROSOFT POWERPOINT 95)

to support work would accept this abbreviated input and automatically change **Don't Build** to **Build**.

It is an intolerant interface that allows the user to type "7/12/94" for a date and then reports "**Invalid Date**" simply because one digit lacks a leading zero. An input field for a date should, ideally, accept almost any format of date the user types, but errors can be reduced or eliminated by the simple expedient of presenting a prototype or example that informs the user how the system is expecting the date (more about this in Chapter 11).

Interfaces can also be made more or less tolerant depending on what data is checked for validity and when. Validating all fields at the end of a data entry screen is a common practice that may sometimes make sense in terms of the flow of work. The system will be far more tolerant if it returns to the screen with the invalid fields highlighted, the cursor on the first field in error, and an informative message on the status line. Worst of all are programs that complete their end-of-screen validation and then kick the user back to the top of a blank screen to try again. Ludicrous as this sounds, we have seen it all too often, including in commercial software.

Data validation may seem like a sound practice, but validation carried to an extreme can reduce usability. For example, in the initial implementation of a college admissions system, all entry fields were validated by the software. The admissions office found the system almost unusable. Many of the fields were unknown when an admission record was first entered, so data entry clerks were forced to make up values in order to satisfy the validation checks. For other fields that were optional or not used officially, validation was overkill and only served to slow down data entry.

In general, validating unused fields or fields that are not processed by software but are of interest only to other people makes for intolerant software. Assuring, for example, that an optional annotation field contains only alphanumeric text is not just extra programming—it may preclude some potentially worthwhile future uses, such as using special symbols or graphic characters in the annotations to flag records visually.

REUSE PRINCIPLE

> *Reuse internal and external components and behaviors, maintaining consistency with purpose rather than merely arbitrary consistency, thus reducing the need for users to rethink and remember.*

Consistency has been so widely preached that nearly everyone recognizes it as the *sine qua non* of good user interfaces. Consistency in appearance, placement, and behavior within the user interface makes software easier to learn and to remember how to use. It seems remarkable that a principle so highly touted and widely cited should also be so seldom fulfilled in practice. In truth, high degrees of consistency across a complex user interface are not easy to achieve. Furthermore, highly consistent interfaces often achieve their consistency at the expense of other important design criteria.

> *It seems remarkable that consistency, a principle so highly touted and widely cited, should also be so seldom fulfilled in practice.*

Over time, we have been led to conclude that reuse, not consistency, is the key issue. With greater reuse comes greater consistency. Reuse of components and designs within and between systems is advantageous to users because users will have fewer things to learn and remember and because the interface will be more predictable and understandable. Building user interfaces and their supporting internals from reusable components assures consistency not only in appearance but also in behavior. What users have learned before—about this system or from others similarly assembled—is more likely to be applicable whenever they see familiar components or arrangements.

By reusing internal and external components and designs throughout a system, the developer can create not only a more consistent user interface but also, often, a less expensive system. Striving for consistency alone can increase the cost of development and may even sometimes be an inappropriate effort. The goal should be consistency with the purposes of the software and its use, not consistency for its own sake, which may lead to foolish consistency or even to consistently bad solutions.

Many accepted standards and established user interface components and conventions are examples of unfortunate consistency. Standard software platforms may impose on developers conventions that are poorly designed or badly thought out. Common dialogues can set a consistent but low common denominator, and standard shortcut keys are often arbitrary and inconsistent in themselves.

Not only do inconsistent user interfaces lead to less usable software, but they

> *Not only do inconsistent user interfaces make for less usable software, but they also require more programming.*

also usually lead to more programming. The user interface fragments shown in Figure 3-6 all come from the same drawing tool. The fragments in Figures 3-6a and 3-6b both control the same characteristics for text, but where part (a) uses push-buttons to select text alignment, part (b) uses option or "radio" buttons. These option buttons employ the same unfortunate vertical arrangement as does the dialogue box of Figure 3-2, whereas the push buttons are arranged in a natural spatial metaphor. Elsewhere in this tool, yet another variation for aligning objects is used—in the form of option buttons arranged horizontally, as in Figure 3-6c. Although the spatial metaphor is correct, the choice of widgets is unfortunate since the natural impulse is to click on the picture, which, in this instance, is not an active area; labeled push buttons would have been better. Every one of these

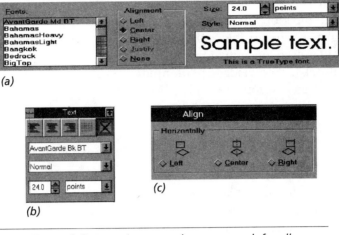

FIGURE 3-6 *Inconsistency makes more work for all.*
(COREL DRAW!)

different interfaces for similar or identical functions had to be designed and programmed. Indeed, we can suspect that they were done by different programmers who not only did not share code but also probably did not even talk with one another.

Even where things are consistent within this user interface, the consistency is incomplete and not necessarily desirable. Text style and size are selected similarly in the first two dialogue boxes, although the vertical order is inverted. In the first case, font selection is separated from font size and style, which represents a structural problem because these are closely related conceptually from a user's standpoint. In both cases, the style options are hidden in a drop-down selection list, which is a visibility problem that forces every change in text style to involve the extra step of opening the drop-down list.

OTHER RULES

The eleven guidelines just described are certainly not the only ones that can assist designers in creating more usable software. Jacob Nielsen, long an advocate of simple and cost-effective approaches to usability, assembled one of the best-known sets of usability heuristics [Molich and Nielsen, 1990; Nielsen, 1993] and later researched the ability of various rules to explain the actual usability problems found in delivered systems [Nielsen, 1994a]. Among 101 specific heuristics, including Nielsen's original ten, 95% of the more serious usability problems were accounted for by the ten rules paraphrased here:

1. Seeing/pointing versus remembering/typing
2. Consistency (same thing, same way)

3. Timely and accurate feedback
4. Salient repertoire of actions
5. Forgiveness (reversible actions)
6. Familiar user conceptual model
7. Feedback (acknowledgment of input)
8. Prevention of errors
9. Easily discriminated action alternatives
10. Modeless interaction

An additional five rules were among the top ten in explaining all problems, serious or not:

1. Speaking the user's language
2. Aesthetic integrity (simple design)
3. Shortcuts and accelerators
4. Real-world conventions
5. Help with error recognition and recovery

All of these "best" rules are clearly implied in one form or another by the five rules and six principles of usage-centered design. Modeless interaction may not be an obvious requirement, but it falls within the Tolerance Principle since modeless dialogues do not rigidly fix the sequence of user actions.

Although a factor analysis of the rules uncovered no particularly strong factors, the top seven factors—covering about 30% of the variance—certainly have a familiar ring:

1. **Visibility of system status** (keeping the user informed)
2. **Match between system and real world** (user language and real-world conventions)
3. **User control and freedom** (easy exits, undo, and redo)
4. **Consistency and standards**
5. **Error prevention**
6. **Recognition rather than recall** (reduced remembering with visible options, actions, and instructions)
7. **Flexibility and efficiency of use** (customization and support for advanced users)

Nielsen added to these three other rules to round out a revised set of ten heuristics [Nielsen, 1994b]:

8. **Aesthetic and minimalist design** (reduced irrelevant or rarely needed information)
9. **Help in recognizing, diagnosing, and recovering from errors**
10. **Good help and documentation**

It is not difficult to see the connection between all but the last of these heuristics and the rules and principles of usability. Help systems and documentation can have an enormous impact on usability, but we see these as simply another part of the interface between the system and the user within which all the broad principles of usability apply. We will have much more to say about help systems in Chapter 11.

In short, designers who learn to apply the basic rules and principles of usage-centered design are probably standing on firm turf. These eleven simple heuristics are well grounded in what is known about human–computer interaction and are supported by extensive experience and study. Together, they cover a lot of territory. Consistent application to design decisions and to identifying usability defects stands a good chance of leading to substantially more usable software.

DETAILS, DETAILS, DETAILS

Highly usable software does not, ultimately, emerge from principles or rules, but from thinking. Usability engineering is not rocket science, but it does require a thoughtful approach with attention to detail. And it requires a willingness to return, again and again, to the work, reconsidering decisions and revising results, tracing consequences and interactions.

Small details can make or break a user interface. Attention to detail can transform an acceptable design into a great one. Good ideas with great potential can be ruined by small matters overlooked or considerations rushed to conclusions.

> *Usability engineering is not rocket science, but it does require thought.*

For one example, Microsoft's Office 95 (and 97) provides a shortcut bar to give immediate access to the user's choice of applications, files, or folders. For such an application launcher to function as a central dispatch point, it must be instantly available from anywhere at any time. To save screen real estate and to avoid visually intruding on the user interface of applications, Office provides a clever mechanism in which the shortcut bar can, in effect, be hidden behind a narrow gray strip at the edge of the screen, popping out as needed whenever the mouse pointer passes over the strip. Unfortunately, this technique leads to the bar repeatedly popping out of hiding when it is not wanted. Whenever the user goes to select something near that edge of the screen where the shortcut bar lurks, it springs out, first obscuring the desired target and then taking its time to roll back into its lair.

The problem, well understood by anyone with any knowledge or training in human–computer interaction, is that the pointer almost always overshoots the intended target but is so quickly reversed to settle onto the right spot that most people are unaware of their brief, automatic correction. For the hide-and-seek mechanism to work perfectly, all that is required is a slight delay before triggering the bar to leap from hiding. If the mouse pointer has moved back out of the narrow strip before the delay is up, nothing happens, much as with the little hints or "tool tips" that pop up only when the pointer pauses over an icon on a toolbar. Ironically, through its overzealous responsiveness, the reclusive shortcut bar penalizes the very users it should most help. The faster the mouse is traveling, the greater the pointer overshoots the target. Power users—who work quickly, expect rapid access to numerous applications, and often value clean and uncluttered screens—are precisely those who are most likely to trigger the pop-out inadvertently. The lesson learned in so meticulously working out the optimal delay for popping up tool tips was lost, forgotten, or ignored by the designers of the shortcut bar (and the Windows Task Bar, which offers the same mechanism). Getting this right does not require elaborate testing, advanced mathematics, or sophisticated analyses; five minutes of actual use and a few minutes of careful thought reveal the problem and its solution. It is not rocket science.

The evolution of pop-up hints or tool tips itself offers another illustration of the importance of details. Apple introduced them in the form of "balloon help" on the Macintosh many years ago, but they also goofed on the technique chosen to activate the pop-up. When balloon help was enabled, balloons would pop up instantly as the pointer passed over objects anywhere on the interface. Most users, finding the effect not only disconcerting and distracting but also unhelpful, soon turned it off. The basic idea was sound, but the all-or-nothing implementation made it nearly useless. Once again, careful thought about the needs to be served by balloon help would have made clear the problem and the needed behavior. Throughout this book, we will have numerous other examples illustrating how good user interface design involves details, details, and more details.

> *Developers become better designers as they become better users—as they become more aware of interaction and more observant of how they and others interact with systems.*

In our experience, developers become better designers as they become better users—as they become more aware of interaction, more observant of how they and others interact with systems of all kinds, and more thoughtful about alternative ways to support interaction. They start noticing usability problems in doors that do not open as expected and in highway signs that are hard to interpret. They begin to see usability principles manifested in good designs all around them and violated in unusable systems of every ilk. They become increasingly intolerant of poor design. Eventually, they are able to observe and criticize their own work in terms of usability. Slowly, they come to realize that better design does not have to cost more or be more difficult to implement, but it does usually demand more thought. User interfaces that punish users are often the product of knee-jerk, thoughtless design. Usability is improved through mindfulness.

ESSENTIAL MODELS
FOR USABILITY

USERS AND RELATED SPECIES:
Understanding Users and User Roles

OF USE AND USERS

If we are going to build better tools, how do we know what tools to build? Before we can even start designing a user interface, we must know something about what it interfaces, about what will be on either side of that interface between the software and the user. We do not have to know everything, but we do need answers to a few basic questions:

- What will the users of this software be doing?
- What will they be trying to accomplish?
- What do they need from the system to accomplish it?
- How should the system supply what they need?

As we develop a system and it evolves through successive refinements or releases, we are also interested in the answers to some additional questions:

- What in the system is not working or is ineffective?
- How could the system be made more effective in supporting use?

Answers to these questions can be sought in various ways. Some developers, alone in their cubicles, seem to wait for divine inspiration or clues from the cosmos that might help in creating requirements out of nothing. Others look to other software—previous versions or competing products—for clues. Some will talk with the marketing department or the manager down the hall who seems to know a thing or two. Some may conduct surveys or

> *Some developers wait for divine inspiration or clues from the cosmos that might help in creating requirements out of nothing.*

analyze customer complaints. Some development groups make the radical move and go directly to the source—the users themselves—bypassing altogether the indirect channels and secondary sources.

If, as we suggested in the previous chapter, user interface design is a kind of dialogue between designers and users, then both parties need to be involved. The body of this dialogue takes place through the medium of the user interface, which embodies and presents to users the designer's understanding of the user's needs. To build that understanding and to build interfaces that communicate effectively with users and support them in their work, designers need, at some point, to deal directly with the users on the other side of the user interface. Although we are advocating a move away from purely user-centered approaches to software design, this does not mean that those who use the software are unimportant or are to be ignored.

REAL USERS AND OTHERS

The users whom we need to reach and understand are the real users of the software—that is, the end users who will have actual hands-on interaction with the software. These people are the ones doing the work, the ones employing our software systems as tools, whether to run a payroll report or to be entertained by outwitting warlocks in a fantasy forest.

End users are the primary and ultimate source of information to guide usage-centered design, though they are not necessarily our only resource. Some of what we need to learn about users and usage can be gleaned from other sources, ranging from supervisors and experts to trainers and technical support staff. Nevertheless, it is important not to confuse any of these others having information or an interest in the software design with the real thing—the end users.

ERSATZ USERS

Real users, the end users of software, are easily confused with certain others who, though they are not themselves users, may still have a legitimate voice in software design. Most notably among these "related species" are customers and managers.

Customer voices. Customers and clients are the people who buy software or contract for its production, but they may or may not actually use it. We do need to know and understand our customers if we are to stay in business and keep our jobs, but, to build more usable software, we need to know and understand our users even more so. Customers and clients pay the bills, which gives them clout and lends weight to their opinions, but their opinions and ideas may often have little to do with the actual use of software.

Listening to the voice of the customer is a touchstone of modern business practice, but the voice of the customer can also be a siren song that leads software developers astray. The heart of usage-centered design lies in giving people what they need rather than what they want—a sometimes subtle but always important distinction that is crucial for long-term success.

The very best designs anticipate rather than follow markets. Merely responding to customers leads to reactive designs. No market surveys of television viewers in the 1960s would have uncovered a customer base clamoring for video cassette recorders, yet the latent and unfelt need was there in the way viewers were trying to make use of their sets.

> *The very best designs anticipate rather than follow markets. Merely responding to customers leads to reactive designs.*

In our view, delivering the best value to customers means giving the users the service and products they need to be more effective. At times, this may even require convincing the customer that they do not want to spend money on an approach that will not work. At times, it even means declining business or turning down a project. Perhaps we might say that it is important to listen to and be responsive to your clients, but not to let them dictate your delivering less than your best.

Managing managers. Managers of end users and upper management within client organizations are among those who commonly raise their voices to be heard in the design dialogue. Such managers are, in some sense, indirect clients and do need to be listened to by developers. Project managers and other managers of software development also often have strong opinions about what users need or should get. They are our bosses and cannot be ignored.

In general, however, only the people who actually do a particular job really know what it entails and will readily recognize what will best support or improve it in practice. Managers of end users and clients who intercede for them are not generally reliable sources of information for good user interface design.

In one company, a group of developers, newly committed to a user-oriented approach to applications development, was asked by the manager of one of the research laboratories to develop a system for use by the technicians who conducted tests and tracked samples. When the developers showed up at the lab to talk with some of the technicians, they were stopped by the manager, who told them not to bother the busy staff. He told the developers to sit down, listen, and take notes: Everything they needed to know he could tell them in 20 minutes! The developers delivered the new system as requested, but, when it was installed in the lab, the technicians complained aggressively and refused to use it. The manager bemoaned his uncooperative staff and belittled the applications developers for delivering a bad system, but he never learned that he was the problem.

When managers stand in for users or stand between designers and users, the information received is generally incomplete and often distorted. Managers may sometimes be pushing a political or an organizational agenda that is quite apart from matters of good user interface design. If they are granted undue influence, the design will suffer.

> *Managers of end users and clients who intercede for them are not generally reliable sources of information for good user interface design.*

None of the foregoing is to say that user or client managers are always a problem or that they should be ignored. The vital lesson for the designer is always to remember that such people are not the same as end users and that input from them should be treated distinctly and separately from that originating with end users.

USER SURROGATES

User surrogates are people who, though not themselves users, may be able to serve as effective stand-ins for some purposes. If no end user is readily available, it is better that developers talk with a user surrogate rather than manufacture requirements out of a vacuum by talking with no one at all. User surrogates include former users of a system or similar system, application domain experts, trainers, and user supervisors.

Domain experts. **Domain experts** have knowledge about the broad general domain to which a specific job, task, or application belongs. In many cases, they can offer useful perspectives on the needs of end users. Domain expertise is not the same as direct knowledge of the work to be supported, however. For example, a professor of accounting—a domain expert—may know a great deal about the field of accounting and financial control but not understand the demands of the job or the daily dilemmas facing a bank teller.

The perspectives offered by domain experts complement and augment those of end users. Domain experts can, in many instances, help complete the bigger picture or suggest overlooked needs that must be supported.

Trainers. Trainers are another potentially valuable indirect source of information about users and uses. They may be responsible for training people in specific aspects of a job or in the use of specific software, such as earlier versions of a new system to be developed. Trainers tend to have some familiarity with both broad principles and practical issues. As teachers, they are often keenly aware of the complexities of software systems and of the work these are intended to support. They are likely to know a lot about what has made a system difficult to learn to use or inefficient for some tasks.

Supervisors. Managers who directly supervise end users can sometimes be a knowledgeable source of information about users and uses, but only if they are relatively close to the work and if their own agendas do not distort or color the information. Supervisors who have little daily contact with the work, who do not understand their subordinates well, or who have a markedly different perspective on the work than those who work for them are not likely to be good informants.

INFORMANTS AND INTERPRETERS

Many people and groups may stand ready to tell designers about user needs or to interpret for the absent or inarticulate user. Most common among the potential informants or interpreters are marketing and sales staff, supervisors, and technical support staff.

Marketing. Marketing departments become involved in product design in various ways. They may participate by request, but, as often as not, they insist on having a role in shaping the software and its features without waiting to be asked. When asked, they are typically queried what users really want or need. Marketing personnel may have some insights into what users want, but they rarely understand what users need, nor do their jobs equip them to understand. This limitation seldom prevents marketing people from rendering strong opinions, offering up survey results, or summarizing the findings from consumer focus groups.

The problem with marketing folks is that they understand markets, not users. Concerned with market share and the position of their products in the market compared with the competition, they tend to focus on features—the more the merrier—and on release schedules—the sooner the better—and on price points, not on user needs, usage, or usability.

Marketing can sometimes serve as a bridge to users, but experience has shown that marketing more often becomes a block preventing or restricting access to users. Marketing people want to build market share, and this agenda colors their abilities to serve as informants or interpreters. To their credit, good marketing people may have a larger vision of the potential for a product or line that can be useful for designers to understand. Unfortunately, their insight into work and usage is likely to be even more limited than their knowledge of users.

> *Marketing can sometimes serve as a bridge to users, but it often becomes a block preventing or restricting access to users.*

For practical and political reasons, inputs from marketing must be taken into account in designing software, but these inputs must never be confused with the needed information about users, user needs, and uses. In many companies, marketers may have more clout than developers, which means the adroit designer must become adept at not only the pragmatics of usage-centered design but also the politics of product planning.

Sales. In many respects, the story regarding salespeople is similar to that of marketing. Like marketing, sales is more interested in customers than customer needs. Whatever makes the sale is a good feature; what happens afterward in actual use is often of somewhat less importance to the salesperson.

Nevertheless, salespeople are more likely than marketing people to have direct contact with customers and even, in some cases, with end users. Building a good relationship with the sales staff can make it easier for developers to get access to customers and users when access becomes necessary.

Technical support. Technical and help-desk support staff can be a good source of information about users and usage. Their jobs bring them into direct contact with end users on a regular basis. On the one hand, through the questions and help requests they field from users, technical support people often develop a deep knowledge of poor user interface design and problems in using software. On the other hand, they are likely to know less about the normal course of users' work and what succeeds in user interface design.

Their problems and interests in supporting software can be markedly different from those of users, however, and these differences must be kept in mind when weighing information from support staff. Features that enhance usability may sometimes make a system harder to support. For one example, user customization of screen layout enables the end user to tailor an application to particular needs or work habits but can be maddening to technical support people trying to talk a user through a problem over the telephone.

Documentation specialists. The technical writers and specialists who write user manuals and create help files can sometimes be a rich source of information about users and uses, but they are more often consumers of this information, which they need to produce their pieces of the end product. Their skills in communicating can be an asset in dealing with users, however, and they may sometimes be brought into the dialogue with users for this reason. In all cases, designers should work closely with documentation specialists to ensure the overall usability of the system with its documentation. Obviously, the work of designers, developers, and documenters should be closely coordinated; ideally, all should be integrated into a single team.

INDIRECT SOURCES

People are not the only source of information and input that can help guide the design work. Just as archaeologists can glean much about a culture from the remains of its cities and villages, the perceptive designer may be able to learn from the objects and artifacts of modern business.

Manuals. Ask some users what they do and how they do it, and they will immediately point to a thick ring binder on a bookshelf. Standards and procedures manuals are commonly used to define jobs and the processes by which various tasks are carried out, but such official descriptions seldom correspond closely to actual practice. Such manuals do not so much describe work as serve as references or repositories to resolve disputes or to guide the handling of rare or exceptional circumstances. They also may be used to avoid responsibility ("It's not my fault. I went by the book.") or to fix blame for unsuccessful or questionable actions ("She did not follow procedure in this case.").

The incongruence between written standards and practices and actual work in so many organizations can be viewed from different perspectives. One Australian organization includes a full-time staff position of "process rationalizer" whose job it is to follow up on engineering and software development work after the fact to make sure that all the forms and documentation have been completed with the right boxes checked off in conformance with the organization's stated and duly certified processes. In their view, doing the work well is a process quite apart from reassuring the government or certifying authorities. A quality assurance specialist who carries out ISO 9001 certifications was shocked to hear this story, but most people who work in the industry know that such practices are common even if the job title is not. The point is, of course, never to trust official descriptions of procedures and practices without comparing the written word to observed behavior. In our experience, the thinner the manual, the more likely it is to bear some resemblance to the work that is actually conducted.

> *Standards and procedures manuals serve as references to resolve disputes, to guide the handling of rare or exceptional circumstances, to avoid responsibility, or to fix blame.*

Formal standards and procedures manuals are more important and are likely to reflect reality more accurately in some application domains and some industries. A good medical lab is likely to follow chapter and verse of the standard protocols for blood tests, for example. Defense contractors are more likely to go by regulations than are commercial game developers. One of us was once reimbursed in cash for expenses associated with a visit to a military base simply because so many forms and approval steps were needed to cut a check that it would have cost more than the amount of the expenses.

Derived data. Derived data refers to information about users and user needs that is derived from records or information obtained for other purposes or otherwise in the normal course of business. The piles of paper and internal publications that accumulate in any enterprise can be a mother lode of data just waiting to be mined.

Technical support and help-desk logs are often a rich source of usability information. Many technical support groups keep excellent records of problems and resolutions and frequently analyze their own databases to understand patterns in user problems. They compile lists of frequently asked questions (FAQs) that profile the problems users have had. Of course, not all the information from technical support records relates to usability, but a surprising fraction of it will have user interface design implications either directly or indirectly. If users frequently call because they cannot find a particular feature, perhaps there is a major layout and organization problem or perhaps the navigation map needs to be reviewed for possible improvement.

In a similar vein, customer complaints on related products or previous versions or releases of the same product can be of use in designing new systems. Spontaneous feedback or volunteered complaints represent a highly skewed sample. Some people write letters of complaint or make phone calls quite regularly, while other customers, often no less dissatisfied, write or say nothing. Some people have never lodged a formal or informal complaint in their lives. Complainants are often those consumers who have learned that the squeaky wheel gets the grease. Their problems sometimes have as much to do with personality as with product defects and may not necessarily be representative of those encountered by the larger population of users.

> *Spontaneous feedback or volunteered complaints from customers represent a highly skewed sample.*

Even when built-in biases are taken into account, it can often be difficult to interpret complaints and requests for technical help. The implications for user interface design can be quite subtle and buried rather deeply. When a high percentage of users complain that a system is slow, what does that mean? What is making it slow? Is it the way they are using it or the equipment on which they are running it? Perhaps they are not carrying out tasks in the manner for which the system was designed. Do features need to be reorganized or are there important unsupported use cases? It is usually hard to tell, and a detective spirit may be needed to tease the usage-centered implications from such problem-centered data.

The most important limitation of customer complaints and technical support records is that they are one-sided. They do not tell you what worked well, what features people were able to use effectively, and what users liked. Such records

EMPATHY

Many developers try to imagine what users need, but the history of using inference or inspiration to divine requirements is not very promising. Still, when genuine end users are not available for one reason or another, developers may be able to infer some of the information they might otherwise obtain directly from the source. It requires learning to think like a user. Exposure to end users can help, as can mutual participation in critical inspections, such as **collaborative usability inspections**. Some developers become more attuned to the user perspective just by becoming familiar with the rules and principles of usability. Role-taking is another route to empathic understanding of users and user needs.

In role-taking, the goal is to imagine oneself as a software user, to get into the head of the user, so to speak. It helps to think first about some of the defining characteristics of those user roles and role incumbents in which you are interested.

Use what you know about the physical setting in which the user works to imagine yourself there. Ask yourself questions about what it looks, smells, and feels like in that setting. Try to imagine what the state of mind of the user might be when your system will be in use. As much as you can, try to forget what you know as one of the computer elite and as the designer or builder of systems, especially of the particular system you are working on.

Gedanken experiments, or thought experiments, involve imagined use of an imagined system. It can help to have a vividly visual imagination, but a quick sketch of an unimplemented user interface can help even the most concrete thinker. In a *gedanken* experiment, the developer pictures or looks at the interface of some system and then fantasizes the performance of various scenarios that might be a part of everyday work.

"User-think" is difficult, and not everyone can learn to do it well. Even those who are reasonably good at it are bound by the limits of their knowledge and their imaginations.

Empathic inference through role-taking and *gedanken* experiments is probably best suited to truly novel fields of application or for projects that "boldly go where no man has gone before." Even in truly greenfield applications, however, there is nearly always some related system or tool and some related area of application that can be investigated and that can become a source for potential user-collaborators.

may reveal something about what features are actually used, at least insofar as these cause problems for users, but they will not give any indication of facilities that go unused.

Questions. To some groups, user surveys and questionnaires are appealing as an alternative to sitting down in the same room with users and actually talking with them. Questionnaire design is an art and science in its own right. To a considerable extent, you get different answers depending on how the questions are asked. In most surveys, respondents who complete and return questionnaires are a highly selected subset of users.

As a channel for communication from users to developers, questionnaires provide much more limited bandwidth than do face-to-

> *Questionnaires provide much more limited bandwidth than do face-to-face interviews or collaborative modeling sessions.*

face interviews or collaborative modeling sessions. Structured or closed-ended questions with fixed or limited responses can prevent developers from learning about unanticipated needs or issues. Open-ended or essay questions may seem to get around this limitation but are more time-consuming to answer and to analyze.

In general, written questionnaires should be regarded as a supplementary or confirmatory source of information, not as the primary mode of involvement for users. A written survey might answer specific questions about general patterns of use, such as how many users of the current system make use of a particular feature or what percent might find a built-in calendar function helpful.

USER ROLE MODELS

It is clearly advisable that, at some stage in the process, preferably earlier rather than later, somebody from the development team ought to sit down with one or more real users to have a good discussion. Mere conversation is not the objective. We need to model what we learn from our users, to confirm with them and with our clients our understanding of the work to be supported, and, ultimately, to incorporate that understanding into the software we build.

> *We need to model what we learn from our users, to confirm with them and with our clients our understanding of the work to be supported, and to incorporate that understanding into the software we build.*

The basic process is simplicity itself: Listen and learn, build a model, share it with users to get feedback, and then refine the model. Of course, the realities are considerably more complex. What do you say to users? What questions do you ask? How should the conversation proceed? At one extreme is an attitude that we, as professional developers, know what works and what is best for users. Users are ignorant and misguided at the very least. At the other extreme is the attitude that users know best what they need and ought to direct, if not dictate, the design.

In our view, neither extreme leads to the best designs. The dialogue with users is a negotiation, a process of circling in on mutual understanding. Such a dialogue requires a combination of technical and interpersonal skills. In this chapter, we will be focusing more on the technical side, on the models developed from this dialogue, rather than on the dialogue itself. After we have built a more thorough understanding of the technical issues, we will return to the dialogue in Chapter 20, when we explore the subject of how to use users most effectively in the development process.

By whatever route we come to understand them, users are of interest to developers, not as people, but because of the relationships they will have with the system to be designed and built. We may want to help them and to make life better for them, but we do that by delivering well-suited software. Many users may be fine and interesting people, but their lives apart from their relationships with our system are not of interest or importance in usage-centered design.

We represent the relationships between users and systems as roles:

> ■ A ***user role*** *is an abstract collection of needs, interests, expectations, behaviors, and responsibilities characterizing a relationship between a class or kind of users and a system.*

A **user role** is an abstraction; it is played by those users who assume a particular relationship to a system. A user role comprises a collection of common needs or interests, shared expectations, patterns of behavior, and responsibilities assumed by users in relation to some system [Wirfs-Brock, 1993]. Such a collection may be common to any number of users. Different sets of needs, expectations, behaviors, or responsibilities constitute different roles. It is important to remember that a role is an abstraction, not a real person, not a job title, not a position, not a function. It is not even a real group of people, but rather an abstract class defined by a particular kind of relationship to a system.

> *Users are of interest to developers, not as people, but because of the roles they will play in relationship with the system to be designed and built.*

One user role can be played by any number of different people. Conversely, a single user can take on any number of different roles with the same system. For example, we are heavy users of word-processing software. Often, we are playing in the role of writers. In this role, we expect little of the software, other than to transcribe and save what we type and otherwise keep pretty much out of the way. The software should do nothing that might interrupt the flow of creative thought, such as pausing, unbidden, to complete some internal indexing task or beeping on every spelling error. The primary goal is speedy, effortless input supported by the simplest of immediate editing capability.

At other times, either of us may use the same word processor in our role as editors. In this role, the software's capacity to let us change and rearrange the words becomes paramount. Assistance from the software with spotting typos or grammatical errors might also be appreciated. Yet another role in relation to the same software is that of publisher. In the

ACTORS AND ROLES

The concept of user role as used in this book is substantially the same as the notion of **actor** introduced in object-oriented software engineering [Jacobson et al., 1992], with one important difference: Actors, in the original definition, included other nonhuman systems—hardware or software—interacting with the system of interest. Thus, the centralized bank accounting system might be considered an actor in relation to an ATM program. Because usage-centered design is addressed to the needs and interests of humans interacting with a system through its user interfaces, only the human players are relevant.

Many people have found that Jacobson's use of the term *actor* to refer to the role played in relation to a system is confusing. Colloquially, "actor" refers to the person playing a part, and "role" refers to the part being played. Our term, *user role*, means just what it says and distinguishes the concept from the related one in object-oriented software engineering.

role of publisher, say, of a company newsletter, our primary interest is in the layout and appearance of material on the page—what graphics are used, how the text wraps around the illustrations, where the page breaks fall, and whether material fits into the allotted space. The content, the words themselves, are no longer the focus. To support this role, the software should show things as they will appear when printed and allow direct manipulation and rearrangement of the layout.

ROLE MODELING

In its simplest form, a **role model** (or **user role model** as it is also called) is just a list of the user roles to be supported by a system, with each role described in terms of the needs, interests, expectations, behaviors, and responsibilities that characterize and distinguish that role. We give each user role a name that captures the basic nature of the role, typically in the form of two or three concatenated words, and we provide a brief description highlighting the role's most salient and relevant characteristics.

In its simplest form, a user role model is just a list of the user roles described in terms of the needs, interests, expectations, behaviors, and responsibilities that characterize and distinguish them.

We construct a user role model by asking questions—questions of ourselves, of our users, or of the available informants:

- Who would or could use the system?
- What is the general class or group to which they belong?
- What distinguishes how they would or could use the system?
- What characterizes their relationship to the software?
- What do they typically need from the software?
- How do they behave in relation to the software, and how do they expect the software to behave?

Often, we start with a particular user in mind and then generalize toward the abstract role. For example, we might be working on a new package for laptop presentations. We think of one potential user in particular, a fellow in the sales department. More broadly, we think about company sales representatives who need to create slick but simple material for presentation at customer sites. Finally, we realize that there are many different users in many different jobs who have similar kinds of basic needs in using a presentation package. They make frequent use of on-screen presentations, but it is a relatively small concern in their jobs. These users are not likely to be particularly imaginative or artistic, and their uses are relatively unsophisticated. They want the capability of quickly and easily producing simple slides in standard formats, such as ones with a series of bullet points or displays of quantitative information in the form of simple graphs or charts. On those occasions when they might enliven their slides with graphics, they will most likely rely on standard clip-art as supplied with the software. We might summarize this role in a condensed form such as the following:

```
RoutineMinimalistPresenter
frequent use; rapid, easy operation; unsophisticated uses;
simple, standard formats: bulleted lists, bar charts, pie charts,
graphs, etc.; standard clip-art.
```

In our experience, the best approach to constructing a basic user role model is to begin by brainstorming a list of *candidate roles* with a minimum of discussion or detail. (See sidebar, Model Building.) Each role is given a name that typifies the relationship of such users to the system. Getting just the right name is less important than getting the right idea, so you should not debate the choice of names too much, nor should you worry about duplication, overlap, or fine differences among candidate roles. The initial list is just a slate of candidates; no one has been elected yet.

> *Often, we start with a particular user in mind and then generalize toward the more abstract user role.*

Once the initial list of candidate roles has been generated, you should sort through it, arranging similar or related roles into groups, considering ways to simplify and generalize the model, looking for opportunities to eliminate overlap or duplication. Next, you will begin to fill in the details, describing what you can of the characteristic needs, interests, expectations, and behaviors of each role. When describing user roles we want to stay focused on those characteristics of the role that are relevant to design of the software user interface. For example, in the course of analyzing user roles for a ski-lift ticket sales kiosk, we may note that those individuals in the user role of **SingleTicketPurchaser** tend to wear white hats or to own K2 skis. While such information might be of interest to advertising or marketing folks, neither point is particularly useful to us in designing the ticket kiosk's user interface.

As we progress in describing each of the use roles we've identified, we also want to concentrate on those characteristics which most clearly distinguish one role from another. Often, in the process of trying to articulate what it is that makes a role distinct, we discover that we have fundamentally the same role appearing under different names. By combining such similar roles and eliminating trivially different distinctions we keep the role model simple and effective.

Having reviewed the detailed model once more to consider any further simplifications or generalizations, at this point, at least in this most basic or informal form, the role model is considered to be complete. Before we leave it for the next modeling activity, however, we need to identify a set of one or more **focal user roles**.

MODEL BUILDING

Usage-centered design relies on models to guide the design process, including user role models and task models. In many respects, building models is an art form, but the art is easier to master if it is guided by an understanding of the creative process. Even the simplest models can become monstrous when developed for complex and highly sophisticated real-world applications. Thousands of details and hundreds of concepts may have to be catalogued and interconnected correctly. Where to begin and how to proceed?

1. **Separate creation from criticism**. Extensive experience has shown that creative thinking, especially in complex problem solving, is hampered when critical discussions are intermixed with the generation of creative ideas. For example, in brainstorming sessions, the rules for the process typically prohibit the discussion or criticism of ideas as they are being generated. In the absence of such rules, software developers, generally logical and critical by both temperament and training, often derail themselves through premature analysis and debate.

2. **Separate perspective from detail.** Getting a broad overview or perspective on issues is quite a different process from specifying and elaborating the details. Sometimes, the overview comes first and the details are filled in later; other times, the bigger picture emerges only after the details are complete.

3. **Separate generation from organization.** In many cases, bits and pieces of information can be recognized or created apart from any insight into how they are interrelated; in others, understanding the relationships among ideas leads to new ideas. In all cases, the elements themselves and the inter-relationships among them are distinct aspects of the whole picture.

Over many years of experience across multiple application domains, we have found that following an orderly process based on those three basic rules makes model building much easier, especially when undertaken in groups or teams of developers. The model building process itself has four steps:

1. **Compile.** The first step is to generate ideas or pieces of the model, such as user roles, without discussion or debate. Brainstorming or such variants as notestorming [Constantine, 1993e] are used to generate a collection of ideas without worrying about the details. The idea is to capture as many pieces of the puzzle as rapidly as possible.

2. **Organize.** Once compiled, the initial set is carefully reviewed in order to understand the pieces and the relationships among them better. The collection is sorted and organized by groups or categories appropriate to the model being constructed. Redundant or overlapping ideas can be combined or eliminated. The interim results are summarized.

3. **Detail.** Once the compiled concepts or elements have been organized, more specific details need to be completed. Descriptions are developed and elaborated; missing data is incorporated.

4. **Refine.** Finally, the organized and detailed model is studied in order to improve and complete it. The work is closely scrutinized and critiqued to assure that it is comprehensive, consistent, and correct as a model. If necessary, the model may be reorganized at this point.

The entire process is iterative and repetitive. At any point, the modelers may back up or return to an earlier step. Details may reveal hidden relationships; refinement may lead to new ideas or expose the need for elaboration of the basic model.

FOCAL ROLES

Focal user roles play a special part in helping to shape and define the user interface. Some roles are more vital to the user interface design process than others. Some roles are ubiquitous, while others may need to be taken into consideration in the design even if they are quite specialized and rare among actual users.

Focal roles are those few user roles that are judged to be the most common or typical or that are deemed particularly important from a business perspective or from the standpoint of risk or some other technical concern. We may know, for example, that the most common user for a hotel reservation system will be the desk clerk. Or we may conclude that the hospital administrator role, though rare, must be given special attention in designing a new hospital pharmacy system. In most applications, only one or a very small number of roles, two to three, will be designated as focal roles.

> *Focal roles are those few user roles judged to be the most common or typical or that are deemed particularly important from some other perspective.*

In many cases, it is fairly clear what are appropriate choices for focal user roles, but

SORTING CARDS

Card sorting is a simple and versatile technique for ordering and making sense of data. To conduct a card sort, all you need is a stack of standard-size index file cards. Each of the items to be sorted or ranked is written onto a separate index card. If the items are already in digital form, they can easily be printed out onto cards or onto adhesive labels to be stuck on cards.

In one variation of a card sort, an affinity clustering, cards are sorted into groups based on apparent similarity or relatedness. Alternatively, cards can be sorted into predefined categories.

Another variation is to sort the cards in order by some criterion, such as relative importance, degree of associated risk, or expected frequency. This form of card sorting is useful in selecting focal user roles, for example. Items are first sorted on each of several different criteria and then selected in one of two ways: Either the ranks according to each criteria are combined into a joint ranking and the top items are identified, or the top items on each ranking taken independently are selected.

Large quantities of items can be easier to sort using endpoint-anchored ranking. The rater looks through the cards and selects the highest-ranked card on the criterion and sets it aside; then the lowest-ranked card is set aside separately. The process is repeated until the remaining collection of cards—the middle-rated ones—is small enough to be sorted easily into order. The three piles are then combined.

Combining rankings from multiple team members is simple. Each rater sorts the cards independently and then flips the stack over and numbers the cards in sequence on the backs. (Make sure everyone numbers the stack in the same direction.) Afterward, the separate ranks on the back of a card are summed together to establish a joint ranking. (If you are of quantitative bent, you can readily determine the extent of agreement among those independent rankings by computing a coefficient of concordance, such as Kendall's W [Siegel and Castellan, 1988]. You can even determine whether the agreement is significant or not.)

In threshold voting, each rater selects from the collection of cards a set number of cards, which are then marked on the back with a tick. After all raters have made their selections, the N cards with the most tick marks or any card with more than a predetermined number of tick marks is selected. Threshold voting can be a quick way to partition a set of objects into two sets, such as focal and nonfocal user roles or features to be implemented or not in the first version of a system.

The physical handling of the cards is an important part of the card-sorting process, making it easier to shuffle and rearrange ideas and to immediately see the results. Various orders and arrangements can be tried and interpreted quickly. Whereas most people have difficulty rank ordering printed lists of more than a half dozen items or so, card sorting can be used efficiently and reliably with ten times that number. Actual manipulation of objects also draws on alternative thought-modes that can speed and simplify decision making.

Try it!

where there are many roles or information is ambiguous or limited, the choice of a few focal roles may be difficult. In these cases, we find it helpful to use a card-sorting procedure. (See sidebar, Sorting Cards.)

USER ROLE MAPS

User role models as simple lists of roles are simple to develop but fail to capture some important aspects of the roles played by users. A sizable system may have to support users in any number of roles, some of which may be quite similar or closely related. A simple list of roles and characteristics ignores or omits these relationships.

> *The user role map is a way of capturing the big picture; it reveals how all the various roles fit together in defining who will use the system and how.*

The **user role map** is a way of capturing the big picture; it reveals how all the various roles fit together in defining who will use the system and how. It is referred to as a *map* because it represents the interrelationships among all the roles that users can play in relationship to a given system. Within a user role map, roles can be interrelated in several different ways: by **affinity,** by **classification**, or by **composition**. By consolidating details and allowing common descriptions to be reused without rewriting them, user role models employing these relationships are often simpler than unstructured lists. Moreover, compared to the more piecemeal descriptions of individual user roles,

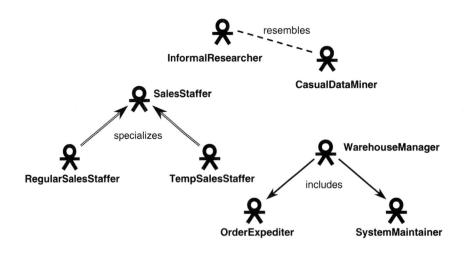

FIGURE 4-1 *Noting relationships among roles.*

the role map better reveals the overall nature of the interface between users and the system.

AFFINITY

The term *affinity* is used in modeling to refer to a recognized similarity or resemblance of an unspecified nature. User roles may be similar in style of interaction, in expectations, or in terms of any of a variety of common characteristics or shared features. For example, for a statistical analysis package, the user roles of **InformalResearcher** and **CasualDataMiner** might have quite similar descriptions. We would say that there is an affinity between these roles and would represent this relationship by a dashed line between the roles on a user role map, such as the one shown in Figure 4-1. In a text-based model, each of the user role descriptions would include a clause referencing similar or related roles. (See Appendix E for an example of a paper-based form employing such a clause.)

CLASSIFICATION

In some instances, a user role is a subtype of another, more general role, and represents a more specialized version of that role. In the course of developing the role model for a retail sales application, we might have identified **RegularSalesStaffer** and **TempSalesStaffer** as specialized variants on a common theme. Although users in these roles will have many functions in common, they are likely to have different levels of experience and skill in using the system and show different patterns of usage. Some information and actions may be of interest in one role and not the other. The common themes can be represented by an abstract role, which, in this case, we might call simply **SalesStaffer**. To represent this relationship of classification into roles and subroles on a user role map we use a double-lined arrow, as shown in Figure 4-1. In this example, the two roles are subclasses of the abstract role **SalesStaffer**. For a textual description, we would say that the subrole "specializes" a named general role.

COMPOSITION

Some roles combine the characteristics or features of two or more other roles and are, in a sense, composed out of these other roles. For example, a warehousing application might need to support an **OrderExpediter** role and a **SystemMaintainer** role, along with a **WarehouseManager** role that includes both of these roles, possibly along with some other unique interests or expectations. We would represent this composition relationship using a simple arrow, as shown in Figure 4-1, and, in text form, would specify that the **WarehouseManager** role "includes" the others.

USER ROLES IN ACTION

To illustrate the use of user role models, we introduce a very simple application—a common productivity "applet"—that will be used throughout the rest of this book as a concrete example of a user interface design problem.

Imagine this situation: You are typing information into a text entry box of some application, perhaps a free-form comment to be saved as part of a database entry. You reach the point where you have just typed the trademarked name of your company's flagship software product. You remember that company policy requires that the name should appear with a little trademark symbol after it, but you are temporarily stymied. The application you are using does not support any special symbols, and you do not have a keyboard that includes the trademark symbol as one of the keys.

You remember that Windows supports a way to enter any character by typing its ASCII code, but you cannot remember the code. Your desktop software collection includes an applet that might help, so you call it up. The applet might look something like Figure 4-2. You find the layout hard to read and a bit confusing. It seems to waste space on a lot of blank characters. You finally locate the tiny trademark symbol, but, when you switch back to your original data entry box, you cannot remember whether the magic code is **Alt+0153** or **Alt+0158**. You try both, but neither of them works because you forget the barbaric legacy of early Windows that requires these codes to be entered from the numeric keypad. Finally, you discover that you can get the desired character into the text entry box through the

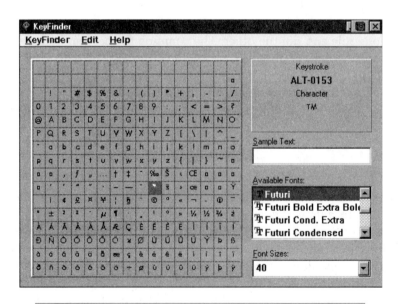

FIGURE 4-2 *A utility to find and enter special symbols?*
(NORTON DESKTOP FOR WINDOWS)

clumsy and complex sequence of double-clicking on the trademark symbol in the grid of the applet, then double-clicking on the character which now appears in the **Sample Text** box to select it, next copying to the Windows clipboard with **Ctrl+C**, then switching back to the data entry application, and finally pasting from the clipboard with **Ctrl+P**. (Although some applications, such as word processors, include their own facilities for inserting special symbols, there is still need, on occasion, for an autonomous, general-purpose capability. Windows 95 supplies a utility called "Character Map," which is similar to the one illustrated here.)

> *It is often a good idea to start modeling with the obvious or with what we already know.*

Surely, we can do better than this! Let's begin the process of building a better applet for this job by trying to understand the roles of the users who might make use of such a utility.

It is often a good idea to begin modeling with the obvious or with what we already know. So, we might begin with the kind of generic user whose primary need is similar to our own—namely the occasional entry of a single special character, such as a trademark or copyright symbol. Let us call this role the **CasualGeneralTyper**. (We eschew the word *typist* here to avoid the semblance of a job title.)

Who else might use such a piece of software? Someone writing a memo for overseas distribution to the German subsidiary who needs an umlauted character here or there might use it. Or perhaps you want to enter a word or two in Cyrillic for your Russian business partner. We might designate this role as the **CasualTranslator**. Why "casual" translator? Because a professional translator or foreign language typist would not use such a primitive utility. Such users would require a special keyboard or a far more powerful and efficient software facility.

Another role of this sort might be the **CasualMathematician**, anyone with the occasional need to enter a mathematical symbol or two. A serious or professional mathematician would not have much use for our simple applet but would use an equation editor or a special mathematics package instead. Along similar lines, we might identify **CasualScientist** and **CasualEngineer** roles.

Sometimes users make extensive use of special shapes and symbols in multiple fonts to enhance the appearance of documents. These potential users of the applet are in the role we might whimsically refer to as the **FancyFontFutzer**, because they continually "futz" with sizable collections of fancy fonts.

We have neglected one more kind of potential user: the programmer wanting to look up the hex or ASCII decimal code for a character or check the correspondence between a code and a printed character in a particular typeface. We can duly refer to this role as the **CasualCoder** because any *real* programmer would have memorized all these codes!

The initial list of candidate roles for our applet is as follows:

`CasualGeneralTyper`
`CasualTranslator`
`CasualMathematician`
`CasualScientist`
`CasualEngineer`
`FancyFontFutzer`
`CasualCoder`

When we look more closely at similar or related roles, we will no doubt conclude that the **CasualMathematician**, **CasualScientist**, and **CasualEngineer** are highly similar, differing largely or only in the particular special technical symbols that they will use. We might note an affinity among these roles, but more careful thought would suggest that these minor variations on a common theme are really subclasses of a **CasualTechnicalTyper** role. Eventually, we might even consolidate them into a single role.

We can next begin filling in some of the details that characterize and distinguish each role. In the **CasualGeneralTyper** role, the user has only occasional use for the utility and is interested in inserting a single symbol from a relatively small set of specified symbols of interest to the user. The exact symbols of interest may depend on the particular user, but they are likely to include such things as the copyright and trademark symbols, some currency symbols, and simple bullets to highlight items in lists. Users in this role will expect simple, efficient operation.

The **CasualTranslator** role differs from the **CasualGeneralTyper** role in that a larger collection of symbols is of interest to the user and the user may need to insert a whole series of special characters in order to complete a foreign word or phrase. Efficient operation will be an even stronger expectation of this role (due to the need, typically, to insert multiple special characters per use). Some such users may even prefer to use keyboard shortcuts or escape codes for frequently typed foreign or accented characters. In such cases, the utility becomes more of interest as a reminder of forgotten shortcuts than as a technique for inserting characters.

In the **CasualTechnicalTyper** role, the user is interested in more than simply inserting a character since mathematical notation and other technical symbols often depend for their interpretation on exact size and positioning. The set of symbols of interest is also likely to be more extensive than for the **CasualGeneralTyper**.

The **FancyFontFutzer** has a similar interest in the size and position of symbols because appearance is important. For this reason, too, the user in this role is apt to want to try and retry several symbols in succession before finding just the right bullet or glyph to create the desired effect.

In the role of **CasualCoder**, the user is not interested in inserting characters at all but is interested in the correspondence between characters and their internal representations as expressed by hex or decimal codes.

In all the identified roles save for the **CasualCoder**, the basic intent of the user is to insert into some text one or more symbols or special characters that are not found on the keyboard. Were the symbols on the keyboard, the user would have no need for the utility. Thus we might conclude that the **essential purpose** of the applet is that of "keyboard extender." In light of this essential purpose, it becomes clear that many utilities, such as the one shown in Figure 4-2, fail fundamentally to support these roles since they waste space displaying characters that are already on the keyboard. They do so because what is displayed is just the ASCII character set in sequence. In a sense, the programmers have merely taken the internal data structure and sprayed it on the screen without any regard for what users may need or intend to accomplish. This is an egregious example of *inside-out design* (What we refer to as: "Your programming is showing.").

STRUCTURED ROLE MODELS

In the discussion so far, the user role model has been considered as a loose collection of named roles accompanied by informal descriptions of the salient and relevant characteristics of each role. The informality of this view speeds the process of modeling, which may be particularly appropriate for smaller projects of relatively short duration or for projects undertaken within streamlined development processes. Such minimalist role models have been used very effectively to help design a wide variety of applications. However, these informal models are not without their limitations. It is often difficult to know what must be included in the description of a user role and what may be safely or preferably omitted. The inexperienced analyst proceeds with little guidance in recognizing relevant features of roles. More importantly, information that first becomes available or that is clarified in the course of defining and describing user roles may not always be captured and preserved in a way that supports good design or that facilitates tracing of requirements later in the development process.

> *Informal user role models speed and simplify the process, but it is often difficult to know what must be included and what may be safely or preferably omitted.*

The **structured role model** evolved as a way to methodically capture, early in the development process, as much relevant information as possible about the relationships of users to the planned system. A structured role model collects and organizes information about users in roles, guiding the derivation of a complete task model in the form of essential use cases and highlighting **operational context** facets of user roles that are likely to be of significance for designing an effective user interface.

ROLE CONTENTS

The structured role model helps us capture information concerning the system's operational context—that is the environment and context in which the software will be used—that is useful for understanding the work of users and for determining the shape of the user interface. This information is organized in the form of a series of collections which we refer to as *profiles* because they do not consist of a single factor or simple value but combine numerous factors and define a range or distribution of characteristics among users within a given role. Operational context profiles may also apply to or be *bound to* individual use cases or an application as a whole, as is discussed in Chapter 13. In the course of creating the structured role model we focus on the profile information insofar as it is associated with particular user roles. This information is then fed-forward into the **operational context model** (see Chapter 13).

> *The structured role model is a way to methodically collect and organize information about users in roles, guiding the derivation of the task model and highlighting operational context facets of user roles likely to be of significance in designing the user interface.*

The profiles that have most often proved relevant to user roles include:

- **incumbents**—aspects of the actual users who will play in a given role
- **proficiency**—how usage proficiency is distributed over time and among users in a given role
- **interaction**—patterns of usage associated with a given role
- **information**—nature of the information manipulated by users in a role or exchanged between users and the system
- **usability criteria**—relative importance of specific usability objectives with respect to a given role
- **functional support**—specific functions, features, or facilities needed to support users in a given role

Several other profiles may sometimes be of significance for user roles in an application, namely:

- **operational risk**—type and level of risk associated with the user's interaction with the system in a given role
- **device constraints**—limitations or constraining characteristics of the physical equipment through which a user in a role interacts with the system
- **environment**—relevant factors of the physical environment in which a user in a role interacts with the system

Incumbents. In sociology, a person who takes on or acts in a particular social role is referred to as a **role incumbent**. The role incumbents for a user role often share common characteristics that need to be taken into account in user interface design. The incumbents in the role of **CasualMathematician** can all be expected to have some knowledge of and experience with mathematical notation, for example. The users in the role of **LocationSeeker** for a downtown information kiosk will be unlikely to have much if any prior experience with that particular information kiosk.

The **incumbent profile** represents the various bits of information about the actual users who are likely to play a particular role in relation to the system. The important information falls into three categories:

- Domain knowledge
- System knowledge
- Other background

Domain knowledge refers to how much incumbents in this role are likely to know about the application domain that the system supports. **System knowledge** refers to how much users in this role can be expected to know about the system itself, how it operates, and how to use it. Bank tellers, for example, may be expected to have fairly substantial knowledge of the bank software system yet only modest knowledge in the domain of bank finance or accounting. Customers using an automatic teller system may typically be quite familiar with ATM systems but are not expected, in their roles as customers, to know much of anything about bank accounting.

Other background information on role incumbents may include any potentially relevant information about the training, education, experience, intelligence, or sophistication of users who might be expected to play in this role. For example, we noted that the **CasualBasicPresenter** was expected to be a somewhat unimaginative and inartistic user of presentation software. It could be important to realize that the **EnvironmentEngineer** role for a building climate-control system is usually filled by janitors who are well trained but typically not well educated. This could influence the terminology used within the user interface and how information is presented to users in this role.

Proficiency. The **proficiency profile** refers to the level of skill (as distinguished from knowledge) in operation of the system by users in a given role. It can range from novice to intermediate to expert levels of usage. The complex matter of how to design user interfaces to accommodate different levels of usage proficiency is the subject of Chapter 11. Role incumbents may differ substantially in their level of proficiency, and, for some systems, little can be said about the average or typical levels of proficiency. In other cases, a profile or pattern might be evident. For example, most bank tellers can be expected to use the banking software at intermediate or expert levels of proficiency because they are trained up to a certain level of skill by the bank and because they use the system almost constantly in their work. By contrast, most users of a public information kiosk will be rank amateurs, and none are reasonably expected to reach advanced levels of skill.

> *The role proficiency profile describes the level of skill (as distinguished from knowledge) in operation of the system by users in a given role.*

Interaction. The **role interaction profile** includes sundry information about the typical or expected patterns of usage of users in this role, including such things as the frequency and periodicity of interaction:

- **Frequency**—How often will the user take on this role?
- **Regularity**—Is there a regular period or is usage more or less sporadic?
- **Continuity**—Is interaction within this role essentially continuous or is it more intermittent?
- **Concentration**—Is usage concentrated into bursts or batches or is it more distributed?
- **Intensity**—What is the rate of interaction?
- **Complexity**—How complex are interactions within this role?
- **Predictability**—Are interactions within this role more or less predefined and predictable or are they highly variable?
- **Locus of control**—Is the interaction driven by the process or by the user?

Where quantitative information on these aspects is available, it can be incorporated in the interaction profile. For example, we may know that the **CorporateDirectoryMaintainer** role involves once-a-month processing of some 80 to 90 change transactions. For this role, interaction is regular, the frequency is monthly, and interaction is concentrated into batches of 80 to 90 events in a single sitting. In other cases, only qualitative or impressionistic information is available. In this role of **CorporateDirectoryMaintainer**, for example, interactions are fairly simple and relatively predictable, although the process will be driven or controlled by the user.

Facets of the interaction profile can strongly influence design objectives and the kind of user interface design that will be most effective. For example, infrequent use may put a premium on remembering how to use a system from one use to the next, while complex interaction may require close attention to interface simplicity and ease of operation.

Information. Where information originates and how it flows between user and system have important implications for user interface design. The **information profile** compiles what is known about the nature of the information being exchanged between the system and users in a role. This includes

- **Input origins**—Where does the input from the user in this role originate? What is its ultimate or actual source?
- **Flow direction**—Does information flow predominantly from or to the user?
- **Information volume**—How much information is available and of interest to the user?
- **Information complexity**—How complex is the information available and of interest to the user?

Information coming from the user may originate in the user's mind, but this is not always the case. The user in a particular role may be listening to someone speaking, either in person or over the telephone. The former would characterize a financial decision–support system used in the role of **LoanApprover**, with the customer seated across a desk from the user; the latter would typify the **TelephoneOrderTaker** role for a catalogue-sales order-entry system. For the **ClaimsEntryClerk** role in an insurance system, the source of entered data might be a paper form. *Aural, visual,* or *mental* origins for the information exchanged each impose different constraints on the user interface design. Visual feedback using on-screen graphics will not work where the user is looking at a paper form rather than the display, for example.

> *Where information originates and how it flows between user and system have important implications for user interface design.*

When information flow is largely *to* the user, a premium is placed on clear, efficient, and understandable display of information, which may be relatively less important when information flows mostly in the other direction. Large amounts of information or particularly complex information impose similar demands.

Usability criteria. Each of the aspects of a user role embodied in the other profiles can affect the relative importance of various design objectives or **usability criteria profile**. In addition to the core usability criteria introduced in Chapter 1—learnability, rememberability, efficiency in use, reliability in use, and user satisfaction—other criteria often come into play. These include accuracy, clarity of presentation, comprehensibility, and flexibility of operation. For example, interaction that is frequent, continuous, concentrated, and intense will place a premium on efficiency and accuracy as objectives in the user interface design. In some cases, even more specific and focused design objectives can be identified based on the user role characteristics. For example, large amounts of information and complex interaction may suggest that ease of navigation needs particular attention in the user interface design. A more thorough discussion of how design objectives are shaped by user roles and other contextual factors appears in Chapter 13.

Functional support. Some user roles may require very specific and identifiable kinds of support from a system in the form of particular functions, features, or facilities. The **functional support profile** includes these functional role requirements. The **CasualCoder** role for the keyboard extension applet, for example, requires the ability to match special characters to their equivalent internal codes, a capability not of intrinsic interest to users in any other roles.

Other profiles. For some applications there are other important factors associated with user roles that have an impact on user interface design and should be captured as part of the structured role model. One example is the **operational risk profile**, an assessment of the potential costs or consequences of error or failure in the use of a system. We find that the issue of operational risk is most often associated with specific use cases, such as **settingRadiationDose**, rather than with particular user roles, but this does not always hold. For example, all aspects of a patient records system in a health care facility entail substantial risks in the event of an error in use. Nevertheless, some user roles, such as **MedicationDispenser**, may carry more risk across the board than others, such as **BillingVerifier**.

BUILDING THE STRUCTURE

Constructing a structured role model is much like building an informal user role model, only in greater detail. The primary sources of information are end users themselves, domain experts, and, to a substantially lesser degree, clients and end-user supervisors. Roles are first identified and listed, the list is reviewed and organized, details are filled in, and the model is reviewed and refined. Forms, such as the one illustrated in Appendix E, can be useful as checklists to make sure all relevant categories are covered and to help designers organize the information.

> *It is seldom necessary to answer all the questions or check off all the categories, but it is important to capture the information that will have some impact on the user interface design and the models on which it is based.*

It is seldom necessary to answer all the questions, fill in all the blanks, or check off all the categories. What is important in each project is to capture the information that will or is most likely to have some impact on the user interface design and the modeling that leads to it. It wastes time and paper to capture and track information that is neither meaningful nor likely to be used.

The role model should include what is known, salient, and relevant about each user role. Categories or profiles that do not particularly distinguish a role or that are unlikely to have any significance in the design can be skipped and flagged as not applicable. However, if there is insufficient information on some aspect of a user role and it is potentially relevant for the particular project, an effort should be made to obtain the answers. Are speed and efficiency likely to be of importance to keyboard extension users in the role of **CasualCoder**? Unlikely, given the expected infrequency of use, but perhaps the opinions of some amateur programmers might be sought.

It appears to be easiest to start with affinity relationships first and then derive the other more specific relationships among user roles where these are identifiable. One of the simplest ways to perform an affinity analysis is through card sorting. (See sidebar, Sorting Cards.) Ideally, the complete role map should be developed, but, when there is insufficient time or inadequate information to construct a detailed user role map, at least the affinity analysis should be completed.

CARRY FORWARD

The information embodied in the user role model is primarily of interest for aiding in the identification and elaboration of the use cases to be supported by a system. User roles are the most important immediate source of information for building the task model. Of greatest help in this effort are the functional support profile, the role interaction profile, and the role information profile, although other profiles within the structured role model may occasionally imply tasks to be supported or provide ideas for elaboration or refinement of the use case model.

> *User roles are most important as the primary resource for building the task model, but they have other direct or indirect influences on various aspects of the user interface design itself.*

The information compiled within a structured role model also has some direct or indirect influence on a number of aspects of the user interface design, including the overall architecture, the user navigation through the various parts, and the layout and detailed design. Although the influence of user roles on design should, in principle, be taken into account more or less continuously throughout design and development, it is usually practical only to return to the user role model at key points in the development process. It is especially important to review this model prior to and during the visual design, when the first paper or active prototype is being developed, and as part of each usability inspection process. The role proficiency profile specifically comes into play when planning for the support of progressive usage, a topic that will be discussed at length in Chapter 12. Other aspects of adapting user interfaces to the context in which they are deployed and used are covered in Chapter 13.

5

WORKING STRUCTURES:
Task Modeling
with Essential Use Cases

WORK, WORK, WORK

Work is fascinating. We could watch it for hours without getting bored! That, of course, is one way to understand the work that people do and how it might be supported in software. To give people better, more useful tools with which to work, we must understand what they are doing and what they are trying to do. Learning the roles that users will play in relation to the system being built is the first step; the second is to understand and model the nature of the work that must be supported within those roles.

In social settings, when we want to know about somebody's work or job, we ask. Usually, we just start with some form of that overworked conversational opener "So, what do you do?" For everyday discourse, a job title is usually about all you need to know. If you do not know what a tuck pointer or a compensation analyst does, a sentence or two will fill you in. When it comes to building software systems to support users in their work, however, we need to know a great deal more. We need to know in substantial detail what users will be trying to accomplish in their work using our system and how they will need to go about it.

> *Most of us do many things quite well without having much of a clue as to precisely how we do them.*

After that first polite inquiry when we meet someone, we do not usually follow up with the question "So, how do you *do* what you do?" This is probably for the best since most work is rather complicated and hard to describe in words, and, more importantly, most of us do not have much of a clue as to how we actually do many of the things we do. How, for instance, do you say the word *work*? Can you

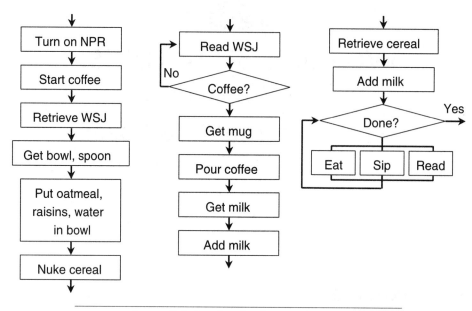

FIGURE 5-1 *Starting the day, step by step.*

describe the process? Could you offer concrete and detailed instructions to some-one who understood English but who had never spoken aloud before?

In the context of software development, simply asking users what they do and how they do it is not going to tell us enough to help us design good software. Ask them directly, and users will most often give you the official story, telling you what they are supposed to be doing, even though that may be worlds apart from what they actually do. They may tell you, in all honesty, what they believe they do, but, if you watch them in their everyday work, you are likely to see them doing quite different things. Or when you ask, they may point to a set of manuals on the shelf above the desk and comment simply that "it's all in there."

Consider our own field of software development. Procedure manuals, stan-dard practice guides, and even textbooks on software development may go into excruciating detail about how some task is supposedly carried out, but a little investigation will almost always reveal that all these volumes are substantially works of fiction. Like literary classics that everybody cites but almost nobody has read, these manuals and guides are referred to in order to reinforce arguments or are opened up on rare occasion to resolve disputes, but otherwise they probably have little to do with everyday work activities.

Learning about what users really need from software to support their work, as distinct from what they want or what they merely think they need, requires a dia-logue between analysts/designers and users in the form of a conversation in which both parties gradually build a joint understanding of the work and how to support it. This joint understanding is embodied in **task models** that represent the structure of user needs—the architecture of use.

TASK MODELING

There are many ways to model work. Most traditional ways to describe work or tasks are variants of the kinds of models that should be quite familiar to software developers. One popular approach is to use some form of flowchart that describes tasks in terms of a logical sequence of events or processes. Even large, complex tasks can be described by breaking them down into a series of small, sequential steps. That is the basic idea behind all computer programs and programming. Flowcharts, finite state machines, workflow models, and data flow diagrams are all forms of sequential models that can be and have been used to model human tasks. For example, Figure 5-1 illustrates a flowchart for the ritual that might begin the day of someone who fancies oatmeal, National Public Radio, and the *Wall Street Journal.*

This sequential approach to modeling human work is detailed and concrete, resembling, in many respects, computer programming. Consequently, it tends to appeal to programmers and traditionally trained systems analysts. As might be expected, flowcharting and its kin may generally be better suited to modeling computer tasks than human tasks.

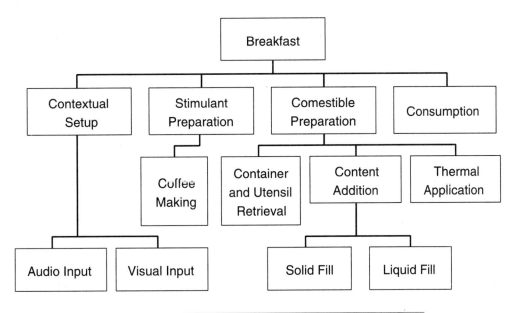

FIGURE 5-2 *Breaking down the start of the day.*

Complex tasks can also be understood through hierarchical decomposition—that is, by breaking tasks into subtasks and decomposing subtasks into still smaller units. Structure charts, work breakdown charts, and other forms of expressing functional decompositions have all been used for modeling the structure of work as well as of systems. Functional decomposition, however, can produce elegant models that have little to do with the realities of how work is accomplished or how users think about what they are doing. Figure 5-2 is a possible work breakdown chart for the morning routine shown in Figure 5-1. Like the flowchart for the same task, a hierarchical model can be fairly fanciful even when conceptually accurate.

> *Functional decomposition can produce elegant models that have little to do with how work is actually accomplished or how users think about it.*

Hierarchical models are conceptual and categorical, leading, when well thought out, to clean and balanced classification schemes. Hierarchical modeling resembles outlining a good journal article or textbook. Not surprisingly, this approach seems to hold special appeal for academics and others with a research or scientific bent.

FROM SCENARIOS TO USE CASES

Scenarios are another way to represent the structure of tasks and work. Scenarios are narrative descriptions of an activity or activities, taking the form of a story, a vignette, or an episode bound in time and taking place within a given context. In various forms, they have been widely used in software design [Carroll, 1995]. Scenarios are scripts for work or interaction and are characteristically rich and realistic. For example, the start of the day (Figures 5-1 and 5-2), in scenario form, might go something like this:

> Enter the kitchen and turn on NPR on FM radio. Prepare coffee if needed (get coffee filter, measure coffee and water) and turn on coffee-maker. Bring in WSJ from driveway. Get out bowl and spoon, then fill bowl with oatmeal and raisins from cupboard. Add water and stir, put in microwave (at high, 2 minutes). Read WSJ until coffee is ready. Grab a mug from shelf and pour coffee. Get milk from 'fridge and add to coffee. Fetch cereal from microwave, and add milk. Take stuff to table, and enjoy coffee and cereal while reading.

Scenario writing is a bit like storytelling, which may explain why the approach is often preferred by more artistic or literary-minded analysts. Although scenarios typically take the form of a continuous narrative, they can also be cast as sequences of images in the form of storyboards.

Scenarios for user interface design narrate the interaction between a user or type of user and a system. In our experience, conventional scenarios have some serious limitations when it comes to user interface design. Their emphasis on realism and rich detail can obscure broad issues and general organization. Because scenarios comprise plausible combinations of individual tasks or activities, they can make it more difficult to isolate and understand the basic kernels of interaction.

In our work, we first turned to a close cousin of the scenario, the **use case**, whose very name suggests some kinship to usage and user interfaces. We briefly introduced use cases in Chapter 2, but we will examine them in more detail here.

The concept of the use case was first applied to software development by Ivar Jacobson as part of his object-oriented software engineering method [Jacobson et al., 1992]. So successful have use cases been that they have since been integrated into virtually every major approach to object-oriented analysis and design. Although developed for use in designing and constructing object-oriented software, there is nothing particularly object-oriented about use cases, and they are applicable to virtually any development approach.

A use case is a case of use, or one kind of use to which a system can be put. A use case is:

- Supplied functionality
- An external, "black box" view
- A narrative description
- Interaction between a user—in some user role—and a system
- A use of a system that is complete and meaningful to the user

As the term is employed in object-oriented software engineering, a use case is a narrative description of interaction between a user—in some role—and some system. Use cases represent an external or "black box" view of the functionality supplied by the system to the user. Use cases can be considered to be part of the specification of requirements. Besides their application to requirements engineering [Davis, 1993], use cases play a central organizing role throughout the development process within some approaches to object-oriented software engineering.

Each use case describes, in narrative form, an interaction that is complete, well defined, and meaningful to some user. Within object-oriented software engineering, use cases can describe interactions with other systems and equipment in addition to interactions with human users. When the objective is user interface design, however, we can safely restrict our view to those use cases that represent interactions between people and systems.

As originally conceived and as used within many development methods, use cases are often expressed in the form of a continuous, linear narrative. We have found that a convention introduced by methodologist Rebecca Wirfs-Brock offers a number of advantages. In this structured form, the narrative is divided into two parts: the **user action model**, which shows what the user does, and the **system response model**, which shows what the system does in response [Wirfs-Brock, 1993]. This form clearly divides the responsibilities and interests of the user from those of the system and its developers.

Consider the process of getting cash from an automatic teller machine (ATM), a problem often used to illustrate use case modeling. Here is the use case for this task as supported by our bank in Australia:

gettingCash

USER ACTION	SYSTEM RESPONSE
insert card	
	read magnetic stripe
	request PIN
enter PIN	
	verify PIN
	display transaction option menu
press key	
	display account menu
press key	
	prompt for amount
enter amount	
	display amount
press key	
	return card
take card	
	dispense cash
take cash	

In this two-column format, the line down the middle represents, symbolically, the system boundary separating the user from the system. It is, in a sense, the user interface. This format also highlights the part played by the user, which is the part most crucial to good interface design.

ESSENTIAL USE CASES

Some developers and methodologists have attempted to employ use cases in their original form as aids to user interface design [Bilow, 1995; Graham, 1994; McDaniel, Olson, and Olson, 1994; Whitehead, 1995] not only with great enthusiasm but also with what must be judged as mixed success. Our own earlier work and experimentation highlighted some major problems and limitations with use cases employed for this purpose. In particular, conventional use cases typically contain too many built-in assumptions, often hidden or implicit, about the form of the user interface that is yet to be designed. As models, they lean too closely toward implementation and do not stick closely enough to the problems faced by users.

The use case for **gettingCash** just shown, for instance, assumes that bank cards with magnetic strips are being used, that there is a visual display, and that the user will indicate responses via a keypad of some kind. It contains many steps that are not part of the user's agenda but which are imposed by a particular user interface and internal design that are already assumed. Unfortunately, these assumptions are not made explicit in the narrative. In this conventional form of use case, some aspects of the user interface have already been determined without necessarily having been designed. These

> *Conventional use cases typically contain too many built-in, premature assumptions, often hidden or implicit, about the form of the user interface to be designed.*

implicit design decisions and the constraints and limitations they place on the ultimate form of the user interface may or may not be the best for supporting the task of getting cash from an ATM. If we design a user interface based on such a concrete and specific use case narrative, we may have already missed many chances for a better design.

The difficulties just described led us to develop a new form of task model, the **essential use case** [Constantine, 1994b; 1995a; Phillips, 1996], by drawing on the concept of essential modeling [McMenamin and Palmer, 1984] introduced in Chapter 2. Ian Graham has described a related form of condensed, abstract use cases and called them *task scripts* [Graham, 1996]. An essential use case is defined as follows:

> ■ An **essential use case** is a structured narrative, expressed in the language of the application domain and of users, comprising a simplified, generalized, abstract, technology-free and implementation-independent description of one task or interaction that is complete, meaningful, and well-defined from the point of view of users in some role or roles in relation to a system and that embodies the purpose or intentions underlying the interaction.

An essential use case is based on the purpose or intentions of a user rather than on the concrete steps or mechanisms by which that purpose or intention might be carried out. Others have recognized the value of incorporating user goals or purposes into use case modeling, but not within the simplifying framework of essential modeling [Kaindl, 1995].

As employed in usage-centered design, an essential use case is a structured narrative consisting of three component parts: a statement of the overall user purpose or intention expressed within the use case plus a two-part narrative comprising the **user intention model** and the **system responsibility model**. Essential use cases are named, and, where possible, the name implicitly expresses the user intent or purpose of the use case.

> *Essential use cases are based on the purposes or intentions of users rather than the concrete steps or mechanisms by which those purposes or intentions might be carried out.*

The notation for essential use cases is very simple. Following the convention introduced by Jacobson, a use case is represented by an ellipse labeled with its name (see, for example, Figure 5-3, which appears later in the chapter). Following the convention devised by Wirfs-Brock, a **use case narrative** is arranged as two parallel columns. For a **conventional use case**, these columns are the "user action model" and the "system response model." In an *essential* use case, the columns are renamed to reflect a change in perspective. The left-hand column becomes the "user intention model" because essential modeling shifts the focus from actions to intentions—that is, to the objective or the "aim that guides action," the "course of action that [the user] intends to follow."[1] The right-hand column becomes the "system responsibility model," reflecting the user's expectations regarding the responsibilities to be assumed by the system.

The difference between a concrete use case and an essential one may seem subtle, but the consequences are anything but. The difference is best appreciated from an illustration. We can rewrite the previous example of **gettingCash** in the form of an essential use case by focusing on intentions rather than actions and by simplifying and generalizing from the concrete use case. We start by asking ourselves why the user would do something as strange as sticking a valuable bank card into a slot in some machine. On the surface of it, this seems like a singularly silly action, especially considering that there is some chance that the machine will simply swallow the card and never return it. Nevertheless, users dutifully insert their cards into slots every day. Why? Because they want to identify themselves to the ATM system. They do this for the simple reason that they do not want anyone else withdrawing money from their accounts. For the same reason, every user has a stake in the system's verifying the identity of each user. The essential use case for this interaction might look like this:

---

1. *The American Heritage Dictionary of the English Language, Third Edition* copyright © 1992 by Houghton Mifflin Company. Electronic version licensed from InfoSoft International, Inc. All rights reserved.

gettingCash

USER INTENTION	SYSTEM RESPONSIBILITY
identify self	
	verify identity
	offer choices
choose	
	dispense cash
take cash	

Once the user's identity has been verified, the system should offer a choice of actions, one of which ought to be "the usual." It so happens that some 70% to 90% of all ATM transactions are cash withdrawals, and some 70% to 90% of cash withdrawals are for the same amount and from the same account as the last transaction by that customer. To support this most frequent use case, the choice of "the usual" should be the first offered or the easiest for the user to confirm, simplifying use and speeding the task.

This essential use case is dramatically shorter and simpler than the concrete use case for the same interaction because it includes only those steps that are essential and of intrinsic interest to the user. Because it is closer to a purely problem-oriented, rather than solution-oriented, view of the task, it

> *Essential use cases are often dramatically shorter and simpler than concrete use cases for the same interactions.*

leaves open many more possibilities for the design and implementation of the user interface. Other than magnetic-stripe bank cards, there are numerous ways that users could identify themselves and have that identification verified. The ATM might employ voice recognition, thumbprint analysis, or even a retinal scan to figure out who is using the system. (We have been using this example in teaching for years. Some manufacturers have now begun experimenting with retinal scan technology for ATMs.) In a high-security installation where everyone is tracked via laser-scanned badges, cash machines for the employee credit union could be designed to know automatically the identity of anyone approaching to use the machine. Yet another possibility opened up by the essential use case is to offer choices or confirm them through voice-response processing.

LEVELS OF ABSTRACTION AND GENERALIZATION

Both concrete use cases and essential use cases are closely related to scenarios. Although some writers define the term *scenario* so broadly as to cover almost any activity in narrative form [Carroll, 1995: 20–21] and some even use the term as a synonym for *use case* [Booch, 1994; Firesmith, 1994; Wirfs-Brock, 1993], we think there are important and useful distinctions that are worth preserving.

As the term is generally employed, a scenario is a concrete and detailed description of a particular sequence of events that is specific, even though it may be intended to be representative of a more general kind of interaction. Nielsen, for example, defines a scenario as "a self-contained description of an individual user interacting with a specific set of computer facilities to achieve specific outcomes under specified circumstances over a certain time interval" [Nielsen, 1995]. It is hard to picture being much more specific and concrete than that.

However, people often use scenarios to talk about and describe general patterns through specific examples. For instance, consider software for a semiauto-mated, computer-supported technical-help facility. In trying to get a handle on how this system should operate to support help-desk users, a developer might offer a scenario something like this:

> It's 4:00 A.M. and Marge Ackerman calls the Tech Support Hotline. No one answers, so the system picks up, and she hears the voice prompt, "Welcome to TechnoWiz. Please key in your customer ID." She keys in "2006789" on the telephone keypad, then hears the menu for software support options, and so on.

Naturally, we do not intend to design a system that works only for customers named Ackerman or that is somehow tailored for optimal operation in the wee hours of the morning. The particulars of the scenario are meant as stand-ins for more generic interaction. One of the problems with using scenarios to guide user interface design is that we must be able to separate the generic from the specific in order to design the user interface to support the broad class of interactions, not just the particular variant expressed in a scenario. In simpler instances, teasing out the general case from the specific or isolating the concrete details to be ignored is not too difficult, but scenarios can also be quite lengthy, embodying not one simple goal or activity, but many. As problem descriptions grow large and complex, incorporating many different scenarios or elaborate ones, the generic and the specific become more conflated and confused. In many projects, these are not successfully kept separated, and the resulting design is based on a muddled mix of generalized and specialized considerations.

Scenarios are often used to talk about and describe general patterns through specific examples, but separating the specific from the general and keeping track of these can be daunting.

A conventional or concrete use case is a reduction or abstraction from a collection of related scenarios. Ivar Jacobson, who coined the term *use case*, says that scenarios are instances of use cases [Jacobson, 1994]. That is, a scenario is a specific embodiment of the general form expressed in some use cases. A use case for the tech support system might read something like this:

> User dials Tech Support Hotline, hears prompt, keys in ID, hears support services menu, and so on.

One simple way to understand the fundamental difference between scenarios and use cases is to think of them as if they were actual program code. Comparing the scenario and use case for the tech support system reveals that scenarios are typically expressed in terms of constants or literal values, such as "2006789," while use cases are expressed in variables or symbolic terms, such as "ID." Thus, although they model interaction with a particular user interface and, of necessity, make direct reference to specific features of that user interface, use cases, as originally conceived, are a more generalized, more abstract form of expression than scenarios. In the tech support example, the use case refers, however indirectly, to vocal presentation with keypad response over a telephone.

For the designer of user interfaces, this adherence to concrete forms of expression constitutes a significant limitation of conventional, concrete use cases. Some of the design decisions regarding the form and features of the user interface have, in a sense, already been usurped and are, by implication, built into the narrative description of the use case.

Concrete use cases intermix requirements with design. By definition, they do not represent user purposes and intentions apart from interaction with some particular kind or form of user interface. The writer of concrete use cases is analyzing and describing requirements imposed by the problem intermingled with implicit decisions about what the user interface is going to be like. Ironically, the very specificity of conventional use cases leads to a lack of clarity in the model.

If we want to get as close as possible to the users' perspective and concentrate on understanding and describing their needs and intentions from this perspective, then we have to turn to a still more abstract model. An essential use case describes interaction independent of implicit or explicit assumptions regarding the technology or mechanisms of implementation. An essential use case corresponding to the scenario and concrete use case described earlier might be something like this:

> Request help, identify myself, select help service, and so on.

This variant of the narrative is stripped of concrete details and is devoid of references to any particular user interface devices or features; hence, it leaves the choice of these open in the final user interface design. Indeed, the very same essential use case could describe use of a help system based on a Web site. The user might request help by clicking on a URL rather than by calling on a telephone. The Web site might employ a "cookie" that automatically identifies users.

This last form of the use case is an essential model in the sense introduced in Chapter 2; it is an abstract, idealized, and technology-free description of a problem with minimal intrusion of assumptions about particular solutions. As such, it is closer than either scenarios or concrete use cases to a direct expression of what users actually need to accomplish with a system. Returning to the programming analogy introduced in comparing scenarios and use cases, the terms in which the essential use case is expressed are abstract superclasses or supertypes to which the variables within the concrete use case belong. Because it is "essential," the essential use case leaves open many more options in terms of the implementation of a suitable user interface. For example, identification and service selection in the tech support application might be accomplished through voice recognition.

> *Scenarios, concrete use cases, and essential use cases are related task models representing successive levels of greater abstraction and generalization that take us closer to user needs and intentions.*

Scenarios, concrete use cases, and essential use cases are related task models that represent successive levels of greater abstraction, simplification, and generalization. Moving from scenarios to use cases to essential use cases takes us closer to a pure and idealized expression of user needs and intentions. Because essential use cases are simplified descriptions of the capability the system must supply, they also pave the way to building smaller, simpler software that nevertheless meets the needs of users.

Scenarios can also be considered to be **enactments** of one or more use cases or essential use cases. An **enactment** consists of the steps taken to carry out a use case with a particular user interface. Obviously, any essential use case can be enacted in a number of different ways, so there are many possible scenarios corresponding to each essential use case.

There are also differences in size and granularity when essential use cases and use cases are compared with scenarios. The storytelling demands of scenarios often require greater length. The more realistic the scenario, the more likely it is to be embellished by color and details, not all of which may be needed to define the work under consideration. For similar reasons, scenarios, at least as used in typical practice to capture and describe requirements or guide design processes, will usually draw on and narrate multiple use cases. Whereas scenarios often typically range from a page to dozens of pages [Weidenhaupt et al., 1998], well-written use cases are seldom more than a page or two in length, and essential use cases are usually expressed in a handful of lines at most.

Essential use cases yield a more compact model in part because of their higher level of abstraction and in part because the activity of essential use case modeling encourages the partitioning of tasks into small, coherent units of description. This fine-grained approach not only compresses the description of tasks but also promotes the reuse of task descriptions, as we will clarify in the next section.

THE USE CASE MAP

Use cases do not exist in isolation. A complete software system may have to support dozens or even hundreds of use cases, and, within any reasonably coherent application, these use cases will be interrelated. Expressing the interrelationships among use cases enables us to describe the overall structure of the work to be supported by the application and its user interface. The **use case map** for a given problem partitions the total functionality of the system into a collection of interrelated essential use cases. By separating out distinct and meaningful interactions and showing how they are related, we can construct a simpler overall model of the supported work and the capability the system should supply.

The complete use case model is expressed as a set of narratives defining the body of each use case and a use case map showing how use cases are interrelated. Essential use cases can be interrelated in various ways, including by classification, by extension, by composition, or by affinity. These relationships allow the analyst or designer to separate out common elements of the supported work, resulting in a simpler task model.

SPECIALIZATION

Some use cases are specialized versions of others. For example, in our familiar ATM application, the use cases for `withdrawingCash`, `depositingFunds`, and `queryingStatus` are all subclasses or specialized forms of an abstract class of interaction that could be called `usingATM`. The relationship between `withdrawingCash` and `usingATM` is called **classification** or **specialization**. The relationship is that one use case "is-a" (or "is-a-kind-of") another use case. This relationship is like the class–subclass relationship at the heart of object-oriented analysis and design.

Specialization allows us to simplify the overall use case model by separating generic or general-purpose forms of interaction from more specialized adaptations to narrower purposes. Thus, we do not have to keep rewriting the more general patterns of interaction but can write them once and "reuse" them by referring to them. As shown in Figure 5-3, a double-lined arrow is used to indicate specialization in a use case map. The line can be labeled "is-a" or "specializes" as best suits the context.

The general case—that is, the **supercase** specialized in a **subcase**—is an abstract class, a use case that, in itself, is never enacted. It does not stand on its own as an

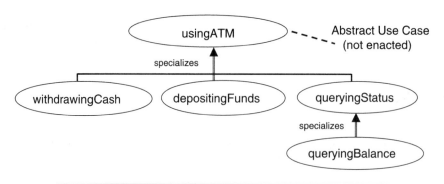

FIGURE 5-3 *Specialization of use cases in a use case map.*

interaction that would actually be carried out by a real user. Bank customers do not "use an ATM." They withdraw cash or deposit funds or query account balances.

Object-oriented programming uses the class–subclass relationship, or **inheritance**, as it is often called, as a means to structure large systems and to support component reuse. The primary purpose of classification in the essential use case model is to simplify the model of usage and build understanding of what the user interface must support. For this reason, it is not absolutely necessary that the use case map be rigorously correct. What is more important is that the model partitions all usage into a reasonable number of essential use cases that make sense to users.

> *It is not necessary that the use case map be rigorously correct, but the model should partition usage into a reasonable number of use cases that make sense to users.*

As a rule, good modeling practice restricts classification to cases where there is a strict type–subtype relationship, where the subcase represents a strict subclass of the supercase. The proper use of inheritance is a subtle and much debated issue in the world of object orientation [Page-Jones, 1995]. For our purposes, if a sentence of the form "every **subcase** is a kind of **supercase**" makes proper sense, then it is usually acceptable to employ the specialization relationship. For example, every **withdrawingCash** is indeed a kind of **usingATM**.

The actual implementation of the user interface and the underlying internal components, though guided and influenced by the use case map, will not necessarily follow the model exactly. Coding decisions are not design decisions, and they are influenced by many factors. Just as usability can suffer when the user interface too closely reflects the code that implements it, so, too, slavishly modeling the internal program structure on the user interface can lead to less durable internal architectures. We will have more to say about these issues in Chapter 19.

EXTENSION

One of Jacobson's inspired innovations in object-oriented software engineering was the notion of **extension** as a relationship between use cases. One use case is said to "extend" another use case if it represents inserted or alternative patterns of interaction within the course of the use case being extended. For example, in the course of carrying out the use case to change the appearance of an item on the screen, the user may have to browse for an appropriate icon among the picture or icon files within the system. The normal or expected course of interaction, called the *basis* or **basis case**, does not necessarily include browsing for additional graphic files. Here, **changingImage** is the basis case:

changingImage

USER INTENTION	SYSTEM RESPONSIBILITY
request change	
	show appropriate images
select image	
	show preview
confirm	
	close

Many different use cases might require browsing for image files; browsing will be needed anytime a desired image is not among those offered by a particular use case. By creating a separate extension use case, **browsingImages**, the narrative for the basis is kept simpler, and the interaction embodied in the extension becomes available to extend other use cases. The interaction of the extension, **browsingImages**, does not appear in the narrative of the basis, **changingImage**; it could occur at any point within the course of the basis. The same is true for any other use case that might be extended by **browsingImages**. Separating out extensions as distinct use cases maintains the simplicity and clarity of the basis cases and encourages a single, common realiza-

> *Extension was an inspired invention of Jacobson, a powerful concept that can substantially simplify use case models.*

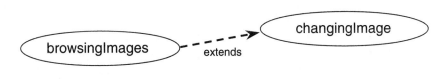

FIGURE 5-4 *Extension cases: alternatives and exceptions.*

tion of each extension in the implemented user interface, thus supporting the Reuse Principle.

Extension is a powerful concept that can make possible substantial simplification of essential use case models. Within the use case map, we represent extension by a dashed line and arrow labeled "extends," as shown in Figure 5-4. In the supporting narrative for the extension, a note can be appended indicating what use cases are extended:

browsingImages	EXTENDS: `changingImage,`
	`insertingImage,`
	`openingImageFile`

USER INTENTION	SYSTEM RESPONSIBILITY

USER INTENTION	SYSTEM RESPONSIBILITY
`request more`	
	`show more images`
`[continue until found]` `select image`	
	`insert image` `close`

COMPOSITION

Use cases can be decomposed into component parts or subcases representing subordinate or included patterns of interaction. The **composition** relationship is designated on a use case map by a simple arrow pointing to the subcase and labeled "includes" or "composed of" or "uses," as shown in Figure 5-5.

The interaction represented by the supercase is carried out using or making use of the interactions within the subcase or subcases, and the narrative for the supercase will refer to any subcases that are used. For example, the use case **loggingJobStart** within a job-tracking program might make use of **authorizingAccess** and **enteringJobParameters**, indicated within the use case narrative with a ">" followed by the name of the use case being used. This way of modeling the interaction separates the independent and largely unrelated subtasks

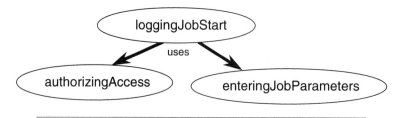

FIGURE 5-5 *Composition: use cases from other cases.*

of **authorizingAccess** and **enteringJobParameters**. As shown next, subcases composing an essential use case can appear in either the user intention model or the system responsibility model, depending on whatever makes sense and leads to the most natural reading of the narrative:

loggingJobStart

USER INTENTION	SYSTEM RESPONSIBILITY
request new job	
	>**authorizingAccess**
>**enteringJobParameters**	
	close

Composition resembles both classification and extension and is directed to similar ends, but there are important differences. With composition, the narrative for the supercase, the one shown as decomposed into subcases, refers to the subcases on which it depends. Similar to a computer program that calls subroutines, the supercase explicitly refers to the component use cases needed to complete the narrative of its interaction. In both specialization and extension, the use case being specialized or extended does not "know" about subcases, and references to subcases do not appear within the narrative for the supercase. The distinction is a question of "visibility," or of which use cases "know about" or contain explicit references to other use cases. Specializations and extensions are not visible to the use cases they specialize or extend, so new specializations or extensions can be freely created to refer back to a common general case or basis case without requiring the modeler to go back and alter the narrative for those cases.

There is no one right way to model the interrelationships among a particular collection of essential use cases. The same problem can often be modeled correctly in more than one way using specialization, extension, or composition. As a rule, composition is reserved for required parts or subsequences, while extension is used for optional interactions; specialization is best for strict subtyping. However, the ultimate criterion should always be parsimony: which relationship expresses the structure of the work in the simplest way, which relationship restricts flexibility the least. In the job-tracking example given earlier, **authorizingAccess** and **enteringJobParameters** are required for **loggingJobStart**, and their timing and order are a part of its definition; hence, composition is preferred over extension because composition permits a simpler and more direct representation of what is known about the task. In other instances, the choice may well be less clear.

AFFINITY

Many times, especially early in the modeling process, it becomes evident that there is some relationship between certain use cases but that the exact nature of that relationship remains unclear. The use cases within an application often fall into meaningful or logical clusters, such as a group of use cases all having something to do with maintaining travel expense information. We use the concept of **affinity** to describe such relationships, which may sometimes be quite unclear or ambiguous. Affinity represents apparent but unspecified relatedness between use cases. We model affinity by grouping use cases into logical clusters on the basis of degree of similarity, positioning them together within the use case map. Use cases may even be shown as closer together or farther apart or overlapping to varying degrees as reflects the degree of apparent relatedness. For instance, we might believe that **withdrawingCash** and **depositingFunds** are somewhat more closely related with each other than either is with **queryingStatus**, even if we are unsure of what exactly these similarities might involve. We can model these use cases as shown in Figure 5-6. When it is convenient graphically to overlap similar use cases, we can do so, as in the cases of **depositingFunds** and **transferringFunds** illustrated in the figure; otherwise, we can connect them using a dashed line without arrowheads. The label can reflect what we do know about the nature of the relationship; often, it merely identifies the use cases as resembling each other.

The affinity relationship is especially useful early in the development life cycle, when the analyst/designer is uncertain and may not want to commit to a particular model because the details are not known or are considered unimportant. Nevertheless, affinity can be a valuable guide to sound user interface architectures because it supports the Structure Principle, steering the ultimate design toward placing similar or related things closer together on the user interface and separating independent or unrelated things.

On occasion, two use cases that represent different user intentions may be virtually identical or equivalent when it comes to modeling the tasks they represent. We connect such use cases by a dashed double line and use "equivalent" or "identical" for the label. In this way, the use case map is kept complete from the user

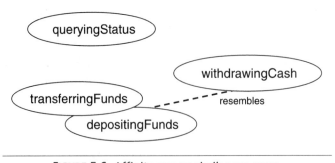

FIGURE 5-6 *Affinity among similar use cases.*

perspective but cues developers not to create separate and distinct implementations.

FOCAL USE CASES

Before the essential use case model can be considered complete, it is necessary to identify one or more **focal use cases**. Focal use cases are the focus of attention around which the user interface or some portion of the user interface will be organized. Focal use cases for the entire system embody the main, central, important, or representative uses of the system. In most cases, focal use cases will support the focal user roles identified in the role model.

For example, in the keyboard extension applet we have explored in earlier chapters, the **CasualGeneralTyper** and **CasualTranslator** roles could be identified as focal. Use cases that support these roles might include the closely related cases of **insertingSymbol** and **insertingPhrase**, which are consequently identified as focal use cases. We indicate focal use cases on the use case diagram by a double ellipse (see, for example, Figure 5-7, which appears later in the chapter).

In addition to focal use cases for an application as a whole, focal use cases may be identified for any subsystem or part of an application. These focal use cases, in turn, help organize the design of the corresponding parts of the user interface.

> *Focal use cases serve as a starting point, but the choice of where to begin is not the whole process.*

Use cases may be identified as focal for various reasons, including importance to the user, importance to the provider, or even business risk. There is no one right answer to the choice of focal roles or focal use cases. As in photography, focusing on one thing necessarily blurs other things. Focal use cases serve as a starting point for deriving an appropriate user interface architecture, but the choice of where to begin is not the entire process. With careful attention to detail and appropriate review and refinement, even an unfortunate choice of focal use cases need not doom a design. The role of focal use cases in user interface design and the methods for identifying them will be considered in greater detail in Chapter 20.

BUILDING ESSENTIAL USE CASE MODELS

IDENTIFYING USE CASES

The logical starting point for identifying use cases is the user role model. From the relationship to the system embodied in user roles, the needs and intentions of users can often be inferred. Actual users who are familiar with specific roles or who will play those roles in relation to the system can, of course, also help with the modeling.

From an examination of user roles, a collection of candidate use cases emerges. With our focus on essential purpose and user intentions, we would typically begin with a few appropriately targeted questions about each role:

- What are users in this role trying to accomplish?
- To fulfill this role, what do users need to be able to do?
- What capabilities are required to support whatever users in this role need to accomplish?

Jacobson also supplies some suggested questions regarding each role [Jacobson et al., 1992: 155].

- What are the main tasks of users in this role?
- What information will users in this role need to examine, create, or change?
- What will users in this role need to be informed of by the system?
- What will users in this role need to inform the system about?

The first of these questions may be a bit unfocused, but the remainder cover fairly familiar territory—largely, the standard concerns of conventional information processing.

The process of developing a complete essential use case model can proceed along various paths. Many developers prefer to brainstorm a list of candidate use cases first, without worrying about exact details or definitions. Each essential use case is noted by assigning it a name and/or identifying an essential purpose. This preliminary list of candidates is then studied and, if necessary, pruned down by eliminating overlap or combining substantially similar or closely related use cases where that seems reasonable. Narratives are then written for the use cases, and the relationships among them are determined. Other developers find it easier to begin with one candidate use case and complete a draft of the use case narrative before moving on to another use case.

Brainstorming a list of candidate use cases first has the advantage of helping to develop a quick overview of the kind of usage a system will have to support. By sticking with quick identification, simple names, and succinct statements of purpose, brainstorming also encourages a more abstract and general viewpoint consistent with essential modeling. On the other hand, starting with the narrative for one particular case can help to focus the analysis early on real issues. In either course, whenever the process bogs down or gets stuck on some issue, switching to the other mode can be useful. If you run out of steam coming up with a list of candidates, just start detailing the narrative for one of them. If it becomes too difficult to fill in the narrative details, just back off and see whether there are other use cases that can be identified.

USERS AND USE CASES

Depending on your preferences as developers and on the software development life cycle model your organization employs, building the task model, like the role model, may be carried out with greater or lesser involvement of users. Some teams find it very productive to include user representatives in brainstorming sessions or even in narrative writing, while others prefer to talk informally with users and then separate from them to do the actual modeling. We favor a collaborative approach called **Joint Essential Modeling** (JEM), which will be introduced in Chapter 20.

In any case, verifying the use case model with users is a good idea. Both use case and essential use case narratives are particularly easy for users to understand and to corroborate. To users, the narrative is just a kind of dialogue in two columns. No particular training is required to understand this convention. If the developers stick to the spirit of the use case model and limit the language to that of users and the application domain, users will have no trouble reading and critiquing use case narratives. Since some users may see essential use cases as oversimplified or as lacking in important detail, it is best for developers to explain that the goal is to represent the purposes of interactions, not the mechanics. For these reasons, too, some developers prefer to work with users through scenarios, which are later transformed into essential use cases through abstraction and generalization. Whether the "essentialized" narratives are verified by users is another choice. Their primary use is as guides to user interface design, but sharing essential use cases with users can provide early feedback on the completeness of the model and its accuracy.

> *To users, use case narratives are just a kind of dialogue in two columns. No particular training is required to understand this convention.*

WRITING USE CASE NARRATIVES

The process of writing a use case narrative begins with identifying the essential purpose or user intent embodied in the interaction. What are users doing? What are they trying to accomplish? Why?

Once an essential purpose has been identified, the use case is given a simple name implying purposeful, goal-directed action. Transitive gerunds, verbs of continuing action with a direct object, make good names for essential use cases. Consider these examples:

```
findingCustomer
verifyingOrder
insertingMathSymbol
```

If the user purpose or intent is not well expressed or fully implied by the name of the use case, an explicit **purpose** clause should be added to the head of the narrative, describing and detailing the purpose or goal from the user's perspective. It is important, especially within team or group efforts—with or without users present—not to get too hung up on the name. Discursive debates on what to call a use case are usually unproductive and miss the point of the process. Getting precisely the right name is less important than writing a simple, clean narrative description. On the other hand, a particularly ill-chosen name can misrepresent the essential purpose of a use case and may make it more difficult to determine whether two use cases are similar or even the same. Names that capture the essence of a use case make it easier to identify the relationships among use cases and to communicate with users. Names that draw too heavily on the vocabulary of programming and information processing can confuse and alienate users and fool developers into thinking they understand when they do not. In training developers to think in essential terms, we usually ban the use of all technical programming terms and data-processing concepts, forcing analysts to paraphrase in the ordinary language of applications and users.

The heart of essential modeling is to return repeatedly to the question of purpose. For every user action, we ask the same question again: Why? Why would a user do this? Why would anyone want to perform this action? What is the user interested in or intending to accomplish at this point? We always endeavor to use language that focuses on the purpose of interaction, not the means. Then, we simplify and generalize.

> *The heart of essential modeling is the question of purpose. For every user action, we ask the same question again: Why?*

As much as possible, the body of the essential use case narrative should be expressed in the language of the users and of the application domain. Programming constructs and computer jargon are to be avoided. Some designers have used various forms of pseudocode or "structured English" to express iterations and conditional actions in narratives. Unfortunately, this practice tends to turn attention away from the problem essentials and too far toward programmed solutions. Narratives that resemble computer programs can also intimidate users and are usually more difficult for them to understand than ones expressed in the ordinary vocabulary of the work being supported. Narratives in geek-speak disrupt the dialogue between users and developers and make it more difficult to verify correctness and completeness of the essential use case model.

In general, we find that informal language, even if sometimes imprecise, is best for writing essential use case narratives. Instead of **do-while** and **else-if** with careful **begin-end** bracketing, we prefer "**continue like this until**

satisfied" or "**optionally try**." As long as a user can understand it and both the developers and users interpret it the same way, then any term or turn of phrase is acceptable.

Some people find it difficult to think in terms of abstract interaction and essential purpose apart from concrete action. One way around this difficulty is to begin by writing out one or two scenarios and then simplify and generalize these into more abstract and essential form. It may even take several rounds of simplification and abstraction before a suitably essential expression is reached. Other people, of course, find it easier to think and write in more general terms. Whichever course is easiest for you is the "right" way.

In any event, one important step—perhaps the single most important step in all of usage-centered design—is to go back and look at what you have written and once more try to simplify it and generalize it. Application and reapplication of this step is a major part of designing systems that are both cheaper and better. The steps within an essential narrative place a lower bound on the simplicity of the implemented interface: Fewer steps make smaller and simpler interfaces possible.

APPLICATION

The problem of the keyboard extender applet introduced in Chapter 4 nicely illustrates the process of essential use case modeling. For an initial try, we will elect the **CasualGeneralTyper** and the **CasualTranslator** as the **focal roles** that typify potential users of the applet. Beginning with the **CasualGeneralTyper**, we start looking for use cases that would support this role. The role was described in terms of an interest in inserting into text a single symbol from a relatively small set of special symbols. The need for this applet arises in the course of ordinary typing simply because some needed symbols are not found on the keyboard.

One use case to support this role might be called **insertingSymbol**. It begins with the user's requesting or asking for specified symbols not found on the keyboard. The appropriate response is for the system to show a collection of symbols from which the user can select. This, of course, should be a collection of symbols in which this particular user is likely to be interested. If the user sees the needed symbol, it is necessary to select it—that is, to indicate to the system which symbol is wanted. And then what should the system do? It should insert the selected symbol. Where? Wherever the user was typing—in other words, at the current position of the text cursor. And then what should the applet do? It should go away since this use case is defined as inserting only one symbol. But if the user does not see the desired symbol, what then? Rather than complicate the use case under construction, we identify the need for a **browsingSymbols** use case, an extension that can no doubt be used elsewhere in our task model. This leaves us with the following essential use case for **insertingSymbol**:

insertingSymbol	
request symbols	
	show specified symbols
select symbol	
	insert it
	leave

To support the role of **CasualTranslator**, we will need another essential use case, which starts out similarly but then diverges. We might call this use case **insertingPhrase**. Recall from the discussion in Chapter 4 that a user in the **CasualTranslator** role might need to intermix a series of special symbols with ordinary typed characters (*Plus ça change, plus c'est la même chose.*):

insertingPhrase	
request symbols	
	show specified symbols
select symbol	
or type character	
	add to phrase
repeat until complete	
	insert phrase
	leave

Although this interaction closely resembles **insertingSymbol**, the differences are very important and present challenges for the user interface designer. In particular, the first use case ends once any symbol has been selected, while, in the latter case, the interaction continues until it is explicitly terminated by the user.

There are, quite possibly, many effective ways to resolve this conflict in required behavior, but a naïve and simplistic approach will probably not be effective. A student once designed a user interface for this problem that started with a dialogue box incorporating several radio buttons. The user was required to select the one corresponding to the intended use, as casual typer, translator, or whatever. This is not part of the interaction from the standpoint of the user. On every use, the user is punished by the lazy and uninspired design of the user interface. Such an approach may be easy to think of, but it clearly falls far short of any ideal. Worse, it fails to recognize that users may not know within which role their current needs fall and that these needs may change in the course of an interaction.

Implicit in both of the preceding use cases is the need for some means by which the system can know what symbols are of interest to the user. It is tempting to start thinking about clever schemes for the program to collect statistics and discern from historical usage what symbols are most likely to be of interest to a particular user. In its simplest form, this approach would present the most recently used symbols. **Adaptive interfaces** that try to second-guess the user and conform to unstated expectations have hidden pitfalls that will be explored in Chapter 12. For now, we will just point out that any such scheme means extra work for the programmers and fails to support an important interest of users in all the identified roles—namely, to be able to tell the system what symbols they want to see. Consequently, we will identify another extension, **specifyingSymbolCollection**, to enable users to specify a collection of symbols of interest.

Leaving aside the extensions for the moment, we might next look to the **CasualArtist** and **CasualEngineer** roles for inspiration. These roles are supported by a somewhat different use case that might be called **tryingSymbol**. This use case resembles both **insertingSymbol** and **insertingPhrase** but might look like this:

tryingSymbol

request symbols	
	show specified symbols
select symbol	
	insert it
optionally retry/reposition until satisfied	
	leave

We have, once again, neglected the poor **CasualProgrammer**. In this role, the user is interested in the relationships between characters and the codes by which they are known internally or by which they can be entered through the keyboard. We could call a supporting use case for this role, **translatingSymbols**:

translatingSymbols

request symbols	
	show specified symbols
select symbol	
	show equivalent codes

This might remind us that the **CasualTranslator** role could also require a somewhat similar facility, **reviewingShortcuts**, in order for the user to be reminded of the keyboard shortcuts for special symbols. The **translatingSymbols** use case also highlights that there is an inverse to this, which might be called **translatingCodes**:

translatingCodes	
request symbols	
	show specified symbols
enter code	
	show equivalent symbol

We can already suspect that here, too, is an opportunity to support more than one use case with the same user interface, but we do not confuse the issue by designing the prototype at this moment.

We still have to detail the two extensions that we identified along the way, **browsingSymbols** and **specifyingSymbolCollection**. Because these are extensions that begin and end within some other use case, the narratives take a slightly different form than the ones already written. The use case needed to browse for symbols might look like this:

browsingSymbols	
request more symbols	
	show more symbols
repeat until found	

The use case to define collections of symbols of interest requires a little hand-waving at this point:

specifyingSymbolCollection	
request specified collection	
	show symbol collection
optionally name or rename add, remove, and arrange symbols as desired continue until satisfied	
	remember collection

The narrative just shown is intended to cover both defining a new collection and redefining or altering an existing collection. For the former, the use case begins with an unnamed and empty collection. This bit of linguistic legerdemain draws on a programming perspective and is representative of exactly the kind of shortcuts that developers are prone to take in use case modeling. Is this wrong? Maybe, maybe not. But it is convenient.

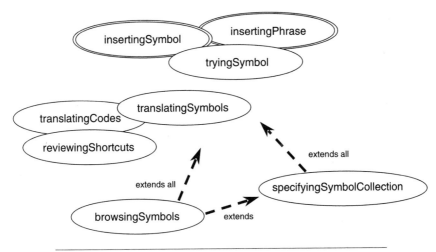

FIGURE 5-7 *Use case map for a keyboard extender.*

The completed use case map is shown in Figure 5-7. This diagram shows close affinity among **insertingSymbol**, **insertingPhrase**, and **tryingSymbol**, as well as among **reviewingShortcuts**, **translatingSymbols**, and **translatingCodes**. This affinity will lead us, eventually, to group the solutions for these design problems together on the user interface. The basis cases and their extensions will also very specifically guide the organization of the user interface, as will be seen in the next two chapters.

6

INTERFACE ARCHITECTURE:
Interface Contents and Navigation

WORKPLACES

Work takes place in context. People carry out different tasks in different places, within suitable contexts in which are assembled or can readily be gathered the tools and materials needed to complete a given task. Tools comprise those things that people manipulate to perform operations on materials, which are the objects of and results of work [Volpert, 1991]. We go to the garage to change the oil in the car and to the kitchen to make a good curry for dinner. To change the oil, we get out the right wrenches, a drip pan, cans of oil, and a new oil filter. For the curry, we get out a skillet and a saucepan, measuring spoons, and a favorite knife. We gather some onions, dried chilies, potatoes, lentils, and spinach. We reach for some good spices, like fenugreek, turmeric, coriander, and others. We would not go to the kitchen to change the oil, nor would we cook in the garage (at least not unless it's for a rained-out barbecue!).

> *The contextual nature of work is so natural and ubiquitous that we are scarcely aware of it.*

The contextual nature of work is so natural and ubiquitous that most of us are scarcely aware of it. Efficient performance takes place in a context in which the necessary tools and materials are immediately available. The dental assistant arrays a different set of tools and materials on the dentist's tray for an extraction than for a routine filling. The plumber and the carpenter both carry toolboxes, but they fill them with different tools.

Good user interfaces are organized to provide a set of distinct **interaction contexts** appropriately equipped for carrying out the sundry tasks of interest to the user. Because of the close similarity between the words *content* and *context*, which are easily confused in aural presentations, we often refer to interaction contexts as the **interaction spaces** within the user interface. In this chapter, we will use the terms interchangeably.

The contents of each interaction space are those tools and materials needed for completing the use cases being supported. Interaction contexts are the places within the user interface of a system where the users interact with all the functions, containers, and information needed for carrying out some particular task or set of interrelated tasks. (Others [Lillienthal and Züllighoven, 1997] have independently reached similar conclusions about user interface design based on tools and materials arrayed in context.) Designing a good user interface architecture thus involves specifying tools, materials, and the spaces to hold these, distributing the total contents of the user interface over a number of distinct but interconnected interaction spaces.

The **interface content model**, or simply, the **content model**, is an abstract representation of the contents of the various interaction spaces for a system and their interconnections. In implementation, each interaction space becomes a recognizable collection comprising part of the user interface—a window, a screen, a dialogue box, or a page within a tabbed dialogue, for example—populated by specific interface components, such as toolbars, datagrids, command buttons, or selection lists.

Some activities are simple enough or sufficiently self-contained to be completed within a single interaction context at one time, but others require moving from one context to another or even visiting some places repeatedly. The complicated annual ritual, **buyingHolidayGifts**, requires the user—the shopper—to navigate among a number of interaction contexts: the various stores and shops. It could take trips to several toy stores, a stop at the wine shop, and a tour of the hardware emporium. The forgetful shopper may end up returning repeatedly to the same store, and the obsessive shopper may go back and forth between stores before finally committing to a choice. For some tasks, such as **buyingHolidayGifts**, there may be a substantial degree of flexibility in the order in which the transitions between contexts are taken, although visiting interaction contexts in arbitrary sequence could turn an unpremeditated shopping spree into an exhausting ordeal. For other procedures, such as eye surgery in a day-patient facility, the navigation through interaction contexts can be quite fixed by nature or even absolutely rigid in practice.

To help us design a well-suited user interface architecture, one that supports smooth workflow and efficient use, we will need to model how users, in role, can navigate from interaction context to interaction context in enacting use cases of interest. For this purpose, we include in the content model a **context navigation map** or simply, a **navigation map**, in order to model the complete structure of the user interface architecture in the abstract.

The process of determining the contents and organization of the user interface—apart from the appearance and behavior of the actual interface components—is sometimes referred to as **abstract prototyping** [Constantine, 1998a]. The advantages of **abstract prototypes** are numerous. Abstract prototypes encourage thinking about what is on the user interface before worrying about how it will look or how it will behave. Instead of making it up as they go along, visual developers will already know what they are prototyping when they start programming. In our experience, designers converge on a good design faster when they create an abstract prototype first, before beginning sketches or other forms of representative visual prototypes.

INTERFACE CONTENTS

MODELING THE CONTENTS

To model the contents of user interfaces, we have found that some of the simplest modeling technology—paper and Post-it notes—works best. Modeling with paper and Post-it notes has no doubt been done by many professionals to various ends, but we were particularly inspired by the work of Karen Holtzblatt and Hugh Beyer, who use what they term the "work environment" model as part of contextual inquiry, their approach to requirements modeling [Beyer and Holtzblatt, 1997; Holtzblatt and Beyer, 1993].

> *Some of the simplest modeling technology—paper and Post-it notes—works best.*

In content modeling, a separate sheet of paper or portion of a large sheet is used for each interaction space to be represented. Interaction spaces are named according to the broad purposes or functions they serve or by the way in which users might think of that part of an application. Figure 6-1 shows an example. We might call an important interaction context within a new real estate system **houseHunting** or **House Hunter Dialogue**, for example. We try to avoid uninformative, generic names, such as **mainScreen** or **workSpace**, which can signal a lack of coherence or a shortage of design deliberation, especially where the names just sound like so much tech-talk.

Within each interaction context, the tools and materials to be supplied to the user are represented by Post-it notes in various colors. Some writers on user interface design refer to this kind of model as a *low-fidelity* prototype because it represents the user interface but not in very faithful detail. True, a little pink Post-it does not look much like a drawing tool, and a big blue one hardly resembles a datagrid, but calling the content model a low-fidelity prototype misses the point. The interface content model is actually a *high-fidelity* abstract model that faithfully and accurately represents—in the abstract—the designer's understanding of how the necessary tools and materials are to be distributed and deployed on the

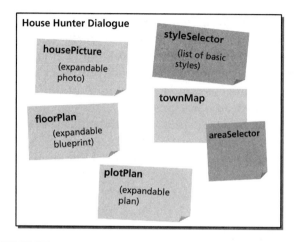

FIGURE 6-1 *Low-tech modeling of abstract interface contents.*

user interface. The content model enables designers to work out the structure and overall organization of the user interface without having to draw pictures and without having to commit to a particular choice of GUI widget. A **lineStylePicker** tool in an interaction space could end up as a combo box, a scrolling pick list, or as a floating tool palette in the implemented interface. The choice must eventually be made, and the choosing should be done well and with good reason, but the important issue early in the design process is that the user interface will definitely offer the user, in an appropriate place, a tool for picking the line style.

> *Calling the content model a low-fidelity prototype misses the point. It is actually a high-fidelity abstract model that faithfully and accurately represents—in the abstract—the tools and materials to be distributed on the user interface.*

The very fact that a Post-it does not look like a real GUI widget is a constant visual reminder to the designer that this is an abstract model, a model that leaves open many options, not only in appearance but also in the behavior of the user interface and its components. By deferring design decisions regarding these details, we are able to retain a focus on the problem, on usage and user needs, over a longer period. In the long run, this patience will pay off. It will help us keep the user interface design simple by keeping it more closely attuned to what is truly necessary. It will help us avoid stereotypes and keep us from settling for canned solutions without having considered what is best within a given context.

Another big advantage of Post-it notes over sketches or drawings is the ease with which major reorganizations of the user interface architecture can be carried out. This ease encourages experimentation and exploration. Does it make sense to put this control over here rather than there? What if we duplicated these facilities in several places? Does it make more sense to split this group from that and add an extra container? Whatever the questions, the Post-it notes are readily moved from one corner to another or shuttled between sheets or regrouped in various ways.

Whiteboards or large sheets of flip-chart paper taped to a wall are an advantage when working in groups, making it easier for everyone to see and to interact with the interaction spaces. However, a word of caution is in order. More than one eager modeler has arrived at work in the morning only to find that the elves of entropy had visited in the night, leaving a vastly simplified interaction context on the wall and half the tools and materials strewn on the floor, an outcome that is

MACHINABLE MODELS

Since the end product of usage-centered design is a software user interface that will be developed on a computer using software development tools, having a model in machinable form is highly desirable. Computer-based models are more easily copied and distributed than are paper-based models, especially multimedia collages like Post-it note interaction spaces, and they better support version control and requirements tracing.

A Windows version of Post-it notes is available (from 3M Software) that offers one possible approach. It emulates versatile sticky notes on-screen and provides "memoboards" on which they can be grouped to represent interaction contexts. Notes and note boards can be printed or converted to text, but file management facilities are not much better than with paper Post-it notes. Aside from being unable to hold them in your hand or throw them at critical colleagues, you can do anything with electronic Post-it notes that you can with the paper ones. We use both kinds extensively in our work.

The software has a fairly clean, even elegant user interface, but it also illustrates how a simple, otherwise commendable design can fail in the details when important use cases are neglected. Throwing away a note, a frequent use case for what is basically a disposable medium, is a nuisance in the software version. Notes must be dragged to a special trash can (the Windows Recycle Bin will not work) or must be discarded from the note menu item **Trash Note**. The access

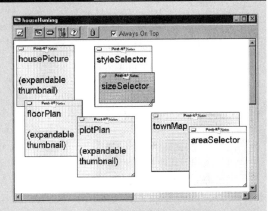

Sample electronic version of interaction contexts.

key for the tiny control button in the upper left corner of the note is not the standard **Alt+Space**, but **Alt+N**, making for an exceptionally obscure shortcut: **Alt+N+R**.

. Some groupings of functions are odd or inconsistent. The vital **Find** tool, for example, is on the toolbar of the "master" Post-it pad but is buried in an **Options** menu reached via the toolbar on a memoboard. It escapes us why, with only four colors available, the user has to go through a clumsy color-change via that irritatingly minuscule menu button rather than, more naturally, being able to click directly on a pad of the chosen color on the memoboard toolbar.

Is 3M listening?

hardly in the spirit of "simplify, generalize." Never leave a Post-it model alone for long.

Content models are as useful for interacting with actual users and user representatives as they are for collaborating with colleagues. When users see carefully drawn visual prototypes or on-screen simulations, it is easy for them to think of what they see as the actual user interface, even when they have been told otherwise. The more realistic the rendition in the prototype, the more prone users are to reification. A bunch of green and yellow Post-it notes on a sheet of newsprint, on the other hand, will never be mistaken for a real user interface. Users will be less likely to perceive such an abstract model as a fixed commitment to a particular design. Along with the designers, they will be encouraged to stay focused on the basic questions of whether everything needed is present on the interface and well organized into various contexts for use.

> *The more realistic the prototype, the more likely users are to see it as the actual user interface, even when they have been told otherwise.*

Once they get the hang of abstract user interfaces, users often become perceptive critics and enthusiastic collaborators in the modeling process. Typically, they will first require a bit of explanation, although not too much ("See, this dingus here means that you'll be able to pick the line style at this point. It's a sort of placeholder. We haven't yet decided what would be the best way to show that—maybe a pop-out tool palette, maybe something else—we'll work out the details for the prototype, but for now we want to leave it open.").

The fact that Post-it notes are themselves tangible objects that can be held in the hand and physically moved from place to place or tossed into a wastebasket is a boon to user interface designers. Modeling through manipulation of tangible objects draws on mental modes and cognitive capacities that augment critical analysis and logical thinking. Physical models also encourage play and exploration and facilitate group interaction. This added dimension of using tangible stand-ins for abstractions is at the heart of numerous analysis and design techniques, including the popular and highly successful CRC cards used in object-oriented analysis and design [Wirfs-Brock, Wilkerson, and Weiner, 1990] as well as other group-oriented approaches to problem solving [Constantine, 1993e]. Other user interface design tools and techniques, such as CARD and PICTIVE [Muller et al., 1995], also make use of tangible objects to represent concepts and components, but the interface content model differs from these earlier techniques in that its tangible stand-ins are specifically intended not to look like the real components for which they substitute.

CONTENT LISTS

The Post-it form of a content model is a good way to think through problems in interface architecture, but it is not very practical for documentation, communication, or permanent archiving. We find a textual form of the content model works better for these purposes. Interaction contexts are simply listed along with their contents as an indented outline:

```
House Hunter Dialogue
    housePicture
    expandable thumbnail photo
    floorPlan
    expandable thumbnail blueprint
    plotPlan
    expandable thumbnail plan
    styleSelector
    list of basic house styles
    townMap
    areaSelector
    from tool palette?
```

Although less natural and intuitive than playing with Post-it notes, the content model can obviously be constructed in the first place using word-processing or outlining software.

Not only is a text-based version of the content model more compact, but it also can be a better format for communicating with clients. The textual model is easily incorporated into requirements models and makes for easy requirements tracing. Ideally, we would like software modeling tools that would allow us to manipulate abstract tools and materials as visual representations and then switch to the same information in outline form. (Write your favorite vendor of CASE tools or visual development environments!)

SETTING THE CONTEXT

Logically speaking, the interface content model derives from the use case model. What is the relationship between use cases and interaction contexts? How many use cases fit in one interaction context? The initial working assumption is that each use case will be supported by its own interaction context so that, in accordance with the Visibility Principle, it can be enacted completely without any potentially distracting surplus of tools and materials. This starting assumption is most reasonable for use cases that are substantially unrelated. Where two or more use cases are substantially similar or closely related, it may make more sense to support them through one common interaction context. The use case map, representing the relationships among use cases, and the narratives themselves, which can reveal overlapping procedures, are the guides. The more closely two use cases are related or resemble each other, the more reasonable it is to support them with a common interaction context, although combinations should not be formed indiscriminately, without thinking through the consequences for the users in the supported role or roles.

Sometimes, more lengthy or complex use cases may need to be split across more than one interaction context, especially if supporting the use case in one context would result in an overly dense or cluttered interface. The designer must always be cautious about distributing a use case over multiple interaction contexts because too many contexts can confuse or frustrate users and because switching contexts too often leads to inefficient, error-prone interaction.

> *Too many interaction contexts can confuse or frustrate users, and switching contexts too often leads to inefficient, error-prone interaction.*

Special rules apply to supporting extensions and subcases. All the facilities needed to support an extension should normally be located on the same interaction space as the basis use case or on an adjacent space—that is, another interaction space immediately accessible to the user through a single transition. The same principle applies to use cases composed of subcases. Subcase support should be either on the same interaction space as supports the supercase or on an adjacent space. This rule allows users to enact extended or composed use cases with fewer context changes.

To a large extent, developing a good content model is a matter of informed trial and error. It is precisely because of this exploratory nature that a highly flexible medium like Post-it notes is preferred. An effective way to proceed is to start with an informed guess—guided by the use case map—about an appropriate set of interaction spaces. Sheets of paper are posted or areas of a whiteboard are set aside for each interaction space. As the model is elaborated, new interaction spaces may have to be created or existing ones may be combined. Experimentally enacting the use cases with a given set of interaction spaces will often reveal problems in the distribution of tasks among them. The context navigation map, discussed in a later section in this chapter, is also a tool to help refine the organization of interaction contexts and is often developed concurrently for this reason.

TOOLS AND MATERIALS

Each interaction space in the content model is populated with a collection of abstract tools and materials representing the content and capability that will be supplied to the user by the user interface. These **abstract components** are placeholders for the actual visual components in the implemented interface. Their placement and organization within interaction spaces will help guide the design of the corresponding parts within the completed user interface.

Abstract tools supply the functions and active capabilities required to complete a task; materials are the data, containers, displays, or work areas upon which the tools of the user interface can operate. As a rule, it is useful to distinguish tools or functions from data or containers. By convention, Post-it notes in so-called hot colors—pink, yellow, orange—are used for functions, tools, or other active controls; cool colors—blue or green—are used for the more passive elements of the interface representing containers, displays, data, information, or work areas. We are not dogmatic about color coding; this color scheme is simply one we have found to be easy to explain and remember. If all you have is a pad of yellow Post-it notes, don't let that hold you back; if you love

> *Abstract tools supply the functions and active capabilities; abstract materials represent the data, containers, displays, or work areas upon which the tools can operate.*

fluorescent green but hate hot pink, go ahead and establish your own conventions, as long as everyone around you understands the scheme. Having Post-it notes in an assortment of sizes and colors available is useful. The small squares are naturals for simple functions or tools, and larger ones can represent working areas or fairly substantial displays. Input areas and output areas can be assigned different colors, and ad hoc distinctions and conventions can be devised to suit the problem being solved.

THE PROCESS OF CONTENT MODELING

The typical process of content modeling begins with examining the validated use case narratives line by line to determine, for each use case, what tools and materials will have to be supplied within a given interaction space in order for the user to enact the use case. As each required tool or material is identified, a Post-it placeholder is added to the interaction space. The placeholder components can be grouped or otherwise arranged within the interaction space to reflect how they are likely to be used or how they will make the most sense to the user. A collection of tools might be grouped together to one side to suggest a possible floating toolbar. The container for `customerCreditHistory` might be placed just below the `customerFinder` tool. A series of placeholders might be arranged to conform to the most likely order in which they will be used.

It is neither necessary nor practical to work out all the details of layout using the content model—those will be settled in completing the implementation model—but some of the more obvious or broadbrush matters can certainly be explored. The same principles apply whether the problems are explored and resolved in the abstract through the content model or "in the concrete" within the implementation model: The final arbiter is always the fit between the interface and the task at hand. Because problems in layout are often ultimately matters of detail that can depend strongly on the visual appearance of components, we cover these issues more fully in Chapter 7, on layout and visual design.

For each interaction space we first want to consider what information is needed at the user interface for a user to enact the supported use case or set of related use cases successfully. A visual inventory of the required data and data containers is created by placing labeled Post-it notes on the interaction context. In principle, this step could be done in the form of a written list or matrix showing the needed data [Lauesen and Harning, 1993], but we find it convenient to work directly on the interaction spaces. The Post-it notes are labeled with brief descriptive names characterizing the data or container. A container to hold the bitmap image of a house in a real estate application might be labeled as a **propertyPhoto**, for example. If more detail is needed, additional explanatory text can be added to any Post-it note.

As always, we assume the external point of view and adopt the language of the user and of the application domain whenever possible. The vocabulary should be consistent with that used in the use case narratives, which are, in turn, based on the glossary or dictionary of terminology for the project or on the defined domain classes or entities and attributes from the data model.

Once the data demands are identified, the use case or cases being supported are reviewed to identify needed functions or operators. For each such tool identified, a placeholder is added to the interaction context. We label Post-it notes with a succinct name characterizing the general function performed or purpose to be served by the component(s) represented. A tool to display enlarged views of neighborhood street maps might be designated a **zoomingMapViewer**, for example. As in many aspects of usage-centered design, picking the right name or way to represent the concept is not terribly important. What one team sees as a **zoomingMapViewer** tool might be thought of as a **zoomableMapView** container by another. In either variation, the necessary functionality would be present in the model and understood by the team.

> *Once the data demands of a use case are identified, the narrative is reviewed to identify needed functions or operators.*

If additional information is necessary for clarity or desirable for communication, a brief description or annotation can be added. The Post-it abstract component may sometimes be annotated with brief implementation notes about the possible form or behavior of the component once it is realized on the implemented user interface. For example, a designer might have in mind that a thumbnail image can be expanded by double-clicking; a comment to this effect can be written on the Post-it note. Or a proposed icon might be sketched on the Post-it note. Although this practice blurs the distinction between the abstract architectural design and the visual design of the implemented user interface, it is also a reasonable way to deal with the natural tendency of designers to bolt for the barn, as it were, jumping ahead once they reach this late stage in the modeling process. In many cases, such comments about proposed implementation are the most succinct way to carry forward good design ideas.

In addition to those tools and materials demanded by the essential use case narratives, we may consider adding to the interaction space selected optional contents. We want to be cautious in this, lest we become guilty of contributing to feature creep. What we are most looking for are added tools and materials that might simplify some supported tasks or make usage easier for some users. We also want to include tools and materials that are required but only implicit in the essential narratives for the use cases. For this, we might have to turn to other specifications or requirements documents. And, as always, for each interaction context modeled, we pause frequently to try to simplify and generalize the results.

THE CONTEXT NAVIGATION MAP

Typical software tools and applications in the real world will involve numerous interaction contexts. To carry out complex tasks or complete work comprising a number of tasks, users will typically have to move from one interaction context to another. Every abstract interaction space will become a screen or dialogue box or window that must be understood by the user, and every change of context will require a corresponding switch of thinking on the part of the user. Perhaps one of the most important trade-offs in the design of user interface architecture is whether to limit the contents of each interaction space in order to keep it small and simple, thereby proliferating the number of contexts, or to reduce the number of separate interaction spaces, thereby increasing the complexity of each one. Small and simple interaction spaces are likely to be easier for the inexperienced user to interpret but may impose excessive transitions between contexts to carry out any given task. Conversely, consol

> *One of the most important trade-offs is whether to keep each interaction context small and simple, thereby proliferating the number of contexts, or to reduce the number of separate contexts, thereby increasing the complexity of each one.*

idating tools and materials into fewer interaction spaces may speed operation for some users at the expense of overwhelming the less practiced ones.

The context navigation map represents the overall architecture of the user interface by modeling the relationships among interaction contexts. This part of the content model is a diagram in which each complete interaction space is represented by a simple rectangular object. Arrows connecting these objects represent possible transitions from one interaction space to another, such as calling up a dialogue from a command button or switching views through a menu. The map

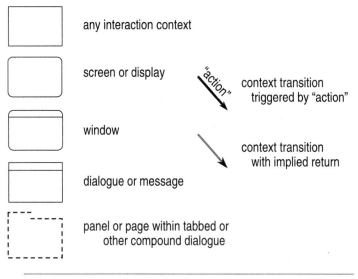

FIGURE 6-2 *Notation for navigation maps.*

models the ways users can navigate through the various interaction contexts within the user interface in the course of enacting use cases.

The notation for context navigation maps, shown in Figure 6-2, is very simple. An unadorned rectangle on a navigation map can represent any abstract interaction space within the content model or any interaction space in the implemented interface. As the design progresses toward implementation, it can sometimes be useful and appropriate to differentiate various implemented forms of interaction spaces. A dialogue box is represented by a barred rectangle, a screen by a rounded rectangle, and a window by a barred, rounded rectangle. The sheets or pages of a tabbed dialogue are represented straightforwardly as tabbed rectangles. Other distinctions are possible and often created more or less ad hoc to fit the needs of particular projects. (See, for example, the discussion of embedded systems applications in Chapter 14.)

As in Figure 6-2, the arrows representing possible context transitions are labeled with the conditions under which transitions occur. A few conventions are sometimes used to simplify representation of common types of transitions within implemented interfaces. For example, the conventional notation for menu selections (e.g., **View|Toolbars**) is pressed into service to label a change of interaction context from an application window to a dialogue through a menu selection. Square brackets indicate a transition triggered by a command button (e.g., **[Apply]**). Angle brackets are used to indicate an icon or a tool selection (e.g., **<Page Width>**). As with the objects representing interaction contexts, new notational conventions can be created to serve particular project needs. One useful shorthand notation is a double-line connector instead of two separate arrows to represent a transition to a modal dialogue or other interaction context having a required but implied return, such as via an **OK** or a **Cancel**.

BEHAVIORAL, ARCHITECTURAL, AND SEQUENTIAL VIEWS

Context navigation maps can be drawn to suit varied purposes. The simplest variation is the *behavioral view*, which models the interaction context transitions associated with enacting a single use case. This view is often the starting point for architectural design. If all the behavioral views for the various use cases in an application are combined into a single diagram incorporating all the interaction contexts along with all possible transition paths, the result is called an *architectural view*.

A less frequently used form of the navigation map is the *sequential view*. When enacted, some use cases will carry the user back to the same interaction space repeatedly. On each return to a particular context, the state of the system may have changed. In the sequential view of the navigation map, a single use case is modeled, and each instance of an interaction space is shown separately, so any one interaction space can appear in more than one place. The result is an extended form of representation that strings out the interaction like a storyboard. This variant of the navigation map is seldom used but, because of its resemblance to a storyboard, may sometimes be of help in communicating with users. It may also be of use with programmers for guiding the implementation of complex use cases. Sequential, behavioral, and architectural views of the navigation map correspond roughly to what others [Apperley and Duncan, 1995] have referred to as Screen Sequence Diagrams, Dialogue Transition Diagrams, and Dialogue Maps.

USES FOR NAVIGATION MAPS

Context navigation maps are useful for a number of different purposes. The navigation map serves as a check on the interaction space portion of the content model, as it can reveal various kinds of problems in how tasks are distributed over the interaction spaces. The architectural view provides a rough overview of how complex the system will be for users. Overly long chains of transitions invite review for possible consolidation and simplification of interaction contexts. Architectures that spread out in an explosion of transitions from some interaction context might benefit from a different distribution of interface contents.

If not constructed concurrently with or preceding the interaction contexts, a navigation map should be developed once the content model is complete and then be carefully reviewed both in overview and on a use-case-by-use-case basis. The navigation map is reviewed through trial enactment of use cases. Enacted use cases that bounce back and forth between contexts or that carry the user through a long chain of transitions may indicate an interface architecture that is inefficient

CLEANING UP THE MODELS

As this chapter and the preceding one have made clear, the role model, task model, and content model are intricately interconnected. Thus, if for no other reason, a concurrent engineering approach, with all three models developed together, is justified by this interdependence.

The strong relationships among the models also make possible validating them against one another. The completed usage and architectural models can be checked against a set of consistency criteria, as follows:

- Every user role must be supported by one or more use cases.
- Every use case must support one or more user roles.
- Every use case must be fully supported within the content model.
- Every interaction context must be used in some one or more use cases.
- All tools and materials must support some one or more use cases.
- Every transition between use contexts should be used in enacting some use case.

A user role not supported by any use cases should be reexamined. It is possible that the role was incorrectly identified or described in the first place. It may have proved to be redundant or irrelevant, with all its needs and implications covered by other user roles. Before eliminating a user role from the models, you should be sure that all its implications for user interface and internal design are reflected in other user roles. Another possible explanation for a user role with no use cases is that the supporting use cases are missing from the task model. The developers should try to identify additional use cases that might support that role.

Use cases not associated with any user role can appear through requirements creep and as the result of inventive model builders who add capability that no user needs. Every such orphaned use case should be carefully reviewed to justify its existence. Some legiti-mate use cases—system administration or housekeeping functions, for example—may not support any user role directly yet may be required to support overall operation of a system. Use cases for which no supported role can be identified could also be an indication that a role is missing. Although use cases drive the user interface design process, an overlooked user role could mean that required use cases associated with that role have also been omitted. When use cases are found that support no user role, the user role model should be reviewed to see whether other user roles should be added and analyzed for supporting use cases.

The system will not work if it does not supply all the required capability to perform all use cases; hence, the content model is checked to verify that it includes everything needed to enact all use cases. Conversely, a user interface that includes interaction spaces or content not required by any use case is an interface that is bigger than it need be. Developers should consider eliminating features and facilities not needed to support required use cases. The same goes for unused navigation paths; they should be considered for possible elimination from the design.

Use cases that are distributed over multiple interaction contexts should also be noted and examined. The architecture may need to be redesigned to avoid forcing users to endure too many context transitions, especially where common or important use cases are concerned.

An interaction context that supports too many use cases could also be a sign of architectural problems, but this is uncommon in practice. Many systems legitimately consolidate most control and coordination into one interaction context or into a small number of them. Well-conceived common dialogues or widely useful extensions may be used in enacting a large number of different use cases. A large system with everything crowded into a single screen and workspace may need to be redesigned, however.

to use and difficult to master. Superfluous layers of interposed dialogues are also often readily apparent from the navigation map.

After all refinements and adjustments to the interaction contexts and navigation map models are finished, a final completeness check should be performed, in which all use cases are reviewed to verify that they could, in principle, be enacted with the abstract interface contents as modeled. The validated interface content

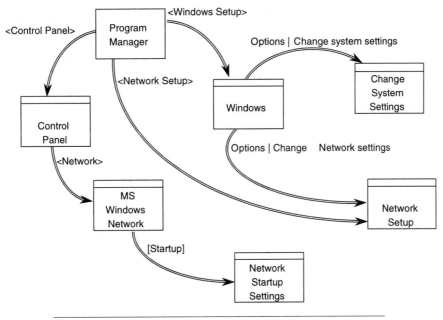

FIGURE 6-3 *Problems in context navigation.*
(MICROSOFT WINDOWS FOR WORKGROUPS)

model will need to be recorded and may need to be converted to machinable form, either as an outline or a diagram (see sidebar, Machinable Models).

Navigation maps are powerful tools for understanding the overall organization of complex software, including software that has already been built. With actual screen shots from an implemented interface substituting for abstract interaction contexts, navigation maps can be used to document software systems and can be particularly helpful for new users looking to get an overview of how a system works or to see where particular features are located.

Navigation maps can also reveal lurking problems in the organization of existing designs and can clarify possible solutions. For example, the navigation map in Figure 6-3 models part of Windows for Workgroups dealing with network log-on procedures. How might the typical user, who is not a network administrator or system programmer, change these? A natural impulse would be to select the **Network Setup** icon within the **Program Manager**, but this leads to a dead end that does

> *Navigation maps are powerful tools for understanding the overall organization of complex software, revealing lurking problems in the organization and clarifying possible solutions.*

not include changing the log-on process. The **Windows Setup** icon is another reasonable option, but, as the diagram reveals, this also fails to lead to the required dialogue. The required path is through the **Network** icon on the **Control Panel** and the **Startup** button on the **MS Windows Network** dialogue. **Network Startup Settings** and **Network Setup** are obviously semantically related; one would expect to find them together or at least interconnected in some way.

The navigation map itself suggests the easiest resolution to this problem: Provide a transition path from the **Network Setup** context to **Network Startup Settings** so that users can find what they are looking for by either path. For visibility, this transition should be accessed from a command button in **Network Setup**. Careful inspection of this navigation map could suggest other structural improvements, such as providing a link from **MS Windows Network** to **Network Setup**, since network setup is certainly a subset of network operation.

As more and more such isolated structural defects are identified, one might conclude that revamping the entire architecture is indicated. With existing software, the trade-off is always between small, easily coded local changes that fail to solve global problems and larger-scale reorganization of the interface architecture that could require wholesale reprogramming. The navigation map makes it easy to experiment on paper with alternative arrangements representing varying degrees of architectural revision. For systems burdened by the legacy of a large installed base of users already familiar with the warts and weirdness of the user interface, localized structural fixes that smooth operation with minimal disruption to familiar look-and-feel may often be preferable to global redesign.

Problems in the interface architecture of implemented systems often result from the failure to consider important use cases or to think in terms of usage. For example, many printers can operate in two modes: one, for draft work, that saves time or toner, and another, for finished work, using higher resolution or denser printing. Even casual observations or forethought will highlight two things about the use of draft and final modes for printing. A switch to draft mode for a quick review of a large or complex document is almost inevitably paired with a later switch back to finished quality. In addition, it is very important for the user to know in which mode a print job will be completed before starting it. Printing in the wrong mode can mean wasting time and ink for a draft that will be discarded anyway or throwing out hundreds of pages and redoing a final report that was inadvertently printed in faint gray.

> *Problems in the interface architecture of implemented systems often result from the failure to consider important use cases or to think in terms of usage.*

In usage-centered terms, the use case for **printingDocument** is extended by **changingPrintModes**, and among the information needed by the user to enact the use case **printingDocument** is the current print mode. Following the norms for handling use case extensions, the support for **changingPrintModes** should either be in the same interaction context that supports **printingDocument** or on an adja-

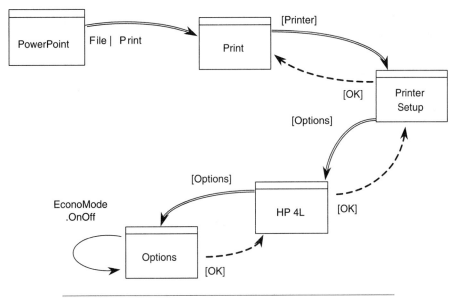

FIGURE 6-4 *Context changes to change print modes.*

cent one accessible through a single transition. Instead, we often get architectures like the one shown in Figure 6-4 for a popular printer as used within a popular presentation package on a popular platform. The user is forced through six context changes and an option button selection merely to set the print mode. The usage-centered approach would lead to an option button or drop-down on the **Print** dialogue, thus satisfying both the need for feedback about the current state and the need to control the state directly. This example often gets a chorus of "but, but, but" from programmers in classes we have taught ("But that's hard to do in Windows!" or "But Microsoft won't let us do that!" or "But the Common Dialogue for printing doesn't support that!"). We usually respond with a "but" of our own ("But that's why you get paid the big bucks—to solve problems.").

APPLICATION

Returning to our running example of the keyboard extender, we would start developing the content model with initial candidates for the needed interaction spaces. It makes sense to try supporting the cluster of similar, closely related use cases—**insertingSymbol**, **insertingPhrase**, and **tryingSymbol**—within a single interaction space. What materials—data or data containers—are needed to support these use cases (repeated here for convenience)?

insertingSymbol

request symbols	
	show specified symbols
select symbol	
	insert it
	leave

insertingPhrase

request symbols	
	show specified symbols
select symbol	
or type character	
	add to phrase
repeat until complete	
	insert phrase
	leave

tryingSymbol

request symbols	
	show specified symbols
select symbol	
	insert it
optionally retry/reposition	
until satisfied	
	leave

Obviously, we will need a **symbolCollection** to display the specified symbols. For **insertingPhrase**, we will need some place to hold the phrase being built; call it a **phraseBin**. These are, remember, only placeholders representing abstract requirements. We have not yet committed to any particular form of display or container. The phrase bin could even be in the document itself if we think we can visually and functionally integrate the interface for the keyboard extender with that of the application from which it is invoked. However, these decisions come later.

Moving from materials to tools, we note that all the use cases refer to selecting a symbol, so we add a **symbolSelector** to our interaction space. We might, at this point or sometime later, consider the needs of those poor users trying to distinguish all those minuscule diacritical variations—like ì, í, î, and ï—displayed on a high-resolution screen. A **symbolViewer** tool to enlarge symbols might be added to the interaction space on the reasonable argument that this tool will make supported tasks easier for many users. Understanding the close tie between viewing

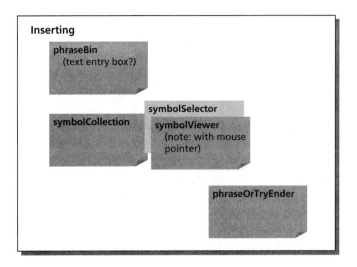

FIGURE 6-5 *An initial interaction context for the keyboard extender.*

and selecting and recalling the Structure Principle, we might slide the two place-holders together, assuring that, in any final design, the components will not end up too widely separated to be practical. Of course, we may "know" that the mouse pointer is going to be the **symbolSelector**, but its behavior in this capacity is not yet determined, nor is its relationship to the **symbolViewer** designed, so, even though the pointer is a standard GUI feature, we include it in the abstract in our model.

To support **insertingPhrase** and **tryingSymbol**, we need one more function allowing users to explicitly inform the system when they are done, as apart from selecting characters. We might add a placeholder called **phraseOrTryEnder** for this function. Some experimentation with layout might lead us to move the **phraseBin** toward the top and the **phraseOrTryEnder** toward the bottom. We might consider combining the **symbolSelector** and **symbolViewer** into a single tool, bringing us to the stage shown in Figure 6-5. Note the implementation comment suggesting that the **symbolSelector/symbolViewer** be associated with the mouse pointer.

We can validate this initial portion of the interaction context by attempting to enact the essential use cases it is intended to support. Missing are the optional functions of repositioning or other manipulation of the special symbol as found in **tryingSymbol**, but these are functions of whatever other application our utility is collaborating with, not the keyboard extender itself. Simple as it is, the interaction context in Figure 6-5 covers everything in these first three use cases.

We also have some extensions to consider next—most importantly, **browsingSymbols**. This extension is so closely related with the focal use cases that we add it to the current interaction context. The contents already include a

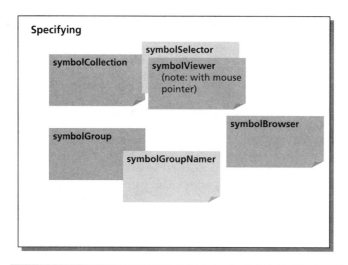

FIGURE 6-6 *An interaction context for specifying new symbol collections.*

symbolCollection, so all we need to add is a **symbolBrowser** tool. If we do not decide at this stage to integrate the use cases, we will have another chance to appreciate the cost of a separate interaction context for **browsingSymbols** when we later build and study the navigation map.

We may not be as sure whether **specifyingSymbolGroup** is better supported within the current interaction context or on a separate one. When we are uncertain, the default assumption is to start with a separate interaction context for each use case. This choice is further supported by the fact that **specifyingSymbolGroup**, as a setup or customization function, is both relatively infrequent and conceptually quite distinct from normal usage of a keyboard extender. Building a separate interaction context for this use case might lead to something like Figure 6-6. Note that, conceptually, two containers for symbols are needed: one to hold the collection being specified and one to hold all defined symbols. Following the Structure Principle, these are assumed to have the same or similar organization, so the implemented interface might incorporate two instances of the same visual component.

The designer might also note the close similarity between the **Inserting** and the **Specifying** interaction contexts. Generally, it is well worth considering whether or not to combine highly similar contexts. In this problem, however, we have already justified supporting the extension in its own interaction context. It might be possible to avoid duplicating features through a creative compromise between fully separate and fully combined interaction contexts; we will return to this trade-off in Chapters 8 and 9, when we complete the visual design for the keyboard extender.

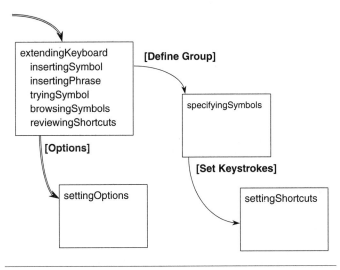

FIGURE 6-7 *A navigation map for the keyboard extender.*

The content modeling would continue in this manner until all use cases have been supported. A proposed navigation map for the utility is shown in Figure 6-7. As might be expected, few interaction contexts are needed for this modest piece of software. In the course of modeling the interface content and context navigation, other use cases and supporting features have been recognized. In analyzing the **specifyingSymbolGroup** use case, one might reasonably conclude that, if users can specify or change the groups of symbols presented by the utility, they may also expect to specify or change the keyboard shortcuts associated with specific symbols. For **reviewingShortcuts** in support of the **CasualTranslator** and other user roles, the system must provide the option of displaying, in some form, the associated keyboard shortcuts along with the symbols. Generalizing on this need, a catchall interaction context for setting options and preferences has been included. This architecture is not claimed to be optimal, only workable. In the usage-centered approach, we will have other opportunities to refine and improve on the design.

CREATING THE VISUAL DESIGN

7

DESIGNING THE DIALOGUE:
Layout and Communication

FROM ABSTRACTION TO EXPRESSION

The essential models introduced in the previous three chapters are not ends in themselves. The role, task, and content models are the maps that guide designers toward a sound user interface design closely tied to the work to be supported. In this and succeeding chapters, we will begin to examine the specifics of how to transform the content model into an **implementation model**, a prototype for the actual system specifying the layout of the user interface and defining the interaction between user and system.

In order to develop an implementation model from the essential models, two kinds of questions must be answered. First, the designer must decide how each abstract interaction space will be embodied in the user interface as an actual interaction context—for example, whether as a screen, a window, a dialogue box, the page of a tabbed dialogue, or in some other form. Second, each abstract component contained in these interaction spaces must be realized as some actual visual component on the user interface, such as a tool, command button, datagrid, text box, check box, or drop-down list. Although these parts of the process are not entirely separable, we will approach them as somewhat distinct topics, beginning in this chapter with some of the broader issues in the layout and organization of interaction contexts. Then, Chapters 8 and 9 will examine in some detail the matter of component design and selection. Finally, having established the requisite background, Chapter 10 will delve into the process of deriving the implementation model and embodying it in a prototype or visual design of some form.

COMMUNICATION CHANNELS

It is easy for developers to slip into the habit of thinking of graphical user interfaces (GUIs) in terms of graphics and miss the fact that software user interfaces support a number of alternative channels or modalities for communicating with users. In addition to graphics, the designer has available text, color, and sound as means for sustaining the dialogue with users. The goal is to present the tools and materials required from the content model in the mode—text, graphics, sound, color, or any combination—that most effectively and economically communicates with the user.

IN A WORD

Any traveler abroad who has tried to get by with gestures alone knows that communication entirely without words is challenging. Text, therefore, is an indispensable part of the dialogue between software and users. Designers of graphical user interfaces should not be afraid to use words and text to communicate with users.

> *One well-chosen word can sometimes communicate more eloquently and concisely than a contrived and confusing icon.*

A picture is not always worth a thousand words. At times, one well-chosen word can communicate far more eloquently and concisely than a contrived and confusing icon. How many users, on first encounter, would even recognize the object shown to the right in the toolbar in Figure 7-1, much less decipher its function?

Extensive Defense Department research long ago confirmed that pictures combined with words were invariably more effective for communication with users than either words or pictures alone. For this reason, graphical symbols should be combined with labels or text, especially for beginners just learning how to use a system. Labels on tools should be a user-controlled option, but the default in most applications should be for icons to be labeled with text. Hints or tool tips that pop up when the pointer rests on an icon are a highly useful feature but do not serve the same function since they cannot be scanned or read by the user when the pointer is not on a tool. Chapter 11 will provide more discussion of this issue.

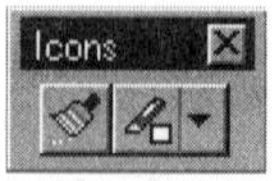

FIGURE 7-1 *What is it? A word or two might help.*
(MICROSOFT WORD 7.0)

Explanatory text can be helpful, but an interface smeared with too many words can be just as daunting as the interface without any. Lengthy messages or wordy prompts are likely to be skimmed quickly or ignored altogether by many users. Software for use should use language with precision and concision. The user's time is valuable, and space on the screen is at a premium. We will, however, have much more to say on this topic in Chapter 11 on help and messages.

Fancy fonts. The flashy layouts of *Wired* and its kith notwithstanding (see sidebar, Wild, Wired World), good design usually avoids mixing too many different fonts (or typefaces), type sizes, or type styles. Changes of font or style can disrupt the flow of interaction and distract the user. This does not mean that everything must be presented to the user in the default normal upright sans serif type used by the operating system. The very fact that a different weight (**bold**, for example) or a distinctive typeface (Bauhaus, for example) attracts the user's attention can be used by the skillful designer to help guide the dialogue. Nevertheless, few design problems are likely to justify using more than two or, at most, three different typefaces in a single user interface, however.

Most discussions on the subject caution against presenting text in all caps or uppercase letters. It is true that text presented solely in capital letters will slow most readers by a slight margin, but this does not mean it should be avoided altogether. Lengthy passages in upper case should be avoided, but headlines, banners, and labels in caps draw attention to themselves and establish their importance. Selective use can help orient the reader and give structure to complex information. One special rule concerns the abbreviation for *okay*, which is always capitalized, thus: **OK**. We mention this in part because it

WILD, WIRED WORLD

Studies of readability and comprehension in print media formed the basis of some important early work on user interface design. It is ironic that, in recent years, a style of typography and graphical design in print has emerged that flouts the hard-learned conventional dictums of page layout and visual design. First modeled by *Wired* magazine but mimicked by many others since, this style of journalistic excess uses busy, blaring backgrounds peppered with a bewildering visual cacophony of typefaces and styles to grab for media awards and for the fleeting attention of a readership raised on MTV and video games. In paper analogues of Web-site links and fancy television scene transitions, stories and features weave in and out among one another across, down, and through the pages.

Is it art? Perhaps. Admittedly, we like *Wired* and some of its kith. Some we read more than others, often dictated by interest or need dominating over preferences. We may read until the page begins to blur from eye fatigue or until we lose the thread of an article once too many times. It can be slow slogging to read a story set in green 9-point Hexotica Extra-condensed against a speckled metallic amber and chestnut backdrop.

The editor of one publication in the computer field defended this kind of design by saying that slowing down the reader was the intention. Is annoying the reader also intentional? Does it exemplify good intentions to make it more difficult for the reader to get needed information—in the case of this particular journal—about user interface design? The editor countered that the practice kept the work exciting for his layout and graphics people. Bravo. These are the magazine layouts and article designs that win awards. Is the object to win awards or to produce a useful and highly usable product? It should be clear where we stand on this one, whether applied to magazines or software, Web sites or remote controls.

is one way that some insiders in the human–computer interaction community distinguish amateurish designs by rank novices.

So-called serif type, such as the one in which the body of this book has been set, incorporates into the letters little decorative elements that enhance readability. It has long been established, at least for the printed page, that serif type can be read faster and with greater accuracy than can sans serif typefaces, such as the example of Bauhaus shown earlier. Strangely, this does not seem to hold true as consistently when it comes to text displayed in tiny dots upon a radiant monitor screen. As a rule, user interface designers are on solid ground staying with simple sans serif typefaces, such as the "System" font used within Windows. In fact, within the context of a conventional graphical user interface, serif type can be distracting, a characteristic that can confound the user or that can be used to good effect if chosen with care.

Italics or a slanted type style, *such as this*, can be especially problematic on graphical displays. Italicized text can seem lighter than surrounding text and tends to recede visually. At common resolutions within current display technology, the more complex shapes of italics often make them appear somewhat jagged and broken compared with upright text in the same size and typeface.

Small fonts. One young colleague of ours often works with half a dozen windows open on his workstation, each displaying a reduced full-screen view of some program or application, replete with tiny, unreadable text. He, of course, can read it all with ease, having not yet reached his thirtieth birthday and still having 20–20 eyesight.

An important rule for successful communication with software users is to avoid "under-forty fonts." The rule does not refer to type that is under 40 points in size, but to type that can be read only by those users who are under forty years of age. Designers who have not yet passed that milestone and experienced presbyopia for themselves either should have their user interface designs reviewed by an older colleague or should use the squint test. If you can still read the text from a meter away through heavily squinted eyes, you are probably safe.

> *For successful communication, avoid "under-forty fonts" that can be read only by those users who are under forty years of age.*

Not every user will be happy with your choice of fonts or styles, so you should, as a rule, support font customization by users. Developers often retort that giving users control over fonts will mess up their carefully planned layouts or cause problems with text that ends up truncated or that spills over into other visual components. As much as possible, message boxes and dialogues should be implemented to resize automatically to accommodate varying font sizes. Although the programming to do this well can be tricky in some languages and development environments, various third-party components offer ready-made support for such resizing. These schemes will not prevent all problems with large or space-hogging fonts, but they do help. In those cases where the end-user customization is exotic enough to undermine even the most flexible schemes, we as designers can do nothing anyway, and users can rightfully be left to suffer the consequences of their own idiosyncratic tastes.

COLORFUL INTERFACES

Modern graphical user interfaces in general and Windows in particular have perpetuated a gruesome gray color scheme that is low in contrast and often bloody boring. Readability is strongly influenced by contrast. Black text on a white background is far and away the most readable, closely followed by white text on a black background. Displaying black text on the medium gray of standard message boxes sharply reduces readability. Using one shade of gray for text against a background of another shade renders text

> *Modern graphical user interfaces have perpetuated a gruesome gray color scheme that is low in contrast and often bloody boring.*

even harder to read. Interfaces implemented entirely in shades of gray can take on a sameness in which no part stands out from any other.

Color provides an added channel that can be used in parallel with other means of communicating with users. Color can indicate items or areas of greater importance. Objects and text can be in color or can be accented through colored backgrounds or borders. Color can also be used to associate or disassociate elements visually on the user interface. Objects of the same color, even when widely separated on the user interface, tend to be seen as related or associated.

In general, large areas of bright, primary, or highly saturated color on a screen can confuse users and cause visual fatigue after prolonged viewing. Some color contrasts, such as green on red or red on green, are particularly hard on the visual system. Except for photographs and full-color graphics, interfaces that use many different colors can appear busy and bedazzling. The ability of color to highlight and emphasize elements of the interface is lost if everything visible is in bright colors. Ironically, color communicates best amidst the sea of gray of conventional graphical user interfaces.

> *The ability of color to highlight and emphasize elements of the interface is lost if everything is brightly colored. Ironically, color communicates best amidst the standard sea of gray.*

Although information and features can be highlighted and distinguished through color, color coding should not be used by itself for any distinction that is important to the user. A remote query system for use by police and other law enforcement officials had to be redesigned after it was learned that many cruisers were equipped with monochrome display laptops. In the original design, red flags indicated major or felony "wants and warrants," yellow indicated minor offenses, and green indicated a clean record. Even in vehicles with full-color displays, bright sunlight could make some colors hard to distinguish.

Not everyone sees the world in full color. About one out of every twelve males and a somewhat lower percentage of females have some form of "color blindness" or color discrimination difficulty. They may be unable to tell the difference between a red flag and a green one, for example.

> *Color should always be combined redundantly with some other cue, such as line weight, text style, or distinctive symbols.*

For more than one reason, then, color should always be combined redundantly with some other cue, such as line weight, text style, or distinctive symbols. An effective use of color coding is to qualify or communicate secondary information, such as status or activity, regarding information presented on the user interface. To take one example, in the list display of a mail-order customer database, red could indicate an exception or condition requiring attention, blue could indicate more detail is available, and green could indicate a new or recently updated entry. A distinctive graphic for each condition or status code, such as the circle, diamond, and triangle shown in Figure 7-2, makes the information understandable on a monochrome display or by a color-impaired user. This scheme is merely an illustration, not a recommendation; the best choice of color codes and symbols will depend on the application.

Color codes, especially ones that are more or less arbitrary, can be particularly difficult to learn, and the more colors used, the harder the learning. From four to seven different colors is the practical maximum for color coding under most circumstances. In any case, an on-screen key for color codes, such as the one illustrated in Figure 7-2, should be used as an aid in learning and use.

SIGNS AND SYMBOLS

Graphical user interfaces, as the very name implies, encourage the use of graphics, and many designers, especially beginners, feel compelled to "do something with graphics" in every user interface. Graphics provide a useful channel of communication that can be cleverly exploited, but graphics can also become a distraction, grabbing for the user's attention and slowing down the interaction. Complex graphical backgrounds can make text hard to read and other graphical elements hard to distinguish. Trying too hard to "say it with pictures" can result in user interfaces that are harder to understand and use than if a few choice words had been displayed.

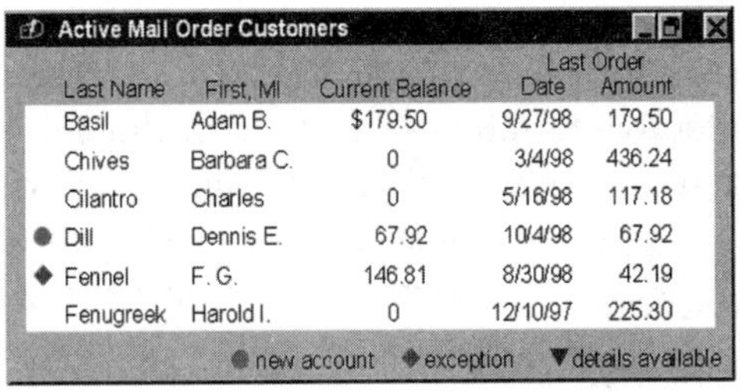

| | Active Mail Order Customers | | | | |

FIGURE 7-2 *Multichannel coding.*

Graphical communication is of no value whatsoever in some applications, such as in a system incorporating high-volume manual data entry from paper forms. In the role of data entry clerk, the user is typing "heads down," not even looking at the screen.

The archetype for inappropriate or irrelevant graphics is what we call "big bozo bitmaps"—oversize graphics, such as the one shown in Figure 7-3, that take up a lot of space on the user interface but have little or nothing to offer to the user. Once limited largely to the "splash screens" that displayed when an application was launched, they have since spread to dialogue boxes and "wizards" that break up interaction into tiny steps, filling each dialogue panel in the interaction with a large but largely meaningless graphic.

Many designers, especially beginners, feel compelled to "do something with graphics" in every graphical user interface.

Although display speed has become less a problem with today's faster processors and more powerful graphic accelerator boards, particularly heavy use of graphics not only is a distraction but also can eat up system resources and slow down the software. This is especially a problem with Web and Intranet applica-

FIGURE 7-3 *Worthless pictures, wasted screen real estate.*

tions, which, with a certain irony, often make extensive use of graphics (more on this matter in Chapter 14 on special applications).

Graphics can be effective for either the static or the animated display of information, especially where it is the relationships among the displayed data that are most important. Graphs and charts can convey progress, emphasize key information, provide easily understood overviews, or highlight relative values.

> *Text and graphics are often best used redundantly. Graphics reinforce and anchor the message conveyed in words, and text elaborates or explains the graphics.*

Text and graphics are often best used redundantly—as parallel channels for communicating a common message. The graphics help reinforce and anchor the message conveyed in words, and the text elaborates or explains the graphics. Skillful combinations of text and graphics make the user interface easier to understand and reduce user errors. A good example of this two-channel approach was illustrated in the color-coding scheme of Figure 7-2 in the previous section.

Another good example is the use of *glyphs* (small, simple symbols) on certain command buttons, such as those illustrated in Figure 7-4. Glyphs on the primary navigation controls—**OK**, **Cancel**, and **Help**—make it easier for the user to spot them and know how to proceed or not, even when these controls are not located where the user expected them. This style of controls, although often associated with Borland (now known as Inprise), the company that pioneered them, deserves wider use. Glyphs on every button clutter the user interface, while selected use satisfies Nielsen's plea for clearly marked exits [Nielsen, 1993]. Not all users like glyphs on command buttons, so this, like labels on tool icons, should also be a user-selectable option.

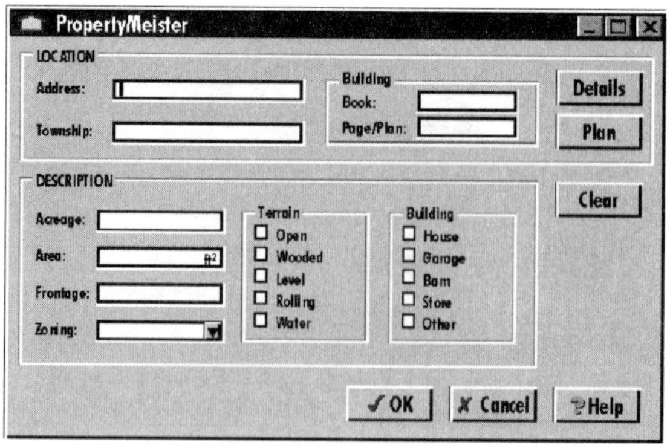

FIGURE 7-4 *Glyphs on command.*

Graphical elements need not be complicated or dramatic to be of value. Some of the most primitive graphical devices, such as simple lines used as dividing rules, frames, or borders, can help organize the interaction context and orient the user.

SOUNDING IT OUT

Sound can be another highly effective channel of communication with users, but, like color, it, too, must be used judiciously; a little can go a long way. Users will learn to ignore sound if it is used too often or for inconsequential or conflicting purposes. Silly sounds in serious applications quickly become tiresome.

It is important to use different sounds for different purposes. If the same sort of beep is used on every occasion, it becomes mere noise since no information is conveyed. The selection of appropriate sounds is like the design of effective icons; the trick is to make the meaning immediately apparent to the casual or inexperienced user. A soft click or other relatively unobtrusive yet reassuring sound can confirm input, for example. A pleasant but more distinct sound, such as a chime, can signal successful completion of a form or task. A minor error might be conveyed by a somewhat less pleasant and more attention-getting sound, such as a brief minor chord or blat of a horn. A European-style tritone siren could be reserved for imminent core meltdown at the nuclear power plant or for catastrophic corruption of a database index.

Different sounds should be used for different purposes. The same beep used for every occasion becomes mere noise.

Sounds need to be chosen to be appropriate to the application as well as the setting in which they will be used. A noisy supermarket and a quiet office may require different approaches to "ear-con" design, and sounds may be completely ineffective or inappropriate in some contexts. These and other contextual issues will be covered in more depth in Chapter 13.

Users should have full control over sounds in most software, but especially in typical desktop applications. This control should not be devolved to the Windows volume control or the switch on a speaker. It is also insufficient to offer a lone check box under user preferences to turn the sound on or off in total. The user may want to hear a chime when a report has been completely generated but not want a chirp on every entry error. True, the clever and sophisticated user can accomplish such selective control through the **Sounds Properties** dialogue of the Windows **Control Panel**, but this clumsy way of offering user control over the audio output of your software is the stamp of lazy programming.

SCREEN REAL ESTATE

The available space on the monitor or display is usually referred to as *screen real estate*. Whether the user interface will be presented in 1.2 million colors on a 30-inch monitor with 1280-by-1024 resolution or will be squeezed onto a 9-inch VGA display, screen real estate is always a limited resource. Effective use of screen real estate requires the designer to manage subtle trade-offs in the placement and ordering of visual features as well as in their distribution over different interaction spaces.

THE FLOW OF WORK

In the context of user interface and interaction design, **workflow** refers to the way the user moves around within and between interaction spaces. The layout and organization of the features on the user interface shape the workflow, determining whether it will be smooth and efficient or slow and awkward.

Attention, attention. Good layout starts with getting the user's attention. Each interaction space should provide an initial focus for the user's attention that is purposeful, not accidental, and useful, not unfortunate.

Some companies, for instance, have internal user interface style manuals or guidelines that call for the corporate logo to appear prominently and in full color on every screen or window. What most commands the attention of the visual system? Motion, then color. Put a large, colorful logo at the top of every screen and what happens? The user's attention is first diverted to the irrelevant logo and then must be redirected elsewhere. Videotapes of users will reveal a telltale glance of the eyes as each screen pops open. Add animation to the logo, as some companies will now do to demonstrate their programming prowess, and the attention-grabbing power is multiplied.

> *Good layout starts with getting the user's attention— purposefully, not accidentally.*

Not only does the colorful logo waste screen real estate, but it also demonstrably slows down interaction. Few regular users within a company will need to be reminded from day to day or moment to moment for whom they are working. This observation suggests that there may be appropriate uses for this device. For example, some firms provide telephone order-taking services under subcontract to multiple catalogue companies. When a call comes in on a particular telephone line, the software automatically displays an order entry screen with the name and logo of the associated company. One minute, the operator may take a call for the Bloom-All Dutch Bulb Company; the next, for Water's Start Clothing. A prominent name and eye-catching logo help the operator make the requisite mental shift and answer the call appropriately. Secondary cues in the form of distinctive color schemes or easily recognized layouts can further help orient the operator.

Good designs will typically draw the user's eye to the initial entry field, to the beginning of a sequence of actions or decisions, or to important data or key information. These starting points will, of course, have been identified in the course of task modeling and content modeling. The user should be able to understand the significant information or most important parts of the interaction context quickly and easily. In mission-critical applications, especially with complex displays, the ability of the user to separate the relevant information from data that can and should be ignored may spell the difference between success and disaster.

> *The ability of the user to separate the relevant information from data that can and should be ignored may spell the difference between success and disaster.*

The designer has available a variety of techniques to attract and direct the user's attention, including color, graphics, animation, borders, highlights, text style and size, line weight and style, and the like. However, if, on any one interaction context, too many techniques are used or too much information is made salient, the user will merely become lost in a visual jumble of another sort.

The visual components and groupings of them should be arranged for a simple logical flow through each interaction context consistent with the focal or most frequent use cases. Generally speaking, the logical starting point for interaction is in the upper left-hand corner, with the focus of attention and interaction proceeding toward the lower right-hand corner. This favors placing the primary navigation controls in the lower right. Microsoft and other major software vendors have begun to favor grouping the primary navigation controls in the upper right, however, which would lead to a U-shaped workflow in well-designed dialogues. This arrangement can allow for a longer path through the interaction context that can simplify some user interface layouts.

In either variation, it is imperative that the primary navigation controls should be consistent in location and appearance throughout the entire user interface. In cases where other considerations may force the relocation of the primary navigation controls for a dialogue, other visual cues, such as the glyphs illustrated in

> *The primary navigation controls should be consistent in location and appearance throughout the entire user interface.*

Figure 7-4, can help the user rapidly locate these essential visual features.

The most difficult interfaces to master and the most error-prone layouts are ones that lead the user on a merry chase around the user interface, with frequent reversals of direction required in order to complete a task. Especially when the visual targets are small, such as option buttons or small tools, this kind of "drunkard's walk" can dramatically slow down use and increase errors.

If a single interaction context supports multiple use cases, it will be more challenging to arrange the layout for felicitous workflow. The temptation is to compromise and derive a design that is equally bad for every case. It is better to organize the interface to support well the focal use cases or those that will be most frequent at the point the user encounters the particular interaction context, sacrificing ease of use or efficiency somewhat for the less important or more unlikely use cases.

Increment by increment. A recent trend in organizing software workflow is to break up a process into very small steps, each one presented on a separate interaction context. At each step, the user typically makes a single choice or enters one bit of information before going on to the next step on a fresh interaction context. In some cases, an additional confirmation step is interposed. To use up what would otherwise be empty space on the screen, each step may be accompanied by a big bozo bitmap, along the lines illustrated in Figure 7-3. We refer to this workflow model as "3I design," for **Incremental Interaction Interfaces**, or, less charitably, as "4I design," for *Idiotic* Incremental Interaction Interfaces. Though not without its occasional valid applications (see, for example, the discussion of wizards in Chapter 11), this interaction model is becoming overused. It can force the user to switch contexts and mental frames of reference constantly and to break up a single and coherent task into too many tiny, time-consuming steps. This sequential, stepwise pattern of workflow can be helpful for complex but infrequent tasks, but it is usually inappropriate for focal or common use cases.

> *4I design (Idiotic Incremental Interaction Interfaces) breaks up a single and coherent task into far too many tiny, time-consuming steps.*

Workbench interaction. Not all tasks or applications lend themselves to a simple and organized workflow, either within interaction contexts or between them. The pattern of usage we refer to as **workbench interaction** typifies a broad class of applications and software tools, including drawing packages, word processors, CASE tools, and programming environments. In workbench interaction, the workflow centering on a focal work area is complex and unpredictable. A single workspace, often larger than the window through which it is viewed, along with an associated collection of tools and controls, supports a variety of use cases and extensions.

To support workbench interaction most effectively, visual features should be organized into semantic groups and by subtasks. In this way, even though the sequence of interaction is not uniform or predictable, components that are thought of together or typically used together are likely to be found together on the user interface.

Effective support of workbench interaction requires a compact, flexible, and feature-laden user interface. Commonly used are floating, dockable palettes carrying numerous tools that are completely customizable by the user.

DISTRIBUTING INFORMATION

Information as well as tools and functions need to be distributed across interaction contexts in ways that reflect anticipated patterns of usage. If information that is used together in enacting a use case is split across more than one screen or dialogue box, for example, the user may be forced to switch back and forth between contexts, reducing efficiency and increasing errors.

Synchronous displays sometimes offer an effective way to organize information and conserve screen real estate. Synchronous displays are linked interaction contexts in which actions within one context are immediately reflected in the other. An example would be linked list and record detail views in a database application. Selection of an entry in the list view causes the corresponding details to appear in the detail view; altering a field in the detail view changes the corresponding data in the list view. Another example would be a linked numeric and graphical display of the same dataset within a statistical program. Synchronized interaction contexts offer users multiple views of the same information and support interaction with either view at the discretion of the user. Information that is shared across synchronized interaction contexts reduces the load on the user's short-term memory.

> *When information that is used together is split across multiple screens or dialogue boxes, the user may be forced to switch back and forth between contexts, reducing efficiency and increasing errors.*

VISUAL ORGANIZATION

According to the Structure Principle, usability is enhanced when similar or related features appear together or in similar form on the user interface and when dissimilar or unrelated things are separated or appear distinct on the user interface. Good visual organization helps the user make sense of each interaction context within the user interface.

Graphical techniques. Visual organization is achieved through a variety of graphical techniques that associate or disassociate visual features. Position and proximity are the most basic techniques for visual association and disassociation. Things

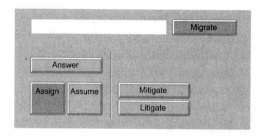

FIGURE 7-5 *Visual organization techniques.*

that are grouped closely are seen as related, while things that are separated are seen as distinct. Simple lines can also group and separate elements independent of their actual distances from one another. A frame around a set of command buttons defines them as a visual unit. Color and shape can accomplish the same purposes. Features in the same color are perceived as related, even if separated by some distance. The same principles apply to components of similar or dissimilar shapes. As Figure 7-5 illustrates, various organizing techniques can be combined in a single interaction context.

Good visual organization avoids the extremes of overcrowded widgets and sparsely populated interfaces. Cramming too many visual components willy-nilly into one interaction context not only is visually unappealing but also confuses users, who get lost amidst the clutter and chaos and miss the important data or controls. The result can be increased stress and errors. At the other extreme, designs marked by vast open spaces waste screen real estate and can lead to inefficient usage.

> *Good visual organization avoids the extremes of overcrowded widgets and sparsely populated interfaces.*

Increasingly popular tabbed dialogues pose some special problems in visual organization. Not only navigation controls but also other fixed controls that are common across all the pages of the tabbed dialogue need to be separated and moved off the pages themselves; otherwise, as tabs are selected and changed, these fixed controls can appear to protrude through the tabs' pages and break the illusion of the tabs as solid objects. The significance of this phenomenon of visual object persistence, which helps users make visual sense of the user interface, will be explored more fully in Chapter 9.

Because all the pages of a tabbed dialogue have the same area, it is not uncommon for some pages to end up looking like a vacant lot while others are crammed with controls. Effective layout of tabbed dialogues may require rethinking the categories by which features are allocated to tabs. The guiding principle should be the use cases being supported. Some seemingly logical categories will unnecessarily separate features that are often used together, leading to clumsier enactments of

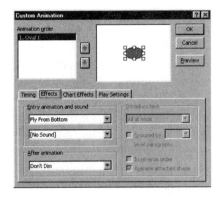

FIGURE 7-6 *Time and motion slowed.*
(MICROSOFT POWERPOINT 97)

use cases. For example, a tabbed dialogue from within a presentation package is illustrated in Figure 7-6. A common task is animating an object, which typically requires setting the motion or style of animation and controlling the timing relative to other events. In this design, the user must always move between two different tabs, **Effects** and **Timing**, to complete the usual task. While this organization may make sense to users in terms of the categories in which they think and reason about presentation problems, it does not reflect how they carry out tasks.

Aesthetic apprehension. Visual organization based on semantic and task considerations is most important for good usage-centered designs, but visual aesthetics can also be a factor of lesser import. As a rule, the primary goal is to achieve a highly usable design. Aesthetic appeal is a secondary concern best approached through polishing the design once a good basic layout has been obtained.

As a holdover from work with the printed page, graphical designers refer to the space between visual features as "white space," even when this space may be gray or black on the user interface. As a rule, graphical user interfaces are somewhat more appealing and may even be marginally easier to understand when white space is approximately balanced and

> *The primary goal is a highly usable design; aesthetic appeal is a secondary concern best achieved through polishing a good basic layout.*

distributed somewhat evenly over the interaction context. For user interface designers with a "tin eye," one guideline is to make the total amount of white space above the midline and below it roughly equal, as well as the white space to the left and to the right of center in the interaction context. The same guideline applies to the number of user interface controls or visual features on either side of the midline and of the centerline. The goal is not perfect symmetry, but something resembling a rough balance. Radically skewed designs are likely to be the most visually disconcerting.

White space is especially important between visual elements and between visual elements and borders or edges. For readability, space is needed between labels and the edges of command buttons, for instance, and controls should not be crowded up against the edges of dialogues or the frames within them.

User interfaces where components do not quite line up can look amateurish, and some research [see, for example, Comber and Maltby, 1994; 1995] suggests that alignment of visual components is more than just an aesthetic matter; it can have some impact on ease of interpretation and use. For a tidy appearance, aligning both the top edges and left edges of visual elements has the greatest effect.

The component size is another visual dimension that can convey meaning and establish associations or disassociations among visual features. Primary navigation controls and other standard command buttons should all be of the same standard size throughout the user interface, but other functions may employ distinct sizes or even different shapes to help the visual organization. However, any one interaction context should not use too many different sizes of controls if it is to appear tidy and well laid out. We will return to this issue of the size and alignment of visual features when we take up quantitative measures of user interface designs in Chapter 17.

8

PRACTICAL WIDGETRY:
Choosing and Designing Visual Components

BUY OR BUILD

As part of the design process, the user interface must be populated with visual components in the form of the actual user interface widgets that will serve as the tools and materials employed by the user. In some few cases, there will be only one obvious choice for the widget, but most of the time, the designer will have to choose among a number of alternatives to find the most appropriate embodiment for some abstract tool or material from the content model. The choices may include not only standard visual components but also the possibility of components that are custom designed for a given application or context.

How do you pick the right widget to solve a particular user interface design problem? In some cases, the choice can be guided by some kind of formula or set of rules. Many designers avoid heavy thinking through the practice of design by imitation—choosing components on the basis of what they have seen before in other systems. Others bow to de facto standards and just do whatever Microsoft does.

> *Many designers avoid heavy thinking either by choosing components on the basis of what they have seen before in other systems or by doing whatever Microsoft does.*

In the usage-centered approach, the design and selection of visual components is model-driven. In every case, we are seeking the most understandable and usable interpretation of the content model and the most efficient realization of the use cases to be supported.

It would be impractical to go into detail about all the assortment of widgets available for modern graphical user interface design, and any attempt to catalogue them in a book would soon be outdated in any event. Instead, we will focus on several categories of design issues that typify the kinds of decision making involved in implementation modeling.

ICONIC COMMUNICATION

Where would graphical user interfaces be without icons? Icons—the graphical symbols on tools and other visual features—are so ubiquitous in modern software that, to many people, icons are a virtual synonym for a graphical user interface. In the inflated language of software marketing, icons make a user interface intuitive. Although icons do not necessarily make a user interface intuitively obvious, well-conceived and well-designed icons can improve both the learnability and the rememberability of user interfaces by promoting easy recognition of features. They are definitely a part of the look-and-feel that helps mark a user interface as contemporary.

"EYE-CON" DESIGN

Like other aspects of good user interface design, creative icon designs can take time. However, it is important to keep in mind that, if it takes you as the designer more than a few minutes to invent an icon, it is almost certain not to be intuitively obvious to the casual user. Anything that takes the user more than a second or two to figure out can never be said to be intuitive or "guessable." Obscure icons not only do not help the user guess their meaning but also can be hard to memorize and may actually slow down the process of learning how to use a system.

Good icon and tool design calls for a simple and consistent style, yet with icons that are readily distinguishable from one another. The selective and restrained use of color can help communicate meaning and enhance apparent differences. A fairly good example is shown in Figure 8-1a, a collection of tools from a presentation package for arranging graphical objects. These icons make use of "minimalist" graphics clarified by selective use of color. Knowing the context in which they are used, it is not hard to figure out what they mean. However, they can be improved somewhat. The tiny arrows in the icons of the first six icons are hard to see and add no information. Thickening the bars representing the points of alignment and highlighting them by making them darker would increase the visual differences

> *Icons are often claimed to make a user interface intuitive, but obscure icons can be hard to memorize and may actually slow down the process of learning how to use a system.*

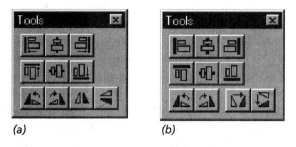

(a)   (b)

FIGURE 8-1 *Tool icons for object arrangement operations.*
(MICROSOFT POWERPOINT)

FIGURE 8-2 *Iconic conventions for abstract and concrete actions.*
(MICROSOFT POWERPOINT)

among these icons, as can be seen in Figure 8-1b. The last two icons—for flipping horizontally and vertically—are clarified by adding small arrows like those on the rotation tools.

Wherever possible, the icon designer should draw on established conventions, prior associations, and accepted standards. Care should be taken not to violate or contradict highly familiar signs. For example, the widely accepted slash-and-circle sign for "no" or "prohibited" should not be pressed into service for "create a wheel" in a vehicle design package.

Objects or concrete nouns are usually the easiest to represent as icons; they are merely depicted directly, often in simplified or abstract form. Actions are somewhat more difficult, but nouns can sometimes stand in for verbs. For example, an image of a printer can stand for "print," or an opened folder can represent "open file." Abstract verbs are the hardest of all to represent as icons. Conventions can help. Representing the concept of "undo" as an icon has long challenged graphics designers, but the hegemony of Microsoft has reinforced the convention of the little counterclockwise loop, shown at the left in Figure 8-2, to the point that it is all but instantly recognizable. Conventions can also collide with other needs and lead to confusion. The differences among the undo, redo, do again, and rotate icons, shown left to right in Figure 8-2, are minimal and somewhat arbitrary.

SEMIOTICS

An icon means one thing to a software designer and something else to a specialist in the study of signs and symbols. Some knowledge of semiotics, the science of signs, can be useful for user interface designers [Callahan, 1994; Constantine and Henderson-Sellers, 1996]. We refer to any graphical symbol on a tool or other visual control as an icon, but, in semiotics, icons are one of three basic categories of signs: indexical, symbolic, and iconic.

> *In semiotics, the science of signs, icons are one of three basic categories of signs: indexical, symbolic, and iconic.*

Indexical signs are associated with what they represent by a necessary physical or logical connection. Smoke is an indexical sign for fire, for example. *Symbolic* signs are arbitrary. The letter *h* in the Latin alphabet has no necessary association whatsoever with the soft puff of air we use to pronounce it in English, nor does the similarity in shape between an *h* and a *b* give any clue to their pronunciation. The sign composed of the letters *h-a-t* does not in any meaningful way resemble the thing we cover our heads with that it represents.

Iconic signs bear some form of similarity or likeness to the things for which they stand. For example, a symbol on a user interface might represent software "tools" with pictures of a hammer and screwdriver. There are many variations on iconic representation that can be used to create software icons, including direct depiction of objects, analogy and metaphor, synecdoche, and homonyms.

Analogies and metaphors can be a rich source of icon ideas; a magnifying glass can be used to signify "search," for example. However, analogies and metaphors that are too clever or creative can create problems for users, especially when they are based on inside knowledge or a programming perspective. One system used an image of a globe to represent user preferences or options. A programmer from the software vendor justified this design by pointing out that such preferences were "global" parameters. This is a graphical example of inside-out design, a form of software malpractice in which geek-speak becomes the visual language at the user interface.

> *Homonyms or visual puns for icons often work only in one particular language and culture.*

In synecdoche, a part is used to represent a whole, the specific represents the general, or vice versa. A telephone or a telephone connection might be represented by an image of a handset, for example.

Many programmers are such avid punsters that homonyms or visual puns can be particularly appealing to them. However, homonyms and puns are particularly risky for user interface design because they "work" only in one language and often only within a particular culture. For example, one system used a picture of a dog, a golden retriever, to represent "retrieve from database." Not only does the user have to recognize the breed of dog, but also, in some countries, the same image might remind the user of dinner time. For another example, the button to "file" a document in one system pictured a nail file. Corny but cute? Perhaps. Helpful? Probably not.

TOOLBAR ORGANIZATION

The Structure Principle applies to the organization of tools or icons as much as to any other part of the user interface. Robust modern user interfaces will almost invariably provide for some form of customization by the user (see Chapter 12), but this is no excuse for not thinking through the best organization for the factory-fresh defaults that the user sees after initial installation.

Good tool organization is based on what tools mean and how they are used. Perhaps because it is easy to think of tools in terms of categories or types, software developers typically rely heavily on semantic organization. Drawing tools are placed in one collection and arrangement tools in another, for instance. Sometimes, though, even simple categorical collection can seem obscure to users. Why would the free-rotation tool be with the drawing tools in MS PowerPoint while the tools for 90° left and right rotation are among the arrangement tools, yet they are all together under **Rotate/Flip** on the **Draw** menu?

Tools should be made available to support the use cases, but this does not mean that each use case should have its own unique tool or icon. In many kinds of applications, especially those characterized by workbench interaction, the proliferation of tools could lead to a bewildering and less usable interface. Efficient support for common use cases is usually best achieved through refinements or modifications to layouts to bring together tools that will often be used together.

> *Tools should support the use cases, but this does not require that each use case have its own unique tool or icon.*

For an example, consider the problem of aligning graphical objects within a drawing or presentation slide. Objects can be aligned vertically or horizontally; they can be aligned vertically along their left edges, vertically along their right edges, or centered; and there are three variations on horizontal alignment. In principle, these tasks could all be supported with one tool or menu entry that calls up an alignment dialogue, but this just makes each and every alignment operation take two extra steps (open dialogue, close dialogue).

In addition to the simple cases, there are combinations of alignment operations that arise frequently in graphical design, such as centering a bunch of objects both vertically and horizontally. We may decide against providing an added tool button for such a use case, but we do not want to make it unduly difficult either, especially if it is fairly common. The collection of alignment tools illustrated in

(a)   (b)

FIGURE 8-3 *Aligning alignment tools for multiple use cases.*

Figure 8-1 groups the tools into two categories for vertical and horizontal alignment and fortuitously brings together the two centering tools for a quick click-click realization of the use case. However, when the tools are arrayed on a toolbar, such as the vertical one shown in Figure 8-3a, paired operations like "center all" or "align upper left corners" become considerably clumsier. The arrangement of Figure 8-3b still makes visual and semantic sense, but brings together the tools for paired operations. It speeds up the paired operations without slowing down the single-step use cases.

MENUS

Menus are not as "sexy" as icons, but they are versatile and vital potential contributors to usability in modern software. Menus play roles other than just granting access to functions and features. Alan Cooper (1995) refers to menus with the somewhat pedantic term *pedagogical vector* to suggest that menus can be a means to help users learn what they can do with a system and how they can do it. Many users start out with a new system by opening one menu after another to see what is available and to understand something of how functions are organized within the software. Nested menus promote the exploration of available features. Unlike nested dialogues, menus display the navigation

> *Many new users start by opening one menu after another to see what is available and to understand how functions are organized within the software.*

hierarchy, so users can see directly how they reached a particular point. Unlike tools and command buttons, menus defer action; they can be opened and examined without triggering any processing as long as a final selection is not made by the user. The user's faith that a menu can be opened without effect should not be undermined by menus that behave in unexpected ways. (See sidebar, Bang, Bang.)

Menus are not for beginners only. Well-designed menus can promote the transition between menu operation and the use of tool buttons or keyboard shortcuts. For skilled or advanced users, access or accelerator keys based on selected letters from menu and item names help speed production use, and menus serve as quick reminders of these keyboard shortcuts. Simply opening a menu to check the keyboard equivalent for some operation is much quicker than searching the help system.

MENU ORGANIZATION

Menus should be organized by semantics and by task structure, which, again, obligates developers to have some understanding of the categories within which users think about their work and a deeper understanding of how tasks are organized in practice. The names of menus and the items within them should follow common naming conventions or should reflect the vocabulary of users and of the application domain.

Some conventional assignments to menus are execrable from a human factors perspective. The worst common offender is also the most ubiquitous: the omnipresent **File** menu. Under it are all kinds of things that have nothing to do with files or filing as most people think of them. By historic conventions that we are probably stuck with, printing and exiting are thrown in alongside opening, closing, and saving files. If you follow the rules strictly, even an application that uses no files,

---

BANG, BANG

Now and then, you will see a word on the menu bar with an exclamation point after it. This is not an indication of importance or an invitation to open the menu. It should be read as a warning and, perhaps, as a confession of shame on the part of the user interface designers. If you click on such a marked menu, you will not see a menu list politely drop down. Instead, you are likely to be plummeted into the midst of an operation or to find a dialogue box suddenly thrust in your face. In the shortcut lingo of programmers, an exclamation point is called a *bang,* and this sort of menu is often referred to as a *bang menu.* Aptly named. Bang, bang, you're dead—or in some other undesirable state.

Bang menus violate the reasonable expectations of users regarding well-mannered interfaces. By hindering the casual and comfortable exploration of the user interface, bang menus reduce the value of menus as learning devices. If an action is to be triggered on selection, it should appear as an item within a menu or be accessed through a tool or command button. Some programmers protest and say that their system would require a menu with only one item beneath, perhaps with the same name as the menu itself. This dilemma should be taken as an invitation for redesign and reorganization of the menus.

The only thing worse than a bang menu with a bang after the title is a bang menu without a bang. Both should always be avoided.

---

*Some conventional assignments to menus are execrable from a human factors perspective; the worst common offender is the ubiquitous **File** menu.*

as such, would have to include a **File** menu to serve as a placeholder for **Exit**. Users have become so accustomed to this abuse that many manage to make sense of a **File** menu even in contexts in which it is nonsense.

The big software vendors have perpetrated some of the most illogical organizations and then perpetuated them through successive releases in the name of supporting the installed base. A widely familiar example is found in a popular word-processing program that puts most formatting control under **Format**, where a logical user would reasonably expect to find it, but requires going through the **View** menu when it comes to headers and footers on pages and to the **File** menu to set page margins and some aspects of headers and footers. Go figure. There are logical, *programming* arguments and historical reasons for all these placements—we've heard them all—but they still make little or no sense from the standpoint of the users and their tasks. If some misguided style guide says **Page Setup** has to be under the **File** menu, nothing prevents the intelligent interface designer from also putting it under **Format**.

Nearly all application windows with a menu bar will support a core set of menus that includes **File**, **Edit**, and **Help**. Conventional menus that do not apply in all circumstances include **View**, **Insert**, **Format**, and **Window**. Other common but not universal menus include **Tools**, **Options**, and **Preferences**. Because there are guidelines for all of these more or less standard menus and because users have built up expectations regarding their contents and interpretation, designers should avoid using them for unconventional purposes or placing unexpected items within them.

Special precautions apply to menus like the last group listed: **Tools**, **Options**, and **Preferences**. These are sufficiently vague as to invite the inclusion of all manner of design detritus. Although there are legitimate definitions of what constitutes a tool and what distinguishes options from preferences, in practice almost anything can be force-fit under any rubric. We refer to these as "garbage menus," pseudorandom collections of miscellany and misplaced functions. They are often used as dumping grounds for all those functions the designer was too lazy or uninspired to put into a better home. Sometimes the collections are so loose the menus might as well be labeled **Stuff** or **Junk**. Certain menu names are usually clues to a lack of design or forethought. Common offenders include **Services**, **Special**, **Facilities**, **Functions**, and **System**. These are not always meaningless, but, even when they subsume reasonable collection of items, their names provide little clue as to what they contain.

> *"Garbage menus" are pseudorandom collections of misplaced miscellany, dumping grounds for all those functions the designer was too lazy or uninspired to put into a better home.*

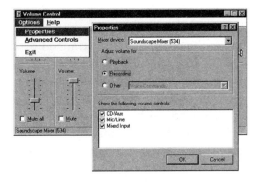

FIGURE 8-4 *Example of a garbage dump menu used to bury functions.*
(SOUNDSCAPE)

For unbridled lunacy in the use of garbage menus, it is hard to top the example in Figure 8-4. For a sound-enabled computer, two kinds of volume settings are required: those controlling playback and those controlling recording. In the utility shown in the figure, the default configuration displays playback controls. To get access to recording controls, the user has to go under **Options**, select **P̲roperties**, then, within the dialogue box, click on the option button for **Recording**, and then close the dialogue box, thereby revealing the same primary dialogue again, but suddenly transformed.

Like dialogues, toolbars, and other features, menus should be organized by semantics and by the structure of tasks. Items that are thought of together or used together ought to appear together or near one another. Items that have little or nothing to do with one another ought not to be tossed onto the same menu. The names of menus should clearly suggest the items included, and item names should describe the functions to which they grant access.

Good menu design, like most other aspects of good user interface design, is based on striking balances between different forms and sources of complexity. The menu bar for an application window should surface the primary categories or collections of tasks at the top level so that the user has a high probability of making the correct guess and finding a desired feature or facility on the first try, without having to search through an entire menu hierarchy. In general, too few or too many menus represents a problem in structure. Too few menus can mean that too many features are buried and that the menus themselves may be too long or nested too deeply; too many menus that divide features among too many categories will confuse some users and make it harder to find

> *Good menu design, like most other aspects of good user interface design, strikes balances between different forms and sources of complexity.*

what is needed to complete tasks. Typically, well-designed menu structures will spread from 3 to a maximum of 12 menus across the menu bar. The width of the menu bar when the application window is maximized establishes a good upper limit, but 6 to 9 menus will suffice for most software.

The number of items within each menu should also be kept within reason, but more items per menu with fewer levels of nesting generally promotes quick understanding and navigation. The vertical height of the display screen places a sharp upper bound beyond which the designer must resort to confusing multicolumn arrangements. Well-organized menus rarely have more than 15 to 20 items at the top or first level; submenus should probably be kept more limited, having never more than 7 to 9 items. The designer should specify both full or long versions and abbreviated versions of menus. Abbreviated menus, which are often the default condition for software when first installed normally, should incorporate all the core or basic features but can omit more advanced, esoteric, or infrequently used entries.

Nested or cascading menus, in which selecting a menu item opens another menu of items, can particularly tax the ability of users to make visual sense of and navigate through available options. Two levels of nesting should be considered the maximum under normal circumstances; three should be regarded as an absolute limit. Most users are flummoxed by the seemingly endless right and left cascading of menus off the Windows **Start** menu.

To promote explorability and predictability of the menu system, menu items should follow the conventions for differentiating immediate actions, dialogue activation, and menu cascading. In Windows 95, for example, the convention is to indicate a dialogue with an ellipsis and a submenu with a small triangle.

KEYBOARD ACCESS

Menus serve as an alternative means of access to features not only through point-and-click operation but also through keyboard entry. Anything that can be done through tools on a toolbar should also be accessible through menus. Because some users have a strong preference for immediate access through tool buttons, the converse rule applies to tools as well.

A cardinal rule of graphical user interfaces is that it should be possible to carry out all operations with the software using only the keyboard.

A cardinal rule in the design of graphical user interfaces is that it should be possible to carry out all operations with the software using only the keyboard. The keyboard is the instrument of last resort and the preferred mode for many advanced users. A system should be fully usable using the keyboard alone. More advanced users concerned with performance often prefer toolbars and keyboards to mousing through menus. Some users also have difficulty with pointing devices or lack the dexterity needed for precise point-and-click operation. Some pointing devices, such as those found on many laptop or notebook computers, are barely adequate for all but the most rudimentary tasks. In some situations, a pointing device may be inoperative or unavailable.

One way to provide keyboard access to menus is through what are now referred to as *access keys*. These are the underlined alphabetic characters in Windows menu names and menu items that are typed in sequence after pressing the `Alt` key, such as `Alt+E+C` for **Copy** or `Alt+E+P` for **Paste**. Access keys were once referred to as *mnemonics*, meaning memory aids, but the subsequent change in name reflects the real shortcomings of access keys as memory aids. It is not hard to remember that **EC** is short for **Edit|Copy**, but what about **OY** to apply text style? Of course, it is short for **Format|Apply Text Style**.

The problem is that there are only 26 letters, and certain of these are used in common words and computer terms much more frequently than others. The **F** of **Format** is already used as the access key for the **File** menu, and the **A** of **Apply** is already taken up by the **Alignment** item in the **Format** menu.

.Access keys need to be chosen carefully if they are to be anything other than arbitrary nonsense strings that will be hard to remember and easy to mistype. Methodical and meaningful design of menus and access keys not only permits simpler keyboard operation but also facilitates the sort of progressive learning by which slow beginners become fast experts.

> *Access keys need to be chosen carefully if they are not to be arbitrary nonsense strings that will be hard to remember and easy to mistype.*

If the normal rules for assigning access keys are followed, the first results can sometimes be little better than random letter combinations. As menus cascade and spread across an interface, devising effective access keys becomes more and more challenging. The thorough designer may need to rename and reorganize menus through multiple revisions to achieve an acceptable compromise between simple menu structure and simple keyboard access.

To illustrate how such design issues are worked out in practice, consider a document management system that employs a tabbed dialogue for access to an in-box, an out-box, a log of faxes sent and received, and an on-line telephone/address book. Across the top of the window are to be the usual menus for **File**, **Edit**, **View**, and **Help**, with their customary access keys, plus menus for user preferences or options and for various tools. A hasty or ill-considered design might end up as shown in Figure 8-5a, sticking the user with learning to type `Alt+P` for **Phone Book**, as well as the inconsistent `Alt+I` for **In-Box** but `Alt+U` for **Out-Box**. The out-box is likely to be used far more often than the more specialized **Options** menu, so why not use the second letter for **Options**, thus freeing up the `Alt+O` for use with the **Out-Box** tab. Unfortunately, this swap usurps the **P** from **Phone Book**. The next unique letter in **Options** is the sixth one, which is uninformative. Better

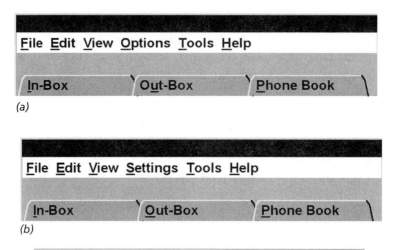

FIGURE 8-5 *Initial and final designs for initial letter access.*

to access the telephone/address **Book** by the **B**. In the interest of using only first initials for mnemonics, we might substitute the term **Preferences** for **Options**. If **Settings** is a better term for this menu (with **Preferences** and **Options** as items), we can again use the **P** for **Phone Book**, resulting in Figure 8-5b, an interface with both reasonable names and straightforward first-letter access keys for all menus and tabs. Not every problem in every application can be solved in this manner, but the attempts follow a similar process.

There are only 26 letters in the Latin alphabet, and Microsoft has reserved some for specific purposes; nevertheless, designers have an obligation to think carefully and do their best to define good shortcuts and access keys. Omitting access keys for menu items is inexcusable and punishes any user with a preference or need to use keyboard functions. The "center all" alignment operation described in the discussion of tools and icons takes a minimum of 11 keystrokes to perform from the keyboard with the menus shown in Figure 8-6, which strangely omits obvious first-letter access keys from the submenu. Were access keys incorporated, the operation would reduce to 6 keystrokes: **Alt+D+A+C**, **Alt+D+A+M**. For good reason, advanced users of drawing tools are likely to prefer a well-organized toolbar!

CONTEXT MENUS

Context menus are those brief menus that pop up on right mouse button click or when **Shift+F10** or the "Application" key (on a Windows-style keyboard) is pressed. The menu that appears depends on the object that is currently selected or clicked upon.

FIGURE 8-6 *Awkward alignment through menu manipulation.*
(MICROSOFT POWERPOINT 95)

Context menus can be a powerful and versatile addition to a user interface, but not all users will avail themselves of the advantages. The main advantage of context menus is that they offer the user access to many more commands or operations without taking up any screen real estate until they appear. On the other hand, it seems to take users longer to learn how to use context menus precisely because the menu is not located at a stable point on the user interface and the contents vary depending on the object clicked. The results can be a momentary surprise requiring a quick reorientation that is awkward for some users. In practice, context menus are more likely to be used by advanced users, and many users, especially relatively casual or inexperienced ones, almost never touch them and may even be unaware of their existence. On the other hand, some users employ context menus for a wide variety of tasks and use them almost constantly.

> *Some users employ context menus almost constantly, while others almost never touch them and may even be unaware of their existence.*

The rules for organizing context menus are similar to drop-down menus, except that menu items should be limited to only those operations that apply to the selected object. Long menus, with more than seven or eight items, are out. The preferred ordering is by expected frequency of use. Microsoft [1995] suggests that so-called primary commands (such as **Open**) be placed first, followed by transfer commands, other commands, and then a **Properties** entry to cover everything else. The wisdom of duplicating the effects of a double-click on the highly accessible first entry of a context menu is questionable, however. As the users of context menus are apt to be the more skilled ones striving for speed, they are highly unlikely to perform the awkward dance of a right-click, slide of the pointer, and then right-click again when a quick and almost instinctual double-click will do the same thing.

FAST FOOD MENUS

Mousing around takes time. Every point-and-click operation can take another full second or two. The time it takes to click is always about the same for any given user, but the time it takes to point to a visual target is governed by Fitts' law [Fitts, 1954]. The math is seldom important to the practicing developer or designer, but the basic relationship is that the farther the pointer has to move and the smaller the visual target, the longer it takes to point to something. Fitts' law suggests two strategies to increase the speed of point-and-click operations: (1) Bring targets closer and (2) Make more distant targets larger.

One small, simple change can dramatically speed selections from lists of all kinds. Compared with standard drop-down or pop-up menus that open in only one direction, the average distance the pointer has to travel to reach an item is halved for lists or menus that open out in both directions from the current selection point. The research supporting the advantages of pop-out lists or menus is so solid that it is surprising they were not made standard long ago. Users understand these menus without instruction and quickly become accustomed to them. Although users may not be conscious of their increased efficiency, the gain is no less real.

Solid research supports the advantages of two-directional pop-out lists or menus; it is surprising they were not made standard long ago.

So-called Fitts-ized (not "fit-sized") menus take advantage of another consequence of Fitts' law. It takes longer to point to more distant visual targets primarily because the pointer always overshoots the target and must be adjusted and must settle back in before a selection can be made. By making more distant targets larger, the average time for selection is reduced. An example of a Fitts-ized menu is shown in Figure 8-7. Such menus can reduce average selection time markedly. Improvements are also possible by making "sticky" borders (the heavy edges in

FIGURE 8-7 *Menus fitted for efficiency.*

FIGURE 8-8 *Hypothetical context menus to reduce average selection time.*

Figure 8-7) that keep the pointer inside the list or menu unless the pointing device is pushed beyond the margin by a preset distance. This compensates so subtly for the innate tendency to overshoot that most users remain unaware of the mechanism when it is operational.

If menu items are arrayed equidistantly around the current pointer position, average selection times would be reduced even more dramatically. This has been used effectively for pop-up context menus and tool palettes [Lyons et al., 1996]. Although menus that differ radically in appearance from conventional ones may be resisted by users, the basic principles can be applied in small variations that can achieve many of the same benefits. For example, conventional context menus can be altered only modestly into an effective compromise form, as shown in Figure 8-8, to reduce expected selection times.

SELECTING SELECTION WIDGETS

When it comes to user interface components through which users express choices, the variety facing the designer can be almost bewildering. The basic variations, however, are simple, being represented by two classic user interface components: option buttons and check boxes. Option buttons, once known as *radio buttons*, allow the user to select exactly one choice from among a set number of alternatives. Check boxes allow the user to select any number of choices from among a set of alternatives. Even for these standard cases, *1 out of N* and *0 to N out of N*, a

> *The variety of selection widgets can be almost bewildering, but the basic variations are simple.*

variety of components are available. Getting the best one for a given problem may require several iterations and certainly will require careful thought. It is not just a matter of grabbing something off the tool palette in a visual development environment. Each of the available widgets behaves a little differently and has its own advantages and disadvantages. Some take up more screen real estate or are less efficient in operation than others; some are more awkward than others when used

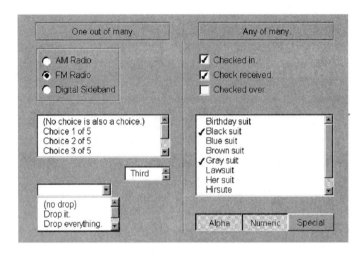

FIGURE 8-9 *Standard visual components for selection.*

from a keyboard. No formula or table can cover all the trade-offs that might have to be considered, but here are some general guidelines.

ONE OF MANY

The conventional user interface components for selecting *1 out of N* include, as shown in Figure 8-9, option buttons, spin boxes, fixed selection lists, and drop-down lists, as well as fixed-list combo boxes and drop-down combo boxes. Each of these will be favored under somewhat different circumstances.

Option buttons. Option buttons are best for selecting among a fixed set of alternatives as long as the number is relatively small. They have the advantage that all options are visible—which makes visually scanning the choices fast and easy—but, for selection within large sets, too much screen real estate is used. Option buttons are rarely used where the number of options must vary because either the amount of screen space taken must also vary or all options have to be shown, with unavailable options grayed out.

Spin boxes. Spin boxes are most often used to set a numerical value over a relatively small range, but they can sometimes be used for selections from among other kinds of sets. With non-numeric values, the number of options must be relatively small and must fit into some natural and readily apparent order, or the user will never find the desired choice. The advantages of the spin box are simple operation and compactness; the main disadvantage is that the available options are not visible, although they are implied by the ordering of the selection set.

Fixed lists. A fixed selection list is fixed in its visible size but not in the number of items it can include. This means that fixed lists support more options and a variable number of options in less space than do option buttons, but only at the expense of requiring scrollbars. Visibility is thus reduced, and scrolling to search the nonshowing options reduces efficiency.

Drop-down lists. Drop-down selection lists trade speed and convenience for screen real estate. They take up even less space than fixed lists because drop-down lists show only the currently selected item until dropped open. Initially, none of the available alternative options are visible, and an extra step, to open the list, is required on every use. Drop-down lists can be made more efficient for data entry and for use through the keyboard, however, by having the list drop down automatically when it receives focus. Such nonstandard behavior will not be the best choice in all situations, so it must be evaluated on a case-by-case basis. User testing with a working prototype may be needed to resolve some decisions about the optimal appearance and behavior of this versatile component.

> *Both fixed lists and drop-down lists have some irritating characteristics that reduce ease of use.*

Both fixed lists and drop-down lists have some irritating characteristics that reduce ease of use. When scrolling through a list without changing selections, the selected item can disappear outside the visible range, and once the focus (highlight) moves to another item, the former selection is no longer identified in any way. With a drop-down list, the common user action of trying a series of selections can be particularly awkward and time-consuming since the user has to drop down the list, scan or scroll to an option, select it, then reopen the list, scan or scroll again to the next option, and so on.

Combo boxes. Combo boxes combine a text entry field with a fixed or drop-down selection list so that the user either can select from among the options directly or can type the selection into the text box. This combination can serve two different purposes: either to allow the user to enter new selection items into the list or to provide a shortcut selection procedure. In the hands of skilled users working from the keyboard, combo boxes can be particularly efficient since the user need type only enough characters to identify the desired selection within the list. When the detailed behavior of the combo box in this role is closely fitted to the supported use cases, the results can be substantial increases in efficiency.

SOME OF MANY

The choices for selection widgets narrow when it comes to allowing the user to select *0 to N out of N* alternatives.

Check boxes. Check boxes are the traditional widget for choosing any number of items from a set. They are most effective when the number of alternatives is modest, but they are sometimes used with larger collections of options. When there are many options to choose from, check boxes are best arranged in logical groups based on either semantics or function or both. Check boxes are not particularly efficient when it comes to screen real estate. For much the same reasons as applied to option buttons, check boxes are seldom used where the number of alternatives is large or can vary.

Extended-selection fixed lists. Extended-selection fixed lists allow the user to select more than one item from within a list, which can be longer than the visible list space and can include a variable number of items. A check mark of some kind indicates which items within the list have been selected. Although extended-selection drop-down lists are possible, they are little used, and with good reason, since each added selection requires reopening the list and the list must be opened to see all the selected entries.

Toggle buttons. Tool buttons can also be used to support some cases of either *1 out of N* or *0 to N out of N* selection. In the toolbar from a popular word processor shown in Figure 8-10, the tools are all toggles: Click once and the button depresses and stays depressed; click again and it releases. In the left group—bold, italics, and underlined—the toggles behave like check boxes, while the right group—controlling justification—behaves like a set of option buttons. Nothing in their appearance communicates this difference, although the semantics imply it. The user is clued into the precise behavior on first trying the widgets. In one group, depressing a button has no effect on others in the group; in the other group, depressing a button releases the previously depressed one.

> *A standard visual cue might be helpful to signal which behavior to expect from a group of buttons, but most people do quite well without it.*

Although some human–computer communication experts decry this sort of lack of visual communication, most users have, in practice, little difficulty learning the differences since each use reinforces the distinction. It might be helpful to have a standard visual cue that signaled in advance which behavior to expect from a group of buttons on a GUI, but most peo-

FIGURE 8-10 *Tool buttons as check boxes or option buttons.*
(MICROSOFT WORD 7.0)

ple do quite well with the often unannounced variations in the behavior of buttons on stereos and cameras and VCRs. In the absence of a standard solution, some designers prefer to put some kind of frame around a set of toggle tools functioning as option buttons, thus highlighting their interdependence and behavior as a group.

SPECIAL CASES

The variations represented by option buttons and check boxes cover a lot of typical selection cases, but other cases crop up from time to time. You may have a situation in which a user must make some selection but can choose any number of the available options—in other words, a *1 or more out of N* selection. For an example, consider the problem of checking spelling: At least one dictionary or set of spelling conventions must be selected, but more than one may be required to proof a document that mixes languages.

Bruce Tognazzini recounts at some length his attempts to devise an effective design for "one-or-more" style buttons on the Apple Macintosh [Tognazzini, 1992]. What is the proper behavior of such a control and how is it shown on the user interface? The central problem is to decide what should happen when a user tries to uncheck or turn off a one-or-more button when it is the only one checked in a group. If the last button on simply refuses to turn off or chirps an error, many users never figure out the real one-or-more behavior of the group; they just assume that the particular button cannot be turned off. The solution developed at Apple, but rarely if ever used, was to flip the adjacent button on. It almost does not matter what such buttons look like (although Tognazzini obsessed on this); users catch on quickly to the behavior.

Of course, still other variations on selection are possible. Sometimes, the choice needs to be *0 or 1 out of N*, a variation on the option button theme allowing for none being selected. More often than not, this case is covered by adding an extra option button labeled **None** or its equivalent. More challenging are such exotic cases as *exactly 2 out of N* or *no more than M out of N*. For example, a program compiler for machine tools could handle no more than three target controllers on one project. The original solution was to use multiple sets of repeated option buttons, as in Figure 8-11a, a somewhat space-hungry and inelegant approach. One might consider just telling the user what can and cannot be done by heading a set of check boxes with an admonition to "**Check no more than 3 target controllers**." However, this does not allow setting the priority among targets. If priority is relevant and the selection process is infrequent (as it would be in such a configuration setting), a better scheme might be to use a set of drop-down lists, with a (**none selected**) choice as the first option, as illustrated in Figure 8-11b. This scheme has the advantage of making it easier to see at a glance what the current settings are.

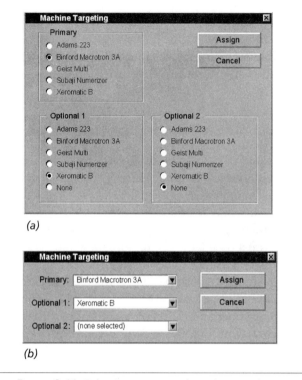

(a)

(b)

FIGURE 8-11 *Selecting no more than three options.*

In the further reaches of selection problems, we start running into limitations of standard widgets and conventional interaction idioms. In some cases, we may want to consider creating new and unique solutions, a topic we will explore in more depth in Chapter 9.

MENUS AS SELECTION WIDGETS

Menus are sometimes pressed into service as selection devices to set options or preferences. Menu items for this purpose can be set or reset just like option buttons or check boxes, and the same glyphs—a small dot and a check mark—are used to indicate the set state. Examples can be found on the **View** or **Window** menus of many applications. Menus work better for the *1 out of N* option button variant than when used with checked items to select *0 to N out of N* because the menu closes after every selection, making it inconvenient to set a series of conditions.

9

INNOVATIVE INTERFACES:
Creative Interface Engineering and Custom Components

CREATIVE ENGINEERING

According to the chorus in Steven Sondheim's *Sunday in the Park with George*, art isn't easy. Neither is engineering, we might respond. Good art and good engineering both demand creativity. Perhaps because of its graphical elements and the early involvement of graphic design professionals, user interface design is often thought of as an art [Laurel and Mountford, 1990]. An overemphasis on artistry and artistic merit can be unfortunate, however, because art does not have to be practical. The ultimate test of software usability is how a user interface works in practice. Because the user interface has to work, effective user interface design is really a form of engineering, not one of the graphic arts. Unlike art, engineering is constrained by practical goals and measured by performance.

Engineering can also be both creative and artistic. A bridge must be long enough to span the river and wide enough to carry the traffic. It must support the largest anticipated loads, must be stable under the force of anticipated winds, and must survive the largest tremors expected in an area. However, a bridge, such as the Anzac Bridge shown

> *Effective user interface design is really a form of engineering, not one of the graphic arts.*

in Figure 9-1, can also be an elegant and aesthetic work, a creative expression of functional beauty.

Usage-centered design, through its application of abstract models and its emphasis on the fundamental goals of users, encourages and challenges designers to devise creative and original solutions to user interface problems. Standard components and conventional layouts may suffice in many cases, but often it becomes clear at some point in development that standard solutions are less than optimal.

FIGURE 9-1 *Creative engineering: the Anzac Bridge in Sydney, Australia.*

In this chapter, we will look at how practical and creative concerns can be combined to engineer innovative user interfaces.

WHY INNOVATION

In usage-centered design, every transition from a content model to a visual design is an opportunity for innovation. What is the best realization for a given abstract component? Typically, the designer will compromise by selecting some standard component, but there are times when no standard widget fits well or when other factors favor custom design. Sometimes, the accepted components or techniques fairly beg for improvements.

> *Every transition from a content model to a visual design is an opportunity for innovation.*

Custom user interface components and configurations are developed for many reasons and to serve varied goals. The developers may want to shave the time taken to complete particular use cases, or they may want to improve input reliability. They may be looking to reduce support costs or to create a more competitive product through dramatically better or different user interfaces.

The initial assumption for any visual design is that it will conform to accepted standards using conventional components and familiar forms of user interfaces. Sometimes, however, the standards are simply stupid. Graphical user interface standards and style guidelines are peppered with rules and conventions that run

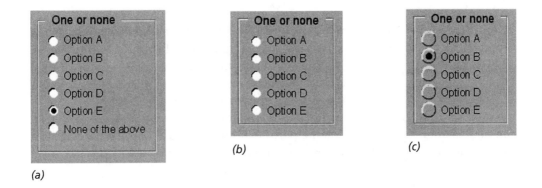

(a)

(b)

(c)

FIGURE 9-2 *Three solutions to the one-or-none selection problem.*

counter to experience and to established principles of software usability. Status-line support for tool-tip help, to pick one example, puts key information at the least noticed part of the display and separates it from related information and the user's focus of attention. Standard but stupid.

Sometimes, there is no standard solution. For example, option buttons and selection lists force the user to select one out of a number of choices, whereas check boxes and extended-selection lists allow the user to select any number of items, from none at all to all. What if the problem involves selecting one or none? What about one or more? At least two?

The one-or-none case, for example, can be supported with conventional components and standard behavior by using option buttons with an added **none of the above** option, as shown in Figure 9-2a. A nonstandard option button, like the one in Figure 9-2b that, when it is on toggles to off if clicked, more compactly supports the one-or-none case. Unfortunately, these nonstandard buttons look just like the plain vanilla kind; the user has no way of knowing, a priori, that they toggle, like real radio buttons. Perhaps the nonstandard solution shown in Figure 9-2c might be considered.

Sometimes, of course, the standard solutions are of no help because they do not apply. Perhaps the application domain is new or unusual; perhaps the standards are incomplete or obsolescent. Windows 95 or 98 standards may make sense on the desktop but can be completely inappropriate for a Windows-based system for use on the factory floor of a bottling plant.

Standard, easy solutions, conceived with care, will be good enough in most cases, even though they might not yield dramatic results. Sometimes, though, "good enough" is not enough, and only dramatic gains in usability will suffice. At such times, only a genuine breakthrough can deliver the substantial improvement needed to have a standout product. Mere novelty will not suffice.

Creatively engineered user interfaces do not always pay off for the innovators, however. Even dramatically better interfaces may not be accepted among users or within the marketplace. Innovations using custom components and nonstandard layout face a tougher standard than ordinary user interface designs. For many users, only dramatic improvements will be enough to justify coping with novelty.

To innovate or to imitate? The trade-offs may involve many nontechnical issues—marketing, timing, corporate image, executive ego, and the like. Better design does not always triumph. Technical improvements may tend to win out in the long run, but the short run may be dominated by other factors, and the long run may take longer to arrive than a particular company can wait. We will return to these messy management issues in the final chapter of the book.

WHAT INNOVATION

Innovation in user interfaces can affect visual components or their combination and layout. Innovations may lie in appearance or behavior or both. Broadly considered, interface innovations can be classified in terms of

- Aesthetics
- Form
- Behavior
- Function
- Architecture

Innovation in aesthetics is about the surface appearance or nonfunctional characteristics of the interface. A new, animated splash screen to appear on application launch would be an example. Aesthetic innovation appeals to so many development and marketing groups because a new look-and-feel can make software appear to be new without demanding genuine invention. Web sites are hotbeds of aesthetic innovation, where conventions are few and components can look like nearly anything.

Unfortunately, aesthetic innovation seldom improves usability and often degrades it. Command buttons that resemble pill cases or doorknobs may look cute in a brochure, but they are likely to confuse and slow users. Sleek control panels that resemble black-anodized aluminum stereo components can perpetuate the same usability problems that plague consumer electronics.

> *Aesthetic innovation seldom improves usability and often degrades it.*

Innovation in form is about the functional or consequential aspects of appearance—shape, color, shading, and aspects of appearance as they affect usability. Using shading and shadows to differentiate controls and aid recognition is an example of innovative form that is not merely a matter of aesthetics.

Innovation in behavior—in how interfaces and interface components act—may offer more potential for improving usability, but behavioral innovation is typically harder to achieve than innovations in appearance. Unless skillfully engineered, custom visual components or combinations that act differently from conventional ones often pose problems for users.

Functional innovation means that software offers new capability. Because it can pay off with a new bullet point in an ad, functional innovation is also much sought by marketing people. New functions can also be relatively easy to concoct, especially if they do not have to be needed or useful functions. The disease of creeping featuritis is the all-too-common result of such easy innovation.

Innovative user interface architecture is the biggest innovation of all. It involves novel and effective reorganization of conventional or familiar user interface elements. Architectural innovation probably poses the biggest challenge for developers, but it also may offer the largest potential gains in software usability. Architectural innovation can be, and often is, combined with functional, behavioral, and even aesthetic innovation. Visual programming, the core concept of modern visual development tools, is an example of an innovative user interface architecture that should be familiar to most software and application developers. Visual programming does not merely present a better code editor; it alters the way code is created.

THE PROCESS OF INNOVATION

Over the years, we have had clients who have challenged us to devise user interface designs that were not merely good, but were genuinely original. In one case, we even agreed to come up with a breakthrough in user interface design within a short time frame and on a fixed budget. It was close, but we managed to deliver on our promise.

When we thought about how we went about solving such old problems in new and more effective ways, we realized there was a pattern to how we worked. The approach we were taking integrated engineering and artistry, combining creativity with pragmatism in a cyclic or iterative process.

ITERATIVE INNOVATION

There is more than one way to look at this process. On a grand scale or from a bird's-eye view, iterative innovation looks like the graph in Figure 9-3, alternating between expansion and contraction, between unbridled creativity and critical analysis. First, the number of possibilities and the scope of the solution are expanded without much if any regard for practicality or whether proposed ideas are realizable or will work effectively. Then, the results from the round of expansive creation are reduced through critical analysis. Our thinking is brought back down to earth and made practicable by considering practical limitations and

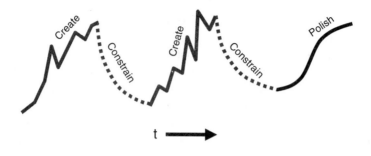

FIGURE 9-3 *Creative expansion and critical contraction in the process of innovation.*

testing our ideas against the harsh realities of the real world. Art may thrive on pure and positive creativity, but engineering needs the power of negative thinking to succeed [Petroski, 1994].

Alternately creating and constraining the solution continue until we run out of time or are satisfied with the basic results. We then finish off by refining details and polishing the design. This polishing process often involves not only filling in design details and resolving outstanding technical problems but also making aesthetic enhancements that preserve the engineering results already achieved.

Getting started on a creative engineering process can sometimes be difficult. If you are stuck for ideas or do not know where to begin, you can kick-start the whole cycle by blowing holes in a competitor's product or attacking an earlier version of the proposed system. A vigorous round of criticism, especially applied to someone else's work, never fails to stimulate ideas.

The process of creative user interface engineering seems to work most efficiently when practical constraints are applied in layers, one or a few at a time. With each new layer of practical constraints, the design is refined to meet the constraints, and the results are critiqued and analyzed. After a few layers of constraints have been applied and met by refining the design, a new round of creative elaboration and rethinking can be initiated.

BOTH–AND DESIGN

A common barrier to creative new ideas is the human tendency to think in terms of dichotomies, of irresolvable opposites or mutually opposing forces. Such either–or thinking tends to lead to design compromises or to uninspired combinations. The most innovative interfaces often integrate elements or aspects of alternative designs through new approaches that go beyond mere trade-offs. For example, a design group with roots in both Open-Motif and Windows might debate whether the vertical scrollbar really belongs on the left or the right of a window. A strict compromise would lead to the absurd option of putting a scrollbar right down the middle. A simpleminded combination might put scrollbars on both sides. A creative synthesis that preserves screen real estate while supporting ambidextrous operation would make scrollbars dockable like toolbars.

Both–and thinking looks for a creative synthesis of apparently opposing ideas or seemingly exclusive alternatives. Rather than compromise, it seeks to incorporate the best of both worlds and to satisfy conflicting goals simultaneously. An organized process can make it easier to find both–and solutions:

1. Separate and list the features of the alternative approaches, proposals, or ideas.
2. Separate and list the advantages or strong points of each alternative.
3. Separate and list the disadvantages or weak points.
4. Make note of and question any assumptions regarding mutual exclusiveness or incompatibility.
5. Try combining the best features and advantages of the alternatives into a single solution.

One of the tricks that makes both–and thinking work is the belief that a creative synthesis is possible. Always assume that opposites or opposing ideas can be integrated or combined effectively and then force yourself to think creatively.

The same kind of idea generation and elaboration process used for modeling can be applied to innovative engineering. As introduced in Chapter 4, the basic steps are

1. Compile or create
2. Organize or structure
3. Detail or elaborate
4. Refine or reorganize

> *Either–or thinking leads to design compromises or to uninspired combinations. Both–and thinking looks for creative syntheses incorporating the best of two worlds.*

For creative engineering, the objective is to produce a model or description of a novel approach for a user interface design.

THINK ABOUT IT

Some of our best work has come out of pretending to use systems that do not exist. *Gedanken* experiments are trials or experiments played out in the laboratory of the mind. *Gedanken* experiments can be a solitary game or a group activity. They can be used to generate ideas or test them out.

Typically, you start out trying to get a clear mental picture of some user interface. It helps to close your eyes. Some people find that starting with a sketch of a design on paper helps them to form a clearer mental image, but you should then close your eyes or set the drawing aside and stare into space, whichever makes it easier to imagine the user interface before you. You next imagine yourself enacting

---

VISUAL THINKING

Some people are better than others at imagining designs or fantasizing interactions, but nearly everyone can improve visual thinking with practice. Here is a little exercise we use when teaching visualization and creative design. You need to close your eyes, so someone will have to read the following directions to you, one at a time. (Don't cheat and read ahead; it will spoil the fun!)

1. Close your eyes
2. Picture a standard drop-down, scrolling selection list for selecting one item out of many. The list starts out closed.
3. Imagine that the current selection reads "yellow."
4. Imagine yourself selecting "brown."
5. Now select "purple."
6. Open your eyes and describe what happened.

Could you picture the discrete steps of the process? Did you see the list open when you clicked on it and close when you made a selection? How was the list organized? What difficulties did you have? As the result of this experiment, what improvements come to mind that would make it easier to find the color you want in the list?

Now, try to imagine an improved design. Carry out some additional mental experiments to see how your improved design works. Finally, make a sketch or drawing of the best design you can devise.

some use case with the imaginary interface, pointing and clicking and typing your way through the steps. In the course of imagining the interaction, problems typically become immediately apparent, and you may find your mental image of the interface actually changing, even as you try to use it. In a group, everyone should try to perform the same task independently and then share and discuss the experiences.

The big advantage of *gedanken* experiments over real usability testing is that nothing has to be created to be tested. In fact, the design does not have to be practical or even possible; it only has to be imaginable.

RADICAL EVOLUTION

Bill Buxton, of Silicon Graphics, has described an approach to innovation he calls "radical evolution." Radical evolution is a form of creative engineering in which the aim is for modifications that are substantial without being revolutionary. Radical evolution is accomplished within the status quo while introducing incremental but significant alterations in interface or interaction design.

One promising source of inspiration for radical evolution is to look to the real world of work and everyday experience. People have substantial know-how and many learned skills that are unrelated to computers or software user interfaces. This knowledge and these skills can be exploited as the basis for interface innovation through radical evolution.

The idea is to innovate but not emulate, to be guided by physical models and real-world actions but not be constrained by attempting to simulate or replicate them exactly. The interface innovator is seeking new applications, within software user interfaces, for old idioms and established skills.

Know-how and many learned skills that are unrelated to computers or software can be exploited as the basis for interface innovation through radical evolution.

Buxton has described how he evolved a radical redesign of the interface for a computer-based drawing system used by professional graphic artists. Artists who work with acrylics or oil paints typically use a brush and a palette. The palette holds dabs of the colors currently being used, and the brush applies the colors to the working surface. The palette is not set aside on a table or placed in a drawer while in use. It is kept in hand for ready use whenever a new color is needed. The artist holds the brush in one hand, and the palette in the other, always keeping the palette near the work and near the brush. This two-handed operation is an efficient skill already well learned by any professional artist.

Conventional software drawing packages give artists only one-handed operation, forcing them to move the pointer and their attention away from the work and the current point of interest in order to select a different color from some tool palette at the edge of the screen. Conventional floating tool palettes do not solve this problem because they are invariably floating in the wrong place and must constantly be shoved around to keep them out of the way but handy. The innovative solution devised by Buxton exploits externally learned skills to give the digital artist two-handed operation: The artist controls the "brush" with the mouse in the preferred hand and moves a floating palette with a trackball using the other hand. This seemingly complicated interface, because it draws on established real-world skills, is mastered almost instantly by experienced graphic artists, who also almost invariably find it more productive than the conventional one-handed software interface.

What can we do if special hardware solutions are not available or not allowed? The real world can still inspire interface improvements. As always with usage-centered design, the key questions are about user intentions. The objective of the two-handed brush-and-palette approach is to keep the color palette instantly available wherever the artist is drawing. How about a pop-up palette that appears at the pointer when the right mouse button is clicked?

How do we turn this idea into a workable design? The first creative impulse might be to display a simulated artist's palette at the current pointer, but this seemingly solid object will be suddenly thrust in the artist's face, obscuring the very point where the artist is looking. Maybe we put a big hole in the middle of the palette. In fact, a circular or elliptical menu not only resembles an artist's palette but also is more efficient than a linear list or rectangular array. However, the artist does not have independent control over the position of such a pop-up palette once it appears, so even as an annular menu with a hole in the middle, an important part of the work may be obscured. A semitransparent pop-up palette might be a reasonable compromise. After another round or two of refinement, we might end up with a design like the one shown in Figure 9-4. For high-efficiency, a full spectrum of colors or a graphical brush selection menu should be reachable either through the color palette or directly by a key-shifted right-button click.

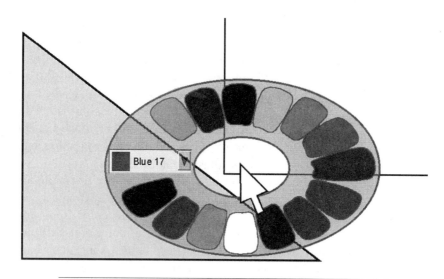

FIGURE 9-4 *A translucent pop-up elliptical color palette for the pro.*

Field observations of graphic artists at work can yield other inspirations. For example, some artists tend to switch back and forth between brushes or pens of different width. Rather than always requiring the user to go through one of the context palettes, a "swap tool" key could be programmed.

INSTRUCTIVE INTERFACES

The ideal set by the Access Rule points us toward user interface designs that require no help or training to be used effectively. This may be a difficult yet still attainable goal for familiar forms and conventional components, but it would seem to retreat beyond reach for anything novel or innovative. The secret to innovations that do not require reeducating the entire populace is to make interfaces that teach users how they are to be used.

The secret to innovations that do not require reeducating the entire populace is instructive interfaces that are inherently self-teaching and are built on consistent extensions that are intuitable and explorable.

Instructive interfaces are user interfaces that, through clever construction and design, are inherently self-teaching. Instructive interfaces rely on intrinsic characteristics rather than external help or prompting to show the user how to use them. Instructive interfaces are [Constantine, 1997c]

- Intuitable
- Explorable
- Consistent

Popular literature often refers to *intuitive* user interfaces, but no interface is intuitive in the sense that psychologists use the term. *Intuitable,* meaning capable of being guessed, is a better word for user interfaces [Raskin, 1994]. An intuitable interface or feature means that the user's best guess about what something is or what it does will probably be correct. In intuitable user interfaces, familiar or standard components behave as expected, and new features have reasonable and understandable behavior.

To be guessable, interfaces often make use of theme and variation. The user is presented with old components used in new ways or with interfaces that resemble conventional ones but with a creative twist or two. As in music, theme and variation in user interfaces present things that are simultaneously both new and yet already familiar and understandable.

For example, a common user interface problem involves setting two numbers to specify a range. Spin boxes can be an effective way to set such values, especially where the maximum number is not too large. However, conventional spin boxes make for a visually disjointed interface. Simply shifting the spin buttons for the starting value to the left improves the layout, as shown in Figure 9-5. Although nonstandard, these left-handed spin boxes are instantly recognizable by users as small variations on standard themes.

Interfaces are explorable if they impose no penalties on the user for looking. In explorable interfaces, it is possible to activate most controls or dialogues without effect, so the user can look them over without actually doing anything. Explorable interfaces offer straightforward visible navigation through the various interaction contexts of the user interface. The user can see what is available and possible and how to get from here to there and back. As mentioned in Chapter 8, well-designed

> ### JUST GUESS
>
> Intuitability is remarkably easy to verify in practice. All you need to do is ask a number of users to guess what something is or does. You need subjects who have never seen a particular feature or facility before, so you first ask potential subjects whether they have seen your brilliant innovation before.
>
> For those subjects who pass the first cut, you ask them what they think or would guess the object of interest is. Next, subjects are asked to describe what they think it would do or how it would function. It can be useful then to ask subjects what would be their next guess about the meaning and behavior if they were told their first guess was wrong.
>
> You should set a target threshold for acceptable intuitability. For example, you might aim for 60% of users guessing the correct meaning and function on the first guess or for 90% guessing correctly on either the first or second guess.
>
> With intuitability so easily tested, claims of "intuitive interfaces" that are not backed by data should be laughed off the market.

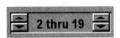

FIGURE 9-5 *Spinning double numbers through theme and variation.*

menus are examples of conventional user interface features that promote exploration.

To support users' exploration of features and learning by trial and error, actions need to be perfectly reversible. Every dialogue must have a **Cancel** button, and canceling should be the functional equivalent of never having entered the dialogue. All actions should be reversible through multiple-level undo and redo facilities. For database operation, simple and safe rollback needs to be supported to allow files to be restored to a known prior state.

Consistency is a simple goal with many facets. Internal consistency among the various parts of a user interface is always important, but, for interface innovations, consistency with standards and conventions and with preexisting software has the greater impact on both usability and user acceptance. The overriding objective in novel designs is not to maintain absolute consistency with other software or with prior approaches, but to avoid major inconsistencies. Contradictions and conflicts are the killers. When most software acts one way and your design does the opposite, however clever or efficient you may think the scheme to be, you will have created problems for your users.

For instructive interfaces, behavioral consistency is usually more important than consistent appearance. In many cases, unconventional looks are less challenging than unconventional actions. For successful innovation, predictability may be far more important than consistency. Even utterly original components with unusual behavior can be acceptable to users if they behave predictably—that is, initially as expected and consistently over time.

AFFORDANCES AND CONSTRAINTS

Among the many contributions of usability guru Donald Norman is a pair of terms that have become part of the working vocabulary of user interface specialists around the world. *Affordances* and *constraints* are the twin pillars supporting instructive interfaces.

Affordances are how interfaces or objects of any kind invite or facilitate particular uses or actions. The most popular examples of affordances are from physical objects and systems. A round, knurled handle atop a valve affords twisting. A vertical bar on a door affords pulling, while a horizontal one, especially with a flat plate, affords pushing. Violate affordances, and you end up with frustrated users attempting to do the undoable, tugging on levers that must be turned or pushing doors that must be pulled. Failure to use affordance is often signaled by ordinary and familiar objects bearing signs that we humorously refer to as "instruction manuals." Opening a closet door should not require training, but in one hotel we encountered the handle illustrated in Figure 9-6. The doors were no doubt instruction-free when the hotel first opened. One can sympathize with the hotel operators who had to cope with countless complaints of stuck closet doors from the first

FIGURE 9-6 *New twist on unusability: a door handle with an "instruction manual."*

guests. Although the magnetic catch was quite strong, the actual operation of the door was trivial. The real problem was that the affordance of the handle—for twisting—is deceptive. No matter how hard it is twisted, the handle stays frozen.

Constraints are the flip side of affordances. Constraints are how objects limit or restrict possible actions or uses. A lever in a horizontal slot is constrained to move back and forth, for example. Both affordances and constraints are communicated by associations that may be physically or logically inherent but are, as often as not, merely part of the learned culture.

For graphical user interface design, designers must think in terms of visual affordances and visual constraints. The objects on the screen are, in a sense, illusions. There is nothing actually three-dimensional about the modern "3D look-and-feel," yet the illusion of shading and other visual affordances and constraints can inform and guide the user as effectively—or ineffectively—as can bathroom faucets or emergency door handles.

> *On-screen objects are illusions, yet visual affordances and constraints can inform and guide the user as effectively—or ineffectively—as can bathroom faucets or emergency door handles.*

A common example of visual affordance is the "push affordance" of command buttons and of tools on toolbars. Square or rectangular shapes on the screen, shaded to appear to protrude from the surface, afford pushing. Whether this is intuitable or only learned, push affordance says to typical users, "You can click here to make something happen." The affordance is reinforced when the visual component appears to depress into the surface when first clicked upon.

In this sense, the recent trend toward flat, Web-style active components evidenced in Microsoft Office 97 is a step backward in usability. An important visual cue to help users scan and make sense of a new user interface is lost when any

FIGURE 9-7 *Vertical sliding affordance reinforced by visual and behavioral constraints.*

part of the visual field could trigger an action. The presence of little "instruction manuals" ("Click here.") on Web sites is evidence that something is wrong. Without the hints, the user has to search because only when the pointer passes over an object is its affordance communicated, either by its apparently popping out from the surface or by a change in the cursor.

Push affordance is perhaps the most ubiquitous, but modern graphical user interfaces can communicate other kinds of affordances. Triangles and arrows can communicate direction of user action or effect. The widget in Figure 9-7 invites the user to try to slide the little rectangle up and down. The visual "slot" and the widget's programmed behavior reinforce the affordance by constraints.

For another example of visual constraints as a communication to the user, consider modal dialogue boxes, in which the user is required to take some action within the dialogue box before continuing with any other task. How can this "instruction" be communicated to the user?

One way is by effectively disabling the pointer whenever it is beyond the boundaries of the dialogue box. In most systems, an attempt to click outside a modal dialogue box results in a chirp or ping signaling the user that the action is not allowed. However, this technique communicates the constraint only after the user attempts some action, not when the pointer moves outside the box.

It might be tempting to communicate the constraint directly, simply by preventing the pointer from being moved outside the dialogue box. This approach has two major drawbacks. First, in a multitasking environment, other applications might be active and might legitimately be interacted with even before the user responds to the modal dialogue. Second, users hate the sudden loss of control over the pointer and may incorrectly think that something has gone wrong with the mouse or trackball.

A more common technique for communicating this constraint is to have the cursor change shape when outside the modal dialogue box. This is a reasonable choice for feedback, but the common practice of changing the pointer to the wait cursor (an hourglass in the default Windows 95 configuration) is flawed. The wait cursor communicates the wrong message to the user; it says the system is busy. If it happens that the cursor lies outside the box when the dialogue first opens, the user may be fooled into waiting for an operation to complete when no operation is

FIGURE 9-8 *Drop-kick zone with visual affordance.*

under way. We have known users who left to get a cup of coffee and returned, only to find the system still apparently busy.

As with all communication to the user, the rule is to say what you mean. If you mean that operation outside the modal dialogue box is disallowed, just say "no" to the user directly by changing the cursor to a backslash or an X inside a circle.

Affordances and constraints can be used to inform users about what to expect of new components. For example, one user interface we designed for a client required a single component that served both as the target to which documents could be dragged and as a control that could be clicked by itself to trigger an action. We needed a "drop zone" and push button all in one. An earlier design had used a slight visual well or depression to convey "drop affordance" to users, a widely used but not universal approach that most new users quickly understood. However, this appearance gave no indication that the target could also be clicked to launch an activity. The design trick to make this component succeed is to combine drop affordance with push affordance to make a "drop-kick" zone, like the one in Figure 9-8, whose behavior users are more likely to guess correctly.

Another example of using affordances and constraints to make instructive innovations is that of selection lists embedded within data-display grids. Many modern data-display grids provide for in-place editing, in which fields in columns can be edited directly without opening a separate editing dialogue. If a field within the data display represents a selection from within a list, it is a natural extension of in-place editing to program the field to function as a drop-down list. Without a visual cue, however, the user has no way of knowing, *a priori*, which fields are just text entry and which will function as drop-down selection lists. A small rectangle, as seen in Figure 9-9, with push affordance and resembling the

FIGURE 9-9 *Extensions made visible through affordance: embedded drop-down lists.*

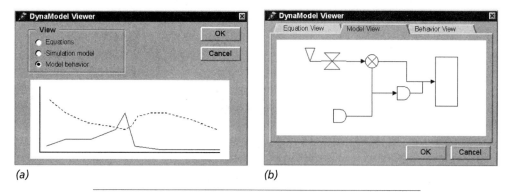

(a)   (b)

FIGURE 9-10 *User interface stability through visual persistence.*

button of a drop-down list makes the user interface more understandable. Even the naïve user who has never seen embedded drop-down lists will almost certainly guess how they work.

VISUAL OBJECT PERSISTENCE

Infants live in the ultimate WYSIWYG world. When a toy ball rolls behind a box, it ceases to exist. With time and experience, infants acquire what psychologists refer to as *object persistence,* the realization that objects continue to exist in the same form, even when they are moved or disappear from view. Object persistence helps us to see solid objects in the real world as stable and enduring, even as our view of them changes or is wholly or partially obscured.

Visual object persistence is a property of good visual components and user interfaces that helps the user make sense of the interface and follow what is happening. For example, the two interfaces shown in Figure 9-10a and Figure 9-10b are functionally equivalent—in either case, a click on a visual element switches to another display—but the user experience is quite different. When a dialogue box suddenly changes appearance, the behavior violates common everyday experience of the world that our brains evolved to explain. When a tab within a tabbed dialogue is clicked, the user perceives a page being brought forward while other pages drop behind, but nothing has been created or destroyed or suddenly transformed. With visual persistence, the interface becomes easier to parse visually and is more readily understood, even where it employs novel features or behaviors.

> *Visual object persistence helps the user make sense of novel interfaces and follow what is happening.*

Clever use of visual object persistence can make even complex or completely unfamiliar interfaces easy to interpret. Violation of visual object persistence can

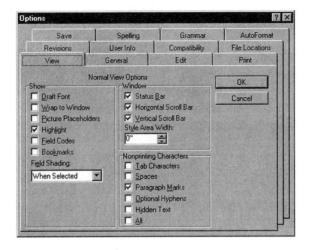

FIGURE 9-11 *Failed attempt at visual object persistence.*
(MICROSOFT WORD 6.0)

make even simple behavior hard to follow. For example, when the tabs of a tabbed dialogue are arranged in ranks, as in the infamous dialogue shown in Figure 9-11, most users find the visual behavior bewildering. A click on **General**, **Edit**, or **Print** behaves in a familiar and easily understood way, but clicking on **Spelling** results in a reshuffling that is visually confusing and disconcerting to most users, despite its logical simplicity. Visual object persistence has been violated.

The new component shown to the right in Figure 9-12 is a pop-out list. One of the advantages of pop-out lists is visual object persistence: The list just appears to open out both upward and downward, with the currently selected value remaining stationary in the middle. In a drop-down list, the list suddenly appears, and the selection focus jumps from the unopened field to some point within the list. The pop-out list in Figure 9-12 employs a double-triangle glyph to suggest on first encounter that this is like a drop-down list, but not exactly. Theme and variation again.

IDIOMATIC EXTENSION

Interaction idioms are familiar, stylized gestures and modes of interaction used in communicating with a user interface [compare Cooper, 1995]. Like the idiomatic expressions of speech and writing, interaction idioms do not convey meaning literally. They are neither intuitable nor intrinsically meaningful; they assume meaning strictly as a matter of convention. Interaction idioms are basic components of the dialogue between users and user interfaces whose syntax and semantics must be learned by every user.

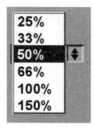

FIGURE 9-12 *Pop-out list: visually more stable than a drop-down list.*

For example, consider the simple and very basic interaction idiom "select." We often speak of selecting an object on the screen, but how do we do it? This notion is actually communicated through a gesture that involves sliding or pushing or rolling a pointing device until the visible pointer appears to be within or over the visual object and then depressing a button on the pointing device. Experienced users do not think in terms of these fragments of the interaction; they think of selecting something through the entire gesture—the interaction idiom.

Not only are interaction idioms conventional language for using software, but they also are a tool for interface innovation. They can be generalized, extended, or applied in new ways or within new contexts. For example, the drag-and-drop idiom for moving files and other data objects has been extended within some software to allow moving tools within and between toolbars. Instead of awkward dialogues to redefine toolbars, the user enters a special customization mode and then uses conventional mouse techniques to add or rearrange tools. The interaction occurs in place, at the toolbars themselves, using familiar interaction idioms.

Unfortunately, in many of the systems supporting drag-and-drop toolbar customization, menu customization is typically handled by awkward, out-of-context interaction in a separate dialogue. Why not extend conventional interaction idioms for menu customization? For example, once in customization mode, menu names and items could be editable in place just by double-clicking. Menus could be reordered by selecting and then dragging.

MOVING INTERFACES

Animation is for more than just a matter of wait-state cartoons and flaming wastebaskets. Although many developers think of animation as a form of entertainment, animation has a variety of legitimate uses in innovative interfaces. Of course, animated elements can be used to make user interfaces more interesting and exciting, but animation can also contribute directly to software usability.

Effective animation is informative, like the familiar blue progress bars that tell users how a file transfer is proceeding. Interface innovators should consider animation for other meaningful applications. For example, process control software might give the flow rate in liters per minute numerically but also picture animated liquid flowing through a transparent pipe at a speed proportional to the actual rate.

Animation can also be distracting. A grinning paper clip that keeps wiggling and changing expressions may be cute for the first few minutes but soon becomes an irritating distraction. Motion commands the highest priority for visual attention, so it is hard to ignore animation on the screen. In order to concentrate, some users will even use their hands to cover an animation that cannot be turned off [Spool et al., 1997]. The ability to grab the attention of the user can be used to advantage to convey information of crucial importance through animation.

Because it so commands the attention of the user, any animation can slow down performance of tasks. Users may unconsciously wait for an animated sequence to be finished before continuing with their work, even when waiting is unnecessary. Silly animations, like the famous flaming wastebasket of a popular PIM, not only contribute to frustration but also can

> *Animation can direct the attention and guide the eye, establishing visual and mental linkages that help users understand and keep track of what is happening.*

significantly eat into productivity. Even worse and harder to ignore are random variations in motion that keep surprising the user, such as the exploding, shrinking, flying, and vanishing acts that accompany deleting an electronic Post-it note in one program.

Animation can direct the attention and guide the eye, establishing visual and mental linkages that help users understand and keep track of what is happening within the user interface. For example, when the results of an operation are to connect components in a graphical display, showing the line draw itself from one shape to the other is better than having it suddenly appear from nowhere. Animation can be especially effective for helping users sort out visually complex displays, such as the prototype design tool illustrated in Figure 9-13 [Noble and Constantine, 1997]. Use case enactments are displayed as arrows superimposed on a

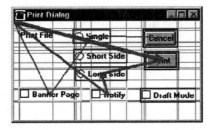

FIGURE 9-13 *Dynamic feedback for designers.*
(VUEIT PROTOTYPE)

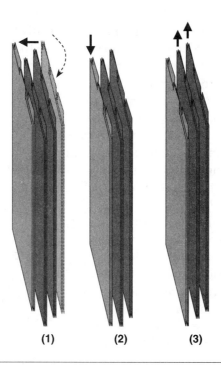

(1) (2) (3)

FIGURE 9-14 *"Side view" of tabbed dialogue animation.*

dialogue layout. As a static picture, more than a few of these enactment paths make for a bewildering network, yet experiments show that the confusing tangle suddenly becomes meaningful when the paths are animated to act like rubber bands as the designer moves components around within the layout.

We solved a long-standing and perverse problem with tabbed dialogues through animation. As mentioned earlier, tabbed dialogues with tabs arranged in ranks are visually ill-behaved. By carefully animating the movement of tabs within ranks, a visually confusing interface suddenly becomes obvious. For this instance of radical evolution, we took our cue from physical action in the real world. The important thing is to have the tabs and ranks appear to move in ways that always leave no doubt in the users mind as to what has happened.

Referring back to Figure 9-11, let us say the user selects the **Spelling** tab in the back rank. We first make it appear that the back rank simply moves straight forward, with the selected tab in front. The whole rank then appears to drop down in front, after which the other ranks slide up into place behind it. Viewed from the side, this apparent motion looks like Figure 9-14.

Carefully thought out, not only does the animation make it easy for the user to follow what happens as various tabs in various ranks are selected, but it also supports exploration. Conventional Windows behavior reshuffles the tabs when the mouse button first goes down. Scanning through the various pages of a tabbed dialogue then requires separately clicking on each page of interest, and a selection cannot be canceled by sliding the pointer off the tab. With the animated behavior just described, a page comes forward on button down but does not reposition until the button is released. This allows the user to just slide the pointer over the tabs to see them all in succession; sliding the pointer off a tab simply cancels the selection and leaves everything as it was.

APPLIED INNOVATION

SCROLL WORK

Just because a component or technique is widely used or long established does not mean it is a good idea. Even old standards can benefit from creative reengineering. Some standard features of modern graphical interfaces are really bad when it comes to usability. Scrollbars are a good example of bad design [Constantine, 1992c; 1994c]. From the standpoint of established usability principles, it is hard to imagine a worse way to move around within a two-dimensional drawing or document.

There are two basic use cases for graphical navigation: `viewingOverThere` and `viewingSomewhereElse`, the problems of local navigation to nearby spots and global navigation to distant or unknown locations within the graphical space. Scrollbars support neither very well. Simple intentions, such as shifting the view to see something off-screen somewhat to the upper left, can require a series of alternating actions on the upper right and lower left. Only moves that are exactly vertical or exactly horizontal are relatively simple, and these require an unnatural mental and visual shift: To move vertically, the hand and eye must first move horizontally off the drawing or working area, and vice versa to move horizontally.

A number of competing and superior schemes have been devised to solve the graphical navigation problem [Constantine, 1994c], including the viewfinder navigator engineered by one of us many years ago to solve a client's problem. The design objectives are efficient and direct movement in any direction, the pointer and visual focus remaining within the working area, and rapid learning based on extension of established skills.

The viewfinder navigator represents radical evolution and draws on established real-world experiences and skills using such things as cameras, binoculars, and camcorders. An escape sequence, such as chording and holding down both mouse buttons or a special keyboard action, shifts operation into viewfinder mode. A simulated camera viewfinder, such as the one shown in Figure 9-15, is superimposed over the working area to provide a familiar visual cue and frame of reference. The pointer remains visible but fixed at its location on the screen. The mouse now controls the apparent movement of the viewfinder (and pointer) over the drawing surface, exactly as if the user were scanning a landscape with a

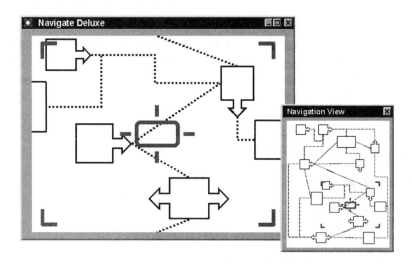

FIGURE 9-15 *The viewfinder navigator scheme in viewfinder mode.*

camera or binoculars. Users find this operation completely natural and master it almost instantly for simpler and faster navigation. A release of the mouse buttons or mode-shift keys returns the view to normal pointer control.

For better support of global navigation, the `viewingSomewhereElse` use case, a map view or zoom-out mode is helpful. One way to provide this is with a navigation window, such as the one shown in Figure 9-15. The map view should be visible always, never, or whenever in viewfinder mode, at the user's option. Other effective graphical navigation schemes have also been described [Constantine, 1994c].

OVERLOADING

Another technique that can be used to create radical evolution is active overloading. The designer starts with passive visual components and then loads them with active behavior. The technique is referred to as *overloading* because a control ends up with more than one meaning and function. With careful, methodical design, active overloading can yield versatile, function-packed interfaces without overcrowding. Do it well, and you win new friends and customers; do it badly, and you merely leave them confused and unimpressed.

> *With careful, methodical design, active overloading can yield versatile, function-packed interfaces without overcrowding.*

One familiar example of active overloading is found in the evolution of column headers for data displays. Every column in a datagrid needs a label so that the user knows what the data represents. There are also certain common operations and actions that are needed for each and every column. Passive labels, which are merely fixed output fields at the top of columns, just sit there and do nothing. Turning passive labels into active controls makes possible new behaviors without taking up more screen real estate. Give them push affordance, and you have properly informed the user that these are not your old-fashioned do-nothing labels. There are a number of use cases potentially to support:

`selectingAll` (where column selecting makes sense)
`sortingUp`
`sortingDown`
`resizingColumnDisplay` (wider, narrower)
`hidingColumnDisplay`
`movingColumnDisplay`

Active overloading of the column label gives us only one button at the top of each column. Clicking or pushing on this header cannot easily support every one of these use cases. The Windows Explorer double-overloads the column header as a toggle to support sorting in either order—the second and third use cases.

To cover all use cases, other interaction idioms will need to be exploited. If a click on the header sorts the column, a double-click is a natural for `selectingAll`. The Windows Explorer and other systems cleverly support the `resizingColumnDisplay` and `buildingColumnDisplay` use cases through one fairly natural idiom: dragging the boundary between columns. A column can be hidden by simply squeezing it down to nothing. The Explorer informs the user of the presence of a hidden column through a change in the cursor, but this is usually too subtle. A visual ridge—the graphical remnant of a vanished column—is probably a better choice because it is always visible.

The Explorer-style header that toggles ascending and descending sorting on the column has some significant usability defects. A multicolumn list might be sorted on any column, and there is no obvious feedback to the user as to either the selected column or the order of sort. Users may have to scan the lists in several columns before deciphering the sorting; many users routinely re-sort grids even when unnecessary to avoid the error-prone and sometimes painstaking scanning. Of course, the header button could be programmed to remain depressed to show the selected column, but this still leaves the user in the dark as to the sort order.

> *Some of the best innovations in user interfaces are small and come about from worrying over and refining small details.*

Some of the best innovations in user interfaces are small and come about from worrying over and refining small details. A small glyph, such as the one shown in the first column of the display in Figure 9-16, flags the column on which the list is sorted

FIGURE 9-16 *Creative overloading at the top of columns.*

and the sort order—down or descending in this instance. A canted triangle is ideal for this sort of glyph; it will not be confused with a drop-down, and its meaning becomes clear to the user on the very first use.

Multilevel sorting on multiple columns (e.g., **Sales** within **Supervisor**) can be supported through other simple extensions of common interaction idioms. Shift-click, which is used for extended selection in lists, is a natural. Hold the **Shift** key down, click on **Supervisor**, then click on **Sales**, and then click again, and the result would be as in Figure 9-16.

The remaining use case, **movingColumnDisplay**, can also be supported by a straightforward and natural extension of another interaction idiom: drag-and-drop. The simplest approach would simply have the user click on and drag the column header to move the column to another position, but this is apt to be prone to accidental column moving, which could be very disconcerting for the user. A safer but still reasonable approach would require the user to select the column first by double-clicking. This behavior also matches common behavior within word processors: You double-click to select text and then drag to move selected text.

> *Heavy but reasonable overloading yields a display that is completely customizable by the user, at any time, solely through familiar interaction idioms and without a separate configuration or formatting dialogue.*

The end result of this heavy but reasonable overloading is a display grid that is completely customizable by the user, at any time, solely through familiar interaction idioms and without going through a separate configuration or formatting dialogue. Although much of the extended behavior is hidden, it is easily described. You can almost see the ad copy: "Drag-and-drop resizable columns: Click the label to sort, double-click to select, drag-and-drop to rearrange. And more! Fully customize displays to fit your needs and tastes."

COMPLETING THE DESIGN

10

EXPRESSING SOLUTIONS:
Implementation Modeling and Prototypes

FUN STUFF

This is the fun part. For many designers, the real fun finally begins when it is time to produce the paper prototype or visual design for the user interface. Not surprisingly, some are inclined to rush it, just as programmers are prone to plunging into cutting code without waiting for a complete design.

Constructing the visual design for the user interface is, without a doubt, one of the more interesting and creative activities in the entire process. Here, the designer is challenged to find effective, practical ways to realize the various requirements reflected in the essential models and their supporting documentation. Now, the developer draws upon knowledge of human–computer interaction, graphical design, widget selection, and layout to balance competing objectives and to trade off among conflicting constraints. This is the best chance to be truly creative and constructive.

> *For many designers, the real fun begins with the paper prototype or visual design for the user interface.*

It is possible to skip over the visual design and proceed directly from the content model into programming the software, especially when using visual development tools, such as Visual Basic or Delphi. Certainly, skilled and sophisticated developers who are intimately familiar with essential modeling can program directly from the abstract models. This can sometimes be an appropriate shortcut, especially for small, one-person projects to develop simple systems. For most programmers, however, the gap between content model and the design of an on-screen form can be rather large—too much to cross in a single step.

In our experience, better results are obtained when programming is guided by an **implementation model**, a visual design that more closely resembles the final implemented interface. Those analysts and designers who completed the essential models are in the best position to create the implementation model. They have the best grasp of the models, they understand the user requirements, and they are likely to have the clearest ideas of how to support these in practice.

> *For most programmers, the gap between content model and the design of an on-screen form can be too much to cross in a single step.*

An implementation model is a representation of what the final implemented user interface will look like and how it will function. It can take many forms, but, most commonly, it is a simple sketch and supporting notes or documentation. In usage-centered design, the essential models are the primary supporting material since they capture the most important functional and operational requirements in relation to the user interface.

Although often documented with a pencil sketch or other visual representation, strictly speaking, an implementation model is more than just a layout and a selection of widgets for each interaction context, just as a working program is more than just its user interface. To implement the content model and support the use cases, the system must not only look right but also act right. Simulations and working prototypes can, if done well, capture both appearance and behavior,

> *An implementation model is more than just a layout and a selection of widgets since the system must act right as well as look right.*

but simple pictures and other passive or non-working models need to be tied to behavioral models. Where the essential use cases are inadequate for these purposes, state-transition diagrams or flowcharts can be pressed into service to document complex cases.

Whatever its form, the implementation model is a chance to work out the finer details of the user interface design without having to cut code. It also provides a particularly effective medium for review and communication with users and clients.

PROTOTYPES AND PROTOTYPING

PROTOTYPE ARCHETYPES

Prototypes come in many different forms: active and passive, high- and low-fidelity, horizontal and vertical. Each variant has its problems and peculiarities as well as its most appropriate applications.

Action. Prototypes can be active or passive. A **passive prototype** just sits there and does nothing. A sketch on paper or a drawing in PC Paint or MS Draw is a passive prototype. A passive prototype may be as primitive as a quick pencil sketch on the back of a placemat or as sophisticated as a nonworking mock-up created in a visual programming language. A passive prototype may even sometimes be a precise and detailed simulacrum that is all but indistinguishable from a real user interface but that, like the figures in a wax museum, will not act like the real thing.

> *A passive prototype, even a precise and detailed simulacrum, is like a figure in a wax museum: It may look real, but it does not act like the real thing.*

An **active prototype** is an implementation model that actually functions to some degree or another. Whether simulations or partial implementations, active prototypes act like the real thing, at least within some specified range of operation.

Fidelity. A prototype that closely resembles the user interface it depicts is referred to as a **high-fidelity prototype**; one that only vaguely looks like the real thing is called a **low-fidelity prototype**. As noted in Chapter 6, some people refer to content models with their abstract components as low-fidelity prototypes.

High-fidelity prototypes are not necessarily better; they just look better. For some purposes, such as communicating with end users, low-fidelity prototypes may actually be more effective, while, for others, such as making a pitch to upper management or potential investors, the high-fidelity approach may be more appropriate.

Orientation. Prototypes can also be described as horizontal or vertical. A **horizontal prototype** is a thin slice off the top, a superficial representation of most or all of the user interface with little or nothing behind the screen. Even in active form, a horizontal prototype will usually exhibit only minimal activity: Dialogues may open and close, but little else will function. A horizontal prototype is typically highly expressive regarding appearance but largely silent on behavior.

A **vertical prototype** is, by contrast, a narrow slice through a system, representing the more or less complete design for one segment of the user interface and its underlying functions. The term is most often applied to active prototypes, although passive prototypes may occasionally be drawn up for such a vertical segment. In an active form, a vertical prototype will present all the interaction contexts and simulate all the behavior associated with but one or a few use cases.

A hybrid tactic can be used to create what has sometimes been called a *deep-and-wide* prototype. Such a prototype is a shallow realization of the entire user interface along with a full simulation or implementation of selected use cases. Deep-and-wide prototypes are especially effective for demonstrations and presentations to management because they can create a convincing illusion of an actual working system. Everything looks and works right so long as the user does not wander off the narrow, predefined trail demarcated by the fully featured vertical slice.

> *Deep-and-wide prototypes can create a convincing illusion of an actual working system so long as the user does not wander off the narrow, predefined trail.*

PASSIVE PROTOTYPES

Passive prototypes include paper prototypes, computer drawings prepared with graphics software, and nonfunctioning mock-ups created using programming tools of one sort or another. So-called paper prototypes, simple drawings of user interfaces, are probably the most widely used form of user interface prototype. Since not all paper prototypes are on paper, the term *static visual design* may sometimes be more accurate. **Visual designs** can be created in a variety of media on a variety of materials, from standard letter or A4 copy paper to flip-charts or whiteboards.

Paper prototypes in most any medium are relatively easy to produce and revise. You do not need to be a Rembrandt to draw a usable paper prototype. Simple, quick pencil sketches often serve quite well, even when they only marginally resemble any actual software user interface. Accuracy and graphical detail are generally less important than the overall structure and visual organization of each interaction context.

> *You do not need to be a Rembrandt to draw a usable paper prototype. Accuracy and graphical detail are generally less important than the overall structure and visual organization.*

For reports or presentations to clients or for final review of a highly refined design prior to implementation, high-quality visual representations prepared using computer-based drawing tools, such as Freehand or Corel-Draw!, are probably preferred. Even these may not in all cases be highly accurate renditions of the appearance of the final interface, but at least the lines will be straight. Screen shots of an active prototype or mock-up can also be used for this purpose.

Visual development tools have gotten so good that some developers find it easier to create a nonfunctional interface implementation in a visual development language than to draw one using a graphics package. Nonfunctional programs have the advantage of high-fidelity representation and can sometimes be used as the basis for active prototyping or even system development later. However, they restrict the visual design to whatever widgets and features are available within a particular development tool and its libraries. For new or innovative designs, it is often easier just to sketch or draw what you mean.

Passive prototypes alone are not enough to express the implementation model. Layout and appearance must be connected with behavior and interaction. All forms of passive prototypes can hide behavioral, performance, and operational problems. Eventually, the development team must be able to demonstrate real behavior and functional capability, either in an active prototype or the delivered software.

ACTIVE PROTOTYPES

Active prototypes, also called *functional* prototypes or *working* prototypes, can take a variety of forms, each with its uses. These include

- Software mock-ups
- Simulations
- Limited implementations

The term *mock-up* usually refers to a prototype of limited fidelity and performance constructed in a software medium other than a full-blown programming language or the target language for implementation. Various general-purpose tools have been used to create such simulations, including PowerPoint and Macromedia Director. Computer-based mock-ups can usually demonstrate basic logic and limited behavior, such as changes in appearance or the interactions among user interface components. Simulations typically act more like real programs, demonstrating a wider range of behavior. Rather convincing simulations can be created even with relatively simple tools, such as PowerPoint or some other presentation package, but simulations are also often created in conventional programming languages.

> *Rather convincing simulations can be created even with relatively simple tools.*

Simulations are most often developed using programming languages that favor quick and easy implementation, including rapid application development tools, visual development environments, or specialized prototyping tools. General-purpose tools often used for this purpose include such systems as PowerBuilder or the venerable Visual Basic, as well as Delphi, Tcl, or even, occasionally, such heavyweight programming systems as Visual C++. For special purposes, specialized tools are available, such as Emultek's Rapid for embedded systems programming.

Simulations are seldom intended to become actual delivered software, even when written in conventional programming languages. In contrast, a limited implementation is some part of the actual final system in the final programming language—for example, a partially functional Delphi realization of the user interface for a system to be developed in Delphi.

Active prototypes are not always constructed in software. The so-called Wizard of Oz paradigm has been widely used to prototype and test out user interface designs of many kinds, but most especially for exotic or unusual configurations. In this approach, the behavior of a system is realized through behind-the-scenes manipulation. For example, the development team may want to try out a telephone-based interface that mixes limited voice recognition with telephone keypad responses. The behavior of the system is simulated by a person on the other end of the telephone line.

Working prototypes and simulations are not finished software, although they can sometimes seem like it to users. And users are not the only ones who sometimes forget that prototypes are not the real thing. Programmers may be tempted to try and save time by expanding and refining a prototype into a full-featured system. However economical this approach may seem to be on first consideration, except for relatively small applications with a sharply limited expected life span, it is a path fraught with dangers.

Software is the only engineering field that throws together prototypes and then attempts to sell them as delivered goods. Initial prototypes and final products are built for different purposes and often through dramatically different development practices. Prototypes are seldom a good foundation for finished software. Prototypes tend to be hacked and pasted together with little attention to architecture or good programming since the object is to create something as quickly as possible that sufficiently resembles the anticipated system.

> *Software is the only engineering field that throws together prototypes and then attempts to sell them as delivered goods.*

Working prototypes have their uses, aside from embodying the design of the user interface. Prototypes make the most sense when used for proof of concept or a test of feasibility, and such are their primary uses in every engineering field save software. If you do not know whether a particular design will be workable with real users, a functional prototype is a good idea. Perhaps you are unsure whether a screen full of information can be refreshed quickly enough over a busy network to support telephone query operators. Perhaps some question remains about whether users will be able to discern the functioning of your clever new selection widget. Build a working prototype or good simulation.

Working prototypes are also a good choice for communications with customers, both committed and prospective. A screen that fills with little graphic bits and then re-sorts its contents is likely to be both more convincing and more easily understood than a drawing that has to be explained ("If you click here, all the little triangles and squares pull apart and arrange themselves in chains.").

Even the best and most carefully programmed of working prototypes can still obscure usability issues and performance problems. Prototypes are expected to be slow, which may hide the revelation that the working system could also prove unacceptably slow. Display grids that work fine for a handful of test cases may be visually overwhelming when fully populated with real data. The efficient and simple operation implied by a wizardlike simulation of a voice-processing application may never be repeatable with the speech-recognition algorithm that will be used in practice. Prototypes are seldom able to factor in such influences as network performance or database organization that can have a strong impact on usability.

INTERFACE PROTOTYPING

The great advantage of prototypes is that prototyping is easier than programming. Prototypes that are overly ambitious or that are too fussy in form defeat the purpose. The best implementation model is the simplest and easiest one to construct that is still sufficient to work out and document the design. For the majority of software, a paper prototype is more than adequate.

> *The great advantage of prototypes is that prototyping is easier than programming. Prototypes that are overly ambitious or fussy defeat the purpose.*

When prototyping is part of a process of successive or iterative refinement, you should always limit the number of iterations lest the project turn into a never-ending story. Users will always find something wrong or something more they want or something they do not want, regardless of how many times they are shown a prototype. Successive versions, therefore, do not always improve a design, and the iterative process does not always converge on some best or most workable solution. Often, it can be difficult for even experienced designers to tell whether a new design is truly better than the previous one or merely different. This difficulty is one reason why quantitative measurement often plays such a central role in software usability. Numbers are unambiguous; either they get better or they do not (see Chapters 17 and 18).

Whatever the medium, always be sure to keep earlier versions of prototypes. For many reasons, you may have to revert to an earlier version. If pencil sketches are revised on the spot in meetings with users, make sure there is always an unaltered copy to fall back upon in the event that users change their minds.

Prototypes in any form are not a substitute for good analysis and design. Thinking on paper is acceptable, but not thinking is not. All too often, active prototypes can become an excuse for precipitous programming. Developers are frequently pressured by managers or customers into massaging a prototype into delivered software rather than using it as it was intended—as a model for the separate design and development of the final system.

> *Prototypes in any form are not a substitute for good analysis and design.*

MAPPING THE MODELS

Translating the content model into an implementation model is not a simple matter of establishing correspondences or substituting real components for abstract ones. In some cases, for easy problems or where the models have been developed with particular care or insight, the process may resemble some loose mapping from one form of representation into another, but that is a lucky and uncommon happenstance. As in translating between natural languages, even though the rules may be well defined, good translation is an art. Sometimes, the translation is straightforward, but a straightforward translation sometimes turns out to be nonsense.

> *Producing a good implementation model cannot be reduced to a handful of brief rules applied in a few simple steps.*

The complexity of the design issues detailed in the previous three chapters is testimony to the complexity of this final design activity. Producing a good implementation model cannot be reduced to a handful of brief rules applied in a few simple steps.

Three general classes of issues must be resolved to complete the implementation model:

- **Contexts**—What are the implemented interaction contexts?
- **Components**—What are the user interface components within contexts?
- **Composition**—What is the layout and organization of components in each interaction context?

The designer must choose what form of interface context on the implemented user interface will realize each interaction context in the content model. The designer must select what software user interface components will serve for each of the abstract materials and tools in the content model. The designer must also develop an effective arrangement of the user interface components within each interaction context.

These are neither sequential nor independent decisions. The interactions are such that, to a large extent, all three kinds of issues must be addressed simultaneously.

INTERFACE CONTEXTS

Although programmers may tend to think primarily in terms of windows and dialogue boxes, modern graphical user interfaces provide a substantial range of choices to implement interaction contexts. Unfortunately and all too often, none of the standard choices available is quite right for a particular problem. Designers should not be afraid to consider hybrids that amalgamate features or characteristics of more than one form of interaction context if this will speed or simplify use or make a system easier to learn. For example, the strict rules for Windows 95 place menu bars on primary application windows but not dialogue boxes and associate primary navigation controls, such as **OK** and **Cancel**, with dialogue boxes but not application windows. Users, however, seem to have few if any problems with dialogues that include menus or application windows with an **Exit** button when this makes sense in terms of the organization of their problems.

> *Programmers tend to think primarily in terms of windows and dialogue boxes, but modern graphical user interfaces provide a greater range of choices to implement interaction contexts.*

It is not possible or practical to discuss in detail all the options and the issues these entail. Many of the details are platform-dependent and may even differ somewhat from one development environment to another. The important point is for designers to familiarize themselves with the available options [see, for example, Microsoft, 1995] and consider alternative schemes for organizing user interfaces into interaction contexts. Primary and secondary interaction contexts include

- Screens
- Primary or application windows
- Child windows
- Fixed dialogue boxes
- Resizable dialogue boxes
- Tabbed dialogues or notebooks
- Tab or notebook pages
- Pop-up panels
- Drop-down or open-out dialogue panels
- Floating tool palettes
- Wizard-style succession panels

Focal interaction. The first major question facing the designer of the implementation model is, What is the user looking at most of the time when interacting with the system? What form will be used to realize the **focal interaction context** or contexts? The focal interaction context is the primary point of interaction between the user and the system. Typically, it will support the focal use cases; often it will support other use cases as well. In workbench-style interaction, the focal interaction context may support a large number of use cases in whole or in part. The implementation of the focal interaction context is often intimately tied with the overall organization of the user interface architecture. The alternatives available include

- Full-screen models
- Single-document models

- Multiple-document models
- Multiplex models
- Tabbed notebooks
- Dialogue boxes

Although sometimes considered outdated, the full-screen interaction model should not be written off out of hand. In this model, all or most of the interaction between user and system takes place in one or more separate screens. On the plus side, the full-screen model maximizes available screen real estate and minimizes window management overhead. On the minus side, the user will have less flexibility, and full-screen context changes can be more abrupt and disorienting than changes that preserve visual object persistence.

> *Although sometimes considered outdated, the full-screen interaction model should not be written off out of hand.*

For some problems, resizable windows or movable dialogues offer no advantages and may just complicate and slow down use. For example, in a telephone order-entry application, the operator is dealing with only one customer at a time and probably using no other application concurrently. In such applications, the cleaner, all-or-nothing approach of full-screen operation makes the most sense.

The so-called Single-Document Interface (SDI) is the classic approach to windows-style applications, with a single document or file open in a single application window. If the user has any need for working with more than one document, multiple instances of the application will need to be supported. Single-document models are simple to use and, relative to more advanced models, easier to program.

Multiple-document models include a number of common variations that allow one application to operate on a number of documents or files at a time. The standard Multiple Document Interface (MDI) under Windows may have an uncertain future. In its orthodox form, it can be difficult at times to interpret, especially for beginners. Even old hands may find themselves disconcerted by tools and controls that vanish and reappear as the focus shifts from one child window to another. Other variants, such as the window management model Microsoft refers to as *workspaces*, overcome some of the problems of standard MDI but introduce their own peculiarities.

In many applications, tabbed notebook pages are much easier for users to understand and work with than are multiple child windows. Tabbed notebooks or "workbooks" dramatically reduce window management overhead at the expense of some flexibility. Where it is neither reasonable nor necessary for the user to see more than one view or document at the same time, the visual object persistence of tabbed pages can offer significant gains in ease of use.

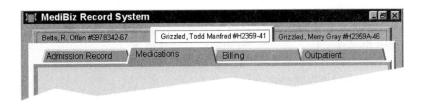

FIGURE 10-1 *Tabbed visual design for patient record interface.*

The tabbed page visual metaphor does not solve all problems, but it is a versatile way of organizing the focal interaction context. For example, a word processor can display all open documents as tabbed pages, keeping the names of all open documents visible on the tabs across the top of the window. Another example is a hospital patient record system that may sometimes require an admissions clerk to have records on two or three patients open at a time. Each patient record also may have a number of views or sections. It is vital that the clerk not confuse one patient with another and not confuse one view with another. It is also important to present available functions in a consistent way that reduces mistakes. Window management overhead could be both a distraction and a source of errors. A nested tabbed notebook arrangement, such as the one modeled in the abstract in Figure 10-1, might satisfy these requirements.

Yet another useful model has no universally accepted name. Microsoft refers to it as the *project window management model,* some people call it the *open desktop model,* and we have called it a *multiple single-document model.* The approach turns each of a number of documents or views and any number of collections of facilities into free-floating, separate windows on the desktop. It works best for complex, workbench-style applications, like software development environments, where it has become almost conventional.

Some applications are sufficiently restricted in size or scope that the focal interaction context may best be realized as a dialogue box rather than an application window. The keyboard extension applet we have been using as a design example is a prime candidate for this treatment.

Goal lines. Several broad goals should be kept in mind when organizing the user interface into interaction contexts.

Perhaps the most important objective should be to reduce context switching as much as possible and eliminate gratuitous context changes. Whenever reasonable, the design should allow for completion of use cases without switching interaction contexts. One of the most common architectural mistakes in user interfaces today is to require the user to switch interaction contexts unnecessarily. Every action takes the user to a new

> *Most important is eliminating gratuitous context changes and reducing context switching as much as possible.*

dialogue box and, from there, to a subdialogue. Like little fleas on bigger fleas, the nested dialogues multiply, until the screen looks more like a mosaic tile floor than an organized desktop. In one system we were called on to evaluate for a client, the dialogues were nested seven deep at one point, which was enough to cause a system error in the beta release software.

Designers should be cautious about interposing interaction contexts ahead of the focal interaction context. Start-up dialogues that require extra steps or specifications from the user are often evidence of knee-jerk design. It is all too easy with some development tools to throw in a standard security log-on dialogue, replete with password protection and periodic mandatory password change.

Another vital but often neglected goal should be to reduce window management overhead. Window management overhead is all that time you spend moving and resizing windows—dragging, tiling, cascading, untiling, minimizing, restoring, and the like. Each such operation may seem to take little time, but, over the course of a day, the overhead accumulates. Heavy users of multiple, complex applications can waste as much as 10% of their time on window management. Many users get so fed up with becoming confused trying to find a hidden window or dialogue that they work only with maximized applications.

> *An often neglected goal is reducing window management overhead—all that time wasted moving and resizing windows.*

The solution is not to banish resizable windows, but to make more intelligent use of available features and mechanisms. We remember a demonstration of a sophisticated and very expensive CASE tool in which every window opened in the middle of the screen at the same default size. Every time the demonstrator opened another window or view, she started out by resizing it and moving it to another location on the screen. Even for this agile and experienced user, the time spent fiddling with windows was a significant part of the total time of the demonstration.

User efficiency with this CASE tool could be improved in more than one way without radical reprogramming. One simple scheme would just remember the settings from the last instance of a particular view or dialogue. If another instance were already open at the same point, an offset could be created to cascade the windows. More promising might be to look at how developers were using the software and size and position windows appropriate to the use. One could either gather field data on actual use, or simply do a careful and thoughtful analysis. In fact, since the windows were invariably increased in size by the user, just increasing the default size substantially would have been a help.

This example also highlights the importance of observation as a part of good design. Although the developers and designers had all seen their tool demonstrated on many occasions, they had never noticed this simple and consistent pattern. Why? Because they were watching but not really observing. Observation is a state of mind, not a position of the eyes.

INTERFACE CONTENTS

In populating the implemented interaction contexts with visual components, the designer is always striving for simpler and easier operation. We start with the simplest assumptions and abandon them only as necessary. In the first try, each abstract component is realized by a single, separate user interface widget. The first rendition will typically employ only standard widgets in conventional arrangements [Constantine, 1998a].

> *Start with the simplest assumptions—each abstract component realized by a single widget, standard components in conventional arrangements—and abandon them only as necessary.*

If the results are good, the job can be considered done, but a careful examination of the initial design will often expose one or more problems or suggest possible improvements. We review the visual design from the perspective of basic user interface design principles. More importantly, we once again make test runs to enact the supported use cases, only now with the implementation model.

On occasion, one abstract component may best be realized as more than one widget. A common example is where an abstract component actually models a collection of operations or set of alternatives—for instance, a component to **SetTextStyle**. This may become a set of tool buttons to set bold, italic, underlined, or strikeout, for example. We should, however, always heed the advice of William of Ockham and avoid the needless multiplication of widgets.

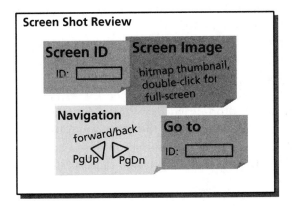

FIGURE 10-2 *Sample content model awaiting creative realization.*

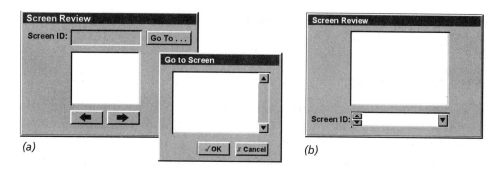

FIGURE 10-3 *First and second tries.*

More than one abstract tool can sometimes be combined into a single user interface widget, thus saving screen real estate and often simplifying the user interface. In some cases, the needed combination is just a standard component—for example, a scrolling list display to implement both an **AddressList** container and an **AddressListBrowser** tool. However, the designer should be prepared to think creatively about nonstandard combinations.

In Figure 10-2, part of the content model for a software development tool is shown. Here, the user has the ability to browse forward or back through a series of screen images or to select a specific image by name, number, or other identifier. The identifier of the current image is to be shown along with the image.

A simpleminded initial design for this part of the problem might look something like Figure 10-3a. The screen identifier becomes a labeled display field; the screen image becomes a thumbnail bitmap holder, as planned; and the navigation tool is split into a pair of buttons to page forward and back. Direct access to a particular screen is through a dialogue box with a fixed scrolling list box. This sort of uninspired design is common when systems are developed directly with visual development tools. The focus of attention bounces around within the interaction context, an extra context change is required to select an image by name, and related elements are not brought together.

To devise an improved design, we might start by noting that the functions of displaying the current screen identifier and of paging through screens can be covered by a single widget: a spin box. We might next consider bringing the selection list back up to the main dialogue. To save screen real estate, the fixed scrolling list could be replaced with a drop-down list. We might now note that the identifier display function is duplicated by both the drop-down list and the spin box, suggesting the potential for a creative combination of the two widgets. This leads to the more elegant and efficient tentative design represented in Figure 10-3b.

INTERFACE COMPOSITION

Layout on the interface cannot be wholly separated from the choice of visual components. The need for a large list display or drawing area may constrain the choice of widgets to implement other facilities. Conversely, widgets that closely fit the structure of the problem can make screen real estate available, as the example in Figure 10-3 illustrated.

The principles of workflow introduced in Chapter 7 are called upon to establish an initial composition for each interaction context. With one eye on the supported use cases, we lay out the widgets to allow a smooth progression through the interaction context.

It can be worth reminding ourselves now and then of the Structure Principle. Not only do we want to group together those components that are thought of together or are used together, but we also want to make tools and materials that are similar or related appear to be similar or related on the user interface.

In general, displaying more data of a given type is better than displaying less. Users can usually find what they are looking for much faster by scanning a list or grid visually than by performing a search or by scrolling or paging through data. The human eye and brain form a remarkably efficient search engine.

In our experience, it is best to begin by assuming that screen real estate will not be a problem, that there will be plenty of space for everything you want to include. For those cases where there is sufficient room, you will have a good design without having wasted effort on cramming in widgets or reducing the size of data displays. If screen real estate becomes a problem, as it often does, you will also be in a better position to make reasonable compromises, having already devised a no-compromise design.

There is no substitute for playing around with various arrangements and choices of widgets. Truly fine designs are achieved by reviewing and refining the implementation model not once or twice but repeatedly. Although this may appear to be time-consuming, it is far faster to put a visual design through several revisions than to build, test, and rebuild a working system or even just a functional prototype.

IMPLEMENTATION MODELING ILLUSTRATED

Based on the discussions in this chapter and the previous three, we are in a position to devise an implementation model or a visual design for our keyboard extender applet, starting with the central interaction context supporting the focal use cases of **insertingSymbol** and **insertingPhrase**.

Some of the translations from the content model that was shown earlier in Figure 6-5 are relatively straightforward, but others involve some subtle trade-offs.

An initial design can be developed with little difficulty, but arriving at a really good design is a bigger challenge that may require several tries. We begin by assuming that standard components in conventional arrangements will suffice.

EXTENDER DESIGN ONE

Although this utility will function as an independent applet, in light of its simplicity, an application window with a menu bar would be overkill. In terms of overall layout, the primary issue is that we would like to maximize the amount of space for displaying available symbols without turning the dialogue into a screen hog that will cover up too much of the application from which it has been called. A menu bar would mostly serve to waste space. For compactness, we might want to array any command buttons along with the primary navigation controls across the bottom.

The heart of the utility is the **symbolCollection** plus **symbolBrowser**, realized together as a scrolling box. For the one-of-many selection required to implement a **collectionBrowser**, we might consider a fixed selection list, a drop-down list, or a spin box. The fixed list makes more fonts or user-defined symbol collections visible at one time, while the spin box is more efficient for viewing a succession of collections or fonts because scrolling and selecting are combined into a single operation. The drop-down list combines the disadvantages of both spin boxes and fixed lists. A good first try would place a fixed selection list beside the scrolling symbol display.

For visibility, the **phraseBin** would go at the top, above the **symbolCollection**, just as in our original content model. The **phraseBin** can be implemented as a simple text box or edit box serving as both a display of an assembled phrase and also as a text entry field, thus cleverly supporting the **insertingPhrase** use case, which may intermix both keyboarded and special symbols. Using a standard text box also makes the contents fully editable by the user.

The placement, behavior, and labeling of the primary navigation controls entail trade-offs. The function of an **OK** button will be to insert a selected character or the contents of the text box into the original application at the current selection point. Although it would be nonstandard, we might consider labeling it **Insert**, which better communicates its function. Some users might expect this to insert without closing, but that is likely to happen only once. In any event, for efficiency reasons, the navigation buttons are not expected to be the primary means of interacting with the utility. They need to be present to provide familiar defaults, but they are unlikely to be used by any regular user.

We are still left with the question of how we efficiently support both **insertingSymbol** and **insertingPhrase**. One way would be to employ different interaction idioms for the actions of adding to a phrase and inserting a character or phrase—for example, having a single-click select the character and add it to the

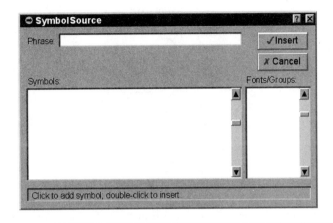

FIGURE 10-4 *First version of the keyboard extender visual design.*

phrase and a double-click insert the character, along with anything accumulated in the phrase. In other words, the user double-clicks on the last character to insert and close the utility. Although this paired idiom approach is quickly mastered in practice, it is hidden behavior. The effect of a single-click is likely to be discovered spontaneously, but, in the presence of an **Insert** button, the double-click may remain undiscovered indefinitely. We might leave open the final decision but temporarily elect to prompt the user with an initial status bar message such as "`Click to add symbol; double-click to insert.`"

Eventually, we might arrive at a preliminary design such as the one shown in Figure 10-4. The design of the interaction context to support `specifyingSymbolGroup` has been deferred.

EXTENDER DESIGN TWO

One of the problems in the initial visual design is with the behavior of the scrolling selection list used to set the font or user-defined group. When scrolling through a long list looking for a particular item, the current highlighted selection scrolls out of view, and it is easy for users to forget precisely what they are looking at in the synchronized character view to the left. In addition, to scan the contents of a series of fonts or sets, each must be separately selected in turn, which can require an awkward and time-consuming sequence of scroll, select, look, scroll, select, look, ad infinitum.

We want to keep the selection point in view and have it change automatically as the list is scrolled. No standard widget has the desired appearance and behavior. The widget shown in Figure 10-5 is one possible design. It resembles a standard scrolling list, but a "cursor window" appears to be affixed solidly to the dialogue surface; whatever is under it is automatically selected. The spin buttons, though in an unexpected context, suggest their obvious function.

FIGURE 10-5 *A novel selection widget: a spin list?*

We have not yet addressed the problem of defining user-specified groups. In developing the content model back in Chapter 6, we raised the issue of whether one interaction context or two were needed. There is a substantial overlap between the focal use cases and **specifyingSymbolGroup**; both require a **symbolBin** and a **symbolBrowser**. In addition, **specifyingSymbolGroup** needs a bin to hold a group being constructed or changed and a place for the name of the group. We could create a separate subdialogue to support **specifyingSymbolGroup**; a very conventional approach might look like the example in Figure 10-6.

Recognizing the functional overlap in the primary and secondary dialogues, we might be tempted to find a way to crowd everything into one dialogue box, but this wastes screen real estate with relatively infrequently used facilities. We could eliminate the overlap by using a floating window, as shown in Figure 10-7. The problem is how to add characters into the group from ones found through

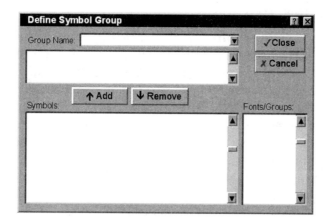

FIGURE 10-6 *A conventional approach to user-defined symbol collections.*

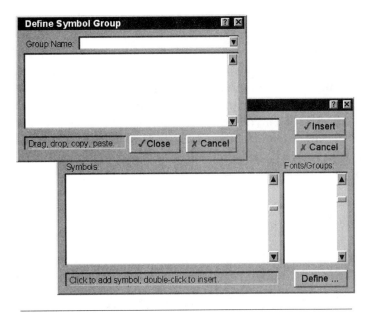

FIGURE 10-7 *Eliminating redundancy in facilities for defining symbol collections.*

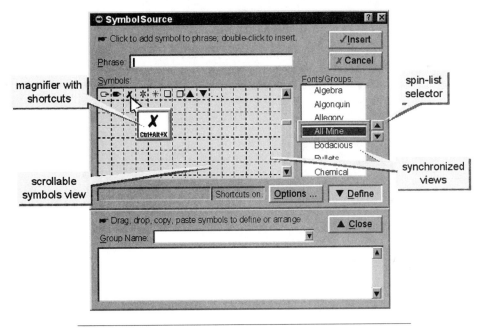

FIGURE 10-8 *An improved design for the keyboard extender applet.*

browsing with the main dialogue. The drag-and-drop idiom is a natural, but it seems less obvious for dragging characters between windows.

A drop-down panel, as shown in Figure 10-8, is probably the best option. A banner message at the top of the panel prompts the new user regarding the hidden behavior. A sound design would also support reasonable generalizations, including extended selection of multiple characters, plus copy, paste, and delete from menus or the keyboard. The design shown in Figure 10-8 is an amalgam of ideas from numerous classes we have taught. It is not in any sense the ultimate design, but it is a far sight cleaner, more efficient, and more flexible than where we started in Chapter 4.

11

HELP ME IF YOU CAN:
Designing Help
and Helpful Messages

EVEN EXPERTS NEED A LIFT

It is a common experience: You have forgotten exactly how to accomplish an infrequent but necessary task with software you are using, so you reluctantly turn to the on-line help system. You look under one term, then another, and then work down through three levels of nested entries. Nothing, zilch, nada. You give up and ask your office mate. He doesn't remember either, but, before calling the tech support line, the two of you try several things that don't work. Your final desperate call to tech support is put in a queue, so you hang up and head down the hall to see Jeanine. Jeanine knows *everything* about Windows! As you finally return to your work, you try not to think about what this little misadventure has cost when you add up everybody's wasted time.

The help that software provides—or fails to provide—can have a profound effect on the usability of a system. Well-written, well-organized, and accessible help can compensate to a certain degree for limitations in software. Good help will not turn a sow's ear of an interface into a software silk purse, but it can help. Poor on-line help and documentation, on the other hand, can reduce a marginal system to utter unusability. Although the Access Rule challenges us to design so well that even beginners will need no help, we know this to be an unachievable ideal. Thus, the design of help systems and documentation are as much a factor in software usability as are dialogue design and screen layout.

> *Poor on-line help and documentation can reduce a marginal system to utter unusability.*

Help systems serve many purposes. When they work, they can answer those isolated questions that crop up sporadically in the use of any system: What is this?

How do I do that? Where do I find it? They can offer tutorials and encouraging support for novices, serve as a safety net for experts, and promote continuous learning among improving intermediates. Good user manuals and help files can prevent work from grinding to a halt every time the user is lost, confused, or uncertain. They can reduce the need for peer support and cut technical help desk costs.

Badly designed help, vacuous manuals, and unhelpful help files can also be instructive. They teach users not to bother turning to these ready resources, but to give up or to rely on other sources instead. Every time users fail to find an entry for a subject they are seeking, they learn not even to try the help system. Every help file that is itself inconsistent, convoluted, or confusing discourages users from trying to cope with complex and bewildering interfaces. Many users, conditioned by past failures, almost never consult the on-line help. User manuals and help systems are turned to only as a last resort. Software vendors and technical support people may want to shout "RTFM" (Read The Friggin' Manual) to their customers, but the manual, like the help files, is often unreadable, uninformative, or both.

> *Badly designed help, vacuous manuals, and unhelpful help files teach users to give up or to rely on other sources instead.*

Writing good documentation and help files requires special skills that the average developer or user interface designer is not usually expected to have, but that does mean that the issues are separate or separable. Increasingly, forward-thinking development teams are integrating documentation specialists and technical writers into development teams. Developers and documenters need to understand how their work interacts and how it affects software usability. In this chapter, we examine software help from a usage-centered perspective.

USE CASES FOR HELP

Obtaining help is a task, a sometimes necessary step in the completion of other tasks. Referring to help can be, in task-modeling terms, an extension to almost any use case supported by a particular piece of software. If we analyze requests for help in terms of user intent, we recognize that help can serve varying ends, and, depending on the user intent in seeking help, different responses are required from software. Some **help cases** (use cases for help seeking) are generally supported in on-line help, while others have been largely ignored or poorly implemented at best. Table 11-1 summarizes the most common of these help cases.

TABLE 11-1 *Essential use cases for help seeking*

User Question	Use Case		Implementation Notes
	USER INTENTION	SYSTEM RESPONSIBILITY	
What is this?	`seekingIdentification`		
	`indicate object`	`brief description`	Pop-up tips, context help; available for everything
How do I...?	`seekingInstruction`		
	`identify task`	`operational sequence`	Possible demonstration or walk-through
What should I do?	`seekingSuggestion`		
	`request`	`hint`	Often first step or next step
What do you mean?	`seekingClarification`		
	`request`	`different explanation`	Not details or advanced since user is confused
Tell me more.	`seekingElaboration`		
	`request`	`details or advanced`	
Remind me about...	`seekingReminder`		
	`identify feature/task`	`brief synopsis`	
Where is...?	`seekingLocation`		
	`identify feature`	`give place, routing`	Possible map, animation
What can I do?	`exploringFeatures`		
	`request`	`overview, topic map`	"See also," "Other," and "Related topics" helpful; typical table of contents or outline seldom useful

HELP CASES

Just as users' questions to helpful colleagues will vary, diverse intentions underlie the use cases for on-line help. Perhaps the two most common reasons for seeking help are to find out what something is and learn how to do something: What is this? How do I do that?

The help case **seekingIdentification** is reasonably well supported in most modern software through pop-up "tool tips" or context-sensitive help. The most common failing in supporting these help cases is that identification help is potentially needed for various features, so pop-up hints should be available not only for tools but also for menu items and other active elements of the user interface. The entire user interface should not be enabled for tool-tip style help, however, because this leaves the user with no place to rest the pointer without becoming annoyed or distracted by one of those little yellow messages. Of course, identification help on all features should be available on request, such as the context help accessed in Windows 95 through **Shift+F1** or the question mark tool typically found on the title bar of dialogue boxes.

> *Just as users' questions to helpful colleagues will vary, diverse intentions underlie the use cases for on-line help.*

The help case **seekingInstruction** is less well supported in typical systems, but the situation has been improving in recent years. In seeking what is technically referred to as *procedural help* (help with how to perform a task), users want much the same response as they would get were they to ask a colleague to show them how to do something. Step-by-step narratives in a help file can work reasonably well for relatively simple tasks or for more advanced users, but they also suffer from significant disadvantages. For tasks that are complicated relative to the sophistication of the user, the user will be forced to switch back and forth between the help file instructions and the parts of the user interface within which the task must actually be accomplished. This requires switching mental contexts and operationally switching interaction contexts. Subtle or complicated procedures or instructions may force the user back to the help context repeatedly just to understand and correctly execute one step in the process. Whether the help system display is "always on top" and blocks part of the screen or can be hidden by the active window, a substantial amount of window management may be required of the user.

> *Complicated tasks require the user to switch repeatedly back and forth between the help file instructions and the user interface.*

For some purposes, animated help that demonstrates a process or that steps a user through the sequence within the actual interaction context for the task is better than passive narrative instruction (more on this later).

A highly specialized variation of `seekingInstruction` is the help case `seekingSuggestion`, which covers a myriad of circumstances in which the user does not know how to start or what to do next. This predicament is common in everyday work, but the help case has rarely been addressed by help system writers and is not directly supported in most graphical user interfaces. Ideally, this help case ought to be supported by its own dedicated mechanism or tool. In some circumstances, the user may not even know that help is needed. This is most typical on system start-up or on entry to a dialogue box or window. When the user does not know that help is required, the help case must be initiated by the software or by inaction on the part of the user, which is an example of what might better be termed `offeringSuggestion`.

Several help cases commonly serve as extensions for other uses of help systems, notably `seekingClarification` and `seekingElaboration`, but also sometimes `seekingInstruction`, especially in the sense of requesting an actual demonstration. So common are these needs that well-planned help entries should routinely provide a set of three buttons or links—**Explain**, **More**, and **Show**—to give users access to another explanation, advanced or detailed information, and a demonstration or assisted walk-through, respectively.

Users who have some experience with a system but are still learning often need brief reminders about features or facilities that they have used before. The help case `seekingReminder` is best supported by providing brief synopses or digests of more elaborate help, especially instructional help. Help that is written in an appropriate style, starting with an overview, will tend to cover this case without additional attention (more about help style in a later section on writing help).

Features that are needed but that are not visible pose challenges. Especially for infrequent tasks, the user may remember a feature and even remember how to use it but may not know where to find it among the interaction contexts of the user interface. Procedural help that shows how to accomplish a task sometimes omits where the user must go to start the task. The help case `seekingLocation` should be answered by the system by pointing or by tracing or showing a route to the desired feature.

Finally, the help case `exploringFeatures` is typical of beginning users, but more experienced users who are ready to discover and try new things are also interested in this form of help. The typical table of contents or topic lists within help files are seldom effective for this purpose. Tutorials and automated "tours" of software tend to focus too much on basics and do not, typically, leave the user free to wander around the user interface to get a feel for its structure and contents. We have seen users scan through menus and lists of custom components in their attempts to satisfy this help case.

FIGURE 11-1 *Procedural help contents organized by use cases—almost.*
(MICROSOFT EXCEL)

ORGANIZING HELP BY USE CASES

A problem for users seeking procedural help, the **seekingInstruction** help case, is telling the system what it is they want to accomplish. Finding the needed help is facilitated by extensive, well-conceived indexing, and quasi-intelligent searching mechanisms, such as Microsoft's "Answer Wizard," can be useful if implemented well and supported by rich help files. However, some very simple approaches can make finding procedural help easier and more reliable.

Procedural help is most helpful when it is organized by use cases that are titled and written in the ordinary language of the users and the application domain and that are well indexed. Use cases are a natural for organizing and providing access to help because they represent the basic interests of users. Each essential use case is a complete and well-defined task based on something a user might try to accomplish. If the essential task model has been well constructed, then it will reflect how users think about and conduct their work. Each use case becomes an entry in the help file. The use of more or less standard forms and naming conventions facilitates users in finding what they need. This has already become a common practice for the contents of

> *Essential use cases are natural for organizing and providing access to help because they represent the basic interests of users.*

many help files, as, for example, in the partial contents shown in Figure 11-1. Many of the entries shown might as well be the names of use cases.

For another example, from our now familiar problem of the keyboard extender applet, the user would expect to find help under headings such as these:

```
Defining
    new collections of symbols or special characters
Inserting
    single special symbol or special character
    phrase or series of symbols or special characters
```

The first two entries should also be listed under **symbol, Inserting** or **character, Inserting**, and the last entry should also be reachable by requesting help on **phrase** or **string**.

ACCESS AND PRESENTATION TECHNIQUES

Modern graphical user interfaces provide a variety of mechanisms for the user to gain access to on-line help and for the system to present help. Both access and presentation techniques should fit the specific help case. Available modern access techniques include access by fly-over, on pause, by indication, by index, and by search. Presentation techniques include display in a separate window, on a status bar, or at the current pointer position.

DISPLAYING HELP

On-line help can be presented in a number of different ways at various points within the visual display:

- At the cursor or pointer
- On the status bar
- As a hint or panel within an application window or dialogue
- In a separate, independent window
- In "cue cards" or autonomous messages

The current position of the cursor or pointer is, of course, the most likely focus of the user's attention. Help messages that pop up at or near this position are effective for both identification help and, in some instances, for procedural help. For example, so-called tool tips or hints that pop up to identify active visual objects on the user interface have proven both popular and effective for the **seekingIdentification** help case.

Status bar messages are a standard feature of Windows-based systems. They are most often used to provide context help on menu items or to augment identification help on tools or other features. In either capacity, the status bar has problems. Its position at the bottom of the screen places it in the least noticed part of the visual field. The reduced contrast of standard color schemes, which place thin, black text on a medium-gray background, makes it even more likely that help displayed in this position will be missed by the user. In fact, some users remain permanently and blissfully unaware of the helpful messages being intermittently supplied by software on the status bar. This should be regarded as a defect of the status bar as a bearer of significant messages, not as a sign of user ineptitude.

> *Some users remain permanently and blissfully unaware of the status bar messages hidden at the bottom of the screen.*

Status bar display is also sometimes used with good intentions to supply a helpful starting hint as a default when the user first launches an application or opens a dialogue box, which supports the help case of **seekingSuggestion** or **offeringSuggestion**. This use can be especially appropriate where there is some important hidden behavior or feature about which the new user might not otherwise become aware. However, the user is perhaps only slightly more likely to notice and read a message on the status bar when a window first opens than later in the course of ongoing interaction. An apparent need for a starting hint may be a good indication to the designer that an alternative design should be sought. Panels or frames within a dialogue or window often provide a better place to present essential hints, such as a hint on how to get started. An example is illustrated at the top of Figure 11-2. Another alterna-

> *An apparent need for a starting hint may be a good indication to the designer that an alternative user interface design should be sought.*

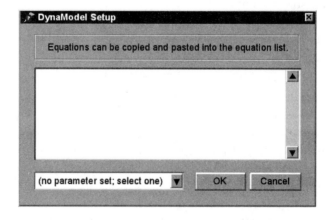

FIGURE 11-2 *Hints for getting started.*

FIGURE 11-3 *Cue card that offers a way of providing procedural help.*

tive is to present hints in context—for example, by utilizing the empty state or null value of a field to suggest appropriate action, as illustrated in the lower left of Figure 11-2.

As first mentioned in Chapter 3, if you must use the status bar and you want to assure that the user attends to the help being proffered, you might want to consider using color or apparent motion to attract the user's attention. Start-up hints on the status bar could be flashed once when a dialogue first opens, but a still better practice would be to establish a standard and distinctive color for start-up hints that differentiates them from other messages on the status bar. Dark red is a good candidate. Such start-up hints are more likely to be noticed by a first-time user without being terribly distracting to more advanced ones.

Conventional help files typically display their contents in a separate window independent of the active window. In practice, such help often seems to be consistently in the wrong place at the wrong time, either blocking parts of the screen that are of interest to the user or, conversely, dropping behind the window of interest when the active focus is switched. Status bar help has at least the advantage of appearing in a fixed location as part of the active window. With conventional help displayed in a separate window, window management can become a significant factor in reducing the usability of the help, especially for the **seekingInstruction** help case, where the user needs to follow a series of instructions.

Cue cards, as in the example shown in Figure 11-3, display as autonomous messages on top of the active window. Typically, cue cards support the **seekingInstruction** help case, presenting the user with successive steps to be performed to complete a task.

ACCESS TO HELP

Help can be activated through a variety of mechanisms that should be chosen to suit the help case and to fit with the rest of the user interface design. A number of techniques put activation wholly or partially under control of the software. These include

- Static, permanent display (e.g., fixed hints or prompts)
- Automatic display on system start-up (e.g., "tip of the day")
- Automatic display on window or dialogue opening (e.g., first-step hint)
- Automatic, spontaneous display by algorithm or analysis (e.g., "tip wizards")
- Automatic display on feature use (e.g., transition hint of keyboard shortcut)
- Automatic display on time delay (e.g., tool tips)

Other activation techniques require explicit user action. Examples include

- Key press
- Menu selection
- Tool selection

Help activation can also be modal or nonmodal. For example, in many systems, clicking on a question mark tool will change the cursor appearance and put the software into a context help mode. Pointing at an on-screen object yields a brief pop-up message defining, describing, or explaining the object and its uses. Modal help may be persistent, remaining on until explicitly turned off by the user, or it may function for only a single use or query. Occasionally, persistent and nonpersistent modes are mixed in one modal help facility, although the effect can be disconcerting. For example, the context help tool in Word for Windows 7.0 is persistent when used to query about objects within a document but is nonpersistent if used on a tool or other active interface element.

The majority of users probably think of software help in terms of the content of separate help files reached via the **F1** key or the **Help** menu and accessed through an index or by searching. However, this form of help can be too cumbersome for simple questions regarding visible features within the current interaction context. It works best for more extended queries, such as the help cases of **seekingLocation** and **seekingInstruction**, or for ones involving objects that are not visible and cannot be pointed to. The success of the user in getting the needed help will depend in large measure on how well the help files are organized and indexed. Organization by use cases with extensive cross-referencing, paraphrasing, and alternative terms will make it easier for users to find what they seek.

Conventional "context help," such as obtained with **Shift+F1** in Windows, gives access to help by indication; the user merely clicks on the object of interest. Its most obvious and appropriate use is to answer the question, What is this? Often it is also appropriate for the software to provide an answer to the related question, How do I use this?

Apple's original "balloon help" on the Macintosh, mentioned in Chapter 3, was an example of fly-over activation, in which the pointer passing over any enabled feature triggers a brief pop-up message. The activation-on-pause technique that later became common for tool tips is much better for the **seekingIdentification** help case, but fly-over help may yet have some appropriate applications. The **exploringFeatures** help case is not well supported by pop-up-on-pause help because the pointer has to rest on something before the hint appears and because the help messages are often far too brief. Some implementations of pop-up tool-tip help will display successive hints as the pointer moves to other tools, but this trick works only as long as the pointer moves slowly enough and does not pass over a visual component for which no pop-up help is available. Context help, activated by point-and-click, also does not work well for exploring because most implementations allow the user only one selection before the pointer reverts to its normal shape and function. To explore with the context help pointer, the user would have to keep turning it back on either with **Shift+F1** or by going back to the toolbar.

> *Neither pop-up tool tips nor context help work well for exploring user interface features.*

Exploration would be better supported by a form of modal fly-over help that allowed less experienced users to wander over the interface with the pointer shifted into "exploring" mode, getting explanations and suggestions regarding anything they pass. This help mode should be easily and instantaneously turned on or off, and the pop-up tips or descriptions should be brief but not as terse as typical tool tips. Windows conventions provide some help of this sort on the status bar coupled to tool-tip pop-ups and to menus. However, help displayed on the status bar is unobtrusive to a fault, so unnoticeable that many users remain unaware of it even after extensive experience. Bouncing the gaze from pointer to status line and back is so inconvenient that most users make little or no use of the facility, especially for **exploringFeatures**.

Fly-over help that pops up spontaneously in context, at the location of the pointer, is far better suited to exploring the interface. The problem is how to turn such fly-over help on and off. Tool tips and other pop-up help use a triggering mechanism almost perfectly tailored to **seekingIdentification** because the user need do nothing to discover and use the capability. Just doing nothing is precisely what brings up a tool tip.

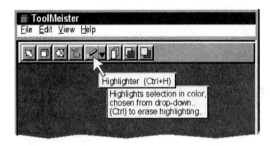

FIGURE 11-4 *Visual design of cascaded "tool-tip" help for* **seekingElaboration** *help case.*

Designing the perfect access technique for fly-over exploration will probably take research and laboratory testing, but a workable scheme would be a modal variant of conventional context help. A tool button on the toolbar would turn on fly-over help and then turn it off when clicked again. Software targeted for rank novices might initialize with fly-over help enabled, along with a static message saying how to turn it off, but this is another trick that could backfire and alienate first-time users, so laboratory testing and market research would be desirable.

Sometimes, users want more information than is typically provided by tool tips or fly-over help. The **seekingElaboration** help case might be supportable through added information displayed automatically after a longer pause. For this to be effective, it is important to maintain visual object persistence. The original "balloon" and its text should not be replaced—the user might still be interested in the contents—but extended. A cascading display, such as shown in Figure 11-4, has the right behavior and visual properties. Here again, laboratory and field testing would be needed to determine the optimal delay time for such cascaded help, but it is probably in the range of 1 to 3 times the initial time-out for the tool tip to appear.

The trick of activating help after a time-out has still other potential uses—in particular, to support **seekingSuggestion** or **offeringSuggestion**. For example, when a dialogue first opens, if the user takes no action within a reasonable period of time, the software might display a pop-up hint about where to start or what to do next. Such a hint would be dismissed by any subsequent action by the user. To avoid annoying the more experienced user who is merely taking time to think, the delay could be increased after the first display of a given hint.

SPECIAL TECHNIQUES AND MODALITIES

SOUND AND SLAPSTICK

Both sound and animation can have their uses in providing users with help. Sound appears to be a promising channel for presenting procedural help, the `seekingInstruction` help case, especially for intermittent or infrequent users of systems. Audible help could offer several advantages over written text that must be read from the screen by the user. Aural input is concurrent with vision; while audible help is playing, the user can still see the entire screen and can carry out actions being described. The user does not have to remember written instruc-

> *Audible help is concurrent— the user does not have to remember written instructions while attempting some task.*

tions while attempting some task. Audio playback supplementing visual presentation can make direction easier to understand. On the other hand, for most users, reading is much faster than spoken words. Recorded instructions are also difficult for users to review. Rewinding a playback to listen again is considerably clumsier than just shifting the eyes and rereading a sentence. Furthermore, even with the best of current compression techniques, audio-supplemented help files can grow enormous. Of course, disk space is becoming ever cheaper and more abundant, and improvements in speech synthesis from text could make audible help practical in a wider range of applications.

Although sound would seem, in principle, to have an edge over displayed text for procedural help, in practice, many experienced software users are reluctant to change work habits to listen to help. In fact, users typically read along from written text as they listen to spoken instructions, so the potential efficiency of concurrent activity is often lost [Reeves et al., 1996].

Animation, like sound, is probably most effective for procedural help. An animated demonstration can either point to successive steps for the user to perform, simulate performance, or actually carry out complex tasks. To be most effective, animated help needs to be fast and used selectively. Silly or inconsequential animation, such as animated faces, are even more annoying when the user is seeking help than at other times.

Based on how people learn to perform tasks, the animated methods of supporting `seekingInstruction` can be ranked in terms of their expected effectiveness for complex tasks. For simple tasks, the differences between user-paced coaching and demonstrating may be inconsequential, since the user can easily recall the demonstrated sequence to enact it. In any case, directions or explanations can be presented in pop-up messages, aurally, or both:

1. Indicate and explain successive steps, paced by user performing each step.

2. Indicate successive steps, without explanation, paced by user performance.

3. Demonstrate and explain successive steps at preset pace.

4. Demonstrate, without explanation, successive steps at preset pace.

5. Actually perform and explain successive steps for user at preset pace.

6. Actually perform, without explanation, successive steps at preset pace.

7. Perform entire operation for user without demonstration or explanation.

In truth, most people learn to perform tasks most quickly and thoroughly by actually doing them. Some users may prefer to be walked through their first attempt, while others may prefer to see something demonstrated before trying it, but no one really learns how to do something by having other people or software do it.

> *Software wizards that simplify complex tasks by performing them magically behind the scene are of little or no value as teaching agents.*

For this reason, "wizards," or software subsystems that simplify complex tasks by performing them magically behind the scene, are of little or no value as teaching agents. Such wizards are best used to automate infrequent tasks that users will be unlikely to perform manually.

TUTORING

Software-based tutorials provide yet another mode for offering help. Tutorials present extended instruction, most often on a group of features, possibly on an entire system. They are typically and appropriately directed toward first-time and less experienced users. Even well-done tutorials are ill-suited to finding help regarding a specific feature. Like other forms of procedural help, tutorials can be interactive and adaptive to user input or merely fixed presentations with no participation by the user.

> *Software tutorials are often little more than demos to show off florid features or the programming prowess of the developers.*

On-line tutorials can be considered a special application of computer-based training, a broad area of educational technology with great potential. Software can provide branching, conditional instruction that adapts to the pace and specific problems of each user. Regrettably, tutorials incorporated into software applications are often little more than demos that show off florid features of the software or the programming prowess of the developers better than they teach the untutored user. The boundary between demonstration and tutorial is so often blurred that many users do not even bother to try the tutorials that accompany major soft-

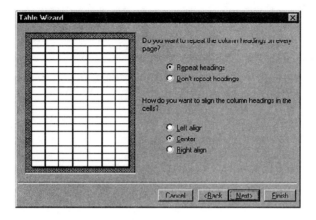

FIGURE 11-5 *Tables by wizardry.*
(Microsoft Word)

ware packages. Even when consulted for an introductory overview, a tutorial is unlikely to be revisited by the same user.

Like prototypes, tutorials can be implemented as software in conventional programming languages or in more limited or special-purpose media. Assembling a good tutorial can be a major development effort in itself, drawing on expertise in training, programming, and writing. In light of the heavy development investment compared to the limited uses, tutorials are not a high priority for good help system design.

SOFTWARE MAGIC

Wizards have become a popular feature of desktop software, especially in feature-laden productivity tools and office suites, but they have also begun to pop up in software development tools and even in some more narrowly focused applications. A wizard typically prepares and carries out some task for the user based on the user responses to a series of questions.

Wizards are a special form of the incremental interaction interface model. In this model, complex tasks are broken down into a sequence of small steps presented as a succession of panels, each panel replacing the previous one. Figure 11-5 shows an example. Each step requires, at most, a decision or two or a few simple responses from the user. Normally, the user has only the option of going forward or back one step or of canceling the task altogether. Wizards are clearly distinguished from ordinary dialogues not only by the succession

> *Instead of fixing usability problems, some developers just stick a wizard on the front end and call it an advanced feature.*

FIGURE 11-6 *Irritating interruption from a useless wizard.*
(MICROSOFT WINDOWS 95)

of small steps but also by the way in which they perform their apparent magic. As a rule, the wizard waits until all user information and input is obtained before carrying out a task behind the scenes.

Well-designed wizards can hide, or at least disguise, messy or complex interfaces. For this reason, wizards have too often been used to avoid or delay needed revision of badly conceived and poorly constructed interfaces. Instead of fixing usability problems, some developers just stick a wizard on the front end and call it an advanced feature or selling point. Unfortunately for the user, using a wizard to paper over a messy interface at best only improves usability for the specific problem covered by the wizard. Users of wizards seldom learn how to perform the task themselves, so they remain dependent on the wizard and restricted to its narrow capabilities. As for the rest of the user interface, users will be left on their own.

Used appropriately, wizards enable users without detailed or advanced knowledge to accomplish complex, obscure, or seldom performed tasks, such as preparing a document master template or configuring a network card. Wizards can also implement specialized enhancements or extensions to applications, such as the construction of a special-purpose spreadsheet. In their simplest implementations, wizards do little more than impose an order on an intrinsically unordered, multidimensional specification process, as in the example in Figure 11-5. In such cases, the simplification is usually achieved at the expense of making the process much more lengthy and involved.

Unfortunately, being fashionable, wizards have sometimes been used merely for showing off or for pointless purposes, such as the irritating interruption provided by the wizard shown in Figure 11-6, which appears when a Windows 95 Briefcase is first used. The folder should merely initialize itself quietly behind the scenes and not annoy the user with a blocking message offering no choices.

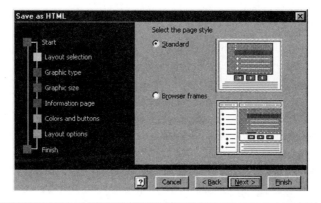

FIGURE 11-7 *Well-behaved wizard.*
(Microsoft PowerPoint 97)

Designing the magic. All of the principles of good user interface design apply to wizards, of course, but it can be helpful to keep some special considerations in mind. Navigation is a significant problem; in working through the successive steps of a wizard, users can become lost not knowing what they are getting into, where they are in the process, or how far they have to go before they are done. Wizards should start by providing an overview of the process—what it will accomplish and what it will entail—at the outset. The user should be kept informed of progress in functional terms instead of by arbitrary indexes, such as percent complete or "step 2 of 5." An exemplary wizard in this regard is shown in Figure 11-7, which provides an overview, shows progress, and gives the user direct access to specific steps through the same active widget on the left. Note the inclusion of a help button.

Many real-world wizards throw users an occasional curve with some bit of technical jargon. As with other kinds of dialogues, wizards should use simple, nontechnical language or the language of the application domain. Questions and choices should be expressed in terms of the user's intentions and goals so that the consequences of particular user actions are evident. It should be easy for users to see the effects of their choices. The wizard should make clear what is being asked and why, as well as how the user should respond. When launched, the wizard should tell the user what it can and will do as well as what it cannot do.

> *The wizard should make clear what is being asked and why, as well as how the user is expected to respond.*

A common problem is that most wizards either do the whole job or do nothing at all. If interrupted, they have to be restarted from scratch. The user may have already gone through half a dozen steps only to discover that a requested bit of information is not available or that some change in a document needs to be made first. It should be possible to suspend and restart wizards, using already entered settings.

While active, wizards should allow users to carry out normal activities and interaction, such as file maintenance, searches, and the like. Most importantly and often omitted, wizards should support full access to the help system.

> *Wizards function best as tutors when they carry out tasks by the same means available to users and actively demonstrate how these means are employed to accomplish the tasks.*

Watch Mr. Wizard. Wizards can also be used to tutor users in how to use advanced features, but this kind of application requires special design considerations. To be effective at providing help, wizards must not do all the work by magic behind the scene. The questions to the user and the steps taken by the wizard should be fairly obvious and simply related to the direct methods by which the user could carry out the same task.

A wizard that utilizes facilities that are not otherwise directly available to the user will not be teaching the user anything. For example, Windows 95 has the ability to automatically configure hardware and set properties, but this capability is available only through the **Add New Hardware Wizard** and only if the user lets the wizard take the lengthy, redundant, and sometimes risky course of searching for all hardware. Users who choose to install a specific piece of hardware by name must do all setting manually, even though the correct settings may be known to the operating system. Wizards function best as tutors when they carry out tasks by the same means available to users and actively demonstrate how these means are employed to accomplish the tasks.

> *Technical writers are better prepared to create readable help expressed in user-oriented terms, but documentation and on-line help are probably best created through close cooperation between writers and developers.*

Unfortunately, even the sophisticated kind of animated-help wizards provided by high-end office software, such as Office 97, are often more significant for their sales appeal than for their ability to support real work. Many users find the continuous animation in some of these wizards a serious distraction.

HELPFUL WRITING

As with all writing, the writing of good help files, help messages, and help system entries requires a certain degree of talent and skill. For the most part, programmers are not the most successful help writers not only because they may lack writing skills in general but also because their perspective is inside-out and deeply colored by

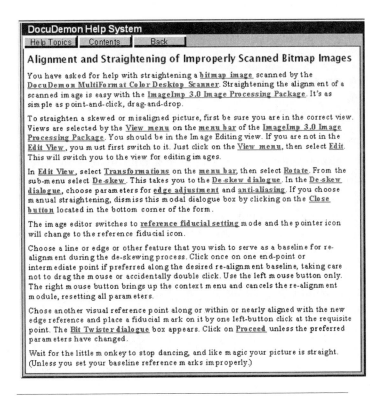

FIGURE 11-8 *How to straighten a picture the hard way.*

their familiarity with the code and the internal structure of the software. Instead of writing in the language of users, they tend to write in geek-speak.

Technical writers or trainers are better prepared to create readable help expressed in user-oriented terms, but, left on their own, they can sometimes fall short in other ways. Some systems have been delivered with well-written, well-organized, but useless on-line help; it was simply wrong. The help writers may have misunderstood technical issues, or some features may have changed without their knowledge. Without close and continual communication between developers and technical writers, the help and documentation often do not match the system, which can make for help that can be worse than no help at all.

Both documentation and on-line help are probably best created through close cooperation between developers and documenters. Documentation and help system creation should proceed concurrently with the rest of the development processes, with frequent coordination and cross-checking.

All too often, documentation and help are written in a mix of techno-babble and phony friendliness that just takes up time and file space. The example in Figure 11-8 is typical. It begins with an introductory paragraph that, in this context, is pure noise. The bewildered user has to wade through the contentless introduction just to get to the wordy but still nearly worthless content. The surfeit of links just adds to the visual and conceptual clutter.

ELEMENTS OF HELP STYLE

How do you write good documentation and on-line help?

- Get to the point.

People seek help because they are trying to accomplish something. Their work is already interrupted. Help should not waste more of their time with long introductions, empty fill, or distracting side discussions. Users just want to get the answers to their questions and then get back to work.

The very best help is written in the style of classic newspaper journalism. The traditional advice to newspaper reporters is

- Tell the whole story in the headline.
- Tell the whole story in the first sentence.
- Tell the whole story in the first paragraph.

Wherever readers may stop reading, they will already know the whole story. With this format, readers are free to choose how much detail or depth is appropriate to their needs and interests. Some readers will just scan the headlines. Some may read the lead of some stories and peruse others in full. Help file entries written in this journalistic style give the user control and require only the time needed by a given user to answer a particular need.

> *Help written in traditional journalistic style leaves users free to choose how much detail or depth is appropriate to their needs and interests.*

Good documentation and help uses an absolutely consistent vocabulary. If you call a thing a "reference fiducial" in one place, don't refer to it as a "baseline mark" in another. "De-skewing," "straightening," "re-alignment," and "baseline rotation" may be interchangeable terms to the programmer, but using them interchangeably in help text will only confuse the user.

As with every aspect of the user interface, the vocabulary of documentation and help should be primarily that of the users and the application domain, augmented with ordinary, everyday language. Specialized terms, concepts, or usage applicable only to a particular software package should be kept to a minimum. Marketing people love to devise their own proprietary terms for everything, preferring neologisms that can be trademarked to simple language. This practice

> *Users are abused when everyday features are given specialized names or branded labels.*

may seem to serve business needs, but it does not serve users who, in effect, may have to switch languages every time they switch packages. Genuine innovations perhaps warrant original terms, but it is better for users if we simply call a thing what it is. Users are abused when everyday features like draft-quality printing are given special names like "EconoMode." Help files and documentation are not advertisements. Rhapsodizing the wonders of the software merely encourages cynicism and distrust from users and gives them one more reason not to consult the help system.

Another rule of writing good help is

- Tell users something they don't know.

Simple language does not have to be simplistic or simpleminded. Help that merely restates the obvious is no help and discourages future use of help. In one system, a request for help from within a font setting dialogue yielded this useless tidbit:

This is the Font Change dialogue. It is accessed through the Preferences selection of the Special menu.

Keeping in mind that your users are working, avoid being overly cute or too "user friendly." Help should be succinct without becoming abrupt.

DOCUMENTATION VERSUS HELP

Documentation and help serve different purposes. Documentation is not a substitute for help, even though documentation is sometimes turned to for help. Documentation records or documents; help helps. On-line help files and printed documentation should agree, but printouts of help files make inferior

BROWSING HELP

Modern help file organization and operation discourage browsing or exploration. In most systems, there is no simple way to page through successive pages or entries in the help file, even though the help files may have been generated automatically or semiautomatically by processing the document files for printed manuals.

The human eye and visual cortex form a remarkably efficient search engine and pattern recognition system. Many people can flip rapidly through a book to find a particular page with some distinguishing visual characteristic, such as text in a particular shape or font or a page with a vaguely remembered diagram in the middle. In these high-speed visual searches, much of the information is processed almost unconsciously. Experienced copy editors can often spot misspelled words in the middle of a page even as they riffle rapidly through a book or manuscript.

Browsing is also a good way to find things of interest or to get an overview of the organization of a system. Flipping through a manual often gives a better sense of what a piece of software is about than reading a summary or outline.

Modern help systems have specific characteristics and features that make casual exploration or scanning exceedingly clumsy. First, information is broken down into many small, separate articles. Second, these are arranged in a hierarchy and interconnected by interposed links that must be traversed to move from one small piece to another. To appreciate fully how maddening this seemingly reasonable organization can be, try reading through the on-line help for Windows, starting with the **Contents** page of the **Help Topics** tabbed dialogue reachable from the **Start** menu. You will find yourself bouncing up and down and flipping back and forth between windows, drilling down multiple levels, and then trying to back up without losing track of where you are and where you were trying to go.

A more usage-centered help dialogue would include a toolbar that incorporates a **Next** tool to trace through the contents hierarchy one topic at a time. Holding the tool button down might page continuously through the topics at a reasonable page-turning pace.

manuals, and help files generated automatically from the document files for manuals are often less than helpful.

The industry trend may be away from bound reference manuals and user guides, but printed documentation has numerous advantages over on-line help. A manual can be read anywhere without special hardware or software. The batteries never wear out on a manual. Printed text is easier to read than on-screen displays. A manual can be read or referred to without covering any part of the screen. In a surprising number of cases, information can be found more quickly by flipping pages of a manual than by expression-searching through an on-line file. (See sidebar, Browsing Help.)

Software vendors prefer to ship everything on a CD-ROM. It saves paper and postage and can simplify production and version control. As long as the different functions and desirable characteristics of documentation and help are kept straight, there is little inherently wrong with this practice. Ultimately, the marketplace will decide how much customers want and are willing to pay for paper documentation. To some extent, it is a matter of price points. The retail purchaser of a home office product who spends less than $100 may accept just a jewel case with a CD-ROM, but the corporate buyer of a $5,000 software package may expect to get a big box. As consultant Tim Lister has often said, people like stuff. A box with a CD-ROM, two thick manuals, a loose-leaf notebook, a plastic template, and two pocket summary cards can have far more perceived value than a CD-ROM in a cardboard sleeve.

EFFECTIVE HELP

What form of help works best? It depends on what you mean by help and what you mean by best. One reasonable index of success is cost effectiveness. Having your own personal PowerPoint trainer and consultant may yield efficient help, but it is not very cost-effective.

For procedural help—finding out how to do something—Jared Spool and his colleagues have ranked various sources of help in terms of cost effectiveness. Independent of other factors, help sources were ranked from least cost-effective, relatively most expensive, to most cost-effective as follows:

- Live support from peers
- Trained technical support staff
- Printed tutorials
- On-line tutorials
- Printed reference manuals
- Printed user guides
- On-line help files
- Active on-line help (e.g., instructional wizards or cue cards)
- Instructive interfaces

In-person support from one's professional peers may be convenient and dependable, but it is also relatively expensive when all costs are factored in. Specialized technical support is somewhat more efficient. Printed and on-line tutorials may cost less in themselves, but they are time-consuming for the user. Printed reference manuals and user guides are also cheap to produce but typically yield answers more quickly and efficiently than tutorials. Wizards and cue cards, when well designed for instructional purposes, are considered by Spool and his colleagues to be more cost-effective than traditional on-line help files.

> *The most cost-effective help is in the form of instructive interfaces that use affordances, constraints, visual object persistence, and consistency to guide users.*

Most cost-effective of all are instructive interfaces, as described in Chapter 9. Instructive interfaces are intuitable and explorable. They employ visual object persistence along with affordances and constraints to guide users implicitly in using a system. Through consistent extension and idiomatic elaboration, they enable users to learn new features and facilities almost unconsciously. In other words (surprise, surprise), the cheapest and most cost-effective help is achieved when no help is needed!

How effective help is in practice depends on how it is used, and it is not always possible to anticipate either the needs of users for help or how they will try to meet those needs. Help systems need to be tested and refined from experience.

The standard approach to usability testing subjects the user interface to a workout but not the help system, which is often not available until just before the shipping date. In the lab, the testers end up simulating the help system themselves. Beta versions are almost always released with incomplete or missing help files.

We favor help and documentation development as concurrent activities in parallel with software design and programming. Help systems should be properly field-tested along with early-release versions.

HELPFUL MESSAGES

A programmer concentrating on tracking an elusive bug does not want to be interrupted by unimportant phone calls or distracted by email announcements popping up on the screen. On the other hand, the same programmer would probably want to be told that the server was about to be shut down or that the building was on fire.

> *If the user either does not know what is happening or is constantly interrupted by messages, it will be harder to accomplish work.*

Although the Feedback Principle (Chapter 3) exhorts the user interface designer to keep the user informed, good design strikes a balance. If the user does not know what is happening within the software or is, at the other extreme, constantly interrupted by verbose or uninformative messages, it will be harder to accomplish work reliably and efficiently. Feedback given through various messages is an important factor in how supportive and helpful a software system will be. This is especially true of error messages, but the presence or absence as well as the content and style of all manner of feedback to the user will influence usability.

MESSAGES AND MEDIA

Most programmers think of communicating with users as something to be accomplished through dialogue boxes or explicit messages displayed on the status bar or in message boxes, but feedback comprises any and all information conveyed to the user through the user interface. Feedback takes various forms and can be

- Intrinsic or extrinsic
- In context or out of context
- Blocking or nonblocking

When the user presses the **Del** key, some object on the screen disappears, visually confirming that it has been deleted. Such *intrinsic* feedback communicates with users through the natural, logical, and apparently direct consequences of their actions. For example, changing the size of an object within a drawing package—whether through a dialogue box, with a spin button, or by dragging the object's "resizing handles"—does not require confirmation through a message box announcing "**Object successfully resized.**" That the object has been resized is communicated intrinsically as a result of the operation itself and its effects on the display. Intrinsic feedback is often the most efficient way to communicate with users. *Extrinsic* feedback, in which the message is conveyed through some independent carrier, such as a message box, is more likely to interrupt the flow of work.

> *Information displayed in context where the user is working and where the information applies is more likely to be interpreted rapidly and correctly by the user.*

Information can be conveyed to users either *in context* or *out of context*. In-context communication places information within data displays and work areas where the user is working and where the information applies. For example, the cursor may change shape, letting the user of a drawing package know that the software is operating in line-drawing mode. In modern word processors, for another example, misspelled words can be automatically flagged within a document by a red squiggle or some other distinctive marking. This is in-context feedback. Alternatively, a spell checker can display a separate dialogue, out of context, that gives a message about each misspelled word. As a rule, in-context information is more likely to be interpreted rapidly and correctly by the user than information presented out of context. Out-of-context presentation is more likely to interrupt the user's work, which can be a shortcoming or can be used to advantage, as in those circumstances when it is important—to the user—to grab the user's attention.

Intrinsic/extrinsic and in-context/out-of-context forms of communication can be mixed. A rotating hourglass is not an intrinsic indicator of processing, but it is likely to be in context. Animated documents flying across the screen are a more or less natural representation of a file transfer, but the feedback is not intrinsic and the dialogue box appears out of context.

Another way to categorize messages is whether they are communicated by *modal* or *nonmodal* mechanisms. A modal message requires a user response before the message goes away and allows user interaction or processing to continue. Nonmodal messages go away on their own, either after a set time period, once some particular kind of event has taken place, or upon some other action by the user. For example, context help typically displays a nonmodal identification message that disappears as soon as the user clicks on another object or types something.

From the user's standpoint, however, the issue is not the form of dialogue or message display, but whether the message, in itself, prevents or permits further interaction by the user on whatever is of interest. In other words, is the feedback *blocking* or *nonblocking*? Modal messages are sometimes referred to as "blocking bulletins" [Cooper, 1995] because they block the user from continuing with a task, but the ubiquitous "wait state" cursor can also be a form of blocking feedback. Nonblocking feedback is any form of communication that does not interrupt and prevent continuation of work until the user makes some specific explicit response, such as closing a dialogue box or tapping the **Enter** key.

MESSAGE MODELS

Software messages can be categorized depending on the kind of information they are intended to convey. Messages are commonly used to communicate:

- Errors
- Alerts or warnings
- Progress
- Completion
- Confirmations

Error messages inform the user that an error has been found in data or has occurred in the course of processing. Alerts or warnings are intended to be informative, bringing to the user's attention some condition—short of an outright error—presumed to be of interest or importance. Progress messages, such as the familiar animated **File Copy** in Windows, communicate to the user the progressive performance of some relatively prolonged task. Completion messages inform users when some protracted action or process of indeterminate duration has finished.

Error messages are quite possibly the most common form of message to users, and therein lies a problem. They are probably too common. Programmers often solve programming problems by sending an error message. A buffer overflows, a loop takes an exceptional branch, or an unexpected value is found in a field: The programmer sets an error flag and throws up a message box. Typically, the message itself is conceived and written from the perspective of the programmer or the program itself: "**Error 125.6: Deferred action buffer overflow.**" The results, all too often, are annoying, confusing, or meaningless to users. In any case, they interrupt the work and prevent the user from continuing until after the message is dismissed.

> *Programmers often solve programming problems by sending error messages that are annoying, confusing, or meaningless to users.*

Equally bad are so-called error messages that are not errors at all, but only the result of programming without thinking. For example, consider the poor users of client software for one on-line service. If you change your mind about picking up email and click on the **Stop** button, you must first confirm that you really meant to do what you did. Then, with insult added to interruption, you are blocked again by the totally pointless and misrepresentative error message shown in Figure 11-9, which basically tells you that you were mistaken in your deliberate and confirmed action. If you foolishly fall for the offer of more information, you get a vacuous help file entry that says, in effect, you are wrong, stupid:

> **Your connection was aborted, or canceled, before it was completed. Please try to connect again.**

Duh.

In reaction to the overuse of error messages, Alan Cooper [1995] has proposed a radical position: Error messages should be eliminated. They block the progress of work. They indicate a failure of the software to interpret information or handle

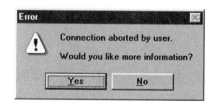

FIGURE 11-9 *Malignment by message.*
(COMPUSERVE 3.0.2)

a situation. They are evidence of failure on the part of programmers to analyze problems adequately and solve them effectively. Systems that are truly usable and well-designed have no need for error messages.

In usage-centered design, we take an engineering perspective on error messages, recognizing the inherent trade-offs in handling errors. The objective of usage-centered design is to reduce both user errors and error messages (more regarding both these objectives later in this chapter).

In many instances, it may be important but not essential that a user know that a particular action has been performed or that a process has been completed. In these cases, the system should reasonably try to assure that the user is aware of the condition, yet it need not require that the user acknowledge receipt of the message. This type of alert may best be handled by a message that, like context help, is displayed and remains "on top," in the visual foreground, until the user takes any action, such as clicking on a control or resuming typing.

> *Confirmations almost universally fail to protect users from the consequences of dangerous or irreversible actions.*

Confirmations are modal messages that require a user to confirm that an initiated action is intended. In an effort to protect users from unfortunate consequences of their own actions, accidental or intentional, confirmations have been used to ensure that dangerous or irreversible actions were actually intended. It must be recognized that confirmations almost universally fail to achieve this purpose. Users quickly learn, for example, to erase a disk by typing **Alt+D+E+Enter** to trigger the operation and immediately dismiss the confirmation dialogue.

In recent years, it seems that confirmations have proliferated, appearing for operations that are trivial or inconsequential. Sometimes, the messages lie, warning of dire consequences that are effectively imaginary, as in Figure 11-10, where the link alone will merely be sent to the recycle bin. Confirmations interrupt the progress of work and annoy users. Nearly all confirmations are unnecessary or ineffective. Reversible operation is far better than confirmation. Tolerant interfaces that support undoing most or all actions are far more usable.

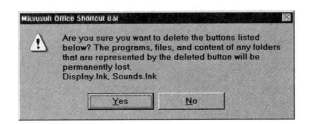

FIGURE 11-10 *False alarm.*
(MICROSOFT OFFICE)

FIGURE 11-11 *Say what?*
(SUN PC-NFS)

Some confirmations are so obscure that no ordinary person can be expected to make a reasonable interpretation. For example, in Figure 11-11, neither option makes much sense.

Confirmations are most appropriate under circumstances where the use case implies that the user can reasonably be expected to want to be informed of a condition or where no particular assumption on the part of the program is consistently reasonable and safe. A classic example occurs in the course of copying a collection of files where some of the files already exist at the destination and the creation details—file size, date-and-time stamp—do not match. Note that there is no excuse for a confirmation message when the files not only have the same name but also have the same file details. The program should go ahead and overwrite the file at the destination. (Overwriting may seem to waste time, but it is more consistent with the user intent—which is to copy—than is skipping. Overwriting also covers some uncommon but important specialized uses, such as being able to overwrite a corrupted copy of a file with a correct copy.)

> *Confirmations are most appropriate where the user can reasonably be expected to want to be informed of a condition or where no particular assumption by the program is consistently reasonable and safe.*

When confirmations are justified, it is especially important to help the user to make the right choice quickly, reliably, and safely. The designer should always ask, What is the important information for the user? How can it be presented to reduce the probability of error? The two confirmation messages from Windows 95 shown in Figure 11-12 are particularly poorly designed. One of these represents a risky situation, in which the user is about to overwrite a new file with an old one; the other represents a normal operation, in which an old file is being updated to a newer version. Which is which? They look alike. Important information is buried. Should the user click **Yes** or **No**? Only a very careful reading of the displayed file details will help the confused user decide correctly.

The redesigns shown in Figure 11-13 illustrate a number of the principles of good communication with users. They are much easier to interpret quickly and

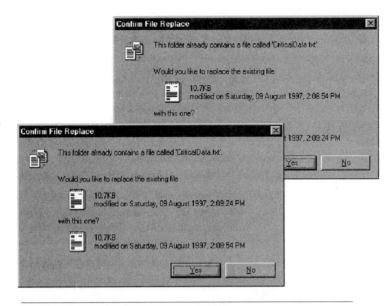

FIGURE 11-12 *Confusing and risky confirmations:* **Yes** *or* **No**?
(MICROSOFT WINDOWS 95)

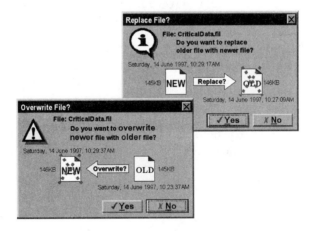

FIGURE 11-13 *Confirmations redesigned for rapid and reliable recognition.*

correctly because key information—the direction of transfer and which file is the older—has been highlighted and the differences between the two messages have been emphasized redundantly. The user does not have to study the file details to make an appropriate decision. In each case, should the user reflexively hit **Enter**, the default action will be the most reasonable and least risky.

ERROR PREVENTION

It is far better, whenever possible, to prevent user errors rather than to report them. As the preceding example illustrates, good communication can reduce user mistakes. Entry errors can be reduced through a variety of other means, including

- Formatted fill-in fields
- Displayed models or formats for input data
- Flexible parsing of input
- Automatic fill-in from codes or abbreviations
- Automatic completion of entries (e.g., combo boxes)
- Displayed codes and translation tables
- Selection sets (drop-down lists, option buttons, etc.)

To illustrate the various issues in reducing errors and reporting errors, we will take the process of entering a date as an example. The poorest form of user interface would merely prompt for a date or have a simple text entry box labeled **Date**. The user who enters an invalid date or one that cannot be interpreted might get a message like this:

> *It is far better to prevent user errors than to report them.*

Syntax error. Unparsable date field or invalid date.

The user does not know from this techno-babble whether the problem was with using dashes instead of slashes or with the order of entering month, day, and year. Any of the formats in Figure 11-14 is an improvement because at least the user knows what is expected. Users often prefer the first variation perhaps because it is more familiar and does not visually fragment what is often thought of as a single entity, but the second form is more common in current interface designs.

Even a free-form entry field can be improved by better, more sophisticated parsing that recognizes varied entry formats and may even be tailored by the

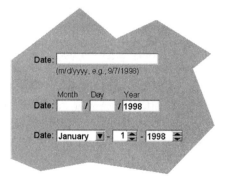

FIGURE 11-14 *Cueing the user to prevent input errors.*

global system settings for the user's preferred date format. Typing "9Aug97" into a data field should not result in a slap on the wrist to the user for entering alphanumeric data into a numeric field. In all cases where the interpretation is unambiguous, the program should do the required translation into the internal format and continue without bothering or interrupting the user.

In many instances where the user types an ambiguous entry or one that invites an unexpected interpretation, the best way to inform the user of how the program interpreted the input is simply to show the results in context by replacing the user's input with the formatted internal interpretation. For example, the user might type "20/11/97" into a date field. Instead of a put-down message box informing the user of the obvious fact that there are only 12 months in the year, the program could merely display **November 20, 1997** in the entry box, perhaps flagged in some way, such as with a distinct background, colored underlining, or a question mark.

> *Often the best way to inform the user of how input has been interpreted is simply to replace the input with the interpretation.*

Another way that can be used in some applications to reduce input errors and error messages for this example of date entry is to use a pop-up calendar widget and allow the user to select a date or dates by point-and-click. This technique eliminates a whole class of entry errors, such as typing "11/31/97" when the end of November is intended. As a rule, selection from among a displayed set of options—via check boxes, selection lists, combo boxes, or option buttons, for example—is more reliable than free-form text entry because typing errors are eliminated.

Where codes or abbreviations—such as item numbers, sales regions, and the like—are to be entered, entry errors can be reduced by several schemes. On-screen tables can help users remember codes, although typically, if there is enough screen real estate for a table, a selection list or option buttons might be a viable alternative. Feedback to the user showing the translation or interpretation of an entered code can also reduce errors. For example, the user might be called on to enter one of eight regional two-character sales codes. The software could respond by displaying the full name or definition of the region, which is readily verified visually by the user:

`MA - Mid-Atlantic States: NY, PA, NJ, DE, MD`

In the event a code cannot be interpreted, the user can be informed in the same way, through in-context feedback within the entry form rather than through a separate error message. For example, if the user mistyped "WR" as "QR," the field might be filled with

`QR? - Unrecognized sales region.`

Depending on the operational context, this "error message" might be reinforced both visually and audibly, for example, by setting the background of the field to a distinct colored pattern and sounding a quiet "ding."

RESISTING THE URGE

Within the program itself, developers should try to correct detected errors or faults, overcome them, or work around them rather than take the lazy way out and cast up an error message at every detection. More often than not, a bit of thought will reveal that there is some reasonable assumption the program can make that will yield reasonable, acceptable, and predictable results. Avoiding superfluous error messages requires the programmer to

- Make reasonable assumptions
- Take appropriate action
- Communicate the interpretation or action taken

Giving feedback to the user about how input was interpreted does not require using a message box at every turn. So-called informative messages interrupt the work every bit as much as error messages and are often even more annoying. In the sales region example, the invalid code **QR** might have only one probable match: **WR**. The program might interpret it as **WR** and flag it suitably as a guess.

WRITING MESSAGES

Filling in the content of useful error and exception messages is an art akin to writing help file entries. Good error and exception messages are

- Polite
- Informative
- Helpful

Writing polite error messages does not mean using "please" and "thank you" or taking up the user's time and attention with loquacious expressions of regret over some unfortunate occurrence. Well-written error messages are polite in that they do not imply that the user is at fault or has done something wrong. The language should certainly not imply that the user is stupid, ignorant, or careless. Error messages should be written from the perspective that it is the program that has a problem. All too many programs spew out insulting or demeaning messages, such as

```
Incomprehensible input. Type more carefully.
Repeated selection error. Re-enter your choice correctly or
seriously consider another career.
```

Fatal syntax error in command line. Where did you learn to program?

Programmers may think such messages are humorous, but most users are not amused, and some will be offended or discouraged from purchase or further use of the software.

Good error messages are also informative. They say exactly what happened and why it happened. They say it succinctly and in the language of the user, the application domain, and ordinary discourse. They eschew technical jargon and obscure terms.

Effective error messages are also helpful to the user. They not only tell what happened but also specify what the user can or should do in order to correct or overcome the problem:

> *Polite error messages do not use "please" and "thank you" or take up the user's time and attention with loquacious expressions of regret.*

CRITICAL COMMUNICATION ERROR

The server is not responding or the local system has become unstable.

Save all work in all active applications, then restart the system by pressing Ctrl+Alt+Del. Any unsaved work will be lost.

The absence of access to help in a modal error message is one of the most common and unhelpful shortcomings of error messages. Just when the user is most likely to need help, access to contextual help is blocked. All error messages should provide a help button leading to context-sensitive help.

As with help, the best style for messages begins with a banner head that states what happened, follows with a synopsis, a short sentence or phrase that summarizes or characterizes the error or condition, and finishes with an explanatory sentence or paragraph. Some writers and users prefer so-called telegraph style for the synopsis because it emphasizes content by suppressing "noise words. For example:

CRITICAL COMMUNICATION ERROR

Server not responding or local system unstable.

Save all work in all active applications. Then press Ctrl+Alt+Del to restart system. Any unsaved work will be lost.

All introductory clauses or stock phrases are noise and should be eliminated. Remember, the user just wants to understand what happened and get back to work as quickly as possible. It wastes disk space and user time to start off with

CRITICAL COMMUNICATION ERROR

A major operational problem has been detected by the communication protocol subsystem. A program condition has occurred that the

```
communication protocol subsystem is unable to interpret or correct
at this time...
```

No kidding. You have just used two full sentences—nearly 30 words—to say absolutely nothing of interest or value to the user. Just get to the point.

To most users, technical detail will be just techno-babble and serves no purpose other than to promote confusion, frustration, and anxiety. This sort of thing is the antithesis of usage-centered design:

```
FATAL ERROR ID# A137

Exception flag COMPRO33LVL raised by object BQ17890:0673 with
illegal value. Queued operations aborted. Initiate data recovery
and reboot.
```

In truth, error message are often called on to serve two very different categories of users: the ordinary users of the software and the maintenance and support staff. Often, technical support or help desk staff will ask a user to specify exactly what a message said or will request the "error code" or "sequence number" of the message. Including coding details or partial dumps in error messages generally does not work. Users often make mistakes in remembering or copying down messages.

A favorite example of useless technical detail is found in some fatal exceptions that can occur under Windows and that provide a scrolling dump. The error message tells the user to call technical support if the same message occurs again. And how is the user supposed to know if this particular gibberish is the same as something that appeared last month? Further, there is no readily apparent way to print out or save the contents of the scrolling dump in the message.

The various programming and technical support functions sometimes crammed into error messages to users are best supported by a completely separate mechanism. There is no reason why all software should not always maintain some form of record of serious or suspect errors and exceptions that would allow maintenance programmers and technical support staff to figure out what happened. A moving window could be used to keep such a file from growing too large; only the most recent entries will be relevant in most cases anyway.

12

ONCE A BEGINNER:
Supporting Evolving Usage Patterns

BEYOND BEGINNERS

The knowledge, skill, and experience of users affect how they use systems of all kinds. As introduced in Chapter 4, role incumbents can vary in several forms of expertise or ability: in knowledge of the application domain, in knowledge of the system supporting that domain, and in proficiency in using that system or application. In this chapter, we will look more closely at the user interface design implications of system knowledge and proficiency.

Beginners, first-time users of software, have been among the most abused and neglected constituency in information technology. They are also among the most catered to and coddled. The revolution in software usability that began with the Xerox Star project and continued with the original Apple Macintosh was primarily aimed at improving the lot of hapless novices. Over the decades, collective insight into what makes systems simpler to learn and easier for newcomers to use has developed and deepened through research and application to the point that the primary issues are well understood even if not always well addressed. The Great Law of Usability, the Access Rule (see Chapter 3), has remained the brightest beacon in the search for usability, guiding designers on their perpetual pilgrimage toward better systems. Perhaps they do not always design systems that are easy to use from the outset, but it is not because they do not know how.

The problems of users as they advance in experience and expertise seem to become progressively less interesting to designers and developers. Most users are rank beginners for but a short time with any particular system. With regular use, they move on to more sophisticated patterns of usage and more skilled forms of interaction. As they do, they are increasingly left to their own devices. Usability testing, which can reveal so much about first impressions and the mistakes and miscues of first-time users, is less suited to investigating interface designs in the hands of trained experts. In order to try out a new design, cadres of test subjects must be trained on the software under test to advanced levels of performance, which is a time-consuming and often prohibitively expensive process (see Chapter 18).

For truly high-volume production systems, usability engineering has evolved techniques, such as the GOMS technique to be described in Chapter 17, for counting keystrokes and shaving milliseconds off user task performance, but, for many software tools and routine applications, the best that more advanced users can hope for is a few keyboard shortcuts or hot-keys haphazardly thrown into the interface almost as an afterthought. Scripting languages or macro facilities have sometimes been added more as a convenience to third-party developers than as a real extension to usability for advanced users. Indeed, some standard features of modern GUIs, such as scrollbars, may substantially hinder advanced users [Constantine, 1994c].

> *You are a first-time user only once.*

The illogical logic of this neglect appears to be that expert users, being experts, do not need good design. Power users, so it seems, should be able to master arbitrary keystroke combinations, such as **Alt+A+P** as a keyboard shortcut to split cells in a document table. (After all, it makes perfect sense since it is the **Split Cells** item in the **Table** menu!) Perhaps this practice is a transplant from the macho/macha mystique of DOS and Unix, where "real" programmers deal in the arcane tokens of inconsistent and obscure commands laced with hidden and undocumented parameters.

An even more neglected and disenfranchised constituency of software users is found among those vast numbers who are no longer beginners but have not yet become old hands with a system. You are a first-time user only once. For most software, but especially for the tools and systems that you rely on to support everyday work, you do not remain a novice for very long. On the other hand, in typical applications, it can take considerable time to reach expert levels of proficiency, and not everyone makes it to the most advanced levels of skill. In the meantime, which may be most of the time, the typical user is in a limbo somewhere between beginner and boffin, with little support from the user interface and no understanding from interface designers.

> *The typical software user is in a limbo somewhere between beginner and boffin, with little support from the user interface and no understanding from interface designers.*

SKIING THE INTERFACE

Sport is often considered a source of lessons for living. Recreational skiing is a sport that offers some useful ideas for designing better user interfaces [Constantine, 1993b; 1994e]. Anyone who skis knows that skiers and ski slopes come in different grades. For those who are just learning to ski—novices—there are the relatively friendly and forgiving slopes designated in North America by a reassuring green circle. For those who have mastered the fundamentals but whose technique and abilities are still developing, there are intermediate slopes marked with a neutral blue square. Finally, for the expert skiers or for those who prefer to think of themselves as experts, there are the challenging black-diamond and double black-diamond trails and slopes.

The majority of recreational skiers are what ski instructors refer to as "improving intermediates." Improving intermediates have advanced beyond the basics of staying upright, stopping, and turning and have developed some finesse and facility in their skiing technique. The classic improving intermediate gets a little better every year. Whether in the flush of confidence from a particularly good run or through failure to heed the signs, intermediate skiers will even take the occasional black-diamond run or turn down an expert-level chute into a mogul field. However, throughout most of their careers, improving intermediates will remain on the upward curve without ever

Most skiers—and most software users—are improving intermediates.

reaching the pinnacle of expert skiing. They are the bread-and-butter skiers who keep the resorts in business, the eternal learners who line up for lessons every season and buy the books and videos in between.

The best ski areas and resorts provide trails for the needs and interests of all three kinds of skiers. The trails are clearly marked according to the level of difficulty, forming an interconnected network that allows skiers to move freely from one trail to another as suits them. An expert skier might warm up on a blue or green trail before heading for the top, an improving intermediate might practice a particular technique on a novice trail, and a novice might push the envelope a bit on an intermediate slope.

Both slopes and skiers vary. Expert slopes tend to be steeper or narrower or bumpier; novice slopes are broader and less steep. Novices, intermediates, and experts use different techniques. Beginners first learn to turn through the safe but inelegant snowplow technique but gradually move on to stem turns. Intermediates and experts ski parallel. Beginners often use their poles incorrectly or not at all, while experts guide and time their turns with them.

Really good user interfaces are like the best laid out ski areas. They are based on an understanding of the changing patterns of usage as users build experience with a system, and they provide distinct but interrelated facilities to support these varied patterns as they evolve. In fact, the best user interfaces help novices to become intermediates and intermediates to advance toward expert usage. This may seem like a tall order, but understanding the basic characteristics and issues in novice, intermediate, and expert styles of usage can help the designer to find economical ways to accommodate them all.

PROGRESSIVE USAGE

The **progressive usage model** or **triphasic model** [Constantine, 1994g] is the technical guide to designing user interface architectures in keeping with the ski-slope metaphor just described. It recognizes that patterns of usage evolve as users build experience with a system's features and facilities and that supporting these progressive patterns requires specific and somewhat different facilities within the user interface architecture [Constantine, 1994g]. The patterns of usage are referred to simply as **novice usage**, **intermediate usage**, and **expert usage**, and the user interface features that support them are, respectively, **acquisition facilities**, **transition facilities**, and **production facilities**.

Acquisition facilities are those that the inexperienced user needs to see on first encounter with the software. Good acquisition facilities enable the novice to gain immediate access to features needed to perform useful work. Production facilities make it possible for an experienced, fully trained user to produce sophisticated results with high efficiency. In between are the transition facilities, helping the improving intermediates among software users to progress beyond the slow and sloppy point-and-click of the beginner and, eventually perhaps, to make the transition to high-production expert usage.

At the ski lodge, skiers gather to talk of skiing and skiers. They speak with praise of expert skiers they have known or complain about novices who slow traffic when they take to the intermediate slopes. To refer to the various breeds of skiers, they invoke colorful names ranging from "snow-bunnies" to "hotdoggers." However, the truth is that most skiers are uneven in their abilities. The hotshot on the moguls might have an unpolished turning style on the smoother, gladed slopes, or a rank beginner might be capable of a perfect skating stop. It is the skiing, not the skier, that defines the difference. Even expert skiers may begin their day on the slopes with a warm-up run on the easier slopes, and, when the legs turn to rubber and the knees begin to scream after hours of hard skiing, the smartest skiers of every ability will turn again to the easier runs.

> *For designing better interfaces, it is the differences among patterns of usage— novice, intermediate, or expert—that make the difference.*

When it comes to software, users are not usually at the same level of skill regarding every feature of a system. Because users will have more ability in some areas than others, it is more useful to think in terms of novice, intermediate, or expert patterns of usage than to think of a user as being of some one type or another. For designing better interfaces, it is the differences among these patterns of usage that make the difference.

NOVICE USAGE

By definition, novices are presumed to have little or no experience with the features and facilities of a system. At the same time, like all users, they will have something to accomplish even when they first encounter a particular piece of software. They start out unfamiliar with what it can do and how it is organized. Despite a lack of training and experience, they reasonably expect to make effective use of the system. Their needs may often be limited to the simpler and more basic tasks, yet they are likely to need substantial guidance and support from the software. Novice users may also need reinforcement and encouragement to persevere in learning the system. To summarize, novice usage is generally characterized by

- Relatively simple, basic, or standard tasks
- Dependence on help, structure, or guidance
- Responsiveness to reinforcement or encouragement
- Exploration, trial and error, and tentativeness
- Mistakes and misuses
- Unskilled, slower operation
- Limited use of options or alternatives

INTERMEDIATE USAGE

It can be relatively more difficult to define intermediate usage than to recognize it when it happens to you. You become an improving intermediate when you first experience an already familiar user interface as becoming as much a hindrance as a help. When you start to be annoyed by the very dialogues that helped you learn the system and feel frustrated by the slow pace of point-and-click navigation through layers of dialogue, you have become an intermediate. Intermediate usage is not merely an interim phase or a murky mix of novice and expert patterns, but a distinct pattern characteristic of a large community of users.

Intermediate usage is marked by steadily expanding needs as users build experience and undertake more complex, extensive, or variable work with a system. Compared to novice usage, intermediate usage is grounded in a better and more complete understanding of the capabilities of a system and how these capabilities are organized. With this understanding comes a growing awareness of limitations and shortcomings within the system. As users become more proficient and take on more challenging applications of a system, they are more likely to be slowed by some features of the acquisition interface and to find it a source of escalating annoyance. Nevertheless, these progressing users may sometimes need to fall back on features of the acquisition interface or to turn to help systems for reminders regarding less frequently used operations.

Most importantly, intermediate usage represents constantly changing, steadily evolving work habits and interaction styles. It often involves bolder and more extensive experimentation with how best to use a system to accomplish various tasks. What seemed effective one day may have to be changed the next and reverted to again on the day after. In the same vein, the intermediate user at any time might need to refer back to already forgotten features or to fall back on the more basic operations of the acquisition facilities. In other words, intermediate usage is characterized by

- Experience-based use, with awareness of system limitations
- Expanding needs and growing complexity of tasks
- Continually evolving, changing patterns of interaction
- More extensive and less tentative experimentation
- Being slowed or annoyed by acquisition facilities
- Intermittent need for help or access to acquisition facilities

EXPERT USAGE

Experts are expected to know what they are doing and why, based on extensive experience with a system. Expert usage is grounded in "knowledge in the head" more than "knowledge in the world," as Donald Norman [1988] puts it. Experts do not so much depend on the configuration of the user interface or the information it presents to guide their usage as they do on the sophisticated mental models they have constructed through prior experience. They know, without being reminded, how the software works and what it can do. Nevertheless, as people say on the ski slopes, even experts need a lift. Expert users of software, too, will still need occasional hints or help, and they may even turn now and then and here and there to the intermediate or even the novice facilities.

> *As they say on the ski slopes, even experts need a lift. Expert users of software, too, will still need occasional hints or help.*

The primary focus of expert usage is on productivity and efficient use. More functions of a system will be used, especially including more of the advanced and specialized features or options. Expert-level usage may involve highly varied and specialized needs and rather idiosyncratic or personalized ways of using features. As usage reaches the expert level, it becomes more complex and is likely to incorporate more variations and options and to demand greater flexibility from the software. Systems are likely to be employed in nonstandard ways or even for purposes neither anticipated nor intended by the original developers. Expert users are those who devise clever work-arounds to overcome system limitations or to cover cases unsupported by the software. In fact, employing a work-around to get some system to do something it was never designed to do is a definite indicator of expert usage. In summary, the expert pattern of usage is characterized by

- Basis in extensive experience with the system
- Primary concern with efficiency and productivity
- Idiosyncratic style and mode-dependent patterns of interaction
- Full "knowledge in the head" regarding system operation and organization
- Complex, sophisticated tasks and nonstandard or unsupported uses
- Use of numerous features, especially advanced and specialized ones
- Intermittent need for help or access to transition and acquisition facilities

USAGE PROFILES

Since users are novices only when they start out and typically reach expert status only after extended experience and practice, most users, throughout most of their usage of most software, will be improving intermediates. Improving intermediates are the great neglected majority among users [Constantine, 1993b]. For many kinds of software, then, intermediate usage is likely to be by far the most common pattern. There are many important exceptions, however, and user interface designers have a responsibility to understand the proficiency profile—how levels of skill and experience will be distributed among users—for the systems they design.

Design objectives and user interface details will be different for a system whose users mostly continue to rely on intermediate patterns of usage—so-called perpetual intermediates [Cooper, 1995]—than for one whose users will essentially remain novices. People whose use of a system is intermittent, infrequent, and discretionary are likely to be perpetual novices, who each time approach and use a system much as if they had never seen it before. If you use a system or a particular feature only on rare occasion, you are effectively a beginner each time you see it. A forecasting program that is used once a year and a specialized tool for recovery from catastrophic disk error are examples of systems whose users are nearly all and nearly always novices. In such systems, acquisition facilities are the critical part of the user interface and warrant special attention in the design. At the other end of the spectrum are applications used in production environments that require all users to attain high proficiency before they are allowed to go "on-line." For air traffic control software or for telephone order processing, to take two examples, efficient support of expert usage may dominate the user interface design.

While all aspects of the user interface should be designed well, for most ordinary systems, the greatest gains in usability are likely to stem from better support of intermediate users and usage. Even the most expert user of a system may regularly employ only 10% to 20% of available features. For the other 80% to 90%, the expert may effectively be an intermediate or even a novice.

The proficiency profile in terms of novice, intermediate, and expert patterns is associated with individual user roles. For a given system, not all the roles taken on by users will exhibit the same profile of usage. Information and insights developed in the course of modeling user roles are carried forward to refine the user interface design as it evolves.

SUPPORTIVE INTERFACES

Just as a ski resort is made up of a number of interconnected trails of differing difficulty, so a well-designed user interface consists of a variety of facilities or features, some of which are better geared to expert usage and others more suited to supporting novice usage. The resulting architecture is not three different interfaces, but a single interface with interconnected facilities. An effective architecture allows users to move freely from one set of facilities to another, rather than forcing users to think and operate in one particular mode across the board. We refer to these three parts of the user interface architecture as "facilities" because they are really collections that facilitate different kinds of usage either by presenting different features or by supporting different modes of interaction with the same features.

> *An effective architecture allows users to move freely from one set of facilities to another, rather than forcing them to think and operate in one particular mode across the board.*

The worst sort of realization of the progressive usage model would be a user interface that operated in one of three modes—expert, intermediate, or novice—depending on the setting of an option in a user profile or set of user preferences. Not only would this scheme force the user into making a self-assessment based on an artificial distinction, but it also assumes that everything a user does during a given interaction will be in the same mode or style. For the progressing user, it would force a discontinuous jump when the friendly support of the acquisition facilities must suddenly be left behind for the alternative features of the intermediate facilities. This is a little like telling skiers that, once they graduate to the intermediate level, they have to stick to the blue trails for the rest of their stay.

ACQUISITION FACILITIES

Those parts of the user interface that best support novice usage are referred to as *acquisition facilities.* The design of good acquisition facilities is driven by some of the core principles of software usability. The first priority is maintaining high visibility in the user interface without overwhelming or confusing the user. At any point in the course of interaction, users should be able to see all the relevant functions and the requisite materials needed to complete the immediate task without being overwhelmed by extraneous or irrelevant facilities. The design will be guided by the concept of WYSIWYN (What You See Is What You Need) introduced in Chapter 3, which will be a lot easier to achieve when the designer is working from essential models and understands what the user is trying to accomplish. Feedback to the new user—on the changing status of the system and on its actions as the interaction progresses—needs to be generous and cast in the simplest possible language consistent with the user's presumed knowledge of the application domain.

The aesthetics of the interface are more important for novice usage than for more advanced levels, as an attractive interface invites interaction and can motivate both initial exploration and continued use. For more experienced users, the graphical design and artistic elements may soon fall beneath notice, and decorative elements can even become a distraction for some more experienced users. To encourage continued use, the interface presented to the new user should be attractive and appealing without being cloying, cute, or overly "friendly." Interfaces that cross the line from encouragement into cuteness or that insult the intelligence of users will backfire. To avoid undue frustration and discouragement in the new user, good acquisition facilities need to be highly tolerant and forgiving, accepting varied inputs and responses without unnecessarily correcting or restricting the user.

> *An attractive interface invites interaction and can motivate both initial exploration and continued use by the novice.*

In keeping with the more basic needs of beginners, the acquisition facilities of the user interface should concentrate on supporting the ordinary, typical, or standard cases. As not everything can be made simple, the objective should be to make normal operation as straightforward as possible. This objective is met by initially presenting users with only limited options and restricted variations tailored specifically to the needs posed by standard cases and basic operation. The designer has a responsibility to know what these simple, basic cases are and what is minimally needed to support them. Task modeling through essential use cases and identification of focal use cases will assist the designer in meeting this responsibility.

Novice skiers also need access to more challenging terrain if they are ever to become better skiers, and sometimes a cautious traverse of a steep slope may be required to return to the comfort of a novice trail. Clearly marked routes and warning signs at the entrances to dangerously steep stretches protect novices from accidentally turning into a trail beyond their abilities. Similarly, novice usage of software may also demand carefully controlled or assisted access to selected features at the more advanced levels, although users should be protected from accidental exposure to the expert-level features of the production facilities. Access to transition facilities is necessary if the user is ever to progress to intermediate skills. Advanced features probably need to be buried in the system in ways that avoid

> *Novice users should be protected from accidental exposure to the expert-level facilities of the interface.*

accidental use or disconcerting surprises to the naïve user. The beginner suddenly confronted by a screen full of options cast in arcane technical terms is discouraged from exploring further. Still worse, such a user may inadvertently take actions that are counterproductive at best and outright foolhardy at worst. The new user of a simple application can feel like a novice skier facing an ice-choked ravine if presented with a message like "**Abandon file or destructive modify of file linkage pointers?**" To abandon or to destroy? There seems to be no reasonable way out of such a software canyon.

For all these reasons, navigation through acquisition facilities is typically via nested dialogues and menus that present only a restricted view of the possibilities open at any given point. As represented in Figure 12-1, the user interface architecture of acquisition facilities is characterized by numerous relatively simple use contexts within a rather narrow, deep hierarchy having relatively long navigation paths, especially for less frequently used or more specialized operations. The novice user is carefully led through a series of simplified interaction contexts that cover the most likely cases.

> *What is most often taught as user interface design is probably more accurately described as the design of facilities to support novices.*

From the foregoing analysis of acquisition facilities, it is clear that much of what has classically been preached in the name of good modern user interface design primarily serves the needs of novices. In some textbooks and courses, what is taught as user interface design is probably more accurately described as the design of acquisition facilities.

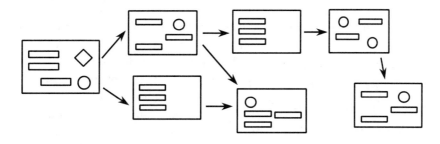

FIGURE 12-1 *Deep hierarchy, the architecture of acquisition facilities.*

TRANSITION FACILITIES

The *transition facilities* that support intermediate usage are a distinct subset of the interface architecture. In a sense, transition facilities connect the acquisition facilities to production facilities, providing a natural migration path for users as they gain experience and skill. Well-designed transition facilities help users to improve their performance and broaden their abilities more or less continuously in the course of using the system. For poorly designed systems, users progress in usage only through determination that overcomes the lack of support from the system.

Effective transition facilities are meaningfully related to the acquisition facilities on which they are built but differ in three important aspects. First, as user needs expand, the user interface should offer more immediate and straightforward access to a larger number of the software features. Second, transition facilities serve as a smooth "mapping" or bridge between the features and operational characteristics of the acquisition facilities and those of the production facilities, thereby supporting steady user progress toward greater proficiency. Third, transition facilities should support continuous customization or tailoring by the user to fit changing patterns of usage. In all of these areas, the watchword is continuity.

What do we mean by a smooth mapping between acquisition facilities and production facilities? Novice usage is often built around point-and-click use of cascaded menus, nested dialogue boxes, and toolbars with large icons and text labels. As usage progresses, the labels on tools become less necessary, and users may turn them off to allow room for more tools. Eventually, even point-and-click can come to seem too slow, and many users will want keyboard alternatives that allow them to accomplish more work with less arm movement. (See sidebar, The Mouse and the Keyboard.)

Well-designed transition facilities supply users with a simple, visible, and easy-to-learn mapping between acquisition facilities and production facilities. In many applications, the mapping from menu selections to keyboard alternatives is confusing and can seem to users to be almost arbitrary. The placing of alternative keyboard sequences beside an entry on a pull-down menu is of marginal help. The visual cue is present for too short a time, user attention is focused not on the shortcut but on the menu item itself, and there is no immediate opportunity for practice or reinforcement since the user will invariably just complete the menu selection. For some "shortcuts," such as using **Ctrl+5** on the numeric keypad to select everything in a document, nothing short of dogged practice and memorization will help. Even when based on highlighted or underlined letters from the menu titles and entry names—what Microsoft now refers to as "access keys"—the resulting shortcuts are often an alphabet soup with little or no mnemonic relationship to the tasks. The typical mapping between access keys and the toolbar or menu equivalents is complicated, is inconsistent, and does not build on prior knowledge or skills, so each keyboard shortcut has to be learned independently.

> *The relationship between toolbar or menu bar operations and their keyboard equivalents is often complicated and inconsistent. Keyboard shortcuts do not build on prior knowledge or skills, so each has to be learned on its own.*

To facilitate continued learning, transition facilities should provide hints, help, and reminders regarding shortcuts or alternative methods for accomplishing tasks. These aids serve as local trail maps, revealing connections between the "novice slopes" and the "expert trails" of user interfaces. For example, toolbar buttons might, at the user's option, be labeled with the equivalent keyboard shortcuts.

Providing quicker access to more features requires menus and dialogues that are organized, as illustrated in Figure 12-2, into a broader, flatter hierarchy that reduces the length of navigation paths and makes more features directly accessible from any particular use context. Effective transition facilities balance the apparent contradiction between these necessary organizational differences and the need to provide continuity with the familiar working environment of acquisition facilities.

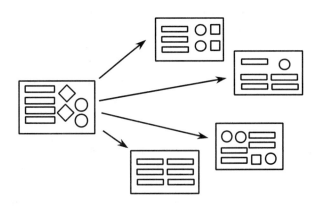

FIGURE 12-2 *Shallow hierarchy, the architecture of transition facilities.*

Proponents of modern GUIs extol the virtues of the virtual desktop and direct manipulation while power users of the old school still argue that nothing is faster than typing a command and a parameter string with wildcard characters. Who is right? It depends, of course, and it depends not only on the specifics of the application but also on the user and the user's level of experience.

The claim that mouse operation is faster than keyboarding for many routine tasks was especially popular among the pontiffs of the Macintosh world, and some investigations actually seemed to support this view [Tognazzini, 1992]. On the other hand, it should not be too surprising that Macintosh users and Apple employees confirm that mousing around the desktop beats pounding the keyboard.

Mouse manipulation can be a faster mode, but mainly for beginners. When users are first learning to employ hidden features—ones like **F6** for **Bold** or **Ctrl+X** for **Cut** that are not visible on the interface—it can take them a moment or two to remember the "shortcut." When newcomers use a word-processing program based on keyboard shortcuts and function keys, a distinct pause will be evident each time the user tries to recall the right keystrokes, and often the user will make mistakes that then have to be corrected. Add it all up, and these costs of awkward keyboarding can exceed the 2.5 to 3 seconds it takes the typical user to move from mouse to keyboard, identify and locate the **Bold** button, click on it, and then return to the keyboard.

On the other hand, once users are trained up to full proficiency, the picture reverses. The master mouse handler gets somewhat faster, but the expert key pounder gets a lot faster, and, over the long run, the function key can be expected to take a small fraction of the time needed for the toolbar button.

However, toolbar buttons marked by well-chosen icons are easier to learn in the first place. The learning curve for point-and-click interfaces initially rises faster than for systems based on command lines or hot-keys. Becoming proficient at using arbitrary escape sequences takes time and is usually fairly unrewarding at first, but good design can help.

Users are more likely to remember their own associations, mnemonic or arbitrary, than the ones set by the designers, so letting users easily change shortcuts and reassign function keys is one way to assist. Another is to give feedback that supports learning the keyboard shortcuts. For example, the little button on the toolbar marked by a bold "**B**" might push itself whenever the user types **F6** or **Ctrl+B** or whatever toggles boldfaced text. Fly-over hints or tool tips and pop-up suggestions can offer keyboard alternatives for point-and-click operation.

In Windows applications, access keys for menu selections are typically indicated to users by underlining the appropriate letter of the menu name and item within a menu. Unfortunately, underlines are often hard to see, and nothing particularly draws the user to notice them, much the same as with shortcut key suggestions that are listed unobtrusively alongside menu items. Progress in usage would be better supported by making such accelerators more apparent without shoving them in the user's face. For example, highlighting shortcuts and access keys each time a menu is used would make them more visible and apparent without intruding on the user too much.

Good practice in user interface design favors allowing all operations to be performed either from the keyboard or with the mouse or other pointing device. This practice not only supports progressive usage but also accommodates varying personal preferences as well as the interests of users with special needs. Not everything is equally suited to both keyboard and pointing devices. Some tasks, such as drawing or diagramming, are inherently better suited to pointing devices, while others are far more efficiently accomplished by typing. To some extent, it depends on the context. If your hands are already on the keyboard, switching to the mouse and back can exact a penalty of about three-quarters of a second. Repeated operations that must be applied to an entire series of cases are often accomplished much faster and more accurately through the keyboard.

Where a mouse or other pointing device is a necessary or preferred mode of control, there are still techniques that can help power users. Greater efficiency for the proficient user is possible with two-fisted input, in which the keyboard and mouse are used simultaneously. Mode-shifted mouse operation using **Ctrl**, **Alt**, and **Shift** keys is one approach. Tool selection via function keys can allow the user to switch tools without moving the pointer off the drawing or working surface to pick a tool from a palette or toolbar. Each such operation that requires moving to and selecting a small target and then precisely repositioning the pointer back to the same point on a working surface may take several extra seconds, even by the most practiced user. Our observations of users of drawing and modeling tools that provide for two-handed control show that advanced users often prefer this mixed mode to the simpler but less efficient mouse-only technique.

Intermediate usage evolves continuously and typically incorporates increasingly more varied and less predictable uses than does novice usage. To support these evolving patterns, the user interface should be readily customizable and extensible in virtually every aspect. Although the need to modify and customize is on-going and continual in intermediate usage, the process of customizing itself is something that occurs sporadically as new needs emerge or old arrangements prove less workable. For this reason, the mechanisms by which the interface is tailored by the user should be simple, straightforward, and self-documenting. Rather than specialized customization dialogues or option-setting procedures, the most effective interfaces allow intermediate users to customize through already familiar features and standard interaction idioms. We will have more to say about user customization and configurable interfaces later in this chapter.

PRODUCTION FACILITIES

Good *production facilities* incorporate various conventional and familiar techniques for making usage more efficient for the experienced user. These techniques include such things as hot-keys that take the user instantly from one part of an application to another, accelerators or access keys that provide keyboard alternatives for point-and-click use of menus and tool buttons, and built-in or user-defined macros and scripts that allow elaborate, user-defined sequences to be triggered with a single click or a few keystrokes.

Since experts are expected to be familiar with the interface, production facilities may present toolbars with unlabeled icons or buttons labeled only with abbreviations, at the option of the user. Because experts make use of many and varied features, they often favor small tool buttons with simplified icons, allowing them to pack more tools onto toolbars to be kept readily at hand. Multiple toolbars that float over working surfaces and can be docked along any edge of the window or can be hidden at will are another approach supporting more advanced usage patterns. While floating, dockable, configurable tool palettes have become relatively common within office suites and programming tools, they have yet to be fully exploited in many other kinds of applications and software.

In many types of systems, such as applications involving drawing, composition, or manipulation of objects, working areas are at a premium. Some of the most advanced users prefer to have larger, less cluttered working spaces in order to make room for more complex projects. It is sometimes the most expert users, for example, who are likely to prefer to see a relatively unadorned blank screen in a word processor or drawing package. Production facilities may make more features

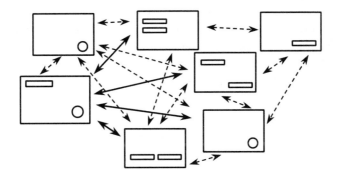

FIGURE 12-3 *Invisible lattice, the architecture of production facilities.*

accessible yet present fewer visible features on the user interface. Effective performance using many features will depend on implicit knowledge that the user is expected to remember without visual cues or reminders.

For efficient user access to more of the features of a system and use in more varied and unpredictable ways, production facilities need to support quicker and more flexible navigation among the various interaction contexts. In effect, the expert user may need to go directly from any part of the user interface to any other, and, in many cases, the path from one interaction context to someplace else may not be visible on the user interface but will depend on a shortcut or other secret code known to the expert. The navigation map for production facilities is typically a complex network with many implied paths, as suggested by Figure 12-3.

Production facilities need to support operation in multiple modes that can be tailored for efficiency on a variety of tasks. The configuration of the user interface may need to be changed frequently to fit highly particular demands of the task at hand. Obviously, switching from one configuration or mode to another needs to be a quick and simple operation in itself. In a similar vein, messages should be terse—often in condensed form and sometimes just in brief codes. Likewise, online help for expert usage needs to be brief and to the point, without covering basic or background information that experts are presumed to have mastered.

> *Experts need interfaces that operate in multiple modes tailored for efficiency on a variety of tasks and that can be changed frequently and easily to fit highly particular demands of the task at hand.*

Except for those applications where production usage is rather simple and very well understood, the ability to customize to specialized uses is essential for effective production facilities. The ideal is for all features of the entire interface to be fully customizable, including all defaults and initial settings as well as the layout of screens and dialogue boxes.

On occasion, even the most expert user may need to fall back on transition facilities or rely on facilities designed for the beginner. These facilities and modes of operation also need to be immediately accessible at the click of a mouse or a few taps on the keyboard. However, it is important to remember that this need for flexibility is not met by providing some kind of mode switch that causes the interface as a whole to revert to more simplified transition or acquisition facilities. Rather, the specific individual features or operations of these other facilities should remain accessible through some straightforward mechanism, even after extensive customization of the interface by the expert user.

DESIGNING FOR PROGRESSIVE USAGE

Some of the more vexing and challenging problems facing user interface designers involve how to continue to support users as their usage evolves and how to devise user interface facilities that change yet preserve visual and functional continuity across different modes or styles of operation. In this section, we will take a closer look at some of the issues involved in supporting experts and improving intermediates without disenfranchising novices.

MAPPING THE SHORTCUTS

Consider keyboard shortcuts—sequences of shifted letters and numbers that substitute for mouse operations. The details of how shortcuts are provided to more advanced users have a lot to do with how usable they will be in practice. In conventional Windows-style software, these take two forms: (1) shortcuts, such as **Ctrl+A** for **Select All** or **INS** for **Paste**, that operate with one shifted or unshifted keystroke and (2) access keys, which begin with the **Alt** key and consist of a series of selected letters or numbers from within menu and menu item names. The letters or numbers used as access keys in menus are indicated by underlining. For example, the access keys for **Select All** on the **Edit** menu are typically **Alt+E+L**, which is not exactly a memorable mnemonic. Well-designed interfaces provide a

> *Making the interface easier for more advanced users who take shortcuts should not make it harder for less advanced users who methodically use point-and-click.*

smooth mapping from acquisition to transition to production facilities, which means offering users shortcuts that are meaningfully rated to the longer methods they learned as beginners and improving intermediates. As was shown in Chapter 8, sometimes creative naming or rewording may be necessary to make shortcuts more sensible and easier to remember. Of course, it is important that making the interface easier for more advanced users not make it harder for the less advanced user who picks items from the menu with a mouse.

Even for tasks that inherently rely heavily on a mouse or other graphical input device, keyboard alternatives can help advanced users. For example, practiced users of graphics applications, such as drawing packages or CASE tools, are slowed by having to move off the drawing surface to select or change drawing tools. Instead, many prefer to use one hand on the keyboard to switch tools while the other hand stays on the pointing device for positioning. Keyboard alternatives are typically not visible on the user interface because they rely on mnemonics or somewhat arbitrary function-key assignments.

In some applications, the position of buttons on toolbars or palettes can be mapped by position to the placement of keys on the keyboard, as suggested by Figure 12-4. Such spatial mapping allows the intermediate or advanced user to select the correct key without shifting the eyes and the attention off the screen. The displayed toolbar itself becomes a visual reminder of the position of the shortcut key on the keyboard, facilitating the user's transition from one-handed point-and-click to two-fisted keyboard-and-mouse operation. Such a scheme would not work for all applications, but it

> *The migration path from novice to expert use is smoothed by visible reminders about alternative ways for accomplishing tasks.*

highlights the importance of designing a smooth "migration path" from acquisition to production interface features. The path is smoothed by visible reminders about alternative ways for accomplishing tasks. Other examples will be given when we discuss transition help in the next section.

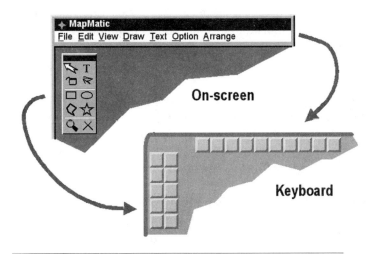

FIGURE 12-4 *Transition facilities supported through spatial mapping.*

There are many other possibilities. Consider, for example, a drawing package. While the user is using a line tool to draw with one hand on the mouse, the other hand could use number keys to control line width and could set line style with keys based on visual mnemonics, such as a colon for dotted, hyphen for dashed, and equal sign for a double line; arrowheads might be toggled using the less-than and greater-than keys. Such mode-dependent operation can be difficult and disconcerting for beginners, but, in the hands of a skilled draftsperson who is well trained with the software, the results can be dramatic increases in productivity and satisfaction.

TRANSITION HELP

Transition help involves help that supports progressive usage, aiding beginners in moving beyond novice usage and supporting the continuous learning of improving intermediates as they progress toward expert usage. Transition help can take many forms. Labels on tools can help beginners learn the meaning of icons. Labeled icons should typically be the default, out-of-the-box configuration, although it should be easily switched. For users who have already learned what the tools are, labels might display the keyboard shortcuts or access keys. However, more advanced users may resent the screen real estate taken up by tool labels since they typically prefer small icons in order to have more tools accessible and more workspace available.

To save screen real estate, transition help offering keyboard shortcuts to users can be presented dynamically. For many years, we suggested that pop-up tips or hints could support improving intermediates by including the equivalent keyboard shortcuts along with the identification that appears when the mouse pointer passes over or rests on a tool or an icon. Some of the Microsoft people in our seminars must have been listening because Word 7.0a finally offered the option to have tool tips include shortcut keys for toolbar functions. As with most aspects of transition facilities, these help mechanisms should be options under the control of the user since, once shortcuts are learned, labels or hints are no longer needed and become a distraction.

However, pop-up hints or tool tips are less than optimal for this purpose because they appear under the wrong circumstances. Hints or tool tips are activated on pause, appearing when the mouse pointer rests for a brief period on a tool or an icon. This behavior is reasonable for informing an unknowing novice about the function of a tool, the **seekingIdentification** help case (see Chapter 11), but a more advanced user, whose mouse maneuvers are speedy, might never activate the hint. The moment when an intermediate user needs prompting about a quicker alternative is precisely when a particular tool is used. The best way to prompt, if not on the tool button itself, is within a pop-up hint that appears *when the tool is depressed.*

Transition help can be thought of as supporting the **seekingSimplification** help case, a specialization of the **seekingInstruction** case. The user is looking for another way—a shorter, simpler, or faster way—of accomplishing a task. In some cases, the user may have learned one method and be unaware that there is any other way. Many modern systems try to support this help case through sophisticated wizards and other forms of simulated software magic that attempt to analyze usage patterns and anticipate user needs for alternative methods. Often, however, the simplest techniques can promote progressive usage. For example, arranging tools into well-organized and visually distinct collections can make learning how to use them easier.

Progressive usage is also promoted by simple relationships between menu selections and their alternatives. For example, menu items can be arranged in the same order as tool palettes and enhanced by glyphs that match those on tool buttons. Figure 12-5 shows an example of a menu that can support learning to use a toolbar—or comfortably shifting back to menu selection. (We did not realize until after incorporating this particular illustration into our teaching materials that the factory default configuration does not look like the one shown in the figure. Without thinking, we had rearranged the toolbar to match the menu! What designers get wrong on the user interface users will often correct—if users are able to customize the interface sufficiently.)

Some well-designed facilities, such as the "Tip Wizards" in Excel 95, have proved effective with helping some users learn more efficient or advanced patterns of usage. In a sense, however, much of the simulated intelligence of tip wizards or "office assistants" is wasted. Users know when a task begins to seem irritatingly long. At that point, they might reasonably turn to the help system,

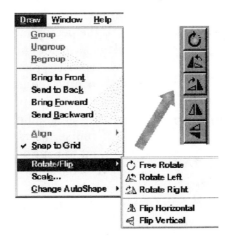

FIGURE 12-5 *A simple relationship between menu structure and toolbar organization.*
(MICROSOFT POWERPOINT 95)

demonstrate a task, and ask, "Is there an easier way to do this?" Another direct support for **seekingSimplification** would be to provide a **Shortcut** button within help file entries to supply a context-dependent **Shortcut** tool that offers a shortcut for the last action performed, if one is known to the software.

The possibilities for clever transition help are boundless. The most important transition help, however, is probably just a well-organized and well-integrated user interface architecture.

ADAPTABLE AND ADAPTIVE INTERFACES

In devising interfaces to support varied and evolving patterns of usage, two fundamentally different strategies can be taken: adaptive interfaces or adaptable interfaces. *Adaptive* interfaces are user interfaces that learn, or at least appear to learn, automatically adapting the configuration or contents of the user interface based on a user's actions. *Adaptable* interfaces are user interfaces that can be configured or changed under control and direction of users to fit their individual requirements.

Adaptive interfaces can be based on mechanisms as simple as last-used or most-frequently-used lists or as sophisticated as inference engines or neural nets that try to analyze what users are trying to do and provide automated shortcuts to accomplish those things. The promise of artificially intelligent software continues to intrigue users and programmers alike. Wizards and agents and hidden engines that work interface magic have been proliferating within commercial software products without necessarily delivering much of value to users [Constantine, 1994j].

One problem with adaptive interfaces is that, in the name of empowering users, they actually rob users of control. The notion of user control is one of the sacred themes of usability, a subtext underlying much that has been written on good user interface design. The desire for control or the perception of control is a basic psychological need, and, when software behaves in ways that wrest control from users, the results can be reduced usability purchased at the expense of sophisticated and, typically, expensive programming.

> *Quasi-intelligent interfaces that analyze usage patterns and modify the user interface accordingly are not only difficult to program but also less satisfying to users than direct user control over configuration.*

Of course, users want control over things they want to control and are more than happy to leave to the software those things that do not interest them. Only the user knows which is which. No piece of software can ever understand your work or what you are trying to accomplish anywhere near as well as you do.

User control is a key to providing both reassuring familiarity and accommodation to changing and growing needs. Good designs let users choose and change how to interact with the system as their needs and working habits change. Quasi-intelligent interfaces that analyze usage patterns and modify the user interface accordingly are not only more difficult to program but also less satisfying to users. All users are disconcerted when familiar interfaces change form suddenly and beyond their control. Even such simple devices as last-used or most-frequently-used lists can sometimes seem unpredictable and unusable to many users. Having just gotten used to a drop-down list that opens with one name at the top, the user suddenly finds the list reordered when next it is opened. What is simple from a logical or programming perspective can seem mysterious to users.

The recent access list on a Windows **File** menu can be extremely useful for resuming work started in another session. However, simple and logical though it is, because it reshuffles entries on every use, it can seem erratic or hard to use for such a simple task as starting a session with the same three files loaded in the same order as used in the previous session. This has a logical but counterintuitive solution. The moderately experienced user might be tempted to type something like **Alt+F+1**, **Alt+F+2**, **Alt+F+3**. However, this loads the files in the reverse of their last used order. (Try it!) The correct solution is not **Alt+F+3**, **Alt+F+2**, **Alt+F+1** either. (Only an inveterate programmer would think to type **Alt+F+3** three times in succession.)

> *Let users choose and change how to interact with the system as their needs and working habits change.*

What users need most is not artificial intelligence to analyze their usage patterns but broad and straightforward control over the configuration and behavior of the interface. Users can then customize the interface to fit their expanding needs and unique and changing patterns of usage as they become aware of these.

CONTINUOUS CUSTOMIZATION

The goal in customization is to allow the intermediate or expert user to simply and flexibly modify the user interface using only the ordinary skills and operations of regular usage. For some problems, this can be as simple as appending to selected dialogue boxes a check box or control that assigns current settings as the default or initial values. For other problems, more creative solutions may be required.

Tool trays. One of the most important forms of customization for more advanced usage is the ability to reconfigure the set of tools and features that are visible at the top level for immediate access. Although metaphors are easily misused or misapplied in user interface design [Constantine, 1993c], this is an area ripe for new metaphors, such as the "tool tray/tool drawer/tool chest" metaphor [Constantine, 1994e]. This metaphor is a straightforward but powerful extension of current user interface techniques based on observations of how people organize and carry out complex tasks.

If you take the time to observe work in varied settings, you will find a common structure to many skilled activities that depend on a variety of tools and materials for completion. The worker begins by selecting a set of tools and materials from a tool chest or inventory of parts and supplies. These are typically then arrayed on or within a temporary holding device, such as a tray, cart, tabletop, drop cloth, or tool belt. Tools are used from this functional tool-tray collection. The collection may be dynamically reconfigured as the worker finds that additional tools or parts are needed or as ones that are no longer needed are returned to the tool chest or to storage. This pattern of work can be seen among artisans and professionals ranging from automotive mechanics, to dentists, draftspersons, and cooks.

> *As practiced, many skilled activities that depend on a variety of tools and materials for completion exhibit a common structure.*

Similarly, the toolbars or palettes for software need to be dynamically and temporarily configurable to any task at hand. Fixed toolbars or ones that can only be reconfigured more or less permanently through a separate dialogue do not fully meet the needs of intermediate or advanced users.

Users need to be able to open at any time the "tool drawers" of a standard "tool chest" containing a large assortment of potentially useful tools and materials that can be either picked up directly or first dragged-and-dropped onto a "tool tray" for repeated use at some later time in the task. Because the collections are implemented in software, any number of tool trays for common operations can be created, labeled, and stored as tool drawers for future retrieval and use. The content of trays could be altered temporarily over the course of a session or permanently for future use. Tool trays would normally behave as temporary holding areas, disappearing at the end of a session unless added by the user as new tool drawers in the permanent portion of the user's tool chest. New tools, such as purchased applets or macros created by the user, could also be added to the tool chest. Behind the scenes, but readily accessible to the user, would be a factory-supplied tool chest with all the standard tools in standard drawers, allowing for selectively restoring individual tools, drawers, or even the entire tool chest at any time. Figure 12-6 illustrates one possible form for the tray/drawer/chest model. In the figure, a master tool chest is shown with one drawer open. The user is dragging a tool to a temporary tool tray. An alternative model based on a notebook or other visually persistent metaphor might also work. Function and behavior, not appearance, are the important matters in this model.

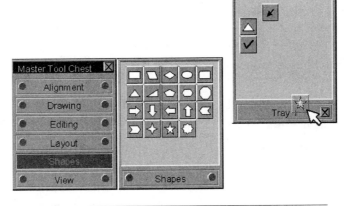

FIGURE 12-6 *Toolbar successor: tray, drawer, and chest.*

In principle, the sort of behavior described for tool trays, drawers, and chests can be simulated with the floating, dockable, configurable toolbars found in many modern software development environments and office suites, but creating, reconfiguring, and switching among collections of tools are typically too clumsy to encourage their dynamic use as a technique for organizing work. The tool chest with its labeled drawers needs to be at ready, top-level access. Selecting a series of temporary trays for use should be as simple as clicking on them. Adding tools should be as simple as opening a drawer and dragging them to a tray.

In a somewhat different way, this same tool-tray metaphor can serve the needs of novices simply by offering them a few small, preset trays of tools for general-purpose use and informing them that other tools can be found tucked in the drawers of the tool chest. Creating a newly customized tray can be merely a matter of opening an empty tray and beginning to fill it with tools.

Layout. The layout of the user interface should also be customizable using the ordinary operations of direct manipulation, including selection and drag-and-drop. Being able to drag a tool button from a palette and place it on a toolbar has become common in the user interfaces of high-end commercial products, but there is no reason this operation should be restricted to tool buttons. Following the principles for innovation introduced in Chapter 9, the improving intermediate should be able to take any feature, wherever it lurks within the user interface, and surface it, bringing it to the top level for immediate access. A user may be deep within some nested set of menus and dialogue boxes when it is realized that a circuitous route has been repeatedly traversed just to change the print quality from draft mode to high resolution, for example. It is at that moment that the user would like to be able to switch modes and literally drag the radio button or the menu item or whatever to place it on a floating toolbar or on a more convenient menu. This sort of capability, although long recognized as a desirable feature, is still rarely implemented. It is gratifying to see that direct drag-and-drop menu configuration has finally appeared in some commercial software, notably Office 97.

Generalization of interaction idioms is a vital source of useful innovations. Configurability should ultimately be extended beyond just reconfiguring toolbars.

> *Layout of the user interface should be customizable using the ordinary operations of direct manipulation.*

To take but one example, it is generally acknowledged among human–computer interaction experts that the status bar is probably misplaced in its conventional position at the bottom of the screen where it is least likely to be noticed and read, yet the standards exhort developers to put it there. There is no reason why the status bar should not itself be a dockable user interface feature that could be dragged to the top of the screen by those users who prefer to get feedback where it is more usable.

A similar argument can be made for ruler bars, scrollbars, and other common features of windows. Vertical scrollbars on the left are preferred by some users and can offer an advantage in certain applications or for certain tasks. This degree of configurability is harder to accomplish in some programming languages and environments than others, but it still should be considered more often by designers.

Defaults. Default settings and initial values for fields are another aspect of the system that the advancing users will typically want to be able to customize. The right default settings can radically reduce the number of steps needed for complex and repetitive tasks and can simplify use by beginners. Rather than requiring the user to alter default settings and initial values by editing an **.INI** file or through specialized and often complicated setup dialogues, interfaces should support setting

> *The right default settings can radically reduce the number of steps needed for complex and repetitive tasks and can simplify use by beginners.*

default values of fields and parameters using the same features and interactions by which those parameters would normally be set in regular use. This goal is often easier to achieve than it might sound. For example, consider setting the default type font and style for any new text entered by the user. As shown in Figure 12-7, a simple check box or button, within whatever dialogue or tool palette is used to set these normally, serves this purpose.

For data entry and transaction-processing applications, various simple schemes can facilitate speedier entry through user control of defaults. A menu item to **Save as Defaults** can preserve current field values on a form or screen as the starting default values. Alternatively, a separate **Change Defaults** dialogue can be used that replicates the layout of the normal entry form, opening up with the current settings or last-entered values. These approaches lend themselves to many

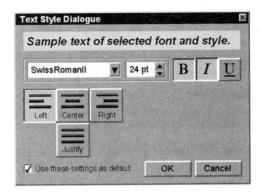

FIGURE 12-7 *Setting defaults from standard dialogues.*

different kinds of conventional data entry, query, and data manipulation applications and do not require elaborate or sophisticated programming.

In principle, almost any parameter or feature within the software should be customizable, including many of those that might not otherwise appear at the user interface. User customization and configurability can sometimes make up for serious design mistakes since the user is given a chance to correct or overcome what the designers may have messed up on or missed. For example, the auto-hide feature of the Windows Task Bar and Office Shortcut Bar mentioned in Chapter 3 would be far more usable if the user could easily increase the delay before these pop out of hiding. Of course, although customization can be a major factor in usability, it should not become an excuse for poor design or lack of thought. Developers have the obligation to design well and carefully and to deliver a preset configuration already well suited to the typical starting user of their software.

Interface configurations. The values of default settings are among numerous aspects of the software and user interface configuration that potentially can require changes under varying conditions of use. Improving intermediates may experiment with different default values and toolbar arrangements as their usage evolves, and experts may want to alter configurations temporarily to fit a specific project or to make a particular repetitive task easier. Each user may prefer a unique set of defaults to make the usage seem easier and more natural.

Interface configuration management schemes can be ordered in terms of increasing sophistication and increasing support of progressive usage. At the bottom end of the scale is an interface that cannot be configured in any meaningful way by the user. More advanced forms of configuring include:

1. Single permanent configuration—All changes become permanent.
2. Single optional permanent configuration—User has option on exit to save or discard configuration changes made during a session.

3. Single revertible configuration—User can discard all accumulated changes and restore factory-preset standard configuration at any time.
4. Dual alternative configurations—User has choice between last-saved configuration and factory-preset standard configuration.
5. Multiple stacked configurations—User has choice between factory-preset standard configuration and multiple levels of previously saved configurations.
6. Multiple named configurations—User has choice among previously named and saved configurations or factory-preset standard.
7. Context-dependent multiple configurations—Configuration automatically depends on company, logged user, and specific project or data.

The option to save or discard any changes made during a session (scheme 2) should always be offered; users, especially improving intermediates, often make mistakes or change their minds about configuration changes. Many commercial software packages allow customized configurations to be restored to the original factory settings (scheme 3), but this primitive capability, though highly desirable, is unnecessarily inflexible and seldom is adequate to meet real customization needs. Typically, the user loses all customization if the factory settings are restored. There is no excuse for not allowing the user to switch back and forth between standard and personal configurations (scheme 4); the added programming required for this capability is insignificant once revertible configuration is supported. If configuration files are supported, providing multiple configurations (scheme 5) and access by names (scheme 6) is straightforward. User-defined and -named interface configurations support safe and manageable evolution of personal configurations for improving intermediates and rapid configuration switches for advanced experts. Having named configurations (scheme 6) also supports multiple users of a single installation, as well as configurations customized for specific projects or data. The most "advanced" level of configurability—automatic context-dependent configuration (scheme 7) is far more difficult to program and is less versatile for users.

> *There is no excuse for not allowing the user to switch back and forth between standard and personalized user interface configurations.*

For nearly any shipping software product, the combination of optional configuration saving on exit (scheme 2) with revertible switching between factory and custom configurations (scheme 4) should be the absolute minimum supported. It offers the user a great deal of flexibility with little added programming. The factory conditions can be restored, configurations can be set temporarily, or experimental setups can be tried, all without losing established configuration settings.

All settings of preferences or defaults need to be easily accessible. User configurability is best supported by two forms of access to preferences and defaults: contextual and consolidated. In many cases, preferences and defaults are most conveniently set in the context of using the functions to which they are most closely related. In other cases, however, it is more convenient to users to be able to go to one place and take care of a collection of various defaults and preferences all at once. Tabbed dialogues provide a convenient and sensible mechanism for organizing defaults and preferences to provide both forms of access. A common tabbed dialogue consolidates all settings into functional groups, each on its own page of the shared dialogue. Whether invoked from a menu or by a command button within a dialogue, the **Settings** tabbed dialogue should open with the requested page faced. Regardless of how the user gets there, any page of settings can then be selected by the user and changed from that one central dialogue. Windows 95 uses this technique for several purposes.

FEATURE ACCESS

As usage becomes more advanced and sophisticated, more immediate access to more tools becomes desirable. Menus that have short and long forms are one possible mechanism for extending feature accessibility, provided there is a readily apparent relationship between the two. Adding new menu items at the bottom of menus preserves the existing structure so that the position of familiar features does not have to be relearned, but this approach can also disrupt the structure of menu sections and the sort order of items. Split menus that divide items into sections have been shown to support higher performance [Sears and Shneiderman, 1994]. Adding new items to the end of sections might be a reasonable compromise between preserving existing structure and integrating new features. The user should have the final say, so the end of menu sections might be the default where new items are initially added, with the user free to move them if desired.

Other ways to allow easy access to more features without overwhelming less experienced users include "stitch-and-rip" panels and dockable dialogue boxes. As represented in Figure 12-8, a dialogue box might have an optional drop-down panel that can be opened up for access to advanced features. Novices can stick with the simple dialogues of the software as it comes "out of the box." Improving intermediates may begin to make occasional use of advanced facilities by clicking on the **More** control (which changes to **Less** once the drop panel opens). When users reach the stage where they prefer to see all the controls or settings all the time, the **Always show options** check box tells the system to leave the panel permanently attached so that it is already open every time the dialogue is opened. Such a drop-down panel functions like a subdialogue for the beginner but appears as an integral part of the dialogue as viewed by the more advanced user. Because the panel opens out from the starting dialogue rather than appearing on top of it, as a separate dialogue would, this technique maintains visual object persistence. By not requiring the user to open an additional modal dialogue that must be

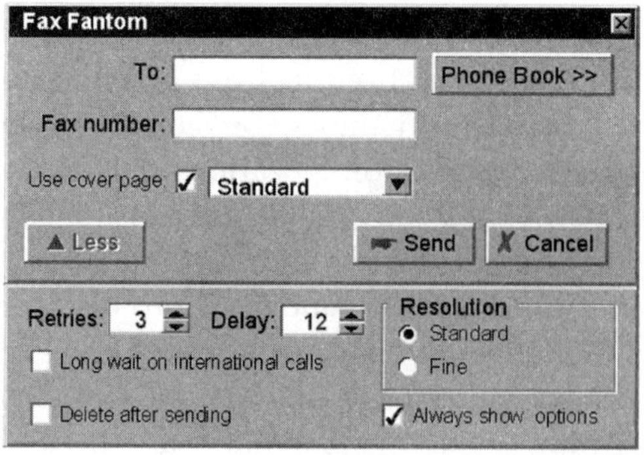

FIGURE 12-8 *Stitch-and-rip: configurable dialogues through extension panels.*

closed before finishing the primary dialogue or taking other steps, the attachable panel improves efficiency.

The stitch-and-rip concept can be extended to allow subdialogues to be "docked" on other dialogues, much as toolbars can be docked to windows. This can be a difficult feature to program without improved support at the operating system level, and it is not useful in all situations. Nevertheless, dockable dialogues can be helpful in supporting broad customizability within some applications.

At the advanced intermediate or expert level, a user may potentially want to invoke any feature, use any tool, or reach any part of an application directly from anywhere in the system. Providing such access through visible controls in every form or dialogue is usually neither practical nor desirable. Interfaces can become cluttered and complicated, making it more difficult to learn and to remember how to use them. Carried to an extreme, all parts of the user interface begin to look more or less alike, reducing the number of visual cues available to help users keep track of where they are within the larger task or interaction. Interfaces cluttered with tools and controls also waste screen real estate, reducing the size of working areas and distracting the user from the immediate focus on a particular part of a task. At the other end of the scale, if most of the direct or alternative access paths are only implicit—hidden rather than visible on the user interface—the user may have too many things to memorize.

> *If you make all tools and options visible everywhere, all parts of the user interface begin to look more or less alike.*

A central "switchboard" or dispatch point can resolve this conflict. The user has to remember only one shortcut "formula"—how to get to the central dispatch point. From there, the full array of features is made visible and can be reached. Modern graphical user interfaces, such as Windows, provide standard methods to switch from task to task or from window to window,

FIGURE 12-9 *An example of a central visual dispatch.*
(MANAGING YOUR MONEY, MECA SOFTWARE)

but these offer only coarse access to a limited number of major components or activities.

A good visual metaphor can provide an effective way to help organize a centralized dispatch point, simplifying both initial learning and continuing use of features. For example, some commercial products have incorporated a "virtual office," such as the one in Figure 12-9, to serve as a common launching point. The virtual office might show a desk with labeled drawers and a calculator, checkbook, and diary lying on top. Bookshelves might hold ledgers and books identified as catalogues, telephone books, and the like. A calendar, bulletin board, and various charts and graphs might hang on the walls. Clicking on any object gives immediate access to the corresponding feature or tool. In usability testing, power users especially seem to like such a virtual office because every part of the program is accessible from a single screen.

Such a visual map may not always be entirely "intuitive," as product brochures often claim, but can promote rapid recognition and early exploration of features for novices. For more advanced users, the most important aspect of this approach is that it simplifies and speeds spatial learning of how to make rapid transitions among features. Instead of row upon row of identically shaped buttons, the user is presented with a rich but stable visual environment containing a host of diverse and readily distinguished controls, thus making it easier to find things in the first place and remember where they are thereafter.

PROGRESSIVE USAGE APPLIED

The keyboard extender applet offers some opportunities to support progressive usage. Although all usage is likely to be somewhat sporadic, usage may be skewed to more advanced levels for users in some roles, notably the

CasualTranslator, since each use is likely to entail a series of uses or selections. The **FancyFontFutzer** role, because of the kind of users likely to assume this role, also implies a bias toward more advanced usage. To promote progress toward advanced usage in these and other roles, the default setting for the **symbolSelectorViewer** ought to include display of keyboard shortcuts.

The first-time user of the **insertingSymbol** use case would, without help or prompting, most likely select a character and then click on the **Insert** button. The shortcut using a double-click, as described in Chapter 10, remains hidden behavior. The **offeringSuggestion** help case might best be supported with a status bar prompt that flashes once each time the dialogue opens until the user first employs a double-click. A similar attention-getting prompt could be used with the drop-down panel that supports defining and modifying groups.

Keyboard-only operation also needs to be supported, not only for the advanced user with a strong preference for the keyboard but also to cover those circumstances when a pointing device may be awkward or unavailable. It is natural and conventional to have the cursor keys operate within the symbol display. Another possibility, suggested by a team in one of our classes, would number the rows and columns of the symbol display to allow keyboard input to shift the pointer directly to a given symbol. Such an unusual feature should probably be submitted for usability testing and user feedback before a commitment was made.

The interface design described in Chapter 10 would be customizable in several ways—most importantly, through user-definable collections of symbols. The basic scheme was discussed in Chapter 10, but some issues remain.

From the standpoint of progressive usage, the most important question is how the user gets a custom-configured set of symbols in the first place. Imposing a setup dialogue that forced new users to set up a collection before the first insertion would be a sure deterrent to many of them. On the other hand, a typical user might never get around to customizing the symbol set. The default set of displayed symbols should probably be, therefore, a user-defined group, preloaded with a modest collection of commonly used, general-purpose symbols. This group, named **My Symbols** or something equally innocuous, would draw the user's attention to its being tailorable. Other predefined collections could include sets for **Chemistry**, **Math**, and other technical areas, as well as a general **Languages** set and sets for various specific languages, such as **Danish**, **French**, **German**, **Greek**, and so forth.

The dialogue window and symbol display area should be resizable, but there is no need to provide a separate dialogue or special mechanism for this. The dialogue window should directly support resizing, communicated by a standard resizing handle in the lower right corner. When resized, the symbol display and phrase box should adjust accordingly.

In addition to specifying the contents and manipulating the arrangement of symbols in collections, the user should also be able to set custom keyboard shortcuts for symbols. Other preferences or options under user control might include, among other things, display of shortcut keystrokes, display of row-column numbers, single or multiple-line phrase display, and "always on top" display of the whole dialogue box.

13

IN PLACE:
Fitting the Operational Context

UNSOUND CONTEXT

Since we were already in the bank that handled our corporate accounts, we decided to take care of a routine transfer of funds in person. On the other side of the big mahogany desk, the young bank officer helping us typed in the transaction until, suddenly, his terminal beeped. Curious, we leaned around to peek at the terminal. An error message was splashed across the screen.

With a look of slight embarrassment, the bank official said, "No problem. I can fix this," and quickly typed another entry. Another beep and another message left him clearly flustered and us definitely amused. "Something is wrong here, but I can take care of it," he said as he immediately resumed typing. "I can use an override to force it through." There were no more beeps, but now he looked crestfallen. It seems that, in his rush to avoid embarrassment, he had inadvertently forced through an overdraft to our business account with several zeros too many.

There was nothing to worry about, he assured us. The error would be corrected automatically when the end-of-day balancing was performed. We were not satisfied, however. Until midnight, we would be unable to draw on any funds, and any routine inquiry regarding our assets would show us to be hundreds of thousands of dollars in debt. We insisted that the erroneous overdraft be corrected on the spot. Not possible, we were told. Once a supervisor override was effected on a transaction, it could not be undone. No, not even the bank president could change it, or so we were told.

This exchange highlighted a number of usability issues. The error message displayed for the bank officer may not have made the cause of the warning sufficiently clear. One can even question a system design that makes it so easy to initiate an exceptional transaction that cannot be undone. However, the problem would probably not have occurred if the bank officer had not become rushed; he would not have become rushed if we had not embarrassed him by looking at his screen; and we would never have known to look at the screen were it not for the loud beep in a quiet bank office. The use of audible feedback was ill-suited to the environment in which this system was being used.

OPERATIONAL MODELING

Truly usable software is highly attuned to its environment. The user interface and the overall architecture are designed with the **operational context** in mind. Just as we would not use the same database design for a pet store as for an auto repair shop or build the same set of object classes for a telephone switching system and a point-of-sale application, we cannot approach the design of a system's user interface with a one-size-fits-all mentality.

> *Truly usable software is highly attuned to its environment. We cannot approach the design of a system's user interface with a one-size-fits-all mentality.*

This is the Context Rule. Systems of all kinds need to be fitted not only to the work that they support but also to the context in which that work takes place. Systems that are deployed and used in different environments or different settings may require different solutions to user interface design problems. Similar capability deployed in varied settings may require divergent user interface solutions. Different constraints apply for a query system on a factory floor, in a kiosk within a busy shopping mall, or on a desk in an executive office suite.

Not all aspects of the actual work environment will necessarily have an impact on user interface design. That a factory floor is noisy will probably need to be taken into account in designing a system for process control, but the fact that the walls are painted green is almost certainly irrelevant. Those aspects of the operational context that are most likely to affect user interface design decisions constitute the **operational context model**, or, more succinctly, the **operational model**. The operational model is a collection of various operational and contextual influences that can play a role in usability. We refer to these collections as *profiles* because each is itself a compilation of a somewhat messy mix of factors that can shape the user interface design [Lockwood, 1994]. Operational factors that can affect user interface architecture and detail design include

- Characteristics of users and user roles
- Aspects of the physical work environment
- Features and limitations of operating equipment and interface devices
- General and specific operational risk factors

ENVIRONMENTAL ADAPTATION

In a sense, the operational model serves as a repository for potentially significant information about the operational context. It is typically compiled through accretion. Although much of the information may become available quite early in the software development cycle, it can be quite acceptable and workable to continue to expand and refine the operational model as other models—and even the design itself—are being developed. As the operational model becomes more complete and detailed, its consequences are carried back into the other models—role model, task model, and content model—and forward into the implementation model.

The profiles of factors within the operational model can influence user interface design in more than one way. Commonly, the operational context can have an impact on the relative importance of various design objectives, such as speed of operation, accuracy, ease of learning, readability, and the like. In some cases, the operational context may have a direct impact on highly specific design decisions and details, such as the appropriate use of sound or color or even the placement of controls within interaction spaces. The impact of the operational context may be reflected either directly in the design process or indirectly, such as the way in which the operational context may need to be taken into account in the development and revision of style guides and working standards. For example, we might recognize that a substantial part of the equipment base on which a particular system is to be deployed utilizes monochrome displays. The project style guide might require that text be readable and that graphical displays be easily interpreted when presented in gray-scale.

> *The operational context can have an impact on the relative importance of various design objectives, such as speed of operation, ease of learning, and the like, and on highly specific design decisions and details, such as the use of sound or the placement of controls.*

We view the process of adapting a user interface design to the operational context, not as a separate step or a phase of the overall development effort, but as a continuous activity that proceeds concurrently with other design efforts. Traditional approaches to user interface and interaction design often begin with a primary focus on the work environment and operational context, but, in our experience, better designs result from a focus first on the work and secondarily on the work environment. Aspects of the operational context thus form a backdrop against which user interface design decisions are made. Each of the emerging contextual factors in the operational model is reviewed to ascertain its potential impact on the user interface design:

- How does it affect the design objectives?

- What implications does it have for specific aspects or parts of the design?
- What impact does it have on the project design guidelines and user interface standards?

BINDING CONTEXT

Much of the information constituting the operational model becomes available relatively early in the development process as part of requirements gathering and user role modeling. As discussed in Chapter 4, a structured role model serves not only as an input to task modeling, but also as a repository for holding operational context information associated with user roles. When creating the structured role model we speak of profile attributes being *bound* to a specific user role or group of roles. But not all operational context information is closely bound to user roles. Often we find that the context information is most pertinent to an individual use case or a group of related use cases. Sometimes the operational characteristics apply to the system as a whole. In any case, the operational context information serves not only to help shape our decisions in designing the implementation model, but also to prioritize our usability objectives and focus our resources on those aspects of the user interface design that will have the greatest impact on producing efficient, effective, error-free use of the system.

Here again is the list of profiles introduced in Chapter 4:

- **Incumbents**—characteristics of the actual users who will play a given role
- **Proficiency**—how usage proficiency is distributed over time and among users in a given role
- **Interaction**—characteristic patterns of usage associated with a given role, use case, or set of use cases
- **Information**—nature of the information manipulated by users or exchanged between users and the system
- **Functional support**—specific functions, features, or facilities needed to support users in a given role or for a specific use case or set of use cases
- **Usability criteria**—relative importance of specific usability objectives for a given role or for a specific use case or set of use cases
- **Operational risk**—type and level of risk associated with a given role or for a specific use case or set of use cases
- **Device constraints**—limitations or constraining characteristics of the physical equipment
- **Environment**—relevant factors of the physical environment

The role of the proficiency profile in user interface design was thoroughly covered in the previous chapter. Here we will take up several of the other profiles and look at the implications such information has on interface design.

INCUMBENT PROFILE

The incumbent profile includes various characteristics of the actual users who will occupy a particular role in relationship to a system. It may not be possible in all cases to know in advance what sort of people are likely to make use of a system, but, in many instances, reasonable assumptions can be made, whether based on prior experience, user surveys, general knowledge, or merely informed guesses. Among the characteristics that may play a role in user interface design are such things as

- Knowledge of the application domain
- Knowledge of the system itself
- Level and nature of training
- Age
- Educational background
- Work and other relevant experience
- Cultural and social background
- Specific abilities or disabilities

The incumbent profile takes into account the knowledge that users can be expected to have about the broad domain of application and about the system itself. Domain knowledge and system knowledge may go hand in hand, but role incumbents in many cases are more highly knowledgeable in one than the other. For example, a supervisor filling in during a busy period at an airline ticket counter may have a thorough knowledge of the vagaries of modern airline ticketing practices and yet be relatively unfamiliar with the current software supporting those practices. Deep domain knowledge usually implies familiarity with vocabulary and concepts that can ease learning and use,

> *It may not be possible in all cases to know in advance what sort of people are likely to make use of a system, but, in many instances, reasonable assumptions can be made.*

but such familiarity can also carry expectations about how information and capability will be presented. If such expectations are not met by the design, usability will be reduced for some users.

Where most users can be expected to have thorough training and knowledge of a particular system, designers may have increased latitude in how to organize the user interface for greater efficiency. Especially where the application is used by

FIGURE 13-1 *Ineffective accommodation to users.*
(MICROSOFT BOOKSHELF 97)

itself, nonstandard solutions may be more acceptable in the interest of speed, safety, or other objectives.

Very young or elderly users may need special accommodation. Enlarged visual targets and large, highly readable fonts may be appropriate for these populations, as well as for the visually impaired. If the recommendations for customization discussed in Chapter 12 are followed, one basic system operating under different profiles might be able to accommodate the needs of highly diverse populations. Once again, omitting user control over even one part of the interface can completely defeat the objective of customizability. For example, Microsoft Bookshelf 97 allows users to select type size—from three sizes, as shown in Figure 13-1—but this affects only the display of entries from the reference databases. The tiny, nonstandard type used in the rest of the interface remains stubbornly fixed and, contrary to recommended Windows 95 practices, does not conform to user display settings, such as when custom fonts have been specified for menus.

> *Omitting user control over even one part of the interface can completely defeat the objective of customizability.*

Age, educational level, and cultural background are obvious factors influencing the designer's choice of appropriate vocabulary and usage within the user interface. Even where role incumbents may vary widely or where few assumptions can be made about these factors, designers should consider what might be an appropriate target for vocabulary and reading level within the planned user interface and how cultural issues might be relevant.

INTERACTION PROFILE

The interaction profile compiles a variety of information regarding how users in particular roles or for specific use cases can be expected to interact with the system being designed. Each of the following aspects of the interaction profile can have a substantial influence on user interface design:

- Frequency of use
- Regularity or periodicity of use
- Continuity (continuous versus intermittent use)
- Intensity (rate of interaction) and volume (total amount of interaction)
- Concentration (batches or distributed use)
- Complexity of interaction
- Predictability of interaction
- Locus of control (process-driven or user-driven)

If a system will be used relatively infrequently or sporadically, retention of learning assumes greater importance as a design objective. Either the interface must be designed such that its features and behavior are easy to remember from one use to another, or it will need to be tailored to novice usage since each use will be more like a fresh start. For example, over our years as PC users, we have on numerous occasions needed to format and partition a hard disk. The time between uses is long enough that, given the poorly organized user interface of the ancient software, we tend to fall into the same traps each time.

> *A system used infrequently or sporadically must be designed with features and behavior that are easy to remember from one use to another, or it will need to be tailored to perpetual novice usage.*

For systems that are used frequently and regularly, learnability and retention may become less important as design objectives, while efficiency of interaction rises in significance. Users who are involved in continuous interaction with a system can have somewhat different needs from those who use a system only intermittently.

With high rates of interaction, efficiency can become a dominant concern, as will accuracy. A telephone order entry system that must cope with hundreds of orders per day for each operator should be streamlined for efficient implementation of the focal use cases and designed to reduce costly and time-consuming entry errors. Very high rates of interaction—where users are working under pressure, for example—may require interfaces that are particularly fault tolerant or that are designed to minimize user errors or to reduce the consequences of errors.

Although high rates of interaction are often associated with large amounts of interaction, this is not always the case. A system with many users may process tens of thousands of queries a day even though each user may account for only one or a few transactions. From the standpoint of the individual user, speed of operation may seem inconsequential—an extra second or two completing a use case may hardly be noticed. Yet, to the entire community of users, the company as a whole, interactive efficiency may emerge as a major design objective.

Another possibility is that interaction may be concentrated into batches or bursts of activity. Concentrated interaction may cause efficiency to become a significant objective even if the total volume and rate of interaction are not particularly high. Such bunched interaction—entering a whole series of changes to a database, for example—can delay the user from getting on with other work. Moreover, users become more aware of the time needed to perform a task when they have to repeat it over and over again. Users can end up irritated and impatient and hence more prone to making mistakes. User satisfaction can also be adversely affected.

It is the high end of the scale of interaction rate and volume that most strongly affects user interface design; lower rates and volumes usually do not require special attention. If only some roles or some portions of an application involve particularly high interaction rates or volumes, those parts of the user interface can be tailored for performance. Ideally, software would be optimized for every task supported, but, in the real world, there is simply not enough time and resources to perfect every task supported, and optimizing one area often means detuning another. Reviewing the operational profile as a whole can help designers to make intelligent trade-offs in usability. A system that is awkward or slow to use in a task performed only once a week can be considered more usable than one that poorly supports a task performed 20 times daily.

> *High interaction rate and volume most strongly affect user interface design; lower rates and volumes usually do not require special attention.*

Interaction intensity and volume can be considered properties of use cases as well as of user roles. Where there is substantial variance between use cases, ones with exceptional interaction patterns should be flagged for special attention in fitting the user interface design to the operational context.

Highly predictable interaction can simplify the design of the user interface, but it puts the onus on the designer to be aware of and understand the expected pattern of interaction in order to tailor the organization and workflow to this pattern. Highly predictable interaction makes it easier to optimize an interface for efficient use. When the content and sequence of interaction are highly variable and unpredictable, it can be much more difficult for designers to find the best layout; hence, learnability and flexibility in operation assume greater importance.

For example, the role of `claimsEntryClerk` in an automobile insurance application may be associated with high predictability. Most likely, there is only one form, and much the same pieces of information are entered from each form. In contrast, an executive using a decision support tool for financial analysis may bring up one set of data, then switch to a different set, produce a graph, and then filter the dataset and run a report. The next day he or she may look at completely different data, produce three reports, and do no graphing. All actions with the system are ad hoc and changeable.

The question of who is in charge can be an important one in user interface design. We use the psychological term *locus of control* to refer to this aspect of the interaction profile. Do the software and the process it embodies essentially drive the interaction, or is the user in control? Free-form interaction with the user in the driver's seat can place more demand on the user to retain "knowledge in the head" and more demand on the designer to promote ease of learning and retention. Interfaces that take charge and walk the user through a set scenario are acceptable solutions for predictable interaction that is process-driven but are less effective for highly variable interaction where the user needs to be in charge. Of course, some fairly predictable interaction may still leave the user in control of the process. The `claimsEntryClerk` may have substantial control over the process in terms of the order of entry, what fields to skip, when to add clarifying comments, and the like, even though the overall task is fairly fixed and repetitive.

> *Free-form interaction with the user in the driver's seat can place more demand on the user to retain "knowledge in the head" and more demand on the designer to promote ease of learning and retention.*

INFORMATION PROFILE

Closely related to the interaction profile is the information profile, which includes four factors regarding the information available to and received from users:

1. Input origins
2. Flow direction
3. Information volume
4. Information complexity

To the source. The information obtained from the user comes from somewhere. Either it starts in the user's mind, with thoughts and ideas, or it reaches the user through one of the senses. Most commonly in software applications, information originates with one of three channels: (1) visual (such as a paper insurance form), (2) aural (such as a customer's voice over the telephone), or (3) mental (such as the ideas generated by an artist using a photo-editing application). In exceptional cases, other senses could play a role. An inspection mechanic might use touch to identify defects in machine parts, which are entered into logging software through a headset microphone; an oenologist might enter details of the bouquet of a new vintage using the keyboard of a handheld terminal.

The ultimate origins of information flowing from the user to the system can be of crucial importance in fitting user interface design to the operational context. Since more than one channel may be used in some roles or some applications, we need to identify the dominant modality in each case. If the user is reading data values from a form or observing nonverbal behavior in a discussion group, it is highly unlikely that the user is also going to be looking at the display screen. Most of the time, such users would not be looking at the screen, and, when they do look at it, they must first reorient themselves within that visual context. Clearly, the user interface in such contexts cannot rely solely or primarily on visual feedback for error or warning messages. In these cases, sound might be much more effective. In contrast, if the user is listening to a customer through a telephone headset, a computer beeping away can be an annoying distraction to both user and customer or may even go unnoticed by the user. Where information originates in the thoughts of the user, the user interface should help users quickly capture ideas or thoughts and make it easy for them to change directions, revising their input or undoing their actions.

Data entry from paper forms and data entry over the telephone present an interesting contrast in the influences of information origin on user interface design. A paper form cannot talk back. You cannot ask it for a correction if an error is flagged. For this reason, careful attention must be paid to handling the exception cases covering missing or incomplete information when designing systems for input from paper sources. The telephone source is, by contrast, interactive, so the person on the line can be queried for corrections or more information.

In the interest of efficient and reliable input from paper forms, the input process needs to mirror the layout of the paper form. The screen layout best resembles the form layout when it comes to the fields of interest, and the tab order of screen fields should correspond with the order in which information appears on the printed page. Why? Visually skipping around the page takes time, and each visual skip has a chance of landing the attention on the wrong line. The entry task is made slower and more error-prone, and training may take longer since the user must learn how to zigzag through the form. In some applications, redesigning the form to facilitate data entry may be part of the user interface design problem.

> *For efficient and reliable input from paper forms, the input process needs to mirror the layout of the paper form; in some applications, the form may need to be redesigned to facilitate data entry.*

With a telephone source, the input process need not follow a fixed sequence, although there may be advantages to following a script that sets the entry order ("May I have your telephone number, area code first?" "May I have your last name? Your zip code?"). In some applications, the system may display the script on-screen as a memory aid, especially for new entry operators.

When it comes to flagging errors or exceptions, beeps and buzzes may not be a good idea with a telephone source since the two streams of sound compete and the customer on the other end of the line may be able to hear the computer. In contrast, sound may be preferred to signal messages in paper-source data entry. Such applications are often known as "heads-down" data entry because the clerk is looking, with head down, at the paper form. If the software simply puts up a message box with no audible attention-getter, the user may not become aware of what has happened until he or she hears the "chirp-chirp-chirp" of the keyboard buffer overflowing.

In and out. Flow direction reflects the importance of taking into account whether interaction between the user and the system is predominantly organized around acquiring information from the user or providing it to the user. In an insurance forms-processing application or in a simple graphics paint program, the process is built around transcription or communication from the user. With a financier using a stock analysis system, the process is more focused on providing information to the user. Decision support and performance support systems are clearly organized around providing information to the user, while transaction-processing systems more typically focus on recording data from the user. Naturally, if the main focus is recording data, then the user interface should facilitate the input process. If the focus is on providing information to the user, then the emphasis within the user interface design should be in aiding data comprehension and helping the user build understanding out of data. Different parts of an application may have differing emphases on acquisition versus provision of information.

Deep and wide. Information volume and information complexity are distinct factors that can have similar influences on design. *Information volume* refers to how much information is potentially available or of interest to the user. Trying to display large quantities of information can, in itself, present design challenges. Information may have to be divided among multiple screens or pages. How is this best achieved? If divided, navigation and visual linking of different parts of the user interface emerge as critical design issues. If too much information is crammed into a single interaction context, readability can become a problem. If clever schemes for condensing data are used, ease of learning or of interpretation may be compromised. Systems with high information volume need to provide users with effective tools and aids for subdividing, grouping, and navigating what would otherwise be an unmanageable amount of information.

Information may be complex in many different ways. *Information complexity* encompasses such issues as the number of time periods represented or the number of subgroups within the information of interest—for example, figures from the

London office, the Chicago office, and the Sunnyvale office. The number of different data types, the number of entity attributes, and so forth, can also affect information complexity. Applications with high information complexity need to help users keep track of which among subgroups are being viewed or manipulated. Designs will need to help the user tame the complexity and turn complicated data into useful information. Within applications with substantial information complexity, clarity of presentation, comprehensibility, and layout assume great importance.

It is important to keep in mind that the information profile reflects operational aspects associated with particular user roles or specific use cases. Users in some roles may, for example, be dealing with inputting a large amount of relatively simple information, but users in other roles may be analyzing and interpreting the more complex results from reducing that high volume of data.

ENVIRONMENT PROFILE

In what type of location is the user located? In a private office? At a kiosk in a public square? Amidst machinery on a factory floor? A mixture of environments? Many aspects of the actual physical working environment within which systems are used may need to be taken into account for effective user interface design. These include sundry things such as the level of ambient noise, the lighting conditions, and environmental factors such as temperature and humidity of the setting, or the presence of vibration. We capture information about these these types of factors in the **environment profile**.

A key element here is the level of distraction due to the physical environment. Distractions can be physical—a noisy fan, repeated phone calls, or an office mate who keeps interrupting, for example—or mental, such as trying to keep track of multiple tasks or trying to remember to do something that must temporarily be postponed. If the distractions are frequent, users may need extra help from the user interface in particular areas, such as in returning to tasks, figuring out where they left off, or easily switching among several tasks.

> *If distractions are frequent, users may need extra help from the user interface in returning to tasks, figuring out where they left off, or easily switching among several tasks.*

The ambient noise level of the environment needs to be taken into account quite apart from whether the noise is distracting. Users can become habituated to a high noise level, for example, but that does not mean they will be able to hear a quiet warning beep amidst the clanks and rattles of a bottling plant. On the other end of the spectrum, low ambient noise must also be taken into account. A raucous squawk from software announcing an imminent appointment might bring a smile in a home office but produce frowns in the halls of a conservative law firm.

In many cases, only site visits to the actual workplace will make the developers aware of what operational conditions may need to be accounted for in the design. Designers may need to consider a variety of aspects of the work setting. The physical layout can be important. If users working collaboratively on shared work are near enough to one another, plain old-fashioned talking may be one way to coordinate some of the work, but, if users are widely spaced or spread over multiple floors, electronic messaging may need to be an integral part of the user interface design.

> *In many cases, only site visits to the actual workplace will make developers aware of what operational conditions may need to be accounted for in the design.*

Outdoor settings can impose design constraints that are dramatically different from those in a conventional office. (See sidebar, Lift Ticket Interface.) Extremes of temperature and humidity, whether outdoors or in interior settings, may need to be taken into account. A system intended for field use by archaeologists may need to cope with the presence of dust, with dirty fingers, and with bright sunlight, for example.

Vibration can be a complicating issue in some user interface designs, such as the control panel of a car stereo where the vibration, bouncing, and swaying of the car can make it more difficult for the user to press the right target button, a problem that is exacerbated under the low-light conditions of night driving.

DEVICE CONSTRAINTS PROFILE

Device constraints are limitations or constraining characteristics of the physical equipment on which a system is deployed or through which the user interacts with the system. The **device constraints profile** identifies equipment characteristics associated with specific roles, use cases, or the system as a whole. There may be limitations on the input side, the output side, or both. These constraints include screen size, resolution, and color depth; keyboard or keypad size and layout; and special controls such as sliders, toggle switches, rotary knobs, or the like. In some projects, the user interface designers may have wide latitude in specifying input and output devices; in others, the devices may be fixed by fiat, economics, or the user community. Monochrome displays limited to a few short lines of characters are still common in many industrial control systems. Even some PC-based software may need to accommodate to a substantial installed base of older monochrome screens with only VGA resolution. As mentioned in Chapter 7, this was found to be the case with software developed for deployment on laptops in police cruisers. Although not all the target computers were monochrome, the software had to be usable on the oldest and least capable systems that were still in wide use.

LIFT TICKET INTERFACE

For an interesting design challenge, consider the operational context issues for a system to operate under rather extreme conditions: an automatic credit-card ticket machine to dispense lift tickets at a ski resort. What are the salient aspects of the physical environment and conditions that may need to be taken into account for a successful design?

- Exterior location, exposed or partially exposed
- Cold, possibly windy conditions
- Presence of ice, snow, water, dirt
- Possible bright sun, direct or reflected

We can anticipate other important aspects of the operational context model. Some users, regular skiers, may become experienced with the system, but it must also be easy for the complete neophyte to use quickly and efficiently without instruction. The transactions are all relatively simple, with little variation. Speed of completion is somewhat important because long lines irritate customers. If processing through automated lines is too slow, users may shift to the staffed ticket windows, defeating the main business purpose of the automated system. Usage will tend to be concentrated at particular peak periods, especially at the start of each day.

Some of the design consequences and conclusions can be quite subtle and may require considerable creativity. For example, consider the fact that the user either will be wearing gloves or mittens or will probably have cold fingers. What does this imply about the design of the keypad, touch screen, or other input device? It means the targets need to be large and relatively small in number so that the correct one can be pressed even with a gloved finger. It suggests simplifying operation and reducing errors through an incremental interaction model.

Users will also be trying to handle credit cards. What can go wrong under these conditions and how might it be avoided or prevented? How can the process be simplified or accelerated? Handling the card will be awkward, and slipping it into a slot the wrong way could result in more user frustration and greater delay than under more ideal conditions. Thus, the card-reading mechanism should accept a card regardless of which way it is oriented. What kind of card reader is indicated? One where the card is swiped through a projecting track or is slipped into a slot? Which will be easier for the user to manage with cold or gloved fingers? These questions may have to be submitted for objective testing. We may also have to do preliminary field observations before we will know what percentage of users will remove their gloves or mittens before trying to use the system. Which reader system will be more prone to mechanical failure? The track has no moving parts but actually projects out into the environment. Which will be more vulnerable to clogging with dirt or snow? Either might be equipped with a wiper or self-cleaning mechanism that brushes or squeegees the card as it is swiped, but the consequences could be more severe if the slot mechanism fails and dirt or snow gets into the interior of the machine proper. A slot system does not in itself convey any affordance regarding in which of the four possible orientations the card is to be inserted, while the track system narrows the alternatives to two since the vast majority of users already understand that the magnetic stripe needs to be read by the machine.

Compared to, say, a warm, well-lit, relatively clean supermarket, the chances that the skier will drop the credit card are much higher. If the card is dropped, it will be more difficult to retrieve, and it is more likely to end up dirty, even unusable. Thus, the goal should make it less likely that the card will be dropped and less of a problem if it is. For example, the terminal could provide a projecting shelf or netting to catch the card if it is dropped in the course of use.

Based on all these considerations, we probably would select the surface track reader. The reader mechanism should correctly read the card with the magnetic stripe oriented either way, swiped in either direction, at almost any speed. This saves the user from having to turn the card if it is oriented the wrong way and also reduces the need for repeated swiping of the card. However, note that the interface succeeds in helping the user and speeding up the line only if the user knows about this feature, so the terminal should prominently announce, "Swipe card up or down facing either way."

We may include under the heading of device constraints physical barriers or impediments between users and a system. For example, the most logical, well-planned keyboard shortcuts will not help the factory worker who is wearing heavy, heat-shielding gloves. Keypad or touch screen used under these conditions may need to be heat and abrasion resistant and have oversized controls.

As one might expect, the most interesting and extreme limitations are often in embedded systems applications, which will be discussed in more detail in the next chapter. For some applications, input may be limited to one or two buttons and outputs to a single line of text or even a small number of LEDs. For example, a laboratory test instrument is to be built into a case the size of a fountain pen. Under common conditions of use, the user will often need to be looking elsewhere once the instrument is inserted into a sample. The system has to be able to convey six messages: testing in progress, testing complete, sample nominal, sample high, sample low, and instrument error.

How can the designer deal with such severe operational constraints? An LCD or LED display is impractical for this application. Sound is the only available channel, and the sound-generating device already chosen for engineering reasons can emit only two tones: one high, one low. In one possible design, the messages are combined into five and communicated as follows:

1. Testing in progress: ' ' ' ' ' ' (rapid ticking made with very short pulse)
2. Complete, sample nominal: ‾ ‾ ‾ (three short, high tones)
3. Complete, sample high: _ ‾‾‾ _ ‾‾‾ (short low, long high, repeated)
4. Complete, sample low: ‾ ___ ‾ ___ (short high, long low, repeated)
5. Instrument error: _ _ _ _ _ _ (rapid repeating low tone)

Although such an interface may not be completely intuitive, it is likely to be easy to learn and to remember how to interpret it.

OPERATIONAL RISK PROFILE

Operational risk refers to what is at stake if the user and the system fail in the correct completion of tasks. What are the consequences of an input error, a failure to complete a transaction, a system lockup, or a delay in processing? In some cases, an error may be inconsequential; in others, disaster may loom.

In far too many applications, designers fail to consider operational risk in connection with particular roles or use cases or fail to think creatively about how errors might be controlled or reduced. Seemingly small input errors may compound and result in substantial consequences. Countless customer databases are riddled with duplicate entries resulting from typing errors during order entry. The bogus records do more than just waste storage space and processing time; they can cost money in mailings and give a distorted picture of sales and the customer base that can lead to bad management decisions. Recognizing this, designers can incorporate soundex or nearest-match searching that makes it easier for an operator or entry clerk to spot whether a new entry matches an existing customer.

Improving accuracy and reliability can also increase efficiency. Good validation and error checking on entry mean less information needs to be reentered and fewer bad transactions need to be corrected later.

Ironically, many techniques for improving accuracy and reliability also increase efficiency of use. For example, a system can automatically generate the city and state from an entered ZIP code, thus reducing errors and speeding entry. In general, good validation and error checking on entry mean less information needs to be reentered and fewer bad transactions need to be corrected later.

Even the appearance and layout of a display can have an impact on errors. Controls that serve radically different functions should not be too similar in appearance or be located too closely. The visual differences between the adjacent controls in Figure 13-2 are too limited for controls that have the opposite effect. In this case, the operational risk is small, especially since the effect can be easily undone, a risk-reduction technique of wide applicability.

Although some applications may be associated with elevated operational risk across the board, there are usually differences from use case to use case. The software controlling a nuclear power plant involves significant operational risk in all its aspects. However, the inherent risk is much higher in using a special command to override a safety feature than in requesting a routine plant status overview.

Where operational risk is higher in connection with particular roles or use cases, special attention needs to be paid to mechanisms that assure accuracy of input and accurate interpretation of output. Confirmation procedures need to be carefully considered.

Confirmation messages were covered in Chapter 11. It is important to remember that, as a rule, confirmation affords only relatively weak or nonexistent protection from error. If an operation is in fact potentially catastrophic, merely

FIGURE 13-2 *Adjacent, nearly identical controls, with opposite functions.*
(MICROSOFT WORD 97)

requiring the user to click on an **OK** button is not enough to significantly reduce risk. High-risk use cases require more definitive and unambiguous assurance that the user's action is intentional. Some systems have used cascading confirmations, but users can keep clicking **OK** or hitting **Enter** faster than the eye can follow. A lesson might be lifted from the pages of weapon systems design. Two separate keys must be turned simultaneously to arm a warhead. An analogy on a graphical user interface might require the user to confirm an irrevocable action with simultaneous pressing of two specified keys while also clicking on a big red **Delete System Image** button. Reversibility, of course, is always highly desirable but not always completely possible or practical.

In most cases, the best the designer can do is reduce the probability of error, not eliminate it altogether. Take the simple and common case of using an ATM to handle a deposit or withdrawal. The typical ATM asks the user to confirm each step in the process. To reduce the chance of the user's confirming reflexively by just hitting the same **Enter** or **OK** key without even reading the display, most ATM software varies which key is used for confirmation. Each screen or menu requires the user to press a different key, forcing the user to look at the screen and thus increasing the likelihood that he or she has read and understood the confirmation request. However, there are no guarantees. With practice, a user could learn to tap the right sequence of keys without thinking, thus defeating the design and someday, perhaps, withdrawing $500 instead of an intended $50.

> *Where risk is high, confirmation procedures need to be carefully considered, but confirmation affords only relatively weak or nonexistent protection.*

There are inevitable trade-offs in managing operational risks. Attempting to reduce or control one risk almost invariably heightens others or has some other impact on usability. The ATM user interface presents a classic example. Most ATMs in Australia and many other countries dispense cash only after the user retrieves the ATM card. This virtually eliminates the chance of the user forgetting the card in the machine, but it also makes it much more awkward and time-consuming to perform multiple transactions on the same visit to the ATM.

PUTTING CONTEXT IN PLACE

To make use of the operational model, designers need to fill in the blanks in terms of the various operation profiles it comprises. Using information from various sources, including the structured user role model, information about each of the many factors is identified. A checklist or simple form, such as the one found in

Appendix E, can serve as a convenient way to assure that all potentially significant aspects have been considered. For this purpose, we are interested in aspects of the operational context that are salient—that stand out—and that are relevant. This requires a certain amount of judgment and filtering on the part of the designer. Once the salient and relevant aspects of the operational context have been identified, each is reviewed for its possible implications in terms of the user interface design, the design objectives, and the design guidelines. To understand this process better, let us compare and contrast two applications that differ rather sharply in their operational profiles.

DimTel Products Order Taking

It's after midnight on Australian television, and the commercials begin to change in character. All of a sudden, the screen is alive with a familiar figure making a frenetic pitch. It's Tim, the DimTel man, hawking a set of razor-sharp kitchen knives for a paltry $19.95 plus postage and handling: "But wait, there's more. If you order now, we will include this set of six steak knives with fabulous faux ebony handles absolutely free. But that's not all. Especially for the viewers of this program, we will throw in this solid maple cutting board, hand-stamped with the legendary DimTel symbol of quality, at no extra charge. That's right, the four incredibly sharp kitchen knives, the six luxury steak knives and this beautiful, hand-stamped cutting board, all for just $19.95 plus postage and handling. Be among the first 100 callers, and the shipping and handling is on us. That's right, absolutely no charge to you. So, ring now and be ready with your credit-card details. Our trained telephonists are standing by to take your orders." Similar scenes are familiar to late-night television audiences in many countries.

Those telephone order takers, standing ready to cope with the surge of callers, need to be supported by good order entry software. What can we say about the operational context that might need to be taken into account in our user interface design? First, this is a high-volume application that is used frequently, more or less continuously, and at a high rate of interaction. Each order is separate and much the same as the last one. The information source is aural, and the volume of information displayed or of interest to the operator is quite small, with only a few different kinds of data. The primary flow of information is into the system. With so many order takers crammed into the "boiler room" operation, the setting is likely to be quite noisy. Sounds generated by the software will only make matters worse.

> *In order processing, high job turnover can mean many novices in training, but, after one shift of processing hundreds of orders, almost everyone reaches expert-level usage.*

The end users of this application may represent an interesting population. In telephone order processing, job turnover can be quite high, meaning that novices in training will be fairly common. However, novices quickly become experts in this context. After a two-hour training and one shift of processing many hundreds of orders, almost everyone reaches expert-level usage. So, the proficiency profile is one of mostly experts and novices. Order takers are unlikely to have much knowledge of the marketing and telephone sales domain, and, although they soon know one part of the software intimately, their systems knowledge is likely to remain rather narrow and restricted.

What do we conclude from this review of the operational context? Speed and accuracy of operation are crucially important. The system should be easy to learn and to master quickly. Flexibility of operation and adaptability of the interface are not high priorities. The design will need to focus on efficient workflow within a simple layout. The interface should be optimized for keyboard operation, with careful consideration of the tabbing order by which focus moves from field to field. Careful attention should also be paid to the choice of widgets to improve performance. For example, we might employ drop-down combo boxes to allow the operator to type only the first few characters of a product. The system could automatically fill in the city and state from the zip code, not only saving typing but also enabling the operator to validate the address ("That's in Georgetown, Maryland, correct?)."

BANKINVEST PORTFOLIO ANALYSIS

The BankInvest software is to be used by bank officers to review and analyze the investments of small investors seeking recommendations. The software must allow the bank official to examine the client's portfolio of investments and look at its performance over different time periods in light of the investor's goals. The user may want to make various "what-if" comparisons, substituting a different mutual fund, altering the mix, or changing the strategy. Since each portfolio and investor is different, it is difficult to say in advance what analyses may be useful and in what order they might be performed. The total volume of use is relatively low despite moderately frequent use. The application is apt to be used nearly every day, but not continuously since the targeted bank personnel will have other duties and use other software as well. In this case, the interaction is clearly directed by the user and is highly variable, originating with the particular thoughts and ideas of the bank analyst. The flow of information from the system is the most important to the user, and the information of interest may be both quite extensive and moderately complex.

Most users of BankInvest will be classic improving intermediates who can be expected to have a moderate knowledge of the BankInvest system coupled with substantial domain knowledge regarding investments and banking practices. They work in a relatively quiet office setting with comparatively few distractions. As they use the system, they may or may not consult paper sources, but they can be expected to be watching the screen fairly closely.

In this application, flexibility of operation and comprehensibility of the output become the driving forces. Being able to view information in various forms—tables, charts, graphs, and so forth—will be valuable. Easy linkages to other systems, such as databases of funds and fund performances, will be essential. Integration or interoperation with other supporting applications, such as calendars and specialized calculators, can help simplify operation.

For efficiency as well as flexibility, it would be desirable to allow users to define and save entire sequences of analyses and reporting for later reuse. Keeping in mind the incumbent profile, something more creative than a typical programmer-oriented macro facility would be needed.

14

SAME GAME, DIFFERENT FIELDS:
Special Applications, Special Issues

THEME AND VARIATION, AGAIN

Everyone believes his or her own problems are special. There is always a certain foundation of truth to this belief, even when the problems are prosaic. On the other hand, common concepts underlie the design of doorknobs and digital imaging systems, kiosks and kitchen timers. The versatile designer is one who knows how to play the game well enough to play it just a little bit differently in different fields.

In this chapter, we will move away from desktop software and look at the application of usage-centered design to a variety of other kinds of system design problems. We will give greatest attention to Web-based applications and to embedded systems applications. Our goal is to be illustrative rather than inclusive.

> *Common concepts underlie the design of doorknobs and digital imaging systems, kiosks and kitchen timers. The versatile designer knows how to play the same game just a little bit differently in different fields.*

WEB DESIGN FOR USE

The World Wide Web has been touted as one of the fastest-growing communications phenomena in history, a medium destined to transform commerce, scholarship, and publication. Whether or not the Web, the Internet, and Intranets represent a profound paradigmatic shift or only another trendy technology, they cannot be ignored. A contemporary book on users and software usability would be incomplete without some consideration of Web-site design.

Usability problems on the Web are ubiquitous but often remain unknown to the site owners for substantial periods of time. Most Web users will not take the time to complain or give feedback, and many may not even be aware of the problems they experienced. Usually, it takes some crisis or dilemma to bring usability issues to the fore. For example, one commercial operation became aware of usability problems only after banner ads elsewhere on the Web failed to generate new business. Potential customers were clicking through on the banner ads and then giving up before completing any business on the labyrinthine site.

Small matters can also make big differences in Web-site usability. A classic example took place at a university in Australia that had converted to Web-based registration for subjects. Instructors began to suspect problems when large numbers of unlisted students, all claiming to be duly registered and waving copies of forms, began showing up for lectures. It seems that the subject registration form on the Web included two action buttons. One allowed students to print a final copy of their completed schedule. Most students did that and then left, never even noticing the other button marked **Confirm**. Absent the confirmation, all subject registrations were canceled.

> *Web designers more often speak of "compelling" Web sites than of usable ones. They seek to enhance the quality of the "user experience" but consider user performance of lesser import.*

It would be an understatement to say that usability is not always given a great deal of attention on the Web. Among contemporary Web sites are some of the most unusable software systems we have ever encountered. Graphic designers working on the Web more often speak of "compelling" Web sites than of usable ones. They seek to enhance the quality of the "user experience" but consider user performance of lesser import. In truth, usability is always a factor—an experience is unlikely to be compelling if you cannot find your way through a site—even though this factor may not be acknowledged explicitly by the graphic artists and HTML programmers assembling a site.

PURPOSE PROFILE

Web sites are constructed for a variety of purposes, and, to some extent, the purpose has an impact on the relative importance of usability. Among the sundry justifications for Web sites are such purposes as these:

- Presence
- Public relations
- Advertisement
- Product promotion

- Sales and sales support
- Customer support
- Technical support
- On-line publishing
- Information resource

Many Web sites are constructed merely to provide a business presence on the Web, with little regard for any purpose beyond being there. Having a Web site has become one of the requisite basics for modern business operation, strictly apart from any real value added to the business or its customers. Especially in high-technology fields, Web sites have become like business cards; without them, it is hard to be taken seriously as a real business entity.

Public relations is a purpose akin to a basic presence but more actively concerned with building and maintaining an image with the general public. Advertisement and product promotion are intended, whether directly or ultimately, to generate queries, qualified leads, and, in the end, actual sales. Some Web sites advertise and promote products and services, but sales are actually made through other channels. Other sites attempt to sell goods and services directly. For some businesses, such as an on-line book or music store, the Web may be the primary or only business site for the company. Sales support, such as allowing customers to check on order status, is often integrated with other sales functions and facilities.

A good example of using a site for customer support is the way some common couriers enable customers to track packages through the Web. Web sites can also provide technical support for products already sold, whether via the Web or through other channels. Given the skyrocketing costs of telephone support, this is a particularly promising but underdeveloped application of Web technology.

On-line publishing uses the Web as a channel for distributing information, which is analogous to magazine or book publication but with, potentially, added capabilities. Some material is now published solely on the Web, while other sites, such as those maintained by many major newspapers, augment or duplicate print-media publication. Information resources of various stripes function like reference libraries or librarians, providing access to permanent databases and collections of information on the Web and elsewhere. Among the best-known and most heavily visited Web sites are information resources, including search and indexing facilities such as Yahoo, Alta Vista, Lycos, and others.

For all types of Web sites, content, usability, and aesthetic appeal all come into play, but their relative importance depends on the purpose of the site.

For all types of sites, three major design factors—content, usability, and aesthetic appeal—come into play, but the relative importance of these depends on the purpose. We think of this as a *purpose profile*, as represented in Figure 14-1. For example, usability may rank a distant third after

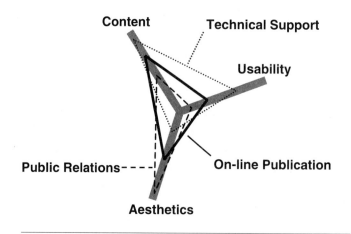

FIGURE 14-1 *Purpose profiles illustrated.*

aesthetics and content for a site aimed to establish a corporate presence or support public relations. For a technical support site, content and usability will far outweigh aesthetics. On-line publishing might need to emphasize all three more equally.

For some purposes, usability may be a factor in the design only in a relatively specialized or limited way. Paper business cards, for example, are not complicated systems from the standpoint of usability. The basic issues are whether the necessary information is on the card and whether it is readable. Web sites intended only for establishing a business presence may require little more in terms of usability than to provide basic content in a recognizable and readable form.

HIT ME

The criterion for success applied to many Web sites is often the hit rate—how many visitors access the site per day or per week. Web design has, consequently, been dominated by graphic artists and others whose concern is for aesthetic appeal or by HTML programmers and other technically focused professionals whose preferences have often leaned toward garish graphics and attention-grabbing animation. Colorful, animated pages are intended to draw more visitors. Interestingly, among regular users of the Web, graphics rates a distant third behind speed of operation and information content as the most important Web-site features [Online Consulting Group, 1997].

Designing a site that appeals because it is fun, attractive, or intriguing is one way to generate hits, but sex-and-sizzle is not the whole story. Good content, apart from presentation, has also proved to be a major draw; necessity is another. Some pug-ugly tech support sites with appalling layout and awkward navigation have achieved astronomical hit rates because they are needed by customers wrestling with complicated or poorly documented products. Building a site that is well organized, well behaved, and well stocked with useful content may be most important for its impact on repeated use. Web users notice inconsistency, sloppy layout, and confusing organization, even if not always consciously. They tend to distrust information that is poorly communicated or difficult to reach and will not return to sites that are poorly designed or filled with fluff, however prettily it may be displayed.

Aside from providing useful and desired content and services, long-term appeal of a Web site depends on a design that is

> *Long-term appeal of a Web site depends on a design that is well behaved, well organized, and interesting—a trio of factors closely related to Web-site usability and to usage-centered design.*

- Well behaved
- Well organized
- Interesting

This trio of factors is closely related to Web-site usability and to usage-centered design. To be interesting, a site not only must hold the interest but also must be related to the needs and interests of users. To be well behaved and organized from the perspective of users, a site must reflect how users think about and carry out their work.

SAME BUT DIFFERENT

Web pages are interfaces between users and a Web site. Web-page design is, therefore, user interface design, and Web-site design is interaction design. Despite claims about a new information paradigm and new modes of interaction, Intranet applications do not cease to be applications just because they are Web-based. Collections of data to be accessed through the Internet or Intranets need to be organized around a sound data model for reliability, efficiency, and ease of access. Information displayed through a Web browser is subject to all the same principles of effective information presentation as if it were shown in any other application window.

The underlying technology available at the desktop may have changed, but the workings of the human eye and hand and their coordination through the human brain are still subject to the same operational prejudices shaped by a million years of primate evolution, all spent coping with a real rather than virtual environment. Designers already know a great deal

> *The chaos and complexity of the Web places a premium on such old-fashioned virtues as making it clear to users where they are and how they got there.*

about how to solve the problems of Web-site design. There is no reason not to draw on what is already well established in terms of graphical design and layout, user interface and interaction design, semiotics, and the like. The need for visual object persistence and the advantages of visibility in the tools and materials needed for successful task completion are not vanquished by HTML or Java applets. If anything, the chaos and complexity of the Web places a premium on such old-fashioned virtues as making it clear to users where they are and how they got there.

HTML, VRML, XML, and their extensions and successors are often heralded by enthusiasts as wonders of the modern world. A close examination of the Web as a medium for implementing tools for people to use quickly reveals that it is, in many respects, a giant step backward. In principle, virtually anything that can be represented on the desktop in stand-alone applications or through client-server architecture can be created on the Web. In practice, many things are found to be substantially more difficult. The repertoire of materials and tools is both less constrained and more limited at the same time. You can make your buttons look like anything you choose, but your users take a hit in downloading bitmaps if you get too grandiose.

Although many Web designers and developers will protest, Web programming is programming, all the long-established principles of software engineering apply

> *Web programming is programming. All the long-established principles of software engineering apply.*

not only to Java but also to HTML, VRML, and XML [Powell et al., 1998]. That some of these make it hard to adhere to good practice only makes sound engineering all the more vital. The issues of database organization and access, user interface design, and program construction are as important on the Web as in desktop applications running under Windows or on any other operating system. Unfortunately, only a minority of people working on the Web realize this. At one recent conference for professional Web designers and developers, we asked for a show of hands of how many in an audience of over 200 had any background or education in computer programming, software engineering, or computer science. Only a couple dozen hands were raised.

Real estate zoning. When you move from desktop or LAN-based client-server applications to the Web, you give up a great deal of control as a designer. The appearance and behavior of pages may depend on the browser in use, screen resolution, user preference settings, and even connection bandwidth. Screen real estate is more limited because the Web browser itself will not get out of the way and typically takes up the entire top of the screen.

If you know what you are doing as a designer, one approach to improving usability on the Web is to take back control over the screen real estate. By laying out Web pages within nested tables and using absolute sizes, the positions and relationships among visual elements can be controlled more precisely and completely. Frames can be used to create areas of visual stability in the apparent interface, limiting what can and cannot be resized, reformatted, and scrolled. Instead of merely throwing information onto Web pages and hoping for the best on the receiving end, designers of Web-based applications should devise the most usable pages in terms of layout, appearance, and behavior and then see how closely this can be approximated using available Web functions.

Of course, seizing more control over what the browser displays can be a double-edged sword. Inept use of tables and frames can sacrifice some of the inherent flexibility of the Web and put users with low-resolution displays at a disadvantage.

> *To improve usability on the Web, take back control over the screen real estate, controlling the sizes, positions, and relationships among visual elements.*

It is important not to give up and forget all that you have learned about good layout and design just because you are designing for the Web, where the browser can rearrange visual elements. For example, one often sees forms laid out as a vertical stack of equal-spaced, equal-sized fields, in complete violation of any intrinsic structure to the information. This kind of naïve layout, illustrated in Figure 14-2, may be excusable within a personal home page constructed by a student for other students, but it is indefensible for a commercial site for use by customers.

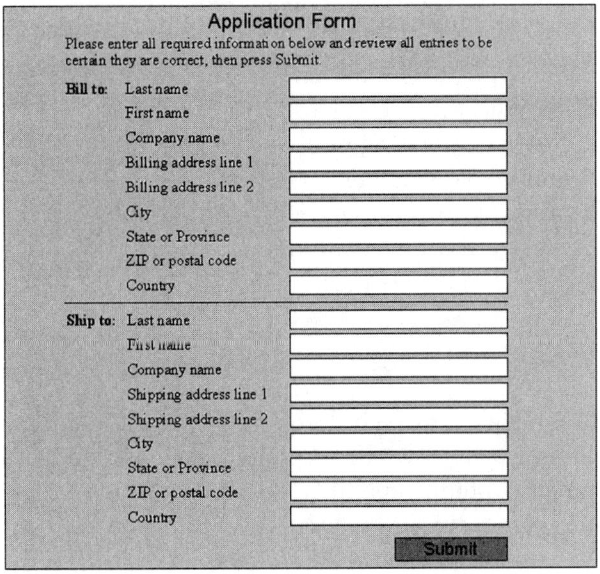

FIGURE 14-2 *Unstructured stacks of input fields.*

Scanning and skipping. Some things are a bit different when users face a browser rather than a stand-alone application. For Web sites, the primary interaction idiom is context switching—going from Web page to Web page by following links. Because context switching is so frequent, navigation can be complex and unpredictable.

Text in various forms and guises is often the dominant form of communication with users, although this is changing as Web browsers and sites are augmented by graphics controls resembling standard GUI widgets in capability if not always in appearance. Web users typically read and scan their way through sites, although it is unclear how much this differs from desktop graphical user interfaces. In many cases, usage is typically focused on content and information, on searching and retrieval activities.

Today's Web sites are far more varied in appearance than typical desktop software in part because of relatively few conventions and a severe shortage of standards. The Web designer can lay out a page in any way he or she desires, give controls any appearance, and use any color scheme, however garish.

Because they operate over networks and the Internet, Web-based systems can be much slower than their desktop counterparts. Naturally, it depends on the kind of connection. Sites targeted to the general public must cope with heavy Internet traffic and 14.4-kilobaud modems, while an Intranet application might be able to count on T1 lines and Fast Ethernet to the desktop.

When it comes to user interface issues, there are far fewer significant differences between desktop and Web-based applications than the Web gurus would have you believe, and some of the apparent differences are disappearing even as you read. Not only are Web weavers borrowing ideas from desktop applications design, but many people talk of Web browsers as the universal client. Web sites designed as Intranet applications for internal use are becoming more and more like their desktop counterparts. Meanwhile, Microsoft has been attempting to integrate its browser into the operating system in a commitment, at least for now, to making Windows and the Web extensions of each other. The Web-style controls in Office 97, as shown in Figure 14-3, and other recent software also exemplify this trend. They are visually flat and communicate their affordance only when the pointer passes over them and they receive focus.

WEB WOES

The most common mistakes in Web design are painfully familiar to anyone with an eye for design and usability. All too often, aesthetic sensibility and graphic design dominate over content, capability, and recognition of real user needs. Web developers, in their own fashion, succumb to feature creep or content creep, creating bloated, busy, baroque Web pages that are slow to load, difficult to read, and impossible to use. It is so easy to add another link or drop in another graphic that

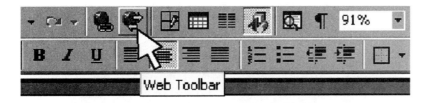

FIGURE 14-3 *Flat-land, Web-style toolbar.*

sites grow like kudzu in a warm climate. Even worse than their desktop software counterparts, Web designers are often slaves to fashion, quick to incorporate the coolest gimmicks and graphics whether these make sense or not. The excessive and inappropriate use of animation is a hallmark of contemporary Web sites.

When not driven by aesthetics, designs may be overly accommodating to implementation details of what is easy or difficult to express in HTML rather than what makes sense or best serves the user. Some simple but powerful interaction modes, such as tabbed dialogues, can only be implemented on Web sites with some difficulty or at a substantial price in terms of performance. Again and again, we hear defensive protests from Web designers and developers that sensible design is too difficult.

In our evaluations of Web-site usability for clients, we do find some recurrent themes that apply especially to Web-based applications. Because of the history and technological limitations of the Web and the habitual biases of many Web developers, some problems are almost endemic.

Page bouncing. A common error is to subdivide information too finely. Because Web developers think in terms of links and pages, they often create pages of links that serve only to reach a series of other pages, such as the one for an advanced training program shown in Figure 14-4. The navigation map for this sort of highly partitioned information structure resembles that of Figure 14-5. Although it might seem to be useful to partition information into small chunks, when viewed in terms of how users try to accomplish common tasks, such pages are often far less than useful. They lead to a problem that might be called *context bouncing*, or, more specifically, *page bouncing*—repeatedly sending users down links only to make them back up again to follow another link. The site visitor interested in finding out information about the course or product or service, perhaps as input to a purchasing decision, must select a topic, read a few lines or a paragraph or two, and then

> *A common error is to subdivide information too finely, leading to the problem of page bouncing—repeatedly sending users down links only to have them back up again to follow another link.*

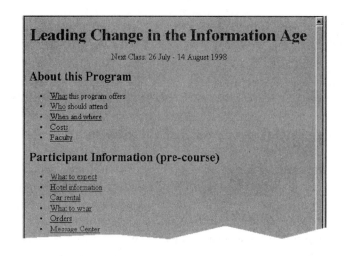

FIGURE 14-4 *Navigating a course of study.*

return to the first page before getting to the next chunk of information by clicking on another link.

The critical design question concerns focal use cases and which cases are more representative or more likely to be frequent. In many situations, a user being interested in one topic or piece of information implies a high probability of interest in other related information. A prospective student in the course being offered in Figure 14-4 is likely to want to know not only what the course is about but also the cost, the venue, and the scheduling, as well as, possibly, other information. To retrieve each bit of information, the user must click on a link, wait for another page to be downloaded from the server, and then return back to get to the next link. This is analogous to breaking up a single cohesive task among multiple modal dialogues. Better task support is achieved by combining closely related

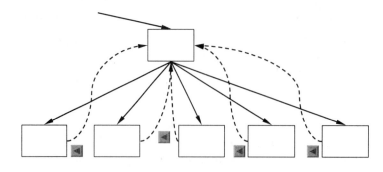

FIGURE 14-5 *Charting a jagged course: the structure of page bouncing.*

information on a single page. Site visitors who are genuinely browsing, scanning for information, would also be better served by this model.

Site visitors who know exactly what they want, who are seeking single pieces of information, and who know how that information is likely to be identified or described may be quite satisfied with the partitioned information model. However, users who are uncertain under what heading the desired information might be found or whose categories and mental models are not well matched by the site will find the context-bouncing approach difficult to use.

Deep drilling. For much the same reasons as give rise to context bouncing, many sites bury pages beneath long chains of links, forcing the user to drill ever deeper to find the information sought or get to the needed form. The problem is exacerbated when link labels and categories do not make sense to the user or fail to match the semantic structure of common use cases. On one frequent-flyer site, for example, the answer to the question of how many frequent-flyer miles must be redeemed for a particular grade of ticket was buried down eight links. Because this site combined such link-drilling faults with page bouncing and confusing link labels, it took following 17 links to find the needed information. The sought-after page contained only a table, with no links or information about actually redeeming accumulated miles, forcing the hapless user to choose between another protracted Ping-Pong tour through the site or a phone call to the service desk. And airlines wonder why their customer service costs are so high!

Some writers on Web usability distinguish *category* links from *content* links [Spool et al., 1997]. Category links describe categories or topics and take the user to collections of information and links to information. Content links specifically identify particular content and take the user directly to that information. The distinction may seem like a valid heuristic, but it obscures the fact that what is at issue is visibility and accessibility of information and features, not the nature of the links. It is easy to see that, like page bouncing, link drilling is a problem of visibility. The information or action to complete a use case is not available where it is needed. Such problems are often avoidable by constructing a navigation map and checking it against the use cases.

> *The natural structure of the information being presented and how it is employed by users should guide the organization of the Web site into pages.*

Linear layout. At the other end of the spectrum of poor design is the site that seems phobic about links and puts everything into lengthy pages of text with few links. Pages that go on and on can have their own visibility problems. Since many users tend to work and think in terms of screens, long pages that require scrolling can increase the chance of users failing to find what they are seeking. Long pages, insofar as they function to users as a single interaction context, can become confusing and overly complex.

The natural structure of the information being presented and how it is employed by users are the basic design issues that should guide the organization of the Web site into pages. It can be helpful to combine into a single page information that is closely related semantically or that, for the user, comprises a single natural structure. The issue is how likely it is that the user will need the information together, either to understand it or to complete a use case.

Putting information together does not necessitate ignoring structure and organization. While some sites are overwhelmed by graphics and animation, others are dominated by a landscape of long narratives and linear series of text blocks unrelieved by graphic signposts or visitor attractions. Making the inherent structure visible to the user can be as simple as separating pages into sections and providing headings and subheadings.

Gone searching. Search engines are almost required features for serious Web sites. They can contribute to usability, but they often amount to token offerings to compensate for other shortcomings of a site. In truth, research by Spool and his colleagues has found that the probability of success in finding information is actually reduced when users resort to site-supplied search facilities. Nevertheless, users have come to expect search functions and may doggedly turn to them despite repeated failures and lost time.

As always, the solution is to fit the function to the problem. Generic, full-text search engines do not take into account anything about the intrinsic structure of the page content being searched; hence, they tend to return too many false positives and overwhelm the user with potential pages. On the other hand, if the lexicon of the site is not tuned to the vocabulary of the user, full-text searching will find nothing, even when the required information is available. Complicating the issue is the fact that users, especially from among the quasi-mythical "general public," seldom know how to formulate effective queries. The more sophisticated the search capabilities on a site, the less likely they are to be used fully or correctly by the casual user. This situation must

> *The more sophisticated the search capabilities on a site, the less likely they are to be used fully or correctly by the casual user.*

be seen as a failure on the part of Web designers and developers, not of Web users.

The best search functions reflect what users are trying to accomplish and are suited to the content. For example, one book club site, in addition to the standard generic access by first letter of title or author, provides drop-down lists for "searches" on author or book title. The advantage of this feature, shown in Figure 14-6, is that it allows visual browsing of the complete list once the drop-down is opened—something you want to make easy and to encourage. Unfortunately, this

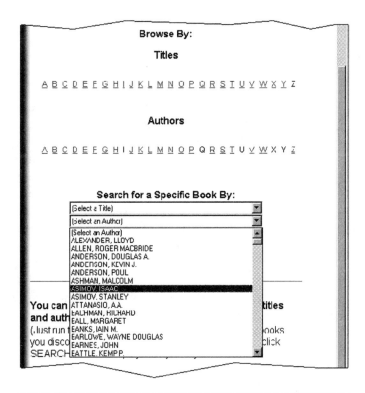

FIGURE 14-6 *Book browsing by title or author.*

example also illustrates usability problems engendered by the Web technology itself because the widget looks like but does not function as a drop-down combo box. The controls are also grouped by similarity of programming function, rather than by user semantics. From the user's perspective, the options here are to seek by author or by title, not to see a list by author (title) starting either with some letter or with some author (title). With the right behavior and organization of the drop-down widget, the access by letters becomes a clumsy redundancy.

The usability of searching is also influenced by what is returned as the search results and how results are presented. For example, a search for books by a particular author on some sites will return a collection of full book descriptions, while others will return a list of links that require drilling down for details.

Even server and browser behavior can influence usability. On the site of one book vendor, each time you select a book to be added to your "shopping cart," the page is refreshed and returns to the top of the page. The contents of the page have changed, but the user is unaware since the relevant message—announcing that an increase in the cumulative number of items selected—is already scrolled out of sight off the bottom of the screen!

WEB WISDOM APPLIED

For Web sites and Web-based applications intended for use, the best way to proceed is to follow the familiar usage-centered trail of abstract prototyping, developing the content and navigation models based on the best support of use cases without

> *Developers can avoid discarding their hard-won wisdom regarding usability by designing first for a conventional graphical user interface and then adapting the design to Web-based deployment.*

out regard to the target environment on the Web. This approach of designing content and organization before appearance and behavior has been applied with marked success to large-scale site design [Sand, 1996]. Some designers have found it productive to design first as if each problem were a freestanding application on a conventional graphical user interface and then to adapt the design to Web-based deployment. At least in this way the designer is made keenly aware of when Web technology is getting in the way and when it can help. It also

helps developers avoid the pitfall of discarding all their hard-won wisdom when it comes to usability.

JUST THE FAQS

The importance of keeping in mind both business goals and user intent in Web-based design can be illustrated with a common problem of page organization and navigation. Many Web sites, especially commercial ones, incorporate a collection of frequently asked questions (FAQs). Effectively written and implemented, FAQs not only serve users but also can fulfill important business objectives since they can divert users from calling overworked customer and technical support lines. Basically, the site operators want customers to succeed in getting the answers to their questions, preferably from the Web site, but failing that, from a customer service or technical support department. Customers should be steered toward finding the answers themselves and should have a high probability of success.

Often, FAQs have been compiled into a single page as one long list of brief questions, each followed by a paragraph or two in answer or explanation. Even if the list is relatively short, finding the answer to a particular problem or dilemma can be difficult. Questions may be in essentially random or inscrutable order. The lists are hard to scan visually because the grammatical structure of questions spreads and buries the key words in which users are likely to be interested—for example, "How do I recover from a disk crash?" Worst of all are those sites that merely list the questions as links to separate pages with the answers, impeding browsing and forcing users into page bouncing.

Some designers consider the browser scrollbars to be enough to support use of FAQs lists. Others may point to a site search engine and claim it as an adequate supporting mechanism. As already explained, such engines are rarely effective in the hands of users, and some are apt to return hits all over the site rather than merely within the FAQs. Expert-level users may resort to the **Edit|Find** function of browsers to search within FAQs or other long text blocks, but this technique is least likely to fall within the repertoire of the very users most likely to need the help of the FAQs.

> *The well-designed FAQs page is organized like a book into three parts: a table of contents or topic list, the list of questions organized by topics, and an index.*

The semantic structure of typical FAQs is fairly simple: Each FAQ has a subject and falls under some general topic or category. For one site, we devised a simple page organization and navigation scheme to take advantage of the inherent structure of FAQs and to maximize the probability that a casual user would successfully retrieve the needed answer if it existed. FAQs are compiled into a single page to facilitate visual scanning. FAQs are listed under broad topics, and each FAQ is headed by a key word or phrase indicating its subject, followed by the question, then the answer. The list is sorted alphabetically by subject within topic. Here is an example:

Subscriptions
Renewing expired subscriptions:
   How do I renew my magazine subscription after it has expired?

   To renew or restart an expired subscription to one of our magazines, simply go to the Subscriptions page and click on the Renew button, then follow the directions at the top of the page. Or just click here.

A well-designed FAQs page is organized like a book into three parts:

1. Table of contents or topic list
2. List of questions organized by topics
3. Index

The alphabetized topic list consists of in-page links to the topic sections, and the alphabetized index consists of in-page links to the subjects, both simplifying and speeding use. A thorough index might include all permutations, such as

   expired subscriptions, renewing
   renewing expired subscriptions
   subscriptions, renewing expired

At the top of the FAQs page is an appropriate heading:

Frequently Asked Questions

To find an answer to your question or problem, select a topic from the list below, scroll through the questions, or check the FAQs index at the bottom of this page.

The index includes an in-page link back to the table of contents.

At the end of the FAQs page, below the index, is another message to the user:

Can't find what you are looking for? Try entering a few words describing the question or problem in the box below and then press the "search" button.

The search returns a page of FAQs in the same format as the main listing and alphabetized by subject. At the bottom of the list is another, identical, search entry box and button, plus buttons to return to the full listing of FAQs or to send email to the customer service department. Although designers might eventually arrive at some similar design by many different routes, the shortest route is to follow the compass of usability rules and principles relentlessly.

THE QUBIT MAKEOVER

On a somewhat larger scale, let us explore the redesign of a commercial Web site. Rather than pursue the complete usage-centered design for this site, we will trace through one thread of decisions and consequences, looking at the modeling, technical, and business issues as they arise.

QubIt Corporation is a fast-growing maker of backup storage solutions based on proprietary compression technology. Sales of their two flagship products, the Quber storage cube for desktop machines and the Quber Libre for laptops, have skyrocketed. Not surprisingly, QubIt is experiencing growing pains. Recently, manufacturing quality control has been slipping, causing a sharp jump in DOAs. As the installed base has grown, more and more hardware and software compatibility problems have also been cropping up.

Technical support has become a nightmare. The waiting time on tech support lines has become so long that callers have started hanging up and clogging the switchboard with calls to other corporate numbers. Most of the calls are from new purchasers with installation and configuration problems. Programmers are being interrupted to field some of the more difficult questions, so productivity has suffered and release of "ArqIt 98," intended to fix some of the installation problems, has been delayed. The Sales and Marketing Group, known to the programmers as "S&M," has been pushing for its immediate release, but the developers are con-

FIGURE 14-7 *Art and function on the home page of QubIt.*

cerned that an early and buggy release will only exacerbate the technical support problems.

QubIt is a forward-looking company that had its Web site up before they had completed the design of its first product. Their whimsical home page, shown in Figure 14-7, reflects the artistic leanings of one of their early programming staff. The hit rate on the site has been good, primarily due to product purchasers looking for technical help. An initial survey by marketing has found that few visitors look at product information and almost none return to the site again.

Everybody has ideas for the best use of the site. S&M is pushing to expand sales, seeing the Web as an inexpensive way to build sales of hardware and software products and to promote awareness of the company. Tech support wants help. The programmers just want to be left alone. The CEO wants to leverage staff and resources by restructuring and redesigning the Web site for greater business advantage.

> *Many Web-site projects make the mistake of starting with wish lists of contents and features and then proceeding directly to graphical design.*

Many Web-site projects make the mistake of starting with wish lists of contents and features and then proceeding directly to graphical design. The various QubIt constituencies have already proposed a list of contents for the revised site:

- Company news and product announcements
- Product spec sheets
- Lists of hardware and software products
- Lists of media supplies
- On-line product and supply order forms

- FAQs regarding the products
- FAQs regarding technical problems
- On-line copies of reference manuals

The tech support staff has pointed out that 9 common configuration issues account for nearly 60% of help desk calls. They argue that lists of FAQs on technical problems—they have compiled nearly 100—should constitute the main content.

A usage-centered Web design does not start with content, however. Usage-centered design is driven by the business case and the purpose profile and develops content and presentation from user roles and use cases. In this example, the business agenda has been set by the CEO, who wants to relieve the crisis in tech support, which is also beginning to drag down sales. The purpose profile therefore emphasizes content and usability.

A joint modeling session, with representatives from both tech support and S&M, brainstormed this list of candidate user roles:

stalledInstaller
> has a focused, specific inquiry; is impatient and dissatisfied; is likely to give up on product or try to reach tech support but unlikely to switch roles

productSeeker
> has specific inquiry; is probably satisfied

supplySeeker
> has specific inquiry; is probably satisfied

befuddledUser
> has a confused, uncertain inquiry or multiple interests; is dissatisfied and unlikely to switch roles

potentialBuyer
> has diffuse interest, potentially in several products; may switch roles but is likely to give up easily

informationForager
> is just looking, probably not buying; is generally interested but might switch roles

Based on the business objectives, the two related roles of **stalledInstaller** and **befuddledUser** are chosen as focal roles.

A list of candidate use cases is next brainstormed and sorted by priority:

gettingHelpWithInstallation
gettingHelpWithOtherKnownProblem
gettingHelpWithUnknownProblem
browsingFAQs
contactingTechSupport
gettingProductSpecs

```
orderingProducts
orderingSupplies
reviewingUserManual
```

The first two are nominated as focal use cases in part because they have the greatest potential for reducing the tech support load.

One interpretation of the use case map for this much of the problem is shown in Figure 14-8. This map shows **browsingFAQs** as an extension to an abstract use case, **gettingHelp**, which serves as shorthand for extending all of the specializations of **gettingHelp**. Strictly speaking, **contactingTechSupport**, which gives access to email and displays the 800 number for tech support, might be considered an extension to all use cases, but business issues must be balanced against usability. Users may be interested in the easiest direct access to tech support staff, but this accessibility is not in their best interests if tech support lines are always busy and email takes weeks for a reply. The model reflects the objective of having the user attempt some resolution via the Web site before being offered the option of contacting tech support directly. The use case map in Figure 14-8 makes **contactingTechSupport** an extension to **browsingFAQs** and **seekingAnswers**. An idea might be fed forward for implementation to consider hiding access to tech support until after the user attempts something, including using the search function to find "email" or "tech support" or the like. Another possibility might be a humorous warning about telephone tech support being swamped, with encouragement to consult the FAQs first.

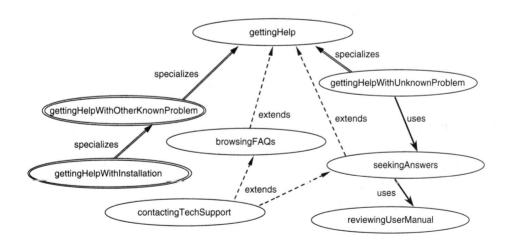

FIGURE 14-8 *Use case map for technical support.*

Starting with the focal use cases, the Web redesign team would write out essential narratives:

gettingHelpWithInstallation

USER INTENTION	SYSTEM RESPONSIBILITY
request help	
	show list of installation problems
select	
	show solution

This narrative can be further simplified. If the use cases are not so simplified here, there will be a second chance for simplification when visibility issues in the content model or in the actual visual design are considered later:

gettingHelpWithInstallation

USER INTENTION	SYSTEM RESPONSIBILITY
request help	
	show list of installation problems with solutions

Similarly, the other focal use case can be expressed very straightforwardly:

gettingHelpWithOtherKnownProblem

USER INTENTION	SYSTEM RESPONSIBILITY
request help	
	show list of all problems with solutions

The rest of the use cases would be similarly narrated.

> *The home page should include support for the focal use cases or clearly evident access to that support.*

Just as in the design of any other application, the next step in redesigning the Web site is to derive an abstract prototype in the form of a content model by starting with the focal use cases. As a rule, within the home page, one would expect to find either support for the focal use cases or clearly evident links or other access to that support. If installation problems are a major motivator for improving usability of the Web site, the home page ought to feature them prominently.

However, we have known sales and marketing types to argue vehemently against any such visibility because it "communicates the wrong message" about

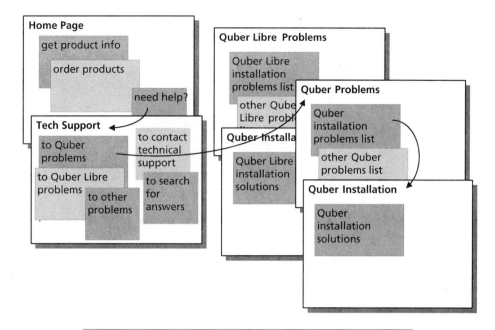

FIGURE 14-9 *First try at a content model for the QubIt site.*

the company and its products. From their perspective, the home page should push product information, build corporate image, and provide prominent links to the on-line sales pages. A compromise is to feature the information and sales links but include a link to technical support, putting help only one link away for the site visitor. This is reasonable because most Web users expect a home page to be largely populated with links to other pages.

One design team working on this problem came up with an initial content model that looked like the one shown in Figure 14-9. This model illustrates the common impulse to categorize and partition information, burying sought-after information and often leading to the problems of page bouncing and deep drilling discussed earlier in this chapter.

Pushed to improve usability, this team refined their model to give more immediate access to the most common problem solutions, thus increasing the chance that site visitors will resolve their problems without intervention from tech support personnel. The content model shown in Figure 14-10 is still a long way from a final graphical design and implementation, but a better architectural foundation has been laid. You might try your hand at sketching out a design for the three pages modeled in Figure 14-10, perhaps along with closely related pages. This might be an appropriate place to "borrow" the FAQs presentation solution described in an earlier section.

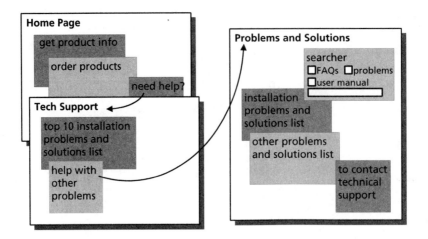

FIGURE 14-10 *Improved content model for the QubIt site.*

MODIFIED MODELING

For the most part, the modeling in usage-centered design for Web-based applications proceeds along much the same lines as for any other product. However, differences in content and structure favor some variations in approach and technique. Web sites can have vast numbers of pages linked by a multitude of paths. Accepted practices, such as providing a set of links at the bottom of every page, can make site navigation easier for the user while complicating the architecture. Even when reasonably well planned, the navigation map for a modest site may be more complicated than for a large-scale desktop application.

For content modeling, we find that the text-based format introduced in Chapter 6 is particularly useful for Web-site design, especially when the number of page types or layouts is large. In this form, we adopt obvious notation, such as underlining page links. We have also incorporated some ad hoc extensions to the notation for navigation maps to make them more succinct and expressive. Figure 14-11 shows examples of some of the notation we have found useful.

EMBEDDED SYSTEMS APPLICATIONS

Boeing's 777 commercial jet has been hailed as a triumph of both engineering and engineering management [Sabbagh, 1996]. Most people see it as an airplane, but insiders have described this state-of-the-art, fly-by-wire vehicle as two-and-a-half million lines of Ada flying in close formation—not so much an airplane as a complex software system packaged and shipped in an airframe.

In truth, the vast majority of the computers in the world do not even look like computers; they are hidden inside cars and trucks, telephones and televisions,

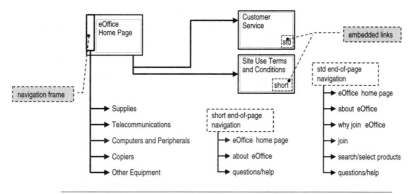

FIGURE 14-11 *Notation for Web-site navigation.*

microwaves and clock radios. The typical modern automobile contains a dozen or more separate computers. The average middle-class family may unknowingly own hundreds of computers. And all of these hidden computers, these embedded systems, had to be programmed. The software in a digital watch may be only a few thousand bytes. A modern laser printer may have several million lines of code.

For embedded systems, usability is a particularly complex stew of many ingredients. Software is seldom, if ever, the entire story. Mechanical engineering, electrical engineering, packaging, and even printing and graphics can all conspire to make life tough for users or can cooperate to make it easy. The user interface design problems in embedded systems applications can be considerably more complicated than on the desktop, not alone because of sundry engineering and pragmatic issues. Embedded systems development crosses functional lines in companies and spans multiple professions. The politics can be messy. A watch may have been created by a famous fashion designer, who will allow on *his* watches only two buttons through which all functions must be performed. Automotive engineers may set the size and shape of the faceplate for a car stereo, industrial designers may lay out the front-panel display, electrical engineers may plan the circuits, while mechanical engineers may devise the tape-transport mechanisms. The software may have to communicate with displays and with push buttons, frequency synthesizers, motors, and solenoids. Who is responsible for the user interface? For usability?

> *The vast majority of the computers in the world do not even look like computers; they are hidden inside cars and trucks, telephones and televisions, microwaves and clock radios.*

Embedded systems span a dizzying variety of applications, from medical technology to consumer appliances, from entertainment electronics to industrial controls, from avionics to telecommunications. The usability of all these varied products is affected by the same influences as desktop software and is heir to essentially the same ailments. Creeping featuritis, for example, infects cell phones no less than spreadsheets. For some 85% of cellular phone users, mobiles are just another telephone for placing and receiving calls [Bransten, 1998]. The many so-called advanced features programmed into these devices—from address books to email access—remain mostly unused, no doubt for good reason. The same basic principles of usability and usage-centered design apply to cellular phones and ATMs as to Windows-based database applications for the one simple reason that on the other side of the user interface is a human eye and human hand coordinated by a human brain. Feedback, visibility, structure, tolerance, simplicity, reuse—they all necessarily apply. It is just as incumbent upon embedded systems developers to understand the tasks to be supported as it is for designers of desktop applications.

HARDWARE AND SOFTWARE

Usage-centered design for embedded systems applications, however, has to span a wide range of technical decisions to take into account such things as the size and shape of displays; the placement of buttons, knobs, and other physical controls; the color of printed overlays; and even the design of mounting hardware. Consider, for example, the control panel for industrial equipment represented in Figure 14-12. The substantial distance between the displayed labels and the push buttons around the panel can slow down operation and even lead to pressing the wrong button accidentally. In this design, the problem begins with the manufacturer of the LCD display panels, who placed the electronics and connectors

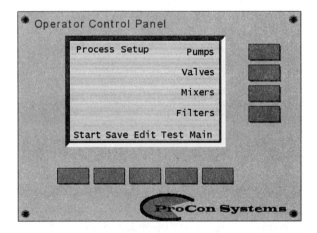

FIGURE 14-12 *Schematic for too-remote controls on operator panel.*

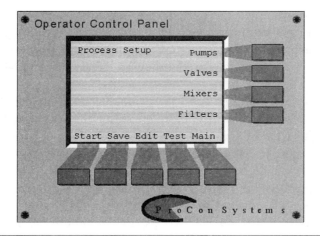

FIGURE 14-13 *Visual mapping to improve operator panel control.*

around the edges of the panel, forcing the buttons to be mounted too far from the display.

It is not difficult to see how user interface design for embedded systems is under a variety of influences from a range of constituents and stakeholders whose interests must be taken into account and whose actions can shape usability of the final product. Manufacturing considerations and production costs must be factored in, as must programming complexities and marketing issues. Even printing and packaging can be part of the user interface. Clever screen-printing on the face of the panel, as shown in Figure 14-13, can ameliorate, though not eliminate, the problems of button and menu alignment.

> *Embedded systems involve three kinds of user interface design problems: (1) strictly hardware problems, (2) software problems, and (3) hardware/software problems, in which there are trade-offs and interdependencies that may potentially be influenced by software developers.*

INTERFACE PROBLEMS

From the perspective of embedded software developers, three kinds of user interface design problems can be distinguished: (1) strictly hardware problems, in which the software has no control or influence over usability; (2) software problems, in which most or all of the factors in usability are determined by programming and software design; and (3) hardware/software problems, in which there are trade-offs and interdependencies that may potentially be influenced by software developers [Constantine, 1993f]. It is incumbent on the developers of embedded software to understand all three variations.

Consider, for example, a so-called "user-friendly" menu-operated universal remote control for a set-top cable box, TV, and VCR. The layout of the buttons and the labeling screened onto the remote may be outside of software control, but how these buttons are used and interpreted may be largely or completely a matter of programming.

The same buttons could be used in various ways to navigate through multi-level menus with very different consequences for the user. For example, menu items might be selected by first using up-and-down channel buttons to position a highlight and then selecting with another button. Alternatively, the user could be prompted to press the number corresponding to a menu item. The latter requires, on average, fewer steps, but it also makes the user note and remember an arbitrary number and then look down at the remote to press the correct button. There are still other possibilities that are even worse, such as prompting the user to press 1 to move up, 2 to move down, and 3 to select.

The remote control will need to enable the user to select cable channels by number. To accomplish this, there are four different schemes in common use:

1. Toggle (with -/- - button) between single-digit and two-digit entry
2. Have separate buttons for 10, 20, and so on
3. Require a leading zero for single-digit channels
4. Treat a number followed by a specified delay as a single-digit channel

The first two options not only are clumsier to use but also require additional buttons; with cable boxes now offering hundreds of channels, these schemes become increasingly impractical. The third option, requiring a leading zero, is the typical choice of unreformed coders, a mild but irritating form of "Your programming is showing." Only the last option is fully generalizable to N digits and also fits the use case.

Thoughtless embedded programming can dramatically reduce usability, however. If the time-out interval following the first digit is set too short, users will feel rushed and become irritated. They will frequently get the wrong channel because of not keying the second digit quickly enough. On the other hand, if the time-out is too long, every access to a single channel is slowed. In the brain-dead remote control supplied with our cable box, the time-out is programmed to be so long that it took months of use before we accidentally discovered one could enter a single digit without a leading zero. One does not need laboratory testing to pick a reasonable delay; a few minutes thought and a *gedanken* experiment or two will put you in the ballpark.

Most commonly, there are hardware/software design trade-offs determining the usability of embedded systems. On a remote control, for example, separate buttons might be used to access each of the various specialized menus for setting options on a TV and VCR, or one unique "Menu" key might be used to bring up a list of submenus. The number of push buttons on the remote control can be reduced through single-button operation, and initial learning may be marginally easier because the user has only one button to push. On the other hand, all operations of all functions are thus made more complicated by at least one extra step. How is the designer to know which is "the best" design, and how is it identified or specified? To answer these questions, we use the simple modeling tools already established: role models, task models, content models, and navigation models.

MODELING FOR EMBEDDED APPLICATIONS

Design modeling for embedded systems often begins with engineering diagrams based on valued features. For a usage-centered approach, we need to back up somewhat and begin with user roles [Constantine, 1996d].

For a fax machine, we might distinguish several roles, such as **CasualCommunicator**, **FaxPublisher**, and **FaxAdministrator**. In the **CasualCommunicator** role, the user is basically

> *For usage-centered design of embedded systems, we need to begin with user roles.*

interested in just sending faxes and receiving them as simply and as quickly as possible. In the **FaxPublisher** role, the user may be interested in setting up lists or groups of targets or even in using facilities for automated fax-back service. The **FaxAdministrator** role may encompass reviewing logs, blocking out certain numbers, changing system parameters, and the like.

Consider resetting the clock on the fax machine to switch to or from daylight saving time. This use case supports the **FaxAdministrator** role. It has a low expected frequency (twice per year) but a very high probability of use (almost certain). A concrete use case for this might look like this:

resettingClock

USER ACTION	SYSTEM RESPONSE
select SET	
	display SETUP menu
select CHANGE TIME	
	show current time
advance cursor to hours	
enter new time	
	show changed time
select SET again	
	confirm (beep)

Note that some, though not all, details of the user interface implementation are implicit or assumed by this concrete use case. Nevertheless, compare the somewhat generic use case just given to the enacted scenario required on one fax machine owned by the authors:

resettingClock

USER ACTION	SYSTEM RESPONSE
press to open access panel	
press FUNCTION key	
	display menu
press 6 for SETUP SYSTEM	
	display menu
press 1 for DATE & TIME	
	display YEAR: XX
enter 2-digit year	
	display MONTH: XX
enter 2-digit month	
	display TIME: XX:XX
enter 4-digit 24-hour time	
	show entered time
press SET key	
	show menu
press STOP key on main keypad	
	show menu
press STOP key again	
	blank menu display
close access panel	

This machine was advertised as having user-friendly menu control, and one suspects its programmers counted themselves clever for placing all control in a common menu structure. Nevertheless, the enacted scenario reveals major usability defects. Most obviously, it is long and complicated, taking 16 keystrokes and two additional steps with 13 separate user actions merely to bump the clock by one hour. The user is forced to engage in actions, such as reentering the date, that are unrelated to incrementing the clock.

Even in this simple case of the user interface to support the **resettingClock** use case, there are interesting hardware/software trade-offs. The designers of the fax machine probably wanted to avoid creating a special feature just for switching between summer and winter clock times. Perhaps they figured that, as long as users can change the clock setting at all, the use case is supported. In the design just given, however, there is no way to change only the clock time since time and date setting are combined into a single function. One could argue that abusing the user is acceptable in this instance because it occurs only twice a year, but, with this design, the user is punished every time the clock needs to be changed for any reason since the entire scenario must be enacted in every case. Even worse, the implementation invites error since it requires the user to remember and correctly reenter the date, note the current time, remember it, and then add (or subtract) an hour and reenter it correctly. This may not be rocket science, but it does foster mistakes.

The essential use case for this problem is, by contrast, strikingly simple. The user knows it is either spring or autumn and time to reset the clock appropriately. The clock time is to be either increased or decreased by exactly one hour:

resettingClock

USER INTENTION	SYSTEM RESPONSIBILITY

"spring forward"
  OR
"fall back"
	add 1 hour
	  OR
	subtract 1 hour
	display new time

Although product designers may not want to dedicate two buttons to a once-a-year task, it is easy to see that incrementing or decrementing is broadly useful for changing the time. In fact, there is no real reason why fax machines could not use the same sort of hour and minute setting buttons as are familiar on clock radios, microwaves, or other common appliances. Almost as good would be to require users to enter the time from the number keys but give top-level access to this capability with a "set time" button.

Since embedded systems programmers, like most of their kin, have a tendency to solve problems by doing more programming, they often propose to solve this problem with no buttons at all simply by complicating the program. One approach would build in tables for automatic resetting of the internal clock for summer and winter times, but it is important to remember that daylight saving time is a political rather than an astronomical phenomenon. After Windows 95 was first introduced, hundreds of thousands of Australians relying on PCs found themselves off by an hour because the autumn changeover had been changed by some state parliaments after the software tables had been constructed.

> *Embedded systems programmers have a tendency to solve problems by doing more programming.*

Another buttonless solution often proposed by participants in our training classes is for the fax machine to use the telephone line to poll or accept a coded signal from a master source. The folly of this networked solution is its capacity for bringing the telephone system to its knees twice a year. Variants on this theme might be practical, however. A class in Europe recently proposed using inexpensive single-chip modules now produced that accept a coded broadcast time signal available throughout the European Union (EU). Not only does this resolve the twice-yearly switch to and from daylight saving time, but it also assures that the fax clock is always correct. Strictly speaking, this feature does not preclude the need for a scheme of manual override and clock setting. Absent some manual control, should the clock ever fall out of sync for any reason, there may be no recourse short of returning the entire system to the factory or scrapping it.

As on the desktop, fully automated solutions, in which the embedded software wrests control from users instead of supporting efficient usage, are always somewhat more prone to failure and generally tend to be more expensive. Another example where this is true is in the area of digital-data display systems for projecting computer output onto a wall or screen. We make extensive use of computer visuals and demos in our presentations and classes around the world. The trend in recent years has been toward autosensing schemes where the embedded program in the data projector analyzes the incoming signal from the computer, figures out the resolution, refresh frequency, and interlacing, and alters its display accordingly. Every once in a while, however, we encounter a projector that is unable to correctly decipher the output of a laptop computer that has always worked fine with other projectors. Either the display flickers or part of it is chopped off or some other anomaly mars the picture. Even a clumsy scheme for controlling resolution and synchronization is better than none in these circumstances. Without recourse to manual setting of the display characteristics, we have sometimes been forced to switch projectors, computers, or venues or even, on occasion, had to work without visuals.

> *Fully automated solutions, in which embedded software wrests control from users instead of supporting efficient usage, are generally more failure-prone and expensive.*

Of course, there is another side to this manual–automatic design trade-off. At the other end of the scale are some digital projectors whose controls are so obscure and badly organized that experienced audiovisual technicians have trouble getting them to behave. One well-known line of pricey European-made projectors has one of the worse-designed embedded systems interface we have ever encountered, a singularly blatant example of "Your programming is showing." In principle, almost every aspect of the display is controllable; in practice, we have watched trained technicians sweat for the better part of an hour trying to perform relatively simple modifications through its obscure menus, elaborate tables, and Unix-like file handling, editing, and saving.

EMBEDDED INTERFACES

Although most of the models and methods of usage-centered design apply as straightforwardly in the world of embedded systems as elsewhere, like Web-based applications, embedded systems applications also have their own peculiarities and special constraints. Perhaps most importantly, because of the combination of hardware and software design and hardware/software trade-offs, good user interface design for embedded applications may be especially hard to achieve.

Users and uses. Users of embedded systems tend to cluster in two profiles. For many applications, users are likely to be relatively unsophisticated and nontechnical. Proficiency profiles are apt to be weighted toward the novice end. Such is the case, or at least the first-order assumption, for virtually all consumer products. At the other end are embedded systems for use by specialists of one ilk or another, from automotive mechanics to geologists, surgeons to lab technicians. For many of these special-purpose applications, most users may be expected to be technically sophisticated and proficient. While not true for all users in all applications, we have found these two clusters of characteristics are typical in many embedded systems design problems.

> *Because so many embedded systems are the tools of everyday work or living, they tend to be heavily used, and many carry substantial operational risks.*

Because so many embedded systems are the tools of everyday work or living, they tend to be used frequently or at high rates. Many systems, including industrial, medical, and scientific ones, are also critical applications, with substantial operational risks associated with some, if not all, user roles and use cases.

These aspects of users and usage in many embedded systems translate into an elevated importance attached to the usability criteria of efficiency and reliability in use as well as transparency or intuitability.

Perhaps the most important guidance we can offer to embedded systems developers is to keep the use cases in mind. For example, the set-top box for our cable TV service includes a "sophisticated" on-screen program guide. Unfortunately, using it is a perpetual irritant. Besides a clumsy layout for the remote control itself, the embedded programming is ill-suited to the more common use cases.

One common usage scenario involves browsing through the TV listings until something looks interesting, checking out the channel for a minute or two, returning to the listings and scanning further, looking at another channel, and so on, until a suitable show is found. But every time the button is pressed to return to the program guide, the display starts out again at channel 2, with the listings shown for two hours forward of the current time. Either the programmers never thought about how the control would actually be used, or they were too lazy to save the pointers from one use to the next. The automatic two-hour advance on the displayed listings is particularly perverse since, for most viewers, the `wonderingWhatElseIsOnNow` use case is almost certainly far more frequent than `lookingForSomethingToWatchTwoHoursFromNow`.

Thinking in terms of task modeling and use cases can often reveal shortcomings of current solutions. For example, a task analysis for the control panel and software for controlling multiaxis milling machines and other complex factory tools revealed some long-overlooked opportunities for automating common sequences.

Input and output. In many cases, the user interface for embedded systems is more fixed and restricted, not only on the input side but also on the output side. Displays are likely to be smaller and less flexible. Input controls may be restricted to a handful of specialized buttons—or less.

On the other hand, in many areas of embedded systems development, the differences from the desktop are steadily lessening. As already mentioned in Chapter 13, the trend is toward larger, finer resolution and even color displays for commercial and industrial embedded applications. Factory automation controls that once employed eight-line monochrome LCD displays and were running on proprietary operating systems are now using full-color screens under Windows. Similar but less dramatic trends can be seen on the input side. Some factory tools are getting full-sized alphanumeric keyboards that enable operators to enter labels and customer information along with tool coordinates and speed settings. Nevertheless, limitations persist. A cell phone may be given a color display panel, but the screen must still be no bigger than a couple inches across. A $200 microwave will not be likely to sport a 14-inch diagonal screen or a full-sized keyboard anytime in the near future.

> *In many areas of embedded systems development, the differences from the desktop are steadily lessening.*

Control overloading. Panel space is often a major limitation on the input side as well as the output side of the interface. Often, the number of buttons or keys is severely limited, and the only way to support all the necessary use cases is to overload the controls, pressing each button into service to perform multiple functions. The secret to successful overloading is to separate frequent or primary functions from less frequent or secondary ones and to organize overloaded functions carefully and logically.

There are two principal techniques for overloading controls: shifted overloading and modal overloading. The former uses one key or button to shift the function or interpretation of others. Such keys are likely to be labeled something like **Function**, **Shift**, or **Alternate**.

Shifted overloading works best where functions can be arranged in a hierarchy or into groups based on frequency, priority, or particular conditions. Just as keys and buttons should be grouped logically, shifted functions assigned to the keys should also form logical groups or be associated with particular keys on some logical rather than arbitrary basis.

It can be tempting to put two closely related operations as the unshifted and shifted functions of one key, but care must be used in doing this, especially where the operations are alternatives at essentially the same level. We have even seen a system that set timed operations using a single button to increment a counter—unshifted to bump seconds, shifted to bump minutes—leading to frequent operator errors.

Modal, or state-dependent, overloading changes the function or meaning of controls when they are used at a particular time or in a particular sequence. Modal overloading works best where some functions become meaningless or useless in certain modes or conditions. For example, while a machine tool is operating under programmed control, manual movement controls do not make sense and may be inoperative.

The common kitchen-timer interface shown in Figure 14-14 illustrates typical problems in control overloading for embedded systems user interfaces. On larger scales, we have seen this kind of problem repeated in many embedded systems. Here, panel space is tight and manufacturing cost is critical, so the number of buttons is severely limited. Modal overloading is used to extend the functions of the available controls. The START button means "pause" when the timer is running and "start" when it is stopped. In other words, it functions as a simple toggle. The MIN button, which normally increments minutes, stops the alarm if it is ringing. Although this is an odd and arbitrary assignment, it causes few problems so long as the user actually reads the labels. The CLR function, which resets the timer to zero, is another matter because the HR button operates in this mode only when the timer is paused. This means that, if a mistake is made while setting the time, the user must carry out the extended and nonsensical sequence of pressing START twice and then pressing CLR.

Obviously, no one thought this through, although millions of timers based on this chip have been sold. Thinking it through yields some interesting answers. Figure 14-15 shows a redesign of the timer control panel with a more sensible

Figure 14-14 *Overloaded timer controls.*

Figure 14-15 *Improved usability through reorganization.*

overloading. Because the counter is already zero when the alarm sounds, there is no real need for two different controls to pause and to stop. It is best simply to let users do what they would impulsively do, which is to hit this button anyway when the alarm is beeping at the top of its battery-driven lungs.

To clear the counter, a number of possibilities are open. Some designers have proposed a further overloading of the START/STOP button by having press-and-hold mean to reset the counter. Logically, however, setting the time to zero is more closely related to setting the time than to starting or stopping the timer, so, following the Structure Principle, we would want to use the HR and MIN buttons for this function. Pressing both buttons simultaneously is a reasonable scheme. Although slightly awkward, it is less awkward and more logical than the modal overloading of the original design. Note that usability has been improved without changing hardware; only the printed labels and the code are changed.

Layout and behavior. Just as on a monitor screen, the controls of embedded systems user interfaces should be laid out logically, based on both semantics and workflow thus fitting with how users think and how they work. The layout should make the logical structure of the controls apparent, as in the line separating the time-setting controls in the kitchen timer.

> *The controls of embedded systems user interfaces should be laid out logically to fit with how users think and how they work, and the layout should make the logical structure of the controls apparent.*

Interaction contexts in embedded applications can take many forms. An interaction context may comprise a display plus a keyboard, a freestanding control panel, or a set of switches hidden behind a locked access door. For example, in one factory automation system, the normal operator controls included two separate and differently configured control panels on the main console, plus a third more limited set of controls hanging from a cable in the vicinity of the machine tool being controlled. Context switching for embedded systems can, therefore, involve more than just simple changes in a display, as in desktop or Web-based applications.

Menus and soft keys. Menu-driven interfaces have found their way into many embedded systems applications. On-screen menus were the biggest part of the shift to "user-friendly" VCRs. Menus offer flexibility, put more of the control over the interface into software, and provide a simple and consistent mechanism for access to a variety of features. Unfortunately, menus do not in themselves increase usability. Menus can offer a single, simple structure for accommodating a wide range of features and functionality, or they can become an excuse for not thinking through problems. We have too often seen them become a substitute for careful thought, with nested menus thrown together all but willy-nilly.

The main issues in menu organization (covered in Chapter 8) apply equally well to menus in embedded software. One big difference is that menus under Windows or other desktop environments are highly standardized in appearance and behavior, while numerous design issues may remain open in embedded applications. The designer may have to decide whether menus are arranged vertically, horizontally, or in two dimensions, as well as how menus are navigated, how items will be selected or confirmed, how the selection point is fed back to the user, and the like.

Menus may be navigated with cursor or "arrow" keys or with a simple cycle control that moves to the next item when pressed. Alternatively, numeric or "function" keys can be used to pick one of N displayed items. If a full alphabetic keyboard is available, mnemonic letters are also an option. Of course, touch screens offer the option of direct selection by pointing. The operational context must also be taken into account. For example, selection by numbers or function keys can be awkward in dim light or where users must repeatedly look from display to key device to work through nested menus.

Soft keys function as a variant of menus. "Hard" keys or buttons are arranged adjacent to a display that shows the changeable functions associated with each key. As with menus, the functional assignments to soft keys should be grouped semantically and for support of common use cases and scenarios. As a rule, designs should avoid the complexity of too many soft keys and too many different assignments. Because soft keys, like full-screen menus, do not provide a visual navigation trace, nesting can be confusing. Users need to be made aware whenever the assignments change. Often, it is not enough merely to change the labels. Animation, graphics, sound, and color changes can draw attention to changed assignments and aid users in navigation.

Parallax is a special problem with soft keys. If the displayed labels are too far from the actual keys they identify and are not in the same plane, the apparent

Figure 14-16 *Printer panel minimalism.*
(HP 4L)

association may not be clear to the user and may depend on the user's position. This is a common problem for particularly tall or short users of some ATMs.

Feedback and communication. Effective communication with users through the limited bandwidth of simple embedded system user interfaces can be challenging, as suggested in the pen-case lab instrument described in Chapter 13. For another example, consider the modern minimalist approach to user interfaces illustrated in the printer control panel of Figure 14-16. Absent the labels, most people find the icons extremely difficult to interpret. Even with the labels, not everything is clear. The light labeled "Paper" indicates either a paper jam or an empty paper cassette. However, a call to insert paper in the manual feed slot is indicated by a flashing "Data" light!

> *Effective communication with users through the limited bandwidth of simple embedded system user interfaces can be challenging.*

For the confused or forgetful user, the vendor cleverly supplies a hidden "help file" printed on the underside of the top cover. This minimanual supplies the following translations:

Error:	Steady	Top door open or cartridge not installed right.
	Blinking	Recoverable error. Briefly press button.
Paper:	Steady	Paper cassette empty.
	Blinking	Paper jam.
Data:	Steady	Data still in printer. Briefly press button.
	Blinking	Manual feed. Insert paper or press button.
Ready:	Steady	Printer is ready for data.
	Blinking	Printer is processing data.

Although the designers seemed to be attempting to keep the number of LEDs to a minimum, the available ones are not even used to best effect. All the flashing is at the same lazy, half-second-on-half-second-off pace, sometimes indicating a problem and sometimes indicating that all is well.

A flashing light is more attention grabbing than a steady one, and blinking indicators are, by convention, usually associated with alarm or exception conditions. But, in this example, a flashing "Error" indicator is less serious than a steady glow. Indeed, a flashing "Error" light turns out to be the hardware equivalent of the blocking modal messages described in Chapter 11. Here, the work is interrupted for what appears to be no reason at all, and the user is reduced to functioning as a slave, serving as a subroutine of the hardware, as it were. On first seeing this, users have been known to ask, "Why doesn't the printer press its own darn button then?"

How do you communicate effectively with the user through so few indicators? As always, the secret is to fit the message to the meaning. For example, when a modem or network link is passing data, its indicator usually flutters rapidly, visually suggesting the rapid flow of data over the line. Our classroom surveys indicate that most users recognize this condition and would find a rapidly fluttering light more reassuring than a slowly blinking one as a way for the printer to indicate it is receiving and processing data.

> *The secret to effective communication is to fit the message to the meaning, as in visually suggesting the rapid flow of data by a fluttering indicator light.*

This following design is a refinement of the work of a number of classroom teams that have tackled this problem. Although it still may not be perfect, this design proved to be more readily intuitable and more easily remembered. It also saves an extra LED!

ERROR	PAPER	READY	
steady			data still in printer, press start briefly
pulsing			door open or cartridge not installed correctly
	steady		manual paper feed
	blinking		paper cassette empty
pulsing	pulsing		paper jam
		steady	printer ready
		fluttering	receiving or processing data

Note that the "Paper" light by itself always just means the system needs paper, while a paper jam, a "paper error," is appropriately indicated by synchronized pulsing of the "Error" and "Paper" indicators. Our classroom surveys indicate that this scheme is easier to explain and more easily remembered than the original one. Once a condition is satisfied, such as by feeding paper or clearing a paper jam, the printer should continue where it left off without requiring redundant confirmation from the user in the guise of pressing the one button on the panel.

OTHER SPECIAL INTERFACES

A wide variety of other specialized applications and operational contexts might be discussed here. For example, information kiosks have started to appear everywhere in airports and shopping malls, in museums and on street corners. With the use of touch screens by members of the general public, kiosks can pose some interesting challenges. Even purely "passive" information displays, such as the arrivals and departures displays at rail stations or airports, can be analyzed in terms of user roles, use cases, and content, navigation, and operational models. A thorough discussion of many of these special contexts not only would be beyond the scope of this book but also would quickly become repetitive. To wrap up this chapter, we will look briefly at only one additional area of application, an increasingly common form of user interface with some unique twists.

SOUND INTERFACES

Although most of our discussion of user interface design issues has been focused on manual input and visual output, the same basic principles and techniques apply to vocal interfaces. Vocal interfaces include systems with either voice input or voice output or both. Because vocal interfaces depend on retention in short-term memory, voice menus must be more sharply limited in both the number of options presented at each level and in the number of levels. As a rule, experience suggests that 2 to 4 choices is a practical limit, although we encountered one foreign embassy phone system that offered 9 choices at the first level and took us through 4 levels of nesting before we reached the right department. The line was busy.

Voice menus do have their special rules and considerations. All prompts should be kept as brief as practical without becoming ambiguous or brusque, especially for services that must be called frequently or used repeatedly. Users hate wordy voice menus with long introductory phrases. Loquacious, so-called "user-friendly" interfaces are even worse when the user seeking tech support has to wait through the whole spiel for a third or fourth time. At least on the desktop, one can click **OK** or **Cancel**. There is no excuse for the kind of verbose introductory baggage that greets callers to one vendor's tech support lines: "Hello, howdy from frigid North Country. We are so glad you chose to use our products and services. We just love to take care of our customers. Let me tell you about the laptop our knowledgeable technical sales people helped me pick out. I am just so thrilled with it." Thrilled, indeed!

After a very short introductory clause, selection prompts should be issued in some kind of logical order or by expected frequency. Experience favors giving each selection prompt first, followed by an action cue: "For desktop system technical support, press 2. For notebook and portables, press 3." Allowing the user to interrupt at any time to enter a choice rather than having to wait for the end of an item prompt is now generally acknowledged as good practice. Good voice menus also incorporate escape routes that can be used at any time, such as 0 for an operator or * to repeat a menu.

> *Users hate wordy voice menus with long introductory phrases.*

Needless to say, the navigation map for voice systems is a critical design model. More often than we would care to admit, we have become trapped in voice menus with loops in them.

CALLING TECH SUPPORT

For a brief example of a voice-processing problem, we might revisit the QubIt Corporation and consider a telephone-based support system as an alternative to the Web site described earlier in this chapter. The purpose of the system would be to accelerate the processing of technical support calls and take some of the load off the tech support staff. The design objectives are rapid call processing, prompts arranged by priority, and diversion of calls from staff. An initial script for selected menus might look something like this:

Main Menu
Welcome to QubIt Corporation's automated customer support system.

For technical support, press 1 or say "Yes" now.
For product information, press 2 or say "Yes" now.
To order systems or supplies, press 3 or say "Yes" now.
For all other calls, press 0 at any time or wait for an operator.

Tech Support Main Menu
This is QubIt Technical Support.

If you are having problems installing your QubIt system, press 1 or say "Yes" now.
If you have other technical problems, press 2 or say "Yes" now.

Tech Support Other Problem Menu
If you know what your problem is, please choose from the following list.

Problems with lost data? Press 1 or say "Yes" now.
Slow backup or a chattering drive? Press 2 or say "Yes" now.

Problems restoring files? Press 3 or say "Yes" now.

Problems installing software? Press 4 or say "Yes" now.

Questions about "backup sets"? Press 5 or say "Yes" now.

To speak with a technical support associate, press 0 or wait for an operator.

Slow Backup Response

Slow backup or a tape drive that makes a chattering sound?

This can usually be fixed from the ArqIt Options menu, a procedure also described in the online help under Options. From the main screen, just select Options, then Parameters. Click on the Reconfigure button in the lower left corner. When the Configuration dialogue appears, click the box marked "Conservative" and then click on OK. Once the reconfiguration is complete, try another backup.

To repeat these instructions, press 1 or say "Yes" now.

For a faxed copy of the detailed instructions for handling this problem, just enter your fax number, with area code first, now.

The "0 for operator" option is always available, but below the Main Menu, the call is actually diverted to technical support lines. The menu selections already made would be automatically communicated on-screen to the support associate who answers.

15

USAGE-CENTERED DESIGN APPLIED:
The TeleGuida Case

SCALING UP

The basic elements of usage-centered design, as presented in the preceding chapters, have been applied effectively to problems of widely varying complexity and sophistication in a variety of fields. The same concepts and techniques that have been illustrated with smaller examples along the way apply in much the same manner to much larger problems. In order to illustrate usage-centered design at a somewhat larger and more realistic scale than in the previous examples, we introduce in this chapter a somewhat more substantial application and follow through the entire process of model-driven design, from initial conception through final implementation modeling. In various of its incarnations, this case study has been tackled by many hundreds of professionals during workshops and training programs held around the world. Its various twists and turns and traps are quite well understood and quite typical of the sorts of issues encountered in practice. The case study takes as its inspiration the very kind of system that many developers have over the years chosen for their first "real" application in a newly learned programming language or development environment: the company telephone directory.

> *The same basic concepts and techniques of usage-centered design illustrated with smaller examples apply in much the same manner to much larger problems.*

In order to make it easier for readers to try their own hands at the problem, we have included a series of "pause points," practice breaks before the discussion continues with the results of modeling and design.

TELEPHONE TAG

Wombat International, Pty. Ltd., is a multinational electronics engineering company with offices in three countries and headquarters in Melbourne, Australia, Milano, Italy, and Frankfurt, Germany. For years, the company has been publishing its own internal telephone book every six months. Not only have the printing and distribution of this directory become a major production, but, unfortunately, the printed version is often substantially out of date shortly after each new printing. Currently, Wombat has roughly 4,200 employees in total, divided more or less evenly between its three main sites. The number of employees has been growing at a modest but sustained rate of 8% to 10% each year, and the company currently experiences about 80 to 90 changes to the directory each month, including staff departures, new hires, internal transfers, and various other changes.

The proposal has been advanced to convert the company telephone directory into an on-line system, a new software-based directory that will include every employee at Wombat International. This is practical because nearly all Wombat employees have immediate access to or work on PCs. The earlier decision to make Windows 95 the standard desktop platform will simplify deployment of a software system. The company is fully networked, with leased high-speed links connecting its three national offices.

As programmers are wont to do, members of the project team quickly generate a long wish list of added features and escalate this modest problem with ambitious plans for direct integration of the new application with email and fax. They want to include additional information, such as email and postal addresses, plus numerous advanced features, including a variety of personal information management functions, such as maintaining diaries, scheduling and coordination of meetings, contact tracking, and mail-merge capabilities. Fortunately, the project leader has decided to take a usage-centered approach beginning with a basic core of essential features on the first release cycle. To keep it relatively simple, the "TeleGuida" system, as it has been dubbed, is intended to be a basic computerized telephone directory to replace the printed edition. The objective is to support flexible and efficient everyday use through a well-designed user interface and carefully selected features. The first question facing the project team is to decide what constitutes the core of essential features.

> *As programmers are wont to do, project teams quickly generate long wish lists of added features and escalate modest problems into ambitious undertakings.*

GATHERING REQUIREMENTS

The project team has started out with a contextual approach to requirements gathering [Beyer and Holtzblatt, 1997], observing actual usage of the printed telephone directory, talking with employees in their offices, and extending their sample by surveying a random subset of employees. After gathering a considerable amount of information, they sorted and categorized the various bits they had learned.

Much of what they learned would be representative of telephone book users and usage in many companies. Following are some of the highlights gleaned from their inquiries.

PRACTICE BREAK

Before reading further, you might want to make some notes that might furnish useful guidance for design of the TeleGuida system based on your own observations and insights regarding ways that people actually use paper-based company telephone directories.

---

1. Most people marked up and annotated their printed directories with supplementary information about the person, such as indicating membership on a particular committee or participation in a certain cross-functional project team.

2. Annotations also frequently included or pointed to the main telephone number of the person's department or the number of a secretary.

3. Most employees used the covers and blank pages at the front and back of their printed directories to record additional entries. Many of these added entries were of personal interest and included details for people outside the company, such as customer contacts and suppliers, as well as friends and family members.

4. Another common use of the inside covers was to create a ready-access list of frequently looked-up numbers (numbers needed repeatedly but not often enough to be memorized).

5. In looking for a particular number, employees might scan through both their added personal entries and the main part of the directory.

6. A particular problem within Wombat is finding the telephone number of someone for whom the country or office in which they work is unknown, such as where the name might lead one to look in the wrong section of the book. For example, many employees with Italian surnames actually work in Germany or Australia.

7. Many of the desktop systems include modems, and employees have said that being able to dial a number automatically would save time and reduce errors, especially for frequent or high-volume users.

8. A high percentage of employees use cellular phones, especially in Australia and Italy where mobiles are ubiquitous.

9. A significant fraction of the sales and technical staff use notebook computers when out of the office. The ability to use the same telephone directory application both on the road and in the office would be advantageous.

In the course of their investigations, the project team learned about some of the problems people experience using the printed version of the internal telephone directory. Many had trouble reaching the correct person in cases where the name was particularly common and there were many duplicate entries, such as for Ian Smith in Melbourne (17 entries), Mario Rossi in Milano (21), or Hans Meier in Frankfurt (16). Some had developed personal tricks or schemes for coping with duplicate names, such as highlighting specific entries called in the past. One informant talked about the difficulty in finding a particular Mario Rossi whom she recalled worked "in accounting or finance or payroll or something like that in Milano." Fortunately, she remembered that there was something peculiar about the telephone number, and, when she saw it, she recognized the correct entry by the three eights at the end of the number.

The team reached several conclusions from these findings. First, if the software telephone directory is to replace the paper telephone directories, it should be at least as flexible and as easy to personalize and customize as the system being replaced. In principle, a software system should be able to provide improved support for the sorts of personal uses evident with the paper-based system. Second, the directory needs to include multiple telephone numbers associated with a given entry, including linked numbers, such as the main department or secretary's number. While the original printed version of the directory was physically divided into three sections, one for each country, further identification of employees by department (e.g., Advanced Mobile Systems Support Group) and actual location (e.g., Bldg. G-1, Room 4-321) would facilitate locating the right person more quickly and extend the usefulness of the software system.

> *New software should be at least as flexible and as easy to personalize and customize as the systems being replaced.*

Effectively, three subgroups of a telephone database need to be maintained. One, a master corporate database comprising entries common to all employees, will need to be maintained in a controlled manner from a central location. A private database of personal entries is unique to each user and mirrors the structure of the shared directory. Finally, a personal list holds for ready access a relatively small set of entries specified by each user. The master corporate directory will need to be updated monthly to reflect cumulated changes. Individual users of the system will be responsible for maintaining their own personal database and ready-access entries. The entries in the databases should include at least the following information:

- Full name of employee
- All telephone numbers associated with that employee
- Department and division
- Location (office and country)
- Ad hoc flags or categories

Telephone numbers within the system should include not only the individual's direct office line but also the main departmental line, the secretary's number if applicable, and mobile/cellular phone if available. Home numbers may also be included in some instances, but it should be possible to code such entries as "published" or "unpublished." Unpublished numbers are to be displayed only to appropriate and approved users.

Ad hoc flags or categories may be added to any entry by the individual user to indicate the status of the entry or membership in a particular grouping of interest to that user. For example, a user might want to create a "Usability Task Force" category and flag the directory entries of five colleagues as indicating the members of that group. Such groupings are analogous to departments or divisions but are created ad hoc for varied and varying purposes. Note that the individual user may thus annotate any entry, including ordinary entries in the companywide directory, but that such user annotations are unique and of interest only to the individual.

From the users' standpoint, what is important is that the system exhibit the right behavior; the implementation is largely irrelevant. For the three databases, the desired behavior, though not necessarily the implementation, is as follows: The main corporate database and personal database behave as if they were integrated, although it is always possible for the

> *From the users' standpoint, what is important is that the system exhibit the right behavior; the implementation is largely irrelevant.*

user to distinguish and separate personal entries from company ones. In other words, the system behaves as if each person has a private copy of the directory, just as each formerly had a personal copy of the printed telephone directory. All personally made additions or annotations appear in the expected places within the listings, but only in that employee's own copy. To the user, the ready-access list is like a special page of selected listings.

Access to and the ability to modify information in the databases is to be controlled. All users can, of course, make any changes to their personal database, but only those authorized for database maintenance can modify entries in the companywide database. Managers and their designated secretaries or support staff may have access to all home numbers in the companywide database. Secretaries and other support staff may need access to and the ability to alter the personal databases of other users to which they have been granted designated access. For example, a boss may need to grant such access to a secretary. With this exception, personal databases can normally be accessed or altered only by the owner of the personal database.

These requirements translate into the need for four different levels or categories of security or access control: normal, support, manage, and maintain. The access privileges for each of these levels are given in Table 15-1.

The project team is acutely aware that the system is likely to be enhanced in the future. A sound architecture that can readily be expanded is a major design objective. Some future possibilities that have been discussed without making any firm commitment to implementation include:

1. Email addresses
2. Integration with internal and external email systems
3. Mailing address, including street address, mail-stop, and so on
4. Nicknames or aliases

A usage-centered approach to this project would involve the following activities:

1. Model the user roles.
2. Model the essential use cases.
3. Develop a content model with navigation map.
4. Develop a paper prototype.
5. Conduct a collaborative usability inspection of the paper prototype.
6. Revise the visual design, and develop a working prototype using a suitable visual development environment.

Each of these activities will be discussed in turn.

TABLE 15-1 *Privileges by access level for TeleGuida*

Access Privilege	Normal	Support	Manage	Maintain
Own personal DB	Read/Write	Read/Write	Read/Write	Read/Write
Personal annotations to company DB	Read/Write	Read/Write	Read/Write	Read/Write
Company DB	Read	Read	Read	Read/Write
Unpublished home numbers		Read	Read	Read/Write
Other designated personal DB (as authorized by owner)		Read/Write		

GETTING AHEAD

Most developers exhibit, in varying degrees, strong tendencies to get ahead of themselves. Despite abundant evidence of the time-saving contribution of appropriate design models, many programmers remain convinced that it is much faster just to build a system than to waste time on modeling. No doubt, many developers who do not follow a model-driven approach might at this point begin to sketch or prototype designs for the user interface. As it turns out, one programmer on the Wombat project team, a real visual development whiz, has already cranked out a working prototype.

> *Most developers tend to get ahead of themselves, and many remain convinced that it is much faster just to build a system than to waste time on modeling.*

PRACTICE BREAK

Before reading further, you might try sketching a conventional, quick-and-dirty solution for the focal interaction context that will be faced by most users in most of their usage of the TeleGuida system. Save your work for later comparison.

The programmer is quite proud of the prototype design, which incorporates a modern-looking tabbed datagrid widget for the directory display. Rather than discarding this solution outright, risking alienating the programmer, the project leader has realized that the team might learn some valuable lessons if the

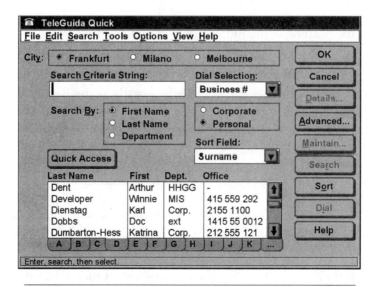

FIGURE 15-1 *Quick-and-dirty visual design for a telephone directory application.*

prototype is treated as a "straw man" design. A collaborative usability inspection is to be made of this TeleGuida prototype, shown in Figure 15-1.

The interactive phase of the inspection is to be guided by several representative scenarios:

Scenario 1

Telephone Mario Rossi on his mobile number. You will recognize the correct Rossi when you see it.

Scenario 2

Telephone the woman in payroll or accounting with a name like Grant or Grandi or Grandt or something like that, city unknown.

Scenario 3

Telephone the Ian Smith in Melbourne who is a member of the Usability Standards Committee.

The inspection begins with first impressions.

PRACTICE BREAK

Before reading further, make a quick list of usability problems that are readily apparent to you from your own first impressions of the visual design shown in Figure 15-1. If you have already sketched your own proposed visual design, try to identify readily apparent defects within your design and then compare these to those you listed for the design of Figure 15-1.

Here is a list of some of the immediately obvious issues:

- Screen real estate—wasted; small display area for results of any search
- Visibility—few listings showing; cannot easily scan visually for listing being sought
- Terminology—**Search Criteria String** and other geek-speak
- Inconsistent terminology—**Surname** and **Last Name**; **Office** and **Business #**
- Structure—**Dial Selection** separated from number field and **Dial** control
- Clarity—numerous controls; some with vague or uncertain meaning, such as **Advanced**; many grayed out
- Keyboard access letters—not all defined; some obscure

The group then begins the interactive inspection process based on the three test scenarios.

Before reading further, try, through a gedanken experiment, enacting all three scenarios with the visual design shown in Figure 15-1, keeping track of usability defects as you encounter them. Try to infer how the user interface might behave based on reasonable assumptions. If you have sketched your own tentative visual design, try enacting the same scenarios with your design, keeping track of usability defects as you proceed. Compare these defects to those identified for Figure 15-1.

The group starts the first of the three test scenarios—Telephone Mario Rossi on his mobile number. You will recognize the correct Rossi when you see it—by selecting **Milano** with the option button. ("Why do we have to do that. Extra step. We just want Rossi. What if we don't know where he is?") "Rossi" is typed into the text entry box, and **Sea_rch** is clicked. A message about "null search results set" comes up. Oops, they missed the fact that the **Sea_rch By** was set to **First Name**. Another defect is noted: confusing, problematic workflow. They notice that the **Corporate** database needs to be selected. ("Extra step. What if we want both? Two separate searches.") Now the Rossies appear in the display, starting with Angelo. ("Do we have to scroll down to find the Marios? What happens if we now do a first-name search on Mario? Oh, we'd get all the Marios and have to scroll to the Rossies.") Someone suggests trying the alphabetic tabs. It takes two clicks on the end tab before the R's appear and then minutes of scrolling to get to the Rossies. ("The tabs are just bells and whistles, fashion that doesn't work in practice.")

Once the Rossi entry is found, all that shows is his office number. ("Visibility problem. How do we see his other numbers?" "You can select **Mobile** in the **Dial Selection**," says the programmer. "But that changes the visible number for all displays. We're only interested in the mobile number for Rossi; most of the time we will want the office number." "Well, you can click **Details** for the full record view.") They click on **Details**, bringing up a dialogue displaying all the information for Rossi, in a different format from the "list view." ("We see his mobile number, but what if we want to automatically dial it?" "Oh," says the programmer, "You have to do that from the main screen using the **Dial Selection** widget." "Arrgh!")

The group quickly finds the second scenario to be almost impossible to accomplish based on what they know how to do so far. ("Inefficient, slow, clumsy.") The programmer tells them they should do that through the **Advanced** search option, which takes them to a screen with multiple drop-down lists separated by "and" and "or" operators. They give up. ("Obscure, geek-speak, awkward.")

They make one try on the third scenario, first searching for and then scrolling through the Smiths, finding that they must select and then display details on each record in succession. ("Hopelessly inefficient!") The inspection is ended with a long list of defects and the programmer's promise to fix them. The project leader convinces everybody to return to a usage-centered approach and to begin modeling.

TELEGUIDA USERS AND USES

Having met with users and had some opportunity to understand the range of potential users for the new software system, the project team is in a good position to start with the user role modeling.

> **PRACTICE BREAK**
>
> *Before reading further, try brainstorming your own list of candidate user roles. If you get stuck, go for the simplest, most obvious, or most familiar examples first, and then expand from there. Review your list for completeness.*

USER ROLES FOR TELEGUIDA

Following is one example of an initial list of candidate user roles, along with some explanatory comments offered during the project team's brainstorming session. The list is typical of the work of numerous teams that have tackled this problem, including reflecting the tendency of software professionals to start off with data administration issues even before considering the common user and everyday uses:

databaseAdministrator
handles the corporate "CRUD" (Create, Read, Update, Delete)

casualSeeker
your ordinary, everyday employee

social/GroupCoordinator
needs to keep contact with various people in groups

secretarialSupport
looks up for others and uses boss's or others' databases

receptionist/Guard
sits at entry desk and calls people being visited

telephoneOperator
gets numbers for people and connects them

salesStaffer
laptop user

fieldTechnician
> technically oriented laptop user

techo
> "real nerd" power user; always in a hurry; wants command-line operation and query entry in SQL

dataEntryClerk
> the one who enters the listings in the first place

The initial identification of a role does not require that the role will be fully supported in the final delivered system. For example, it might be a strategic management decision *not* to support the **techo** role not only because of additional work to support such a role but also because there may, in some applications, be risks associated with allowing users too much direct control.

Another user role that might be dropped is the **dataEntryClerk**. This role has rather specialized needs for what is essentially a one-time use—namely, generating the initial company database. Is this within the scope of the TeleGuida application? It is certainly within the scope of the project, but it might be supported through a separate application altogether, such as an off-the-shelf facility for database creation or a special application created solely for this purpose. In some cases, it might be reasonable to provide an appropriate user interface within the TeleGuida application itself. The **dataEntryClerk** role has some overlap with the **databaseAdministrator** role; it is even possible that one set of cleverly designed facilities could support both roles.

> *Identifying a role does not require the role to be fully supported in the delivered system. It might be a strategic management decision not to support a particular role.*

Here, we will make the reasonable assumption that the initial corporate database will be derived by file conversion from the stored version of the printed telephone directory, merged with data from other corporate files, and followed by manual correction and addition as necessary. This puts an extra premium on efficient support of the **databaseAdministrator** role. Note that this is a role, not a job title, and different incumbents might act in this role for initial file generation and routine monthly maintenance.

The initial user role model as brainstormed needs to be elaborated and refined. On closer examination, some roles are closely related and might be combined. The roles will need to be described in more precise detail.

PRACTICE BREAK

Before reading further, describe each role in some detail regarding typical or expected patterns of usage. Considering the similarities and differences among roles, identify specializations and combine roles as appropriate.

For example, how do the needs, behaviors, and expectations of a telephone operator differ from those of someone serving as a receptionist or entrance security guard? In most ways, these are similar. Both are high-volume users who make frequent lookups of many different targets; hence, speed and simplicity of operation are vital. In both roles, the parties being sought are unknown to the user, and the information origin is aural: They hear the name spoken. This means they will not necessarily know the correct spelling and may need the ability to see all listings that sound like the one entered.

In principle, the **telephoneOperator** role might need to be supported by an additional specialized function: the ability to dial automatically the number being sought, transferring the incoming call to the outgoing connection. This would require a software-controlled, hardware-level interface with the company telephone system, which will differ in the three countries of operation. The project team concludes that this one, seemingly small enhancement, although nice, could be extremely complicated and difficult to implement. They note that, under the present scheme, the telephone directory is not integrated with the telephone switching equipment; the operator looks up a number, keys it into the telephone equipment, and then manually triggers the dialing and call transfer through the telephone switchboard. Not trying to automate the dial and call transfer in the initial release of the TeleGuida software is both reasonable and expedient. On the other hand, the user role model is more viable for future versions of the software if the role is left in, which is best expressed by specialization or subclassing in the user role map.

The revised and expanded user role model, in informal but semistructured form, might look like this:

casualSeeker
 occasional and sporadic use, from few times per week to few times per day; typically seeks single number from among relatively small subset of all listings; usually seeks by name of person but also from other, possibly more vague information; ready-access listings important

social/GroupCoordinator
 interested in user-defined groups and categories; use may be concentrated, as in calling all members of group in succession or defining new group; likely to be concerned with more different listings than **casualSeeker**

secretarial/SupportStaff

frequent and regular daily use; target listings are varied and more likely to be unknown to incumbent; needs access to other's personal databases [over network?]

maintainer

special functional support: the usual CRUD (Create, Read, Update, Delete) for listings

corporateAdministrator

specializes **maintainer**; infrequent and periodic (monthly), batched, moderately high volume (80 to 90 changes); special functional support: direct access (by employee number or ID or record ID), ability to set access levels; criteria: efficiency, reliability, rememberability

personalAdministrator

specializes **maintainer**; infrequent, sporadic, low-volume use; CRUD (Create, Read, Update, Delete) for personal entries only

dataEntryClerk

[NOT SUPPORTED] specializes **maintainer**; very high volume (4,200 records); one-time use; special functional support: direct access (by employee number or ID or record ID), enter/modify all fields; criteria: efficiency, accuracy, learnability

intermediary

gets numbers for others; many, highly varied targets, unknown to incumbents; information origin: aural

receptionist/Guard

specializes **intermediary**; frequent, fairly high volume use; in-person source; may be interested in physical location, route to location

telephoneOperator

specializes **intermediary**; very high rate, high volume, continuous use; headset source; special functional support [DEFERRED]: autodial and call transfer through interface with telephone switching equipment

roadWarrior

special functional support: synchronize laptop and desktop databases

techo

[NOT SUPPORTED] technically oriented power user having high system and platform knowledge; expert usage patterns; special functional support: command-line, SQL entry; criteria: efficiency, flexibility

The effective use of role specialization is clear in this user role model. The abstract roles of **maintainer** and **intermediary**, which have no incumbents, serve as placeholders for information common to multiple roles. Combinations of roles are expected, but, because an incumbent may act in varied roles, these need not all be modeled as explicit compositions. To illustrate, the actual department secretary for the Advanced Applications Programming Group is quite likely at various times to play in the roles of **receptionist**, **personalAdministrator**, and **social/GroupCoordinator**, as well as **secretarial/SupportStaff** and even **casualSeeker**.

> *Once we have covered all the user roles that the application must support, we can identify the focal roles that will most directly guide the initial design.*

Once we believe we have covered all the user roles that the application must support, we can identify the focal roles that will most directly guide the design, especially at the outset. The selection of focal roles should be based on reasonable evidence and sound judgment. On the basis of expected frequency, there is little doubt that the **casualSeeker** role is likely to be the most common, followed by **social/GroupCoordinator**. Most users will also at one time or another play in the **personalAdministrator** role, which will be needed to make full use of the software. The **secretarial/SupportStaff** role can be very important for normal business functioning, but secretaries and similar support staff represent only a minority of employees, although other employees might occupy this role at times. The **casualSeeker**, **social/GroupCoordinator**, and **personalAdministrator** roles

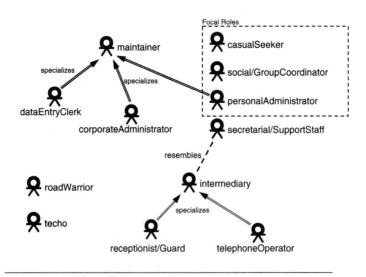

FIGURE 15-2 *User role map for the TeleGuida application.*

from the revised list are reasonable choices for focal roles. The completed user role map for TeleGuida appears in Figure 15-2.

ESSENTIAL USE CASES FOR TELEGUIDA

Beginning with the focal user roles of **casualSeeker**, **social/GroupCoordinator**, and **personalAdministrator**, we can start to brainstorm a list of candidate use cases.

> **PRACTICE BREAK**
>
> *Before reading further, quickly brainstorm a list of candidate use cases. Note only whatever detail or explanation is necessary to distinguish use cases from one another.*

A typical initial list of candidate use cases might look something like this:

findingNamedPerson'sNumber
findingSomebody'sNumber
> where user may know part of the name, perhaps the department, maybe some detail of the telephone number.

findingGroupNumbers
> getting all members of a group or entries flagged by a particular category

dialingNumber
> using modem

gettingReadyAccessNumber
addingEntryToReadyAccessList
deletingReadyAccessEntry
creatingNewListEntry
modifyingListEntry
deletingListEntry
settingAccessLevel
identifyingSelf
> for appropriate access

accessingAnotherPersonalList
grantingPersonalListAccess
definingNewCategory
> new group or annotation

settingEntryCategory
> making an entry a member of a group or category

```
deletingEntryCategory
selectingLanguage
synchronizingListCopies
```
downloading database to laptop or uploading changed database from laptop

This preliminary list will need to be reviewed, refined, and pared down. For example, the first three use cases are very similar, and it is highly likely that a well-designed common search mechanism will satisfy all three. In particular, **findingNamedPerson'sNumber** is a specialization of the more generic use case, **findingSomebody'sNumber**. For that matter, if we consider **findingSomebody'sNumber** to include, potentially, any information known to the user and contained in the databases, then **findingGroupNumbers** is also merely a specialization. The fact that the user will see a list of entries corresponding to the group or category selected is no different than if the user enacting **findingSomebody'sNumber** fails to narrow down the possibilities sufficiently to yield a list with only one entry. If we tackle a whole series of specializations as separate and independent use cases, we risk a design that handles each one in a unique way, potentially complicating the interface and making it more difficult to learn or clumsier to use. We particularly want to avoid the kind of simpleminded, no-brainer interface in which every use case is supported by its own command button, each button launching a unique dialogue.

> *Avoid simpleminded, no-brainer interfaces in which each use case is supported by its own command button launching a unique dialogue.*

It is important to note that the **gettingReadyAccessNumber** use case is quite distinct from **findingSomebody'sNumber**. The sought-after number is either immediately evident in the short list constituting the "Ready-Access List" or it is not; one does not normally create a search for what the eye can scan much faster. On the other hand, we do not want to exclude the Ready-Access List from searches. Why? Because a sought-after listing may exist only in the Ready-Access List and the user might not be aware of this fact. We might want to feed forward an implementation note that the Ready-Access List should always be included implicitly in all searches.

The **settingAccessLevel** use case may be viewed in more than one way. It is unique to the **corporateAdministrator** role, but it can be modeled either as a separate use case or as being included in any complete realization of **modifyingListEntry**. From a strictly logical point of view, the most defensible and transparent modeling might be to represent **settingAccessLevel** and **modifyingListEntry** (excluding access level) as specializations of the abstract use case **modifying**, but this seems to us to be rather pedantic. As a rule, we try for the simplest modeling that is clear to the development team and the collaborating users.

Many beginners will propose uses cases along the lines of **callingSomebody**, which is certainly expressed from the point of view of user intentions but which fails to recognize that the calling itself, taking place between one person and another over a telephone line, is outside the boundary of the software system. On the other hand, optional automatic dialing of a telephone number is recognized as an explicit requirement for TeleGuida. The **dialingNumber** use case is an extension of other use cases. Having found a number, the user may choose to dial it manually, write it down on a note pad, or whatever; having the computer dial a number is an option that may arise at any point.

The **deletingReadyAccessEntry** use case illustrates another issue. This is not so much a separate use case or even a specialization of the more generic **deletingListEntry**; it is nothing more than **deletingListEntry** applied to an entry in the Ready-Access List. We need to remind ourselves to use the same mechanisms for the same operations *across the board.* We show this on the use case map as an equivalence. In contrast, **addingEntryToReadyAccessList** is not a synonym for or variant of **creatingNewListEntry**. Surely, **creatingNewListEntry** should apply to creating an entry in the Ready-Access List from scratch, even as **deletingListEntry** should enable the user to delete an entry from the Ready-Access List. But what if the desired Ready-Access entry already exists, whether in the personal directory or the corporate one? The user should not be punished by having to reenter data already contained in the system. This is the intention of **addingEntryToReadyAccessList**—to copy an existing entry to the Ready-Access List.

> *The user should not be punished by having to reenter data already contained in the system.*

The final list of use cases, grouped into logical clusters of related cases, might be as follows (cases that are equivalent to or have been subsumed under other use cases are shown in parentheses):

```
findingSomebody'sNumber
    (findingNamedPerson'sNumber)
gettingReadyAccessNumber

dialingNumber

addingEntryToReadyAccessList
creatingNewListEntry
    (creatingReadyAccessEntry)
modifyingListEntry
    (modifyingReadyAccessEntry)
deletingListEntry
    (deletingReadyAccessEntry)
settingAccessLevel
```

```
identifyingSelf
accessingAnotherPersonalList
grantingPersonalListAccess
revokingPersonalListAccess

definingNewCategory
settingEntryCategory
deletingCategory

selectingLanguage

synchronizingListCopies
```

The final list of use cases should always be reviewed to see whether it covers all the core capability that will be needed by users in all the identified user roles.

> *Use cases and user roles should be reviewed to see whether any role requires capability that is not represented or fully implied among the identified use cases.*

We ask whether there is any role that will require any capability not represented or fully implied among the identified use cases. Once we are satisfied that the list of use cases is substantially complete, we can create a preliminary use case map on the basis of our understanding to this point, recognizing that, as the modeling continues and we detail the use case narratives, the use case map may need to be revised again. The most frequent use cases for incumbents within the focal roles will most likely be `findingSomebody'sNumber`, `gettingReadyAccessNumber`, and `dialingNumber`; these are good candidates for focal use cases.

PRACTICE BREAK

Before reading further, try expressing the complete use case map in graphical form, using the notation introduced in Chapter 5.

The completed use case map in graphical form is shown in Figure 15-3. Note that use cases that are covered by other use cases are represented in the map but

> *If a simpler model suffices, we would favor it over a more rigorous but more baroque model.*

are shown with dashed outlines. This convention ensures that the capability represented by these use cases is not lost from the model but serves to flag these as requiring a common realization in the implementation model. There are, of course, other ways to model the same basic concepts. For example, the relationship between `deletingListEntry` and `deletingReadyAccessEntry` could be modeled by treating each as a specialization of `deletingEntry`. Although this is, possibly, a

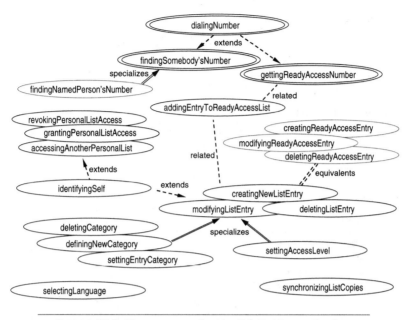

FIGURE 15-3 *Use case map for the TeleGuida application.*

more rigorous model, it is also more baroque. If the simpler model suffices for a particular application in a particular context, we would tend to prefer it.

ESSENTIAL NARRATIVES FOR TELEGUIDA

Normally, we begin with the focal use cases and start trying to write them out in the form of structured narratives, reducing the narratives to essential form as we can. For this example, as with many real-world problems, the essential narratives are remarkably simple, which, ironically, contributes to the difficulty that many developers experience. Convinced that there must be more to the problem, they feel compelled to elaborate or complicate the matter unnecessarily. As explained in Chapter 5, once all the intentions and responsibilities are expressed succinctly in the language of users and of the domain, a use case is complete. For each use case, we ask, "If the user interface allows the interaction described by the narrative to take place, can the user accomplish the objective of the use case?" If the answer is "yes," the essential use case is complete, however brief it may be.

> *Although the essential narratives are remarkably simple for many real-world problems, developers often feel compelled to elaborate or complicate them unnecessarily.*

PRACTICE BREAK

> *Before reading further, write out the narrative body for each of the three focal*
> *use cases in the use case map. Ensure that each narrative is reduced to*
> *essential form and is complete.*

Following are essential narratives for the focal use cases in this application (after studying these and assuring yourself that each is complete and is expressed in essential form, you might try writing out the narratives for other TeleGuida use cases):

findingSomebody'sNumber

USER INTENTION	SYSTEM RESPONSIBILITY

offer whatever is known
  (e.g., all or part of name,
  department, location,
  telephone numbers, etc.)	

	present whatever is found
	  (name, department, location,
	  telephone numbers, etc.)

gettingReadyAccessNumber

USER INTENTION	SYSTEM RESPONSIBILITY
ask for ready-access list	

	present ready-access list
	  (name, department, location,
	  telephone numbers, etc.)

Note that the action of the system in presenting the information completes each of these use cases because **dialingNumber** is an extension (in the event that what the user seeks is not visible within the presented information, the user must necessarily enact another use case; it is not, therefore, part of the narratives for these use cases):

dialingNumber

USER INTENTION	SYSTEM RESPONSIBILITY
indicate number to dial	
	dial it

PRACTICE BREAK

Before reading further, try writing out the narrative body for these additional use cases (ensure that each narrative is reduced to essential form and is complete):

> **addingEntryToReadyAccessList**
> **grantingPersonalListAccess**
> **accessingAnotherPersonalList**

In our experience, the vast majority of use cases for real problems are only a few lines long when reduced to essential form; rarely is an essential use case more than half a dozen user steps in length. Consider these additional use cases, which merit no discussion:

addingEntryToReadyAccessList

USER INTENTION	SYSTEM RESPONSIBILITY
indicate entry to add	
	add to ready-access list

grantingPersonalListAccess

USER INTENTION	SYSTEM RESPONSIBILITY
give name of authorized user	
	add to authorized-user list

When we come to the **accessingAnotherPersonalList** use case, the modeling offers more challenges. In order to complete the use case, the user must be known to the system since the system must verify that the user has been authorized to access the requested personal database. Do we explicitly represent this behavior in the use case? A simpler narrative results if we consider **identifyingSelf** an extension use case that may occur in the course of enacting **accessingAnotherPersonalList** if the user is unknown to the system:

accessingAnotherPersonalList

USER INTENTION	SYSTEM RESPONSIBILITY
request list by name or location	
	make requested personal list available if user is authorized

Many analysts, however, take a more programming-oriented or procedural view and explicitly model the narrative with some form of conditional statement requesting the user's identity. A relatively clean narrative of this form can be constructed by employing the **identifyingSelf** use case as a subcase on the "User Intention" side. Normally, an optional interaction is modeled as an extension, which would not be referenced by name in the use case. The next narrative makes more of the behavior explicit in the use case at the expense of parsimony. Is it wrong? Probably not, although it does play loose with some of the conventions of essential use cases:

> *Many analysts take a programming-oriented or procedural view and explicitly model use case narratives with conditional statements.*

accessingAnotherPersonalList

USER INTENTION	SYSTEM RESPONSIBILITY
request list by name or location	
	request identity if user is unknown
>identifyingSelf if requested	
	verify access authorization
	make requested personal list available

TOWARD A TELEGUIDA PROTOTYPE

Once we have completed the essential narratives for all the use cases, we are ready to start designing the user interface. Taking a usage-centered approach, we begin the design with abstract prototyping through a content model.

CONTENT MODEL FOR TELEGUIDA

We center our attention first on the focal use cases of **findingSomebody'sNumber**, **dialingNumber**, and **gettingReadyAccessNumber**.

> **PRACTICE BREAK**
>
> *Before reading further, try creating a content model with a single interaction context supporting the three focal use cases. Ensure that the content model completely supports the use case narratives.*

From the narrative for **findingSomebody'sNumber**, we recognize the need for a container to hold whatever the user knows about the person whose number is being sought—namely, all or part of the name, department, location, telephone numbers, and so on. Although we modeled this passive "input area" for the user's "search criteria" as a container, some analysts think of this as an active control by which the user inputs whatever is known about the sought-after entry. The line between active and passive is neither hard nor fast, but active abstract components are usually reserved for representing tools that trigger actions or that are used to modify or manipulate data, not for components holding data or serving as input areas.

> *Active abstract components are usually tools that trigger actions or that modify or manipulate data, not input areas or components holding data.*

We will also need to add to the content model a similar container to hold whatever the system finds that fits what the user has specified—namely, the name, department, location, telephone numbers, and so forth. It should be immediately apparent that these two containers are similar, holding virtually the same information. In fact, almost anything that the system could present to the user is potentially something the user could wish to specify in searching for a particular entry. Guided by the Structure Principle, we will want to reflect this similarity by visually associating the two containers, placing them near each other and giving them similar appearance; juxtaposing the abstract components on the content model reminds us of this close association.

Having reached the end of the brief narrative for **findingSomebody'sNumber**, we pause to verify whether the content model is sufficiently complete to support the use case. If we present an interface with a **knownInfoHolder** and a **foundEntriesHolder**, is this sufficient for a user to enact the use case? Absolutely! Although many developers feel compelled to place a search control on the content model, this compulsion is a consequence of thinking in information processing terms; it is not a logical requirement of the essential model. From the user's point of view, there should not be any need to tell the system to go find what is sought; the very act of expressing (entering) what is known suffices as a request. A system that understands this implicit request presents a simpler, more elegant, and more efficient interface from the user's point of view.

It is not hard to see how such a simple interface could be realized in practice. The content model implies a design based on incremental searching. With incremental search, as the user enters information, the presentation of "hits" (found information) is continuously updated to reflect the constraints offered by the user. The user need only type just enough of a name, for example, to be able to see the desired target entry among those appearing in the displayed list, the **foundEntriesHolder**.

In our classes, we always hear a few protests about inefficient queries, network traffic, and database utilization, but these are implementation concerns, and we defer them at this point. We are attempting to describe the simplest and most efficient realization of the use cases. Later, we will either succeed in earning our pay as clever programmers, giving the users what they really need, or else we will make reasonable compromises, but we normally begin by trying to stick to the unalloyed essentials.

> *We begin the content model with the unalloyed essentials: the simplest and most efficient realization of the use cases.*

In considering the relative importance of this particular implementation issue, we should turn to the operational context for guidance. Consider the size of the database. The entire employee telephone directory is a database of modest proportions, small enough to be copied locally on initial use or when updated, even small enough to fit into RAM. Search time will not be an overriding issue in this application.

The **dialingNumber** use case presents a similar lesson to the one learned from **findingSomebody'sNumber**. To select or indicate the number, we must have a **numberSelector** control of some sort. We will no doubt use the mouse pointer, but we put the abstract component on the interaction context as a reminder of this use. Again, thinking too much in traditional programming terms can be a hindrance. Many developers argue that we must also add a **numberDialer** control to the content model, even though this is not required to support the use case narrative. We prefer that the content model reminds us that the best user interface would allow the user both to select a number and to initiate dialing with a single action; that is the golden optimum for which we should strive. How might we achieve this goal? One possibility that occurs to many designers is to double-click on a number to dial it, but this not only is hidden behavior but also usurps for a special purpose an interaction idiom that more often is interpreted to mean "open" or "edit." As always, we will defer the final decision about the best way to implement such a feature on the user interface until we are preparing the implementation model.

Adding support for **gettingReadyAccessNumber** to this interaction context is simple. We will need a control to **showReadyAccess**, but no additional containers are required by the use case since the already available **foundEntriesHolder** serves this purpose admirably. An active abstract component will be needed for the user to choose the "view" that is of interest. This can be considered to be a toggle associated with the **foundEntriesHolder** or some other way for the user to express what listings are of interest. With the addition of a **showReadyAccess** toggle component, the content model to support the focal use cases is complete and might look something like the interaction context shown in Figure 15-4.

Next, we might consider support for the cluster of "maintenance" operations, including the use cases of **creatingNewListEntry**, **modifyingListEntry**, and

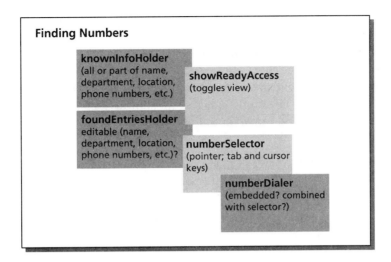

FIGURE 15-4 *Initial content model for TeleGuida focal use cases.*

deletingListEntry. For a start, we might create a fresh interaction context for these use cases. The third of these use cases, **deletingListEntry**, is instructive. In order to get the desired system responsibility of dropping a specific entry, we must be able to indicate the entry to be deleted. In order to indicate an entry, we must have a collection of entries from which to make a selection. We immediately find ourselves replicating the **foundEntriesHolder** and **knownInfoHolder** from the focal interaction context, a strong hint that we do not need to support this use case on a separate interaction context. We need add nothing to the content model to support **modifyingListEntry** if we assume that the **foundEntriesHolder** is an editable container—that is, if we support editing in-place. How we accomplish this is a matter to be resolved within the implementation model. Clearly, there will be some trade-offs in terms of available screen real estate and the visibility of the information present, but the problem does not require that we introduce another interaction context just for this use case. We will need to return to this issue again, however.

The **creatingNewListEntry** use case will require us to add a **newEntryHolder**, which comprises the name, department, location, telephone numbers, and so forth. This new abstract component seems to have the same structure as the **foundEntriesHolder**; it is essentially an **instance** of the contents of the **foundEntriesHolder**. Do we really want a separate interaction context for maintenance, or might these use cases also be handled within the focal interaction

> *Although it is common practice to require switching to another interaction context to create a new record or file entry, operation will be simplified if we can avoid unnecessary context changes.*

context without unduly complicating it? Although it is common practice to make the user switch to another interaction context to create a new record or file entry, this is not always the smoothest realization from the user's perspective. We do not make the user of a spreadsheet application launch a dialogue to insert a new row in the middle of the spreadsheet, for example. If we can avoid unnecessary context changes, operation will be simplified, and we should keep this in mind as we finish the content model and move on to the navigation map.

NAVIGATION MAP FOR TELEGUIDA

The navigation map for this application should not be complicated. Context switching, especially for focal or other common use cases, can make the system inefficient and far less usable.

> **PRACTICE BREAK**
>
> *Before reading further, try sketching a complete navigation map for the TeleGuida application. Pay particular attention to limiting the context switching necessary for enacting focal or common use cases.*

The navigation map in Figure 15-5 would normally be considered tentative at this stage. The focal interaction context is intended to cover a majority of the use cases, with a few of the more special-purpose use cases allocated to separate interaction contexts. Examining the context transitions in the diagram reveals that most of them are taken only infrequently in normal use, with the exception of the transition from the focal context to **Detail View**. The typical user may need to switch frequently back and forth between these interaction contexts, making **Detail View** almost another focal context. This highlights a design problem needing to be addressed in developing the implementation model. The notation for **Selecting Language** as an enclosed interaction context represents the fact that this capability must be surfaced where indicated.

VISUAL DESIGN FOR TELEGUIDA

In the course of developing the usage-centered models, the project team has become inspired to attempt an innovative design solution that will be both elegant and efficient, both for the focal use cases and for certain other high-volume use cases—namely, the maintenance use cases of **creatingNewListEntry**, **modifyingListEntry**, and **deletingListEntry**. They have decided that they will not be constrained by conventional appearance and behavior whenever an unconventional approach will lead to an efficient and easy-to-use system.

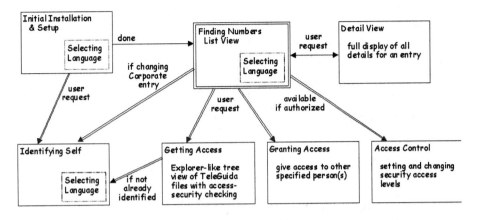

FIGURE 15-5 *Proposed navigation map for TeleGuida.*

PRACTICE BREAK

Before reading further, try sketching a complete visual design for the focal interaction context of the TeleGuida system. Working systematically from the content and navigation models, carefully consider layout, workflow, and creative choices of visual components.

The visual design illustrated in Figures 15-6, 15-7, and 15-8 is a mock-up based on ideas contributed by numerous teams that have participated in our classes over the years. Because it has been revised through iterative inspection, it is more representative of a final design than typical first-cut designs. However, it is not being offered as a definitive or flawless solution—no such solution exists—but as a composite that illustrates some of the problems and possible solutions in the implementation model for TeleGuida.

Many of the most effective solutions share common features and have similar overall organization. We will discuss some of the major features and design trade-offs represented in the design presented here.

Layout. In this application, it is critical to recognize the importance of efficient layout and effective use of screen real estate. One specific objective is to get the largest number of entries displayed and to show as much of each entry as practical. Why? Because the eye is quicker than the hand. Most users can visually scan through a list of entries much more quickly than they can manually scroll or than they can formulate a sufficiently narrow set of search criteria. Since any part of an entry might be necessary or useful in helping the user to recognize the desired entry, the more of each entry we can display, the better. In particular, we want to show multiple telephone numbers and have as many as we can immediately accessible for dialing, whether manually or by modem.

Guided by the content model, it is fairly easy to conceive of the parallel structure for search-criteria entry and for display of the found results as shown in Figure 15-6. This arrangement not only makes it easy for the user to search on any displayed field but also simplifies the layout and makes it easier to interpret. Careful layout can also save screen real estate by eliminating redundant labels; in the illustration, a single set of column labels separates the search entry from results display and identifies both.

> *Most users can visually scan through a list of entries much more quickly than they can manually scroll or than they can formulate a sufficiently narrow set of search criteria.*

This format allows the user to search on anything that is displayed, but that also highlights a potential disadvantage since the user cannot search on a field that is not visible. In practice, this does not seem to constitute a major defect, but a designer determined to "have it all" might try devising a creative compromise.

The tabbed dialogue structure is certainly not the only way to give the user access to multiple views into the telephone lists, but, as long as not too many views are needed, the tabbed metaphor offers rapid view switching along with visual object persistence through a simple and fairly natural mechanism. The

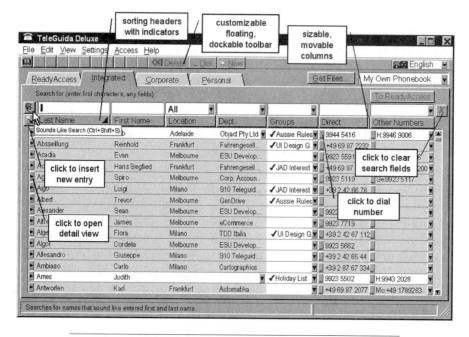

FIGURE 15-6 *Focal interaction context, usage-centered visual design for TeleGuida.*

example design shown in Figure 15-6 extends the tabbed metaphor for accessing the directory files that belong to others. The drop-down combo box to the right of the tabs provides immediate access, if the user is authorized, to anyone else's personal files that have been accessed before. (The same facility would also be available under the **View** menu.) The command button to the left of this widget brings up a short dialogue that obtains access to additional files, if authorized, and adds an entry to the drop-down list. (The same capability would also be available under the **Access** menu.)

Except through cut-and-paste, conventional tabbed dialogues do not support moving data between pages. (An elegant scheme to overcome this limitation is under patent review.) In this design, the use case **addingEntryToReadyAccessList** is supported through a dedicated button to add a selected entry from one of the other tabs to the **ReadyAccess** tab. It has been placed on the tab pages directly because it is not meaningful on all pages.

Efficiency. To achieve efficient implementation of the first focal use case, **findingSomebody'sNumber**, incremental searching is done on multiple fields. As soon as the user starts typing anything, the contents of the display grid are updated to reflect the constraints. So, for example, with the location set to Milano, typing "Rossi" in the first field starts the "Rossi" listings and then "Mario" in the second field narrows it to the Marios. If the desired Mario is not visible, the user can scroll down or narrow the search further based on other fields. If an attempt to locate a particular person fails, the user can click the "sounds like" control to the left of the search entry fields to locate all names that sound like the entered names based on a soundex algorithm.

Want to see all the members of the UI Design Group? Pick "UI Design Group" from the **Groups** combo box. In this design, the **Location**, **Dept.**, and **Groups** fields use drop-down combo boxes, but they could just as well use pop-open combo boxes. Of course, the drop-down fields are also enabled for incremental search. The drop-down box for **Location** includes an "All" entry, the default setting on entry, and could include other plausible combinations, such as "Europe."

Setting of the language needs to be surfaced (in case the user cannot read the interface) but need not be particularly efficient. A separate dialogue would do, but a drop-down box on the toolbar is cleaner. The same widget would reappear in the other interaction contexts under which language can be set.

The tabbed dialogue structure chosen here is one of many mechanisms that can offer single-click access to the Ready-Access List. One design team suggested making it a user option for the Ready-Access List to become a floating, resizable window with an "always-on-top" option that keeps it visible on the desktop. This capability was not directly requested or required, but it would allow the user to keep the Ready-Access List at hand at all times if desired. Although it would be unconventional in both appearance and behavior, this feature could be combined with the tabbed dialogue as shown in Figure 15-7. The Ready-Access List window starts as docked to the tab, where most users might leave it. However, it can be dragged from position like a floating toolbar. If docked at the sides of the screen, it could be given, at the user's option, automatic pop-out behavior like the Microsoft Office Shortcut Bar. (If the **ReadyAccess** tab is clicked when the contents have been floated, presumably the focus would shift to the ready-access contents, wherever they were.) Note that the fields have been customized by the user. Each tab supports its own independent customization of field sizes, placement, and sort order.

In Figure 15-7, the custom data-display widget for **Groups** is shown open. It is an in-place extended selection drop-down that allows for multiple items to be selected. Because it is a combo box, a new entry to the list can be created merely by getting focus to the field and typing the new entry, followed by **Enter**. This is not unusual behavior for a drop-down combo box (compare the "styles" drop-down in Microsoft Word, for example), but it is hidden behavior. When open, the drop-down displays **(new)** as the first entry; clicking on this closes the box and puts focus in the field with the text cursor at the beginning of an empty field. Extended-selection drop-down lists have one operational disadvantage: The drop-

> *Extended selection is inefficient in drop-down lists: To check or uncheck more than one entry, the list has to be reopened.*

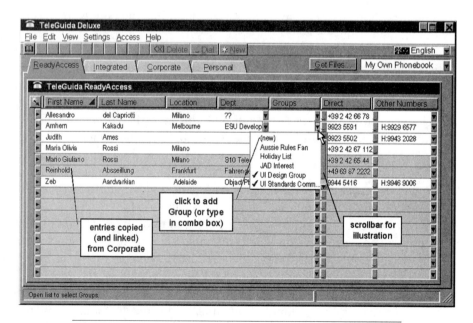

FIGURE 15-7 *Ready-Access List, usage-centered visual design for TeleGuida.*

down closes up once a selection is made. Should the user want to check or uncheck more than one entry, the drop-down has to be reopened. An alternative behavior, in which the drop-down remains open as long as focus stays within it, might better support the use cases. This is one for lab and field testing to see whether the gain is offset by the unexpected operation.

Efficient implementation of the focal extension **dialingNumber** is supported by the small embedded dialer buttons as part of each telephone number field. This makes visible the mechanism by which numbers can be dialed instantly. The embedded drop-down button under **Other Numbers** gives access to all other numbers with only one extra, in-context click. The desired behavior here would be for the system to remember the last-selected number from among these and have it be the exposed number on subsequent uses. The **Other Numbers** widget is intended to be a smart component that automatically includes all numbers that are not visible as columns.

Data display. The most important element of user customization is the customizable data-display grid that uses movable, resizable columns and sorting column headers with sort indicators. Each view (tab) is independently customizable; for example, this user maintains the Ready-Access List in alphabetical order by first name, which is displayed as the first column on the **ReadyAccess** page. Such capability might be challenging to program from scratch but is provided by readily available component libraries. Columns can be collapsed to make room for other information. Notice the thin shaded bars to the left of the first and last fields representing collapsed columns. The former represents the **Employee ID** field for use in the **corporateAdministrator** role to provide immediate and unambiguous access to a specific entry.

All fields within the display support in-place editing. Double-clicking on a field places the field in editing mode for direct modification or replacement. Fields that cannot be modified by the current user as logged in have a gray background, and modifiable ones have a white background. Note that, as required, assignments to **Group** can be added to any entry.

The small "detail" buttons to the left of each displayed entry open the entry with a nonmodal dialogue overlay, as shown in Figure 15-8. This overlay displays the complete contents of the entry and allows modifying any field if the user is authorized. Once opened, successive records can be viewed or modified using "navigator" controls on the dialogue overlay or the **PgUp** and **PgDn** keys. In this way, scanning through details of successive records is easy, and the various use cases supporting the **corporateAdministrator** role are made more efficient. As a nonmodal dialogue, any action outside the overlay will close it, including clicking the "detail" control again. For visibility, a close button also appears in the upper right corner.

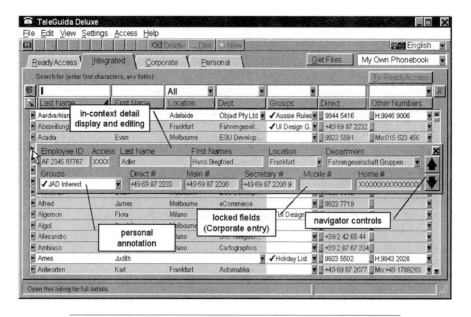

FIGURE 15-8 *Detail display, usage-centered visual design for TeleGuida.*

And furthermore. The visual design presented here is certainly not perfect, but it does illustrate how design features follow from usage-centered modeling. Not all issues have been resolved, and, admittedly, some trade-offs have been struck more elegantly than others. Naturally, one design cannot possibly incorporate all the good ideas that our enterprising students have devised over the years. Space does not permit discussing all the details, such as menu structure or other interaction contexts. Our purpose in going into what detail we have is not so much to solve the problem as to illustrate the process of how such a problem might be solved.

> *One design cannot possibly incorporate every good idea, and some trade-offs will have been struck more elegantly than others.*

PRACTICE BREAK

Before leaving the TeleGuida example, conduct your own design review or usability inspection of the presented visual design. Try to identify potential improvements or extensions that would enhance some aspect of usability. Complete the specification of the menus. Try to complete the visual design, including the support for these use cases:

```
identifyingSelf
grantingPersonalListAccess
accessingAnotherPersonalList
```

ASSESSMENT
AND IMPROVEMENT

16

BETTER NEXT TIME:
Improvement by Inspection and Review

ASSESSING USABILITY

It is all but impossible to get it right the first time when it comes to user interface design. The usability of software depends on numerous aspects of both underlying functional features and their surface appearance in software. The shape and position of icons on a toolbar can make a so-called productivity tool harder to learn and easier to misuse. Even with a simple and transparent menu structure to gain access to page formatting functions, unexpected or awkward behavior in the dialogue can make the cleanest and most intuitive interface layout pointless.

Software can be made dramatically harder to use by the smallest details of placement, sequencing, arrangement, and even labeling. It is very difficult, even for well-trained designers guided by proven principles of usability and supported by effective design tools, to get every aspect of the user interface correct on the first try [Constantine, 1991c]. Highly usable designs tend to evolve only through multiple iterations and successive generations [Norman, 1988].

Without feedback and refinement, even the best usage-centered design is almost doomed to failure. In order to improve user interface designs, the most important thing to learn is where you went wrong. A variety of techniques enable developers to identify the problems and shortcomings in software and software designs. Inspections and reviews, the primary topic of this chapter, offer rapid,

> *In order to improve user interface designs, the most important thing to learn is where you went wrong.*

efficient, and easily practiced means to locate usability problems and help identify potential solutions. Usability inspections and reviews complement good user interface engineering by finding the problems and limitations in otherwise sound designs. Usability inspections are not a substitute for good design and development practices. Like reliability, usability has to be designed in; it cannot be achieved by testing and inspection alone.

EXPERT EVALUATION

When you do not know what you are doing or are unsure of the results, the time-honored technique is to turn to an expert. An *expert evaluation* is a subjective assessment of the usability of a product based on the experience and judgment of an expert or experts in usability. Expert evaluations rely on expertise. The more knowledgeable, experienced, perceptive, and skilled the expert, the better. The expert may be qualified by a background in usability engineering, user interface design, graphics design, ergonomics, computer–human interaction, industrial or cognitive psychology, or software engineering and development. Expert evaluations may be conducted on working software or on designs or prototypes in one form or another.

The expert may use any of a variety of informal or formal methods, but the findings ultimately rest on the judgment of the expert rather than on the methods employed. Most experts will conduct some direct experiments or trials with the product being evaluated. Evaluators may engage in open-ended exploration of the user interface or systematic performance of representative tasks or both.

The results of expert evaluation rest on the judgment of the expert rather than on the methods employed.

Experienced evaluators develop their own kit bags of special tricks. Some of these can be useful for developers to learn. In addition to enacting selected use cases or trying out various scenarios, many expert evaluators do things like playing dumb, stress testing the interface, or conducting an exhaustive exploration. Mastering some of these techniques will not make you an expert, but it may help you do a better job of assessing your own and others' work.

Studied ignorance. Many usability experts develop an ability to look at a user interface from the point of view of a completely naïve or inexperienced user, in effect, forgetting or blocking out much of what they know about software, computers, and user interfaces. Playing dumb is a form of dereferencing [Constantine, 1994b], of stepping outside the frame and seeing a system in a fresh and unspoiled light. For practice, take a look at the three window control buttons on the right end of the title bar in any Windows 95 application. Try to see them as a naïve user might and guess at their functions.

First impressions are essential for effective user interface evaluation, and expert evaluators learn to take note of their immediate impressions of each interaction context before examining it in any detail or experimenting with it. Following the principles of layout and workflow discussed in Chapter 7, whatever is first noticed within an interaction context ought to be, if not the first thing of interest to the user, something important. A dialogue box that seems cluttered at first glance can soon feel tolerable after it has been tried a couple of times, yet the first impression can be a clue to lurking usability problems.

Over the edge. Stress testing involves evaluating a system by pushing it to its limits, such as performing actions out of sequence, skipping or repeating steps, overloading buffers, and the like. Such tactics often uncover important usability problems and may be the only way to expose the software's error handling and error messages, which are so vital to usability. In the situation where a design or nonfunctional prototype is being evaluated, the expert may repeatedly ask questions such as, What happens if I do this? Why can't I do it this way?

Every mountain. Scenarios can be useful for examining a system in its intended use, but scenarios also tend to limit assessments. Typically, they keep to the rather narrow or normal paths, with relatively little in the way of detours or backtracking. The experienced evaluator will try to find some way to at least visit and look at every part of the user interface, trying every tool, control, and command button. In addition to a slow and careful look at each interaction context, the evaluator may spread all the screen shots or dialogue designs out on a table or shuffle through them in various orders to look for relationships or hidden problems.

Results. The outcome of an expert evaluation is typically a list of usability problems and a set of recommendations. Most commonly, the ten or so most serious problems are reported, but some evaluators will deliver complete lists of all problems identified.

Expert evaluations can be remarkably fast, reliable, and cost-effective. Highly skilled evaluators can examine as many as 30 or more screens or dialogues in a day and identify 60% to 70% of the usability problems. Even at outside consulting rates, an expert evaluation can be a bargain. In one study, expert reviews identified four times as many usability problems as laboratory usability testing at a third of the cost [Tognazzini, 1992: 60].

> *Even at outside consulting rates, an expert evaluation can be a bargain.*

Because expert evaluation is essentially a custom service, an evaluation can be undertaken with a variety of objectives other than merely finding usability problems. The evaluator might look particularly for performance problems or concentrate on problems for specific user populations, such as new users making the switch from a competing product.

The biggest shortcoming of expert evaluation is that there is little or no technology transfer. Developers may learn what they did wrong but not necessarily why it is a problem or how to avoid it in the future. Unless the evaluation is also tied to redesign work or assistance, developers may find themselves with a list of problems and recommendations that give insufficient guidance on how to make the needed improvements.

PEER REVIEWS

Another approach to evaluating the usability of a piece of software is to ask someone nearby to take a look at it. Many developers turn to colleagues for informal reviews, and some groups even institutionalize various forms of peer review in the design process. We reserve the term *peer review* for informal and unstructured reviews carried out by developers; structured inspections or walk-throughs are another matter and are considered separately.

Peer reviews are widely used. Peer reviews are easy to conduct and easy to incorporate into almost any development process. No special training is needed. All you need do is take the time to have another developer or a group of developers go over your user interface design or prototype.

Peer review may be better than no review at all, but, ironically, although casual peer reviews are easy to carry out and do not employ costly experts, they can be remarkably inefficient and expensive for what they accomplish. There is little reason to believe that one untrained or unaided developer will be much better at evaluating a user interface or design than any other similarly qualified developer will be.

> *Casual peer reviews can be remarkably inefficient and expensive for what they accomplish, wasting a lot of time in needless debate and discussion.*

The strength of numbers does not in itself assure finding more problems or more solutions. Most commonly, groups of developers who try to do unstructured peer reviews end up wasting a lot of time debating and discussing, discussing and debating, with relatively few problems identified unambiguously and fewer still resolved definitively. Put any two developers together in a room, and you will get three opinions, four if the topic is programming languages. Untrained developers conducting unstructured reviews may even go around in circles just trying to agree on whether something is or is not a usability problem.

Although argument in informal peer reviews may often be vigorous, critical and unbiased evaluation may still be in short supply. It can be a challenge for a team to critique its own work effectively or to look at it without unconscious bias. Very often, vested interest and pride in the current design make it hard for the developers to see the problems.

USER REVIEWS

Software developers with a real commitment to usability eventually turn to users to help assess their designs and products. A *user review* involves end users or user surrogates in reviewing a paper prototype or other embodiment of a design. (User review of working software is called *testing*. Or *sales*.) Like expert evaluations and peer reviews, user reviews are conducted to find usability problems, to identify potential improvements, and to assess the overall level of usability of a system. Typically, users will be asked to examine and comment on a design; they may also be asked to walk through particular tasks or scenarios, pretending to interact with the system to carry out the work. Because they involve members of the development team and the user community, we refer to these sessions as *joint design reviews* or *joint interface walk-throughs*.

Some professionals, among them colleagues of ours, consider such user review processes to be forms of usability testing, perhaps qualifying the term by referring to it as "testing a design" or "paper-prototype testing." In our opinion, this play on words violates the conventional meaning of testing and can be misleading. Testing requires something functional to test. One may test an electronic device or even a working prototype in the form of a breadboarded circuit, but one does not test a blueprint or circuit diagram. One tests software by running it with test cases, but, when a group of programmers step through a listing to verify its logic, it is not called *testing*; it is properly and almost universally called a *code review* or *walk-through*. We reserve the term *testing* for actual trial or experimental use of a working system, functional prototype, or simulation, either in the field or in a usability testing lab (more on testing in Chapter 18).

User reviews are typically scheduled to last a half hour to an hour; occasionally, a really good discussion with a knowledgeable and enthusiastic user may extend beyond the scheduled duration. If user reviews are conducted too often, they can become unimportant or even a nuisance to users. Frequent user reviews can also make it appear that the developers are unsure about their work. A couple of reviews at critical points in the development process can be more valuable than a couple every week.

> *The discussion and interaction between a pair of users as they try to work out solutions together is often a valuable source of insight into usability issues.*

User reviews conducted with users in pairs or small groups have a number of advantages. The best results are achieved when each pair is charged with solving problems jointly. The discussion and interaction between them as they talk through ideas and try to work out solutions together is often a valuable source of insight into usability issues. Input from a larger number of users can be obtained this way without taking more time from developers.

It is tempting to gather even more users, but more than two or three at a time is seldom an advantage. Focus groups—focused, facilitated discussion groups widely used for social science and market research—have also been applied to user reviews of interface designs or product usability. For various reasons, focus groups are more effective for other purposes, which will be looked at in Chapter 21.

Following are a few pointers for more effective user reviews.

Plan and organize. Work out a basic process or protocol for the meeting to make efficient use of your time and the user's. Define what you want to learn from the session and decide on a strategy for learning it. Assemble all the materials you will need. Have sketches or simulated screen shots for all the screens and dialogues you expect to need, but be prepared to do a quick sketch of a new dialogue to cover the unanticipated. If you are using essential use cases or other goal-based user tasks, make sure they are printed out in simple, ordinary language and in readable form.

Ask questions. Be ready with questions for the user, but do not try to cover everything with questions or you may overwhelm the user and overly limit the information you can get. As appropriate, use both fixed-response questions ("Which screen did you find hardest to use?") and open-ended ones ("What are some additional features or capabilities you believe would have made this task easier?").

Look and listen. Even more important than questions are observations. Watch what users do and how. Listen to everything and do not feel compelled to respond. Interested but noncommittal is a good posture that encourages user feedback. To make sure you do not miss anything and can review what happened, audiotape or videotape the session.

Goal-based tasks. Have one or more essential use cases for the user to try to enact with the design. Covering multiple use cases is preferred, but this end can be accomplished either by defining a larger problem or task that incorporates several use cases or by asking the user to try each of several use cases independently. Problems should be pretested with colleagues to be sure they are neither too hard nor too easy for the time allotted. Be careful not to choose tasks that are too closely tailored to the current design; you will not learn much that way.

First and last impressions. Have users comment on each interaction context when they first encounter it. At the end of the session, ask them for any overall impressions, afterthoughts, or additional comments.

Simulated system and help. The developer conducting the review with the user should play the part of the system, simulating the behavior of the nonfunctioning interface. The user should be encouraged to act as if the design or paper prototype were a real working system. The developer should be careful to avoid leading the user, giving hints, or providing help unless requested. Help that is given to users on request should be restricted to simple descriptions or clarification, as for the `seekingIdentification` or `seekingClarification` help cases. It is good practice to limit help to what might reasonably become available in the on-line system help or documentation. Any request for help should be taken as indicating a usability problem in the design. Often, a brief discussion of the reason for the request will help the designer learn more about problems in the design. All signs of hesitation, confusion, or mistakes on the part of users should be noted and discussed.

TESTS AND MEASURES

For quantitative measurement of software usability, developers can turn in either of two directions: to *objective testing* or to *usability metrics.* Usability metrics are a promising new approach to usability assessment that allows some aspects of usability to be calculated from design characteristics rather than compiled from test data. Usability metrics will be explored in detail in Chapter 17.

Testing employs users as subjects to attempt tasks in systematic experiments. Testing, as noted earlier, requires something to test; you cannot test a design or document. Usability testing can be quite complex. It can require specialized equipment and facilities along with well-trained testers to devise, conduct, and interpret the tests. Much more will be said of usability testing in Chapter 18.

INSPECTIONS

Structured walk-throughs and inspections have a long and distinguished history in software development [Gilb and Graham, 1993; Yourdon, 1989]. The goal of all inspections, whether on the factory floor or in the barracks, is to find defects, and software inspections have been applied with great success to this end on everything from requirements documents to code. Many development groups have found them to be one of the most cost-effective and time-efficient ways to improve the quality of software.

We refer to any of several forms of more or less formal, systematic processes for locating usability problems as *inspections* or *structured inspections.* Usability inspections employ developers and/or usability specialists, sometimes in conjunction with users, to identify **usability defects**. Usability inspections, the focal point of this chapter, are very versatile. You can inspect almost anything. Usability inspection techniques of various forms have been applied to requirements documents, design models, paper prototypes, and screen shots. You can also inspect a working system, a functional prototype, or a simulation for usability. Inspections can be conducted at virtually any stage or phase of the software development life cycle and can be used repeatedly in a process of iterative or progressive refinement.

Usability inspections are attractive for software developers for a number of reasons. For one thing, usability inspections are a focused and self-contained activity that can be introduced into almost any software development process without excessive commitments of resources. It is not necessary to radically alter standard development practices or life cycle models to start doing usability inspections and to begin to reap many of the benefits in improved usability. The essential methods and procedures of usability inspections themselves are relatively easily learned. User interface design is a rather complex subject to master, even when simplified by usage-centered models, but almost any developer can learn how to spot usability problems in an inspection session through applications of common sense and a handful of heuristics, such as those introduced in Chapter 3.

> *Usability inspections are very versatile. You can inspect almost anything at virtually any stage of software development.*

Compared to most testing schemes, inspections are faster and simpler. Because they are quick and can be applied to virtually all design models and artifacts, inspections can yield useful information much earlier than can testing. In our opinion, the biggest payoffs come from inspecting an early paper prototype, the finished user interface design, the working prototype if any, and the first working or internal release version of the software.

Inspections are more consistently efficient and effective than peer reviews because of three things:

- organization
- systematic process
- focus

Structured inspections are organized activities, with specific roles and responsibilities. They are carried out in orderly, step-by-step processes that assure important activities are completed and that help keep attention from being diverted. The best inspection processes are sharply focused on identifying usability problems and guided by specific rules and principles.

A number of structured inspection techniques for assessing usability have become well established. In the next section, we will introduce some of these methods.

INSPECTION METHODS

HEURISTIC EVALUATION

Arguably the best-known usability inspection technique is *heuristic evaluation* [Nielsen, 1993; Nielsen and Mack, 1994], a method devised by Jakob Nielsen of Bell Labs and later of SunSoft. It is called "heuristic" because it is guided by a set of general rules or heuristics for good user interface design. Nielsen's ten heuristics were introduced in Chapter 3, but other sets of heuristics can be used. Several evaluators, trained in the method, independently inspect a design, looking for usability problems in the areas covered by the heuristics. Their findings are then pooled.

Evaluators may sometimes be assisted by an observer, a member of the development team who can answer questions about the application domain as well as the software and its intended implementation and who may even offer suggestions or hints to speed the evaluation process. The observer is also responsible for recording or note taking during the evaluation session, which also makes more efficient use of the evaluator's time.

> *Heuristic evaluation, guided by a set of general rules or heuristics for good user interface design, is arguably the best-known usability inspection technique.*

The evaluation is a two-pass inspection procedure. In the first pass, the entire user interface or design is reviewed in order to understand its overall structure and the general flow of interaction. In the second pass, the evaluator examines individual interaction contexts and their contents, assessing them against the criteria of the chosen heuristics. The evaluator does not usually undertake enacting specific use cases or tasks, although the procedure has sometimes been altered to include this.

A heuristic evaluation typically takes from 1 to 3 hours and may be followed by a debriefing intended to elicit the evaluator's suggestions for improvement or redesign. Strong features to be retained or left unchanged may also be highlighted during the debriefing.

Any one evaluator will typically identify only about 35% of the usability defects, but pooling the results of more evaluations improves the percentages because different evaluators will spot different problems. Two independent evaluators will, on average, catch half the problems, and five will account for about 75% of them. Returns diminish rapidly: To catch 90% of the defects, you have to use twelve different evaluators working independently, and the peak of the cost-benefit curve is around three to five evaluators [Nielsen, 1994b: 33–35].

COGNITIVE WALK-THROUGHS

The *cognitive walk-through*, a highly structured group process developed by Lewis and Polson [see Wharton, Rieman, Lewis, and Polson, 1994], is another fairly well known, although less widely practiced, inspection technique. Based on a cognitive theory of skill acquisition, it identifies particular kinds of usability problems in a design by stepping through task scenarios for which success criteria have been defined in advance.

In a cognitive walk-through, the group steps slowly through a task scenario, conducting for every action a detailed analysis of the user's intent, knowledge, thought processes, and interpretations. The focus is on one single facet of usability: learnability. The objective is to find various kinds of potential barriers to learning in the form of mismatches between the conceptualizations of designers and users or miscommunications. As a result of this somewhat narrow focus, the process may miss many kinds of problems and has some tendency to identify only the relatively less severe usability defects.

Although not highly productive when conducted by developers, in the hands of trained experts, this inspection technique can yield acceptable results. Some evidence suggests that, as used by experts, heuristic evaluations find more actual usability problems than do cognitive walk-throughs [Desurvire, 1994].

PLURALISTIC USABILITY WALK-THROUGHS

The *pluralistic usability walk-through* [Bias, 1994] originated at IBM and is an attempt to help developers put themselves in the shoes of users. It is a collaborative process involving end users, developers, and usability experts with all participants expected to play in the role of users. Unlike the cognitive walk-through, it is not based in any specific theory nor is it, like the heuristic evaluation, guided by a set of predefined heuristics. In the words of its originator, the goal of a pluralistic usability walk-through is "coordinated empathies" [Bias, 1994].

A pluralistic usability walk-through is driven by a task scenario chosen in advance and for which has been prepared a storyboard, a series of screen shots or drawings representing the various interaction contexts in their sundry conditions. For each step in the task, all participants independently decide on what action or actions they would take next and note these on their own copies of the storyboard. No discussion takes place until all participants have completed a given step. When the discussion of the step begins, end users—the genuine article, that is—speak first.

This inspection technique has some appealing features, but it tends to be relatively slow. Because each participant must have a personal copy of each panel of the storyboard and everyone must be on the same panel at the same time, in practice the process is limited to a single thread of the scenario that must be completely worked out in advance.

COLLABORATIVE USABILITY INSPECTIONS

A **collaborative usability inspection** [Constantine, 1994a] is a systematic examination of a finished product, a design, or a prototype from the standpoint of its ultimate usability by intended end users. The review process is a team effort that includes software developers, end users, applications or domain experts, and usability specialists collaborating to perform a thorough and efficient inspection. This approach has features in common with both heuristic evaluation and pluralistic usability walk-throughs, and it borrows techniques from expert evaluations, but it was designed to be a faster and more efficient process for developers to learn. Experienced inspection teams have been known to identify as many as 100 usability defects per hour.

Collaborative models for usability inspections have particular advantages in bringing together representatives from both the development and user communities. By drawing representatives of the user community directly into inspections, user-centered perspectives are incorporated into the process, and some of the benefits of more expensive and elaborate objective usability testing can be gained through simple inspections. Collaborative inspections can help build deeper awareness on both sides concerning the interactions between design considerations and constraints and those features and forms that matter in shaping ultimate usability of software. By including usability specialists and applying the principles and guidelines of usability repeatedly on a product or on multiple products, software developers build skills and a steadily growing fund of knowledge about how to make software more usable and how to achieve user interface designs that are better to begin with. For embedded systems applications, collaborative inspections offer the added payoff of enhancing communication between software developers and hardware engineers [Constantine, 1993f].

By including users and usability specialists in inspections and repeatedly applying the principles of usability, software developers build skills and a steadily growing fund of knowledge about good user interface design.

A collaborative usability inspection can be conducted at any point in the product development life cycle. Any development artifact can be inspected for usability defects, including requirements documents, models of tasks and intended usage (such as usage scenarios or use case models), paper prototypes, front-end prototypes, nonfunctional mock-ups, simulations, and alpha or beta versions. Even earlier releases or competing products can be inspected to yield input for a new development cycle. If an inspection is completed on design documents or prototypes, many usability problems can be avoided from the outset. Collaborative inspections can also be repeated at various project milestones or used iteratively to refine a product toward high levels of usability.

OBJECTIVES

Collaborative usability inspections, like structured code walk-throughs, are quality assurance tools. The ultimate objective of the inspection is to improve product quality in terms of usability. To this end, its primary purpose is to identify usability defects and interface inconsistencies in the product, prototype, or design. A closely related aim is to assure that good features that contribute to usability are preserved. To a somewhat lesser extent, an inspection may propose corrections or solutions to usability defects, but the central concern of the process is with finding problems, not with solving them. This requires that problematic features and effective features be differentiated, but the first attention is given to defects.

In our view, an efficient inspection process aims to find as many problems as possible within the time allotted. This requires an organized approach that maintains attention on defects. Freewheeling and open-ended discussions of the merits of one approach or another or protracted debates about the relative seriousness of a particular defect can be singularly wasteful of time. A collaborative inspection is not structured to evaluate overall usability of a system or to compare it with other systems or counterparts, nor is it intended to be a collaborative design process. Defects need to be corrected, and problems may call for new designs, but redesign or reprogramming, whether carried out by individuals or groups, is distinct from the inspection process itself.

Developers must keep in mind at all times that the purpose of the inspection is to identify defects. Finding defects is not a sign of failure but of success. Failure in inspection means a failure to find usability defects, allowing them to pass without notice into delivered products. Identifying a defect does not imply an obligation to fix it, however. The decision to correct a defect or allow it to stand is a technical management issue that can depend on many factors, including the seriousness or severity of the defect, the cost of correcting it, and the availability of resources. The philosophy of a usability inspection is always that it is better to know where the problems are even if it is later decided to defer correction or ignore them altogether.

> *The purpose of a usability inspection is to identify defects. Finding defects is not a sign of failure but of success.*

USABILITY DEFECTS

What is a defect?

■ A **usability defect** is a potential problem in the operation, appearance, or organization of a system that makes a final product less easily used by its targeted population of end users.

The focus is on usability, not just the user interface, on the overall architecture or organization of features and functions, not just their surface realization and appearance.

> ■ Operationally, a **usability defect** is any clear or evident violation of an
> accepted or established usability principle or guideline;
> or it is any aspect of a system that is likely to lead to confusion, error,
> delay, or outright failure to complete some task on the part of any user.

Something is considered to be a usability defect if and only if it can be justified on the basis of one of these two criteria: Either it violates an agreed-upon principle, or it is apt to cause problems for some user or users. Problems for users include becoming confused, making a mistake, being slowed down, or being unable to complete a task. A defect is not simply something that somebody in the inspection is vaguely bothered by or does not like. The fact that a participant dislikes a button or is displeased by a menu ordering does not make it a defect; that someone is confused by it does.

> *A usability defect either violates an agreed-upon usability principle or is apt to cause problems for users. It is not simply something that somebody does not like.*

An identified usability defect can be thought of as having four components in two parts: location and identity of defect, problem and rationale. A defect is identified as a specific feature or facility at a specified location within the user interface and described in terms of a specific problem or difficulty justified by some rationale for why it is a problem. For example, an inspection of a desktop productivity tool might find these defects:

Location/Defect	Rationale/Problem
Customization dialogue: No **Cancel** button	Tolerance Principle: forced selection if dialogue mistakenly opened
Toolbar change dialogue: "Insert" and "Append"	Geek-speak: not meaningful to user
Edit button not grayed	Feedback Principle: misleading to user

FOCUS

An effective collaborative usability inspection requires meticulous attention to detail and a persistent user perspective. The proper attitude is critical. Developers need to maintain the mindset of an impatient and intolerant user. The presence of actual users in inspections helps to catalyze taking the user perspective.

Usability inspection is a little like proofreading in that the aim is to spot the mistakes. It is also like editing, in that the ultimate objective is to find ways to improve communication with the "reader" (the user). Good editors learn to read like readers, and developers need to practice thinking more like users. A usability inspection might also be likened to literary criticism, in that more than just superficial appearance or structure is being considered. The overall organization or architecture of the product is also being examined and critiqued.

Once defects have been identified, well-designed features or aspects of the design that contribute to usability can be highlighted. The intent of noting strong points in the system or design is to provide guidance on what aspects should be preserved in making any corrections or changes. Some engineers and designers have difficulty with the relentlessly critical focus of the usability inspection, so shifting periodically to the strong points of a design can be helpful.

It is important that participants direct their critical attention to the product and not the people who designed or developed it. All comments are about practical usability and the technical aspects of the user interface, not about participants as persons, their thinking processes, or their abilities as engineers and designers. The Lead Reviewer, who moderates the inspection (and who we will describe more fully later in this chapter), must keep the discussion at the technical level and not the personal.

It is particularly important that developers and specialists do not argue with users participating in the inspection. Argument or even defensiveness on the part of the technical participants is likely to cut off further input from users. Maintaining a critical focus and enforcing the special restrictions on software developers participating are considered to be the responsibilities of all members of the inspection team, not just the Lead Reviewer.

> *For inspections, the proper attitude is critical, but criticism is directed toward the product and not the people who designed or developed it.*

It can be useful to cultivate a kind of "practiced naïveté," in which members of the inspection team approach the system as if they were naïve users who had never seen it or anything like it before. It helps to be critical, impatient, and intolerant with the system or prototype, acting more like real end users than like software developers or product reviewers.

As participants in the inspection try out operations or work through usage scenarios, no one should offer help or advice on how to carry out any function. The fact that something is unknown to the would-be user or not obvious is a sign of a probable defect and should be noted as such. Similarly, anyone examining the interface should not be offered help, guidance, or advice in how to use or interpret an element of the interface, except when help is requested. All such requests are signs of one or more usability defects and are so noted. Participants should avoid consulting manuals, guides, or help files, except as these are themselves being inspected critically. As much as possible, every exploration of a part of the interface should be treated as if it were an independent inspection without reference to knowledge of other parts of the system.

Developers who worked on the system are particularly encouraged to distance themselves from their work by setting it aside for a period of time preceding an inspection. They should try to approach it from a fresh perspective, as much as possible forgetting what they know about the system and the process by which it was designed.

Often times, approaching a system with a fresh, even somewhat innocent, perspective can reveal significant defects that make it harder to use. A surprising number of serious problems in delivered products are the sort that would be obvious to nearly any first-time user. It does not take trained usability specialists to spot such defects; it only takes an open mind and a critical eye (Constantine, 1994a).

> *It does not take trained specialists to spot many usability defects; it only takes an open mind and a critical eye.*

Software developers and designers who participate in collaborative usability inspections are subject to some special restrictions. In particular, they must be reminded that it is inappropriate during an inspection to explain their work or defend the rationale behind it. This slows down the process of identifying defects and discourages the critical attitude that has been found to be essential to a thorough inspection.

INSPECTION ROLES

The group carrying out a collaborative usability inspection is referred to as an *inspection team* and consists of software developers, end users or end-user representatives, and usability specialists, plus hardware designers or engineers for embedded applications. Because such a team is necessarily cross-functional and may even involve personnel from multiple companies or business units, it is important to promote a spirit of teamwork in pursuit of a common goal: the production of a better, more usable product.

Inspection teams can range from as few as 3 or 4 to as many as 20 or more participants, but our experience suggests that 6 to 12 is probably the most effective. Because the basic mode of operation can be likened to a specialized form of brainstorming, larger groups may actually have some advantages. On the other hand, large inspection teams may require particularly strong leadership to keep them on track and under control.

The inspection team includes some members with special roles. A Lead Reviewer convenes and moderates the process. An Inspection Recorder maintains a complete log of identified defects. The Continuity Reviewer has a special responsibility for identifying inconsistencies in the user interface.

Lead Reviewer. The Lead Reviewer, who convenes and leads the inspection, should be designated beforehand, preferably by the Project Manager or Project Team Leader. In general, however, it is not a good idea for managers or team leaders themselves to lead inspection sessions, although they may participate as reviewers. The Lead Reviewer is also responsible for preparation to assure that the inspection can proceed efficiently and for follow-up activities to assure that appropriate action is taken on the results of the inspection.

During the inspection, the Lead Reviewer is responsible for keeping the process of the inspection moving, for keeping the group engaged and focused on the inspection, and for assuring that everyone has an opportunity to participate and provide input. The Lead Reviewer enforces the rules and agenda for the inspection.

> *It is not a good idea for managers or team leaders to lead inspection sessions themselves.*

Unlike in traditional structured walkthroughs or code inspections, there is no facilitator as such since the objective is not discussion or analysis but the identification of defects. The Lead Reviewer is not a neutral facilitator but a reviewer who is expected to contribute to the inspection without dominating.

Inspection Recorder. The Inspection Recorder is responsible for keeping a complete record of all defects identified, noting their location in the system, summarizing the problem, classifying it into useful functional categories, and assigning an estimate of the severity of the defect. Because the Inspection Recorder needs to understand the technical details of the discussion, he or she must be a professional developer, not a member of the clerical or secretarial staff. In small inspection teams, the Lead Reviewer or Continuity Reviewer may have to double as the Inspection Recorder.

Depending on the type of product, prepared forms for recording defects can greatly simplify and speed up the recording process. An example of such a form is found in Appendix E. A tape recorder can be useful as backup documentation to settle questions or clarify later uncertainties, but audio recording is not suitable as the primary record of an inspection. Some groups have found that videotapes may have an advantage as a backup record.

The Inspection Recorder not only records defects as they are identified but also must make an initial estimate of how severe each defect is. This estimate gives management and designers a starting point for establishing priorities and making decisions about what to fix when, although it is, of course, subject to revision. We have found that group discussions of severity take too much time and are no better as starting points for decision making. Where necessary, the Inspection Recorder can defer judgment and refer a defect for further evaluation.

Continuity Reviewer. Consistency in user interfaces is an elusive goal. The Continuity Reviewer is an optional role that serves much the same function as the person responsible for continuity in modern feature film production. It is the responsibility of the Continuity Reviewer to watch for inconsistencies among different parts of the user interface and to monitor departures from established standards, guidelines, or requirements. Inconsistencies are not necessarily defects, although they often are. An inconsistency from accepted practices that makes a dialogue simpler and more natural may be justified, for example. Because it is so difficult to monitor and maintain consistency across all interface elements in complex systems, the Continuity Reviewer should give full attention to spotting inconsistencies.

In small inspection teams, the Continuity Reviewer may double as Inspection Recorder, or the role may be omitted and the responsibility for monitoring consistency distributed to the entire team. Where consistency is a major problem or major objective, a separate Consistency Inspection (see later section in this chapter) may be a more efficient means to achieve user interface consistency. If the size of the project justifies, a permanent Continuity Reviewer may also be designated.

SEVERE DEFECTS

Defects are rated in terms of estimated severity based on their likely impact on usability. We have found a four-point scale of severity based on the following descriptions to be workable:

- *4, Critical*—blatantly obvious defect; significantly reduces overall usability or makes the product substantially unusable for some purpose or purposes
- *3, Major*—some task or tasks substantially more difficult to perform or master; significant increase in likelihood of error
- *2, Minor*—some chance problem; impairs performance, impedes learning, or increases error somewhat
- *1, Nominal*—nuisance or annoyance; small probability of error or insignificant delay

The working assumption is that critical defects are the showstoppers that absolutely must be fixed if at all possible; major defects should be fixed; minor defects are ones that it would be nice to fix; and nominal defects are the relatively trivial or cosmetic leftovers that are fixed only if it is quite easy and convenient. Unfortunately and all too often, it is the level-1 and level-2 defects that get taken care of and the level-4 ones that are left alone.

The levels of defect severity are subjective judgments. The numbers assigned to the estimates just make it easier to combine ratings by several judges or evaluators.

Developers. The inspection team should include at least some software designers and developers of the system under inspection. It is also desirable to include some developers who are not involved in the product design and development of the system under inspection. Junior staff members or recent recruits may be especially useful in usability inspections since they are typically eager and enthusiastic and bring a fresh perspective that is not

The Continuity Reviewer serves much the same function as the person responsible for continuity in modern feature film production.

likely to be as saturated with the accepted practices of the development group or their habitual thinking patterns.

All contributors to the product, design, or prototype under inspection are subject to special constraints on their participation in the inspection. They are not permitted to explain, defend, excuse, or rationalize any aspect of their design or the decisions leading to it. Experience has shown that anything even remotely resembling defensiveness discourages participants, especially users, from vigorous pursuit of defects. For the same reasons, arguing with, challenging, or criticizing users is forbidden. It is the responsibility of the entire team, but particularly the Lead Reviewer, to enforce these rules.

> *Developers are not permitted to explain, defend, excuse, or rationalize any aspect of their design or the decisions leading to it.*

Developers should also avoid making implied promises to users. Even a casual comment about something being easy to fix can seem to a user like a contractual commitment.

Some developers bridle at these restrictions, wondering what function they serve if they are not allowed to argue, challenge, criticize, defend, design, or promise anything. Developers and designers of whatever stripe are expected to participate fully—as critical reviewers seeking to spot defects. Anything that diverts their attention from this assignment lessens their effectiveness. Over the long haul, practice with maintaining this critical focus will help developers to see the problems in their designs even before these reach inspections.

Users and domain experts. It is important to remember that developers are not typical users and almost without exception do not and cannot represent the real interests or perspectives of end users. The same is true of clients and customers who are not themselves end users of the actual product. For best results, the inspection team should include at least one genuine end user; more than one is even better. If there is more than one distinct and identifiable end-user community or constituency, representatives of each type of user should be involved. For example, an ATM system may be used in different modes, even through different interfaces, by bank customers, supervisors, and service personnel; all three should be represented.

Domain experts have special expertise in the general area of the application but are not typically end users or representative of end users. For example, in a banking application, accountants or senior bank staff could be domain experts for systems they themselves might never use. Domain experts can be useful members of an inspection team, but they are not substitutes for genuine end users.

It is sometimes necessary to employ user surrogates for an inspection. For the inspection of new software for currency trading, for example, no currency traders were available; they were all too busy in the currency markets. A trainer with some experience with a previous version of the currency software was invited as a user surrogate. If no genuine end user is available, it is especially important that a domain expert participate; otherwise, there may be important questions about actual uses that cannot be answered by anyone in the inspection.

The comments and inputs of users should be given special weight in the inspection process without allowing these to dictate user interface design decisions. It is important to remember that the real usability of a product is **defined** by users, not by developers or "experts." The Lead Reviewer should encourage user participation and protect users from criticism or antagonistic questioning. Users and domain experts should be looked to as authorities but not as arbiters. Following the inspection, developers and designers have the final responsibility for user interface design. During the inspection, they should listen openly to all comments and inputs from users, recognizing that users are not expected to be designers or to make design decisions themselves. Users may sometimes make inappropriate suggestions, unfortunate requests, or see problems where there are none. However bizarre or wrong the ideas and comments may be, all input from users should be noted without discussion ("Thank you very much. We have noted that purple makes you nauseous. Now, any other problems?").

> *If no genuine end user is available, it is especially important that a domain expert participate in the inspection.*

Usability specialists. Usability specialists of all stripes and specialties can be useful contributors to a collaborative inspection. Such specialists might include graphics designers, user interface designers, interaction designers, ergonomicists, human–computer interaction specialists, psychologists, industrial designers, and others. Whether from within or from outside the development organization, usability specialists function in a consulting role, as a source of expertise but not as the final arbiters of interface design decisions. They should be encouraged to contribute but be restrained from dominating. It can be considered a bad sign, however, if they are ignored or overridden too often in an inspection process. It means that the development team is not making effective use of the expertise that is available to it.

INSPECTION PROCESS

Preparation. It is the responsibility of the Lead Reviewer to see that all advanced preparation is completed before convening the inspection. All team members should be briefed on their participation in the inspection. If a finished product or prototype is being reviewed, equipment to run the software should be available in the room in which the inspection will be carried out. This should include a data projector of some kind, a large screen monitor, or several interconnected monitors to make it easy for all members of the inspection team to see the system in operation. Paper copies of actual screen shots for all major screens, menus, and dialogues should also be available because these vastly simplify record keeping and discussion. If a design document or paper prototype is being inspected, a projectable copy of the document or prototype should be prepared, along with paper copies for all participants.

> *Participants are not expected to review materials in advance; it is better to approach inspections from a fresh perspective.*

Unlike code inspections or structured design walk-throughs, participants are not expected to review materials in advance of the inspection itself. In fact, it can be advantageous to have all team members approach the product being inspected from a fresh perspective.

The site of the inspection should be large enough for all participants to work comfortably. It should be equipped with the usual meeting paraphernalia, such as whiteboards, flip-charts, overhead projector and screen, and a supply of markers, masking tape, and Post-it notes (larger sizes are better). Easy access to a copier is also recommended.

Because a successful inspection demands concentration and undivided attention, members of the inspection team should clear their calendars for the duration of the inspection meeting. There should be no interruptions for phone calls or for reasons other than emergencies. The inspection can be launched by briefly reiterating the intent and nature of the inspection process. Inspection efficiency can be facilitated by brief, focused team building. (See sidebar, Inspection Teamwork.)

Interactive inspection. In our experience, usability inspections are best conducted in two distinct passes or phases: an interactive inspection and a static inspection. In the first pass, the *interactive inspection*, the system is actually used (or usage is simulated) to carry out representative tasks. These tasks are prepared in advance as usage scenarios that include typical, characteristic, and critical interactions in normal system usage. The inspection team walks through these scenarios to develop a feel for how the system would work in normal use.

> *The inspection should begin with the initial state of the system—that is, with the application launch, system bootup, or power on.*

The interactive inspection pass should begin with the initial state of the system on first encounter by an end user—that is, with the application launch, system bootup, or power-on conditions as appropriate. As much as possible, the inspection should proceed systematically through usage scenarios as actual users would carry them out, with the team noting defects and inconsistencies as the interaction or simulated interaction proceeds. Errors and exceptions should be dealt with as these arise in the normal course of simulated usage.

The inspection should cover typical or representative tasks as well as a few atypical or exceptional interactions that might be important for one reason or another. Tasks are best expressed in their essential or goal-oriented form from the user's perspective, leaving the detailed actions to be filled in by the users and other members of the inspection team.

For example, an inspection scenario for a telephone directory application might read as follows:

> Find the entry for Mario Rossi, who is one of those working in accounting or finance, and add him and his telephone details to your personal directory file, flagging his entry to show he is the first member of the new "UI Interest Group" that you are just now compiling.

Scenarios for usability inspections should be printed or written out so that they are easy for the entire group to follow.

In enacting inspection scenarios, the user or users should take the lead in suggesting actions or in operating the system or prototype. The first opportunity to comment on a part of the user interface or to note defects should also be given to users, but developers should not expect users to carry the bulk of the responsibility for identifying defects. A collaborative inspection should not be allowed to become a user review with a lot of developers sitting around watching. Putting too much on the users and too little on the developers makes users self-conscious and wastes developers' time. Everyone in the inspection should be looking for problems. In the long run, much is to be gained by developers learning how to spot usability defects in their own work.

As each interaction context is encountered for the first time, the Lead Reviewer should ask for first impressions (problems noticed immediately) before

INSPECTION TEAMWORK

Because inspection participants are expected to function as a team, we usually start with some brief team-building process designed to put people in the proper frame of mind for the inspection. The goal is to generate a collective spirit of enthusiastic criticism and skepticism.

All the participants should be introduced, beginning with the users. The next step is getting everyone on the same page with regard to the inspection process. Even if most of the participants have been in inspections before, it can be helpful to review the agenda and the rules for collaborative usability inspections. A brief overview of the product being inspected should outline the major requirements with respect to usability and user interface design.

To begin with some fun and to encourage a sense of joint responsibility for the process, we explain that any attempt to rationalize or justify any part of the software design is to be greeted by a loud and collective imitation of a truck's air horn. We get the whole group to practice pretending to be impatient truckers, pulling on imaginary cords and making a loud and ugly blast on the air horn.

We also explain that we want people to become critical users, quick to spot problems and eager to let us know. One technique we often use is cheerleading the group in shouts of such things as "Hopeless!" "Cluttered!" "Awkward!" "Confusing!" and "Unusable!" The inevitable laughter sets a good tone for the session.

It can also be useful if the leader helps developers and other participants place themselves in the role of users and take on a user-oriented perspective. The Lead Reviewer might ask users to say a few words about their jobs or to talk briefly about their problems using other software or previous versions, for example.

pursuing the next step in the scenario. After each use case or scenario has been completed in the interaction inspection phase or following each screen or major interaction context, the Lead Reviewer should ask for comments about what features or characteristics of the current design seem to work effectively and should be preserved. These can be noted by the inspection recorder in a separate document or file to be delivered to the developers after the inspection is complete.

Tracking effective and desirable features and characteristics is important to avoid throwing out the usability baby with the defect bathwater.

It is not possible by enacting realistic usage scenarios to inspect all paths through a user interface.

Static inspection. In the second pass, the *static inspection*, the inspection team "visits" or reviews all interaction contexts, independent of the order in which these might be encountered in ordinary use. Generally, it is not possible to inspect all transition paths through a user interface architecture, especially by enacting realistic usage scenarios. For this reason, the inspection team should attempt to inspect every interface composite—the screens, menus, or dialogue boxes of the application—at least once. Static inspection should consider icons, buttons, labeling, layout, messages, controls, interactions, and so forth, in detail. In short, as many of the fine details of the user interface as time permits should be inspected.

Finalization and follow-up. It is important to allocate sufficient time for a thorough inspection of the system or prototype but not to let inspections drag on too long. After a few hours, fatigue can markedly reduce the effectiveness of the inspection team. Small systems may be inspected in as short as an hour or two; large ones may require multiple sessions spread over several days. Very large or particularly complex systems may have to be inspected in sections. Fine details in the user interface can be examined in separate inspections covering subsystems or modules.

Fatigue can markedly reduce the effectiveness of the inspection team.

Before ending an inspection, the Lead Reviewer should ensure that the inspection is complete. If there is time, the inspection team should quickly review the defect list maintained by the Inspection Recorder.

The Lead Reviewer is responsible for following up on the inspection, working with the appropriate Project Manager or Team Leader to ensure that decisions about corrections are made and implemented. Follow-up activities include

1. Estimating the difficulty and cost of corrections for defects
2. Sorting defects by severity, functional category, and estimated cost
3. Reviewing user interface architecture for possible refinement or reorganization

4. Grouping defects for assignment to particular personnel or scheduling for particular releases or versions

5. Completing redesign of affected portions of the interface

6. Implementing changes

Except for unusually complex usability problems with widespread impact on the software, cost estimation for individual defects is usually just an eyeball guess, not a systematically derived costing. It is ultimately a management decision whether and when to address identified usability problems based on the anticipated impact, cost of correction, and available resources. More often than not, some

> *Just because a defect is identified does not mean it will be corrected, but it is better to know of the usability defects than to remain ignorant.*

problems will be deferred until later releases or versions, and some may be ignored completely. The important issue is that such decisions be made rationally rather than merely being left to chance. Just because a defect is identified does not mean it will be corrected, but it is better to know of the usability defects than to remain ignorant. After implementation of any corrections to defects, the Lead Reviewer or someone else charged with quality assurance will need to verify the revised product or design against the original defect list.

FOCUSED INSPECTIONS

CONSISTENCY INSPECTIONS

Consistency may be the hobgoblin of little minds, but it is also a frustratingly elusive goblin. Consistency inspections are one approach that can help deliver on consistency in user interface design.

A *consistency inspection* is a variation of a collaborative usability inspection. In a collaborative consistency inspection, a group of developers reviews all of the elements of a complete user interface to identify inconsistencies across interaction contexts and their contents. Typically, a smaller team—seldom more than three or four developers and usually no users

---

RULES OF THE GAME

The basic rules for collaborative usability inspections have been worked out slowly over years of inspections in order to make the process more effective and efficient in finding usability defects and user interface inconsistencies. Close adherence to these rules will pay off in inspections that are more productive and software that is more usable:

- Everyone participates.
- User input comes first.
- Users enact the scenarios.
- Developers enact the software.
- Everyone finds defects and consistencies.
- Always explain or justify defects.
- Never explain or justify designs.
- Never argue with users.
- Make no decisions or promises.
- Do not design solutions on the fly.
- Note all suggestions and comments and move on.

Although some developers may protest that, if they cannot argue, debate, justify their work, or do redesign, there is little point in coming to an inspection. Of course, the point is to find usability defects, and the rules help developers to stay focused on the point.

or usability specialists—will better serve for consistency inspection. In effect, all participants function as Continuity Reviewers, although one may be designated Lead Reviewer and another will necessarily serve as Inspection Recorder. A jaundiced eye keenly attuned to inconsistencies is more important than any particular expertise.

> *For a collaborative consistency inspection, a jaundiced eye keenly attuned to inconsistencies is more important than any particular expertise.*

Unlike the typical collaborative usability inspection, a consistency inspection is not driven by use cases or scenarios. Instead, interactions contexts are reviewed in groups or collections to facilitate side-by-side comparison. Interaction contexts may be grouped by function or form, such as all error message boxes, or collected to review components or features of a certain type, such as all menu bars. For example, all dialogue boxes might be examined together to compare how layout, appearance, and behavior might differ. Collecting interaction contexts by categories or by contents makes it easier to spot inconsistencies.

Any inconsistencies within a given category are noted by an assigned Inspection Recorder. If an immediate choice of approach or resolution of the inconsistency is possible, the proposed solution will be noted. Otherwise, the noted inconsistency is examined more closely at a later time in order to figure out what one approach will work best in all cases.

Certain categories of user interface elements and features lend themselves to inspection as a group or set. Common groupings include

- Menu bars and menus
- Toolbars and tool palettes
- Dialogue boxes for overall layout
- Data fields and labels
- Command buttons
- Informative message boxes
- Error message boxes
- Status bar and status messages

These categories or sets are inspected for consistency in appearance and layout or ordering of component parts, such as in menus, as well as for consistency in nomenclature or terminology. Where the behavior of components is known to the inspection team or easily inferred, behavioral consistency should also be considered.

For most purposes, static screen shots of windows, dialogues, and messages work best. For example, all error messages can easily be examined as static shots by taping them to a wall or simply sorting through them in order to compare them and look for inconsistencies. Note, however, that some categories will require multiple screen shots of the same part of the interface, as, for example, when comparing menus that will need to be examined in their open condition and in the varied conditions under which some items may be disabled. It is hard to know in general which will be more efficient—screen shots, which must be prepared in advance, or repeatedly moving back and forth between different windows or views to make comparisons. A tool like Lotus ScreenCam may also sometimes be of use in a consistency inspection.

A consistency inspection is strictly focused on locating inconsistencies, not identifying other kinds of usability problems. If attention is diverted to other issues, the inspection process can easily become too slow and inefficient.

CONFORMANCE INSPECTIONS

Another specially focused form of inspection is the *conformance inspection.* A conformance inspection resembles a consistency inspection, but the purpose is to identify departures from the governing user interface standards or style guidelines. For this reason, all participants must be familiar with the applicable standards and style guidelines, and users are not normally included. User interface designers and other usability specialists can be particularly helpful because they are likely to have more intimate and in-depth knowledge of standards and style guidelines.

> *Participants in a conformance inspection must be familiar with the applicable user interface standards and style guidelines.*

Conformance to user interface standards is more commonly verified by conformance audits conducted by an individual auditor working independently. Collaborative conformance inspections confer several advantages, however. Each participant can take primary responsibility for a different portion of the standards or guidelines. This division of labor increases the odds of catching any departures and requires familiarity with a smaller, more manageable body of material.

As with consistency inspections, conformance inspections are focused entirely on one goal: identifying departures from standards and conventions. An inspection team of three to four will probably suffice to achieve this goal in most circumstances.

17

BY THE NUMBERS:
Measuring Usability in Practice

COMPARISON SHOPPING

Your usability inspection identified a number of serious defects in one particular data entry screen. Recognizing the need for a complete rework, the development team has devised two proposed designs. The design team is evenly divided over which of the two proposals will be easier to use, and, after more than an hour of debate over the relative merits, the discussion is at an impasse. Neither analyses of essential use cases nor arguments on the basis of usability principles have broken the deadlock. Sometimes, it does come down to a matter of taste or personal opinion, but is this one of those cases? How do you separate taste from technical issues, opinion from operational advantage? When the choices are tough, how do you choose among alternatives in user interface design?

The most widely accepted approach to resolving usability questions has long been to resort to testing, either in a usability test facility or out in the workplace. Objective or empirical testing is a useful tactic in the usability playbook (more about this in Chapter 18), but testing also has its limitations. Most importantly, you must have something to test. Usability testing requires a working system, a good simulation, or at least a functional prototype. What can you do when all you have is a sketch or a nonworking visual prototype? How do you get beyond subjective impression and qualitative arguments to something more objective?

It would be great if we could compare user interface designs like engine designs. You perform some calculations and conclude that this screen is rated at 231 peak brake horsepower at 3,200 rpm with an efficiency of 17%, while that one will only crank out 179. What we need are ways to attach numbers to designs that give some indications of their relative quality and effectiveness. What we need are usability metrics.

MEASURED QUALITY

Usability metrics are software quality metrics—quantitative indices that measure or estimate some factors or dimensions of software quality. Metrics have a long history of successful application in software engineering [Card and Glass, 1990; Gilb, 1977; Henderson-Sellers, 1996]. Usability metrics are a relatively recent development, an adjunct to essential modeling that can help developers answer some of their unanswered questions. Metrics are not some ultimate solution to software usability problems, but, along with better design models and more flexible and efficient methods, they offer practicing developers an additional tool to help guide them toward more usable solutions [Constantine, 1996e].

> *Usability metrics are a relatively recent development, an adjunct to essential modeling that can help developers answer some of their unanswered questions.*

USES AND ABUSES OF METRICS

Usability metrics have a number of uses, but, from the practitioner's perspective, the most important is that they help answer questions that frequently arise in the course of real-world development projects. We first became interested in usability metrics because of recurring questions like these from developers:

- How good is this design, really?
- Is this approach good enough, or should I keep working at it?
- When we make this change, is the resulting design better, worse, or just different?
- Which of these approaches is likely to be more usable?
- Is the difference between these alternatives substantial or only minor?
- What is wrong with this design and how do we improve it?
- If we do it this way, is it likely to be more efficient or less?
- Is this design probably easier to understand than that one?

Much of the time, once the rules and principles of usability are applied or after the designs are checked against essential models, the answers are fairly clear. However, there is a nagging residue of difficult cases where the answers remain unclear even after protracted consideration. This is especially true when it comes to one question:

- How can I be sure this design is better than the other (or previous) one?

Besides answering questions about the design problem at hand, software quality metrics can serve other purposes, both short- and long-term. They can be used as part of broad, continuing efforts to improve software development processes and product quality. By evaluating the quality of current and competing products through usability metrics, a benchmark is established, a quantitative reference point against which to gauge the success of new techniques or tools. By keeping track of usability metrics and other software quality metrics, managers and developers can get continuous feedback on how well their teams and tactics are working. Metrics can also help development teams deal with management and clients by documenting team performance and product quality. Managers, especially, like to see numbers, and, when the numbers look good, so do the software developers.

Metrics also carry risks; they can be misapplied and misunderstood. No simple number can completely represent anything so subtle and complex as the usability of a software system, but numbers can sometimes create the illusion of understanding. Because they are based on dispassionate computation, they may be given undue weight when balanced against judgment, however sound, and opinion, however well informed. A quick look at the numbers is not a substitute for a careful study of a user interface. Usability metrics should augment and support other forms of design review and evaluation, not supplant them.

> *No simple number can completely represent anything so subtle and complex as the usability of a software system, but numbers can sometimes create the illusion of understanding.*

Groups that make use of metrics should be prepared to ask telling questions about the metrics. What do the numbers actually represent? What do they really measure—as opposed to, What are they called? For example, one user interface design metric in the literature is referred to as "Layout Complexity" [Comber and Maltby, 1995], but, once you plow through the computations, you discover that it really measures how well aligned the various widgets are on the screen or dialogue, which is probably not what most people mean by complexity.

Different kinds of usability metrics have different uses and different potential for misuse. Metrics for usability can be thought of as falling into three broad categories:

- **Preference metrics,** which quantify the subjective evaluations and preferences of users
- **Performance metrics,** which measure the actual use of working software
- **Predictive metrics,** or design metrics, which assess the quality of designs or prototypes

PREFERENCE METRICS

One of the most popular and straightforward ways to assess usability is to use **preference metrics**. You grab a few unsuspecting subjects—users or potential users—and ask them what they think of the system. Subjective user evaluations have both advantages and disadvantages. They can be relatively inexpensive and easy to obtain, but they also do not necessarily give designers the information they really need. Not only are user evaluations subjective, per se, but user preferences also are generally only relatively weakly correlated with actual ease of use or other measures of usability in practice. In some cases, users will say that they prefer particular designs even though those designs are actually harder to use or less efficient. This may be especially true when users are asked to evaluate Web sites [Spool et al., 1997]. Nonetheless, subjective impressions from real users cannot be ignored altogether. User satisfaction is a component of usability and also an important factor in success in the marketplace. Indeed, user preferences may be better predictors of marketability than usability.

> *User preferences are generally only relatively weakly correlated with actual ease of use in practice. In some cases, users will prefer designs that are actually harder to use or less efficient.*

Many developers try to work out their own schemes for assessing user preferences. They may show users two sketches for a screen layout and then ask the users which they prefer. If the developers are more systematic, they might first draw up a list of questions to be rated on a scale of 1 to 5. Custom-designed questionnaires or rating scales can be useful where there are highly particular issues to be settled or where the interface or its domain of application is unusual. For example, a design team might want to get a handle on whether help-line users prefer to give responses verbally or by pressing keys on a telephone keypad. Or potential users of a wearable heads-up display device might be shown simulated displays printed on clear film and asked about their color preferences.

Like user interface design, questionnaire design is both an art and a science with many twists and turns. Subjective assessments made by users can be complex, incorporating any number of factors that may need to be carefully separated and evaluated. Standard forms or questionnaires that have been systematically designed and tested can have real advantages. They can be more reliable than ad hoc surveys, and their validity may already have been established through research or widespread use. Some may offer the bonus of allowing comparisons against standardized scores for other software systems.

One good example of a standardized set of preference metrics is the Software Usability Measurement Inventory (SUMI) developed as part of the ESPRIT project [Porteous, Kirakowski, and Corbett, 1993]. SUMI is a 50-item questionnaire that includes five subscales measuring different subjective aspects of usability similar to the five facets of usability introduced in Chapter 1:

- **Affect**—how much the user likes the design
- **Efficiency**—how well the software enables productive use
- **Helpfulness**—how supportive the software and documentation are
- **Control**—how consistent and normal the software response is
- **Learnability**—how easy the software is to explore and master

The SUMI approach requires a working system or prototype. Subjects try out the system or prototype and then fill out the questionnaire on the basis of their experience with it. Although the approach may seem somewhat complex, using SUMI offers the advantage of software support. In addition to computing scores on the five subscales, the software can compare results to norms and even flag specific questions for which the subjects' answers were highly skewed compared to typical results. SUMI, thus, makes an excellent adjunct to usability testing.

There are, of course, other approaches to evaluating user preferences. For developers interested in a quick-but-not-too-dirty evaluation of designs or paper prototypes, there is the Subjective Usability Scales for Software (SUSS) questionnaire. We originally devised SUSS for our own research on usability metrics. SUSS is a very short questionnaire that typically can be completed in four to ten minutes. Using only ten carefully constructed items, it measures six key elements of user interface designs affecting usability:

- **Valence**—liking or personal preference
- **Aesthetics**—attractiveness
- **Organization**—graphical design and layout
- **Interpretation**—understandability
- **Acquisition**—ease of learning
- **Facility**—overall ease of use

A copy of SUSS is found in Appendix F. The SUSS questionnaire makes use of a novel evaluation technique to obtain more reliable estimates of usability from user evaluations. (See sidebar, Subjective Scenarios.)

The SUSS instrument or other comparable short questionnaires can be used to get a quick reading on a design or alternative designs at low cost. Because it is so short, SUSS can be used to evaluate a number of different parts of a user interface design or be employed repeatedly over the course of a project. It can highlight potential problem areas to be reviewed more carefully, such as where one screen scores substantially worse than others in the same application or when users like one design and rate it as more attractive but consider a different one easier to learn and to use.

SUBJECTIVE SCENARIOS

The SUSS questionnaire uses multiple-scenario, affective-cognitive rating, a form of rating scheme intended to overcome some of the problems and limitations of less sophisticated paper-and-pencil techniques. Simple global ratings of ease of use are notoriously unreliable and often only weakly related to actual ease of use. Ratings of visual prototypes are doubly handicapped because subjects do not have the opportunity to actually try using the interface to be rated. Subjective evaluations of ease of use can also be contaminated by other aspects of the respondent's subjective impression, such as aesthetic appeal.

In the SUSS technique, users are shown a sketch, drawing, or screen shot of a visual prototype and are asked to study it before rating it—first in terms of personal impression and then in estimated ease of use for specific tasks. This scheme separates affective from cognitive evaluation, feelings from rationally informed judgments. The most subjective and personal preferences are expressed first before ease of use is independently rated. The personal impressions are expressed in terms of how much subjects like a user interface, how attractive they think it is, the perceived quality of the graphical design and layout, how easy it is to understand, and how easy they think it would be to learn to use.

Scenario-based assessment in the second part of the SUSS questionnaire presents a series of four representative concrete scenarios devised by the developers or investigators. Ideally, these scenarios are based on typical, realistic tasks representing a range of difficulty. Subjects rate each scenario in terms of how difficult it would be to carry out with the given design. Only after these specific scenarios are evaluated do users evaluate overall ease of use. The validity of this technique is supported by research [Constantine, 1996e; 1997e].

All the SUSS questions use balanced, Likert-style ratings on a scale of 0 to 5—a proven format. With no neutral or middle choice, subjects are forced off the fence in terms of evaluating each item. Besides producing separate ratings on each of the six factors, results can be summed to yield an overall score ranging from 0 to 50, with assessed ease of use accounting for half the total. This score is not an absolute index of quality, but a relative one that can be used to compare alternative solutions for the same problem.

Even task-based subjective usability ratings do not, of course, measure actual ease of use. What they do measure is what users think about how easy it would be to use a particular design once it is implemented, which could be quite different from what actually happens in usage. However, preliminary evidence suggests that a sampling of three to four representative tasks correlates well with differences in actual ease of use between significantly different designs [Constantine, 1996e; 1997e].

PERFORMANCE METRICS

Some questions can be settled only through actual use of a working system, and it is the function of usability testing to simulate the conditions of use sufficiently well to yield dependable answers. **Performance metrics** are indices of various aspects of how users perform during actual or simulated work, which may take place either in a usability testing laboratory or under field conditions at typical work sites. A variety of aspects of performance can be measured, such as time to complete a task or suite of tasks, error rates, or the frequency of requests for help. We will have more to say about performance metrics in Chapter 18.

> *Some usability questions can be settled only through actual use of a working system.*

PREDICTIVE METRICS

Design metrics are objective measures of quality that can be calculated from design artifacts, such as visual designs for screen layouts. They are referred to as **predictive metrics** because they are estimators or predictors of some one or more aspects of the actual performance that can be expected once a system has been implemented and put into use. Valid design metrics will be strongly correlated with actual ease of use, efficiency, freedom from errors, and other indicators of usability in practice. For software and application developers, design metrics offer an alternative to subjective user evaluations or after-the-fact usability testing of functional

> *Design metrics make it possible to evaluate and compare designs quickly and economically without first constructing a functioning system, simulation, or working prototype.*

prototypes or systems. The great advantage of design metrics is that they make it possible to evaluate and compare designs quickly and economically without first requiring construction of a functioning system, simulation, or working prototype.

USER INTERFACE DESIGN METRICS

WHAT TO MEASURE

Design metrics for user interfaces come in several flavors:

- **Structural metrics,** which are based on surface properties
- **Semantic metrics,** which are content sensitive
- **Procedural metrics,** which are task sensitive

The simplest to compute are measures called **structural metrics**, which are based on those surface properties of the configuration and layout of user interface architectures that can simply be counted or toted. Various structural metrics have been devised and tried, including

- Number of visual components or widgets on a screen or dialogue
- Amount and distribution of white space between widgets
- Alignment of widgets relative to one another
- Number of adjacent screens or dialogues directly reachable from a given screen or dialogue
- Longest chain of transitions possible between screens or dialogues

Many of the most straightforward structural metrics, such as those just listed, are oversimplified attempts to measure complexity. It seems reasonable, for example, to assume that a screen with more widgets on it is more complex—therefore harder to use—than one with fewer widgets—other things being equal, that is.

Unfortunately, many simple structural metrics lack a strong theoretical rationale relating them to usability and, in practice, are only weakly correlated with end-product usability. More importantly for practicing developers, structural metrics do not typically address questions of great significance in everyday design problems. User interface designers are confronted with more vexing and substantive problems than how many widgets are on a dialogue box or the amount of white space surrounding them.

Many simple structural metrics lack a strong theoretical rationale relating them to usability and are only weakly correlated with end-product usability.

Unlike simple structural metrics, **semantic metrics** are content-sensitive measures that take into account the nature of user interface components or features in terms of their function, meaning, or operation. Semantic metrics can measure aspects of user interface designs that depend on the concepts and actions that visual components represent and how users make sense of the components and their interrelationships.

Procedural metrics are task-sensitive measures based on aspects of the actual tasks or scenarios that may be carried out with a user interface. Procedural metrics deal with the fit between the various tasks and a given design in terms of its content and organization. In general, we can expect designers to get more practical direction from content-sensitive and task-sensitive measures than from simple structural metrics. In principle, a given metric could be both content sensitive and task sensitive, but, in practice, separate metrics are typically needed.

MEASUREMENT CRITERIA

To be of greatest value to practicing software developers trying to decide everyday user interface design issues, metrics should be sound, simple, and easy to use. Practical metrics should:

- Be easy to calculate and interpret
- Apply to paper prototypes and design models
- Have a strong rationale and simple conceptual basis
- Have sufficient sensitivity and ability to discriminate between designs
- Offer direct guidance for design
- Effectively predict actual usability in practice
- Directly indicate relative quality of designs

A strong, simple conceptual basis means that designers can readily understand the rationale for a metric and see what makes one design better than another in terms of it. One can more easily be confident of results when these are rooted in

OTHER YARDSTICKS

User interface design metrics are not an entirely new idea. Some previous work has been done, although not a great deal has been published. A few measures developed previously may be of some practical use.

Layout Complexity. Comber and Maltby [1994, 1995] derived a measure they call **Layout Complexity**, from earlier work on typographical layout [Bonsiepe, 1968] and screen design [Tullis, 1988]. Layout Complexity is based on the distribution of sizes and positions of visual objects. According to this measure, a layout is considered more complex if there is more variation in the heights and widths of visual objects and in their distances from the edges of the visual interaction context.

Although the original concept was argued to have a basis in information theory, the measure itself has some significant conceptual and practical problems. Virtually the same end results can be achieved without resorting to complicated information-theory formulas merely by totaling the number of visual components plus the number of different top-edge alignments and the number of different left-edge alignments of components [Galitz, 1994].

Layout Complexity is strictly a structural metric, which means that it does not take into account what visual components are placed where, but only how they vary in size and distance from the edges. For this reason, the degree of practical guidance offered for planning and refining real designs is relatively limited. Moreover, although Tullis originally argued that "simpler" designs were more usable, more recent research by Comber and Maltby reached the conflicting conclusion that designs of intermediate Layout Complexity may be better. We consider Layout Uniformity, one of the metrics in the suite described in this chapter, to be an improvement on Layout Complexity.

Layout Appropriateness. Sears [1993] defined a measure called **Layout Appropriateness** that is a procedural metric, task sensitive but not content sensitive. Layout Appropriateness estimates the relative efficiency of a particular screen or dialogue based on the expected cost to complete a collection of tasks. This metric favors arrangements where visual components that are most frequently used in succession are closer together, reducing the expected time (cost) of completing a mix of tasks. Experimental applications have demonstrated improvements in usability when Layout Appropriateness is increased.

The overall Layout Appropriateness for a given screen or dialogue compares the task-weighted total cost for a particular design to the theoretical minimum cost for an optimal layout, which must be computed. Layout Appropriateness *(LA)*, as defined by Sears, is a simple ratio:

$$LA = 100 \cdot \frac{C_{optimal}}{C_{designed}}$$

where

$$C = \sum_{\forall i \neq j} p_{i,j} \cdot d_{i,j}$$

$p_{i,j}$ = probability (frequency) of transition between visual components *i* and *j*

$d_{i,j}$ = distance between (or other index of transition cost) visual components *i* and *j*

To compute Layout Appropriateness, the designer must know how often users will move from one visual component to another, which requires a thorough knowledge of how frequently each task will be carried out and which sequences of visual components will be used. The distance between visual components can be employed as a measure of expected time needed to move between them, or a more complex and potentially more accurate estimate can be used, such as the Fitts Index of Difficulty [Fitts, 1954; Fitts and Posner, 1967], which takes into account the sizes of visual targets and the distances between them.

The formula for Layout Appropriateness also requires that the optimal layout be identified and its expected cost computed, by linear programming or heuristic optimization, for example. For screens or dialogue boxes with a significant number of components, calculation of the minimal cost and optimal layout can present substantial computational difficulties, although software tools can help [Sears, 1995].

Data Cohesion. Coupling and cohesion are two of the software quality metrics of classic structured design [Constantine, 1968; Yourdon and Constantine, 1978]. Coupling is a measure of the strength of interconnection or degree of interdependence between two components. Cohesion is a measure of the strength of the semantic or conceptual relationships among the internal parts of a given component. (See later sidebar, Cohesion.)

(continued)

· OTHER YARDSTICKS (CONT.)

It seems plausible that cohesion, and possibly coupling, might, after suitable translation and adaptation, have some relationship to user interface design quality. Derivatives of both have been developed to measure the quality of screen designs, with mixed results [Kokol, Rozman, and Venuti, 1995]. Most promising was the measure of cohesion based on the extent to which visual elements on a single screen all belong to one or to related data entities. This metric, which could appropriately be termed **Data Cohesion**, is most meaningful for data entry screens, the kind of application for which it was devised. Reductions in error rates and data input times were reported for one project employing Data Cohesion. The basic idea embodied in Data Cohesion was on the right track but got derailed along the way. We will not go into details here because, unfortunately, the metric is not well defined and cannot actually be calculated from the published formula.

more than just numbers. A good conceptual basis makes it easier for designers to understand how differences in measured levels reflect differences in designs. Ideally, the measure and the measurement process itself should guide the designer toward improved designs. Metrics that can be computed solely from visual designs, design models, or nonfunctional visual prototypes will also be more useful than ones that require fully or partially working systems.

One of the questions that is often of interest to designers is how good a certain design might be in some absolute sense. An absolute assessment can be useful in deciding whether or not to invest in further refinement or testing. A metric that generates a number on an arbitrary scale permits comparisons between designs but does not answer the question of how good or bad a single design might be in isolation. Is it near perfect, or is there still plenty of room for improvement? Metrics based on ratios between actual and ideal designs or that indicate goodness-of-fit to some aspect of the supported tasks are apt to be more broadly useful to the designer.

Effective metrics should, of course, reliably predict important aspects of the usability of software in actual application, such as task performance times, learning time, or error rates. User interface design metrics need also to be sufficiently sensitive so as to distinguish between similar designs that are likely to differ in ultimate usability. Ideally, the metric itself or the process by which it is computed should provide information that suggests ways to improve a design.

Essential Usability Metrics Suite

No one metric can capture enough of the subtlety and complexity of user interface design to serve as an overall index of quality. It takes a suite of metrics to cover the various factors that make for a good user interface design. The Interface Metric Project is a research initiative we launched in 1994 to develop and validate a practical suite of quantitative metrics for guiding user interface design. The goal of the project was to devise design metrics that are simple to use, are conceptually sound, and have a clear and transparent rationale connecting them to established principles of good design.

The suite has evolved considerably as research and experience have accumulated [Constantine, 1996e; 1997e; Noble and Constantine, 1997]. Currently, five metrics are included that together cover an assortment of measurements likely to be significant to designers seeking to improve the usability of their software:

1. Essential Efficiency
2. Task Concordance
3. Task Visibility
4. Layout Uniformity
5. Visual Coherence

The first three of these—Essential Efficiency, Task Concordance, and Task Visibility—are procedural or task-sensitive metrics based on essential use cases. These three metrics can be used to measure the quality either of specific parts of the user interface or of complete user interface architectures. The simple structural metric of Layout Uniformity assesses aspects of a single interaction context taken in isolation. The suite is rounded out by a powerful content-sensitive or semantic metric, Visual Coherence, which can be used to evaluate either isolated interaction contexts or complete user interface architectures. With one exception, which will be explained, the metrics are normalized to a range of 0 to 100 so that they can be interpreted like percentages, with 100 meaning your design is perfect or as good as it can get in terms of whatever quality is being measured.

ESSENTIAL EFFICIENCY

The essential use case narrative is an ideal against which the actual interaction with a given design can be compared. In keeping with the Simplicity Principle, short narratives ought to be realized through designs that support brief, straightforward interaction. **Essential Efficiency** (*EE*) is a simple measure of how closely a given user interface design approximates the ideal expressed in the essential use case model. *EE* is just the ratio of the essential length to the enacted length—that is, the ratio of the number of user steps in the essential use case narrative to the number of **enacted steps** needed to perform the use case with a particular user interface design:

> *The essential use case narrative is an ideal against which the actual interaction enacted with a given design can be compared.*

$$EE = 100 \cdot \frac{S_{essential}}{S_{enacted}}$$

Enacted steps are defined by counting rules that govern what constitutes a single discrete user action. (See sidebar, Counting Steps.)

For example, consider the ATM interface introduced in Chapter 5. For the number of essential steps, we just count the number of lines in the left column of

COUNTING STEPS

Many software metrics in common use, including the venerable and widely used Function Points [Albrecht, 1979; Albrecht and Gaffney, 1983], require analysts to count various kinds of the constituents of problems, programs, or designs. To reduce the latitude of judgment and increase the reliability of calculations, counting rules have been developed to define just what counts as what. For comparisons to be valid, consistent rules must be applied. The suite of user interface design metrics requires being able to consistently count several components of interactions and interfaces, including the number of steps required for carrying out tasks. Like most such counting rules, the rules for counting enacted steps are largely heuristic—pragmatic but not grounded in deep theory.

To compute Essential Efficiency, Task Concordance, or Task Visibility, it is necessary to count the number of steps that must be taken by a user enacting some use case in interaction with a particular user interface. What counts as a step? Is every keystroke a step, or does entering an entire name count as one step? Under the counting rules worked out with our clients, each of the following constitutes a single enacted step in the completion of a task using a software user interface.

Enacted Steps

1. Entering data into one field by continuous typing that is terminated by an enter, a tab, or some other field separator
2. Skipping over an unneeded field or control by tabbing or by means of any other navigation key
3. Selecting a field, an object, or a group of items by clicking, double-clicking, or sweeping with a pointing device
4. Selecting a field, an object, or a group of items with a keystroke or series of connected keystrokes
5. Switching from keyboard to pointing device or from pointing device to keyboard
6. Triggering an action by clicking or double-clicking with a pointing device on a tool, a command button, or some other visual object
7. Selecting a menu or a menu item by a pointing device
8. Triggering an action by typing a shortcut key or key sequence, including activating a menu item through keyboard access keys
9. Dragging-and-dropping an object with a pointing device

The objective under these counting rules is to capture basic conceptual units of interaction, rather than the strictly operational or manual units, such as the keystroke level of analysis employed in the GOMS method. (See later sidebar, Good Old GOMS.) In an effort to make them more useful for comparison with the abstract steps of essential use case narratives, enacted steps strike a compromise between conceptual and concrete measurement. For the most part, enacted steps reflect what users experience or think of as discrete actions, such as selecting, moving, entering, deleting, and the like. Because completion times for enacted steps can vary tremendously, they are better indicators of relative interaction complexity than of expected task performance times, although there will be some correlation. Where a more precise and reliable estimate of expected times is of interest, a GOMS-type analysis could be carried out. (See sidebar, Good Old GOMS.)

When there is more than one way to enact a given use case, as there typically is, the steps for the shortest and longest enactment can be counted to estimate a range. In general, the longest enactment will be more typical of novice or untrained users, while the shortest sequence can be regarded as a potential performance for expert or highly trained users.

the essential use case narrative, the "User Intention" model. For the enacted use case, we count the number of user actions according to the counting rules established for enacted steps. The essential use case in this ATM example has three steps (identify self, choose, take money), while the enacted use case illustrated involves eight discrete user actions, which means $EE = 37.5\%$ for the existing system. Without changing to exotic new technologies, an improved interface could be designed that offered the customer the choice of selecting "the usual" to initiate a cash withdrawal from the usual account in the amount usually requested. This would result in only five steps for the enacted use case (insert card, enter PIN, select "the usual," take card, take money) for an Essential Efficiency of $EE = 62.5\%$, a substantial improvement.

Because Essential Efficiency compares enacted steps to the essential narrative, the results are dependent on having a good essential use case model. Sloppy or incomplete modeling can yield numbers that look better than they are. In practice, the use case narratives should be reviewed to see whether additional simplification and generalization are possible before computing Essential Efficiency. Of course, the degree of simplification in the essential narrative will not affect comparisons of alternative designs in terms of EE for the same use cases.

EE can also be computed for a mix of tasks. If the overall efficiency of a design for an entire mix of tasks is of interest, the Essential Effi-

---

GOOD OLD GOMS

A mainstay of mainstream usability engineering is an analysis technique known as "GOMS" (Goals, Operators, Methods, and Selections) [Card, Moran, & Newell, 1983]. GOMS is based on the so-called model human processor, a theoretical model of how people carry out cognitive-motor tasks and interact with systems. GOMS analyses involve breaking a task down into very small cognitive and motor steps needed to perform the task with a particular user interface. The total task time can be estimated by adding up measured times for such operations as shifting the eyes from one part of the screen to another, recognizing an icon, moving the hand to the mouse, moving the pointer to a particular spot, and then clicking the mouse button twice. Years of research have established ranges of times for many different basic mental and motor operations, such as choosing among a set of options, remembering a code, clicking on an icon, or typing a character. (See the sidebar, In Theory, in Chapter 3.)

For an excellent overview of GOMS research and application, see Olson and Olson [1990].

---

ciencies of the various tasks can be weighted by the probability (expected relative frequency) or relative importance of each task:

$$EE_{weighted} = \sum_{\forall i} p_i \cdot EE_i$$

where

p_i = probability (or weighted importance) of task i
EE_i = essential efficiency for task i

In practice, however, designers are often not in a position to make good estimates of the expected frequencies of the various tasks. For this reason, the average Essential Efficiency for the most common or most important few tasks is often substituted.

Computing the weighted EE is especially useful for considering design trade-offs. In most cases, simplifying one task or part of the interface will make things more difficult somewhere else. By considering the average EE or the weighted EE, the overall impact of a change can be evaluated.

Task Concordance

Task Concordance (*TC*) is another metric based on use cases that evaluates support of efficiency and simplicity. *TC* is an index of how well the distribution of task difficulty using a particular interface design fits with the expected frequency of the various tasks. Good designs will generally make the more frequent tasks easier. *TC* is computed from the correlation between tasks ranked by anticipated frequency in use and by enacted difficulty. Task Concordance is the exception to the rule that metrics in the suite behave as percentages; *TC* ranges from −100 to +100%. When a design is perfect in terms of Task Concordance—that is, when more frequent tasks

> *Good designs will generally make the more frequent tasks easier. Task Concordance is an index of how well the expected frequencies of tasks match their difficulty.*

are always shorter than less frequent tasks—*TC* = 100%. If the design is basically backwards, with more frequent tasks taking more steps, then *TC* will be negative, with *TC* = −100% for a completely wrong-headed design. *TC* will be 0% or close to it whenever the design is essentially random or unrelated to the tasks to be supported.

Although *TC* could be defined in a number of different ways, for simplicity we use the rank-order correlation between task frequency and task length employing a statistic called *Kendall's* τ (Greek tau). To compute τ, it is only necessary to list all the tasks in order of their estimated or expected frequency along with their enacted difficulty. Use cases are compared for difficulty according to the number of enacted steps required for completion.

Ranking tasks by expected frequencies has several advantages over trying to estimate actual frequencies. Absolute frequencies of tasks, as required to compute Layout Appropriateness (See sidebar, Other Yardsticks) or weighted Essential Efficiency, are difficult to estimate prior to implementation. Most analysts find it easier to judge whether one task is likely to be relatively more or less common than another, without regard to the actual numbers. For example, you may know with absolute confidence that initializing a new database will be much rarer than entering a new customer and yet have not the slightest idea of the exact percentage of time either will occur. Rank orderings are also typically more

INFINITE INEFFICIENCY

Math mavens will no doubt have noticed that *EE* does not exactly cover the range of values from 0 to 100%. For incredibly inept interface implementations, it can become very small but cannot reach 0% in practice. One arguable interpretation is that *EE* = 0% means a use case is not possible with a given user interface design; it would take an infinite number of steps.

In practice, *EE* could exceed 100% when a clever and highly efficient design supports a poorly worked out essential use case. We would take *EE* >100 as a call to review and refine the essential narrative, but other designers might prefer to let the impressive if improbable results stand.

dependable than absolute frequency estimates, which often have to be pulled from thin air. Use cases can be ranked by expected frequency using the same kind of simple card-sorting techniques that are used to rank user roles and to identify focal use cases (see Chapter 4).

Kendall's τ offers an appealing way to compute Task Concordance because it is a statistic that is simple to understand. In its basic form, it is just the fraction of all pairs of items that are correctly ordered versus incorrectly ordered. More precisely, the formula for Task Concordance is a ratio:

> *Absolute frequencies of tasks are difficult to estimate. Prior to implementation, it is easier to judge whether one task is likely to be relatively more or less common than another.*

$$TC = 100 \cdot \tau = 100 \cdot \frac{D}{P}$$

where

> D = discordance score: number of pairs of tasks ranked in correct order by enacted length less number of pairs out of order
> P = number of possible task pairs

If every task has a different difficulty or enacted length, P is simply

$$P = \frac{N(N-1)}{2}$$

where

> N = number of tasks being ranked

The formula for Kendall's τ gets considerably more complicated if there are ties in either the ranking by expected frequency or by enacted length. We find it generally better to find some way to break ties than to resort to the more complex calculation, although nearly any good statistics software will do the work for you. Ties in rankings by enacted length can be broken by taking into account differences in the complexity of individual steps or in how they are combined.

For user interface designs with lots of tasks, using a program, such as any standard statistical software package, is recommended, but, for simple problems, TC can easily be calculated by hand. Consider a screen with five representative tasks that the analysts figure will probably occur ranked as follows:

Tasks (ranked in order of descending expected frequency)	Enacted Length (number of user steps in enacted use case)
Task A	7
Task E	7
Task B	5
Task D	8
Task C	6

The current design results in the enacted lengths shown in the right-hand column. We start by breaking the tie between the first and second ranked tasks. Let us say that task A is judged to be marginally more difficult to carry out than task E, even though they have the same number of enacted steps.

For each pair of numbers in the right-hand column, we ask whether the pair is in the right order or the wrong order relative to the ranking by expected frequency. For each pair in the right order, we add 1 to the discordance score, D, in the formula for TC; for each pair in the wrong order, we subtract 1. In other words, we compare 7+ to 7, which gives a −1, then 7+ to 5, which gives another −1, then 7+ to 8, which adds 1, and so forth, until we have counted all the comparisons. Adding it all up gives $D = -2$. Then, we find P:

$$P = \frac{5 \cdot 4}{2} = 10$$

$$TC = -20\%$$

The design being evaluated is, all in all, pretty poor since it means the user interface is quite backwards. What if we could improve a bit on the more frequent tasks? We might try to change the design to eliminate a few steps in the two most frequent tasks, only to find that this makes task B, the third ranked, more difficult:

Tasks (ranked in order of descending expected frequency)	Enacted Length (number of user steps in enacted use case)
Task A	4
Task E	6
Task B	7
Task D	8
Task C	6

Computing Task Concordance for the revised design, we get

$$TC = 52.7\%$$

which is probably quite an improvement at the end of the day.

TASK VISIBILITY

Task Visibility (TV) is another relatively simple procedural metric based on use cases. It is grounded in the Visibility Principle, the notion that user interfaces should show users exactly what they need to know or need to use to be able to complete a given task. It measures the fit between the visibility of features and the capabilities needed to complete a given task or set of tasks.

Quantifying visibility is a more subtle challenge than it first appears to be, and several revisions have been required to devise a metric that is simple yet reflective of sound design practice. The visibility of user interface features is a matter of degree. Things that are immediately obvious from looking at the current screen are more visible than those you have to open a menu to find, which are more visible than those located in other interaction contexts. The relative importance of visibility also depends on aspects of the task. It is more vital to have immediate access to those things that are always required to complete a use case than those that may or may not be needed for a particular enactment. It may be acceptable, for example, to place features needed to enact an extension use case one level removed on a separate interaction context, as reflected in the rules for deriving content models covered in Chapter 6.

> *Task Visibility is a metric grounded in the Visibility Principle, the notion that user interfaces should show users exactly what they need to know or to use to complete a given task.*

Ultimately, it proved easiest to define Task Visibility in terms of the enacted steps rather than interface features, separating out those steps that use hidden capabilities or that are taken in order to gain access to features. A feature is visible if you can see it when you need it, so enacted steps performed in order to see or gain access to parts of the user interface must reflect reduced task visibility. The formula for Task Visibility is

$$TV = 100 \cdot \left(\frac{1}{S_{total}} \cdot \sum_{\forall i} V_i \right)$$

where

S_{total} = total number of enacted steps to complete use cases
V_i = feature visibility (0 to 1) of enacted step i

The formula for *TV* is expressed as a percent of the total number of steps because longer, more complex tasks may legitimately need to be distributed across more than one interaction context. Task Visibility reaches a maximum of 100% when everything needed for a step is visible directly on the user interface as seen by the user at that step. Visibility would reach 0% for a workable design only

> *Visibility would reach 0% only under very exceptional circumstances, such as a high-security interface for remote access to highly sensitive information.*

under very exceptional circumstances. One example might be a high-security interface for remote access to highly sensitive information. When the user connects, there is no prompt for name, identification, or password; the user must know how to type these, in what order, and with what separators. Successful log-on is indicated only by the cursor's moving down a line, after which the user must type the correct series of commands on the blank screen without prompting or feedback. In such a command-line interface, every enacted step must be accomplished entirely on the basis of "knowledge in the head" [Norman, 1988], without visible cues or prompting.

Task Visibility can be evaluated for individual use cases or for extended task scenarios that might incorporate any number of use cases. To calculate *TV*, an essential use case or set of use cases is enacted with a given user interface design. The total number of enacted steps is tallied. For each enacted step, the analyst determines whether the enacted step was performed to gain access to features that were not visible on the user interface as it would appear to the user at that point or whether the step used hidden features not visible on the interface. The counting rules for enacted steps have already been covered in a sidebar; the rules for counting feature visibility are presented in another one. (See sidebar, Visibility Rules.)

Task Visibility takes into account only one side of the concept of WYSIWYN, or What You See Is What You Need. It ignores whether things that are *not* needed are also found on the user interface. In principle, we could reduce Task Visibility whenever unused or unnecessary features are incorporated into the user interface. In practice, this refinement makes sense only if all use cases supported by the system are considered in the calculation, which is more often than not quite impractical.

For an example, consider preparing a slide for an on-screen presentation. The presenter wants an object to enter automatically from the right of the screen when the slide first appears. How does one accomplish this in PowerPoint 97?

Enacted Step	Type	Visibility
select object	direct	1.0
open **Slide Show** menu	exposing	0.5
open **Custom Animation** dialogue	suspending	0.0
open drop-down list	exposing	0.5
select **Fly From Right**	direct	1.0
click on **Timing** tab	exposing	0.5
set **Automatically** option button	direct	1.0
click **OK** to close dialogue	suspending	0.0
	Total	4.5

Since there are eight steps in this enactment, $TV = 56.25\%$. Other enactments are possible, but Task Visibility varies little. Task Visibility might be improved in several ways. For instance, one can argue that the conditions under which animation takes place and the style of animation are closely related and ought to be found on the same dialogue tab. Animation could also be considered a property of the object, to be made available on a property inspector instead of within a modal dialogue that blocks other interaction until dismissed.

LAYOUT UNIFORMITY

Not every developer who ends up responsible for user interface design necessarily has a graphics designer's eye for layout. **Layout Uniformity** (LU) is a structural metric that gives a quick handle on one important aspect of visual layout. It was devised as a more practical and simplified replacement for Layout Complexity. (See sidebar, Other Yardsticks.)

Layout Uniformity measures only selected aspects of the spatial arrangement of interface components without taking into account what those components are or how they are used; it is neither task sensitive nor content sensitive. As the name suggests, this metric assesses the uniformity or regularity of the user interface layout. Layout Uniformity—or LU—is based

> *For developers who do not have a graphics designer's eye for layout, Layout Uniformity is a structural metric that gives a quick handle on one important aspect of visual design.*

on the rationale that usability is hindered by highly disordered or visually chaotic arrangements. The influence of regularity on usability is probably not terribly large, but it is one factor. Complete regularity is not the goal, however. Too much uniformity not only can look unappealing but also can make it harder for users to distinguish different features and different parts of the interface. We can expect that moderately uniform and orderly layouts are likely to be the easiest to

VISIBILITY RULES

Feature visibility associated with an enacted step is considered to vary from 0 to 1. In practice, enacted steps are classified according to function and method of performance into one of four categories: hidden, exposing, suspending, or direct.

Hidden. Hidden operations draw on the user's internal knowledge of the application and its use apart from any information communicated by the visible user interface. Hidden steps include

- Typing a required code or shortcut in the absence of any visual prompting or cue
- Accessing a feature or features having no visible representation on the user interface (for example, the Windows 95 Task Bar when hidden)
- Any action involving an object or a feature that may be visible but the choice of which is neither obvious nor evident based on visible information on the user interface

Opening a generic context menu by clicking on blank background with the right mouse button or typing a keyboard shortcut without being prompted is an example of a hidden step. Hidden enacted steps are assigned a visibility of 0.

Exposing. An enacted step is exposing if its function is to gain access to or make visible some other needed feature without causing or resulting in a change of interaction context. Exposing actions include

- Opening a drop-down list
- Opening a menu or submenu
- Opening a context menu by right-clicking on some object
- Opening a property sheet dialogue for an object
- Opening an object or drilling down for detail
- Opening or making visible a tool palette
- Opening an attached pane or panel of a dialogue

- Switching to another page or tab of a tabbed dialogue

Exposing actions have an intermediate effect on task visibility and are assigned a visibility of 0.5, unless they are or must be accomplished using hidden features, in which case they are classified as hidden and given a visibility of 0.

Suspending. An enacted step is suspending if its function is to gain access to or make visible some other needed feature and it causes or results in a change of interaction context. Suspending actions include

- Opening a dialogue box
- Closing a dialogue or message box
- Switching to another window
- Switching to or launching another application

Suspending or context-switching actions that occur as the first or last enacted step of extensions or other optional interactions have an intermediate effect on task visibility since they provide access to features that may not be needed in all enactments; they are assigned a visibility of 0.5, unless they are or must be accomplished using hidden features, in which case they are classified as hidden and given a visibility of 0. Context changes that are nonoptional, that are required in most or all enactments, have a strong effect on task visibility; these are assigned a visibility of 0.

Direct. An enacted step is a direct action if it is not hidden, exposing, or suspending. In other words, direct actions are accomplished through visible features whose choice is evident and which do not serve to gain access to or make visible other objects. Examples of direct actions include applying a tool to an object to change it, typing a value into a visible field, or altering the setting of an option button. Direct enacted steps are assigned a visibility of 1.

understand and to use. Layout Uniformity is defined as

$$LU = 100 \cdot \left(1 - \frac{(N_h + N_w + N_t + N_l + N_b + N_r) - M}{6 \cdot N_c - M} \right)$$

where

N_c = total number of visual components on screen, dialogue box, or other interface composite

N_h, N_w, N_t, N_l, N_b, and N_r are, respectively, the number of different heights, widths, top-edge alignments, left-edge alignments, bottom-edge alignments, and right-edge alignments of visual components. M is an adjustment for the minimum number of possible alignments and sizes needed to make the value of LU range from 0 to 100 (note the "ceiling" function, $\lceil \; \rceil$, which means the smallest integer greater than the enclosed value):

$$M = 2 + 2 \cdot \left\lceil 2\sqrt{N_{components}} \right\rceil$$

Layout Uniformity goes up when visual components are lined up with one another and when there are not too many different sizes of components. The role of Layout Uniformity can best be appreciated by example. In Figure 17-1 are three alternative layouts for a dialogue box. The widgets are left blank because Layout Uniformity does not care what the components are or do. For the layout with no consistency in size or position (Figure 17-1a), $LU = 0\%$, as expected; likewise, for the completely uniform layout (Figure 17-1c), $LU = 100\%$. Neither one of these is typical of good user interface designs. The intermediate design (Figure 17-1b) is more typical of real dialogue layouts, with $LU = 82.5\%$, which, in our experience, is quite acceptable.

To compute Layout Uniformity, some rules of thumb are needed for determining what counts as a visual component and how to judge when components are aligned with one another. These counting rules are discussed in the sidebar, Counting Components.

As a structural metric concerned only with appearance, Layout Uniformity should not be given undue weight in evaluating designs. It can, however, be useful to the designer who lacks an eye for layout to know when a visual arrangement

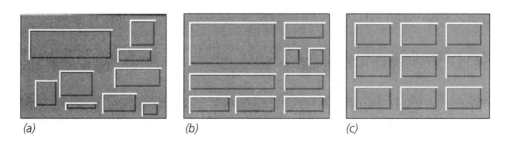

(a)   (b)   (c)

FIGURE 17-1 *Layout Uniformity illustrated.*

Like a good filing system, a well-structured user interface makes it easy to find things because related things are consolidated and unrelated things are separated.

might be improved. A review of well-designed dialogues suggests that, in general, a value of *LU* anywhere between 50% and 85% is probably reasonable, other things being equal. Outside that range, the designer may want to do some thoughtful shuffling of the visual components to make the layout either a little more or a little less uniform.

VISUAL COHERENCE

A well-designed screen or window "hangs together." A good nested set of dialogue boxes collects in one place all those things you think of together and keeps the less related things apart. Like a good filing system, a well-structured user interface makes it easy to find things because related things are consolidated and unrelated

COUNTING COMPONENTS

Both Layout Uniformity and Visual Coherence require counting the number of visual components in an interaction context. A visual component is

- Any user interface widget
- An external label not on or embedded in a user interface widget
- A pane, panel, or frame around any one or more widgets or labels

Simple lines separating one part of the visual interface from another are not considered to be visual components in themselves.

Since the arrangement and alignment of components as perceived by the human visual system are of interest, component edges are considered to be aligned if they appear to the unaided eye to be aligned. Text labels, which can vary in height, are a more complicated matter.

Standard practices in user interface layout allow the top edge of text to be slightly below the top edge of an adjacent component and the bottom edge to be slightly above an adjacent bottom edge. Text may also be centered vertically relative to an adjacent component of similar but not identical height. Both edges of text that are aligned according to these conventional practices can be considered to be aligned for purposes of computing Layout Uniformity.

things are separated. This is just the Structure Principle in operation. **Visual Coherence** (*VC*) measures how well a user interface keeps related things together and unrelated things apart. More specifically, it is a semantic or content-sensitive measure of how closely an arrangement of visual components matches the semantic relationships among those components. Based on the principle that well-structured interfaces group together components that represent closely related concepts, Visual Coherence reflects important and fundamental aspects of user interface architecture that strongly affect comprehension, learning, and use.

Visual Coherence extends to user interfaces the well-established software engineering metric of cohesion (see sidebar, Cohesion), which gauges how closely interrelated are the contents of software units. A strict application of cohesion to dialogue boxes or other user interface composites would be simplistic since the classic notion of cohesion does not take into account the way component parts are arranged or grouped, only whether they are present or not. Determining which features to place on a given interaction context is, of course, one design consideration, but, for the more challenging questions regarding specific layout and visual arrangement of components, the broader notion of Visual Coherence is needed.

For example, the two dialogue box designs shown in Figure 17-2, used in research on Visual Coherence, group visual components very differently by using empty space, lines, boxes, and other visual techniques to define visual groups. The overall Visual Coherence of each design depends on the semantic related-ness among the features or components con-tained or enclosed within each of its visual groups.

To be able to evaluate Visual Coherence, we have to be able to look at any two visual elements on the interface and determine whether or not they are closely related seman-tically. We can do this in more than one way, but for now let us imagine we have a table that we can use to determine whether a particular pair of elements are sufficiently closely related

> ### COHESION
>
> The classic software engineering notion of cohe-sion [Constantine, 1968; Yourdon and Constan-tine, 1978] is a quality metric that gauges the semantic or conceptual interrelatedness of ele-ments within a particular program component or module. The more closely interrelated are the parts, the easier it will be to perceive and under-stand the collection of parts as a unified whole or gestalt. Cohesion is a form of a complexity (or simplicity) metric in that components high in cohesion are simpler to understand, whether for purposes of construction, use, reuse, extension, or modification. The concept of cohesion has been operationalized in a variety of ways and widely applied in software engineering practice and research. Most recently, it has been extended from its original application within procedure-based programming and traditional structured methods into forms usable in modern object-oriented software engineering practice [Embley and Woodfield, 1987; Chidamber and Kemerer, 1994; Henderson-Sellers, Constantine, and Gra-ham, 1996].

to justify putting them in the same visual grouping on the user interface.

Visual Coherence for any particular visual grouping is simply the ratio of the number of closely related pairs of visual elements to the total number of enclosed pairs. We compute this ratio for the innermost visual groups, and then we just repeat the same thing for the next level outward, until we have covered the com-plete interaction context. In determining what is related to what at outer levels, we

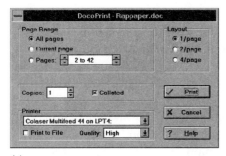

(a)

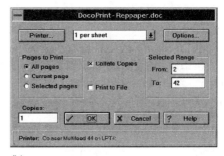

(b)

FIGURE 17-2 *Same problem, different Visual Coherence.*

may end up comparing visual groups to other visual groups or to simple visual components grouped at that level.

Total Visual Coherence of a design for an interaction context is computed by summing recursively over all the groups, subgroups, and so forth, at each level of grouping:

$$VC = 100 \cdot \left(\frac{\sum_{\forall k} G_k}{\sum_{\forall k} N_k \cdot (N_k - 1)/2} \right)$$

with

$$G_k = \sum_{\forall i,j \mid i \neq j} R_{i,j}$$

where

N_k = number of visual components in group k

$R_{i,j}$ = semantic relatedness between components i and j in group k,

$0 \leq R_{i,j} \leq 1$

In practice, semantic relatedness can be simplified to just two values: $R_{i,j} = 1$ if components i and j belong to the same semantic cluster and are, therefore, substantially related; $R_{i,j} = 0$, otherwise. This formulation reduces the calculations to counting the substantially related pairs and appears to work quite well in discriminating real designs. It has the correct behavior as a metric in that it favors organizing user interface components into subgroups, but only so long as those groupings make sense—that is, enclosing substantially related components associated with a cluster of closely related semantic concepts.

> *Semantic clusters, being invisible and intangible, must be discovered; a good starting point is the glossary, domain object model, entity model, or data dictionary for the application.*

Semantic clusters, being invisible and intangible, must be discovered by the designers. Fortunately, this process of concept sorting need only be done once for a given project. The starting point is the glossary, domain object model, entity model, or data dictionary for the application. A good domain object model is probably the best starting point since the domain classes, their methods, and their attributes define an overview of the semantic organization associated with a given application [Constantine, 1997e].

Each of the concepts in the problem domain, from whatever source, is written onto a separate index card. The concepts are then sorted into clusters of closely related terms using a card sort or affinity clustering technique such as that described in Chapter 4. If desired, the clustering task can be completed collaboratively, or several people can complete the task and then discuss and resolve differences in their clusters. Including one or more users among the sorters is desirable. Once the semantic clustering is complete, each cluster can be given a name or heading and the whole collection converted to a list.

To evaluate Visual Coherence, the list of concepts is scanned to determine with which concept each visual component or group is most closely related. If two components or groups are both determined to be most closely related to concepts in the same cluster, then they are considered to be substantially related and are assigned an $R_{i,j} = 1$. If they are associated with concepts from different clusters, then $R_{i,j} = 0$. For a finer-grained measure, components that are closely associated with concepts in separate but related semantic clusters can be assigned an intermediate value for $R_{i,j}$.

Ultimately, it should be possible to derive semantic clusters directly from a complete domain object model, with the strength of semantic relationship based on the nature of the object relationship, such as superclass-subclass, method-of, attribute-of, and so forth. Realization of an object-oriented version of Visual Coherence is under way.

METRICS IN PRACTICE

An important factor in the effectiveness of any metrics initiative is how the numbers are put to use. Utilized inappropriately, metrics can take on an exaggerated significance and may come to dominate design decisions. For example, the effect of immediate feedback on design quality has been investigated at the University of Technology, Sydney [Noble and Constantine, 1997]. Some design metrics can be computed automatically within a visual development tool for user interface layout. Given instant numeric feedback on their layouts, designers can sometimes unconsciously work to maximize their scores rather than derive the best design. The result can be good-looking numbers but poorer interfaces when all factors are taken into account.

The technique of dynamic metric visualization [Noble and Constantine, 1997] was devised to provide "live" feedback during user interface layout without loading the designer astray through a tyranny of numbers. Instead of metrics values displayed numerically or graphically, the designer is shown the underlying basis for the metric of interest. For example, the paths representing enacted use cases can be displayed overlaid on the user interface layout. The designer sees how the lengths of these path lines are affected by the placement of visual components. Tasks that are more frequent are represented by thicker path lines, visually reminding the designer of the relative importance of different use cases. Similarly, the basis of Layout Uniformity can be communicated through light grid lines along the edges of visual components, thus highlighting misalignments. Semantic relationships among components can be displayed by colored lines or highlights. In this way, the conceptual issues of task efficiency, visual alignment, and visual coherence are made apparent without creating a tyranny of numerical scores. By updating the feedback dynamically as the developer places and moves components, the development environment can help support sound user interface layout.

In the absence of such next-generation visual development tools, software developers should be wary of allowing usability metrics to cloud their judgment. Quantitative comparisons can be helpful so long as they do not begin to substitute for thought, careful design, systematic review, and judicious testing.

> *Software developers should be wary of allowing metrics to cloud their judgment. Quantitative comparisons are no substitute for thought, careful design, systematic review, and judicious testing.*

For the greatest value, metrics should also fit with the management agenda and political climate of an organization. For example, a suite of three customized metrics was constructed specifically to meet the needs of one client, an internal application development group serving the needs of a large financial institution. Feedback from end users in the organization had highlighted usability problems in several areas. Users had complained that earlier systems had been inefficient and unreliable in use largely because too many screen changes were required in the course of completing a transaction, data frequently had to be reentered in multiple places, and input errors were common because incoming data were not validated appropriately and effectively.

With the threat of outsourcing hanging in the air, it was especially important in this organization to be able to monitor and demonstrate improvements in usability compared to previous systems. The three metrics we developed evaluated usability in terms of simplicity, efficiency in use, and reliability in use. They were simplified and expressed negatively to make it easier for end users to understand and compare new systems to earlier versions. **Excess Context Changes**, as the term implies, was an index of unnecessary changes in interaction context as a percentage of user steps, a simplified variant of Task Visibility. **Entry Redundancy** assessed duplication of entry data as a percentage of total data fields. **Validation Inefficiency** was the percentage of data entry values not supported by immediate validation or some other means of reducing input errors. With simplified definitions and counting rules, end users could readily see how their interests were being taken into account by the development group and how much the software was improving in these terms.

18

TEST SCORES:
Laboratory and Field Testing of Usability

HISTORY TESTING

For good and sufficient reasons, usability testing has long been the foundation of modern usability engineering. The usability lab was where "real" data was gathered from the interactions of real users with real systems. Data from laboratory study not only resolved practical design problems for developers but also provided a growing body of insight into the general nature of human-machine interaction.

In a sense, the story of usage-centered design begins in the test lab. Early in our work on software usability, we were struck by a seeming contradiction. Various software vendors had publicly declared a commitment to user-friendly development, visibly demonstrating their commitment by constructing gleaming new usability testing labs equipped with the latest technology and staffed by cadres of Ph.D.-bearing specialists. Still, these very companies continued to churn out software products riddled with glaring usability defects. Something was going wrong. Between the intention and the execution, some part of the process was breaking down.

As we learned more about how many of these development groups worked, we realized that a central problem was the excessive reliance on usability testing to identify user interface design problems. The typical strategy, somewhat oversimplified, was to plunge ahead into coding with little regard for user interface design and minimal understanding of the needs of users. Once a working system was ready, it would be turned over to the usability testers, who were expected to find the problems. The testers were, of course, doomed. The problems were invariably too numerous, and the time and budget were consistently too limited. Such usability problems as testing did uncover were often left uncorrected, for it was usually already too close to the planned release date, and the required fixes were often too complex, too widespread, or too fundamental to be effected.

Not all the blame could be placed on the role of usability testing; many parts of the process were failing along the way. Developers were usually too focused on programming problems. They were working without adequate models or effective tools. The process itself often left no time or place for end-user involvement. Nevertheless, the central fact is that many of these companies believed that, through usability lab testing, they had created an effective software usability program and were delivering usable products. Their customers knew better.

If the truth be told, usability testing has too often been employed as an ineffectual substitute for good design and careful thought. Effective usage-centered design is a demanding process, a continuous occupation throughout a project from inception to delivery. In contrast, usability testing, as typically practiced, is an event—a single step that may often be deferred until quite late in a project. Usability testing can be turned over to someone else, the testers, while design usually falls squarely on the shoulders of the development team itself.

> *Usability testing has too often been employed as an ineffectual substitute for good design and careful thought.*

To a certain extent, usability testing is becoming a commodity service. The techniques are well established and widely taught. One well-equipped and competently staffed lab is likely to be about as good as the next one. The procedures are not particularly difficult to understand and apply, and there are many good sources of basic information. Without slighting the skills and contributions of professionals specializing in usability testing, designing a good usability test protocol is usually easier than designing a good user interface in the first place. Many companies have taken what amounts to the easy way out, at least in the short run, putting their faith in testing and shortchanging on design.

Ironically, the greatest benefits from testing accrue when it is preceded by thorough and effective design. Indeed, usability testing fits particularly well with a usage-centered development approach driven by user roles and essential use cases. Here, we will cover only some of the basics of usability testing, especially as these relate to usage-centered design; other sources should be consulted for more details [see, for example, Nielsen, 1993; Rubin, 1994].

TESTING, ONE, TWO

Usability testing comes in two major variants: laboratory testing and field testing. At times, the distinctions may not be entirely clear. Field testing may even sometimes attempt to replicate laboratory conditions in the field, using essentially the

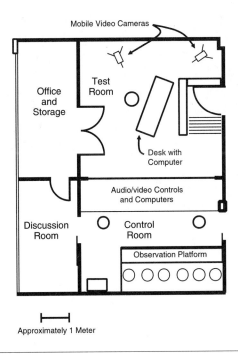

FIGURE 18-1 *Floor plan for a usability testing laboratory.*
(University of Technology, Sydney, Australia)

same methods and much the same equipment simply packed into road cases and rolled into customer offices.

LABORATORY SCIENCE

Laboratory testing involves tests conducted in a fixed setting specifically configured for usability testing. The exact floor plan and configuration may vary considerably, but the usability lab diagrammed in Figure 18-1 is representative. The typical lab has one or more areas in which subjects will try using the system under test plus one or more areas where testing staff can monitor and observe the proceedings. The subject area is often furnished to resemble a comfortable office setting, as shown in Figure 18-2. It must be equipped with whatever computers and operating platforms are required to run the software under test, but it may also be configured with special software to monitor keyboard and mouse operation or screen activity. Video or audio equipment records sessions for later review and analysis. The observation area is typically separated from the subject area to avoid disturbing test subjects. The former is outfitted with monitors, mixers, and recorders, as well as computers and other equipment for event logging and

FIGURE 18-2 *User subject area in a usability testing laboratory.*
(University of Technology, Sydney, Australia)

analysis. In many installations such as the one in Figure 18-3, a one-way mirror permits easy observation of the session by numbers of observers.

The main advantage to such an arrangement is that it provides a controlled and consistent environment in which to evaluate software. Comparing the results of different tests, different users, or different systems is easier and more defensible under these conditions. Findings from a series of tests can be confidently combined for statistical analysis. Laboratory testing offers another advantage to companies that invest in it: Usability testing facilities serve as a visible, bricks-and-mortar demonstration of a company's commitment to its users and to enhancing usability. We suspect this motivation factors into the decisions of many companies, whether they are willing to acknowledge it or not.

FIGURE 18-3 *Observation room in a usability testing laboratory.*
(University of Technology, Sydney, Australia)

The capacity to observe test sessions is an important and sometimes under-appreciated feature of the usability testing lab. It can be an instructive and hum-bling experience for software developers to watch a user struggle with their software during a test session. As they see the uncomfortable consequences of their user interface design decisions, developers frequently find themselves developing deeper empathy for end users. The immediacy of watching a session "live" seems to enhance the impact, but videotapes of sessions can also be informative.

> *A usability test lab provides a controlled and consistent environment in which to evaluate software. It also offers a visible, bricks-and-mortar demonstration of commitment to users and to enhancing usability.*

The principal problem with laboratory testing is that the consistent and controlled conditions that are its greatest strength are also a weakness. However comfortably furnished, the lab is still an artificial setting quite distinct from the usual context in which everyday work takes place. It is well known that subjects act differently in such settings than they do at work. They will approach problems in ways that differ from the tactics they would use in their accustomed work environment. Although all test conditions are necessarily contrived in one way or another, taking users out of the office and into the laboratory adds to the unnaturalness of the situation and reduces the generalizability of the conclusions reached from testing.

> *However comfortably furnished, the usability lab is still an artificial setting in which subjects will act differently than they do at work.*

OUT IN THE FIELD

Field testing takes the usability tests into the workplace. Conducting usability tests *in situ* does not necessarily mean that user-subjects will be observed working at their own desks on their familiar workstations. More often than not, some attempt is made to control and monitor the process, largely for the convenience of the testers and to enrich the results. Usually, the test staff is in another room or is separated by a partition from the user. Generally speaking, users are brought one by one to a common room, such as a conference room, that serves as a temporary test site.

In its most minimalist incarnation, usability testing in the field requires only a trained observer outfitted with a notepad. More often, video cameras, microphones, data loggers, and recorders, mixers, and monitors are trundled about in road cases. Fully equipped portable usability testing systems are available for purchase as off-the-shelf units. In practice, a great deal of effective testing can be accomplished aided by no more than an inexpensive camcorder on a tripod plus an adjustable mirror.

Field usability testing with portable equipment can be less expensive than lab testing. Often, the equipment is more modest, and there is no need to construct and furnish a permanent suite supported by full-time staff. However, the greatest advantages of field testing are in its greater realism and comfort for users. Typically, users are in more or less familiar surroundings using familiar equipment and configurations.

> *Realism and natural settings, the strengths of field testing, are also shortcomings because testers have less control over test conditions.*

Realism and natural settings are also shortcomings of the field-testing approach because testers have less control over test conditions. Noise, interruptions, and other distractions can interfere with test protocols. A telephone may ring in the middle of a test scenario, or a subject may be called away for a meeting before a test is concluded. It is sometimes possible to turn such problems into an advantage, however. If the environment is representative of the conditions under which a system will be deployed, a design that is robust enough to cope with interruptions and distractions may be vital. Test protocols can even be designed with planned interruptions to evaluate the ease with which users can return to a task and remember how to proceed.

BETA-TESTING

In addition to systematic usability tests conducted in much the same manner as laboratory tests, many companies consider beta-testing as a form of field evaluation of software usability. So-called alpha and beta releases have become linchpins of the software development process. An alpha release is, of course, typically an early version of software intended for internal release. It is a working version but only a rough cut, often erratic in behavior and performance and missing some important features—hardly the kind of thing you would want outsiders to see. Indeed, the alpha release is often the focus of near-heroic efforts to achieve a stable system through integration testing.

> *Within some of the largest software houses, beta-testing often substitutes for careful design, review, and debugging.*

Although it may be less robust and efficient than the final shipping version, a beta release is assumed to be essentially complete and fully functional. Historically, many user interface problems are not discovered or corrected until the beta version is released. Within the sorry excuses for software development processes practiced by some of the largest software houses, customers using the beta release are effectively exploited as debuggers and usability testers, substituting for the careful design, review, and debugging that the vendors should have done themselves.

Asking your customers about what problems they had using the beta version of your software may seem like a relatively inexpensive and friendly thing to do, but it will not necessarily get you good information. Relying on spontaneous feedback from beta test sites is even more unreliable. Those people who note problems and communicate them are a self-selected subset of users at the beta site. Like those who complain to customer relations departments or who write letters to the editors of newspapers, they are not necessarily representative of that vast majority who never complain directly. Unfortunately, that majority may suffer in silence only to go with a competitor's product when given the opportunity.

Developers will hear of only a small fraction of the usability defects encountered by beta users, even when feedback is actively sought. Even the most motivated users neither remember nor record all the usability problems they encounter. Especially with early beta

> *Even when feedback is actively sought, developers hear of only a small fraction of the usability defects encountered by beta users.*

releases that are particularly unstable and unpolished, the typical user will uncover so many problems that they will not have the time to write them down on forms. When surveyed regarding usability problems, these users will remember

TESTING REALISM

One of the appeals of beta-testing is that it not only is conducted in the real place of work but also represents testing with real work, as opposed to testing with typical test cases or scenarios. The objectives of realistic testing can be achieved in almost any test format and setting, however.

Developers, reviewers for magazines, and users of beta releases share a certain tendency to "play around" with a new system rather than putting it to the test of doing real work. A feature that seems clever and friendly when you first try out a user interface may become a major headache and an impediment to productivity after the fortieth use.

Some tests may need to have users complete not a few or a dozen tasks, but hundreds of examples. We have even found that developers can become remarkably insightful about their own software if, instead of "playing user" for a few minutes, they actually do real work on it for several hours or complete several hundred entry operations.

Field testing should also include at least some use under typical working conditions. This means testing within environments that replicate or resemble the operational context in which a system will be deployed, in terms of noise, lighting, vibration, distractions, and the like. Real-world testing may also require trying to use the system with realistic load factors, such as

- Full network traffic loads
- Nearly full hard disks
- Large or highly fragmented files
- Corrupted or incomplete datasets
- Multiple applications running
- Slow processors with limited RAM or disk space

Such load factors may have unanticipated effects on performance that can substantially reduce usability in practice.

Extensive testing under realistic conditions can be expensive and difficult to plan, which is one reason why many companies rely so much on beta-testing. On the other hand, not everything will need to be tested under all conditions when tests are planned with sufficient care based on good knowledge of expected and intended usage patterns. The impact of various load factors on infrequent or highly specialized use cases may even be substantial and yet be of little consequence in the larger scheme of things.

only the most recent ones or ones that stand out in memory for one reason or another, but these are rarely the most important problems to know about. Even worse, users often attribute usability problems to themselves and to their inexperience with a new release. Under laboratory or field test conditions, a mistake will be noted by an observer and will be tied back to some feature of the user interface. Users working on their own with a beta release will most often just try something else and continue, unaware that that their mistake was really your error in design.

TEST PROTOCOL

Usability testing is a job for trained professionals, but the basics are relatively straightforward. Testing employs users as subjects who attempt to carry out specific tasks using the system being tested. Test conductors observe, monitor, and record users in their attempts to enact assigned use cases or scenarios or in the course of performing real work. The observations and recorded results are analyzed for indications of usability problems. The testers may analyze performance in terms of speed, accuracy, number of mistakes, number of retries, and the like. They will also look for signs of confusion or hesitation on the part of the user-subjects. Perhaps the greatest appeal of usability testing is that it can yield empirical data that is both quantitative and objective.

True usability testing requires some form of working system with which users can attempt to perform assigned tasks. The system does not need to be working software in its final delivered form. Alpha and beta release versions of software are frequently the target of usability testing. Testing can also be conducted with a functional prototype or simulation in one form or another, which may be the preferred scheme since it makes possible earlier feedback from testing.

We consider the distinction between testing and inspection to be an important one. You can inspect or review a paper design or other document; you cannot test it. Without stretching meanings beyond recognition, there is no reasonable way to evaluate user performance on a stack of paper. Nevertheless, useful feedback can be obtained from users who are led through a review of a visual design or paper prototype. As discussed in Chapter 16, such joint design reviews or joint interface walk-throughs are more accurately described as forms of inspection than as testing.

Usability testing is an established discipline with established techniques, and training in the methods and procedures of usability testing is widely available. Although it does take knowledge, experience, and intelligence to carry out usability testing, it rarely requires great inventiveness.

UNDUE INFLUENCE

One of the cardinal rules of all usability testing, wherever it might be conducted, is for the testers not to influence the subjects. Developers, in particular, find it difficult not to help users with conscious or unconscious hints. It can be as subtle as a glance toward a mouse or an almost imperceptible nod as the user moves toward the right menu. It can be as blatant as saying, "Why don't you try the **View** menu?" In one test, a loud gasp was heard as the user approached a debugging control inadvertently left in the test version.

> *One of the cardinal rules of all usability testing is not to influence the subjects, but developers find it difficult not to help users with conscious or unconscious hints.*

Allowing test subjects to proceed unimpeded and uninfluenced by the developers or the testing staff is a prime motivation behind the common use of video cameras and remote observation. Putting observers in another room on the other side of a one-way mirror is good assurance that they will not deliberately or unintentionally prompt or guide the test subjects.

Keeping one's distance under field conditions can be more difficult. It takes great discipline and much practice to be able to sit beside or in the same room with a user and not cough or grunt at the wrong (or right) moment. For this reason, portable testing equipment often relies on remotely controlled video cameras to allow observers and test subjects to be in separate rooms.

In all fairness, some testing approaches rely explicitly on interaction between tester-observers and user-subjects. In some techniques, the tester functions as a coach, presenting the tasks in a piecemeal fashion and drawing out the user with questions or suggestions as the test progresses. This more active style of testing may work best with children or with users who are reluctant to undertake tasks or who are hesitant to talk about their efforts [Nielsen, 1993; Rubin, 1994].

TALK TO ME

In much usability testing, the user-subjects are encouraged to "think out loud," maintaining a running monologue about what they are doing as they are doing it. The purpose of this running commentary is to gain access to what users are thinking about and what their intentions are as they try using the system. Here is an example:

> Okay, so now I think I want to set the parameters for the controller. I don't see any tool for that, so I'll try the **System** menu. Oops, nothing there. Ah, here it is under **File**. Never would have expected that. Now I'm confused. Why are all the controls grayed out? What do I need to do first?

Without access to this kind of information, testers may find it difficult or impossible to figure out why a user became confused at a particular point or what part of a screen led to taking the wrong action. Testers may be forced to speculate or to advance conjectures that will need testing through further experiments.

Unfortunately, most people work differently when they are asked to think aloud than when they simply go about a task in whatever is their usual manner. Some subjects find it awkward and have difficulty sustaining the commentary. For some, it can become a major distraction, shifting their attention from the task to commenting upon it. Many subjects are aware of "editing" their commentary as they report it. There is often a tendency to "censor," mentally correcting mistakes of logic or reasoning without reporting them. Almost always, the tasks are completed more slowly when carried out with a running commentary than without it. Not only does this impediment invalidate some performance data, but the slower and more thoughtful pattern of use also may actually hide significant usability problems that would show up only when users are working quickly and without forethought, as they are more likely to be doing in the course of normal, everyday work.

> *Unfortunately, most people work differently when they are asked to think aloud, and many subjects are aware of "editing" their commentary as they report it.*

Thus, with or without the running commentary, important information reflecting on system usability may be lost. The *paired-subject strategy,* also sometimes called *constructive interaction,* is one way to deal with this difficulty, offering some of the benefits of a running commentary in a more natural and familiar process for completing tasks. In this approach, user-subjects are assigned to two-person teams and charged with completing the tasks together. The pairs are directed to talk over what they are doing as they do it. Typically, one person will handle the keyboard while the other deals with instructions and documentation. For many people, this is a more natural process than sustaining a monologue on their own performance. It has proved particularly effective with subjects from certain cultures that do not encourage talking about or drawing attention to oneself. However, the paired-subject strategy may slow performance even more than having a single subject think aloud, and it requires twice as many subjects for the same number of tests.

Another innovative approach to this problem is the *deferred-reflection* strategy we developed based on previously unreported work first done at Boston State Hospital. In the course of refining techniques for training psychotherapists, it was found that the recall of earlier thoughts while viewing videotapes was facilitated whenever a person's own face was visible on the screen. Both the richness of the narrative and its accuracy when checked against verifiable information were enhanced.

To apply this strategy to usability testing, it is only necessary to videotape the subject's face along with a view of the monitor and keyboard during a test session. Two video cameras or camcorders can be used for this purpose, or an adjustable mirror can be placed so that the subject's face is within view of a single camera aimed over the subject's shoulder at the screen and keyboard. In the deferred-reflection technique, subjects work at their own pace and in their own styles, without having to maintain a running commentary. In this way, testing sessions more closely approximate normal usage.

> *Using deferred reflection, subjects can work at their own pace and in their own styles, but the later recall of their "inner dialogue" is excellent.*

After a session is over, the videotape is reviewed and analyzed by the testers, who look for signs of puzzlement, hesitation, and the like. Selected segments are then shown to the subject, who is asked, "What were you thinking just then?" or "What happened right there? Do you recall what you were trying to do at that point?" Recall of the subject's "inner dialogue" is excellent using this technique.

BEFORE AND AFTER

What is said to subjects at the outset of testing and following each session can shape the validity and value of the results of usability testing. Users should be made to feel welcome and comfortable in the test setting and, as appropriate to the test plan, should be familiarized with the equipment and procedures. It is most important to make clear to all subjects that they are not being tested or evaluated; it is the system that is being tested, and the subjects are considered as collaborators in exposing weaknesses and enhancing the quality of the product. Often, the setup itself can be intimidating and will make some users feel anxious and self-conscious. In some situations, failing to put subjects at ease could invalidate some of the findings.

> *Particularly for internal clients, building and maintaining good relationships with end users should always be a subtext of the post-testing debriefings.*

Most testing plans include a debriefing or post-test interview with each subject. Subjects are typically thanked for their participation and reassured about their performance.

In the debriefing, subjects are usually asked for feedback, reactions, and suggestions about the tests and about the design being tested. Asking for their input and ideas usually makes users feel better about their participation. Particularly for internal clients within the same company as the developers, building and maintaining good relationships with end users should always be a subtext of these dialogues.

Often, users will have very specific criticisms or complaints about the user interface, and some may even say how they think it should be designed. All such feedback should be reviewed and considered carefully, even if it may be of relatively little value in many cases. Occasionally, a strong trend or consistent pattern emerges from the post-test feedback that will augment or qualify the test results. Users may also volunteer additional insights into the sources of confusion or the causes of mistakes during the test session that can save considerable detective work on the part of testers. Just as in collaborative usability inspections, users are treated as a source of potentially useful input but are not expected to be designers, nor is any one user regarded as an authority on the user experience.

MEASURED PERFORMANCE

Performance metrics quantify and summarize important aspects of actual usage either under controlled laboratory conditions or within an ordinary work environment. Performance metrics provide convenient ways to summarize findings from usability testing. Through repeated and consistent use of appropriate standard metrics, varied products and projects can be compared, and process improvement over time can be gauged.

The quantitative approach to usability testing advocated by Nigel Bevan [Bevan and Macleod, 1994] in England is both simple and effective. This approach is based on a suite of summary performance metrics. The choice of measures and the relative importance attached to any given measure depends on the established goals of the usability tests. This collection includes six measures of performance:

1. Completeness
2. Correctness
3. Effectiveness
4. Efficiency
5. Proficiency
6. Productiveness

For consistency with the predictive design metrics introduced in Chapter 17, we define these metrics as percentages.

Complex, extended test scenarios with vague criteria for correctness or completion will require subjective judgments that can erode the objectivity of any conclusions.

The metrics compute aspects of the actual performance of each test subject using the system being tested. The quality of the system is estimated by the average scores over a number of subjects. The metrics require that it be possible for the testers to determine the extent to which assigned scenarios were completed and whether or not they were performed correctly. This requirement is easy to meet when the test protocol is based on a series of small tasks of comparable difficulty. Complex, extended scenarios with vague criteria for correctness or completion will require subjective judgments on the part of the testers, which can erode the objectivity of any conclusions.

Completeness is simply the percent of total assigned work completed within the allotted time. We would expect that software that is easier to use would enable users to accomplish more. *Correctness* is the percent of completed work that was correct, and *Effectiveness* is correctly completed work as a percent of total work—namely, completeness times correctness. In general, one wants to improve both the amount of work completed by users of a system and the accuracy of that work. However, for some applications, lower levels of productivity may be acceptable if errors can be reduced.

Efficiency is defined here as Effectiveness per unit time—in other words, the percent correctly completed per unit time. Efficiency corrects for differences in time spent in different test sessions by different subjects, such as if some subjects using an improved version of a system should finish early or if field tests do not always allot the same time to each subject.

In order to compute what Bevan terms *Proficiency*, it is necessary for at least one subject to gain enough practice to become highly proficient at the assigned tasks. This defines an expert level of Efficiency, which may often be a measure that is of interest in itself. Proficiency is then defined as the average level of Efficiency expressed as a percentage of the Efficiency of the expert user. This performance metric evaluates the difference between novice performance and expert performance. It may also be indicative of the steepness of the learning curve to be mounted as users progress from novice to expert usage.

One way to speed and simplify the calculation of Proficiency is to train some test subjects to expert-level performance on only a small subset of representative tasks. Selected test subjects practice these tasks until performance begins to level out, indicating that performance has peaked. Their trained performance on these tasks can then be compared to the average for untrained subjects.

Although no single measure has much chance of capturing usability in a truly global sense, one metric devised by Bevan, the *Productive Period* or *Productiveness*, is quite sensitive to a variety of aspects of user interface design that can influence usability. Productiveness is simply defined as the percent of total subject time spent productively:

$$\text{Productiveness} = 100 \cdot \frac{T_{total} - T_{unproductive}}{T_{total}}$$

where

$$T_{total} = \text{total time spent on tasks}$$
$$T_{unproductive} = \text{unproductive time}$$

Unproductive time includes all time spent seeking help from test administrators or others, using the help system or referring to documentation, and searching or scanning for needed features or functionality. It also includes time spent undoing actions or redoing actions that had been canceled, negated, or rejected earlier. For a finished product in which software performance is realistic, unproductive time may include time waiting for results or for the completion of software operations.

> *Productiveness, a useful one-number index to get a quick handle on overall quality, is quite sensitive to a variety of aspects of user interface design that can influence usability.*

Productiveness is particularly sensitive to problems in visibility and structure. Violations of the Visibility Principle will lead to more time spent searching or scanning for features. Failure to adhere to the Structure Principle will be reflected in greater search time as well as more false starts needing to be corrected or undone. Poorly designed help will also lower Productiveness. So long as improvements are not achieved at the expense of Efficiency, Productiveness can be a useful one-number index of approximate usability. It can be used to get a quick handle on the overall quality of a design or to track the impact of changes over time.

Various other quantities of interest can be measured. For example, where retention or rememberability is of particular interest, the number of features remembered or correctly described during a post-session debriefing could be taken as an indication of system quality. Alternatively, a questionnaire administered at a later date could be scored for correct recall. Subjective evaluations, such as the preference measures discussed in the previous chapter, are also often coupled with usability testing.

TESTING TACTICS

The process of usability testing, whether conducted in the field or restricted to a testing laboratory, requires essentially the same activities in much the same sequence:

1. Define the goals and objectives of the test.
2. Specify a suitable setting and framework for testing.
3. Determine observational criteria and factors to be measured.
4. Specify or clarify the nature of the targeted user population.
5. Devise test cases or task scenarios suited to the target users and the testing objectives.
6. Recruit representative test subjects.
7. Conduct tests with observation and measurement.
8. Summarize and analyze results.

9. Formulate conclusions and recommendations.

10. Compile and communicate findings.

Some of these activities are nearly self-explanatory, but some warrant further discussion.

PLANNING GOALS

Good usability testers are dedicated detectives, determined to ferret out the lurking problems. The best may even set out to break the products they test. One of our clients, facing mounting negative reports from the marketplace, submitted a specialized software development tool to the company's internal usability labs for comparison with competing tools. The lead tester created a brilliantly targeted scenario for the tests that particularly highlighted some of the major weaknesses in the product. While academics or research-oriented usability professionals might question this approach or consider it biased, it was, in practice, a highly successful test program because it exposed so many crucial usability problems in the product and stirred the software development group to action.

The goals of usability testing need to be set realistically. Usability testing, as typically conducted, can find problems only within the framework established by the basic user interface architecture. It can identify points at which users become confused or dialogues that require too many steps, for example, but it can seldom reveal that the thinking of the designers was completely off target.

> *Usability testing can find problems only within the framework of the basic user interface architecture; it seldom reveals where the thinking of the designers was completely off target.*

For example, the tool vendor mentioned earlier, being very serious about improving the usability of its software, not only sent the system off to a usability lab for testing but also retained consultants to conduct an expert evaluation of the same software. The testers at the lab did identify an assortment of specific problems, many of which were also cited in the report from the experts, but the testing failed to recognize significant architectural problems requiring substantial reorganization of the user interface.

Whenever practical, the goals of testing should be translated into quantitative terms and objective measures. For example, a design team may have set out to create an instructive interface that obviates the need for tutorials or elaborate help files. Among the quantities to measure might be the number of requests for help, references to the draft manual, and accesses to the help system. An observational goal might be to note the subtasks and parts of the interface associated with the most help requests or references.

SELECTED SUBJECTS

Effective usability testing hinges not only on the skill of the testers but also on the choice of the subjects. On some measures, average performance of the top quarter of subjects may be double that of the bottom, and the best subjects may do ten times better than the worst [Egan, 1988].

The choice of test subjects is guided by two general rules: representation and range. Subjects should be representative of the actual population of users for which the system is targeted. Subjects should also include a range of abilities and experience typical of the variance among targeted users. Even where only a few tests will be run, the value of testing can be enhanced by careful selection of a mix of subjects.

The structured user role model simplifies the selection of test subjects because it identifies classes of users and characteristics of typical role incumbents.

Groups practicing usage-centered design are at an advantage in selecting test subjects because the structured user role model identifies classes of users and characteristics of typical role incumbents. At a minimum, test subjects should include representatives of the various levels of platform, domain, or system knowledge anticipated in the targeted roles.

The test plan should clearly specify the target population and how representative subjects will be chosen. A new productivity tool aimed at professional programmers need not be tested with new computer users. Software that will be deployed on only one platform may not need to be tested with users who are unfamiliar with that platform.

Be prepared to pay subjects enough to motivate them to keep appointments and to participate fully and enthusiastically. For the vast majority of tests, fewer than a dozen subjects will suffice, and the total fees paid, even if generous, will be small change compared to the full testing budget. One no-show that wastes the time of the entire usability staff and leaves the facilities idle will cancel out any savings from scrimping on subject fees.

Significant problems may emerge only after tasks are repeated a large number of times or only among highly practiced users.

While most subjects will be newcomers to the system being tested, for most systems it is highly desirable to conduct tests with at least one subject who gets extensive exposure and practice with the system. Significant problems may emerge only after tasks are repeated a large number of times or only among highly practiced users. (See sidebar, Testing Realism.) The proficiency profile of the structured role model should be a guide. There is little or no justification for testing a public information kiosk with trained users, while the interface of the search engine and display for the technical database used by telephone technical support operators may require testing with numerous users who are given extensive practice.

TEST CASES

Constructing appropriate tasks for usability testing is another art form to be mastered for effective usability testing. Like the scenarios employed in collaborative usability inspections, usability test cases are readily derived from use cases. Composite scenarios are formed from collections of use cases selected to represent user intentions appropriate to the defined testing goals and to provide sufficient coverage within these goals. For example, tests of a keyboard extender application targeted for users in multinational firms might focus on the **CasualTranslator** role. The initial list of candidate use cases might include **insertingSymbol**, **insertingPhrase**, and **reviewingShortcuts**. Scenarios are then constructed to include enactments of all the chosen use cases. Testing is more effective when tasks are both representative and relatively realistic, or at least plausible. For this example, the test might involve three tasks:

> *Like the scenarios employed in collaborative usability inspections, usability test cases are readily derived from use cases.*

1. Typing a memo that includes several phrases in a few different languages with accented characters
2. Looking up the keyboard shortcuts for all the special characters used in the German language
3. Attempting to type a memo in German by using the keyboard shortcuts

Usability test cases are often longer or more elaborate scenarios than those used for inspections, which must be short enough to allow extra time for defect identification and interpretation. Alternatively, shorter tasks may be repeated several times during a single test session, an approach especially appropriate for repetitive tasks on production systems, such as order entry or claims processing. Tasks will usually need to be adjusted to make effective use of the test time allotted. The expectation is that the average subject will be able to complete the task or tasks during the session. This usually requires some actual pretesting followed by rewriting of test scenarios.

Constructing usage-centered tasks for usability tests is a multistep process:

1. Identify targeted user roles.
2. Select supporting use cases.
3. Combine use cases into realistic or plausible scenarios.
4. Expand into fully enacted form with the user interface under test.

5. Revise and express as a sequence of subgoals or steps for the user, leaving the enactment open.

Generating plausible scenarios from collections of use cases is one place where the art comes into testing. These composites are then expanded into enacted form to verify coverage and the exact features of the user interface that will be exercised. Occasionally, the trial enactment may uncover a step in the scenario that cannot be accomplished, either because of a design failure or because a partial prototype does not support the needed feature. The fully enacted form is information for the test designers, not the test subjects. Test subjects might be instructed to locate a particular folder and open it to inspect its contents, verifying whether or not it contains a specified fax file; subjects would not ordinarily be given a scenario that directed them to double-click on the little picture at the bottom of the list in the upper right corner of the screen.

WHY TEST, WHY NOT

Because usability testing plays such a prominent role in the business of software development and because our view is not uncritically positive, it is worth summarizing the issues. Here is an overview of many of the pluses and minuses, the payoffs and the problems in usability testing.

Usability testing is best used for specific purposes and with specific goals in mind. Handing over a system with a vague request to "see how usable it is" will be unlikely to yield highly useful information or to be very cost-effective. Because it is difficult or impossible for usability tests even to approach full coverage of the user interface of most systems, only a small fraction of the usability defects in a system are likely to be uncovered by usability testing. For this reason, test cases must be constructed to investigate identified issues and evaluate selected portions of the user interface.

Because only a small fraction of the usability defects in a system are likely to be uncovered by usability testing, the most effective tests are aimed at answering specific questions.

Usability testing has proved to be particularly effective at uncovering subtle or unanticipated defects, the kind of defects that tend to be overlooked in inspections or missed even by experts. In general, usability testing reveals fewer usability problems than well-conducted collaborative inspections or competent expert evaluations, but the defects uncovered during testing tend to be more severe or of a more serious nature.

The most effective usability tests are aimed at answering specific questions, such as whether a novel user interface feature will work as anticipated. Testing is also appropriate for comparing alternative design solutions for the same problem.

It can be useful on both practical and political grounds for resolving subtle and highly contentious disputes about design details.

For example, one design team wrestled with how best to increase the efficiency of a data entry process. They concluded that selected use of drop-down combo boxes could potentially reduce the amount of typing, but some members of the team argued that the standard default behavior of such a widget could actually slow down a clerk working from a keyboard. Normally, once a drop-down list receives focus, a separate user action is required to open it prior to making a selection. A nonstandard component that opened immediately on receipt of focus might save keystrokes and speed processing. Other team members maintained that this behavior would be sufficiently disruptive to slow down operation overall. A targeted usability test with a working prototype could resolve this issue fairly quickly and at far less cost than releasing the wrong version only to have to backpedal later.

As already highlighted in Chapter 16, the primary downside of testing is the need for a working system or functioning prototype of some sort or another to test. For this reason, usability testing tends to come relative late in the software development life cycle or after a considerable investment of resources has been made to construct the working prototype or system. The process of designing tests, conducting them, then analyzing and interpreting results, and reducing these to recommendations can be time-consuming. By the time usability tests are completed, there may be little time for redesign and implementation.

Often, the most serious defects are discovered to be virtually hard-coded or embedded fairly deeply in the structure of code, and changing them is found to be too costly at such a late stage. Usability testing conducted on alpha or beta releases can come at particularly critical points in the overall release cycle when delays are likely to be costly. Although the results of limited and highly focused testing can sometimes be turned around in a matter of days by crack labs, delays of a week or more are common.

Usability testing is not as effective for finding some kinds of usability problems or addressing certain usability questions. Subjects are almost invariably relatively naïve or inexperienced. Testing for problems encountered at expert levels of usage is possible but difficult.

Usability tests are also better at finding local or isolated usability defects than at recognizing fundamental flaws in the overall architecture or organization of the user interface. Test cases are limited and are constructed within the assumptions framed by a design and by the questions of the designers. Without a comparison system to test in parallel, it can be difficult or impossible to recognize from tests that a user interface architecture is essentially backwards or inside-out in its organization. Instead, testers will report the large number of small and localized problems that stem from fundamental flaws. Fundamental architectural issues are best addressed by design and explored through abstract modeling. In our experience, expert evaluators are far more likely than usability testers to identify problems in the architecture or overall organization of user interfaces.

Usability testing is at its best when it is coupled with usage-centered design. Indeed, to get the most value from usability tests, the design should be almost right going into the testing process. When the design and architecture of the user interface are sound, usability tests can focus on answering lingering questions and looking for localized hidden "gotchas," which is what testing does best.

> *Usability testing can be an important and useful tool in service of enhanced usability, but it is never sufficient in itself to deliver highly usable software.*

Our own view of usability testing is that it can be an important and useful tool in service of enhanced usability so long as it is recognized as only one specialized tool among many. Particularly in the absence of good models or methods for design, usability testing is indispensable. Testing, however, is never sufficient in itself to deliver highly usable software.

ORGANIZING AND MANAGING THE PROCESS

19

CODE AND YOU'RE DONE:
Implementing Interfaces

OBJECTS AND INTERFACES

Programmers love to program, which is fortunate—after all, you cannot invoice customers with the paper prototype for a billing system anymore than you can drive the engineering blueprints for an automobile. Designs are not ends in themselves, but routes to superior software solutions. Even an excellent plan can be spoiled by inept execution, however. Construction techniques matter no less when it comes to software than in building airframes or office buildings. In this chapter, we will explore some of the issues in implementing usage-centered designs.

How does one implement good usage-centered designs? What is the best, most effective internal architecture for the code that supports the user interface? The best architecture for the user interface is, as we have argued, one closely molded to the structure of whatever work is to be supported. The best internal architecture for the programming behind the scenes is one that is, in turn, simply and systematically connected with the externally defined needs. It is integrated with the user interface architecture, although separable from it. It contains the least amount of code

> *The best internal program architecture is simply and systematically connected with externally defined needs and integrated with the user interface architecture yet separable from it.*

that will suffice for the fullest support of user requirements. Internal components and interface components are easily related to one another, and there are no superfluous components at or behind the interface. How does one achieve this systematic integration? This is where object-oriented development enters.

It is not our intention to explain object-orientation or get into detail about object-oriented design techniques. For those unfamiliar with the subject or wishing a deeper understanding, many excellent books are available. Among these, one that we might particularly recommend is the concise and practical introduction by Page-Jones [1995]. What we want to do here is explore some connections between object-orientation and good usage-centered design.

What has object-orientation to do with user interface design, much less software usability? If we look at the literature of object technology, we might conclude that it has little if anything to do with these. Although some products have been laying claim to object-oriented user interfaces for decades, the world of objects has paid scant attention to users, usability, or user interfaces other than to offer libraries of graphical user interface classes to programmers. For example, of more than 6,000 pages of text in 15 popular books on object-orientation, only 161 pages deals with users, usability, or user interfaces, and most of that is found in just a few books [Constantine, 1996c].

Object-orientation promises many things, among them a seamless software development process that uses a consistent vocabulary and a single set of concepts throughout, beginning with the outside world, the so-called real world of the problem domain, and proceeding smoothly and without discontinuity all the way through to code. An important term or concept that might appear in the requirements specification will be reflected in the analyses and design models and will even be found in the code itself. The classes of objects and use cases comprising the problem definition will structure the internal software architecture, shape the user interface, and organize the code. Anyway, this is the fantasy. The reality is, of course, always a rougher road with more gaps and detours [Constantine, 1997d].

> *Object-oriented software construction has become one of the genuine success stories of modern software engineering.*

True converts and charismatic gurus of methods have hailed object-orientation as a programming panacea, the salvation of software development, and the answer to the "software crisis." Hype and hope aside, the simple truth is that object-oriented software construction has become one of the genuine success stories of modern software engineering. Not everyone is a convert, of course. Good work can still be created using classic structured methods, and junk continues to be cranked out under the newly raised banner of object-oriented analysis, design, and programming. Nevertheless, as a rule, object-orientation is a Good Idea, more beneficial than harmful, more utilitarian than irrelevant.

OBJECTS FOR IMPLEMENTATION

Whatever the elaborate philosophical and pedagogical raiment in which the object-oriented programming paradigm may sometimes be dressed for sale, the naked truth about objects is really remarkably simple. **Objects**—strictly speaking, object **classes**—are convenient chunks of programming. Objects allow programmers to package into a single, comprehensible collection, a number of operations along with the data upon which these operate. Well-conceived object classes are powerful, readily comprehended components that bring together only the most strongly associated bits of function and data [Constantine, 1995d]. Because well-designed objects effectively hide their inner details and support simplified use through messages from the outside, they promote component-based construction and reuse. Naturally, success in software construction through reusable components depends on much

> *Object-oriented development based on reusable objects can be a major contributor to user interface consistency.*

more than just the choice of language or programming model [Constantine, 1992g], but having the right model for the programming infrastructure definitely helps.

Software objects can be first-rate packages for implementing good user interfaces. Because they hide implementation by encapsulating data with associated operations, objects become a convenient package for facilitating reuse of both interface and internal components. To the extent that object-oriented programming is used effectively for component-based development, it can be a major contributor to user interface consistency through the Reuse Principle. Reuse is, we maintain, far and away the most effective route to achieving consistency in user interfaces.

OBJECT-ORIENTED USER INTERFACES

You will no doubt encounter the term, so it is probably necessary to say something about *object-oriented user interfaces*. What is an object-oriented user interface? Some have suggested that it means any user interface implemented with object-oriented programming. Object-oriented programming, however, merely describes the internal construction techniques, and these are, or should be, invisible to the user anyway. Others have claimed that object-oriented user interfaces refer to point-and-click, drag-and-drop on-screen manipulation of objects, but these interaction idioms are just the standard fare of all modern graphical user interfaces. Some even associate object-oriented interfaces with representations of physical objects from the real world on the interface, but we already know that the appropriate use of icons and other graphics has to be suited to the intended communication between system and user and guided by the tasks performed, not predetermined by the programming paradigm [Constantine, 1993c].

One detailed definition has been offered based on three characteristics of object-oriented user interfaces [Collins, 1995]:

1. Users perceive and act on objects.
2. Users classify objects based on how they behave.
3. All the interface objects fit together into a coherent overall conceptual model.

The first characteristic is about users, not user interfaces, and about aspects of users that may well be hard-coded in the human brain, at least when it comes to ordinary everyday objects. If we are considering software objects, then we are only characterizing software developers working within an object-oriented framework. The second characteristic, also about users and not interfaces, is almost certainly not true across the board. People classify ordinary objects in terms of many features and factors other than behavior. You might, for example, observe that all politicians seem to act pretty much alike but that you have a friend who *looks* like Bill Clinton. As to the third so-called characteristic of object-oriented user interfaces, by this point in the book, it should be obvious that it merely describes a well-organized user interface of any variety that fits the work and conforms to the Structure Principle.

SUPERFICIAL OBJECTS

Yet another view of object-oriented user interfaces is that they bring to the surface of the interface the constructs and interrelationships of the object-oriented paradigm, presenting users with objects and class hierarchies and with methods and messages as the medium of exchange between users and systems. This view is, perhaps, more defensible as being strictly object-oriented, but it may also lead to some unfortunate designs. In its most rigorous interpretation, users would be forced to interact with an object-oriented interface by moving little messages around from object to object on the screen, which is unlikely, in most applications, to have much to do with effective support of the relevant use cases [Constantine, 1997c].

Ordinary users would never describe what they do with a graphical user interface as "sending messages to objects."

An obsessive preoccupation with making everything object-oriented can lead the user interface designer astray. For one thing, work is behavior. It is made up of actions, steps, and activities interconnected by other activities. At its heart, work is operations, not objects, which is one reason why use cases are so effective for modeling work.

THIS DO!

Object orientation is sometimes associated with a distinction in the grammar governing the interaction between users and user interfaces. Old-school command-line interfaces most often employed an action-object grammar. A command (action) was followed by a series of arguments or parameters specifying the target (object) of the operation and the conditions or qualifications: Copy this to there, filter this by that, and so forth. In the action-object grammar, the user first selects an operation such as an application or a tool, and then selects an object to act upon such as a file or a shape. The object paradigm, as well as the much-touted document-centered design model, favors the reverse order: An object is selected, and then the operation is chosen.

The same dichotomy in thinking is reflected in many parts of graphical user interfaces and in common patterns of usage. Many user interfaces utilize both action-object and object-action metaphors for different tasks. For example, a drawing program may expect the user to choose the fill tool and then apply it to part of the drawing but to select an image object before picking up a cropping tool.

Different users may have different preferences for working, or the same user may employ different patterns at different times. For example, one can launch an application and then use **File|Open** to pull in working documents, or one can first select files and double-click to launch the associated application. In our observations, many regular computer users do some of each, depending on what is convenient at the moment or what fits best with their thinking about the problem at hand.

A preference for one grammar over another may be dependent on native language and even culture. In English, we say, "Copy this page!" but "This page copy!" rings false in the ear. To speakers of languages like German, where verbs are often deferred to the very end of sentences, the object-action grammar might well feel more natural in a wider variety of contexts.

Tools and operators that work either way, depending on the temperament or technique of the user, are often the best solution. It is stubborn code that forces the user to select a drawing object before applying a new line style, for example. Flexible, tolerant interfaces would allow the user to select the line style and then click on an object, or vice versa. Only careful investigation can confirm whether such ambidextrous operation makes sense in your user interface problem, but our observations reveal that even experienced users of production tools inadvertently attempt to interact using the "wrong" grammar with surprising frequency.

Object class models can be useful for representing a domain of application but not usually for the work to be carried out within that domain.

Ordinary users would never describe what they do with a graphical user interface as "sending messages to objects." Only a programmer whose mind has been warped by too many years of small talk with object-oriented programming systems would conceive of interaction in this way. Users do not send messages to objects. They do things with and to those objects by means of various interaction idioms. (See sidebar, This Do!)

Nevertheless, it is legitimate to wonder whether it ever makes sense to expose any of the machinery of object technology at the interface with end users. For the most part, inside-out design, when the logic and structure of the program show on the user interface, is a sign of failure. Outside-in design, by contrast, means that the internal components and their external manifestations both reflect genuine user needs rather than programming preferences.

Some object-oriented constructs may serve as inspiration for new visual components, however. One example that may sometimes be useful is the concept of "factory objects." A factory object is one that **instantiates** other objects of another

FIGURE 19-1 *Factory object for new notes, software Post-its.*
(3M)

class when sent the appropriate message. Visual components that when clicked or swiped create new instances of a class might be a useful addition to the repertoire of visual design concepts. For example, a "pad" of "software notes," as illustrated in Figure 19-1, can be clicked to open a blank note ready for completion and placement on the desktop or within a document. Such a component may be consistent with the trend toward document-centered user interfaces, but not everyone will be sold on the power of objects. To the user, there may be little difference between dragging-and-dropping from a factory object and selecting **F̲ile|N̲ew** or even just typing **Ctrl+N** to get a new instance of a class.

OBJECT ARCHITECTURE

Object technology also supports separating the interface from supporting internals while keeping them interrelated through an appropriate "object glue." The key to this "separate-but-integrated" implementation architecture is the use of collections of objects separated by function into interface objects, control objects, and entity objects. Such distinctions are now referred to as **object stereotypes**. Interface, entity, and control stereotypes were introduced by Jacobson and colleagues [Jacobson et al., 1992]; other stereotypes have been described by Wirfs-Brock [1994].

> *Object technology supports separating the interface from supporting internals while keeping them interrelated through an appropriate "glue" composed of control objects.*

Interface objects model the interfaces and interactions with users, mediating between users and the software. They encapsulate capability that is specific to particular interface devices or to particular kinds of users. **Entity objects**, also sometimes referred to as **domain objects**, model the tangible or conceptual objects within the application domain, holding the information retained by the system over time. **Control objects** model complex behavior that involves multiple objects, especially behavior not naturally tied to any other objects in isolation. They are especially useful for encapsulating policies or procedures spanning many objects or for managing the interaction among other objects.

When first introduced, control objects were controversial. Purists saw the use of components of this ilk as a corruption of object-oriented concepts by the intrusion of outdated and superceded notions from procedural programming and classic structured design. The important issue, however, is not the purity of the paradigm or of the motives, but the simplicity of models and the resulting code. Control objects and other specialized object stereotypes may look more like functions or collections of functions than like well-conceived objects, but, used appropriately, they can simplify software. Fortunately, sanity has slowly prevailed, and fewer and fewer fanatics rail against the use of "procedurelike" objects.

The separation of responsibilities into three groups of objects proposed by Jacobson bears a close resemblance to another well-established architecture: the model-view-controller pattern [Krasner and Pope, 1988]. Both concepts serve to separate internal information (the model, the entity objects) from the various ways in which this information may be presented or manipulated (the view, interface objects), with separate responsibilities for coordinating the relationship (the controller, control objects).

Object stereotypes (and the model-view-controller architecture) help to localize the impact of any subsequent changes in the design and implementation. The appearance and behavior of the user interface can be changed without having to change the underlying data model. Changes in the data model can be restricted to only the affected parts of the interface. Changes in the relationship between presentation at the surface and the underlying data can be made within control objects. This, of course, is the ideal situation; in practice, a good architecture, at best, reduces the odds of any given change being reflected in too many different places within the code.

> *Object stereotypes (and the model-view-controller architecture) help to localize the impact of any subsequent changes.*

Use cases typically include elements related to all three kinds of stereotypes, so the capability represented by use cases has to be distributed among various objects. The partitioning of the bits and pieces of use cases into object stereotypes proceeds in steps. Functionality that is directly dependent on the environment and that is specific to the user interface or to users is first allocated to interface objects. Anything dealing with information storage and handling or with the fundamental classes or entities of the application domain that does not naturally fit into interface objects is allocated to entity objects. Functionality that is specific to only one or a few use cases, that requires communication or coordination with multiple objects, and that does not fit naturally into entity objects or interface objects is placed within control objects. In other words, the first preference is to stuff things into interface or entity objects, using control objects only where there is no natural fit with either of the other stereotypes. In this way, control objects are not unnecessarily proliferated.

ACCELERATED DEVELOPMENT

Modern software development is not only shaped by technology but also driven by the need for speed or at least by the prevailing perception that the pace of change keeps escalating [Constantine, 1994d; 1995e]. To meet the pressure to deliver more in less time and, often, with fewer resources, various streamlined software development life cycles (SDLCs) have come into popularity as models for accelerated software development. Rapid application development (RAD), rapid product deployment, time-boxed development, and "good enough" software development have all been proposed and tried.

The common feature of most accelerated development strategies is a spiral life cycle model, whereby development cycles through a series of activities or phases, converging on the delivery of a working system. With each complete cycle, a more expanded or refined version of the software is delivered, but even the first completed system is usable. In such an iterative environment, use cases can be a formidable aid to organizing the delivery cycle and ensuring that maximal value is delivered at each successive iteration.

CONCENTRIC CONSTRUCTION

Essential use cases can serve many functions, not only in organizing the user interface and even the internal architecture but also in organizing the implementation process itself. Use cases become the appropriate unit of product delivery because each use case represents one useful piece of work, one meaningful task to some users. Phasing the construction and delivery of systems based on use cases and collections of related use cases assures that users receive the most useful collection of features and capabilities with each release. Basing versions and releases on features rather than use cases can result in systems that incorporate superfluous, little used, or unused features or, worse, can lead to delivering a system where some use cases of interest cannot be enacted because of missing features.

Using essential use cases, it is fairly simple to stage the implementation process, starting with a central core of basic capability and expanding outward.

If the relative priority of use cases has already been established earlier through Joint Essential Modeling or otherwise, it is fairly simple to stage the implementation process, starting with a central core of the basic and most important capability and expanding outward from there. This kind of staging can be used for planning successive releases or as insurance against project overrun or premature cutoff of resources. Concentric construction from core capability outward ensures that, whenever development is stopped, the last working version is maximally likely to be usable.

Multiple versions of the same system are also readily configured based on use cases. The "lite" edition of a software package may cover a fully usable subset of use cases, while the "professional" edition might incorporate various extension cases as well as advanced uses. This is often the most economical way to realize multiple versions since the deluxe variation is just a superset of the economy system. Less typically, the same use cases may be implemented in basic and deluxe forms within different versions. For some products, this may have the greatest appeal to users and in the marketplace, but it should be recognized as needing more programming than versions based on subsets of use cases.

Thinking of versions and editions based on use cases and user roles helps developers and marketing folks to target different user populations and markets more successively. Use case analysis can avoid serious misallocation of features and resources to successive releases or to low-cost and expanded versions. For example, one manufacturer of equipment for factory automation wanted two versions of a programming system for certain parts of the control systems. A stripped-down version of the software was to be offered at a reduced price to purchasers of the least expensive control systems. One approach considered was to provide all the functionality of the advanced software, supporting the same range of equipment, for example, but with a more primitive user interface that required users to program in what was roughly the equivalent of raw machine language. Looking more closely at the low-end users made it obvious that they were precisely the ones who most needed the more advanced programming facilities that would simplify the design and setup of their programs. A better marketing strategy was made possible by providing both versions with the same more advanced programming interface, but restricting the low-cost version to supporting only the less expensive target equipment and leaving out some functionality. In this way, both versions had appealing interfaces, yet the advanced version was clearly a superset with added capability to justify its higher price tag.

ARCHITECTURAL ITERATION

Entropy is the enemy of all software. After a certain point, as software continues to be revised, refined and expanded, the code inevitably becomes more convoluted, more chaotic, and more complex. The forces of entropy that plague all programming are no less powerful when software is developed through rapid iterative prototyping or any other form of successive refinement.

At the outset of all software projects, the developers must make some basic assumptions and establish an overall framework within which to construct the system. To begin with, the basic internal architecture, the core assumptions on which the program is organized, may be sound and well suited to the problem being solved. In iterative development, the problem being solved is, of course, the first version or the first release of the software. Smart developers will draw on their experience and their best crystal-gazing powers of projection to try to anticipate evolving needs. They will establish a sound data model and a robust object architecture, make a good partitioning among application layers, devise a versatile messaging structure, and invent the necessary internal languages and protocols that might be needed to support the immediate and subsequent programming needs.

Nevertheless, with each successive round of iterative refinement, as the application grows and the requirements grow and change, those early assumptions will fit less and less well. It will become harder and harder to shoehorn in new features, to accommodate new data types, or to find a place to plug in new components. Eventually, all evolving software—which is all software—reaches a point of brittleness and instability where almost any attempt to revise or even correct one part of the software brings the whole thing crashing down, where nobody even knows the complete structure anymore. To remain responsive to user needs and competitive in the marketplace, it becomes necessary to start over, with a new architecture and fresh code.

Is it possible, if not to repeal, at least to suspend temporarily the laws of entropy and delay the onset of architectural collapse? It will not do to require that developers must anticipate in more depth and detail in order to arrive at the best long-term solution at the outset of the first iteration. We would once again risk inflicting upon programmers that endemic affliction of old-style waterfall development life cycles, the dread disease of analysis paralysis.

> *In architectural iteration, the basic software architecture is reviewed and revised on each round to ensure its continued viability.*

The solution, we believe, is to refine, repeatedly, the architecture along with the code that is based upon it [Constantine, 1996a]. In this approach, which might be termed *architectural iteration*, on each round of refinements, the basic architecture of the software is reviewed to ascertain its continued viability. The developers reexamine a variety of basic architectural decisions, such as the structure of the code, the partitioning into packages, the organization of the database, the form of internal messaging, the class hierarchy and use of foundation classes, communication techniques, client-server partitioning, and distribution of methods among classes.

Wherever the developers call into question the continued validity and viability of earlier architectural choices, they will then need to consider possible redesign and revision. Thus, the job for the next release cycle or round of iterative refinement consists of two parts: In addition to those corrections and functional enhancements that would otherwise be part of the project, any requisite refinements to the architecture are included. Perhaps some additions need to be made to the reusable component library, and some existing code needs to be updated to make use of the new components. Perhaps the internal file format for preserving user preference profiles needs to be elaborated. Perhaps the partitioning among client software, middleware, and server should be refined. Perhaps some new entity classes or data types ought to be introduced and reflected in the code. Whatever is indicated as of immediate and long-term value is added into the pot for design and implementation. Although this adds to the effort in the next development iteration, it ultimately makes the software more robust and more amenable to further refinement, thus reducing the cost of future iterations.

Architectural iteration will not lead to eternal software, but it can stave off the day of reckoning when the underlying assumptions fail and the foundation crumbles. Legacy systems have been kept pliant and efficient by architectural iteration. Instead of having to be rebuilt from scratch every two or three years, software products may continue to be successfully refined and polished into contemporary competitiveness for many more years.

VISUAL DEVELOPMENT OF VISUAL DESIGNS

In recent years, a revolution has taken place in the tools and techniques used for developing software. Revolutions are common in software. They are being declared at every turn by journalists, methodologists, and public relations people. On closer examination, especially in retrospect, most such "revolutions" or "paradigm shifts" turn out to be little more than old wine with new labels or a minor reformulation in the mix of vintages. Scholars might argue the details yet agree that the genuinely revolutionary article is rare—the advent of high-level languages, the structural revolution that gave us structured programming and structured analysis and design, and the object-oriented paradigm, to name some of the pivotal ones.

The emergence of visual development environments is one of the most creative and energetic strands in the skein of current development practices and products [Constantine, 1995c]. *Visual development* refers not only to the technology, the software development tools

> *Visual development environments are among the most creative and energetic strands in the skein of current development practices and products.*

themselves, but also to the way in which these tools are used. Just as nail guns and power handsaws do not change carpentry but do change how carpentry is carried out, visual development tools lead to a new style of software development and to new development processes.

The tools used to construct user interfaces matter a great deal. Primitive tools not only lead to clumsy interfaces but also encourages developers to avoid revisions or refinements. Where programmers must tailor messages and procedure calls to display user interface elements one at a time, even small improvements to layout or to the appearance of components can require significant reprogramming and testing. Hampered by inadequate tools, programmers for one of our clients repeatedly omitted recommended changes to user interfaces, for example.

Among the oldest and best known of the modern tools are Visual Basic and various graphical application builders, such as PowerBuilder. The idea of visual development is not entirely new, of course; academics have been devising visual programming schemes for decades. One could even say that the commercial fore-runners of modern visual development tools were early report program generators that allowed much of the programming of simple applications to be done through forms that were laid out to look much like the printed pages of the desired report. This may seem to be a far cry from advanced tools like Visual C++ or J-Builder, but the idea is the same—programming driven by arranging the interface as it appears to the end user.

Visual development environments allow developers to create complete working systems largely or exclusively by moving visible objects around on a monitor screen. Instead of writing out the code to display and activate all the components in a dialogue box, the programmer merely selects visual controls from a toolbar and drags them into place on the dialogue box being created. Earlier, screen-painting techniques had taken over some of the clerical overhead but still required programmers to enter absolute screen coordinates to place fields, labels, and command buttons. Direct manipulation of visual components is an all-but-obvious improvement for designing graphical user interfaces, but, with many of the early tools, once the surface appearance was shaped, the programmer was forced to dig behind the scenes into the messy backstage chaos. There often lurked some of the ugliest Basic or scripting language imaginable, strewn around in an undisciplined clutter of references and messaging that interconnected all the scattered bits of functionality hung on the back of user interface widgets and forms.

Such early approaches were merely the first skirmishes in the revolution. The true revolution, which we have been predicting for more than a decade, is based on two additional innovations that are now being glimpsed in the more advanced tools. To make development truly and completely visual, the developer needs to be able to manipulate elements of the design models right along with the components of the user interface, and they need to be guaranteed the equivalence among the various views into the software. In other words, modeling capability needs to be fully integrated into the visual development environment [Constantine, 1995c]. File import and export is not enough. Switching between a CASE tool and a visual programming system, for example, is not enough. It is not application switching, but view switching, that is called for.

In a completely integrated visual development environment, all the various views of the software under development would be maintained together and in perfect correspondence. Not only could the developer instantaneously switch from one view to another, but any change in one view also would be immediately reflected in the underlying software model and, hence, in every other view. Change the code, and the interface changes; change the interface, and the properties are updated.

> *To make development truly and completely visual, developers need to be able to manipulate design models right along with components on the user interface and to be guaranteed the equivalence among the various views into the software.*

Some currently available products realize parts of the full visual development paradigm. Borland's Delphi and successors maintain synchronization between a code view, an interface design view, and an object property inspector. IBM's VisualAge line of products incorporate visual representation and direct manipulation of some aspects of object models. Third-party vendors have provided file swapping to "integrate" Rational's Rose and Borland's Delphi. All of these products or combinations still fall somewhat short of what is possible and needed, although the trend is clearly established. (See sidebar, Galactic Dimensions.)

MODEL OR NOT

Many programmers have argued that, using visual development tools, they can actually create a working prototype or even a fully functional system in less time than they could build a content and navigation model. In some cases, for relatively simple problems that have already been thought through by a skilled and experienced programmer, this may well be true, although content modeling by experienced practitioners is also a pretty speedy operation.

Facile manipulation of the visible user interface, however, is both a strength of visual development tools and a liability. Because it becomes so easy to grab a visual component and drop it onto a form or dialogue box, because visual components are so readily moved around on the interface design, visual development tools can encourage a kind of visual hacking in which just any old control is selected and thrown onto the interface without benefit of design or forethought. Sometimes, the design at best, may be given a little spit and polish to bring the interface controls into alignment and to correct spelling errors in labels.

> *The abstract models of usage-centered design impose a thoughtful order on what can be a chaotic frenzy in accelerated development.*

More often than many die-hard "coding cowboys" would like to admit, the fastest way to solve a problem is to slow down and work more methodically and

GALACTIC DIMENSIONS

A fully integrated visual development that interconnects and synchronizes analysis and design models with implementation and implementation models represents a change in tools and a change in metaphors. Traditional computer-aided software engineering tools are based on a metaphor that has been referred to as the "glass drawing board." Back in the 1980s, we began calling for progression to a new and more powerful development metaphor, better suited to the way human beings actually solve problems and better supporting a flexible and accelerated development process.

The earliest cathode-ray tube (CRT) monitors were sometimes referred to as "glass teletypes" because they mimicked the appearance and behavior of the still older teletype machines they replaced. Text was displayed character by character, and, when the bottom of the screen was reached, text scrolled up and off the top. Until programmers began to transcend that metaphor and use the capabilities of CRT displays more creatively, applications did little more than imitate paper-based teletype interaction.

The glass drawing board metaphor captures the way early CASE tools reflected the assumptions of their developers, who thought in terms of paper-and-pencil drawings of such things as data flow diagrams or flowcharts. Most CASE tools were based around drawing editors, sometimes a different one for each type of drawing, that merely represented two-dimensional paper models on the glass surface of a monitor or terminal screen. Since these drawings typically were too big for the screen, mechanisms for graphical navigation over the drawing surface needed to be devised.

The newly proposed metaphor was dubbed the "glass galaxy," a multidimensional problem-solving space in which developers could drill down into objects in one view or dimension and be taken via software "worm holes" through to related or equivalent objects in another view or dimension. Every surface or view of this polymorphous space was a projection of a common underlying implementation model of the software being designed and constructed. Rather than leading to nothing but a new twist on CASE tools, this metaphor argued for full integration of modeling into visual development environments.

Full integration facilitates not only problem solving but also tracing of requirements. A click on a term within a use case will take the developer to its definition in a glossary. If it is the name of a class, the class definition is equally accessible, both in a class model and in code. Select a use case, and see where in the content model that use case is supported; select a line within the use case, and see what tools and materials within the content model support it or what visual controls in the user interface are used to enact it. Even documentation is merely another view of the software. In an integrated visual development environment, entries in help files and printed documentation are linked to the use cases described and the user roles supported and, in turn, to code and to user interface designs. A change in any part of any view either is immediately reflected in all other views or else triggers a cascade of messages telling the responsible parties or respective owners that a review, reconciliation, or refinement is necessary.

When the basic model was presented as part of a 1989 conference on the future of CASE, the audience was neither amused nor inspired. Rethinking the fundamentals was not in fashion. Fortunately, development tools, unhampered by history, have slowly abandoned outmoded metaphors and have moved steadily closer to the glass galaxy.

---

thoughtfully. The abstract models of usage-centered design impose a thoughtful order on what can be a chaotic frenzy.

Time pressures have often been cited as excuses just to start cutting code, ignoring requirements, skipping over analysis, and omitting design, which is particularly ironic because savvy managers have been proclaiming for decades the time-saving value of modeling. The less time there is, the more important it is to build the system right to begin with by thinking before leaping into the code. The weight of experience is on the side of modeling and smart managers [Constantine,

1994d; 1995e]. When the meter is running and the deadline looms large, an hour spent modeling can save days of disorganized programming.

The usage-centered design activity model, introduced in Chapter 2, is adaptable to a variety of implementation strategies, including so-called RAD approaches and rapid iterative prototyping. Under extremely tight delivery cycles, say, of 60 to 120 days, several tricks can help get the maximum leverage from the time spent in usage-centered modeling. It can be useful to time-box any modeling, allocating a fixed amount of time for each activity. It is also vital to keep the modeling process moving without getting bogged down in lengthy discussions or debate. The focus should be on the immediate project needs without getting off into speculation or futuristic fantasies.

When push comes to shove, the core of a usage-centered approach is the task model. Essential use cases are easier to identify and to detail when the groundwork of role modeling has already been completed, but, for some small systems developed on short schedules, starting with the task model may suffice. Developers already proficient in usage-centered development may also be able to create good working prototypes or operational software directly from use cases using modern visual development tools. The very best and most experienced developers may even be able to model and design in their heads as they code with their hands. For the rest of us mortals caught in the panic of impossible deadlines, we would paraphrase an old Yiddish proverb: When there is no time to think, at least stop and think.

20

USING YOUR USERS:
Users in the Development Process

USE OR ABUSE OF USERS

Who are our users anyway? Where do they fit in the development process? Unlike earlier user-centered and user-oriented approaches, usage-centered design places the work above the worker, but this does not mean that users are not important. End users have vital roles to play in the development process.

Users are, of course, the ultimate consumers of information technology, even when they do not make purchases or sign contracts. In a sense, our users define the business we are in and the reasons for existence of the systems we design. They are the ones who do the real work that keeps our enterprises and the economy going.

In fact, users are the sources of many of the things that can determine the success or failure of our development efforts on their behalf. They are sources of much of the information that will help us to identify and understand the basic requirements for the system to be

> *Users are the ultimate consumers of information technology, even when they do not make purchases or sign contracts.*

built. They are sources of feedback on our interpretations of their problems and on our designs to solve their problems. They are also sources of trouble. They bring changes at every turn and introduce chaos into projects. Not surprisingly, developers and users have long engaged in a conflicted relationship that has ranged from a disengaged respect to open warfare. Like neighboring tribes who speak different languages, users and developers often do not understand each other nor do they always trust each other. The models of usage-centered design can be a tool for translation and communication between these tribes.

An honest history of software and applications development would document a long history of end users being abused at the hands of developers who ignored them or rode roughshod over them to deliver systems that may have worked but were often hardly fit for human endeavor. Having left users on the periphery for much of the discussion, we will now bring them to the center and, in this chapter, consider how best to use users as resources, as allies, and as contributors to the development process.

USERS IN THE CYCLE

One of the basic premises of this book is that software users and software developers are two very different kinds of creatures. Users are experts on use, and developers are experts on development. As developers, we should not abdicate our professional responsibilities to users anymore than we should arrogate their rights to usable systems. Users can, however, play a greater or lesser role in the actual design and development of software.

Waterfalls and whirpools. In the traditional "waterfall" life cycle models—linear, sequential stage-by-stage—users were, at best, attended to in the earliest stages of the process and then actively avoided until the finished package was thrust at them upon completion. In the interim, the sight of a user walking down a hall could send a developer scurrying into a conference room for cover. Users were seen as the bearers of bad news because they were perpetually changing their minds and repeatedly coming up with new requirements.

The advent of rapid iterative prototyping and user-centered design has not necessarily or in all cases improved things for users. Users might be heavily involved for initial discussions and planning, but they are then ignored until needed for prototype review and then ignored again until needed for final acceptance, at which point the whole cycle starts anew. Within some organizations with extended histories of iterative, user-centered development, users and others on the client side get tired of the pace. Their input and participation always seem to be needed immediately, and the commitment of meetings and reviews becomes a substantial burden that is repeated on each of multiple iterations within a major development cycle. In one financial institution, the user community reached the point where they refused to meet with systems analysts except very briefly at the outset of a project. They had learned that the too-frequent meetings with developers were either boring or contentious, often repetitive, and invariably inefficient and unproductive.

> *Users can get tired of too-frequent meetings with developers that are boring or contentious, often repetitive, and invariably inefficient and unproductive.*

Let users do it. At one extreme in a continuum of user involvement is so-called end-user computing, or user design, in which software is designed, or even sometimes built, by users themselves. Often, developers and users have very different perspectives on users doing design. For some developers, the fantasy is to let "them" do the work. Since users are impossible to satisfy anyway, why not have them just design the screens themselves? In a parallel fantasy, some users dream of dumping the analysts and programmers altogether, thus ending their dependency on the priests of technology.

To both factions, making the impossible dream into reality merely requires an adequately powerful and sufficiently user-friendly programming language or development environment. This is an old fantasy. In the dim digital past, COBOL and report generators like RPG and Fargo were introduced as means for ordinary people, using simple forms or everyday English, to program their own applications. Yeah, right. Then, of course, 4GLs were touted for many of the same reasons with many of the same fantasies. Visual Basic was the visual way for nonprogrammers to program. So it goes. The fantasy persists, but the goal remains elusive.

This is not to say that no end user ever creates successful software. Small, stand-alone applications created by end users for special analyses or reporting can be found in use in almost every setting. If these are not created with tools like Visual Basic or Access, they may be cobbled together from a spreadsheet linked to a word processor. In fact, the fantasy of end-user computing fits best with small, simple, straightforward applications in which there is a wide latitude in terms of solution quality and little or no need for integration or interoperability with other systems. However, where users act out the fantasy with some frequency, the proliferation of autonomous systems with no consistency or central quality control can exact a cost to the organization that, though difficult to measure, is not insignificant. For complex problems requiring large-scale integration and sophisticated design, end-user computing is a rarely attempted invitation to disaster.

> *There will probably always be a certain amount of end-user computing, just as there are still amateurs who assemble their own stereos or build their own small aircraft.*

The truth is that there will probably always be a certain amount of end-user computing, just as there are still amateurs who assemble their own stereos or build their own small aircraft. This does not make them audio or aeronautical engineers, however, nor are such amateur efforts a dominant factor in either industry.

Full participation. By contrast to end-user design, which is, by its nature, a solitary and unorganized activity, participatory design is a movement. Having roots in the Scandinavian approaches to job design and worker participation, participatory design is as much a political philosophy as it is a body of technique. It is often closely tied to workplace democracy and worker empowerment. In terms of user involvement in the design process, the basic model might be described as one of inviting users to move in for the duration of the project to share your office and the work.

As can be expected, participatory design places high demands on both users and developers, although it also promises high rewards in terms of superior designs closely fitted to actual usage. Of course, participation can be practiced to varying degrees short of all-out continuous collaboration. Many user interface designers make it a practice to sit down with users for collaborative review and refinement of paper prototypes, for example.

There are many difficulties with fully participatory design. Users, other than the occasional exceptional one, have basically no knowledge of user interface design, limited insight into usability issues, and little understanding of the technical trade-offs inherent in system design. As we have noted before, users are prone to ask for and describe features and facilities that they have already seen or used before. Rather than designing to needs, users have a tendency to fall back on the familiar and prosaic or to take off into flights of impractical fantasy. In end-user design of single-user applications, only the user-designer will suffer in either course of events. For the best results on more ambitious systems, however, both pulls need to be resisted.

Joint design reviews, as introduced in Chapter 16, draw users into collaboratively reviewing a visual design or prototype that has already been constructed by the developers. Feedback from the joint design review is then fed into the next cycle of independent design followed by joint review. This compromise level of user involvement in design is probably far more common today than is fully participatory design.

USERS IN USAGE-CENTERED DESIGN

We have come to the conclusion that users are best viewed as experts on their work and on their own system usage. Developers, on the other hand, should be the experts on software and usability engineering. These two domains of expertise are complementary, and both are required for successful usage-centered design. However, just as developers cannot be expected to do the job of users, end users should not be expected to do design. In our experience, far better results are obtained when users are intensively involved in setting requirements and in other carefully targeted activities, such as collaborative usability inspections, but are not heavily involved as participants in the actual designing of the user interface.

> *Just as developers cannot be expected to do the job of users, end users should not be expected to do design.*

In a usage-centered approach, users are not of interest for themselves but for the roles they play in relation to the system under development, for the uses they have for that system, and for the tools and materials they will need from it.

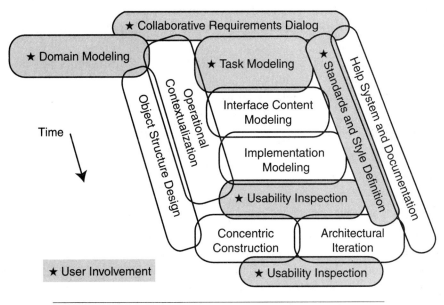

FIGURE 20-1 *Usage-centered design activity model.*

The most effective use of users involves them at a small number of very specific points in the development process toward very specific ends. It aims to make efficient use of their time and of the developers' time. The usage-centered activity model introduced in Chapter 2 and repeated here in Figure 20-1 is user-involved rather than user-centered. It draws in members of the end-user community for tightly focused activities where and when their participation is likely to yield the greatest payoff for the project and all its constituents.

We have already discussed in Chapter 16 the role of users in collaborative usability inspections; the matter of standards and style guides will be discussed in Chapter 21. Here, we will concentrate on the involvement of end users and others from outside the development community in the early activities of requirements definition and modeling.

REQUIREMENTS DIALOGUE, REQUIREMENTS DANCE

You may have heard the following sad tale retold as a kind of urban myth, but this particular story is true. In order to avoid some of the estimation problems and cost overruns of the past, one of our clients in Australia, a producer of communications systems, had decided to improve their requirements gathering process. At the start of their next project for one of the major telecommunications companies, they scheduled a series of meetings to learn about the customer's needs and objectives. The customer's representatives emphatically told the engineers that, because of the tight delivery schedule, specifying requirements was a waste of everyone's time. Instead, the engineers should get to work immediately on the design for the new system!

Although the coding cart is often put before the requirements horse in software and applications development, more typically it is not the users or customers, but the developers, who want to plunge ahead into design and implementation without pausing to determine what it is that they are designing and implementing.

> *The coding cart is often put before the requirements horse in software and applications development.*

At the top of the activity model in Figure 20-1 is, appropriately, a collaborative requirements dialogue. Whether it is called "requirements definition," "requirements gathering," "requirements analysis," or "requirements engineering," this is the activity that determines, at least initially, what the system to be designed and built must do. Are we building satellite navigation software or a personal accounting package? If the name of the game is accounting, what accounting practices must be supported and with what other systems must our system interface? Defined requirements are the foundation of design as well as the basis for quality [Gause and Weinberg, 1989].

Some analysts approach requirements definition as if it were archaeology. The needed information is presumed to be already all out there, buried in documents and dusty tomes, hidden in archives, or cached away in people's offices. The job of the requirements analyst is to dig it out, unearthing the needed information. Some analysts seem to approach requirements definition as if it were astrology, a matter of divining the needs of users by oracular revelation or osmotic transfer. Just hang around clients and users long enough, mumble the right incantations, and the specs will come to you.

In truth, the activity of gathering and analyzing system requirements is often rather subtle and sophisticated. To do it well can require not only skill and good tools but also sensitivity. The best analysts

> *Requirements engineering is not a form of archaeology or history and certainly not astrology.*

have always known that settling requirements is neither a matter of simply finding out from users or clients exactly what to build nor a matter of our simply telling them what it is we are going to do for them. The requirements dialogue is not a sermon or a selling job either, but a dialogue, a process of mutual exploration and negotiation in which consensus is reached between developers on the one side and users and clients on the other.

ESSENTIAL REQUIREMENTS

An "essential" approach to the requirements dialogue is one that emphasizes intention over action, in congruence with the essential use case model. Maintaining an emphasis on objectives, goals, and intentions helps keep the attention focused on real needs and primary requirements. We find it helpful to begin with a discussion or brainstorming process centered on the basic purpose or purposes of the proposed system. The results from this activity should be consolidated into a statement of essential purpose—not a mission statement for the project, but a description of the raisons d'être for the system itself. The dialogue is sparked by questions like these:

> *An "essential" approach to requirements emphasizes intention over action, maintaining an emphasis on objectives and goals to keep the focus on real needs and primary requirements.*

- What is the primary purpose of this system?
- How would you expect to use this system?
- What would you expect to accomplish with such a system?
- What is the reason for doing this particular task?

In trying to understand the work of users, it is important to go beyond work as formally defined or documented to how things are actually done in practice. In defining the purposes of tasks, the analyst must keep in mind that the goals and objectives of users are not necessarily the same as those of the organization. Both should be identified and distinguished from each other. For example, users may want to correct an account entry as quickly and efficiently as possible, but it may not be in the organization's best interest to make it too easy to change certain fields or kinds of information.

Needs and wants. One of the most important responsibilities of the requirements analyst is helping to separate needed functions and features from desired ones. If programming were free and instantaneous, we might try to satisfy every desire, but coding costs, so it is necessary to triage needs from wants. The priority in systems development is to meet needs before satisfying wants. Every user has the right to his or her own fantasies about a system, but it is not necessarily the developers' responsibility to turn fantasy into reality.

> *Every user has the right to his or her own fantasies about a system, but it is not necessarily the developers' responsibility to turn fantasy into reality.*

The requirements process is concerned with four basic categories of information:

1. Function
2. Form
3. Criteria
4. Constraints

The analysis should also carefully distinguish function from form and criteria from constraints.

Functions represent the basic capability of a system, while form refers to the realization and appearance of functions within a system. Although the Bauhaus dictum that form must follow from function can be carried to counterproductive extremes, it still makes basic sense. Form is designed; function is defined. Exceptions abound, but as a rule, it is important to define functional requirements without overdefining the form in which these are realized. Criteria refer to desired system attributes or characteristics, the objectives or goals by which the success of the system might be judged. These might be expressed in terms of performance or quality measures. Constraints are the limitations on possible or acceptable solutions, which may be expressed in terms resembling criteria or in functional terms.

Although users are not encouraged to view the requirements activities as an Aladdin's lamp for exotic systems, in novel systems or "green-field" applications where everything is new and yet to be determined, it can be useful to encourage a certain amount of fantasy and "what-if" thinking. In the case of additions to legacy systems or makeovers of systems already in use, users and clients may be quite reluctant to fantasize or speculate. Usually, they will show a certain amount of resistance to change; they will recite the familiar lines and request the familiar tools ("We want the screens to look just like the old system.").

Conservatism on the part of users is both understandable and often defensible. Intuitability is tied to familiarity [Raskin, 1994]. An interface that has already been mastered is the easiest of all to learn. In truth, all successful systems will change the work for which they are employed and the organization in which they are deployed. A certain amount of work redesign or process reengineering is an inevitable part of good systems design.

Organizational realities can often rear up in unexpected places. The analysts working on an investor services application for a bank division did their homework and devised a prototype design for a new system that would substantially cut the time needed by bank personnel to complete customers' transactions. It was rejected by the client. It so happened that the manager's status and compensation in part depended on the number of people he supervised. Such greater efficiency through a much improved user interface might become a justification for layoffs or transfers out of the division.

We suggest that the requirements activities should gather as much information as practical. Although there may be a certain risk of inundation from a surfeit of information, in our experience it is usually better to know than not to know it. One can always ignore or set aside irrelevant or unwanted information. Some of the frills and more fanciful ideas should be assembled, as long as these are clearly distinguished from essential needs. In many cases, it may be found that certain additional features can be provided at very little cost, which can be important for allocating features to development iterations in the interest of delivering the most value. Some rather important features might even be deferred until later versions in trade for immediate availability of less difficult extras.

> *It is usually better to know than not to know. Even frills and fanciful ideas should be assembled, as long as these are clearly distinguished from essential needs.*

Creeping and leaking. Having an explicit, systematic process for establishing requirements has many advantages, the most important being in managing requirements creep and requirements leakage. *Requirements creep* refers to the expansion of system scope beyond the initially agreed-upon requirements. *Requirements leakage* refers to requirements that enter a project by the back door, becoming part of the delivered system without benefit of whatever procedures for acceptance or review of requirements may have been established. Both requirements creep and requirements leakage can become major management headaches, making it more difficult to meet deadlines and to constrain costs and contributing to the proliferation of bloated, feature-laden systems.

GOING TO THE SOURCE

Not surprisingly, users themselves are probably the best source of information about what they do and what they need in order to do it better. Whole books could be written on interviews and the art of interviewing—and they have been. Here, we will only hit some of the high points of the art as applied to usage-centered modeling and requirements capture.

FACE TO FACE

Interviews and discussions to define requirements, like all task-oriented meetings, tend to be more effective and efficient when they make use of a certain amount of defined structure. The techniques of effective meeting management [Doyle and Strauss, 1982] can be useful in optimizing requirements activities. Three issues should be attended to in advance or as part of every such encounter:

1. Defining the agenda
2. Defining the purpose
3. Defining the relationship

The need for an agenda is obvious. It can take the form of a broad outline or a detailed protocol of topics and questions. The important thing is to think about what you are going to do and how you are going to do it in the allotted time. To a large extent, the agenda depends on the purpose, which should be the starting point for structuring any interview. What are the purposes of the meeting? Meetings in service of requirements engineering can be based on any or all of these purposes:

- Information gathering
- Model building
- Negotiation
- Approval or sign-off
- Auditing or validation

In any case, the analysts or designers have a choice of just how much structure to use in any interviews. At the one extreme is an essentially free-form, conversational style; at the other is a meeting consisting of a series of predefined discussion topics or questions. Set questions or topics can sometimes be more time-efficient, but their use may also lead to leaving out important asides or overlooking vital input that does not happen to fall into one of the predefined categories. To users, ticking off a long list of questions can make a meeting seem more like an inquisition than a collaboration. A more conversational approach organized around specific parts of a system's models or a series of general topics is more conducive to a cooperative atmosphere.

Ticking off a long list of questions can make a meeting seem more like an inquisition than a collaboration.

It is important to have the right participants, participants who are committed, cooperative, and knowledgeable. In one company, when the time came for a requirements capture meeting, the only person who could be "spared" from the user department was a new hire who knew nothing of the old system being replaced and little of the reinsurance business in which the department was engaged.

If possible, where multiple meetings are needed, the same people should participate in each meeting. Changing membership makes it more difficult to build and sustain teamwork. The process is slowed by having to bring new participants up to speed on the process and the work to date. Changing participants can also lead to a complete lack of convergence on consensus since each incoming participant can bring another set of prejudices and priorities into the discussion.

User participants, as well as developers, should understand what the expectations are for their involvement in the requirements activities. The process and the resulting work products need to be suited to the relationship between users and developers and the assumptions on which it is based. Is the user viewed as an informant in an ethnographic or researchlike process? Is the user an assistant to the development team or the client calling the shots? Are users considered ultimate authorities or viewed as collaborators in a joint exercise?

MEETING MECHANICS

The typical requirements dialogue takes place in an office or conference room with the users and the developers facing each other from opposite sides of a desk or conference table. Users and developers come to the meeting armed with separate agendas and carrying their own private notes. More often than not, the meetings are either overly long, stiff, and formal or entirely too brief, unplanned, and unfocused.

Our backgrounds in systems therapy and organizational dynamics make us acutely aware of how small matters concerning the seating and the setting can have a major impact on how a meeting proceeds and how well it succeeds in its objectives [Constantine, 1993d]. Context is especially important for promoting a spirit of collaboration. Before the meeting, prepare a reasonable agenda jointly and distribute it in advance for comment.

> *Small matters concerning the seating and the setting can have a major impact on how a meeting proceeds and how well it succeeds in its objectives.*

Allocate enough time to complete the agenda, or plan for multiple meetings. Do not try to cram too much into a single session, and do not feel the need to pad out a plan to fill an hour. Meetings that are either rushed or dragged out will discourage later participation. Whatever you do, resist canceling or rescheduling meetings. Every time a meeting is called off or postponed, it sends a message about the unimportance of the discussions. People who have moved other meetings or cleared their calendars to take part will resent having to accommodate a new schedule. Every time a meeting is postponed, it will become harder to reschedule.

For the meeting itself, rather than sitting across from your users, sit beside them, facing shared notes and models. You might even sit with users and developers interspersed to highlight the fact that everyone is on the same team and participating as individual contributors to a joint endeavor. For the same reasons, take all notes openly, for the collective good, using flip-charts, whiteboards, or newsprint spread on the tabletop or taped to the wall where everyone can easily see them and amend them.

Neutrality. Successful requirements sessions require good leadership. The meeting is best led by a facilitator who can involve everyone, promoting the free exchange of ideas and helping to build consensus. The best leaders for technical discussions, modeling, and decision making are neutral and nonpartisan. They maintain the focus and keep the meeting on track with the agreed-upon agenda. Meeting leaders with a private agenda to push or with supervisory authority over some of the participants are a problem. Intentionally or not, they have a certain tendency to steer, stifle, or dominate discussions in ways that lead to less effective group performance. Managers from either the developer or the user side may start meetings but, as a rule, should not lead them. Groups often unintentionally defer to authority figures or rebel against them. Leaders who do no more than jump in too soon with their own opinions can compromise the results of group decisions and solutions [Constantine, 1992d].

Punctuation. The beginnings and endings of meetings set the tone and can go a long way toward making the most of the time spent together as well as the time spent afterward. It may seem silly to some people, but every session should be clearly punctuated with a distinct beginning and definite end. Do not just drift into discussion or taper off into silence with participants wandering off at will. Always be sure to welcome and thank everyone. These common courtesies may not always add much, but omitting them is all but certain to put off at least someone.

> *The beginnings and endings of meetings set the tone and can go a long way toward making the most of the time spent together as well as the time spent afterward.*

Begin by reviewing both the purpose and the agenda for the meeting and consider changes to these. If the meeting is begun by the project lead or a manager, he or she should do no more than the opening courtesies and the declaration of the start of the session before turning it over to the appointed facilitator.

On the other end, the wrap-up can be vitally important. The facilitator should finish with a summary of the conclusions and results of the meeting. The group should go over any action items or next steps that have been generated. Someone should take on or be assigned responsibility for each such item. If not already planned, the next session should be scheduled since it is far easier to do that with all participants still together in one room than to do so through long rounds of telephone tag.

WATCHING WORK

Observation of users at work, whether doing the real thing in their usual places of work or carrying out a simulation in an experimental setting, reveals a great deal. We strongly recommend that all software development professionals spend some time just watching users doing work both with the developers' software and with existing or competing systems, including manual ones. It is invariably instructive. For example, technical draftspersons are often seen with both a pen or pencil and

---

LEADING LIGHTLY

Process facilitation is a grand art about which many books have been written, but the basic concepts are relatively few and simple [Constantine, 1992b; 1992d; 1992f]. The group leader needs to be prepared to guide as needed without dominating. Facilitators who talk a lot are not doing their job of getting the group to talk. The neutral facilitator is everyone's friend and ally, trying to draw out each participant's best contributions. Skilled facilitators consciously help to build agreement and consensus but do not push for premature closure.

It is not the facilitator's job to avoid or squelch conflict. Disagreement and disparate views are fuel for creative problem solving and effective modeling. In fact, the most successful group leaders do not shy away from disagreement but rather heighten and clarify differences to build better understanding of issues before helping the group to reach acceptable conclusions [Constantine, 1992b; 1993a].

Some very simple techniques tend to contribute to collaboration and consensus building [Constantine, 1992b; 1992f]. For example, all contributions should be acknowledged and validated ("Thanks. Useful comment."). Facilitators need to listen actively and paraphrase comments and arguments. Building technical consensus can be helped by polling for the "sense of meeting" ("Where do we stand on this? How many accept this view?"). Polling is not voting; it is merely a way to make the level of agreement or disagreement visible and open for discussion. Asking discussants to summarize results and conclusions helps keep ownership of the outcome in the group, where it belongs.

Good joint problem solving and modeling are based on clear distinctions—on keeping separate things separate. Such distinctions include

- Separating the content from the contributor
- Separating the objective from the subjective
- Separating independent or separable issues
- Separating the evaluation from the generation of ideas
- Separating decision criteria from the decision itself
- Separating here-and-now matters from there-and-then concerns
- Distinguishing process (how) from content (what)

Some people are better facilitators than others, but our experience shows that what it takes most of all is practice. Rotating meeting leadership can spread the skills and improve the long-term success of developers and users.

---

an eraser in one hand. Some may even grip both a pen and a small electric eraser at the same time—no mean trick—and switch back and forth between them. It is less common for them to place an eraser to the side where it must be retrieved before making a correction. What does this say about the requirements for the user interface of a CAD tool to support such work?

Difficulties encountered on the job and how they are handled often furnish clues for understanding the normal course of work. Skilled analysts not only watch for the typical or normal procedure but also look for how standard procedures fail, where communication breaks down, or when and how problems arise.

> *All software development professionals should spend some time just watching users doing work both with the developers' software and with existing or competing systems, including manual ones.*

USING USERS

While the notion of using users may seem to run counter to concerns for user empowerment, we believe that using them well is a laudable objective, even as we would want ourselves as developers to be used well. The challenge is how to make their involvement in development as useful and as painless as possible.

> *Managing user and client expectations is a vital part of the job of software development.*

MANAGING EXPECTATIONS

Managing user and client expectations is a vital part of the job of software development. You can deliver a perfectly adequate system, but, if the users expected more or something else, they will be disappointed.

CONTEXTUAL INQUIRY

Contextual inquiry is an approach to requirements gathering and definition that grew out of work started at Digital Equipment Corporation. Although there has been some dispute over early history and appropriate credit, there is little doubt that its most visible and active proponents have been Karen Holtzblatt and Hugh Beyer [Holtzblatt and Beyer, 1993; Beyer and Holtzblatt, 1997]. In tune with a current business trend, contextual inquiry (and contextual design, which is based on it) is said to be directed toward *customer-centered* systems.

Contextual inquiry comprises a fairly elaborate body of techniques and tools for requirements capture and product definition. The basic philosophy is that the structure of work is best apprehended in the workplace—in context, that is. Information is gathered through a basically ethnographic process of observation and interviewing of workers in their everyday work settings.

Collected information is consolidated into a series of models that help clarify both the context and the content of work. To model work, contextual inquiry uses no less than five models, four of which are strongly tied to the emphasis on context: A flow model represents how activities are coordinated through communication, a sequence model captures task scenarios, an artifact model focuses on physical objects involved in work, a cultural model deals with organizational culture, and a physical model centers on the physical work environment. Although much of the same content is represented in contextual inquiry and usage-centered design, the relative prominence of information in contextual design is quite different.

Contextual design takes what we have referred to as *consolidated modeling* approach. The various work models and design models are intended more for consumption of the design and development team than for customers or users. Although paper prototypes are expected to emerge eventually from the process, far more attention is given to understanding work in context than to designing systems with suitable user interfaces. The methods and models of contextual inquiry support analysis and requirements engineering more than software and user interface design.

Under the right circumstances, contextual inquiry could be combined with usage-centered design as a "front-end" process, although the results might well be overkill for all but the most ambitious undertakings. Some of our clients have reported that the ethnographic orientation of contextual inquiry makes it far better suited to automation of manual systems and to reengineering of legacy applications than to "green-field" applications where there is little or nothing to observe and no established context within which to observe it.

In all dealings with users, developers must make clear what the relationship is and what is expected from users. Users need to understand that you are trying to understand what they do, how they do it, and what they need from the system being designed. You are not trying to tell them how to do their jobs. Most importantly, you are not designing a new system for them right then and there.

Many of the "rules of the game" introduced for inspections (see sidebar, Rules of the Game in Chapter 16) are suited to managing user expectations. It is vitally important not to make promises during discussions or reviews with users. Promises—expressed or implied—should be considered to be part of the contracting and negotiation process, not part of the modeling or review process. This distinction must be kept in mind to control and limit requirements leakage, a major cause of requirements creep, which is a contributing factor in the dread disease of creeping featuritis.

It is all too easy for a gung-ho GUI designer to draw another widget on a paper prototype without careful consideration of how that might expand the scope of the project. Whenever it becomes necessary or convenient to change a prototype during discussions with users, it can be helpful to add a reminder that this is not a final commitment but merely a trial for purposes of exploration. Each meeting should be wrapped up with a review of proposed changes and discussion points, followed by an appropriate disclaimer.

> *Never ask users how they like a particular design. The question implies that you are there to please users rather than to serve them.*

Users need also to be reminded that working models constructed for the sake of discussion or to capture understanding are not designs or prototypes. Similarly, even prototypes do not necessarily fix the delivered features or their form.

We sometimes warn developers never to ask users how they like a particular design. The question implies that developers are there to please the users rather than to serve them. If you ask, users might tell you they do not like your design, and you will feel some obligation to change it, even if it is the best solution to the presented problem. Asking the question also invites a shift of attention from needs to wants, away from what works toward wish fulfillment. Collaboration with users can maintain a highly practical and businesslike focus without preventing it from being fun. In our experience, the power of unbridled creativity is better reserved for devising design solutions to requirements once the real requirements have been determined.

COPING WITH CHAOS

Users are admittedly a major source of chaos in the development process. However careful developers are in gathering requirements or in conducting collaborative modeling, they can expect requirements changes. This is simply the reality of software development. We can only do so much to limit changes. Perhaps we should just recognize them as in the nature of the beast. Indeed, instead of trying to contain, control, or even eliminate changing requirements and user-generated chaos, perhaps we would be better off to prepare for, plan for, and allow changing requirements. Indeed, we should have life cycle models, management tools, and development environments specifically tailored to the reality of changing requirements [Hawryszkiewycz and Gorton, 1996].

> *Instead of trying to contain, control, or even eliminate changing requirements and user-generated chaos, we should prepare for, plan for, and allow changing requirements.*

This is part of the motivation behind emerging strategies of adaptive development [Emery, 1998; Highsmith, 1998] in which requirements are defined but are recognized as necessarily tentative, incomplete, and evolving.

To manage expanding user expectations, both capability and facilities need to be prioritized. Most systems are best deployed with an initial set of features that satisfies the most critical requirements first, saving additional features for future refinements that can benefit from experience and the perfect perspective of 20-20 hindsight.

Users and clients are better able to accept an early but scaled-down release when they know they can count on the development team to deliver quality and to deliver it regularly. Norm Kerth has suggested [Constantine, 1998b] that the goal should be to establish a culture of commitment, with regular, reliable releases on a 3-to-6-month cycle. Not only does this model meet the users' need for timeliness, but it also gives developers a tool to manage requirements creep. Instead of expanding the scope of the current project, late breaking requirements are deferred to the next revision cycle, which clients know will also be completed on schedule because its scope will also be actively controlled.

> *You must have a final commit date when requirements specifications become effectively frozen for the duration of the project or iterative cycle.*

It may require several rounds of refinement and release before client confidence is sufficient, so developers need to take the long view of educating their customers.

Even when using highly adaptive development strategies, rapid iterative prototyping, or time-boxed accelerated development approaches, you must have a final commit date when requirements specifications become effectively frozen for the duration of the project or of the iterative cycle. Any emerging or changed requirements after that final commit date can only affect the next design/build iteration, not the current cycle.

It is also crucially important to limit the number of iterations in the refinement of requirements models and designs. Developers should decide in advance that, say, three rounds of refinement will be undertaken before finalizing a user interface architecture. Without a limit on iterations, even rapidly prototyped projects can stretch on indefinitely.

In any event, be sure to keep earlier versions of all analysis and design models. If you fail to, you can count on your users suddenly telling you they want to go back to the version of three weeks earlier because the analysis has drifted from the core capability or the design has become corrupted by peripheral considerations. Effective version control is as essential for models as for code.

Perhaps one of the most important steps developers can take to cope more effectively with the chaos of changing and expanding requirements is a purely technical one. All the best practices of modern software engineering apply. The software needs to be designed and built on a robust architecture that can readily accommodate unanticipated modifications or additions. The better the architecture of the code and the data, the easier it will be to make changes to it. At the detail level, code should be flexible and highly parameterized. The code should be organized into well-designed component parts that are highly cohesive in themselves and loosely coupled with one another. The system should be built around a sound class hierarchy or data model.

USERS AND PROTOTYPES

Interacting with users through paper prototypes is popular among user interface designers. Users like the medium because they can see what is meant by a particular design or can understand by visual comparison the trade-offs inherent in choosing between alternative designs. User interface designers like paper prototypes because it allows them to interact through what they know best—designs.

Because they are concrete, paper prototypes can also contribute to unvoiced and unrealistic expectations on the part of users. The designer may have said, "It will look something like this," but the user hears it as, "It will look just like this." For this reason, hand-drawn paper prototypes are often preferable to high-quality graphics or screen shots when interacting with users. The makeshift and ad hoc appearance can prove advantageous. Paper prototypes do not look like software or even final designs. They communicate unambiguously the tentative and preliminary nature of the design. With pencil drawings or sketches, users are less likely to fixate on unimportant details, and they will not be misled into thinking that the decisions are all made and the design is already coded in concrete. Even so, quick sketches and on-the-fly editing of paper prototypes in the presence of users can sometimes be interpreted as firm commitments. Moreover, even sketchy paper prototypes can draw some into preoccupation with excessive details, such as the form of scrollbars or the appearance of icons on the toolbar. For such cases you might try substituting a content model populated with abstract tools and materials.

> *Hand-drawn paper prototypes are often best because users are less likely to fixate on unimportant details and will not be misled into thinking that decisions are already coded in concrete.*

Let's pretend. As in joint design reviews (introduced in Chapter 16), when passive prototypes are used for communication with users, developers should enact the system and the help functions while users enact the use cases. The trick works best if users and developers pretend that the prototype is a fully functional, working user interface. Careful language used during this process can help prevent unrealistic expectations at later points in development. For example, developers should use expressions like "what might happen next," "one way this dialogue might open would be," and "we are considering having it work like this." Users may need to be reminded repeatedly that the prototype is not the system and that design decisions reflected in prototypes are not final.

In general, we think trying to capture or define requirements through paper prototypes or screen designs is ill-advised. Requirements represent problems to be solved; user interface designs—even rough sketches—represent solutions to prob-

> *Trying to capture or define requirements through paper prototypes or screen designs is ill-advised. Requirements represent problems to be solved; user interface designs represent solutions.*

lems. Defining requirements based on tasks to be supported and, if necessary, the contents of the user interface to support those tasks is less risky than fixing requirements by offering designs. User roles and use cases are the models most concerned with requirements and user needs. Implementation models are closest to the final solution. Content models can be thought of as the pivot point between problem definition and solution design. As such, content models can go either way, expressing problem requirements as well as the content of solutions.

JOINT ESSENTIAL MODELING

There are many routes to understanding what users need. In addition to the sources and schemes already discussed in this chapter, more formal and systematic techniques can be applied to developing the core models of usage-centered design. Some of the most effective approaches bring users and developers together in a collaborative effort.

Several different approaches to the process of model building can be distinguished. In **consolidated modeling**, analysts or designers conduct independent interviews and carry out separate observations and then join together to compile and merge their findings. Out of this consolidated information, usage-centered models are constructed. The consolidated approach separates the information gathering and interaction with users from the interpretation and model building. It makes efficient use of the information-gathering resources of the team because team members can work in parallel before consolidating their findings. This approach characterizes the technique of contextual design [Beyer and Holtzblatt, 1997]. (See sidebar, Contextual Inquiry.)

In **collaborative modeling**, users and developers work together to develop some or all of the models for defining requirements and specifying a system. Collaborative modeling can make effective use of the distinct perspectives that users and developers bring to modeling. The give-and-take of immediate interaction between the two groups can often answer questions and resolve issues more quickly and creatively than if developers build models on their own. Collaborative modeling could also follow after an independent data-gathering process and consolidation of results.

> *Concurrent modeling becomes most efficient when undertaken in teams or groups.*

In Chapter 2, we introduced the idea of concurrent engineering as a way to organize usage-centered design for efficiency. In **concurrent modeling**, the various necessary models are developed more or less simultaneously, moving back and forth among role, task, content, navigation, and implementation models. Concurrent modeling becomes most efficient when undertaken in teams or groups. Individuals or small subteams can each work on a particular model while also interacting and sharing information. This is the basis of the system-storyboarding approach, in which various system views are constructed on the different walls of a room [Zahniser, 1990; 1993].

Of course, consolidated, collaborative, and concurrent modeling approaches can be intermingled. Combinations are likely to be even more efficient and effective, and this is the premise of the technique covered in the rest of this section.

JOINT EXERCISES

Joint Essential Modeling, or **JEM**, is a structured process for collaborating with users to develop usage-centered requirements specifications through concurrent modeling. Joint Essential Modeling somewhat resembles its ancestor, *Joint Application Design* (JAD), a well-established collaborative method that brings together developers, users, and their managers to accomplish systems analysis, requirements definition, and high-level exterior design [Wood and Silver, 1989]. The JAD approach, originally developed in 1977 by Chuck Morris at IBM in Canada, has been widely and successfully used in a variety of settings for many and varied applications. The strength of JAD is that it is not a series of meetings or discussions, but a highly structured, facilitated process of collaboration.

A hallmark of the JAD process is the requirement that users outnumber developers. JAD sessions, lasting from as little as half a day to as long as five days, are preceded by substantial advanced research and preparation and followed by systematic documentation and follow-up.

The JAD session is modeled on basic principles of meeting management [Doyle and Strauss, 1982] and relies on three process roles: facilitator, scribe, and sponsor. The *sponsor*, typically the responsible manager from the user or client side, starts and ends the JAD sessions but does not otherwise conduct the meetings. Sponsors may participate as contributors but are enjoined from dominating the activities or exercising decision-making authority during the JAD process. The *facilitator* actually leads the sessions, sustaining the process and drawing on all participants to complete the work collaboratively. The *scribe* is responsible for recording not only the information and models as these evolve but also the process through which they are developed [Constantine, 1992e]. We will have more to say about these process roles in the context of Joint Essential Modeling.

JAD has been shown to accelerate design and improve system quality. Perhaps the greatest advantage of JAD is that it can substantially increase the sense of ownership and "buy-in" of both users and developers. Over the long term, the increased involvement and influence of users and clients improve the relationship between these communities and software development groups.

> *Although screen design is frequently incorporated, neither methodical user interface design nor a focus on usability is part of Joint Application Design (JAD).*

JAD is well proven with typical or conventional information systems applications in business and industry. Without modification, however, it may not be as suitable for more advanced or exotic projects. Although screen design is frequently incorporated into the conventional process, neither methodical user interface design nor a focus on usability is part of the JAD approach.

Using JAD can place some heavy demands on both users and developers. As traditionally practiced, it concentrates user involvement early in the software development life cycle. As the work progresses into more detailed design and implementation, users may be ignored or even excluded from participation in development and decision making.

FROM JAD TO JEM

Joint Essential Modeling is a structured, facilitated, collaborative process for concurrent usage-centered modeling. JEM was itself a collaborative construction, drawing on our own work as well as ideas and experiences contributed by our colleagues Todd Wyder and Ellen Gottesdiener.

JEM is tailored to usage-centered design preserving some of the strong features of JAD while updating the process to fit better with modern work products and a usage-centered focus. In Joint Essential Modeling, users and developers join in a collaborative effort to define the essential models and reach agreement on core requirements. The objective is to reach consensus on the tasks to be supported in the delivered system. As Wyder has described it, the process proceeds from model creation through examination and on to consensus. Although other models may play some part—including user roles, content models, and even paper prototypes—the principal medium of exchange is use cases, in either concrete or essential form.

> *Joint Essential Modeling (JEM) preserves some of the strong features of JAD while updating the process to fit better with modern work products and a usage-centered focus.*

The primary deliverables from the JEM process are

- User role model
- Use cases, with narratives in concrete form
- Focal use cases

Deliverables that are desirable but optional include

- Essential use case narratives
- Use case map
- Use case prioritization
- Glossary

Jointly developing the user role and use case models is the basic objective of JEM. In its most ambitious form, the collaborative approach can be continued forward into abstract prototyping with users to develop a content model or even into paper prototyping to devise an implementation model. In our view, these become collaborative design activities rather than collaborative analysis. Although collaborative or participatory design can be effective, it is less time-efficient for both users and developers than collaborative analysis followed by independent design with feedback from users.

The efficiency of JEM owes to its structure. JEM is based on carefully delineated roles for participants and highly focused activities for the collaborative sessions.

PARTICIPANT ROLES

The roles in JEM are similar to those in JAD. A sponsor—who may be a customer, a user supervisor, or a project manager, depending on politics, organization, or availability—is desirable. As in JAD, a participating sponsor begins and ends modeling sessions but does not actually conduct them.

Users. Without a doubt, the most important JEM participants are users. Because of the usage-centered focus, every effort is made to assure that user participants are representative of the range of actual end users. In most cases, at least one user at either end of the knowledge and experience spectrum should be involved so that the range of usage patterns and domain expertise is represented. In addition, once candidate user roles have been identified, all nominated user roles should, if possible, be represented among the participating users.

> *Once candidate user roles have been identified, all nominated user roles should, if possible, be represented among users participating in Joint Essential Modeling.*

Process roles. Similar to both JAD and other structured teamwork models [Constantine, 1991a; 1993a], three process roles are employed within the JEM approach: facilitator, scribe, and lead analyst. A *lead analyst* can be designated to assure appropriate technical leadership and expertise in usage-centered modeling. The lead analyst is expected to be familiar with essential models and experienced in the practice of usage-centered design. The lead analyst serves as a consultant and resource to the group on technical matters concerning modeling and usage-centered design. The role is optional; a team of highly experienced modelers might forego designating a lead analyst.

The *facilitator* functions as a neutral process leader, much as in JAD. As in JAD, the *scribe* is far more than mere functionary [Constantine, 1992e]. To be effective, a scribe must have a background in software development as well as knowledge of the conventions of the joint modeling process and familiarity with the models being developed. An ordinary secretary or office-staff person will not be effective in this demanding role. The scribe must track the full process of modeling and decision making, not just note down the results.

Other potential participants. If they are interested, motivated, and available, other professionals can be useful participants in the JEM process. Depending on the project and available personnel, other useful contributors might include quality assurance staff or testers, user interface designers or other usability professionals, trainers, and documentation specialists.

There are also some people who, by the nature of their perspectives or responsibilities, may not be as helpful as participants in Joint Essential Modeling. In our experience, marketing or sales staff, however intelligent and well motivated they might be, often bring to joint modeling sessions an agenda or position that can have a negative effect on the modeling process. Especially in market-driven companies, marketing or sales representatives may aggressively dominate analysis and decision making to the detriment of the technical quality of the product solution. Of course, it depends on the individual as well as the company context. In companies with technically-trained marketing staff who view themselves as part of the corporate team rather than as the driving force, marketing might supply effective collaborators for Joint Essential modeling.

If the joint modeling process becomes embroiled in organizational politics, posturing, or jockeying for position, obviously less work will get done on the essential models. We would probably be hesitant to include representatives of formally constituted user groups, who may be committed to pressing forward an official agenda. For the same reason, union or labor representatives could turn a technical discussion into a labor–management standoff. This is not to say that anyone who belongs to a union or who participates in any formal user organization must be excluded.

> *Some people—marketing or sales staff, for example— by the nature of their perspectives or responsibilities, may not always be helpful participants in Joint Essential Modeling.*

The important issue is that they participate as individual collaborators, not as official representatives. People who can separate their various roles and interests from one another are better candidates for participation in Joint Essential Modeling.

Naturally, all systems evolve within a social and an organizational context that includes official constituencies and political factions. Successful projects take these realities into account, but, in our opinion, the political issues are best handled apart from the modeling process. If these issues are allowed to muddle the models, the result is more likely to be both bad design and bad politics.

ACTIVITY OVERVIEW

In overview, the JEM process consists of five basic activities that are carried out in a series of one or more meetings:

1. Premodeling and consolidation
2. Role modeling
3. Task modeling
4. Model auditing
5. Feature allocation

The preparation and consolidation process prepares materials and an agenda for the subsequent sessions and also generates a candidate list of user roles used as a guide to participation in subsequent joint modeling. Following the development of role and task models, these models are audited for completeness, correctness, and consistency. To complete the process, use cases are prioritized and allocated to successive software versions or project iterations.

These activities are carried out in a series of sessions, which we refer to as follows:

1. Framing session
2. Modeling session
3. Review session

As time permits and for modest projects, the modeling and review phases can be combined into a single session. In some cases, such as when participants must travel some distance to the JEM sessions, a single marathon meeting might combine all three phases; at the other end of the spectrum, a large-scale project might require spreading each session over more than one meeting. Each session begins with an explanation of the JEM method, a review of the purpose and agenda for the meeting, and an introduction to the models being developed. Obviously, the depth of explanation needs to be tailored to the participants, and later sessions will not need as thorough and detailed coverage as earlier ones. These opening overviews, however brief, should always be included.

FRAMING SESSION

The purpose of the initial or *framing session* is to establish the framework within which the joint modeling sessions will operate. The framing session is a preliminary planning meeting that may not involve all the same participants as those in the modeling sessions. The purpose of the framing session is to collect and consolidate available information, both in preparation for modeling and in order to generate a list of candidate user roles. The deliverables from this process are

- Draft statement of essential purpose for system
- Preliminary list of candidate user roles
- List of participants for subsequent modeling sessions

The framing session is quite limited in scope and can be quite brief in many cases. A formal framing session is optional; all that may be necessary on some projects is for some members of the project team to get together, talk about what they know of the application, and brainstorm a list of candidate user roles. This activity may be carried out conjointly with user participants or more or less independently by members of the development team with input from one or more users. If conducted as a formal collaborative meeting, the framing session should include the sponsor and user representatives who can be expected to participate in the actual modeling sessions.

The framing session usually follows a period of initial discussion, exploration, and observation during which developers familiarize themselves with the application, operational context, and domain. Prior to the framing session, the relevant and available background information is collected and consolidated. Such information may include contracts or informal agreements, memoranda, minutes of meetings, documentation from prior versions, interview summaries, survey results, or models developed by some systematic process such as contextual inquiry. This information is reproduced and distributed to all participants in the framing session, who will be expected to be familiar with the information prior to the meeting.

> *The framing session collects and consolidates available information, both in preparation for modeling and in order to generate a list of candidate user roles.*

The work of the framing session begins with the creation of a draft statement of essential purpose. Next, a candidate list of user roles is created by brainstorming. This list of candidates is then reviewed and pared down. Participating users are polled to see how many candidate user roles are represented among them. For candidate user roles not represented among participating users, other participants must be sought. A suggested list of additional participants for subsequent sessions is drawn up by the group.

During the framing session, the group may identify missing data or encounter questions that cannot be answered from available information. All such gaps should be noted in the records and steps planned to fill in the blanks before the next session.

Before the framing session is ended, it is desirable to schedule the first of the modeling sessions and arrange to invite all participants. If conducted as a formal meeting, the session should be ended by the sponsor.

MODELING SESSIONS

The actual joint modeling takes place in one or more *modeling sessions*, during which complete user role and use case models are developed collaboratively. It is convenient to describe the process as two separate phases, although these may be run together into a single meeting in some projects. Two separate sessions will probably be needed for role modeling and task modeling if a structured user role model is being developed. The appropriate level of detail and degree of structure in these models depends on the scope of the project and the sophistication of the participants.

The deliverables for the role modeling phase include

- Final statement of essential purpose
- User role model (informal or structured)
- User role map (optional)

In addition to reviewing the JEM method and the agenda for the session, the facilitator should be sure that everyone understands the concept of user role and the basic structure of a user role model. A short presentation on user role modeling may be needed.

The draft statement of essential purpose is presented to the group for discussion, review, revision, and agreement. The list of candidate user roles from the framing session is reviewed and revised. The group looks for missing or redundant roles and checks to see that all roles are represented among user participants. The model is reviewed, role by role, to fill in descriptions and clarify relationships. If a structured user role model is being developed that includes contextual information, forms or checklists (see Appendix E) can be helpful to assure that all issues are covered.

The task modeling phase is intended to identify all use cases. The deliverables from this phase include

- List of use cases with essential purpose identified
- Use case narratives (in concrete or essential form)
- Use case map (optional)
- Identification of focal use cases

Use case narratives can be developed in either concrete or essential form, although the essential narratives will ultimately be needed by developers to complete the content and implementation models. Some users may have difficulty with the abstractness of essential use case narratives. The joint modeling can begin with concrete narratives and then reduce the narratives to essential form by abstraction and generalization. Alternatively, the developers can independently derive the essential narratives as a separate activity at a later time. One advantage of dealing directly in essential use cases is that it helps maintain a focus on the intentions of users and the purposes of use cases, on the essential

> *Developers will eventually need essential use case narratives, but some users may have difficulty with the abstractness of essential narratives.*

rather than the physical system. Especially in working with internal clients, educating the user community to think in terms of essentials can be advantageous.

If the users find it easier to think initially in terms of complex scenarios of usage, these should be decomposed into subcases, and extension cases should be extracted in order to develop a cleaner use case model. The use case map is an optional but highly desirable deliverable. Working out the precise interrelationships among use cases not only enhances understanding of the application but also provides a better model for auditing in the next phase of joint modeling. Building the use case map typically begins with an affinity clustering to identify logical clusters of use cases. Classification, composition, and extension relationships are then identified. In the course of evolving the use case map, it will often become necessary to revise some of the individual narratives as extensions or subcases are extracted.

The identification of focal use cases is a preliminary to a full prioritization of use cases in the final phase of joint modeling. Focal use cases are those that are

- Typical or representative
- Most common or frequent
- Most important to the user
- Most important to the provider (based on a business case)

In some applications, use cases may be designated as focal because of their importance from the standpoint of risk to the business. For most applications, a small collection, seldom more than half a dozen use cases, is identified as representing core capability.

> *In some applications, use cases may be designated as focal because of their importance from the standpoint of risk to the business.*

During the process of task modeling, the user role model may need to be revised to reflect new insights or information. In a single combined session, the group may move freely back and forth among the user role model, user role map, use case narratives, and use case map.

REVIEW SESSION

The purpose of the *review session* (or sessions if necessary) is twofold: auditing and allocation. First, the group reviews the models to ensure that they are complete, correct, and consistent. Second, use cases are sorted to identify which capabilities are to be supported and when.

Auditing. In auditing the role and task models, the models are first cross-checked to verify consistency with each other. All user roles should be supported by one or more use cases, and all use cases should support one or more user roles. (See sidebar, Cleaning up the Models, in Chapter 6.)

The task model is reviewed in sets of interrelated or interconnected use cases, beginning with focal use cases. Each narrative is checked for accuracy and completeness in itself and for consistency with other use cases. In the process, the group should identify and eliminate any contradictions between different parts of the model. They should also try to locate and consider eliminating any redundancy. The goal is to simplify the model—hence, the design—while maintaining completeness and correctness.

> *The goal of auditing is to ensure completeness and correctness while also simplifying the model.*

Allocation. In the final step of Joint Essential Modeling, the group allocates use cases to specific versions of the product or to successive refinement iterations. The primary purpose of allocation is to decide what features and capability will be immediately implemented in the system and which might be deferred to later releases or even permanently omitted. The allocation process resembles one of the essential decision processes in the popular technique of *Quality Function Deployment* (QFD) [Zultner, 1992], although various procedures may be employed. Prior to the actual prioritization, three pieces of information are needed regarding each use case: expected frequency, business importance, and expected difficulty or cost of implementation.

> *The primary purpose of allocation is to decide what features and capability will be immediately implemented in the system and which might be deferred to later releases or even permanently omitted.*

To help prioritize use cases, their expected frequencies need to be determined. In some cases, historical or empirical data may be available. It may be known, for example, that 83% of ATM transactions at a particular bank are cash withdrawals. Quantitative estimates can be agreed upon in many situations, either in terms of an expected rate ("A reasonable guess is 15 to 20 times a day.") or as a percentage ("About half the transactions are new orders."). The goal is not an absolute or objective index of frequency for all use cases, but an approximate rank ordering. In many cases, it will be sufficient merely to note that certain use cases are rare. Card sorting is an effective technique for rank ordering use cases based on frequency.

In addition to expected frequency, the relative business importance of each use case needs to be judged. A simple four-level rating suffices:

1. Unimportant
2. Useful

3. Central
4. Critical

Collective ratings are easily generated by averaging over the group. A list of use cases can be generated and reproduced for all members, who then assign a number from 1 to 4 for each one on the list. A quick way to do individual ratings is to use a card sort, with each use case written on a separate index card. The cards are then sorted into one of four piles based on the business case for the capability represented by the card. With a small number of use cases, not more than 15 or 20, consensus on frequency appraisals and business importance can be reached through polling and discussion.

Difficulty ratings or rankings can be generated in similar fashion. Use cases can be rank-ordered or rated on a four-point scale of difficulty:

1. Trivial
2. Simple
3. Difficult
4. Very difficult

Once all three pieces of information have been established for all use cases, they can be prioritized either through another card sort or through distributive voting. (See sidebar, Vote Gathering.) Card sorting can be used to sort use cases into piles for implementation on first, second, or later releases, for example. If use cases are rank-ordered by card sorting or by distributed voting, the top-ranked use cases are targeted for implementation in the first version of the system.

VOTE GATHERING

Distributive voting is a method for group selection from among a collection of objects, such as proposed features or use cases to be supported. It is often used for selections made under multiple criteria or constraints—for example, ratings or rankings of cost, business risk, business value, importance to users, expected frequency, or the like.

In distributive voting, each participant is given a certain number of votes, often expressed as a set amount of metaphorical money. The votes (or money) are to be distributed or allocated by each participant among the objects, such as proposed features or functions. Each participant must "spend" or allocate all his or her votes. To avoid any one participant's exercising undue influence over inclusion of some pet feature, there is usually a rule that votes must be spread. For example, each participant may have $100 to "spend" on features, with a rule against spending more than $30 on any single feature.

A set threshold may be established in terms of a minimum number of votes, or the top N vote-getters might be selected. Following the distributive voting, the results are reviewed by the group for reasonableness and practicality. Sometimes, ties must be broken. Occasionally, a feature or function considered relatively unimportant by all voters will garner enough votes for inclusion even though, on reflection, the group consensus is that the feature can or should be omitted. Conversely, a vital feature or function may be overlooked or omitted because everyone assumed it would draw sufficient support from others.

Distributive voting, which is used in the technique of Quality Function Deployment [Zultner, 1992], is generally considered to be a fair way of reaching consensus on selections made under complex and competing decision criteria.

21

GETTING ORGANIZED:
Usability in the Larger Context

ORGANIZATIONAL UNITS

The usability of software reflects the nature of the organization developing the software as much as it does the methods and models applied in the process. The structure and the culture of an organization, its operating rules and units, as well as its values, can have a significant impact on its ability to apply usage-centered design effectively. In this final chapter, we will look at the messy boundaries where the technology and technical issues of usage-centered design meet the organizational realities of current practices and politics.

There are many ways to organize to achieve improved software usability. The first and most basic questions concern whose job it is. Who is responsible for software usability? Who is responsible for user interface design? Who is expected to have the expertise and capability to carry out these responsibilities?

If it is no one's job, if usability is not part of the job description of at least one person, it is unlikely to be achieved [Constantine, 1994h]. The responsibility needs to be broadly shared. One of our European clients, producers of factory automation systems, initially brought us in to train the developers and designers of their PC-based control software. They next realized that the product specialists who turned customer requests into product requirements could increase their effectiveness through familiarity with usage-centered design. We developed a customer-focused training program to help them think in terms

> *If usability is not part of the job description of at least one person, it is unlikely to be achieved.*

of user needs instead of technology solutions and to communicate those needs to developers in terms of use cases and user roles. Finally, the client realized that technicians working on the programmed-logic controllers connected directly to the machines could create better internal code if they understood the connections between machine tool functions and operations and the needs of human operators. Another custom training was developed for them. This is the ideal—making usability a part of everyone's job. Short of the ideal, everyone involved in designing and developing a product should at least speak the language of usage-centered design.

Although formal chartering is not always necessary, some organizations will prefer to designate a recognizable organizational unit to address the problem of usability. Among the varied official entities that might be charged with all or part of the responsibilities for software usability are these prototypical groups:

- Usability Standards Group
- Usability Testing Group
- Software Usability Assurance Group
- Usability Consultancy or Center

As might be inferred from the names, these groups can be expected to function in various ways. A Usability Standards Group is typically assigned the job of setting and sometimes enforcing standards for usability and user interface design. The ubiquitous Usability Testing Group, by whatever title, carries out usability tests of the sort discussed in Chapter 18. A Software Usability Assurance Group is analogous to a Quality Assurance Group. Such a group may engage in standards setting, testing, auditing, and reviews in the interest of assuring that a certain minimum level of usability is maintained. A Usability Consultancy or Center serves as a repository of knowledge and expertise on software usability and user interface design. Of course, the functions of various kinds of organizational units might be intermixed in any number of ways to meet the needs of a particular company.

Regardless of the form of official organizational unit that might be utilized, some questions will need to be answered. What is the mandate or charter of the group? Does the group serve developers only in an advisory or consultative capacity, or do they have some authority? Do they set standards? Do they have the authority to approve or disapprove projects? Is the involvement of the usability group optional or mandatory on each project? Does the group work separately and independently from development teams, or are members of the group integrated into project teams?

> *Which form of organization will work best depends on how your organization approaches change and how it has dealt with comparable initiatives in the past.*

Often, we are asked which form of organization works best. The best answer depends on your organization, how it approaches change and new problems, and how it has dealt with comparable initiatives in the past. If your company already has had success with a separate software quality assurance group that is responsible for acceptance testing, for example, then software usability might be incorporated into the responsibility of that group. Alternatively, a Software Usability Assurance Group with testing capability and approval authority might work well in your organization. On the other hand, if your company has experienced a distinct testing group as a formula for internecine warfare, then a Software Usability Assurance Group is hardly recommended. The trick is to make the organization of usability fit the organization, and we will have more to say on this matter later in this chapter.

STANDARDS AND STYLE GUIDES

Many organizations approach change through declaration and definition. They try to make things happen by setting rules and establishing procedures. Although rules and defined procedures are important parts of how some—though not all—businesses operate, organizational change by fiat probably fails more often than it succeeds.

When it comes to software usability, it is particularly tempting to establish and reinforce a commitment to improved software usability by setting forth a formal set of usability standards or writing a corporate user interface design style guide. In our experience, however, it is better to build experience first before standardizing; otherwise, you run the risk of possessing standards that are not observed or of trying to enforce standards that do not work for you. If standards are imposed too soon, developers may fail to see the point of following the various design specifications and guidelines and, not understanding the rationale behind them, will be less inclined to conform.

> *If standards are imposed too soon, developers may fail to see the point and will be less inclined to conform.*

User interface standards and style guides overlap to a considerable degree. Usually, standards are conceived as more specific and absolute. It might be a standard, for example, that all modal dialogue boxes must have both an **OK** and a **Cancel** command button. Style guides are often conceived more broadly and cast in terms of general recommendations. It might be a part of the corporate style to avoid modal dialogue boxes whenever workable alternatives are available, for example. Style guides may also invoke broad principles, such as promoting user control or tolerating user errors.

CHANGING STANDARDS

We believe that the most usable end products result when both user interface standards and style guides are viewed as evolving and adaptive guidelines rather than as rigid prescriptions. Standards are not set once and for all but evolve through a continuous, adaptive process that proceeds concurrently with the work of every project. This does not mean that standards and style guides are changing all the time; it merely means that they are being critically reconsidered in terms of their continued support of good practices in usage-centered design. At a minimum, at the outset of each new project, the operative standards and style guidelines should be reviewed to assure that they are valid, relevant, and up to date.

> *Standards and style guides should be reviewed periodically to assure that they are valid, relevant, and up to date.*

Good user interface standards and useful style guides emerge from user requirements and from experience in designing to meet requirements. As can be seen in the activity model of Figure 21-1, established standards and style guides affect a number of modeling and design activities, which, in turn, provide input to the ongoing review and refinement of standards and guidelines. In the course of the initial requirements dialogue, role modeling, and task modeling, the relevant standards and style guides will be examined and, if needed, amended. In some projects, special conditions may prevail that require new guidelines or exceptions

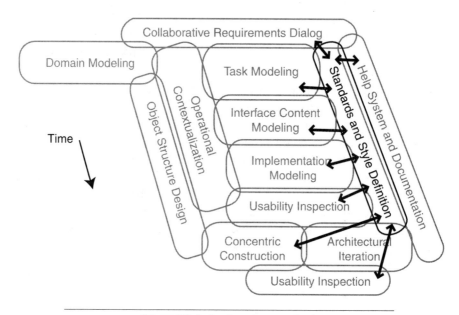

FIGURE 21-1 *Setting the standard.*

to normal treatment; such changes are essentially temporary accommodations to irregular project needs. In some cases, the weight of accumulating experience may dictate the need for more lasting revision. From content and implementation modeling through usability inspection and construction, standards and style guides will need to be actively consulted as sources, but experience in applying the standards and guidelines during these activities may also call for altering the official definitions or favored interpretations.

Because they can have such broad impact on numerous projects, standards and style guidelines need to be developed with care. Assistance from experts is highly recommended, if not in the development, at least in evaluating and refining draft standards.

Some standards and style guides designate particular components or exact layouts for use in specified dialogues or windows. Sometimes, these standards are supported or enforced by standard components, software forms, or templates. The use of standardized components and templates can be a powerful way to achieve consistency not only within a system but also across all applications used in an organization or all products in a line. However, this means that even greater care and thoroughness must be exercised in their design and evaluation than for a single product or application.

USABLE USABILITY STANDARDS

User interface standards and style guides should be viewed as systems in their own right and assessed in terms of their usability by developers. Once an initial set of standards and/or style guidelines has been established, they should be thoroughly evaluated. One can, of course, evaluate a set of standards merely by reading through them, but more systematic approaches are likely to yield better results. The quality of standards can be evaluated in terms of a number of criteria, including

- Conformity
- Coverage
- Convenience
- Consistency
- Compliance

Conformity is evaluated by checking entries in the standards or style guide against accepted usability rules and principles; it can be expressed as the percentage of entries that conform. *Coverage* refers to the thoroughness of standards and guides: What percentage of the questions raised in the course of a project or an evaluation can be answered by reference to the standard or style guide? *Convenience* is an index of ease of use, the usability of the standard or style guide. It can be assessed either as the percentage of questions that can be answered by reference to the standard or style guide within a set time period or as the time it takes developers to find an entry or to conclude that the matter is not covered. *Consistency* is probably most easy evaluated by conducting a consistency inspection (Chapter 16) of the standards or guidelines.

> *The ultimate test of any set of user interface standards or style guidelines is how they affect the usability of end products.*

The ultimate test of any set of standards or guidelines is how they affect the usability of end products. Introduction of standards and style guides should have a measurable or recognizable impact on the usability of software developed with their aid. *Compliance* refers to the extent to which the standards or guidelines set are actually reflected in delivered software. It is assessed by auditing finished products for compliance to standards and guidelines, but rather than taking this as a measure of the quality of the product, it is taken as an indicator of the usability of the standards and guidelines as published. Absent formal and direct measurement, subjective reports from developers should be solicited.

STANDARDS DEVIATIONS

Deviations from the set standards can come about for a number of reasons, and understanding these causes can be useful in creating the standards. Developers may not realize that a standard exists or applies, they can make mistakes in interpreting standards, and they may deliberately choose to depart from standards [Löwgren and Laurén, 1993]. Each of these failings can be minimized with appropriate attention. Standards should be written clearly in the first place and then thoroughly reviewed and edited for understandability. They need good organization and thorough indexing to facilitate locating relevant entries. The need for deliberate departures can be reduced through flexible guidelines that conform to good practice and cover a wide range of conditions. On occasion, technical constraints or innovative applications may require nonstandard solutions [Morris and Kettle, 1996], and these should not be considered a failure of the standards unless comprehensive coverage is the objective.

In our experience, a major contributor to nonstandard solutions is that the standards are too hard to use. They are bloated by verbiage, ambiguous, and not internally consistent. The published user interface style guidelines from the major software vendors are prime examples of these problems.

Our recommendations for standards and style guides are to keep them as succinct as practical and to make them as accessible and as easily used as possible. Instead of trying to micro-legislate everything, it is better to focus on a core of central issues of greatest importance to the organization. For practical application, less is more, particularly when the guidelines and standards are a newly added ingredient in the development process.

Design guidelines are most effective when they are available on-line from within the regularly used development environment where developers can get immediate access to them at any time as questions arise. Guidelines should be complete with examples, explanatory documentation, and extensive cross-references. Ultimately, they should be supported with a repository of reusable interface objects for implementing them.

> *Design guidelines are most effective when they are on-line, integrated into tools where developers can get immediate access as questions arise.*

COMPETING CONSTITUENCIES

Many groups and constituencies hold some stake in the outcome of software and applications development projects. In the interest of enhancing usability, we have placed users at the head of the line in providing input to software product design. As we explained in Chapter 20, however, others may also enter the queue and require attention from developers.

For example, technical telephone-support or help-desk personnel may have a different perspective on various considerations in user interface design. The folks in tech help may want to have lengthy error messages with extensive technical detail—a practive that might overwhelm or confuse users. Support staff may have a strong preference for a single common interface that cannot be customized by users. Personalized interfaces can be a nightmare to support, especially over the telephone. Creative combinations that meet the objectives of end-user flexibility and overcome the objections of technical support are usually possible. For example, the interface can be constructed to be easily toggled between the factory default configuration and the current user preferences. Error messages and dialogues can maintain a hidden log file that keeps technical details for use in troubleshooting.

TO MARKET, TO MARKET

Often, among the most aggressive and influential stakeholders are those who will be charged with marketing or selling the product under development. While ostensibly on the same team as the software developers, tensions between development teams and marketing and sales groups can run high, especially in this era of the "voice of the customer" and market-driven product development. Marketing and sales often dominate the thinking of upper management, and the opinions of these groups, well founded or not, can wield heavy influence in shaping the delivered form of systems.

It is especially ironic how often the interests of sales and marketing seem to be at odds with the needs and interests of the very people who use or purchase their products and services. Certainly, designers frequently find themselves pulled between requests or even demands from marketing and the best counsel of usage-centered considerations.

> *It is ironic how often the interests of sales and marketing seem to be at odds with the needs and interests of the very people who use or purchase their products and services.*

In our experience, the competing pulls of marketability and usability can be dealt with creatively. First, it is always important to keep in mind the difference between market forces and market forces as perceived by sales and marketing staff. Furthermore, the marketplace can itself be a dynamic and pliant phenomenon. While many modern companies pride themselves in being market-driven, there are limits to the philosophy of being responsive to the marketplace. Many of the greatest business successes of the modern world have been cases where markets were created by the introduction of new products and new technologies. The best products anticipate demand and lead the market rather than follow it. When videocassette recorders first arrived on the scene, no market survey would have found consumers clamoring for a way to permanently record television programs.

Sales and market share are the lifeblood of any profit-making venture, but that does not mean that design has to start there or end there. In our opinion, the real objective is to make sales by meeting needs, to create highly marketable products that are also very usable, or highly usable products that are highly marketable. Assuming that the basic choice of product is sound and meets real needs, the easiest route to achieving both is to follow a simple maxim:

Design for use; refine for sale.

This is, by no accident, similar to our rule of thumb for handling issues of utility and aesthetics. It is almost always far easier to make a functional but unaesthetic system attractive than to take an attractive but impractical system and make it work.

> *Design for use comes first. Marketability and artistry are not necessarily of lesser import, but they are better achieved by dealing with them in turn.*

In other words, design for use comes first. Marketability and artistry are not necessarily of lesser import, but they are better achieved by dealing with them in turn. This sequence assumes, of course, that the basic choice of what to construct has been initially informed by an analysis of genuine and expressed needs from users or potential users.

MARKET RESEARCH

Most marketing groups rely to some degree on market research, whether to identify market needs or to bolster prior conclusions. Learning about markets from would-be customers is something like learning about requirements from would-be users. Some of the methods favored by marketing are also used by user interface design specialists.

Focus groups are a technique that began as a market research tool, spread to the social sciences, and now is found in numerous niches across modern business practice. Focus groups are facilitated group discussions focused on a particular topic or issue. The facilitator tries to elicit rich responses by promoting interaction among group participants. Usually, there is an agenda or broad protocol outlining the subtopics to be discussed or the issues to be raised rather than a set list of specific questions as might be used in a group interview. Focus groups can be an effective tool for testing the response of potential customers to new product ideas or advertising campaigns. In our experience, they are better used in this capacity than for eliciting requirements. For the latter, interviews and observation or collaborative modeling, such as the JEM approach described in Chapter 20, are likely to be more effective.

As with other forums for learning about end users, simply because a focus group rejects a design does not mean it is an inferior approach anymore than their enthusiasm for another design means it is more usable. At best, focus groups yield preference measures; at worse, they can generate an escalating critique that has little relation to design quality. Caveat emptor.

MARKETS AND USE

When it comes to marketing and usability, we are, as in many things, true believers in the power of both-and thinking (introduced in Chapter 9). By thinking in terms of innovative combinations, creative designers can often satisfy all constituencies.

Here is one example that arose at a conference on embedded systems software. A manufacturer of electronics for the automotive industry was working on an innovative car stereo for inclusion in a luxury line of cars. The system included sophisticated digital signal processing that could simulate a wide range of acoustic environments under software control. The acoustics could be made to resemble almost any physical setting from a small closet to an intimate cabaret, from a modest

> *By thinking in terms of innovative combinations, creative designers can often satisfy all constituencies.*

concert hall to a great cathedral. The design question was how this capability should be controlled by the user. Ideally, one would probably want two buttons:

one to expand the apparent size of the acoustic space and one to reduce it. Unfortunately, dashboard space is extremely limited, and all the designers had been allowed was a single button. Dealer representatives and the marketing department had made very clear how they thought this button should function: It should alternate between small and spacious environments. In this way, a salesperson could persuasively demonstrate the dramatic differences as a car is instantaneously transformed into a vast cathedral, then a jazz cafe, then a concert hall.

However, the user tooling down the highway will have difficulty finding just the right acoustics for a particular piece of music if the effects are intermixed in a seemingly random fashion. The aficionado of on-road music who is the target of such a feature will want to adjust the sound in modest increments until the desired effect is achieved. Again, separate up–down buttons or a rocker switch would best fit the use case, but, if only one button is allowed, it should step to the next larger (or smaller) acoustic environment with each press until the limit is reached, at which it should reverse direction. Provided there are not too many steps, it should be fairly easy for the listener to pick the most suitable acoustics.

At the time this question was posed, the marketing perspective had already prevailed, but we proposed a creative both-and solution. The stereo is to operate in two modes: a normal, or consumer mode, and a special demo mode used in the dealer showroom. To enter the demo mode, the radio must be turned on while entering a "secret code," such as holding down the rewind and AM/FM buttons. This appeals to salespeople, who become privy to a technological secret, while giving the consumer the most usable operation.

Another example from the domain of pure software concerns the famous flaming wastebasket mentioned in Chapter 9. When an object to be deleted is dragged to the wastebasket, it promptly bursts into animated flames with extraordinary realism. Some programmer no doubt spent many hours getting the fractals just right and animating them just so. Most users prefer to just hit a key to delete items from an agenda. Dragging an item across the screen to a small visual target is itself time-consuming, to which must be added the inevitable pause as the user unconsciously waits for the flames to flicker out. Usable or not, many managers who saw this bit of silliness were impressed enough to buy the software and show it off to colleagues.

One of our classes went one better on this marketing gimmick while also improving usability. Their proposed trash can was a software plug-in with an open API to encourage third-party component builders and amateurs to create a full range of animated deletion targets like Oscar the Grouch trash cans, flaming incinerators, Tim the Toolman gas-powered disposals, or a recycling bin or compost pile for the environmentally minded. In this design, the plug-in could be hidden but the **Delete** key was always active, along with **Edit|Clear**, thus assuring both efficiency and visibility. Both-and thinking. It works!

Usability can, of course, be an important selling point for products, especially when greater efficiency or reliability can be both claimed and demonstrated. As a market matures and the consumers for a product gain experience and sophistication, usability will assume increasing importance compared to shear capability or quantities of features.

> *Usability can be an important selling point for products, especially when greater efficiency or reliability can be both claimed and demonstrated.*

Sometimes, it seems all too obvious that the real job of designers is to design successful products and the job of marketing is to market those products successfully. Neither role is ultimately more important than the other to the long-term interests of the company. The goal of developers, then, should be to work with marketing in creative ways that lead to better and more successful products.

WHEN THE CUSTOMER IS WRONG

As noted in Chapter 20, another constituency that may sometimes be at odds with users is customers or clients. The people with the checkbook may not be willing to pay for what the people with the keyboards really need. Customers are always right, it is said, except when customers are wrong, in which case they are also right. What does the designer do when customers are wrong, when they ask for or even insist upon features or arrangements that are not in their best interests?

There is no easy answer to this one. It depends on the relationship between the developers and the client, whether it is an internal client or an external customer, how important the client may be, and a myriad of other factors. Every consultant knows that there are times when one must choose between giving clients what they want and giving them what they need. The risk of not supplying clients' wants can be the loss of clients. The risk of simply delivering what is asked for can be the loss of integrity or credibility.

> *It is not necessarily wrong to give your clients what they insist upon when you know it is not in their best interests, but it would be wrong not to tell them.*

Like all aspects of defining requirements, contractual commitments with clients are best seen as always negotiable, at least within some limits. Software engineers and developers are bound by their codes of professional ethics to be honest with their clients. It is not necessarily wrong to give your clients what they insist upon when you know it is not in their best interests, but it would be wrong not to tell them unambiguously that your own judgment would lead in another direction.

EXPERTS AND EXPERTISE

In order for usage-centered design and enhanced software usability to be put into practice, it is vital to have access to expertise. Both internal and external resources should be identified. Internal sources of expertise should be inventoried. In every company will be found some people with greater experience or superior skills in graphic design, user interface design, usability testing, or other aspects of software usability. With outside resources, such as consultants, trainers, and testers, the important issue is building a continuing relationship with trustworthy providers whose skills complement those within the organization and whose working style fits with that of the developers.

> *The most cost effective uses of outside consultants help developers add to their own knowledge of software usability and their skills in applying the concepts and techniques.*

Consultants and other outside experts can be used in a variety of capacities. The most cost effective uses of outside consultants involve some degree of skills and technology transfer. All of the following not only can improve the current product but also can help developers add to their own knowledge of software usability and their skills in applying the concepts and techniques:

- Collaborative usability inspections of designs or prior systems
- Collaborative development of internal standards and style guides
- Review and refinement of internal standards and style guides
- Training, mentoring, or coaching
- Usability testing, in the field or laboratory
- Review of designs or prototypes

The value of the last of these, outside review of designs or prototypes, can vary considerably. It depends largely on the thoroughness of the feedback and the willingness of the experts to provide the rationale behind their recommendations.

In our experience, the least cost effective uses of outside experts are ones that get the consultants to do all the work:

- User interface design
- Analysis and modeling (user roles, use cases, and the like)

When modeling or design work is turned over to consultants, there is little or no organizational learning. It can be tempting to "farm out" user interface design work to established firms or expert consultants, but, although the immediate problem may be solved, the organization's ability to solve such problems in the future has not been enhanced.

Subcontracting for certain types of user interface design or implementation work sometimes does make sense, however. Especially where these activities involve quite specialized areas of expertise and may have a substantial impact on end-product usability. Promising possibilities include

- Visual component design and construction
- Templates and standard forms
- Icon design

Designing and building good reusable visual components requires special skills and extensive experience. Visual components to be added to libraries need sound architecture and robust coding, in addition to well-designed external appearance and behavior. Although it can be tempting to "roll your own" user interface controls, it is a temptation that should normally be resisted. Homegrown controls, even of a simple variety, are often ill-behaved and nonstandard. The specialized client software for a major on-line service has been through three integer releases and countless interim revisions, and the programmers have yet to get their homemade scrollbars to conform to standards. If the component you need is not available from third-party sources, we strongly recommend you consider getting experts to build it for you.

> *It can be tempting to "roll your own" user interface controls, but truly reusable components need sound architecture, robust coding, and well-designed external appearance and behavior.*

Program templates and standard forms for use with visual development environments are, as we have noted, an effective tool in promoting standardized solutions to user interface design problems. Because they will be reused on many projects, it is worth getting such templates and forms right in the first place. Working collaboratively with outside consultants is one way to get better results while helping to build internal knowledge. Once good designs have been defined, the actual implementation might be completed in-house.

Icon design is another highly specialized activity that requires special skill and experience. It is more than just a matter of getting the right shape or image; the image must be encoded as a small bitmap with a limited color set. A small number of relatively simple icons might be entrusted to in-house graphic designers. However, the designers must remain focused on usability, not on artistry; otherwise, the result can be the kind of complex, prettified, and artistic but uninformative icons illustrated in Figure 21-2.

FIGURE 21-2 *Web-style icons, beautiful, but...*
(COMPUSERVE 3.02)

CULTURAL FIT

By now, you are probably convinced of the value of usage-centered design and you understand the basics of the models and methods. You are ready to start putting what you know into practice. That means change—changing how you and others in your organization carry out the process of software development. There is no such thing as a purely technical change. All change in the workplace is organizational because even the narrowest change in how work is conducted, if it has any impact at all, will affect the people involved.

> *Introducing new practices, tools, or techniques involves two distinct processes: transition to new technology and diffusion of technology through the organization.*

Introducing new practices and processes or tools and techniques of any kind into an organization always involves two distinct processes. The new approaches have to be introduced into the organization and then spread beyond the point of introduction. These two processes are referred to as *technology transition* and *technology diffusion.* How the transition and diffusion are best accomplished depends on the kind of organization into which the new practices are being introduced.

Every software development group is a little bit different from every other one. If yours is a freewheeling development group that has a history of ignoring or undermining officially chartered committees and task forces, then announcing the new usability initiative with an inch-thick manual of user interface standards is likely to trigger more resistance than compliance.

The formula for success is fairly simple to explain, although it can be far from easy to apply:

- Understand your working culture.
- Locate the reservoirs of capability and good practices.
- Identify influential groups and individuals.
- Identify common organizational communication channels.

Organizational culture can be very complex. It includes such things as the way people talk with each other, how they cooperate or do not, the stories they tell, and the roles of teachers, leaders, and heroes in the organization. It includes collective values and ideals, repeated rituals and ceremonies, and forms of reward and reinforcement. Organizations can be formal or informal, flat or hierarchical, rigid or flexible, chaotic or highly structured.

A variety of schemes have been devised to help make sense of organizational culture. In the software field, the paradigmatic framework [Constantine, 1991b; 1993g] has been used with considerable success by the Software Engineering Institute and by various consultants dealing in process improvement and organizational change [Constantine and Lockwood, 1994; Mogilensky and Deimel, 1994]. We use this framework to assess an organization in terms of the overarching model by which its structure and culture are organized and sustained. Once the basic paradigm of an organization is understood, then responses to change can be anticipated, and effective change strategies can be planned. A brief summary of this framework is presented in Table 21-1. For more details, consult the cited references.

One aspect of corporate culture that is particularly important to understand is where the knowledge and expertise that form the basis for current practices reside within the organization. They might be carried only in the heads of individuals or could be part of the folklore or other informal practices of the organization. They might be codified in methods and procedures or reflected in officially established organizational structures. They might even be anchored in the established professional practices of the discipline of software engineering.

Knowing where current practices are grounded makes it easier to focus change efforts. If a company relies solely or primarily on the skill and knowledge in the heads of individual developers, then new practices need to be targeted to persuade and educate these individuals. If practices are embodied in written procedures and methods, then those procedures and methods will need to be amended to accommodate new practices.

> *It is important to understand where knowledge and expertise reside in the organization. Knowing where current practices are grounded makes it easier to focus change efforts.*

Knowing who the technical and practical leaders are can greatly facilitate introducing and diffusing new practices. To whom do developers look for setting the standard? Who are the sources of new ideas? If the official leaders or unofficial gurus are not "with the program," the program is not likely to succeed. If the trendsetters adopt the new practices, others can be expected to follow. With what groups or units do developers identify? If the project team is the basic and

TABLE 21-1 *Summary of organization paradigms*

Organization Paradigm	Means of Coordination	Orgizational Priority	Characteristic Response to Change	Effective Change Strategies
Closed	Hierarchy traditional hierarchy of authority	Secure continuity stability, group	Resist, compensate; counterbalance forces	Obtain executive sponsorship; target institutional units; shake up and settle down; identify and overcome resistance; set new standards and procedures.
Random	Initiative innovative independent initiative	Creative innovation variety, individual	Embrace, escalate; generate own change	Influence, persuade; recruit natural trendsetters; target individuals; sustain change with resources, practical support; form loose multiple guidelines to frame without constraining.
Open	Process adaptive process of collaboration	Flexible pragmatism stability and variety, group and individual	Explore, incorporate; build own strategy	Ensure full participation; engage in collaboration; build ownership and buy-in; join in defining change and strategy; assemble open-ended, customizable guidelines.
Synchronous	Alignment quietly efficient alignment	Effortless coordination harmony, mutual identification	Ignore or deny; amend shared vision	Revise and represent vision; recruit charismatic visionaries; high visibility, symbolic process; target entire organization simultaneously; guide by vision, transcendent purpose and mission.

influential unit of identity, for example, then training and other activities aimed at changing practices should be targeted to each project team as a unit.

Especially when it comes to diffusing new development practices, it is useful to know how word is spread. What are the real lines of communication in the organization? How do developers swap information or pass on new tricks and techniques? What media are ignored and what are attended with great interest? Every organization is a little different. In some, the printed word reigns supreme; in others, what counts is what is said over lunch in the company cafeteria. If company memos typically go from in-box to wastebasket unread, then memos are not likely to be influential in the change process. If developers carry on their most energetic exchanges by email, then email is probably the medium for the message. Once these aspects of the organization are understood, you will need to take them into account:

- Adapt the practices to fit the organization.
- Target the influential groups and individuals.
- Use the natural communications channels.

The new usability practices and processes themselves will often need to be adapted to the organizational culture. What does that mean? The practices described in this book are the technical foundation that needs to be shaped to fit in with the prevailing style of work and of relating in your organization. Take, for example, essential use case modeling. An organization that carries out a methodical, step-by-step software development life cycle supported by CASE tools will need to find a way to plug essential use case modeling into that life cycle at the right point in the process. They will need to obtain a CASE tool that supports essential use cases or that can be adapted to support them. They will need to develop their own outline for step-by-step task modeling. Otherwise, they will be left with a set of ideas in an informal, paper-based process completely at odds with their ways of working.

> *New usability practices and processes will need to be adapted to fit the organizational culture.*

The transition and diffusion strategies should be planned to use the prevailing culture and style of the organization rather than trying to change or work against these. If a group can crank out good software without formal design, then formal modeling and fully documented requirements tracking will be fighting an uphill and possibly unnecessary battle. Informal forms of usage-centered design adapted to the easygoing style of such developers will be easier to get going. On the other hand, content models created using Post-it notes may not go over well in a group that is used to doing everything through computerized checklists and CASE tools. A group with a successful history of using JAD is likely to find it easy to tackle Joint Essential Modeling, but a gang of highly independent individualists who hate meetings will only struggle against the technique.

This does not mean that organizational culture cannot or does not change. However, we find that organizational change proceeds more quickly and efficiently and is more likely to lead to a lasting and an effective resolution when it fits with the prevailing organizational culture rather than fights against it. If practices do not fit with the culture, then the culture may need to be changed first, which can be a long, slow process at best.

INTEGRATING USABILITY

Usability and user interface design can be integrated into the product development cycle in many different ways. The activity model for usage-centered design represents one approach. Other software development life cycle models that involve users and incorporate a focus on usability have also been proposed, among them SOMA [Graham, 1994] and GUIDE [Redmond-Pyle and Moore, 1995]. Effective approaches have in common an organized and flexible collection of activities with goal-oriented user involvement at specified points in the process.

The starting point for incorporating usage-centered design into your software development practices is the current software development life cycle (SDLC) model as it is actually practiced. You should examine the role of users, how processes contribute to or detract from usability, and how, where, and when user interface design is accomplished. You should also try to identify shortcomings or failures in current practices, especially as these operate counter to enhancing end-product usability.

It is often best to start with earlier stages in the current software development life cycle and then gradually expand until usability becomes fully incorporated over the entire life cycle.

In our experience, it is often best to look first to the earlier stages of the current software development life cycle and then gradually, over time, to add downstream elements until usability as an issue becomes fully incorporated over the entire life cycle. Although the route to be taken and the steps along the route will vary from organization to organization, we have found certain common features of successful usability initiatives [Lockwood, 1995].

1. Usability needs to be made an important and visible issue. If it is not emphasized and reiterated by management and by lead technical staff, it will not likely become important to developers themselves. Visibility is more about actions than words. Slogans and pronouncements have less effect than attaching consequences to increasing or failing to increase usability. Consequences can be as minor as a dressing down or a note of recognition and still be effective.

2. The development staff needs appropriate training to develop knowledge and skills. Training needs to be adequate to the task. In our experience, it takes three to five days of intensive, hands-on training to be ready to put usage-centered design into practice. This does not mean that graduates will be accomplished modelers or designers, but they should be ready to start applying the ideas and techniques in their work. Training needs to be timed so that participants can make effective use of what they learn. Usually, this means training members of a development team just before they begin a new project. By itself, training is not enough. (See sidebar, In Training.) Without appropriate follow-up and continuing support, newly learned techniques and concepts can quickly fall into disuse [Constantine, 1995b; 1997b].

3. Inspections, especially early inspections, can raise awareness and become a context for further learning. Participation in collaborative

---

IN TRAINING

Adequate training for professional staff is essential for success in introducing any new practices to a software development group, but many companies waste valuable time and scarce resources by not using training effectively [Constantine, 1997b]. Training by itself is often insufficient to achieve real results, and, undertaken at the wrong time with the wrong participants, it can actually hamper the cause of change.

At the outset, it is important to train the right people, which means professional staff who can put what they are learning into practice, preferably immediately. People without an interest in the topic or the opportunity to use it themselves not only waste their own time but also can detract from the learning of others.

Most training is undertaken to bring about change, to alter how people work. It pays to look at some aspect of actual practice before and after not only to assess or to demonstrate change but also to demonstrate commitment. The very act of surveying or benchmarking something flags it as important and alters how people approach it. Usability metrics or even just an informal inventory of current user interface design skills

and practices can provide valuable tracking for management and send a clear message that software usability is considered important.

Of course, it is worth getting the best training you can afford, but what happens after classes are over may be even more important for getting the most from the investment in training. Follow-up should come at intervals. Shortly after training, all participants should be contacted with congratulations and a request for feedback. Within the first year, participants should be assembled to review progress, raise questions, and discuss any needs for further training.

Regular inspections and reviews focused on usability not only improve products and practices but also keep the topic and its importance alive. A "postgraduate" workshop or other meeting to share experiences, emerging problems, and lessons learned can be a valuable sequel to training.

The real measure of successful training is not knowledge acquired, but knowledge applied. The goal is to assure that new practices are actually put into practice.

---

inspections can help spread the word about software usability, its importance, and how to achieve it.

4. Good strategies for integrating usability into the life cycle fit new practices and old practices together, modifying present practices to incorporate usability into analysis and design processes, while also tailoring usage-centered design to the organization and its practices.

5. Internal design guidelines can help to codify basic design decisions and practices once there is a firm base of knowledge and skill in usage-centered design and activities have been integrated into the full development life cycle. Designers and developers can avoid reinventing the wheel through reference to standard solutions and a consistent look-and-feel for applications can be maintained.

6. There comes a point in the process where the sophistication of the designers and the subtlety of the issues they are trying to resolve warrant introduction of targeted usability testing. This does not have to mean building an elaborate usability testing lab. As Chapter 18 outlined, simplified, low-cost approaches to usability testing can yield useful input to improve usability.

7. If it is worth doing, it is probably worth measuring what you are doing. With a full life cycle process in place, monitoring and measuring results becomes an effective route to refining the process and improving performance of the development team. Monitoring and measurement do not have to entail a full-scale usability metrics program. They can begin with logging and analyzing technical support queries and user feedback.

Measurement and monitoring, like all aspects of improved practices, need to be tailored to fit the needs and working culture of the organization. A group with a loose, informal style of development may choose to rely primarily on joint design reviews and collaborative usability inspections (see Chapter 16). An organization with more formal processes and practices might begin by combining iterative usability inspections with selective and targeted usability testing outsourced to a commercial testing lab. A custom metrics program could serve to monitor and fine-tune the process over time, starting with a simple set of metrics. The modest beginnings for usability metrics might include a single preference measure, such as the Subjective Usability Scales for Software, a performance measure such as productiveness, and a predictive measure such as task visibility (see Chapter 17).

> *Measurement and monitoring, like all aspects of improved practices, need to be tailored to fit the needs and working culture of the organization.*

LATE REMEDIES

What do you do if you are already in the middle of a project, but you want to improve the usability of this product as well as improve your development practices over the longer term? Although it is clearly better to build usability in from the beginning, projects already under way are not completely doomed. Because collaborative usability inspections are worthwhile at almost any point, an inspection is a good place to start. It will at least make you aware of where many of the problems are and how serious they might be.

Once the usability defects have been identified, fix whatever is easily fixable considering the stage of the development process. If it is the night before you burn the CD-ROM master, there may not be much that you can do, but, at any earlier point, the user interface might be improved substantially. For whatever is not fixable within the current release or development cycle, keep a feed-forward bin with possible changes and ideas for improvement in the future.

> *For software already far along in the development cycle, treat the current project as a learning opportunity.*

Most importantly, you should treat the current project as a learning opportunity. You may not be able to incorporate many of the results of task modeling, but you can learn more about how to do task modeling. You may be able to act on only a fraction of the recommendations that emerge from a joint design review, but you can learn some of the things to avoid in the future.

SEPARATE TRUTHS

Usage-centered design did not emerge ex nihilo, complete and comprehensive in scope as originally conceived. It evolved into an integrated approach through the slow accretion of activities and elaboration of details as it was adapted to meet the needs of practicing designers and developers. Although its elements fit well together, they are not inseparable. Many can stand on their own as useful tools for designers and developers [Murdock, 1996]. They may work best within the framework of the complete approach described in this book, but it is not always possible, practical, or advisable for every development group to adopt the complete package.

Some pieces of the puzzle are more easily extracted from the framework than others. In our experience, the parts that are most likely to be useful in and of themselves include

- Usability rules and design principles as guides
- Essential use case modeling
- Abstract prototyping with content models
- Navigation maps for modeling context transitions
- Operational contextualization
- Collaborative usability inspections
- Prioritized concentric construction
- Iterative architectural refinement
- User interface design quality metrics

Many organizations, for example, have started their software usability improvement processes by introducing collaborative inspections. Once inspections become standard practice, other elements of usage-centered design can be adopted. A piecemeal approach to improved processes may not always yield the most benefits for the investment, but practical and political issues may make it necessary.

Conceptually speaking, essential use cases are the heart of the approach. Under extreme time and resource pressures, we would fall back on task modeling as the irreducible core. It is an aid to thinking even when not the basis for complete usage-centered design. On the other hand, it is hard for people who are new to the ideas and techniques to get much benefit from putting task modeling into practice on its own, and beginners may find it very difficult to identify use cases without the stimulating preliminaries of user role modeling.

Without doubt, collaborative usability inspections are the most autonomous activity in usage-centered design. Inspections are quick, easy to learn, and are readily incorporated into nearly any life cycle model practiced within almost any working culture. Effective inspections do assume some knowledge of basic usability principles, however, so these are often the real starting point for learning to do usage-centered design.

Some activities, although separable in principle, are not likely to yield much return on investment apart from other parts of the process. For example, user role models provide little of direct value and much worthwhile input to task modeling and operational contextualization. Although it can be taught and performed as an autonomous activity, abstract prototyping in the absence of essential use cases makes little sense.

> *Under extreme time and resource pressures, we would fall back on task modeling as the irreducible core: an aid to thinking even when not the basis for complete usage-centered design.*

In the final analysis, the important thing is to do something. If usage-centered design as an integrated approach is too ambitious for an organization to adopt, then it is better to practice some part of it than to do nothing to improve usability. If you are already halfway through a project, then inspect what you have and fix what you can. Whatever form your usability initiative may take, it would be wise also to heed the words of Hillel the Elder: If not now, when?

APPENDIX A
Suggested Readings

We are often asked by clients and students what books on user interface design and usability engineering we recommend. There are many books on the subject; some of them are worth reading. The list that follows is intended as a fairly broad survey emphasizing books that have been found useful by practicing software developers over ones of more interest to academics and specialists.

Beyer, H., and Holtzblatt, K. *Contextual Design: Defining Customer-Centered Systems.* New York: Morgan Kaufman, 1997. The long-awaited basic reference on contextual inquiry and design. Elaborate but effective strategy for requirements definition.

Bias, R. G., and Mayhew, D. J. *Cost-Justifying Usability.* Boston: Academic Press, 1994. An indispensable reference for learning how to convince your boss or clients that getting the user interface right is worthwhile.

Constantine, L. L. *Constantine on Peopleware.* Englewood Cliffs, N.J.: Prentice-Hall, 1995. Amidst essays on teamwork, tools, and techniques are collected numerous useful ideas on managing and designing for usability. About a third of the book is on usability and user interfaces.

Cooper, A. About Face: *The Essentials of User Interface Design.* Foster City, Calif.: IDG Books, 1995. One of the very best books, both practical and provocative. Covers everything from buttons to shangles, grapples to gizmos. Outrageously opinionated and invariably insightful, Cooper is right about a lot of things but wrong on a few crucial matters.

Cox, K., and Walker, D. *User Interface Design. Second Edition.* Singapore: Prentice-Hall Asia, 1993. Solid but uninspired introduction to UI design. Good discussion of documentation, an often neglected element of usability.

Galitz, W. O. *It's Time to Clean Your Windows.* New York: Wiley-QED Publishing, 1994. Focused on-screen design for data entry and display, with thorough coverage, albeit a touch excessive and repetitive. Especially for CUI mainframers making the transition to GUI.

Fernandes, T. *Global Interface Design.* Boston: Academic Press, 1995. Light on detail, subtleties, and application, but a good general introduction to globalization and localization issues and the cultural aspects of user interfaces.

Hix, D., and Hartson, H. *Developing User Interfaces: Ensuring Usability Through Product and Process.* New York: Wiley, 1993. Somewhat idiosyncratic treatment of UI design. Includes practice exercises; emphasizes development process, analysis and modeling of user action.

Mayhew, D. J. *Principles and Guidelines in Software User Interface Design.* Prentice-Hall, 1992. Very thorough and detailed. Heavily influenced by Macintosh, but still broadly useful. Peppered with hundreds of very specific rules.

Nielsen, J. *Usability Engineering.* Boston: Academic Press, 1993. Low-cost, pragmatic, "you-can-do-it-too" approach. Emphasizes small number of sound, broadly applicable rules. Covers inspections and testing as well as design.

Nielsen, J., and Mack, R. L., eds. *Usability Inspection Methods.* New York: Wiley, 1994. Well-balanced collection of papers, including Nielsen's "heuristic inspections" and Bias's "pluralistic walk-throughs." Methods comparisons plus good information and arguments on value of inspections.

Norman, D. O. *The Design of Everyday Things.* New York: Basic Books, 1988. Readable, fun, and full of wisdom about usability in systems of all kinds. Covers basic principles with persuasive and familiar examples. A must-have classic.

Preece, J., et al. *Human–Computer Interaction.* Reading, Mass.: Addison-Wesley, 1994. Very comprehensive textbook, replete with interviews with industry leading lights (Hix, Norman, Shneiderman, etc.).

Shneiderman, B. *Designing the User Interface. Second Edition.* Reading, Mass.: Addison-Wesley, 1993. Update of an excellent textbook by innovative thinker on UI. Must-have reference.

Spool, J. M., DeAngelo, T., Scanlon, T., Schroeder, W., and Snyder, C. *Web Site Usability: A Designer's Guide.* San Francisco: Morgan Kaufmann, 1998.

Tognazzini, B. *Tog on Interface.* Reading, Mass.: Addison-Wesley, 1992. Funny, idiosyncratic, Apple-saturated view of UI. Full of good ideas, but take with a grain of salt.

APPENDIX B
Eleven Ways to Make Software More Usable: General Principles of Software Usability

Usability is a complex subject that can hardly be reduced to a few sound bites or pithy rules of thumb. However, certain broad concepts, consistently applied, can go a long way toward improving the usability of software and other kinds of systems. Here are the core principles that we have found are most easily grasped and applied in practice by software developers.

THE FIVE RULES OF USABILITY

These five broad rules provide general guidance and set the objectives for usage-centered designs:

1. **Access Rule**—The system should be usable, without help or instruction, by a user who has knowledge and experience in the application domain but no prior experience with the system.
2. **Efficacy Rule**—The system should not interfere with or impede efficient use by a skilled user who has substantial experience with the system.
3. **Progression Rule**—The system should facilitate continuous advancement in knowledge, skill, and facility and accommodate progressive change in usage as the user gains experience with the system.
4. **Support Rule**—The system should support the real work that users are trying to accomplish by making it easier, simpler, faster, or more fun or by making new things possible.
5. **Context Rule**—The system should be suited to the real conditions and actual environment of the operational context within which it will be deployed and used.

THE SIX PRINCIPLES OF USABILITY

These six specific principles help evaluation of designs and guide decision making regarding specific issues in usage-centered designs:

1. **Structure Principle**—Organize the user interface purposefully, in meaningful and useful ways that put related things together and separate unrelated things based on clear, consistent models that are apparent and recognizable to users.

2. **Simplicity Principle**—Make simple, common tasks simple to do, communicating clearly and simply in the user's own language and providing good shortcuts that are meaningfully related to longer procedures.

3. **Visibility Principle**—Keep all needed tools and materials for a given task visible without distracting the user with extraneous or redundant information: What You See Is What You Need (WYSIWYN).

4. **Feedback Principle**—Through clear, concise, and unambiguous communication, keep the user informed of actions or interpretations, changes of state or condition, and errors or exceptions as these are relevant and of interest to the user in performing tasks.

5. **Tolerance Principle**—Be flexible and tolerant, reducing the cost of mistakes and misuse by allowing undoing and redoing while also preventing errors wherever possible by tolerating varied inputs and sequences and by interpreting all reasonable actions reasonably.

6. **Reuse Principle**—Reduce the need for users to rethink, remember, and rediscover by reusing internal and external components and behaviors, maintaining consistency with purpose rather than merely arbitrary consistency.

More usable software comes from thinking about the user interface, from trying it out, and from successive refinement. It's not rocket science.

(L. L. Constantine)

Great user interface design is like great architecture: It fits beautifully with its environment and its purpose, with room for creative flair and artistry.

(L. A. D. Lockwood)

APPENDIX C
Glossary

abstract component An abstract placeholder for actual user interface components that represents either tools or materials or containers or controls within a *content model.*

abstract prototype A prototype in the form of a *content model* and a *navigation map.*

abstract use case A superclass serving as a placeholder for shared or common sequences inherited by subcases that are specializations; may not in itself be enacted by an actual user.

acquisition facilities Those portions of a user interface supporting novice usage through ease of use, rapid learning, and immediate access to system capabilities; are characterized by obvious and familiar features and behaviors, high feature visibility, abundant feedback, simplified and standard use cases; part of the progressive usage model.

active prototype A user interface design simulated or partially implemented in software.

affinity A relationship between use cases or between user roles based on similarity of an unspecified nature; is indicated in the use case map or user role map by a dashed line without arrowheads or by spatial proximity without any connecting line.

body (of a use case) See *use case narrative.*

class, or **object class** A description of the common attributes and operations shared by a set of objects; a template for instances of the class.

classification A relationship between *use cases* or between *user roles* in which some are subclasses (or subcases or subroles) of another, inheriting characteristics of the superclass (or supercase or superrole); the "is-a-kind-of" relationship known as *inheritance*. See *specialization*.

collaborative usability inspection A group process for identifying usability defects in a user interface design, paper or working prototype, or system.

composition A relationship between use cases where one use case "uses" or depends on one or more other subcases as included sequences or between user roles where a user role may include or be composed of other roles; also called *inclusion* or *subordination*.

concrete use case A use case as originally defined [by Jacobson], representing interaction between a user and a given or assumed user interface; a class describing the common pattern of interaction of a set of scenarios. See also *essential use case*.

concurrent modeling A process for developing two or more interrelated analysis or design models at the same time (e.g., interdependent development of *user role*, use case, and content models in designing user interfaces).

content model An abstract model of the contents of a user interface in terms of abstract components (tools and materials) contained within interaction contexts; may also include the context *navigation map*.

context navigation map See *navigation map*.

contextualization A process for adapting a user interface or user interface design, based on the operational model, to the working context or environment in which it will be deployed. See also *operational model*.

control object An *object* (software component) modeling *use cases* or other complex behavior involving coordination or communication among numerous objects; encapsulation of policies, procedures, or sequences not closely tied to any one object.

dependence See *composition*.

device constraint profile Salient or characteristic aspects or limitations of the physical user interface device or devices affecting user interface design (e.g., screen size, resolution, keypad format, type of input equipment).

domain expert Someone knowledgeable and experienced in a particular application area, profession, discipline, or type of work; is not necessarily a user.

domain language The natural, common, or accepted vocabulary of a given area of application, activity, or work; the language employed by users and application domain specialists to talk about their work.

domain object An *object* (software component) modeling information retained over time, based on the tangible or conceptual entities of the application domain.

enacted use case A *use case* as actually carried out by a user with a particular user interface or user interface design; a use case as instantiated; a concrete scenario.

enactment The steps taken or sequence defined within the use case narrative using a particular user interface or user interface design.

entity object See *domain object*.

environment profile A profile of salient or characteristic aspects of the physical work environment affecting user interface design (e.g., ambient noise, lighting, social interaction).

Essential Efficiency A predictive metric measuring efficiency of enacted use cases as compared with the ideal represented by essential use cases.

essential model A technology-independent model devoid of unnecessary restrictions or limiting assumptions regarding specific implementation details.

essential purpose The core or primary purpose of a use case or of a system or any portion of a system as viewed from the perspective of external users.

essential use case A simplified, abstract, generalized *use case* defined in terms of user intentions and system responsibilities; a technology-independent use case without unnecessary restrictions or limiting assumptions regarding specific implementation details reduced to its minimal form of expression within the language of users and the application domain. See also *concrete use case*.

expert usage A pattern of usage characterized by extensive experience with a system and high levels of skill and versatility, with a focus on efficiency, speed, and productivity; part of the *progressive usage model*.

extension A relationship between *use cases* in which the behavior of one is modified or extended by another; a use case comprising a special or exceptional case or alternative course of interaction within another use case.

focal use case A use case selected on the basis of importance or expected frequency as a starting point in developing a content model.

focal user role A user role selected on the basis of importance or expected frequency for initial attention in deriving use cases.

functional support profile See *role support profile*.

implementation model A description of the appearance and behavior of a user interface, usually in the form of an annotated visual prototype.

inclusion See *composition*.

incumbent profile See *role incumbent profile.*

information profile See *role information profile.*

instance One *object*; a member of a *class.*

instantiate Create an actual instance of a class.

interaction context A context within which interaction takes place; a part of a user interface collecting a particular set of visible or accessible features and elements; an abstract working space within the *content model* offering abstract components and tools for use. Compare *work environment* [Holtzblatt and Beyer].

interaction profile See *role interaction profile.*

interaction space See *interaction context.*

interface content model See *content model.*

interface object An object (software component) modeling the interface between users and the system, encapsulating functions and features of specific user interfaces or devices.

intermediate usage A pattern of usage characterized by increasing experience and skills using a system and continuously expanding and changing needs, with a focus on continued learning and skills acquisition toward higher performance levels; part of the *progressive usage model.*

Joint Essential Modeling A collaborative requirements engineering process in which designers, developers, clients, and end users jointly define user roles and essential use cases for a project; may also develop a content model.

Layout Uniformity A predictive metric measuring the quality of a graphical design in terms of the regularity of visual/spatial arrangement of features.

navigation map A model of user interface architecture showing the *interaction contexts* and the transitions and connections among them.

novice usage A pattern of usage characterized by little experience with a system and limited system usage skills, with a focus on rapid learning, easy and immediate access to system features, and a high need for support, encouragement, and guidance; part of the *progressive usage model.*

object A component of a software system encapsulating a set of attributes along with the operations on those attributes; an *instance* of a *class.*

object class See *class.*

object stereotypes A classification of objects (software components) based on function or usage: *interface objects, domain objects,* and *control objects.*

operational context The actual context, working environment, and conditions under which a system is or will be deployed and used.

operational model A collection of the salient factors in the operational context affecting the user interface design, including profiles captured in the structured role model (e.g., *incumbents profile, proficiency profile, interaction profile, usability criterion profile*) as well as the *environment profile, device constraint profile*, and operational risk profile.

operational risk Consequent or subsequent damages, costs, or other negative impact due to error, misuse, or operational failure in the course of system use; may be associated with specific user roles or use cases; part of the operational model.

paper prototype A user interface design showing layout and organization on paper.

passive prototype A nonworking prototype. See also *visual design.*

performance metrics Quantitative measures of system usability based on actual performance of users working with a system, simulation, or functional (working) prototype either in a laboratory setting or under field conditions in a normal work environment.

predictive metrics Quantitative measures that predict system usability in practice based on countable or measurable aspects of a user interface design, such as a visual prototype or other nonfunctional design model.

preference metrics Quantitative measures of system usability based on subjective evaluations by users and their impressions of a system, including personal preference, aesthetic appeal, comfort, and satisfaction.

procedural metrics Usability metrics that are task-sensitive and dependent on the structure and sequence of procedures or tasks carried out with a user interface.

production facilities Those portions of a user interface supporting expert or advanced patterns of usage by providing an efficient production environment characterized by rapid and customized access to many features based on user preference and "knowledge in the head"; part of the progressive usage model.

proficiency profile See *role proficiency profile.*

progressive usage model A model of system usage based on evolving patterns of use and changing needs of users as they progress from initial exposure through to advanced usage; includes acquisition, transition, and *production facilities*, which are distinguishable user interface subsets of features and capabilities that support novice, intermediate, and expert levels of usage, respectively.

role information profile A profile of salient or characteristic patterns of interaction within a given user role; includes information origin, direction of flow (to or from user), volume, and complexity.

role incumbent The actual person (user) in a particular user role.

role incumbents profile A profile of the background of typical incumbents in a given user role in terms affecting patterns of usage, such as domain knowledge, system or application knowledge, training, education, experience, intelligence, and sophistication.

role interaction profile A profile of salient or characteristic patterns of usage or interaction within a given user role; includes frequency, regularity, predictability, concentration, and intensity of interaction.

role model See *user role model*.

role proficiency profile A profile of salient or characteristic levels of application proficiency within a given user role in terms of progressive usage patterns (novice, intermediate, and expert usage).

role support profile The evident functions, features, or facilities needed to support a given user role.

scenario A concrete interaction between a user and a system; a single usage of a system; an enactment of a use case or of a combination of multiple use cases.

semantic metrics Usability metrics that are sensitive to the content, meaning, or purpose of user interface features.

specialization A relationship between use cases in which one case specializes (is a subclass of) another; a use case that specializes (inherits aspects of) another. See *classification*.

structural metrics Usability metrics that are dependent only on superficial features of user interfaces; are not task-sensitive or content-sensitive.

structured role model A structured model of user roles in terms of specific categories of salient or distinguishing characteristics, including role incumbent profile, role proficiency profile, role interaction profile, role information profile, role support profile, usability criterion profile, and related roles (role map). See *user role model*.

subordination See *composition*.

system response model That part of the narrative of a concrete use case specifying the actions of the system in response to user actions over the course of the use case.

system responsibility model That part of the narrative of an essential use case specifying the responsibilities that user expects the system to assume in response to user intentions in enacting the use case.

Task Concordance A *predictive metric* measuring the degree of fit between the relative difficulty of enacting use cases with a particular user interface design and the expected relative frequency of the use cases.

task model A model of work or usage comprising a collection of use case narratives along with the use case map; a collection of essential use cases and their interrelationships, including affinity, classification, extension, and composition.

Task Visibility A *predictive metric* measuring the extent to which features used to enact one or more use cases are available when and where needed within the user interface.

transition facilities Those portions of a user interface supporting intermediate levels of usage by providing a continuously customizable interface that facilitates continued learning and skills acquisition and provides a migration path for the user connecting novice to expert usage; part of the *progressive usage model.*

triphasic model See *progressive usage model.*

usability Ease of use; a combination of learnability, rememberability, efficiency in use, reliability in use, and user satisfaction.

usability criteria Specific design criteria or objectives in support of usability, including learnability, rememberability, efficiency in use, reliability in use, user satisfaction, clarity, comprehensibility, and attractiveness.

usability criteria profile A profile of the relative importance of various usability criteria for support of a given user role, especially as influenced by other aspects of the user role profile.

usability defect A potential problem in the operation, appearance, or organization of a system that makes a product harder to use by its targeted population of end users; any part or aspect of a user interface that violates or departs from accepted usability principles or user interface design guidelines or that is likely to cause or contribute to delay, confusion, or error on the part of a user or lead to failure to complete a task.

usability metrics Quantitative measures of the quality of a system in terms of its actual or estimated usability.

usage model See *task model.*

use case A single case of usage; a way of using a system that is complete, meaningful, and well defined to the user; an external, "black box" view of one required capability of a system. See also *concrete use case* and *essential use case.*

use case map A model of user interface architecture representing the interrelationships among use cases in terms of affinity, specialization, composition, and extension.

use case narrative The body or description of a use case in terms of the sequence of interaction between the user and the system; a structured dialogue (usually arranged as two adjacent columns) consisting of a user action and system response model or a user intention and system responsibility model.

user An end user; any person who actually interacts with a system; not to be confused with clients, customers, sponsors, or application domain experts.

user action model That part of the narrative of a *concrete use case* specifying the actions of users in a particular role during the enactment of the use case.

user intention model That part of the narrative of an *essential use case* specifying the intended purposes or subgoals of users in a particular user role during the enactment of the use case.

user interface That part of a system with which a user interacts to make use of the system and through which the user understands the system (to the user, the user interface is the system).

user interface architecture The overall organization of a user interface including both form and behavior; the structure of elements of a user interface and their interrelationships and their relationship to underlying functionality.

user role One kind of relationship between users and a system; a collection of user interests, behaviors, and responsibilities as well as expectations in relation to a system; a type of user, abstract and generalized.

user role map A representation of the relationships among user roles in a user role model in terms of *affinity*, *classification*, and *composition*.

user role model A representation of the various user roles and their salient or distinguishing characteristics as these affect use of a system. See *structured role model*.

visual coherence A *predictive metric* measuring the extent to which features within interaction contexts have been organized in a semantically consistent manner, grouping or associating closely related features and separating or distinguishing unrelated ones.

visual design A nonfunctional user interface design showing layout and organization graphically, whether on paper or using a software modeling or drawing tool.

workbench interaction A pattern of workflow characterized by complex, unpredictable interaction centered on a workspace; a focal interaction context, often larger than the window through which it is viewed, supporting a large variety of use cases and extensions through collections of tools.

workflow The succession of moves of the user within and between interaction contexts in the user interface.

APPENDIX D
Forms for Usage-Centered Design

Paper forms can serve as templates to speed usage-centered activities. This appendix compiles several forms that have proved useful over the years. These can be freely copied as needed. Included here are the following:

- User Role Model—Form S3A
- Essential Use Case Narratives—Form 3
- Software Usability Defect Log

The latest versions of these and other forms can be obtained from our Web site: ˉww.foruse.com.

Constantine & Lockwood, Ltd.

USER ROLE MODEL - FORM S3A

FOCAL ROLES

Nbr.	Name:	Includes:
Specializes:		**Other Related Roles:**

SALIENT BACKGROUND (training, education, experience, background, sophistication, intelligence, etc.):

DOMAIN KNOWLEDGE:
__ low __ medium __ high

SYSTEM KNOWLEDGE:
__ low __ medium __ high

PROFICIENCY PROFILE:
____ % low/novice ____ % medium/intermediate ____ % high/expert

INTERACTION PROFILE:
frequency: __ low __ medium __ high
intensity (rate): __ low __ medium __ high
total volume: __ low __ medium __ high

__ predictable __ variable __ unpredictable
__ concentrated (batched) __ distributed
__ simple __ moderate __ complex

__ required __ discretionary
__ irregular __ regular
__ continuous __ discontinuous
__ process-driven __ user-driven

INFORMATION PROFILE: dominant flow: __ from user __ to user __ balanced
origin: __ aural input __ visual input __ mental process __ telephone __ paper __ other: _____
available information volume: __ low __ medium __ high __ very high
data complexity (elements, groups, data types, sources, etc.): __ low __ medium __ high __ very high

SUPPORTING CAPABILITIES (needed functions, features, or facilities):

USABILITY OBJECTIVES (rank or check):
__ efficiency __ accuracy __ reliability __ learnability __ rememberability __ user satisfaction __ clarity __ comprehensibility
__ attractiveness __ other: _____

OTHER SALIENT ROLE CHARACTERISTICS:

Nbr.	Name:	Includes:
Specializes:		**Other Related Roles:**

SALIENT BACKGROUND (training, education, experience, background, sophistication, intelligence, etc.):

DOMAIN KNOWLEDGE:
__ low __ medium __ high

SYSTEM KNOWLEDGE:
__ low __ medium __ high

PROFICIENCY PROFILE:
____ % low/novice ____ % medium/intermediate ____ % high/expert

INTERACTION PROFILE:
frequency: __ low __ medium __ high
intensity (rate): __ low __ medium __ high
total volume: __ low __ medium __ high

__ predictable __ variable __ unpredictable
__ concentrated (batched) __ distributed
__ simple __ moderate __ complex

__ required __ discretionary
__ irregular __ regular
__ continuous __ discontinuous
__ process-driven __ user-driven

INFORMATION PROFILE: dominant flow: __ from user __ to user __ balanced
origin: __ aural input __ visual input __ mental process __ telephone __ paper __ other: _____
available information volume: __ low __ medium __ high __ very high
data complexity (elements, groups, data types, sources, etc.): __ low __ medium __ high __ very high

SUPPORTING CAPABILITIES (needed functions, features, or facilities):

USABILITY OBJECTIVES (rank or check):
__ efficiency __ accuracy __ reliability __ learnability __ rememberability __ user satisfaction __ clarity __ comprehensibility
__ attractiveness __ other: _____

OTHER SALIENT ROLE CHARACTERISTICS:

Constantine & Lockwood, Ltd., 58 Kathleen Circle, Rowley, MA 01969 | tel: +1 (978) 948 5012; fax: +1 (978) 948 5036 | email:
LConstantine@compuserve.com | LLockwood@compuserve.com

Constantine & Lockwood, Ltd.

Essential Use Case Narratives - Form 3

Nbr.	Name:	Purpose:

SPECIALIZES ➡   EXTENDS┈┈▶   USES ➡

USER INTENTION   **SYSTEM RESPONSE**

Nbr.	Name:	Purpose:

SPECIALIZES ➡   EXTENDS┈┈▶   USES ➡

USER INTENTION   **SYSTEM RESPONSE**

Constantine & Lockwood, Ltd., 58 Kathleen Circle, Rowley, MA 01969; tel: 1 (978) 948 5012; fax: 1 (978) 948 5036; email: LConstantine@compuserve.com | LLockwood@compuserve.com

Constantine & Lockwood, Ltd.
SOFTWARE USABILITY DEFECT LOG

Page _____ Product _____ Recorder _____ Date _____

DEFECT ID Location[1]	Interface Feature[2]			Type of Problem[2]			Description/Notes	Severity[3]
-0	button color command dialogue field function OTHER:	graphic icon item keystroke label menu	message page palette screen tool window	awkward complex cluttered confusing distracting error handling OTHER:	hidden feature hidden behavior inconsistent missing nonstandard uninformative	behavior feedback layout tolerance visibility workflow		4-critical 3-major 2-minor 1-nominal ?-evaluate
-1	button color command dialogue field function OTHER:	graphic icon item keystroke label menu	message page palette screen tool window	awkward complex cluttered confusing distracting error handling OTHER:	hidden feature hidden behavior inconsistent missing nonstandard uninformative	behavior feedback layout tolerance visibility workflow		4-critical 3-major 2-minor 1-nominal ?-evaluate
-2	button color command dialogue field function OTHER:	graphic icon item keystroke label menu	message page palette screen tool window	awkward complex cluttered confusing distracting error handling OTHER:	hidden feature hidden behavior inconsistent missing nonstandard uninformative	behavior feedback layout tolerance visibility workflow		4-critical 3-major 2-minor 1-nominal ?-evaluate
-3	button color command dialogue field function OTHER:	graphic icon item keystroke label menu	message page palette screen tool window	awkward complex cluttered confusing distracting error handling OTHER:	hidden feature hidden behavior inconsistent missing nonstandard uninformative	behavior feedback layout tolerance visibility workflow		4-critical 3-major 2-minor 1-nominal ?-evaluate
-4	button color command dialogue field function OTHER:	graphic icon item keystroke label menu	message page palette screen tool window	awkward complex cluttered confusing distracting error handling OTHER:	hidden feature hidden behavior inconsistent missing nonstandard uninformative	behavior feedback layout tolerance visibility workflow		4-critical 3-major 2-minor 1-nominal ?-evaluate
-5	button color command dialogue field function OTHER:	graphic icon item keystroke label menu	message page palette screen tool window	awkward complex cluttered confusing distracting error handling OTHER:	hidden feature hidden behavior inconsistent missing nonstandard uninformative	behavior feedback layout tolerance visibility workflow		4-critical 3-major 2-minor 1-nominal ?-evaluate
-6	button color command dialogue field function OTHER:	graphic icon item keystroke label menu	message page palette screen tool window	awkward complex cluttered confusing distracting error handling OTHER:	hidden feature hidden behavior inconsistent missing nonstandard uninformative	behavior feedback layout tolerance visibility workflow		4-critical 3-major 2-minor 1-nominal ?-evaluate
-7	button color command dialogue field function OTHER:	graphic icon item keystroke label menu	message page palette screen tool window	awkward complex cluttered confusing distracting error handling OTHER:	hidden feature hidden behavior inconsistent missing nonstandard uninformative	behavior feedback layout tolerance visibility workflow		4-critical 3-major 2-minor 1-nominal ?-evaluate
-8	button color command dialogue field function OTHER:	graphic icon item keystroke label menu	message page palette screen tool window	awkward complex cluttered confusing distracting error handling OTHER:	hidden feature hidden behavior inconsistent missing nonstandard uninformative	behavior feedback layout tolerance visibility workflow		4-critical 3-major 2-minor 1-nominal ?-evaluate
-9	button color command dialogue field function OTHER:	graphic icon item keystroke label menu	message page palette screen tool window	awkward complex cluttered confusing distracting error handling OTHER:	hidden feature hidden behavior inconsistent missing nonstandard uninformative	behavior feedback layout tolerance visibility workflow		4-critical 3-major 2-minor 1-nominal ?-evaluate

Usability Defect: Any feature, function, or facet of the user interface or its organization that violates established principles of usability (e.g., visibility, feedback, etc.) or that is likely to lead to user error, delay, confusion, or the failure to complete a task.

[1] Note location of defect by screen shot or document page; identify defect by log page plus ID number, e.g., 0-8, 2-3.

[2] Circle or check all descriptors that apply to the identified usability defect; write in if "other."

[3] Circle or check initial estimate of severity/significance of defect without respect to cost or difficulty of correction.

Form CUI-Defect S/W3.1   © 1995, 1997, Constantine & Lockwood

APPENDIX E
Subjective Usability Scales
for Software (SUSS)

The Subjective Usability Scales for Software (SUSS) instrument, originally devised for our research on usability metrics, has been used by a number of clients and students to evaluate user interface designs. The sample form that follows is a template for the questionnaire that may be copied freely.

To turn the SUSS template into a workable questionnaire, the placeholder at the top must be replaced by a sketch, screen shot, or other representation of the part of a user interface being evaluated. A series of four representative task scenarios must be devised and incorporated into questions 6 through 9.

To score the SUSS, subtract 1 from the response to each question for the first five questions and subtract the response for each of the last five questions from 6. (This normalizes all questions to a range of 0 through 5 since the last five questions are "inverted.") Sum these individual question scores to yield an overall usability score between 0 and 50. Questions 1 through 5 yield scores from 0 to 5 on each of five distinct facets of subjective usability:

1. **Valence** (liking or personal preference)
2. **Aesthetics** (attractiveness)
3. **Organization** (graphical design and layout)
4. **Interpretation** (understandability)
5. **Acquisition** (ease of learning)

The scores for questions 6 through 10 can be summed to yield an overall score for **Facility** or ease of use that will range from 0 to 25. Alternatively, the final question can be used alone as a score for **Facility** with the same 0-to-5 range as the other facets.

Subjective Usability Scales for Software
SAMPLE FORM

Below is a picture of part of the user interface for _____.
Study the picture for a minute, then answer the questions that follow by circling your answers.

> Screen-shot or
> visual prototype
> here.

1. How much do you like this particular design?	hate it						love it
	1	2	3	4	5	6
2. How attractive or aesthetically appealing is this design?	ugly						beautiful
	1	2	3	4	5	6
3. How good is the graphical design and layout?	poor						excellent
	1	2	3	4	5	6
4. How easy to interpret and understand is this design?	hard						easy
	1	2	3	4	5	6
5. How easy is it likely to be to learn to use this design?	hard						easy
	1	2	3	4	5	6

Based on your understanding of the picture above, please rate how easy you think it would be to use this dialogue to accomplish each of the following tasks:

6. _____.

	trivially easy						virtually impossible
circle a number:	1	2	3	4	5	6

7. _____.

	trivially easy						virtually impossible
circle a number:	1	2	3	4	5	6

8. _____.

	trivially easy						virtually impossible
circle a number:	1	2	3	4	5	6

9. _____.

	trivially easy						virtually impossible
circle a number:	1	2	3	4	5	6

10. Overall, how would you rate the ease of use or usability of this design?

	very easy						very difficult
circle a number:	1	2	3	4	5	6

References

Albrecht, A. J. 1979. "Measuring Application Development Productivity." *Proc. Joint SHARE/GUIDE/IBM Application Development Symposium.* Armonk, New York: IBM.

Albrecht, A. J., and Gaffney, J. E. 1983. "Software Function, Source Lines of Code, and Development Effort Prediction." *IEEE Trans. Software Engineering* 9 (6):639–647.

Apperley, M., and Duncan, A. 1995. "Human–Computer Interface Design in the Software Life Cycle." In Purvis, M., ed., *Proc. Software Education Conference 1994.* Los Alomitos, Calif.: IEEE Computer Press.

Bevan, N., and Macleod, M. 1994. "Usability Measurement in Context." *Behaviour and Information Technology* 13 (1–2):132–145.

Beyer, H., and Holtzblatt, K. 1997. *Contextual Design: Defining Customer-Centered Systems.* New York: Morgan Kaufman.

Bias, R. G. 1994. "The Pluralistic Usability Walk-Through: Coordinated Empathies." In Nielsen, J., and Mack, R. L., eds., *Usability Inspection Methods.* New York: Wiley.

Bilow, S. C. 1995. "Defining and Developing User Interfaces with Use Cases." *Report on Object Analysis and Design* 1 (5):28–34.

Bonsiepe, G. A. 1968. "A Method of Quantifying Order in Typographic Design." *J. Typographic Research* 2:203–220.

Booch, G. 1994. "Scenarios." *Report on Object Analysis and Design* 1 (3):3–6.

Bransten, L. 1998. "The Future Calls: Smart Phones Have Lots of Cool Features— But Not All That Many Customers." *Wall Street Journal*, 15 June:R6.

Callahan, G. 1994. "Excessive Realism in GUI Design." *Software Development* 3 (9):36–43.

Card, D. N., and Glass, R. L. 1990. *Measuring Software Design Quality.* Englewood Cliffs, N.J.: Prentice-Hall.

Card, S. K., Moran, T. P., and Newell, A. 1983. *The Psychology of Human–Computer Interaction.* Hillsdale, N.J.: Lawrence Erlbaum.

Carroll, J. M., ed. 1995. *Scenario-Based Design.* New York: Wiley.

Chidamber, S., and Kemerer, C. 1994. "A Metrics Suite for Object-Oriented Design." *IEEE Trans. Software Engineering* 20 (6):476–493.

Collins, D. 1995. *Designing Object-Oriented User Interfaces.* Redwood City, Calif.: Benjamin/Cummings.

Comber, T., and Maltby, J. R. 1994. "Screen Complexity and User Design Preference in Windows Applications." In Howard, S., and Leung, Y. K., eds., *OzCHI '94 Proceedings.* Canberra: CHISIG, Ergonomics Society of Australia.

Comber, T., and Maltby, J. R. 1995. "Evaluating Usability of Screen Designs with Layout Complexity." In Hasan, H., and Nicastri, C., eds., *OzCHI '95 Proc.* Canberra: CHISIG, Ergonomics Society of Australia.

Constantine, L. L. 1968. "Segmentation and Design Strategies for Modular Programming." In Barnett, T. O., and Constantine, L. L., eds., *Modular Programming: Proc. National Symposium.* Cambridge: Information and Systems Press.

Constantine, L. L. 1991a. "Building Structured Open Teams to Work." *Software Development '91 Proc.* San Francisco: Miller Freeman.

Constantine, L. L. 1991b. "Fitting Intervention to Organizational Paradigm." *Organization Development J.* 9 (2):41–50.

Constantine, L. L. 1991c. "Toward Usable Interfaces: Bringing Users and User Perspectives into Design." *American Programmer* 4 (2):6–14.

Constantine, L. L. 1992a. "Consensus and Compromise." *Computer Language* 9 (4), April. Reprinted in *Constantine on Peopleware.* Englewood Cliffs, N.J.: Prentice-Hall, 1995.

Constantine, L. L. 1992b. "Consistency and Conventions." *Computer Language Magazine* 9 (11), November.

Constantine, L. L. 1992c. "Decisions, Decisions." *Computer Language* 9 (3), March. Reprinted in *Constantine on Peopleware.* Englewood Cliffs, N.J.: Prentice-Hall, 1995.

Constantine, L. L. 1992d. "The Lowly and Exhalted Scribe." *Computer Language* 9 (6), June. Reprinted in *Constantine on Peopleware.* Englewood Cliffs, N.J.: Prentice-Hall, 1995.

Constantine, L. L. 1992e. "Negotiating Consensus." *Computer Language* 9 (5), May. Reprinted in *Constantine on Peopleware*. Englewood Cliffs, N.J.: Prentice-Hall, 1995.

Constantine, L. L. 1992f. "Rewards and Reuse." *Computer Language Magazine*, 9 (7), July. Reprinted in *Constantine on Peopleware*. Englewood Cliffs, N.J.: Prentice-Hall, 1995.

Constantine, L. L. 1993a. "Having It All." *Software Development* 1 (9), September. Reprinted in *Constantine on Peopleware*. Englewood Cliffs, N.J.: Prentice-Hall, 1995.

Constantine, L. L. 1993b. "Improving Intermediates." *Software Development* 1 (2), February. Reprinted in *Constantine on Peopleware*. Englewood Cliffs, N.J.: Prentice-Hall, 1995.

Constantine, L. L. 1993c. "Objects in Your Face." *Object Magazine* 3 (4), July. Reprinted in *Constantine on Peopleware*. Englewood Cliffs, N.J.: Prentice-Hall, 1995.

Constantine, L. L. 1993d. "Official Space." *Software Development* 1 (12), December. Reprinted in *Constantine on Peopleware*. Englewood Cliffs, N.J.: Prentice-Hall, 1995.

Constantine, L. L. 1993e. "Software by Teamwork: Working Smarter." *Software Development* 1 (1), July.

Constantine, L. L. 1993f. "User Interface Design for Embedded Systems." *Embedded Systems Programming* 6 (8):43–58.

Constantine, L. L. 1993g. "Work Organization: Paradigms for Project Management and Organization." *Communications of the ACM* 36 (10), October.

Constantine, L. L. 1994a. "Collaborative Usability Inspections for Software." *Software Development '94 Proc.* San Francisco: Miller Freeman.

Constantine, L. L. 1994b. "Essentially Speaking." *Software Development* 2 (11), November.

Constantine, L. L. 1994c. "Graphical Navigation." *Windows Tech J.* 3 (8):44–45.

Constantine, L. L. 1994d. "In-Time Delivery." *Software Development* 2 (7), July. Reprinted in *Constantine on Peopleware*. Englewood Cliffs, N.J.: Prentice-Hall, 1995.

Constantine, L. L. 1994e. "Interfaces for Intermediates." *IEEE Software* 11 (4):96–99.

Constantine, L. L. 1994f. "Modeling Matters." *Software Development* 2 (2), February. Reprinted in *Constantine on Peopleware*. Englewood Cliffs, N.J.: Prentice-Hall, 1995.

Constantine, L. L. 1994g. "Persistent Usability: A Multiphasic User Interface Architecture for Supporting the Full Usage Life Cycle." In Howard, S., and Leung, Y. K., eds., *OzCHI '94 Proc.* CHISIG, Ergonomics Society of Australia.

Constantine, L. L. 1994h. "Unusable You." *Software Development* 2 (4), April. Reprinted in *Constantine on Peopleware*. Englewood Cliffs, N.J.: Prentice-Hall, 1995.

Constantine, L. L. 1994i. "Up the Waterfall." *Software Development* 2 (1), January. Reprinted in *Constantine on Peopleware*. Englewood Cliffs, N.J.: Prentice-Hall, 1995.

Constantine, L. L. 1994j. "Wizard Widgets." *Software Development* 2 (9), September. Reprinted in *Constantine on Peopleware*. Englewood Cliffs, N.J.: Prentice-Hall, 1995.

Constantine, L. L. 1995a. "Essential Modeling: Use Cases for User Interfaces." *ACM Interactions* 2 (2):34–46.

Constantine, L. L. 1995b. "In Training." *Software Development* 3 (4), April.

Constantine, L. L. 1995c. "Shapes to Come." *Software Development* 3 (5), May.

Constantine, L. L. 1995d. "Software Objectives." *Software Development* 3 (6), June.

Constantine, L. L. 1995e. "Under Pressure." *Software Development* 3 (10), October.

Constantine, L. L. 1996a. "Re: Architecture." *Software Development* 4 (1), January.

Constantine, L. L. 1996b. "Usable Objects: Getting the Message." *Object Magazine* 6 (7), September.

Constantine, L. L. 1996c. "Usable Objects: Abstract Interfaces." *Object Magazine* 6 (10), December.

Constantine, L. L. 1996d. "Usage-Centered Design for Embedded Systems: Essential Models." *Embedded Systems Conference '96 Proc.* San Francisco: Miller Freeman.

Constantine, L. L. 1996e. "Usage-Centered Software Engineering: New Models, Methods, and Metrics." In Purvis, M., ed., *Software Engineering: Education and Practice.* Los Alamitos, Calif.: IEEE Computer Society Press.

Constantine, L. L. 1996f. "Visual Coherence and Usability: A Cohesion Metric for Assessing the Quality of Dialogue and Screen Designs." *OzCHI '96 Proc.* Los Alamitos, Calif.: IEEE Computer Society Press.

Constantine, L. L. 1997a. "Usable Objects: New Media." *Object Magazine* 6 (12), February.

Constantine, L. L. 1997b. "These Are Trained Professionals." *Software Development* 5 (9), September.

Constantine, L. L. 1997c. "Usable Objects: The Seams Are Showing." *Object Magazine* 7 (10), December.

Constantine, L. L. 1998a. "Rapid Abstract Prototyping." *Software Development* 6 (11), November.

Constantine, L. L. 1998b. "Real Life Requirements." *Software Development* 6 (5), May.

Constantine, L. L., and Henderson-Sellers, B. 1995. "Notation Matters. Part I: Framing the Issues." *Report on Object Analysis and Design* 2 (3):25–29.

Constantine, L. L., and Lockwood, L. A. D. 1994. "Fitting Practices to the People." *American Programmer* 7 (12), December.

Cooper, A. 1995. *About Face: The Essentials of User Interface Design.* Foster City, Calif.: IDG Books.

Davis, A. 1993. *Software Requirements: Objects, Functions, and States.* Englewood Cliffs, N.J.: Prentice-Hall.

Desurvire, H. W. 1994. "Faster, Cheaper!! Are Usability Inspection Methods as Effective as Empirical Testing?" In Nielsen, J., and Mack, R. L., eds. *Usability Inspection Methods.* New York: Wiley.

Doyle, M., and Strauss, M. 1982. *How to Make Meetings Work.* New York: Jove.

Eagan, D. E. 1998. "Individual Differences in Human–Computer Interaction." In Helander, M., ed., *Handbook of Human–Computer Interaction.* Amsterdam: North Holland.

Embley, D. W., and Woodfield, S. N. 1987. "Cohesion and Coupling for Abstract Data Types." *Sixth Annual Phoenix Conference on Computers and Communication,* 229–234.

Emery, J. 1998. "The Case for Adaptive Software Development." *Software Development* 6 (4), April.

Firesmith, D. G. 1994. "Modeling the Dynamic Behavior of Systems, Mechanisms, and Classes with Scenarios." *Report on Object Analysis and Design* 1 (2):32–36.

Fitts, P. M. 1954. "The Information Capacity of the Human Motor System in Controlling Amplitude of Movement." *J. Experimental Psychology* 47:381–391.

Fitts, P. M., and Posner, M. I. 1967. *Human Performance.* Belmont, Calif.: Brooks Cole.

Galitz, W. O. 1994. *It's Time to Clean Your Windows: Designing GUIs That Work.* New York: Wiley-QED.

Gause, D. C., and Weinberg, G. M. 1989. *Exploring Requirements: Quality Before Design.* New York: Dorset House.

Gilb, T. 1977. *Software Metrics.* Cambridge: Winthrop.

Gilb, T., and Graham, D. 1993. *Software Inspection*. Reading, Mass.: Addison-Wesley.

Graham, I. 1994. *Migrating to Object Technology*. Reading, Mass.: Addison-Wesley.

Graham, I. 1996. "Task Scripts, Use Cases, and Scenarios in Object-Oriented Analysis." *Object-Oriented Systems* 3 (3):123–142.

Hawryszkiewycz, I., and Gorton, I. 1996. "Platforms for Cooperative Software Development." *American Programmer* 9 (8):11–18.

Henderson-Sellers, B. 1996. *Object-Oriented Metrics: Measures of Complexity*. Upper Saddle River, N.J.: Prentice-Hall.

Henderson-Sellers, B., Constantine, L. L., and Graham, I. M. 1996. "Coupling and Cohesion: Toward a Valid Metrics Suite for Object-Oriented Analysis and Design." *Object-Oriented Systems* 3:143–158.

Highsmith, J. 1998. "Order for Free." *Software Development* 6 (3), March.

Holtzblatt, K., and Beyer, H. 1993. "Making Customer-Centered Design Work for Teams." *Communications of the ACM* 36 (10), October.

Jacobson, I. 1994. "Basic Use-Case Modeling." *Report on Object Analysis and Design* 1 (2):15–19.

Jacobson, I., Christerson, M., Jonsson, P., and Övergaard, G. 1992. *Object-Oriented Software Engineering: A Use Case Driven Approach*. Reading, Mass.: Addison-Wesley.

Kaindl, H. 1995. "An Integration of Scenarios with Their Purposes in Task Modeling." *Proc. Symposium on Designing Interactive Systems*. Ann Arbor: ACM Press.

Kokol, P., Rozman, I., and Venuti, V. 1995. "User Interface Metrics." *ACM SIGPLAN Notices* 30 (4):36–38.

Krasner, G. E., and Pope, S. T. 1988. "A Cookbook for Using the Model-View-Controller User Interface Paradigm in Smalltalk-80." *J. of Object-Oriented Programming* 1 (3):26–49.

Lauesen, S., and Harning, M. B. 1993. "Dialogue Design Through Modified Dataflow and Data Modeling." In Grechenig, T., and Tscheligi, M., eds., *Human–Computer Interaction, VCHCI '93*. New York: Springer-Verlag.

Laurel, B., and Mountford, S. J. 1990. *The Art of User Interface Design*. Reading, Mass.: Addison-Wesley.

Lederer, A. L., and Prasad, J. 1992. "Nine Management Guidelines for Better Cost Estimating." *Communications of the ACM* 35 (2):51–59.

Lillienthal, C., and Züllighoven, H. 1997. "Application-Oriented Usage Quality: The Tools and Materials Approach." *ACM Interactions* IV (6):35–41.

Lockwood, L. A. D. 1994. "Customizing User Interface Design to the Application Profile." *Software Development '94 Proc.* San Francisco: Miller Freeman.

Lockwood, L. A. D. 1995. "Managing Development for More Usable Software." *Software Development '95 Proc.* San Francisco: Miller Freeman.

Löwgren, J., and Laurén, U. 1993. "Supporting the Use of Guidelines and Style Guides in Professional User Interface Design." *Interacting with Computers* 5 (4):385–396.

Lyons, P. J., Pitchforth, M., Page, D., Given, T., and Apperley, M. D. 1996 "The Oval Menu—Evolution and Evaluation of a Widget." In *Proceedings OzCHI '96*. Los Alomitos, Calif.: IEEE Computer Society Press.

McDaniel, S. E., Olson, G. M., and Olson, J. S. 1994. "Methods in Search of Methodology—Combining HCI and Object Orientation." In *Proceedings of CHI '94*. New York: ACM Press.

McMenamin, S., and Palmer, J. 1984. *Essential Systems Analysis.* Englewood Cliffs, N.J.: Prentice-Hall.

Microsoft. 1995. *The Windows Interface Guidelines for Software Design.* Redmond, Wa.: Microsoft Press.

Miller, G. A. 1956. "The Magical Number Seven, Plus or Minus Two: Some Limits on Our Capacity for Processing Information." *Psychological Review* 63:81–97.

Mogilensky, J., and Deimel, B. L. 1994. "Where Do People Fit in the CMM?" *American Programmer* 7 (9), September.

Molich, R., and Nielsen, J. 1990. "Improving a Human–Computer Dialogue." *Communications of the ACM* 33 (3):338–348.

Morris, S., and Kettle, R. 1996. "Testing a User Interface Style Guide." In *Proceedings OzCHI '96*. Los Alomitos, Calif.: IEEE Computer Society Press.

Muller, M., Tudor, L. G., Wildman, D. M., White, E. A., Root, R. W., Dayton, T., Carr, R., Diekmann, B., and Dykstra-Erickson, E. 1995. "Bifocal Tools for Scenarios and Representations in Participatory Activities with Users." In Carroll, J. M., ed., *Scenario-Based Design.* New York: Wiley.

Murdock, M. 1996. "Software Design Teams at Iomega," *Interactions* 3 (2):11–14.

Nielsen, J. 1993. *Usability Engineering.* Boston: Academic Press.

Nielsen, J. 1994a. "Enhancing the Explanatory Power of Usability Heuristics." *Proc. ACM CHI '94 Conference.* New York: ACM Press.

Nielsen, J. 1994b. "Heuristic Evaluation." In Nielsen, J., and Mack, R. L., eds., *Usability Inspection Methods.* New York: Wiley.

Nielsen, J. 1995. "Scenarios in Discount Usability Engineering." In Carroll, J. M. ed., *Scenario-Based Design.* New York: Wiley.

Nielsen, J., and Mack, R. L., eds. 1994. *Usability Inspection Methods.* New York: Wiley.

Noble, J., and Constantine, L. L. 1997. "Interactive Design Metric Visualization: Visual Metric Support for User Interface Design." *OzCHI '96 Proc.* Los Alamitos, Calif.: IEEE Computer Society Press.

Norman, D. A. 1988. *The Design of Everyday Things.* New York: Basic Books.

Norman, D. A., and Draper, S. W., eds. 1986. *User-Centered Design.* Hillsdale, N.J.: Lawrence Erlbaum.

Olson, J. R., and Olson, G. M. 1990. "The Growth of Cognitive Modeling in Human–Computer Interaction Since GOMS." *Human–Computer Interaction* 3:221–265.

Page-Jones, M. 1995. *What Every Programmer Should Know About Object-Oriented Design.* New York: Dorset House.

Petroski, H. 1994. *Design Paradigms: Case Histories of Error and Judgement in Engineering.* Cambridge: Cambridge University Press.

Petzinger, Jr., T. 1996. "Female Pioneers Fostered Practicality in Computer Industry." *Wall Street Journal,* 22 November.

Phillips, C. 1996 "Towards a Task-Based Methodology for Designing GUIs." In Purvis, M., ed., *Software Engineering: Education & Practice.* Los Alamitos, CA: IEEE Computer Society Press.

Porteous, M., Kirakowski, J., and Corbett, M. 1993. *SUMI User Handbook.* Cork: Human Factors Research Group, University College.

Powell, T. A., Jones, D. L., and Cutts, D. C. 1998. *Web Site Engineering: Beyond Web Page Design.* Upper Saddle River, N.J.: Prentice-Hall.

Preece, J., Rogers, Y., Sharp, H., Benyon, D., Holland, S., and Carey, T. 1994. *Human–Computer Interaction.* Reading, Mass.: Addison-Wesley.

Raskin, J. 1994. "Intuitive Equals Familiar." *Communications of the ACM* 37 (9): 17–18.

Redmond-Pyle, D., and Moore, A. 1995. *Graphical User Interface Design.* London: Prentice-Hall.

Reeves, N., Mills, S., and Noyes, J. 1996. "Sounds Like HELP: The Use of Voice for Procedural Instructions in GUI HELP." In *Proceedings OzCHI '96.* Los Alomitos, Calif.: IEEE Computer Society Press.

Rubin, J. 1994. *Handbook of Usability Testing: How to Plan, Design, and Conduct Effective Tests.* New York: Wiley.

Sabbagh, K. 1996. *Twenty-First-Century Jet: The Making and Marketing of the Boeing 777.* New York: Scribner.

Sand, D. 1996. *Designing Large-Scale Web Sites: A Visual Design Methodology.* New York: Wiley.

Sears, A. 1993. "Layout Appropriateness: A Metric for Evaluating User Interface Widget Layout." *IEEE Trans. Software Engineering* 19 (7):707–719.

Sears, A. 1995. "AIDE: A Step Toward Metric-Based Interface Development Tools." *Proc. ACM Symposium on User Interface Software and Technology.* New York: ACM Press.

Sears, A., and Shneiderman, B. 1994. "Split Menus: Effectively Using Frequency to Organize Menus." *ACM Trans. Computer–Human Interaction* 1 (1):27–51.

Siegel, S., and Castellan, N. J. 1988. *Nonparametric Statistics for the Behavioral Sciences*, 2d ed. New York: McGraw-Hill.

Spool, J. M., Scanlon, T., Schroeder, W., Snyder, C., and DeAngelo, T. 1997. *Web-Site Usability: A Designer's Guide.* North Andover, Mass.: User Interface Engineering.

Stevens, W. P., Myers, G. J., and Constantine, L. L. 1974. "Structured Design." *IBM Systems Journal* 13 (2). Reprinted in Freeman, P., and Wasserman, A. I., eds., *Software Design Techniques*, Long Beach: IEEE, 1977; and Yourdon, E. N., ed., *Classics in Software Engineering.* New York: Yourdon Press, 1979.

Tognazzini, B. 1992. *Tog on Interface.* Reading, Mass.: Addison-Wesley.

Tullis, T. S. 1988. "A System for Evaluating Screen Formats: Research and Applications." In Hartson, R., and Hix, D., eds., *Advances in Human–Computer Interaction, Vol. 2.* Norwood, N.J.: Ablex.

Volpert, W. 1991. "Work Design for Human Development." In Floyd, C., et al., eds., *Software Development and Reality Construction.* Berlin: Spring-Verlag.

Weidenhaupt, K., Pohl, K., Jarke, M., and Haumer, P. 1998. "Scenarios in System Development: Current Practice." *IEEE Software* 15 (2):34–46.

Wharton, C., Rieman, J., Lewis, C., and Polson, P. 1994. "The Cognitive Walkthrough Method: A Practitioner's Guide." In Nielsen, J., and Mack, R. L., eds., *Usability Inspection Methods.* New York: Wiley.

Whitehead, K. 1995. "User-Oriented Development of Object-Oriented Applications." *Report on Object Analysis and Design* 1 (5):16–19.

Wirfs-Brock, R. 1993. "Designing Scenarios: Making the Case for a Use Case Framework." *Smalltalk Report,* November–December.

Wirfs-Brock, R. 1994. "Adding to Your Conceptual Toolkit." *Report on Object Analysis and Design* 1 (2):39–41.

Wirfs-Brock, R., Wilkerson, B., and Weiner, L. 1990. *Designing Object-Oriented Software.* Englewood Cliffs, N.J.: Prentice-Hall.

Wood, J., and Silver, D. 1989. *Joint Application Design.* New York: Wiley.

Yourdon, E. 1989. *Structured Walk-throughs.* Englewood Cliffs, N.J.: Prentice-Hall.

Yourdon, E., and Constantine, L. L. 1979. *Structured Design.* Englewood Cliffs, N.J.: Prentice-Hall.

Zahniser, R. A. 1990. "Building Software in Groups." *American Programmer* 3 (7–8):50–56.

Zahniser, R. A. 1993. "Design by Walking Around." *Communications of the ACM* 36 (10):114–123.

Zultner, R. E. 1992. "Quality Function Deployment for Software." *American Programmer* 5 (2):28–41.

Index

3M, 129
4GLs, 483
7±2, 46 (sidebar)

A

Abstract components. *See* Components
Abstract models, 26–27
Abstract prototypes, 127–128. *See also*
    Content model
  Joint Essential Modeling and, 501
  TeleGuida example, 378–382
Abstraction, 26–27, 38
  use cases and, 105–109
Accelerated development, 472–475, 497
Access keys, 175–176 (Figure 8-5)
  progressive usage and, 277 (sidebar)
Access, Microsoft, 483
Access privileges in TeleGuida example, 362
  (Table 15-1)
Access Rule, 47–48, 194, 231, 265
Accuracy, and efficiency, 312
Acquisition facilities, 268, 273–275
Acquisition scale, in SUSS, 421
Action-object metaphor, 469 (sidebar)
Activities, flexible staging of, 36–39
Activity model, 33–37, 34 (Figure 2-2), 485
  (Figure 20-1), 514 (Figure 21-1)
Actors and roles, 79 (sidebar)
Ada, 338
Adaptable interfaces, 284–285
Adaptive development, 496, 497

Adaptive interfaces, 121, 284
Advanced features, and novices, 274
Advanced users, 265–266
  context menus and, 177
Aesthetics, 163
  innovation and, 188
  novice users and, 273
  readability and, 151
  utility and, 518
  Web site, 319–320
Aesthetics scale, in SUSS, 421
Affect scale, in SUMI, 421
Affective-cognitive separation, 422 (sidebar)
Affinity
  use case, 114–115
  user role, 85, 95
  notation, 114 (Figure 5-6)
Affinity clustering, for calculating Visual
  Coherence, 440–441
Affordance, 196–200, 207
  "drop-kick," 199 (Figure 9-8)
  sliding, 198 (Figure 9-7)
Age, and user interfaces, 301
Airline ticketing example, 3–5, 8
Albrecht, A. J., 428 (sidebar)
Aligning objects, 170 (Figure 8-3), 177
  (Figure 8-6)
Alignment, visual, 164
  Layout Uniformity and, 437
Allocation process in Joint Essential
  modeling, 508–509

About the Authors

Larry L. Constantine, Professor of Computing Sciences at the University of Technology, Sydney, and Director of Research and Development for Constantine & Lockwood, Ltd., is the original developer of structured design and numerous core concepts and models underlying modern software engineering practice and theory. In a career spanning nearly four decades, he has published ten books and over one hundred and thirty papers and articles, making significant contributions to both computer and human sciences. Recognized internationally as an authority on the human side of software, he is a consultant and trainer who has taught in nineteen countries and keynoted numerous international conferences. He chairs the Software Development Management Conference, edits the Management Forum in *Software Development*, and serves on the editorial advisory boards of *IEEE Software, Communications of the ACM*, and *IT Journal*. Constantine is a graduate of the Sloan School of Management at the Massachusetts Institute of Technology and has served on the faculties of six major universities.

Lucy A. D. Lockwood, President of Constantine & Lockwood, Ltd., is codeveloper of usage-centered design and originator of the concept of operational profiles. A consultant, trainer, and writer drawing on over fifteen years of experience in programming and project management, she focuses on software usability and pragmatic approaches to the integration of people and technology in the software engineering process. A top-rated speaker at numerous conferences, she has also been track chair of Usability and User Interface Design for the Software Development Conference and the Web Design and Development Conference, as well as Conference Chair of the Enterprise Applications Development Conference. Her publications include articles on user interface design, cross-functional teamwork, and project management. She is a graduate of Tufts University and has been a Visiting Scholar at the University of Technology, Sydney.

Constantine & Lockwood, Ltd., (http://www.foruse.com/) is a consulting and training organization whose clients include major corporations throughout the world. The firm specializes in technical and process consulting in the areas of software usability, high-performance teamwork, organizational culture, and change management.

This book is published as part of ACM Press Books—a collaboration between the Association for Computing Machinery and Addison-Wesley Publishing Company. ACM is the oldest and largest educational and scientific society in the information technology field. Through its high-quality publications and services, ACM is a major force in advancing the skills and knowledge of IT professionals throughout the world. For further information about ACM, contact:

ACM Member Services
1515 Broadway, 17th Floor
New York, NY 10036-5701
Phone: 1-212-626-0500
Fax: 1-212-944-1318
E-mail: ACMHELP@ACM.org

ACM European Service Center
108 Cowley Road
Oxford OX41JF
United Kingdom
Phone: +44-1865-382338
Fax: +44-1865-381338
E-mail: acm_europe@acm.org
URL: http://www.acm.org